City for Sale

Other books by Jack Newfield

A Prophetic Minority
Robert Kennedy: A Memoir
A Populist Manifesto (with Jeff Greenfield)
Cruel and Unusual Justice
The Permanent Government (with Paul DuBrul)
The Education of Jack Newfield

CITY FOR SALE

ED KOCH AND THE BETRAYAL OF NEW YORK

Jack Newfield & Wayne Barrett

Updated Edition

PERENNIAL LIBRARY

Harper & Row, Publishers, New York
Grand Rapids, Philadelphia, St. Louis, San Francisco
London, Singapore, Sydney, Tokyo, Toronto

Photographs in the inserts are credited to the following:
1: no credit; 2, 3: UPI/Bettmann Newsphotos; 4, 5: Janie Eisenberg; 6: UPI/Bettmann
Newsphotos; 7, 8: Wide World; 9: Janie Eisenberg; 10: Sally Goodgold; 11: N.Y. Daily
News Photo; 12–14: Janie Eisenberg; 15: Marc Asnin; 16: UPI/Bettmann Newsphotos;
17: Wide World; 18, 19: © 1975/1988 by Jay Maisel; 20, 21: UPI/Bettmann Newsphotos;
22: © 1981 by *Time* magazine; 23: Fred W. McDarrah; 24: Janie Eisenberg; 25: Louis
C. Liotta/*New York Post;* 26: Benjamin M. Haber; 27: Dorothy Low; 28: no credit; 29:
UPI/Bettmann Newsphotos; 30: no credit; 31: Michael Schwartz/*New York Post;* 32:
Don Halasy/*New York Post;* 33: N.Y. Daily News Photo; 34–38: UPI/Bettmann News-
photos; 39, 40: no credit; 41: N.Y. Daily News Photo; 42–46: UPI/Bettmann News-
photos; 47–49: no credit; 50, 51: N.Y. Daily News Photo; 52, 53: no credit; 54: UPI/
Bettmann Newsphotos; 55: no credit; 56: UPI/Bettmann Newsphoto; 57: no credit; 58:
N.Y. Daily News Photo; 59: Michael Schwartz/*New York Post;* 60: Bruce Gilbert/*New
York Newsday;* 61: © 1986 by Kathy Milani; 62: UPI/Bettmann Newsphotos; 63–65:
© 1986 by Kathy Milani; 66: UPI/Bettmann Newsphotos; 67: Ed Molinari; 68: Janie
Eisenberg; 69–71: UPI/Bettmann Newsphotos; 72: Christophe von Hohenberg; 73:
UPI/Bettmann Newsphotos; 74: no credit.

The Library of Congress has catalogued the hardcover edition as follows:

Newfield, Jack.
  City for sale.

  Includes index.
    1. New York (N.Y.)—Politics and government—1951– .   2. Koch, Ed, 1924–
3. Corruption (in politics)—New York (N.Y.) I. Barrett, Wayne. II. Title.
F128.55.N49   1988   974.7'1043   88-45522
ISBN 0-06-016060-8
ISBN 0-06-091662-1 (pbk.)

89 90 91 92 93 CC/MPC 10 9 8 7 6 5 4 3 2 1

For Janie, Rebecca and Joey
—J.N.

To Franny McG., Mac, and
my first editor, Helen
—W.B.

Contents

Acknowledgments

We have both covered the administration of New York's mayor, Edward Koch, since its inception on January 1, 1978. In a sense, we had been preparing to write this book for eight years before we actually began working on it in February 1986.

For this book we conducted more than 500 interviews— some jointly, most separately. Ed Koch, however, refused repeated attempts to be interviewed for this book just as he refused every request from us individually throughout his term in office. Some of our sources must remain anonymous, like the person who gave us the secret report on Bess Myerson.

Others in law enforcement were generous with their time and document archives, while taking care not to violate anyone's constitutional rights. They include Ed McDonald, Bob Pitler, Sid Caspersen, John Pritchard, Tony Valenti, Bill Schwartz, David Zornow, Len Michaels, Ed Gruskin, Bill Kilgallon, John Moscow, Sam Milman, Stan Lupkin, Kevin O'Brien, Robert Morgenthau, Larry Urgenson, Kevin Carroll, Joan Alexander, Gordon Haesloop, Rachel Gordon, Richard Guay, Ed Korman, Paul Pickelle, and Rudolph Giuliani.

Tom Puccio, the defense lawyer for Stanley Friedman and Alex Liberman, was equally helpful in sharing his viewpoint and original insights. Joel Cohen also provided help.

We want to especially thank one colleague, David Schneiderman, who edited our copy at the *Voice* for years and protected us when Ed Koch tried to get us fired. Our journalist colleagues also helped—Joe Conason, William Bastone, Tom Robbins, Jim Callaghan, Barbara Ross, Gabe Pressman, Paul Moses, Larry Bivens, Nick von Hoffman, Sid Zion, Art Browne, Ed Borges, Adam Cataldo, Jon Gill.

Harper and Row's lawyer Jim Fox and the *Village Voice*'s attorney, Victor Kovner, were wise, flexible, and creatively cautious. Two other Harper friends, Bill Shinker and Liz Perl, were marvelously supportive of this project.

This book owes a special debt to six people:

Rick Kot, our editor, was painstakingly penetrating in his reading and surgically sensitive in his editing. (We would also like to thank Aaron Asher for signing the book and believing in it.) His assistants, Elisheva Urbas and Scott Terranella, made everything easier for us.

Frances Goldin, our agent, radiated enthusiasm for the book and faith in us from the start of the project. She was essential to helping us overcome the inevitable periods of frustration and self-doubt.

Paul DuBrul, who died while we wrote this book, convinced us we could do it and inspired us with his courage.

Nick Pileggi read the manuscript in progress and mediated the occasional disagreements between us. He deserves the Nobel Peace Prize and has our gratitude.

J.N. AND W.B.

But do you not admire, I said, the coolness and dexterity of these ready ministers of political corruption? Yes, he said, I do; but not all of them, for there are some whom the applause of the multitude has deluded into the belief that they are really statesmen, and these are not much to be admired.

—Plato, *The Republic*

Corruption is the most infallible symptom of constitutional liberty.

—Gibbon,
Decline and Fall of the Roman Empire

Don't follow leaders
watch the parkin' meters

—Bob Dylan,
"Subterranean Homesick Blues"

City for Sale

CHAPTER ONE

King of the Hill

IN THE BRIGHT COLD SUNLIGHT of January 1, 1986, Edward Koch was in political paradise. On that day he became the third person in the twentieth century to have the honor of being sworn in to serve a third term as mayor of New York City.

At ten minutes before noon, on cue the mayor appeared on the top step of City Hall. The George Seuffert Band was accompanying the La Guardia High School chorus in the urban anthem popularized by Frank Sinatra, "New York, New York." The mayor's entrance was carefully timed to the lines:

> I want to wake up in the city that doesn't sleep
> To find I'm king of the hill
> Top of the heap.

Ed Koch, three weeks past his sixty-first birthday, was the king of this singular city-state that was the finance, media, and creative-energy mecca of the planet.

Spread out below the beaming mayor were three thousand guests, huddled in warm coats with all the right labels, seated in neat rows of folding chairs. They were the meritocracy of the oligarchy: the best and brightest of the party of government, the lawyers who sold access, the underwriters who sold debt, the developers who financed the politicians. These were the people whose success validated one another's values, creating the camaraderie of the privileged. Ed Koch was a Democrat, and New York was a one-party city with a strong mayoral form of government—a political science formula for lengthy incumbency, for a king of the hill.

The most synergistic metropolis on earth, New York was more than the sum of its 7.5 million people, 2.4 million trees, 865,000 buildings, 150,000 restaurants, and 17 million annual tourists. New York was more than ten Bostons, or three Chicagos. Its critical mass made it one of a kind.

On this day, Ed Koch was more than just the top of New York's heap. He had become a national celebrity, a pop-culture character, and the country as a whole had accepted him as the personification of the sassy city that never sleeps. As author of the 1985 book *Mayor,* a number-one bestseller nationwide for twenty-one weeks, Koch had made more money writing about his job that year ($205,000) than he had performing it ($110,000). He was on television so often, on shows ranging from *Saturday Night Live* to *Romper Room,* that he was invited to join the theatrical performers' union, the American Federation of Television and Radio Artists (AFTRA).

Koch had been the subject of a glorifying lead story in *Time* magazine, posing on the cover with his arms over his head, the skyline behind him. In April 1982, *Playboy* featured Koch as the subject of its monthly celebrity interview, the only mayor regarded by the magazine's editors as being of national interest. The same year the *Boston Globe*'s Sunday magazine ran a sympathetic profile of Koch under a cover headline reading: ED KOCH ON THE MOVE: WILL NEW YORK'S MAYOR END UP IN THE WHITE HOUSE?—a theme *Parade* repeated in an article subtitled, "Why Some People Think He Could Become the First Jewish President of the United States." Author Gay Talese had also nominated Koch for president in the course of giving his book a rave notice on the front page of the *New York Times Book Review* in February 1984. Talese had mentioned Koch's interest in the presidency, and asked, "Why not?" Talese claimed, in a revealing hyperbole, that Koch was "the only white man in New York in ten years to talk back to a black man."

Ed Koch had reached this day, attained this peak, through his abilities as a consummate politician, a Teflon mayor, and a world-class showman. As a politician, he was a Jewish Mayor Daley, filled with faith in himself, lust for power, and a sixth sense for what the lower middle class was going to feel tomorrow. And as a performer, Koch had both a mastery of and an infatuation with the media. He regularly held three and four press conferences daily, and two photo opportunities. He often boasted that he had read his name in the *New York Times* every day since he became mayor. Koch bombarded the public with foreign policy pronouncements, restaurant recommendations, opinions on pending court cases, and burlesque put-downs of his critics as wackos and kooks— all delivered in perfect, pithy, thirty-second sound bites for radio and television.

Ed Koch had assumed office in January 1978, at the start of a period of transition from stringent austerity to economic growth. In 1975, under Abe Beame, New York City had accumulated a short-term debt it could not repay to its lending banks, which had led to a general fear of insolvency. A fiscal crisis had compelled the elimination of 65,000 municipal government jobs, a wage freeze for city workers, severe service cutbacks for the poor, a rise in the mass transit fare, and the abolition of free tuition at the City University. These sacrifices had all been completed before Koch came into office on January 1, 1978. He came to power in a city with lowered expectations about municipal government, whose populace was grateful the calamity of bankruptcy had been averted.

With the end of the fiscal crisis, Koch was able to spend public money to consolidate the economic elite of the city behind his personality and their priorities. The establishment became unified to a degree not seen since the Rockefeller period of the 1960s. Ed Koch fashioned a governing coalition of real estate, finance, the Democratic Party machine, the media, and the recipients of city contracts. During the past eight years the city's economy had grown strong, with employment surging in the finance, construction, service, and high-tech industries. Koch had restored the city's credit in the bond markets, reduced its debt service from 17 to 9 percent, and paid back the federal loans a year ahead of schedule. In 1975 the city had a $1.8 billion debt; a decade later Koch had managed to produce a budget surplus.

Koch presided over a building boom in white Manhattan. Between 1982 and 1985, sixty new office towers went up south of 96th Street. Real estate values in gentrifying neighborhoods in Manhattan and Brooklyn went soaring, and the exodus of major corporations from New York was stopped. A new convention center was built, a half-dozen luxury-class hotels were financed with tax abatements, and tourism increased, injecting revenue into the Manhattan economy of theaters, hotels, and restaurants.

On a more subjective level, Koch had improved the city's morale and self-image, which had been so badly damaged during the doomsday rhetoric of the fiscal crisis. He was not only a brilliant cheerleader but had succeeded in bringing the crime rate down each year from 1981 to 1985. Reading and math test scores rose in the public schools.

Koch impressed almost everyone with the quality of the most visible commissioners appointed during his first term: Robert McGuire (police); Nat Leventhal (housing); Robert Wagner, Jr. (planning); Joe Hynes (fire); Gordon Davis (parks); Basil Patterson, David Brown, and Herman Badillo (deputy mayors).

Not surprisingly, all three of New York's daily newspapers had enthusiastically endorsed Ed Koch for reelection in the Democratic primary of 1985. In a one-party city, this figured as the real election, and the dailies seemed to go out of their way to pay tribute to the scandal-free integrity of Koch's first two terms as mayor. The *New York Times*'s endorsement of Koch, published on September 4, 1985, was typical in its praise: "He [Koch] has hired first rate officials, provided honest government, and greatly improved municipal management."

But while all this seemed true, at the same time the poor were getting poorer, for the boom of the 1980s bypassed whole chunks of the city. Between 1977 and 1985, the proportion of New Yorkers officially classified as living below the federal poverty line increased from 17 to 25 percent. The homeless population grew to 60,000; the high school dropout rate rose to 54 percent; AIDS became a plague; crack became an epidemic. Beggars stood outside Tiffany's, while homeless people slept outside the Trump Tower. Manhattan was fast becoming the Ethiopia of the housing market, with a famine of rental apartments for the middle class and the working class starving for shelter. A city of scarce resources, dependent on its government to be honest and frugal, New York increasingly began to resemble a Dickensian city of extreme paradox, of poverty and overdevelopment, with diversity being swept away by the force of wealth.

Not many people were willing to argue with trend, fashion,

and political success, and criticism was made to seem churlish, almost subversive of civic pride. Lowered expectations, puerile boosterism, material accumulation, and a callous careerism were the messages issued by the White House, Wall Street, Hollywood, Madison Avenue, and City Hall. New Yorkers, too, became proficient at stepping around a human shape under a blanket on a cold night without feeling guilty or considering the government's responsibility.

January 1, 1986 was the crest of the Reagan-era ethos of greed-without-guilt, of celebrating private interests over public purpose. The shredding parties and Swiss bank accounts of Contragate had not yet occurred, nor had Wall Street's insider trading scandals, or the crash and panic of October 1987. The Democrats had not yet won a majority of the Senate in 1986 and defeated the nomination of Robert Bork for the Supreme Court, nor had the grotesque decadence of the Reverend Jim Bakker and Tammy Bakker been exposed.

January 1, 1986 was still the apex of materialism and self-indulgence. This was still the era of Ronald Pelton and John Walker's becoming Russian spies for money, not ideology. This was the era when Madonna's "Material Girl" was the number-one hit song, when arbitrageur Ivan Boesky, before he admitted paying bribes carried in suitcases for insider information, said in a commencement address to the business school graduates at Berkeley: "I think greed is healthy. You can be greedy and still feel good about yourself."

The plaza of City Hall was packed with people in harmony with this *Zeitgeist* of Anything Goes. Boesky himself, in fact, had been invited to the inauguration by Koch, as had other symbolic personalities such as Donald Trump, Carl Icahn, Henry Kissinger, and George Steinbrenner. It was such icons of glitzy greed who inspired Jimmy Breslin to write: "The city's symbol is no longer the Statue of Liberty, but instead is a limousine double-parked on a Manhattan Street, as the police dare not tell it to move."

At high noon, with the temperature at thirty-nine degrees, Edward Irving Koch, wearing no overcoat, a blue pinstripe suit, and his favorite "I Love New York" scarf, looked out over his three thousand inaugural witnesses. Here was a poor boy from the Bronx, a loner in school, a fifty-to-one underdog when he first ran for mayor, accepting the cheers and deferential smiles of the entire government and establishment of New York. Ed

Koch was the sun, and they were the planets in orbit around his power.

Then, as still cameras clicked like locusts and video cameras recorded silently, Ed Koch placed his right hand upon a 160-year-old Bible, a book that had been chosen because it had survived Hitler's attempt to exterminate the Jewish population of Europe. At the mayor's request, the Bible was open to a passage from the book of Exodus in which God urged Moses to cease his praying and take the bold action of marching forward into the Red Sea. Koch selected this passage to dramatize his own resolve during his next term as mayor of New York. More than anything else he wanted to avoid the third-term mental and physical exhaustion that had afflicted Mayors La Guardia and Wagner.

The mayor recited his solemn constitutional oath surrounded by monuments and symbols as venerable as the holy book upon which his palm rested. City Hall itself, with its six marvelous white marble columns, was begun in 1803 and completed in 1812. At the top of City Hall's curved double staircase, Abraham Lincoln's body had lain in state for two days in April 1865.

From the mayor's vantage point he could also see the majestic spires of the 102-year-old Brooklyn Bridge, built by Roebling and made mythic in a poem by Hart Crane. A block southwest of City Hall was the elegant sixty-one-floor Woolworth Building, with its soaring lines and richly decorated interiors, which opened in 1913, and was named "the most beautiful building in all the world erected to commerce" two years later. A few blocks farther south was the World Trade Center, towering over the skyline of the island Truman Capote had called "the diamond iceberg."

Directly behind City Hall, looming like a bad omen, was the Tweed Courthouse, the city's enduring symbol of past corruption. Begun in 1861, and finally certified as an official landmark in 1984, this grand Corinthian-style structure cost fifty-six times its original budgeted cost, owing to all the kickbacks, skimming, and double-billing by Boss Tweed and his gang of boodlers—and to the coincidence that Tweed happened to own the quarry from which the stone was purchased to build it.

At the conclusion of the public ceremonies, fifteen hundred invited guests would be treated to a lavish catered brunch with food dispersed over two floors of Tweed's monument to avarice. Spread out tastefully were fifty pounds of cheese, a hundred gallons of punch, two thousand bagels, and eighty gallons of minestrone soup. Every guest was given a souvenir bottle of Great Western New York State champagne to take home, donated by Seagram's. The spread also included generous portions of De Witt Clinton Raisin-Currant bread, which City Hall archivists reported was served at one of the three inaugurations of Clinton.

But on this day, the crimes and achievements of the past were forgotten in the light of two themes that keynoted the mayor's private conversations and public oratory; serenity and optimism. Before the ceremonies began, Koch had invited the press into his office for some relaxed banter. Pointing out that the sun was shining and the blue sky was cloudless, he said, "The weather is reflective of the state of the city." On his desk was a sign that proclaimed, "The best is yet to be."

Shortly after the oath was recited, the person who would introduce Koch to the crowd stepped forward. Bess Myerson, the mistress of ceremonies, was the city's cultural affairs commissioner, running a city agency with an annual budget of $130 million. Myerson was a trailblazing heroine—the Jewish feminist Jackie Robinson. An immigrant house painter's striving daughter who had grown up in the Sholom Aleichem housing project in the low-income Bronx, she attended Music and Art High School and Hunter College, and then, in September 1945, became the first Jewish Miss America. To American Jews of the postwar generation, her selection was an affirmation of acceptance in America at a time the death camps of Europe were being discovered.

But Bess Myerson had brains as well as beauty. She became a television personality during the 1950s as a game show hostess and panelist, and was a much sought-after fundraiser for Israel and lecturer on anti-Semitism. Then, in 1969, Mayor John Lindsay appointed Myerson as the city's commissioner for consumer affairs, a position that enabled her to make the transition from celebrity to power. By every account she did a splendid job. She hired a staff of smart young lawyers such as Philip Schrag, Sy Lazarus, Bruce Ratner, and Henry Stern. In 1970 alone, her agency found 9,900 civil violations and served 1,535 court summonses. Myerson forced the usually indolent city council to pass some of the most advanced pro-consumer laws in the country. And she was, of course, spectacular each time she appeared on television.

In 1977, Bess Myerson, still sexy at fifty-two, had stood next to Ed Koch when he announced his candidacy for mayor with only a 2 percent rating of support in the polls. During the campaign, she walked with Koch through the Brighton Baths in Coney Island, introduced him at rallies in Forest Hills, kissed him in Co-op City. Myerson was also a prized fundraiser for Koch and a magnet who attracted the media whenever she appeared at his side. She was so popular she was given equal prominence with Koch in the basic campaign poster that papered the city, the first non–family member to be treated as a spouse equivalent by political packagers. She conspicuously held his hand in synagogue on Rosh Hashanah. She encouraged newspaper stories that hinted she might marry Koch after the election was over, and she smiled as Koch introduced her as a possible First Lady of New York. It was Myerson who was at his side when he claimed his victory on a delirious election night that November. She was, in effect, the co-candidate, and Koch owed a large measure of his upset triumph to her.

As Myerson stood on the platform in her fur coat she could see her current lover among the dignitaries in the Plaza, Carl (Andy) Capasso. Capasso was twenty-one years younger, born the year Myerson was crowned Miss America. A ditchdigger who had made it to the top, he was president of Nanco Contracting Corporation, which had received $200 million in city contracts for sewer construction and street repaving work.

Capasso was the Nicky Arnstein of the 1980s. His best friend and neighbor was Mafia boss Matthew (Matty the Horse) Ianniello. Capasso had a $1.9 million estate in Westhampton Beach, a $6 million apartment on Fifth Avenue, good paintings, the best cars, and a beautiful wife when he started his affair with Bess Myerson. Capasso was probably the only cheating husband in history who claimed to be spending his nights with a Mafia boss (Ianniello) when he was really having an affair with Miss America.

On the night before the inauguration, Capasso and Myerson had been part of an intimate party of about thirty who witnessed the private swearing-in of Ed Koch at midnight. The couple had a special reason to celebrate on this particular New Year's Eve. A few days earlier Capasso had won his final divorce case against his battered wife, Nancy. Not only had Judge Andrew Tyler awarded Nancy Capasso $4 million less than she asked for, but he had ruled that Bess Myerson didn't have to testify and sealed the entire record as requested by Capasso.

Judge Tyler also decreed that Andy did not have to make any more child-support or alimony payments.

As Bess Myerson took center stage at City Hall, she quieted the expectant buzz of the crowd with her regal bearing and glorious smile. She introduced "our CEO, our chief magistrate" with a boldly confident prediction: "These next four years will be even better years for our city, and for ourselves."

Behind Koch on the speaking platform was a dais filled with about a hundred people with whom the mayor wished to publicly display a personal bond. Most of his own commissioners were not invited to take places in this section.

Among the guests on the dais were two of the city's most powerful politicians, Donald Manes and Stanley Friedman. Manes, Friedman, and Koch had become friends twenty years before, when Koch and Manes were freshmen members of the city council and Friedman was a top lawyer on the council's staff. Now Friedman was the Democratic county leader of the Bronx, and Manes both the Democratic county leader and borough president of Queens. In a one-party city the men who could determine and manipulate the Democratic nominations for elective office were kingmakers. Manes and Friedman held such power through their control of the votes on the city council and the Board of Estimate. Not only could they purge anyone who voted independently; in effect, they forced Koch to deal with them to trade for votes. The county leaders also controlled patronage; and with hundreds and hundreds of city employees, from commissioners to pothole inspectors, owing their jobs to the party bosses, the Democratic organization was the centerpiece of the Koch coalition.

With a front-row seat next to his wife Marlene, Donald Manes, a few weeks short of his fifty-second birthday, was perceived to be the second most powerful politician in this city of power junkies. He was regarded as Koch's most likely successor, in large part because Koch himself had promoted Manes as the next mayor. When Manes was introduced to the crowd by Bess Myerson, he was cheered more lustily than most of the other dais guests. He was likable, undignified, the public man everyone felt comfortable calling "Donny."

Manes liked to call himself "the king of Queens." As both borough president and Democratic county leader, he had a de facto right of approval over every public project, land-use decision, and development plan in his borough. The base of Manes's power in Queens was so secure that the borough of two million people was virtually depoliticized. In 1985, Manes did not even have a challenger in the Democratic primary for borough president, while Brooklyn, Manhattan, and the Bronx had fiercely contested campaigns. In the general election that year, the Republicans put up only a token candidate, and Manes was reelected with 85 percent of the vote. In 1981, the Republicans hadn't even tried to run a candidate against Manes.

Men who would be president, men like Jimmy Carter, Walter Mondale, Gary Hart, and Ted Kennedy, came as petitioners to his office on Queens Boulevard, seeking his county organization's large and disciplined bloc of delegates to national conventions. In October 1985, *Newsday* ran a profile of Manes under the headline: THE MIGHTY MANES MACHINE. BUT IS IT ENOUGH TO BOOST HIM INTO HIGHER OFFICE? The article ended with an ambitious answer from Manes to that question; "I represent two million people, and I think I do that well. There's no reason I couldn't represent more."

Just two weeks before Koch's inauguration, on December 17, 1985, an ebullient Manes gave his annual "State of the County" address. In it Manes boasted, "Queens is the place where the American Dream is still alive."

Manes had entered politics in 1965, running as reformer who stressed honesty and integrity in government. His opponent was Howard Stave, who knew that Manes did not even live in the district he was seeking to represent. Stave's lawyer, Morton Povman (now a Queens councilman) went out to Jericho, Long Island, and interviewed neighbors, who told him Manes slept there each night and his children went to school in Jericho. But Manes was paying rent to his father-in-law as a phantom subtenant in Electchester, a vast housing complex built by Local 3 of the Electrical Workers Union. This housing development was the biggest voting bloc in the council district.

When Povman tried to subpoena Manes's in-laws to a court hearing on Manes's residency, process servers could not find the in-laws. They looked for days in vain. Manes had hidden his in-laws in the Catskill mountains under aliases. Without their testimony under oath, Manes could not be thrown off the ballot for living in the wrong county. Manes won the election by less than 1,700 votes. Then he and his campaign manager, Alan

Gershuny, started a new political club and named it after their liberal hero, Adlai Stevenson.

By the mid-1980s it had become clear to everyone that Manes was a competent and professional borough president. He combined the right mix of negotiating skill, governmental knowledge, and budgetary mastery. He was the mayor's best friend and most loyal ally on the Board of Estimate, an alliance that proved its value annually when the city's budget would be decided by the board in a final marathon bargaining session. It would always end in a private meeting between Koch and Manes, with Manes then going to the other end of City Hall and artfully coaxing the board to agree with the mayor's final numbers.

With such leverage Manes had the potential to be, in certain ways, the most effective borough president Queens had ever had. He had reversed the spreading blight of the Jamaica area by getting the Social Security Administration's massive regional headquarters—housing four thousand employees—to locate there. He engineered the opening of York College, the improvement of the Archer Avenue subway line, and the reconstruction of Jamaica Avenue. Manes also helped Queens prosper by getting for his borough more than its share of capital improvements and publicly funded projects. Through his clout, Queens reopened the Astoria Studios, became the site of the City University's new public interest law school, and transformed the College Point Industrial Park from a virtually vacant development project into one entirely sold or rented.

Yet like so many others who seek and seize worldly power, Donald Manes had a dark side. By January 1, 1986, many of his closest friends and cohorts had already been prosecuted, including Queens councilman Gene Mastropieri, Judge William Brennan, city taxi commissioner Herb Ryan, and city electrical contractor Richard Kashinsky. In 1976 a grand jury investigating Manes's top deputy, Robert Groh, wanted to indict Manes himself. The prosecutor, aided by a judge, had to urge it to indict only Groh, who was eventually acquitted.

Manes also lived with a demon—the memory of his father's suicide. On a November day in 1955, the 21-year-old Donald Manes had gone to the offices of his father's threatened dairy company in Brooklyn and discovered that he had borrowed the payroll clerk's gun. Manes instantly suspected his father's plans, and headed for the family home in Queens, alone and in a panic. When he got there the house was dark and silent. He went down the basement steps to the den. His dad, a large, gentle bear of a man, was on the floor, covered in blood. The gun he had shoved up his mouth was still in his hand. For the rest of his life Donald Manes would not go down darkened basement stairs alone, anywhere.

In the second row of the dais, still tanned from a Christmas vacation in Puerto Rico, wrapped in his own "I Love New York" scarf, sat Stanley Friedman, the Bronx county leader. With his devilish goatee, Friedman suggested a Mephistopheles. Like Koch and Manes, he, too, was at the height of his power.

Friedman had just engineered the reelection of his puppet, Stanley Simon, as Bronx borough president, and was confident that, as part of a deal with Manes, he now had the votes to pick the new majority leader and finance committee chairman of the city council, as well as the new city clerk. His law practice was thriving and based almost exclusively on clients who did business with the city government. In 1985, Friedman had made about $900,000 from these clients, even if his work involved functioning more as a lobbyist than as a lawyer. And Friedman was holding 167,000 shares of stock in a company called Citisource that were worth about $2 million. Citisource had recently received a $22 million contract from the city's Parking Violations Bureau (PVB) to provide handheld computers to parking enforcement agents.

Friedman personally was even closer to Koch than Manes was. Koch had been a guest both at Friedman's wedding to Jackie Glassman in 1981 and at his $500,000 summer home in Quogue, Long Island. Friedman's wife worked in the mayor's office and had participated in the planning of this inaugural ceremony as a member of the mayor's special events staff. Like Myerson and Capasso, the Friedmans had been among the thirty guests present at the mayor's private swearing-in the midnight before, at the East Side home of David Margolis, the chief executive officer of Colt Industries. In his book *Mayor*, Koch had described Friedman as "one of the smartest, ablest, most loyal people I know."

Friedman had known the mayor ever since Koch was elected to the city council in 1966. But their friendship blossomed during the 1977 runoff for mayor, in which Friedman played a central role. He not only helped deliver most of the Bronx organization to Koch; he also persuaded Abe Beame, the incumbent mayor, to endorse Koch, even though much of Beame's inner circle advised against it. Less than a year later, Koch as mayor reciprocated the favor and helped line up the votes to make Friedman the Democratic county leader of the Bronx.

Like Manes in Queens, Friedman was given almost total control over his borough by the mayor. Any businessman who wanted to develop city-owned land, who wanted a franchise, a contract, a permit, a zoning variance in the Bronx had to go to him. Not holding any public office, and thus having no obligations to make financial disclosures, Friedman was free to become a millionaire through his political influence.

Friedman's authority over hundreds of jobs in city government allowed him discretionary decisions that could make a client rich. His patronage was responsible for the appointment of such highly placed individuals as Ted Teah (City Planning Commission), Paul Victor (Conciliation and Appeals Board), Doug McKeon (Taxi and Limousine Commission), Stanley Schorr (Board of the Industrial Development Agency), and Stanley Wolff (Board of Standards and Appeals) who could be susceptible to influence by Friedman.

Stanley Friedman's phone log revealed the vast employment powers ceded to him by the mayor. One caller left a message that he "took the parks job," was "eternally grateful," and would "do his best to fulfill his obligations." Stanley Wolff, whom Friedman put on the Board of Standards and Appeals (which grants lucrative exceptions to the zoning laws), asked in a message "when should he hand in his resignation?" Friedman's notation next to the message was: "Today. Get him a Department of General Services job."

Friedman wielded this governmental power without his name ever having appeared on a voting machine. He was never elected by the people of the Bronx to any public or party office, not even that of a local district leader. His legitimacy came solely from City Hall. Although the Bronx was 75 percent black and Latino, under Friedman every significant position in its government—borough president, district attorney, surrogate, and county leader—was still occupied by a white male.

Friedman did, as even his detractors would acknowledge, possess the qualities of a natural leader. He had the capacity to inspire loyalty; a quick mind and an instinct for reading character and spotting weakness; a rough, witty charm; and a mediating talent to find a common ground where competitors could save face.

Friedman grew up in the working-class Hunts Point section of the South Bronx, where his father was a taxi driver, and the only college he could afford to attend was the then tuition-free City College. Friedman had the backcourt position on the school's basketball team and was an even better competitor in the playgrounds, where the rules were more loosely enforced. In the Bronx schoolyards, Friedman had been known by the wiseguy nickname of "Bugsy." It fit him, and he loved it—an ideal reflection of his self-image of desperado bravado.

It was the style that Friedman took with him into politics. Back in 1972 Friedman had been involved in a parking ticket scandal at the PVB. He was then still a young lawyer on the staff of the city council. He was caught giving three summonses to his father, Moe Friedman, who was then an administrative assistant in the Bronx office of the PVB. Moe Friedman then entered phony entries of dismissal on the PVB's log sheets, disposition slips, and the summonses themselves. By the time this practice was discovered, Friedman's father had died, and Friedman stonewalled the city's Department of Investigations. They suspected Friedman was lying, but he was clever enough to avoid any charges. So early in his career, Friedman had dodged a bullet, just as Manes had when he successfully falsified his residency to win his first election.

Now, even with his place among the select few on the dais, wrapped in his civic booster's scarf, rich, powerful, and healthy, Friedman was still suffering the hurts and deprivations of a South Bronx childhood. Some appetite deep down in Bugsy Friedman hungered for more, needed to find shortcuts, to cut corners.

Conspicuously absent from the dais was the third great pillar of the city's Democratic machine, the legendary 78-year-old Meade Esposito. Brooklyn was the biggest Democratic county in America, and Esposito had ruled the borough's Democratic Party for fifteen years until his resignation in 1984. Although Esposito had been invited to the Koch inauguration, he had gone to his condo in Fort Lauderdale, Florida, instead. But his people were there: Howard Golden, the borough president and party leader, and Esposito's handpicked successor; Anthony Ameruso, the transportation commissioner Esposito had forced Koch to name even though Koch's own screening committee had found him unqualified; Jay Turoff, the chairman of the city's Taxi and Limousine Commission, who still called Esposito "Chief."

Meade Esposito didn't have to endure the cold wind that blew across City Hall Plaza to prove he still had clout. Esposito knew how much Koch owed him, and remained certain that it was his influence that had made Koch the mayor in 1977. In what proved to be the turning point of the runoff that year, Esposito had given the secret backing of the Brooklyn machine to Koch rather than to his fellow outer-borough Italian, Mario Cuomo. And Koch demonstrated his gratitude by letting Esposito dictate the choice of Ameruso and Turoff, keeping all the clubhouse captains on the city payroll and allowing Esposito to expand his shadow government of patronage appointees in many city agencies. In a second Koch book, *Politics,* Koch had publicly acknowledged his debt to Esposito by telling the story of the covert covenant they had made in 1977 and admitting that Esposito "has always been helpful to me."

What made Esposito a legend, beyond the durability of his power, was his exotic personality. He was menacing, funny, smart, tough, obscene, Machiavellian, volatile, sentimental, and quotable. He was devious but acted like a noble primitive, without guile or guilt. He was also capable of taking unpredictably liberal positions, such as endorsing George McGovern at an early stage for the Democratic presidential nomination in 1972, and ordering his hacks on the city council to vote for a gay rights bill. While Esposito made up so many myths about himself that he became, in effect, a character in his own novel, his Runyonesque creation did mask a more sinister side. Yet rumors of Mafia connections only seemed to give him an aura of glamorous mystery, and so many publicized investigations into his activities ended in exoneration or ambiguity that to his cronies he seemed invincible. And to people of innocent good will, he seemed legitimate.

Born in Brownsville in 1906, the son of an immigrant bartender, Esposito dropped out of high school after six months. During the 1950s he was a bail bondsman with many Mafia clients. In 1960 he was elected the Democratic district leader from Canarsie. Like Manes, he ran first as a reformer; he was even officially endorsed by Eleanor Roosevelt and Herbert Lehman.

On New Year's Day of 1986, Meade Esposito was a lion at twilight, but still a dealmaker and kingmaker. During Koch's years in City Hall, he had become a millionaire, his net worth rising from $100,000 to almost $6 million. In 1985, Esposito's insurance company, Serres, Viscone, and Rice, collected more than $2 million in commissions, and Esposito was paid $257,000 in compensation. The mayor's 1985 reelection campaign committee gave its printing business to Esposito's other vessel for legal graft, Beaumont Printing and Offset, to which it paid $117,000. Esposito's patronage appointees in each city agency were likewise expected to do favors for Esposito's insurance and printing clients, steer contracts to his friends, and carry out the duties that proved this vain old lion still had bite.

Today Esposito was in Fort Lauderdale, soaking up the sunshine with his old buddy Mario Biaggi, the senior congressman from New York City. With Biaggi was his mistress, the redheaded divorcée Barbara Barlow; his wife of forty-five years, Marie, was home in the Bronx, undergoing painful chemotherapy treatments for Hodgkin's disease. Biaggi had nearly been elected mayor of New York in 1973. Although his front-running campaign crumbled when he was caught lying about whether he had taken the Fifth Amendment before a federal grand jury, Biaggi had remained a popular figure in the city, the most honored cop in the history of New York's police department, a champion of Irish and Jewish causes. His pronounced limp, a legacy from his career as a cop, evoked sympathy as he marched in ethnic parades and mounted platforms to collect plaques and honors.

What Esposito and Biaggi did not know was that thirteen FBI agents were watching, following, and photographing them; that Esposito's phones in New York had been tapped by the FBI, with court authorization, for the past two months; and that his conversations with Biaggi had been incriminating enough to warrant this surveillance in the sun. They didn't know that the nice young woman who befriended Biaggi's mistress in aerobics class was an undercover FBI agent. The lion at twilight didn't know it, but he had already become a top-secret FBI project code-named Runnymede, the subject of an investigation led by a federal prosecutor who still regarded Esposito as "an untouchable legend."

In the very last row of wooden chairs in City Hall Plaza sat Rudy Giuliani, accompanied by his old friend and Manhattan

College classmate Peter Powers. From his distant seat, the 42-year-old Giuliani gazed at Donald Manes and Stanley Friedman up on the platform, meditating about whether they were corrupt, wondering if he would one day find himself prosecuting them in his role as United States Attorney for the southern district of New York.

For the past eighteen months Giuliani had been getting periodic briefings about a top-secret FBI undercover operation in Chicago. The FBI was audio and videotaping meetings in the office of a collection company that had been bribing Chicago politicians for city contracts. The president of the company also had a New York office, and fragments of conversations on the Chicago tapes had begun to suggest systematic payoffs were being made in New York City's Parking Violations Bureau. Nothing on the tapes would convict the city officials who were named, but they were filled with knowing remarks that sounded true.

Then, five weeks earlier, on November 26, the FBI had taped a lunch in Manhattan where the PVB bagman, a former quack sex therapist named Geoffrey Lindenauer, had taken $5,000 in a urinal.

And only five days before this festive day of oratory, music, and food, Giuliani had hit paydirt. The corrupt president of the collection company, Bernard Sandow, had agreed to plead guilty and go undercover for Giuliani in New York. In his debriefing, Sandow had admitted that he had paid Lindenauer almost $400,000 in bribes for contracts in New York since 1981. Sandow said he believed Lindenauer was passing the money back to Manes, who had gotten him the job at PVB, and told the FBI that Lindenauer had once said to him, while taking money in another men's room, "Donald thinks you're doing a great job."

The night before, a wired Bernard Sandow had recorded a meeting with the PVB commissioner Lester Shafran. But Shafran had been suspicious, wrote notes on paper, and mouthed the words "Are you wired?" to Sandow.

The Sandow sting was still going on. He was working on New Year's Day, trying to arrange a meeting with Lindenauer, trying to set up meetings with other PVB contractors who he suspected were also paying bribes for city contracts.

But this investigation was so secret and sensitive that Giuliani had not even told his wife, Donna, the anchorwoman on

Channel 11's nightly newscast. Its outlines were just starting to take shape in Giuliani's mind. There was still a margin of doubt, that perhaps the tapes contained mere puffing, or that the pay-offs represented an isolated transaction between Sandow and Lindenauer. It was also possible that this was as big as it seemed, that the powerful politicians on the platform were implicated, and that it would turn into the biggest case of Giuliani's still-young career.

Giuliani, the only child of Brooklyn Italian working-class parents, was the first member of his family ever to go to college. His father was a plumber and a tavern owner, and Giuliani attended college and law school on academic scholarships. Until he was twenty he had planned to become a priest, and prepared to enter the seminary until the obligation of celibacy convinced him to channel his strong sense of sin, guilt, and redemption into the law.

In the mid-1970s, Giuliani became the chief of the anticor-ruption unit in the U.S. Attorney's office under Whitney North Seymour. He convicted Brooklyn congressman Bert Podell in a dramatic trial that ended with Podell pleading guilty in the middle of Giuliani's withering cross-examination. This trial marked the first time Giuliani met Ed Koch—when Koch testi-fied as a character witness for Podell.

Giuliani then went into private practice and earned $160,000 one year. But his workaholic rectitude was not ful-filled by financial reward. So he went back into government in 1981, taking the number-three job in the justice department, under Attorney General William French Smith. Then, in 1983, he gave up his Washington job of national influence and media exposure to become the U.S. Attorney in New York, at a salary of $77,500. His mother thought his new job was a demotion.

But for Giuliani the job was an opportunity to return to the city of his birth and affection, to run the biggest U.S. Attorney's office in the country, with a staff of 130 lawyers, and to be his own boss, to feel free to use the office as a pulpit for his ideas about the law and about values.

Giuliani brought extraordinary skills to the job of U.S. At-torney. He had intellect, audacity, creativity, and ambition. It didn't hurt that he was a tough bureaucratic in-fighter, and a convert to the Republican Party, with important friends in the Reagan administration in Washington. His weakness was a tendency toward excess in publicity, a flaw that was offset by the self-corrective of guilt.

The deepest passion of this priestly prosecutor was apprehending crooked politicians, an achievement that gave him a richer sense of satisfaction than even catching drug traffickers, financial finaglers, and Mafia godfathers. "I don't think there is anybody worse than a public official who sells his office and corrupts others," Giuliani once said, "except maybe a murderer." He had a moral comprehension of why political corruption subverted democracy and injured the commonweal. Giuliani regarded corrupt public officials the way Robert Kennedy thought of Jimmy Hoffa; the outrage was personal.

Giuliani's greatest hero was his own father, and until his father's death in 1981, Giuliani doubted whether he would ever live up to his father's exacting standards and expectations.

As his father was dying, Giuliani asked him, "Were you ever afraid?" And his father, barely able to speak, replied with the ultimate, liberating wisdom, "Everybody is afraid."

One of Giuliani's private fears was that he was a failure at personal relationships, especially after his first marriage ended in divorce. He felt guilty over being too much of a perfectionist, who was too impatient with the imperfections of colleagues and who loved work so much he was unfit for love.

But by the time Giuliani came to this inaugural, he had found the measure of inner peace that is often necessary for great public accomplishment. He had remarried, and his son would be born thirty days later.

After the mayor's speech Giuliani dropped by a reception for David Dinkins, who was sworn in as Manhattan borough president and was the only black elected to the Board of Estimate. At the reception Giuliani came face to face with Donald Manes and exchanged greetings. Giuliani could see that Manes was sweating and pale, and his eyes were shifting wildly.

Giuliani's companion, Peter Powers, said, "Manes looked at you real funny."

Giuliani couldn't tell his friend what he was thinking.

Mayor Koch delivered a twenty-minute inaugural address in the noonday chill. It was a literate, humane speech that promised more would be done for life's casualties, a theme noted by the headline on the front page of the *New York Times* the following morning: KOCH PLEDGES AID FOR HOMELESS, SCHOOLS, AND POOR.

"New York City will lead the fight for more housing," the

mayor told his audience. "We won't rest until the housing we so desperately need is built. . . . We will never be satisfied until our schools give young people the best possible education. . . .

"We stopped the old cruelty of uncaring hospitals and now it is time to stop the new cruelty of substituting park benches and subway stations. . . .

"We will never be satisfied until persons afflicted with AIDS receive all the care and the compassion we can possibly provide. We will never be satisfied until the terrible toll of infant mortality has been reduced even more. We will never be satisfied until people are completely safe in our streets and in our subways. We will never be satisfied until we have finally won the fight for economic, racial, and social justice."

Koch also made spines tingle a little more with a lyrical homage to the city-state he led and loved:

"This is not a place of carefree quietude. Our city is not a refuge from reality. New York is what it has always been: it's the world's number-one arena for genius, it's the battleground for new ideas. New York is the city where the future comes to rehearse, where the best come to get better. We are the leading city because we are the city of leaders. If you are trying for the top, you can't top New York."

The final serene and optimistic peroration of Koch's speech would prove to be supreme, unintended irony. Surrounded by Manes, Friedman, Myerson, Capasso, Ameruso, Turoff, and Shafran, Koch shouted with obvious feeling:

"Finally, I have always perceived, and have always said, that public service is the noblest of professions, if it is done honestly and well. And there are so many people on this platform—and in this crowd—who perform superbly as public servants. I am grateful to them, and I know the people of the City of New York are grateful to them."

CHAPTER TWO

The American Dream and Queens County

I**N THE DAYS LEADING UP TO** the public euphoria of Koch's inauguration, the two lives of Donald Manes were on roller coasters rushing in opposite directions. Manes's public life of political leadership was reaching new heights of status and security. But a series of events was beginning in Florida and Chicago that would soon expose his secret life in New York.

Manes had reached the point in his career where he felt he owned the office that voters had, in fact, elected him to for a temporary term. All day long he saw deferential people who owed their jobs to him—his staff, local politicians and planning board members, judges, city commissioners and deputy commissioners. His city car and driver took him to meetings and to dinners at the best restaurants in the city. Civic ceremonies, such as the lighting of the borough Christmas tree on December 12, were structured to make him the centerpiece.

In December Manes attended a round of festive holiday parties hosted by, among others, the *Daily News,* the Board of Elections, Holiswood Hospital, Congressman Gary Ackerman, Councilman Archie Spigner, real estate developer Mike Lazar (who had been elected to the city council in the same election

as Manes in 1965), the law firm of his friend Sid Davidoff, and
Andy Capasso, the president of Nanco Contracting. Capasso's
party was held at SPQR, a garish restaurant in Little Italy
owned by Mafia capo Matty (the Horse) Ianniello.

During this hectic year-end season, Manes also attended
two meetings with Stanley Friedman and Howard Golden, the
Democratic Party leaders of the Bronx and Brooklyn. The
agenda for these summit conferences was the vacant office of
majority leader of the city council. Manes and Friedman had
made a deal to back Peter Vallone of Queens for the job, with
the Bronx getting in return the positions of council finance
chairman and city clerk. Golden resented Brooklyn's exclusion
from the spoils, and would soon make his own pact with the
Manhattan Democrats and wage an aggressive campaign to
install his man, Councilman Sam Horwitz, as the majority
leader. Although under the city charter, the job was to be filled
by a vote of the thirty-five elected members of the city council,
most of the council members in Queens, Brooklyn, and the
Bronx were told how to vote by their county leaders.

On December 17, at 10:00 A.M., Manes gave his upbeat
"State of the County" speech at Borough Hall, which began with
an ironic boast of provincial chauvinism, "I want people everywhere to recognize what we in Queens have known for some
time: Queens is the place where the American Dream is still
alive."

In the same vein, Manes continued: "Personally, 1985 has
been a gratifying year for me. Receiving 85 percent of the vote
and being reelected borough president was enormously satisfy-
ing. But that vote was more than just a vote for me. It was a vote
for Queens. It was a vote for the direction this borough is taking. And I hope it was a vote for the future. . . . During this
holiday season, let us rededicate ourselves to keeping the ideals
of freedom and opportunity alive here in Queens."

Three days later, on December 20, 1985, about 35,000 copies of *Miami/South Florida* came off the presses. The FBI in
Chicago and the justice department in Washington had been
notified that advance copies of this obscure magazine would
start circulating in the city of Miami that afternoon. Its editors
and publishers had postponed running a story by investigative
journalist Gaeton Fonzi for nearly a year.

The story Fonzi had worked on for so long concerned a
man named Burnett. Fonzi thought he was on the trail of a

killer who kept conning the FBI into letting him out of jail in exchange for undertaking secret assignments. In July 1984, Burnett had been working undercover for the Bureau's Chicago office as an employee of Sandow's collection agency. To keep Fonzi from publishing his story and revealing Burnett, assistant U.S. Attorney Vince Connally, at the urging of the FBI, informed him of the sting in progress, and even let Fonzi tape these confidential briefings. While the prosecutors kept buying time, Fonzi kept learning more details of the case: Burnett had been paying off Chicago politicians; he kept promising bigger fish to the federal prosecutors. He taped incriminating conversations with his boss, Bernie Sandow. He recorded tidbits suggesting Sandow was also bribing New York politicians. He let the FBI install a hidden television camera in his office and in his lake-front apartment.

Finally, after waiting nine months, Fonzi and his editors announced they could delay publication no longer. When the U.S. Attorney and the FBI in Chicago realized Fonzi's story was finally going to appear in Florida, a story exposing their unsavory undercover operative, they chose to leak the sting to the Chicago papers. But they would put their own spin on the story to divert attention from Burnett's past, which the Fonzi article exposed in rich detail.

On Christmas Day 1985, both the *Chicago Sun-Times* and the *Tribune* published front-page stories revealing the FBI's sting and possible bribes paid for Chicago collection contracts by Sandow's company. On December 26 both papers made it clear that Burnett was an FBI informer.

A thousand miles away, in New York City, federal prosecutors and FBI agents decided that the time had come to make their move.

At about 2:15 P.M., December 20—the same day the Fonzi story appeared in Florida—49-year-old Bernard Sandow was sitting in his eleventh-floor office at 928 Broadway, in lower Manhattan. He was in a satisfied mood, having just returned from an expensive lunch and several drinks with New York City's deputy director of the Parking Violations Bureau, Geoffrey Lindenauer. The day before Sandow had slipped $3,000 under the table at lunch to Lindenauer's boss, PVB commissioner Lester Shafran, at Johanna's restaurant on East Eighteenth Street.

Everyone seemed to call the magnetic, amoral Sandow "Bernie." He had once posed for a picture dressed up like a 1930s gangster, machine gun in his hand, hat over his eyes, flower in his lapel; but as owner of a successful collection company, Systematic Recovery Service (SRS), he was drawing a $500,000 annual salary, plus an unlimited expense account for travel and entertainment. He had luxury apartments in New York, Chicago, and Miami, and relished life in the fast lane as a gambler, boozer, schmoozer, and lover—with two ex-wives, the last of whom he had beat up and who was suing him. He had reservations on a flight to Miami in a few hours, where a fighter he had an investment in was scheduled to box.

Bernie had come a long way from his days as an only child growing up in the Moshulu Parkway section of the Bronx, where his father owned a candy store on Bainbridge Avenue. When he flunked out of NYU's School of Commerce, he took off for Florida, where he married a wealthy woman when he was just eighteen. The eternal vows were quickly annulled, but Bernie was too worldly to come back to the Bronx and make egg creams with his father.

In 1970, Sandow formed SRS, and by the early 1980s, the company had expanded to 125 employees and had acquired high-class clients such as banks, department stores, and credit card companies. SRS also had a growing number of parking ticket collection contracts with PVB. Bernie was becoming part of the political scene in New York, both as a campaign contributor and through a reputation of being the man to call if a commissioner or politician wanted a "date" or "escort."

Suddenly, at about 2:30, two well-dressed men entered Sandow's office. They did not have an appointment. One was Joe Persichini, an FBI agent working out of New York. The other was Daryl Gencks, an agent assigned to the Bureau's Chicago office. Persichini captured Sandow's attention with an old law enforcement cliché: "This is the most important day of your life."

The two agents informed Sandow that the government had audio and videotape evidence that he had been making payoffs to public officials in New York and Chicago. They said there already was enough evidence to indict him for racketeering under the RICO antiracketeering statute, for mail fraud, and for bribery under the Hobbs Act.

Although shocked and frightened, Sandow had enough

presence of mind to ask the agents if he could take notes and scrawled a few phrases:

> I am not ultimate target. Want my cooperation in
> New York, not Chicago. . . . every phone conversation
> made from here and Chicago . . . videotapes of certain
> of those meetings . . . FBI viewpoint—hell of a case
> against me . . . very large scope . . . I will be indicted.

The agents went on to inform Sandow that they wanted his cooperation, his testimony against the "deputy commissioner, the commissioner, and the borough president," that the government had evidence that he was paying bribes to those three people in New York, that he had been recorded saying, "I'll pay whatever monies I have to pay to get the business." They did not arrest Sandow but made it clear they wanted him to become a secret government informant and wear a concealed microphone against corrupt public officials.

Sandow indicated that he wanted to think things over and get a lawyer. The agents did not pressure him for an immediate decision; they told him that he could fly to Florida for the fight, and that they would be in contact with him or his lawyer after the weekend. They stressed that they would be glad to play a few of the undercover tapes for his lawyer, to help him make up his mind.

The FBI agents had employed some bluff in their conversation with Sandow, for in the hundreds of hours of audio and videotape in their possession, there was actually no hard, legal evidence that Sandow had bribed "the borough president"—Donald Manes. It was a logical deduction, a reasonable inference drawn from the chaotic fragments of colloquial conversation.

The FBI and U.S. Attorney Rudy Giuliani had, in fact, been apprehensive about confronting Sandow at all, fearful that he might run directly to Manes, warn him, and possibly help organize a cover-up. But the FBI and Giuliani had no choice but to take the risk of going overt with Sandow, for the New York operation was just the tail to a giant undercover investigation in Chicago. And the small monthly magazine called *Miami/ South Florida* was about to roll off the printing presses with a story that would almost certainly force the U.S. Attorney in Illinois to terminate a sting in Chicago that would transform New York City's politics, its government, and perhaps its ethics.

After being accurately informed by the FBI that December 20 was the most important day in his life, Sandow spent the next two days in Miami and Fort Lauderdale with his friend Mel Lebetkin. Sandow apparently contacted Lebetkin after the agents left his office and urged Lebetkin to meet him in Florida, where they could talk without fear of bugs, wiretaps, or surveillance. The two men tried to reconstruct the history of the PVB bribery ring. They reminisced. They condemned fate and luck. They sat around Sandow's $200,000 condo and tried to analyze what Sandow should next do.

Lebetkin's trouble matched Sandow's. A Queens Boulevard lawyer who was often seen having lunch with crooked judges, or gangsters trying to pass as businessmen, Lebetkin, too, owned a PVB collection agency that was started with capital from Sandow and was now under federal investigation. But unlike Sandow, who had met Donald Manes only a half-dozen times, Lebetkin was an intimate friend of the borough president.

Both Sandow and Lebetkin had been drawn into the bribery ring by one of the legendary rogues of the boulevard. A bar owner, city marshal, and bail bondsman, Shelly Chevlowe first broached the subject of payoffs with Sandow in late 1980, when the two were riding in Chevlowe's car. Chevlowe told Sandow that if he wanted his PVB contract renewed, he would have to give him monthly cash payments. The only explanation Chevlowe offered was that Donald Manes was a powerful man who frequently talked with PVB's Geoffrey Lindenauer about contracts and the assignments of tickets for collection. Sandow complied with Chevlowe's demands until eighteen months later, when he switched to paying Lindenauer directly.

One day in 1982, Chevlowe had suggested to Lebetkin, who had also been paying him, that they start a second placement collection agency to collect money on unpaid parking tickets. Lebetkin immediately stole the yellow pages from a public phone book in the Queens courthouse and started calling collection agencies to find one that was for sale, even though he knew nothing about the business. He found the Standard Collection Agency, which was located in a rundown storefront, borrowed money from Sandow, and purchased the small, struggling company.

The collection company was purchased through a subterfuge and placed in the names of Lebetkin's and Sandow's girlfriends. The company had five secret partners: Lebetkin, Sandow, the dying Chevlowe, PVB deputy commissioner Geoffrey Lindenauer, and Donald Manes.

Lebetkin's new company—with its secret partners—was awarded its first PVB contract in 1983. Its commissions grew from $59,000 in 1982 to $1,069,000 in 1985, a rate of growth three times faster than that of any other collection agency. Lebetkin, now a big time operator, was able to move his company into the luxury Silver Towers high-rise, the commercial hub of Queens Boulevard, opposite the courthouse.

So Lebetkin must have had a bittersweet laugh when Sandow now asked him to be his lawyer. Lebetkin may have thought he needed a lawyer himself; he couldn't possibly represent his friend in trouble, because he was about to be part of the same trouble.

Instead Lebetkin recommended Ira London, with whom he had served as co-counsel on a case. Lebetkin called London from Florida on Saturday and alerted him that a friend had an urgent problem and might be calling him at his home on Long Island over that weekend. On Sunday Sandow did phone London and asked to retain him.

London remembers that Sandow was "incredibly upset, nervous, and agitated" during their first conversation, and that he advised his new client not to "discuss any details over the telephone because I knew from Mel that the case involved extensive use of tapes." Sandow made an appointment to meet London in his lawyer's office at 189 Montague Street in Brooklyn at 10:00 A.M. on Tuesday, December 24.

When he returned from his Florida weekend with Lebetkin on Monday, December 23, Sandow paid a visit to his office. He had always recorded on an accountant's worksheet a list of the exact amounts of payoffs he had made to city officials, a list he kept locked in the business safe. He now removed these records to his $3,400-a-month apartment on West 55th Street, where he burned them.

By this point Sandow had decided that he was not going to cooperate with the FBI. Fearful that the FBI would come to his office with a search warrant, he destroyed the pay sheets. He was in a fever zone of panic, and perhaps under the stonewalling influence of Lebetkin. Also, Sandow did not yet grasp the extent of the taped evidence against him gathered by Burnett in Chicago.

London and Sandow talked for a long time on December 24 without reaching a decision on what to do. Sandow's main concern seemed to be that if he made a deal with the government his company would not be forfeited, his contracts canceled, or all his assets confiscated. London called a Chicago lawyer he knew to ask what kind of person the U.S. Attorney in Chicago, Vince Connally, was, and was told, "Connally keeps his promises, and you can count on his word."

Ira London was a tough defense lawyer, one who in almost twenty years of practice had never represented a major cooperating witness. He didn't trust federal prosecutors, nor did he "feel comfortable with clients who inform." He had had a law partner who was prosecuted, and another former partner whose phone was tapped because of his closeness to mobsters and crooked cops. Although the federal prosecutors interpreted London's entry into the case as a sign that Sandow might not agree to flip, London reached Connally in Chicago that afternoon and asked for assurance of confidentiality in New York City if Sandow pleaded guilty in Chicago. Connally gave that assurance, but had to call back a few hours later to tell London the whole story was breaking in the Chicago papers that night, and that he had lost control over events.

By the end of the day, London had scheduled a meeting for 1:00 P.M. on Friday, December 27, at the New York offices of the FBI at 26 Federal Plaza. The meeting would include Sandow, London, Vince Connally, who would fly in from Chicago, two FBI supervisors from Chicago, Benito Romano, a top assistant to Rudy Giuliani, and two FBI supervisors from New York.

Until the very moment the bundles of newspapers were cut open by Chicago newsstand dealers, Donald Manes and his bagman, Geoffrey Lindenauer, were busy working. Their labors did not subside out of respect for Christmas, or in deference to personal misfortune.

On the morning of December 23, Lindenauer had had breakfast with lawyer and collection agency owner Mike Dowd at the Blue Bay Diner on Francis Lewis Boulevard in Queens. It was an appointment Lindenauer had to hound Dowd into keeping, for by now Dowd wanted to avoid seeing this fat collector who talked in psychobabble and told everyone how much loyalty he owed Donald Manes. But Dowd came to the reluctant conclusion he could not keep ducking the deputy commissioner who monitored his company's contract with the city government.

Dowd had an office opposite Queens Borough Hall that housed his own parking ticket collection agency, Computrace. Like Sandow, he had paid bribes to his dear friend Shelly Chevlowe to get PVB contracts until Chevlowe went into the hospital to die of cancer. One of the few times Mike Dowd had cried as an adult was at Chevlowe's funeral, at Schwartz Brothers on Queens Boulevard, on May 9, 1983.

After the services Dowd was still lost in sorrow, standing on the sidewalk, when Donald Manes approached him with dry eyes. "Geoff Lindenauer takes Shelly's place," Manes announced, as matter-of-factly as a baseball announcer reporting a pitching change.

For the next year and a half Dowd paid Lindenauer bribes, but fitfully, and with the self-loathing of a former altar boy, until December 1984, when he stopped voluntarily.

In April 1985 Manes invited Dowd to play paddleball with him, and during the game, the gasping, overweight borough president had said: "Maybe we could work something out and you can pay again." On an earlier occasion Dowd had gone directly to Manes's office and angrily informed him that he would no longer pay kickbacks to Lindenauer. Manes said he understood that Dowd "disliked Geoff," and if Dowd preferred, he could have his "partner bring the money over," meaning to Borough Hall.

Dowd just pleaded, "Please don't destroy the company."

By December 1985, Dowd was in a funk about many things in his life. His father was in the hospital awaiting heart surgery for a life-threatening aneurism. In the days before the operation, which was scheduled for December 27, Dowd was trying to reconcile with his father after a long estrangement, not knowing if he would survive the surgery. Dowd himself was recovering from a slipped disc, which he had suffered while reaching for a roll of toilet paper, an absurdity that did not lessen the ache in his back. Dowd was also breaking up with a woman with whom he had had a serious affair, a parting that made him feel like a failure again, since his marriage had ended in divorce. And Dowd feared his business was also about to fail, that Lindenauer and Manes would terminate his contract as soon as it expired in February because he had stopped paying bribes to them. In the midst of his misfortunes, Lindenauer started phoning Dowd again, inviting him to discuss Computrace's "disappointing performance." A judge had granted Dowd a court adjournment because of his father's surgery. But the bagman would tolerate no adjournments.

As Lindenauer and Dowd sat facing each other in the booth of the diner, Lindenauer was not explicit but hinted clearly that his mission was the restoration of the shakedown, to make Dowd start paying again. Dowd responded by setting out on the table the records of his debt collection company; November had been the most productive month of collections yet. But in the practiced code of the bagman, Lindenauer said: "I'm personally disappointed in you."

Dowd replied, "Just do what you gotta do." He felt "raped, violated, impotent" as he left the diner; the meeting left a scar on his memory, not only the impersonal brutality of it but also his own feelings of shame over having once been so "morally inadequate" as to pay $30,000 in bribes.

The next night, Christmas Eve, Lindenauer attended a party at the home of his close friend, the psychiatrist Dr. Jerome Driesen. Bald, twitching, and a chain talker, Driesen drove a Rolls-Royce, wore mink, organized orgies, and was married to a former Miss Ohio. He combined a private practice with work as a psychiatric consultant for sixteen different city agencies. In this role as a city physician he took bribes—either cocaine or cash—to fix disability cases for municipal employees. Driesen also referred private therapy patients to Lindenauer and let Lindenauer run sessions in his East Side office, which was ornamented with a lampstand that was a gold-plated replica of a city parking meter with a bright red VIOLATION signal.

Not surprisingly, Lindenauer had been able to set up Driesen in the collection business, and took payoffs from Driesen's partners or from the doctor himself—after, of course, Driesen had skimmed off his own share. During the party that night, Lindenauer and Driesen slipped into the bedroom, where Driesen handed over an envelope stuffed with cash. The money was a regular payment from another guest at the party, Michael Shaheen, from which Driesen had already removed his 25 percent share.

Lindenauer and his wife drove out to East Hampton, Long Island, on Christmas Day, to spend part of the holiday at the popular Maidstone Inn. New York City almost shut down on the Thursday and Friday after the Wednesday Christmas. Many important people in city government and politics took those days off.

On Thursday, December 26, Lindenauer received two calls at the Maidstone. The first was from Victor Rosen, the director of adjudications at the PVB, who was not involved in the conspiracy. Rosen informed Lindenauer of the Chicago newspapers' reports that the FBI had an undercover agent named Michael Burnett working for Bernie Sandow at SRS.

Lindenauer blinked. Exactly thirty days earlier, on November 26, he had had lunch with Burnett and Sandow. At the start of that lunch, Lindenauer went into the bathroom of Hisae's restaurant and received $5,000 in cash from Sandow.

Lindenauer told Victor Rosen: "There is nothing to worry about. Chicago has nothing to do with us. I'm sure Bernie did nothing wrong."

The next call came from Steve Lipsitz, an attorney for Datacom, a large PVB contractor and a competitor of Sandow's in both New York and Chicago. He told Lindenauer: "As one of your vendors, I feel it is our responsibility to tell you that there was an article in Chicago that said the FBI had an undercover agent working for Mr. Sandow."

On December 26 many phone calls were exchanged between New York and Chicago. Perhaps twenty-five people—individuals at PVB, in the collection companies, and in the Manes orbit of couriers, as well as Bronx Democratic boss Stanley Friedman—must have learned in the course of that day that they were in jeopardy, that a conspiracy kept secret by some of them for seven years might be revealed, if any one of them talked.

The following afternoon, Vince Connally chaired the meeting between Bernie Sandow, Ira London, and the federal prosecutors. Connally began by showing Sandow and London two undercover videos and playing one audio tape.

At the close of the technological display, Connally leveled Sandow with the information that he faced a RICO indictment that carried a maximum sentence of twenty years and forfeiture of all his assets. He also said there would be bribery and mail fraud counts, and that probably Sandow would have to actually serve between five and ten years in prison on whatever sentence he was given after a trial.

Connally said that he wanted Sandow to plead guilty to

three counts in Chicago, and go to work undercover immediately in New York, where the prosecutors felt they had only a week or two before the entire story of the scandal got into the newspapers.

Sandow stated his own concerns: he didn't want to forfeit SRS or give up the existing contracts with the city government of New York. Nor did he want Datacom and Joe Delario to "walk," and inherit the whole market for parking ticket collections. Sandow was still a competitive businessman.

Shortly before 2:00 P.M. the meeting broke for lunch. Sandow and London wanted to go for a walk, eat alone, and make their decision on Connally's offer.

Bernie Sandow decided to cooperate with the government.

The lawyer who had never had a cooperating witness before and the client who had dressed in his fantasy as a machine-gun gangster committed themselves to candor. Their deal meant that Sandow could hold nothing back from the government. It meant he could not protect Lebetkin, even if Lebetkin was his friend and had sent him to London. If he cooperated, he had to go all the way, London told Sandow.

At about 3:00 P.M., Sandow and London informed Connally, Romano, and the others they had a deal. The stories in the Chicago papers and the three undercover tapes played for him convinced Sandow he was caught cold. He told Ira London that although he had destroyed the pay sheets of his bribes, he still had his diaries with notations that could help him reconstruct his payments to public officials and the formulas by which they were computed. Sandow would plead guilty to three five-year counts in Chicago, and cooperate with the prosecutors in exchange for a more lenient sentence. The issues of forfeiture and salvaging SRS, existing contracts, assets, and tax consequences were left vague and deferred.

Time was so short that at about 3:30 that same Friday afternoon, FBI agents Joe Persichini and Ron Jaco started to debrief Sandow, as Connally left for the airport and Romano went back across the street to report to Giuliani on the meeting. Though he had flunked out of college, Sandow proved to have a splendid memory from his years as a gambler and sports nut and from juggling percentage payments to so many public officials. His first narration of the PVB story was precise, coherent, and credible. Sandow told the agents he had started paying Shelly Chevlowe a 2½ percent kickback in cash for his PVB contracts in 1981. Chevlowe eventually told Sandow to make his payments directly to Geoffrey Lindenauer, and Sandow began meeting Lindenauer every two weeks, mostly in restaurants, and paying the kickback either in the men's room or by passing an envelope under the table. During 1983 and 1984, Sandow received more collection work from PVB, a boon that caused his kickback rate to nearly double. For the past two years Sandow had been paying Lindenauer $5,000 in cash every two weeks, $120,000 a year. He estimated that he had paid PVB's deputy director $250,000 to $300,000 in cash since 1981, and additional thousands to the director, Lester Shafran.

Sandow told his inquisitors that Lindenauer had repeatedly implied that he was sharing the money with Donald Manes. Once, Lindenauer recalled, Manes had described Sandow as a "stand-up guy" who met his commitments. And in late 1985, when Lester Shafran had indicated that he wanted to leave PVB, it was Lindenauer who conspired with Sandow to keep him there. Lindenauer had told Sandow that Manes wanted Sandow to begin $5,000-a-month bribe payments to Shafran, and to take the payments out of the money ordinarily paid to Lindenauer and Manes. Though Sandow willingly implicated Lindenauer, Shafran, and Manes, he denied any criminal relationship with his old friend and legal referral agent Lebetkin.

To the FBI, Sandow's account of these conversations had the ring of truth. Their taped conversations with Sandow over the years had contained numerous references to Manes, including plans by the collection companies to create a million-dollar slush fund to finance a Manes campaign to become mayor of New York. The FBI tapes revealed attempts by Sandow to steer Manes, whose addiction to sex was well known, into an orgy where the borough president and Sandow would "have a chance to fuck together and seal up the whole situation." Sandow had explained that Chevlowe and Manes had "fucked together," describing it almost as a bonding ritual that tied someone irrevocably to Manes. Sandow had also talked about cutting Manes in on an Illinois coal venture, bogus real estate deals, and offshore bank accounts. Saying that Manes was "sitting on a pile of money," Sandow had predicted on an FBI tape: "When Koch's term is up in four years, Manes is going to run."

A few days later, when agents Jaco and Persichini wrote an official investigation memo about Sandow's debriefing, they repeatedly misspelled the borough president's name as "Manis"; they didn't really know much about him yet.

Sometime on December 25 or 26, Donald Manes learned about the PVB investigation. It is likely that his source was his secret partner, Mel Lebetkin, who probably alerted him after his Florida weekend with Sandow. The information was sufficient to make the guilty conscience and fragile psyche of Donald Manes unravel and, in effect, begin a kind of nervous breakdown.

On December 26, Donald Manes's intimate friend, attorney Sid Davidoff, read the Chicago papers and learned of Burnett's role in the SRS sting. Davidoff had clients and friends active in Chicago politics, and he called them for an assessment. They told him it was big, that it might go to the mayor of Chicago. Davidoff had figured out by himself that the probe would probably focus on collection contracts for unpaid parking tickets. Aware that the two top jobs in PVB in New York belonged to patronage appointees of Donald Manes (Davidoff, in fact, had been acquainted with Lester Shafran for twenty years, and knew Lindenauer as someone who was always hanging around Manes, nicknaming him "Ditto" after the yes man in the novel *The Last Hurrah*), Davidoff put two and two together faster than any investigative reporter in New York.

Davidoff called Manes and announced he was coming over to his house on Friday night, December 27. Though Davidoff had the "impression" he was the first person to discuss the investigation with Manes, Manes had already reached Lindenauer in East Hampton during the day. He warned Lindenauer, "I don't want you to talk to anybody, absolutely nobody," and then made a plan to meet him the next night in Southampton, Long Island, where they could have a discussion without using the telephone.

Davidoff and Manes talked in the Manes home in the Jamaica Estates section of Queens that Friday night for several hours. Although Davidoff lifts weights and talks like a truck driver, he is a savvy lawyer. In 1972, when he worked in the Lindsay administration, he was memorialized in Richard Nixon's enemies list as "a first class SOB, wheeler-dealer, and suspected bagman."

"Donald was already a little out of it," Davidoff recalls of their meeting. "He was withdrawn into himself. He didn't react much, or respond. He wasn't himself."

On the basis of what he heard from his Chicago contacts, and the sudden remoteness of his friend, Davidoff decided that night that he would become Manes's lawyer, perhaps to protect their conversations with the lawyer-client privilege. Davidoff is not a criminal attorney but a commercial lawyer and political dealmaker, whose expertise was in government access. For example, he represented Warner-Amex when Manes decided that Warner-Amex would win the best part of the Queens cable television franchise. Davidoff was also the lawyer for the company that wanted to build a Grand Prix auto racetrack in Flushing Meadows. Manes had backed the project over the objections of most Queens community and civic groups, and the scheme still seemed likely to go forward at the close of 1985. Even as he was being sworn in for a new term, Manes was freely telling friends that he might not finish it, and if not, he would become a partner in Davidoff's law firm.

Sometime in that first Manes-Davidoff conversation the idea was born that Lindenauer should be steered to Harold Borg as his attorney. Borg, who had been a friend of Davidoff's for twenty years, was a criminal lawyer of the old school whose clients never cooperated. Presumedly, Manes thought Borg would be the ideal lawyer for this assignment because he believed Borg's loyalties would be with the conspirators.

The following night, Manes and Lindenauer finally saw each other face-to-face in Southampton, where they went to a movie theater that showed several films at the same time. The two wives—Marlene and Nancy—were sent to one movie, while Manes and Lindenauer said they would go to a different one. Instead, these two frightened, overweight, middle-aged men reviewed their fate.

"Are you aware of what's going on in Chicago?" Manes asked.

"I did have one meeting with Mike Burnett," Lindenauer remembered, the meeting in which he'd taken $5,000 in the men's room.

"I thought I told you not to talk to anybody," Manes said.

"I told you I was going to have the meeting," Lindenauer reminded him.

"I don't remember. Do you know if he was wired?"

"I don't know," Lindenauer answered.

"Look, this is very, very serious," Manes said. "I'm going to give you the name of a lawyer, and I want you to call this lawyer. If, God forbid, anybody contacts you, you contact this lawyer . . . Harold Borg. Sid Davidoff knows him very well. You and I can't talk directly. So you'll talk to the lawyer, and the lawyer will talk to Sid, and Sid will talk to me."

Lindenauer, the follower in this relationship, the failure who always attached himself to strong father-figures, tried to calm down the panicking Manes with some forced optimism.

"Nothing has really happened yet," Lindenauer pointed out. "I don't know whether we are in as much trouble as you think we are."

Manes blurted: "I don't want you to go out and collect any more money."

"I'm not about to," the collector replied.

Manes and Lindenauer met again the next afternoon, Sunday, in the living room of the Manes family home in Queens. Manes's mind seemed to be unraveling, and in their conversation he suggested that Lindenauer had three ways out—a fugitive's exile, suicide, or taking the heat.

"Are you going to run?" Manes asked abruptly. "Are you going to leave town?"

"What are you talking about?" Lindenauer responded. "Nothing has happened," and then added: "Where would I go? I don't have any money. I just wouldn't do it."

Looking at his friend, Manes said: "If this had happened to Shelly [Chevlowe], Shelly would go like this," and making the shape of a gun with his right hand, pointed it at his head and pulled the trigger finger.

Shaken, Lindenauer repeated, "Donald, nothing has happened yet. God forbid anything happens, I would not turn you in."

"You don't know what you're talking about," Manes said. "You're talking about the FBI, and you're talking about twenty-five years."

Lindenauer replied from his own fantasy realm. "Listen, Gordon Liddy was caught, and he wrote a book, and he made a lot of money. God forbid, if I got caught, I'd write a book, and make money. But I wouldn't give you up."

Then these two tormented souls, feeling their lives falling apart, hugged each other, each with tears in his eyes, clinging to a lie. "Thank you," Manes sobbed, and Lindenauer left.

But the implicit Manes suggestion that Lindenauer kill himself was a betrayal of a pact between the two, both of whose fathers had committed suicide. Lindenauer's father, a criminal attorney with a Manhattan practice, had hanged himself in disgrace after he was convicted of bribing a police officer in a heroin case. These two men, who so often engaged in an almost therapeutic dialogue, with Lindenauer listening endlessly to Manes's "feelings," had promised each other for years that they would never do to their children what their fathers had done to them.

On Monday, December 30, Manes walked through his public schedule of meetings and dealt with the normal load of phone calls. He met with Stanley Friedman on East 68th Street in Manhattan ostensibly to count votes and plan strategy on how to make Peter Vallone the council's majority leader. Vallone's election had to seem meaningless as he meditated on the specter of indictment, prison, disgrace, the loss of all status, the loss of the approval of others that faced him, his wife, and his children.

Manes had always depended upon the external validation of strangers to feel whole, and now he was going to lose that support. He had always contrived to have people around him to avoid being alone, and now he was going to lose the lonely crowd of backslappers. Manes needed respect, and now he could foresee only humiliation. Since the suicide of his father, Manes feared abandonment, and now he anticipated abandonment by everyone.

Manes's mention of suicide to Lindenauer may have been only the projection of his own unthinkable option, but it did have an impact on Lindenauer. On Monday, December 30, Lindenauer visited the office of Jerome Driesen, the psychiatrist. He asked his friend:

"If a person wanted to commit suicide, and did not want it to be recognized as suicide, could you first take a pill, so that it appeared to be a heart attack?"

"What the hell is going on?" Driesen asked.

Lindenauer explained that he feared the FBI was about to arrest him. He said he was thinking of killing himself but that he wanted to spare his wife and children the trauma he had suffered when his own father died.

Driesen said that pills did exist that could disguise a suicide as a coronary, "but if I gave you these kinds of pills the police would find out."

Lindenauer explained the quandary to Driesen. "Donald said that I had two choices. I could stand up and take the heat. Or I could kill myself."

"You have other choices," Driesen said.

"Forget about talking, because they would put a contract out on me." Presumably, "they" meant Manes and/or Friedman. Lindenauer knew they both had friends and contacts in organized crime.

"Well, there is another choice," Driesen said. "You can run. I can contact an attorney and get the names of places where there is no extradition."

"I don't have any money," Lindenauer explained. "I've got two houses, two mortgages, and a son in medical school."

Driesen, a comrade collector for Manes, was incredulous: "What do you mean, you don't have the money?"

"I don't," Lindenauer said. "The big money hasn't come through yet. The other money hasn't been coming through for a period of time. [Probably a reference to Dowd's terminated payments.] I spent it. I have a couple of thousand dollars, but I really don't have the money."

Driesen then came up with a better solution than suicide—extortion hush money. "So you go to Donald. You go to Stanley [Friedman]. And you tell you're going to take off, and you need $400,000."

Lindenauer left Driesen's office even more perplexed by the alternatives facing him, and was surprised when Manes called him at the PVB offices later in the day, in light of his insistence on avoiding the telephone. The call was probably another sign of Manes's desperate and disoriented mental condition. During this conversation Lindenauer apparently made a request for a large sum of money so he could "run away," and the two men agreed to meet on the street in front of Stanley Friedman's law office at 49 East 68th Street at 3:00 the next afternoon.

That same day, Lindenauer went to a pay phone and called Driesen back for more crisis counseling.

"I have a $1,000 gift certificate from Crazy Eddie [the video supply store] that Bernie Sandow gave to me," Lindenauer said. "What should I do with it? It's in my house. I'm afraid the FBI is going to break in."

The psychiatrist offered direct, practical advice. "Tear it up," he said. "Flush it down the toilet bowl."

On December 31, Donald Manes somehow managed to collect $58,000 in cash. He could have had the money hidden in his house—much like Lindenauer, who stashed his bribes in his own home, afraid of creating the paper trail of a bank account or a safe-deposit box. Matthew Troy, Manes's predecessor as Queens party boss, told us Manes once gave him a handful of cash pulled from a drawer in his home. This incident occurred in 1976, after Troy came out of jail and asked for a job. Instead, Manes gave him money to help him out. But Manes could also have obtained the cash from any one of a dozen accomplices of his, and Manes's office phone logs for December 30 and 31 had messages from Lester Shafran, Anthony Ameruso, and Stanley Friedman.

Manes's diary for December 31 listed a 12:30 appointment at "Stanley Friedman's office, with Councilman Vallone." Vallone swears he did not attend the meeting, and says an important bill-signing ceremony at City Hall had forced its cancellation. Although canceled meetings were normally crossed out in Manes's diary, this one was not, so that it would appear that Manes and Friedman met alone as co-conspirators at 12:30. One Friedman confidant who was also a PVB contractor, Marvin Kaplan, told a reporter that Manes sought hush money from Friedman during this meeting, and that Friedman flatly rejected it. In any event, from some source, on short notice, Donald Manes put $58,000 in cash into a large envelope.

At 3:00 P.M., Manes headed for his rendezvous with Lindenauer. As he was crossing 68th Street, the driver of a car asked him where Roy Cohn's office was. (Cohn was Friedman's law partner.) Manes assumed the passing motorist was an FBI agent and became even more frantic.

"Were you followed?" he asked Lindenauer. He was extremely tense and erratic, more so than he had been in his two earlier meetings.

"How the hell do I know if I was followed?"

Manes was too jumpy to talk to Lindenauer, still believing they were being followed and photographed by the FBI, and began walking around in circles, looking over his shoulder.

"We can't talk now," Manes said. "I gotta talk to Friedman. I'll meet you at five o'clock in front of Jerry's office." (Driesen's psychiatric office was on East 82d Street, fourteen blocks to the north.)

When they reconvened at 5:00 P.M., it was already dark, the beginning of New Year's Eve. Lindenauer now told Manes he needed $400,000, from him and Friedman, to run away, just as Driesen had prompted him to say.

"Are you nuts?" Manes replied.

They began walking aimlessly. Several times Manes started

to hand Lindenauer the envelope with the cash, and each time pulled it back, still worried he was being observed.

"Let's go in the car," Manes said, and as they started driving north on Park Avenue, Manes finally relinquished the envelope.

Manes and Lindenauer then engaged in an absurd exchange whose dialogue could have served as a parody of the 1950s film *Marty*.

MANES: Do you want me to go home with you?
LINDENAUER: That's up to you.
MANES: Are there fingerprints on the envelope?
LINDENAUER: I don't know.
MANES: Do you want me to go home with you?
LINDENAUER: If you want to. You don't have to.
MANES: Okay. You can go home alone.

As he prepared to get out of the car, Manes asked again when his friend was going to leave the country. Lindenauer promised he would flee on Saturday, after his son went back to school.

The first thing Lindenauer did when he got home to Queens was hide the $58,000 in his basement, in the same place he had concealed the bribe he had collected on Christmas Eve. Manes pulled himself together and with his wife dropped by a New Year's Eve party at the home of Judge Geraldine Eiber and her husband Bruce. Six or seven judges were present, and they all thought that Manes was behaving strangely.

Appellate Judge Richard Brown, a Manes friend and colleague for more than fifteen years, saw rivulets of sweat roll down Manes's face, heard his voice sounding hoarse and strained, noticed Manes could not concentrate on a conversation, that he had almost no attention span.

But like most of the party guests that night, Brown attributed Manes's odd behavior to the tension of the power struggle over Vallone's election, or possibly to a side-effect from the liquid diet Manes was on to lose weight, or even to the polyp Manes had had removed the month before. Never could this respected judge imagine that Donald Manes was disintegrating under the fear that he would soon be exposed as a lawbreaker.

On New Year's Eve Barbara Ross was working alone at her desk in the almost deserted *Daily News* city room until 11:00 P.M. A versatile reporter in her thirties who had done investigative projects and covered transportation and politics, Ross had recently joined the *News* after years on the *New York Post*. While Manes was paying Lindenauer the money to run away with, as Lindenauer was concealing the hush money in his basement, Barbara Ross sat reading in the empty, well-lighted modern city room and then color-coding the most relevant portions of a riveting document: the typed transcript of the government's briefings of Gaeton Fonzi in Florida, about Burnett's undercover work in Chicago.

Fonzi knew the editor of the *Daily News*, Gil Spencer, and the two journalists admired each other's work. When the Burnett story exploded in the Chicago papers, Fonzi called Spencer, knowing there would be a New York angle to the story. Spencer hired Fonzi as a special consultant and flew him up to New York on December 29.

A team was put together to work on two separate stories—Burnett's criminal past and the corruption of powerful officials in New York. *News* city editor Arthur Browne, who had a law degree and prizes for his own investigative journalism, assigned Washington columnist Lars Nelson, Brian Kates, and Barbara Ross to work with Fonzi in secrecy.

On New Year's Eve Barbara Ross had no idea of the dimensions of the potential New York scandal, and certainly no clue as to which public officials might be involved. As she struggled through the preliminary stages of assembling a puzzle, her eyes went back over page three of Fonzi's August 1985 transcript, and her yellow marker started to work furiously under these words from Fonzi's law enforcement sources:

> . . . There was some thought that something the president [Sandow] has articulated on tape to Burnett that he has been paying fairly important New York officials for the towing . . . and not just towing, but the collection business that covers a variety of things involving cars in New York . . . the New York United States Attorney's office has expressed a great deal of interest. . . . or at the least, the president of the company [Sandow] could be convinced to turn around and help them make cases on their public officials.
>
> And these are people who are fairly significant within the departments that have something to do with

the collection of parking fees. They are not names that would ordinarily be known to you or me, or anybody else out of New York City . . . but that includes, from what the NYUSA [Giuliani] tells me . . . significant people who are in responsible political positions, in the sense that they are among the decision-makers and people higher-up in the hierarchy of politics, and people that they've been interested in taking a look at for a long time because they hear independently that these guys are corruptible.

Barbara Ross returned to her desk on New Year's Day, rereading and color-coding more of the transcripts—and developing a hunch who the person "in the hierarchy of politics" might be who had influence over "the collection of parking fees." She remembered that when she had worked on the *Post*, Stanley Friedman would call the paper with inside information and tip off reporters when any candidate he opposed was a scofflaw with unpaid parking tickets. She recalled that Friedman had been implicated in a ticket-fixing scandal in PVB in the early 1970s, that Friedman had recently made Elbert Hinkson a state judge, and that Hinkson had once had a top job in PVB. She also regarded Friedman as someone who was corruptible.

On Thursday, January 2, Arthur Browne asked Ross to call U.S. Attorney Giuliani for a statement, something the paper could use about PVB. Ross couldn't get through to Giuliani, but she did reach his assistant, Benito Romano, who was directing the still-covert investigation in New York.

"I'd like to talk to you about Michael Burnett and PVB," Ross told him.

"Oh, shit. I'm getting sick," the assistant U.S. Attorney responded, and as he hung up the phone, a panic-stricken Romano said, "I can't talk to you."

Ten minutes later Rudy Giuliani called Arthur Browne. Giuliani knew Browne, and he understood the inner workings of the press. His wife was a television journalist, and in his private practice, he had been an attorney for the *Daily News*, the *Wall Street Journal*, and *Barron's*. He knew all about the First Amendment, the shield law, prior restraint, deep backgrounders, the delicate bond of trust between source and journalist, and the competitiveness on big stories.

"We've got a problem here," Giuliani told Browne. "You're going to mess up a major undercover investigation if you go with a story on PVB. Please come see me tomorrow morning and we'll talk it through."

At 10:00 A.M. on Friday, January 3, Browne and Ross sat down on a couch in the office of Dennison Young, Giuliani's liaison with the press. Giuliani and Romano were also in attendance, although more anxious than the journalists. Sandow was working undercover for them and by now had already recorded one meeting with Lester Shafran. Sandow was trying to arrange meetings with Lindenauer and Joe Delario of Datacom; and Giuliani, with his quarry in sight, was desperate to prevent the *News* from publishing.

Barbara Ross had the Fonzi transcript on her lap and began the meeting by reading aloud the portions that pointed to high-level corruption in New York City contracts. Arthur Browne stated that the *News* could publish a story the next day, based just on the material that Ross was quoting. Giuliani and Romano, however, didn't recognize the document—to Romano, "It looked like some sort of computer printout"—and when Romano asked what it was, Browne refused to tell him.

Giuliani urged, "Please don't print anything for a week," and explained that he and the FBI were conducting a sting and that any story would alert the targets and "help crooked politicians escape accountability."

The meeting had evolved into a cat-and-mouse chase of questions and bluffing. Browne said he wanted to publish a story in the paper of the following Sunday, January 5. Giuliani asked for more time. Browne then started to play an elimination game on who the major targets of the sting might be.

"It's not the mayor or the city council president," Giuliani volunteered.

"Is it the comptroller?"

"No."

"What about the borough presidents?"

"We can't comment."

Eventually, an understanding was worked out. The *News* would hold up the PVB story on a day-to-day basis. If any competing paper got on to it, however, Giuliani promised to call Browne and release him from his holding pattern. Giuliani felt he had gained a few days, without having disclosed any names. Browne felt he could go forward with a major background piece on Burnett, and that no competitor could scoop him on PVB. Unlike Fonzi, Browne was concerned about corruption in

New York, and he was trying to balance the obligations of citizenship and editorship.

Several times a day for the next five days, Browne and Ross called Giuliani's office and asked, in effect, "Did you catch anybody yet?" Each time the answer was no.

Meanwhile, on January 7, the *News* devoted its front page and five inside pages to an exposé of Michael Burnett that perplexed the city. Few people understood the rationale of giving so much space to attacking an FBI operative whom no one had heard of.

On January 9, Rudy Giuliani kept his promise to Arthur Browne. He telephoned Browne and told him that a reporter on the *Post* had called him, asking questions about Michael Burnett and a sting aimed at PVB. Giuliani released him to publish whatever story his staff could put together, disappointed that the Sandow sting had not been more productive. The conversations he recorded were guarded—everyone had already grown suspicious—and Sandow never was able to arrange a meeting with Lindenauer. Giuliani was now prepared to go overt, subpoena records, convene a grand jury, shake the trees, and see what happened.

As Barbara Ross began to work on her story, the first person she decided to interview was Lester Shafran, the PVB commissioner. To prepare herself she had a copyboy bring her the *Daily News* file on Shafran, to better understand his background. The clips were barren of clues as to who Shafran really was, but, like a bottle washed ashore with a message, there was a note in the file written by the late Joe Martin, a Pulitzer Prize winner from another era. Martin was a perfectionist who did all the drudge work (such as write notes to the files in the morgue) that some future young reporter might find useful against a deadline. The page Barbara Ross found was part of a never-printed story dated March 1976 that placed Shafran in the context of the Queens clubhouse:

> Active in Queens' Democratic politics, was assistant counsel in 1968 to State Senator Majority Leader Joseph Zaretski, and was Queens' assistant district attorney for two years ending in 1971. He was Mike Lazar's assistant general counsel with the Taxi Commission and moved to Transportation with him in 1974. A regular Queens Democrat. . . .

The note to the file did more to give texture to Shafran than all the published clips based on press releases and photo ops of pseudo-events.

When Ross got Shafran on the phone she told him she was doing a feature article on Koch administration officials who were leaving for the private sector. Shafran went right into his packaged pitch on how much he had "improved PVB's management and collections" during his tenure as commissioner.

In her way, Ross was a better undercover than Sandow. She asked a series of innocent questions, and Shafran gave answers that were a cram course in PVB's complex operations. When Ross asked, for example, how companies were chosen for PVB collection work, Shafran assured her, "It's strictly a merit system. Those vendors who have the best performance in collecting unpaid tickets get the biggest contracts. We have a tamper-proof mathematical formula."

Ross then eased the interview into the credentials of one particular PVB vendor—Bernard Sandow, whom Shafran gave high marks: "He's professional."

By late in the afternoon of Thursday, January 9, Barbara Ross started writing the first draft of her story about a major federal investigation into contract bribery at PVB, with the assurance of her editor that it would run in the widely read Sunday paper.

During the first week of January, as the *News* was poised to publish and Sandow walked around with a wire, Donald Manes slipped deeper into depression and breakdown. The vote for the new council leader was set for January 8, and he tried to function as one of Vallone's generals in the battle, but he just couldn't.

On January 2, Roger Starr of the *New York Times* editorial board spoke to Manes by phone. Starr was composing an editorial, which was published on January 4, that endorsed Vallone. "Manes didn't seem to care," Starr says of their conversation. "I had expected him to make a forceful case for Vallone, but he didn't give a damn. He didn't respond at all. He gave one- or two-word answers. It was as if I was dragging him back from a distant place. It was as if he were somewhere else."

All those whom Manes met with that week about the vote, including Vallone himself, Council President Andrew Stein, and publicist Marty McLaughlin, got the sense Manes was "sick" or "in outer space." The task of lining up the two deciding votes fell to Stanley Friedman and McLaughlin, who had worked for Friedman and Councilman Robert Dryfoos. Friedman himself had apparently faced down whatever demons lurked in his mind. He enjoyed political combat, which set his adrenaline pumping. He focused on the parliamentary rules, on how to appeal a procedural ruling by the chair. He put pressure on Andrew Stein to vote for Vallone in case there was a tie vote. He smoked cigars and gave cocky interviews to reporters. And he got commitments from the two swing votes—Manhattan councilman Robert Dryfoos and black Bronx maverick, the Reverend Wendell Foster. Friedman functioned at the top of his game as a political boss.

At noon on January 7, 1986, in the overflowing lobby of Queens Borough Hall, Donald Manes was inaugurated for his fifth term as Queens borough president. Mayor Koch was there to administer his oath of office, and a crowd of about four hundred people, mostly from Queens, was there to share Donny's joy.

But Manes could barely function. When Peter Vallone arrived at Borough Hall, he saw Donald Manes "with his whole hand in his mouth, not his fingernails, his whole fist . . . he looked ill." On that morning Burnett's picture had appeared on the front page of the *News,* and by now Manes knew that Lindenauer had not hired Harold Borg and had not fled the country. The day before, in some act of terminal desperation, he had called Lindenauer at PVB and asked him to meet with him and Stanley Friedman. Lindenauer, who had retained Irving Seidman as his lawyer on January 4, told Manes he didn't think such a meeting would be wise. He did, however, come to Manes's swearing-in, where the two old friends had their final conversation.

"Are you going to run away?" Manes asked in a voice so scratchy he sounded as if he had laryngitis.

"Yes," Lindenauer lied. "This weekend."

The mayor, wearing a carnation in his lapel, flattered Manes extravagantly, as was his public habit, before asking him to repeat the oath of office. Manes apologized for his inaudible voice and raced through a prepared text, in which he managed to say:

"As I take this oath, we all share a special feeling of accomplishment and a deep desire to finish what we have started.

While the words of the oath of office, and my commitment to them, have not changed since I was first sworn in as a city councilman in 1965, the condition and position of Queens certainly has."

The next afternoon, the entire Queens, Bronx, and Staten Island delegations followed the discipline of their county leaders and elected Peter Vallone as majority leader by one vote, eighteen to seventeen. Every councilman from Brooklyn and Manhattan voted for Sam Horwitz, with the lone exception of Robert Dryfoos, who only an hour before the vote had pledged his loyalty to Horwitz in a meeting with all his Manhattan colleagues. Councilman Foster of the Bronx, the eccentric critic of Friedman's, voted the way Friedman had asked him, and like Dryfoos, was given the committee chairmanship he wanted.

The next morning, *Newsday* reported:

> Vallone's triumph signaled a shift in power to a group led by Queens, which with nine members, is the largest part of the coalition that elevated Vallone. "It will do some good for the prestige of the county," Manes said as he held court after the vote and accepted congratulations from scores of other politicians and power brokers.

We happened to be standing next to Manes during the roll call, in the rear of the council chamber. His face was blank, and when we congratulated him on his victory, his hand was wet and limp.

After the vote a spontaneous victory celebration was held in Vallone's office. But Manes vanished, slipping out of City Hall after what was perceived to be a significant personal and political triumph for him. During the party Vallone kept asking, "Where's Donald?" He missed Manes so much that he called the borough president's office to find him and thank him. But Manes was not there.

Late that night a euphoric Sid Davidoff reached Manes by phone at home from Florida where he was combining work, leisure, and a visit with his mother. He had been trying to reach Manes since that morning, when he heard that Vallone had been elected. Davidoff was jubilant, not just for Manes but for Vallone as well, and was surprised to find Manes "distant, remote, strange, very tired." Manes had just been sworn in for a new term, and he had just put his man in as majority leader, and yet he was so depressed that he couldn't communicate with his closest confidant and lawyer. Davidoff was troubled, but a thousand miles away.

Thursday, January 9, looked like a routine day on the Manes calendar. He spent the morning at City Hall, primarily at a meeting of the Board of Estimate, during which he lobbied for a smaller homeless shelter to be located on Borden Avenue in Queens. The Human Resources Administration wanted a facility with 475 beds, while Manes wanted less than 200; by the end of the day the matter was compromised at 275 beds.

At three different times Manes poked his head into the new majority leader's office, and each time Vallone was busy or on the phone accepting congratulatory messages. On the fourth attempt Vallone jumped up, invited Manes in, and made him sit down.

Manes was sweating profusely; his armpits and shirt collar were wet. Vallone remembers: "I asked him to please take it easy and relax for a minute. I gave him a cup of coffee."

"I just wanted to see you sitting behind that desk," Manes said.

"Is everything all right?" Vallone asked, and recalls thinking at the time that Manes was going to tell him he was dying of throat cancer.

"Yes," Manes assured him.

At about 1:00 P.M. Manes made a strange call to Sid Davidoff in Florida. While the two busy men spoke several times a week by phone, their conversations almost always had some business to transact, some goal, project, or decision that needed to be discussed. But now Manes began to chat in an aimless fashion, asking in a weak voice, "What's going on? What's happening?"

The blunt, goal-oriented Davidoff was mystified by the call but assumed it was another symptom of Manes's succumbing to pressure.

At about 2:00 P.M., Manes left City Hall and asked his driver, Martin Gans, to take him first home and then back to Queens Borough Hall. It was highly irregular for him to return to his house in the middle of the day. Manes remained in the solitude of his empty home for about fifteen minutes while his driver waited behind the wheel of the Chrysler limousine with BQ 1 license plates. Telephone company records show that Manes did not place any local or long-distance calls during this period, and though Manes told his driver the reason for the stop

was "to pick up some papers," the purpose of the detour remains a mystery.

By the time Manes returned to his office, he was acting like
a man who had an appointment to keep, even though no meeting was listed on his public or private calendar and his wife was
expecting him home. Manes instructed his secretary, Renee
Shepard, to locate a backup car, a dark blue Ford LTD, indicating that he intended to use it that evening. The Ford, an anonymous car that would be less easily recognized, did not have
either the BQ 1, 2, or 3 license plates or a car phone.

At about 4:15, Manes spoke with Manny Behar, a member
of his staff for the past four years, who was coordinating a wine
and cheese reception that afternoon that Manes was hosting for
Dr. Moshe Yager, the new consul general of Israel. Manes asked
Behar when the reception was expected to end, and Behar told
him about seven o'clock.

"I'll have to leave before that. I have a meeting," Manes
said.

At about the same time, Barbara Ross was at her computer
terminal in the city room of the *News,* starting to write the first
draft of her story on PVB.

And at about the same time Barbara Ross was composing
at her terminal, Bernard Sandow was having a miniature microphone taped to the small of his back by two FBI agents. That
evening Sandow was going to have dinner at the Press Box
restaurant on East 45th Street with Bernard Sennett, co-owner
of the collection company Sennett and Krumholz. Sennett
would make admissions on tape that night confirming the PVB
conspiracy.

As City Councilman Morton Povman watched Manes at the
reception, he could recognize Manes was in distress. "His body
language was agitated," Povman noticed. "He was twitching
and sweating and squinting. And he sneaked out before it was
over. Almost always at public events, Manes would let you
know when he was leaving. This time he just left."

Like Povman, State Senator Emanuel Gold could see that
Manes was in serious trouble during the reception.

"His shirt was hanging out over his stomach," Gold says.
"Sweat was pouring down his face and neck. His voice was
cracking. And he kept on talking. I started to give him hand
signals to cut it short, but he ignored me. I finally walked up
behind him and told him to 'Shut up, already.' He leaned over,
smiled at me, and kept right on talking."

Despite his extreme emotional state, Manes was able to make a few jokes as he spoke, the kind of one-liners that helped make him so well liked by acquaintances in the political subculture. He had introduced the reception's guest of honor as "not only a diplomat, but . . . also a substantial scholar." After a practiced stage pause, Manes lifted his eyebrow, smiled, and quipped, "As is your borough president."

Noticing that his voice was cracking, an aide slipped Manes a glass of iced white wine. He took a sip and said, "This is the kind of water I like."

At about 6:40 P.M. Manes and his executive assistant Alan Gershuny left the reception together, while it was still in progress. Gershuny got into his car, which was parked next to the blue Ford LTD, and Manes walked across Queens Boulevard to a public pay phone between an OTB betting parlor and an electronics shop. The borough president, probably wary of using his office or car phones, spoke to somebody briefly, and then went into the adjacent candy store at 120-72 Queens Boulevard, where he purchased a pack of Kent king-size cigarettes and paid for it with a twenty-dollar bill. Donald Manes did not smoke.

Manes then walked back across the Boulevard and told his driver, Marty Gans, an active member of Povman's club, that he was dismissed for the night, that he would take the blue Ford LTD himself. Gans started to drive the limo back to its parking spot at Fresh Meadows, and was directly behind Manes in the Ford. Both cars stopped for a traffic light at Queens Boulevard and Union Turnpike, and both cars made a right turn. After two-tenths of a mile, as Gans veered off to the left for the Van Wyck Expressway he could see Manes driving east on the Grand Central Parkway's service road.

At 1:45 A.M., highway patrol officers Thomas Ievolella and Joseph Byrne, assigned to the Highway 3 Unit, were on routine patrol, driving eastbound on the Grand Central Parkway. They noticed a car weaving unpredictably across all four lanes, as if its driver were drunk. The two officers switched on their siren and lights and tried to force the car over to the side of the road. The driver pulled over at the next exit, 126th Street and Northern Boulevard, near Shea Stadium and not far from La Guardia Airport.

Officers Ievolella and Byrne approached the car in the dark. The driver seemed to be fumbling for his wallet. But because the car had not been put in park, it bolted forward, coming to a stop against a wire fence that runs parallel to the exit ramp. Instead of rolling down the window, the dazed driver opened the car door to hand the police officers his wallet. It was then that Ievolella and Byrne saw the blood.

There was blood all over the steering wheel, the seat, and the floor, and it filled the pocket on the door where maps are kept. The driver's face was smeared with blood, as was his brown suit, white shirt, blue trenchcoat, and brown loafers. A small amount of tissue was on the floor, near the brake pedal.

The two cops recognized Donald Manes's name on his driver's license, and immediately radioed for an ambulance and a backup unit. "That's Donald Manes," Ievolella shouted into the police radio, rhyming the name with "mains."

The next police officer to arrive at the scene was James Fitzgerald of Highway Unit 3. As he applied a gauze bandage to a deep, straight, Y-shaped cut on Manes's left wrist, he asked, "How did you get cut?"

"I don't know," a groggy Manes replied.

A few moments later Fitzgerald tried again: "How did you get cut?"

"I got cut in front of Borough Hall."

"When?"

"About two hours ago."

By this time a police lieutenant and sergeant had arrived, and perhaps assuming they were dealing with a case of drunk driving by an important politician, they ordered the police radio dispatcher to use "land lines"—meaning telephones—rather than open radio lines, which could be monitored by news-gathering organizations. Using telephones would also prevent the official routine recording of these conversations at police headquarters.

"Oh, they don't want the news media," a sergeant at the scene said in response to the "land lines" order.

"Yeah, that's it," acknowledged the dispatcher. "They don't want anything. Tell them not to even mention it, whoever goes down there."

"Okay," the sergeant answered. "I'll tell them on a hush, hush, hush."

At that point, the police radio dispatcher, working out of

the citywide communications room at 1 Police Plaza in Manhattan, remarked to someone sitting next to him: "You know what it is, they're trying to cover this up. And you and I, we would have been jammed up the [inaudible]. Can you believe this?"

Meanwhile, at the scene, after waiting fifteen minutes for an ambulance to respond, police sergeant Louis Cerrotta decided that Manes had lost so much blood that he should drive the borough president to the hospital in his own patrol car. Manes was helped into the police car, covered with a blanket, and rushed to Booth Memorial Hospital in four minutes. He was admitted to the emergency room at 2:13 A.M. As the police were assisting Manes out of his car, they noticed a blood-stained knife with a four-inch blade on the floor of the passenger's side of the car.

Sam Samuels, Manes's press secretary, was asleep in his home in the Riverdale section of the Bronx when his phone rang at about 2:50 A.M. The call was from an editor at the *Daily News,* saying he had received a report from "a usually reliable tipster" who claimed that Manes had been involved in an accident. Five minutes later, a more senior editor at the *News* called back and told Samuels that "police sources" had confirmed Manes had been in an accident and was now at Booth Memorial Hospital.

"I called Marlene at home at about 3:00 A.M.," Samuels remembers, "and she was very upset and irritated. She picked up on the first ring. She had been calling his car phone, the office, and other staff members trying to find Donald. She had expected him home at about 8:30. I told her what the *News* had told me."

In the emergency room, the nurses had to cut Manes's clothes off his body with a scissors; they were so soaked with blood that they stuck to his skin. Manes was in shock from loss of blood, his pulse was barely perceptible. A team of five worked on him: Dr. Carlos Sucre, the attending emergency room physician, Dr. Debbie Federer, and three nurses—Barbara Langer, Joan Compton, and Elaine Burik.

After Manes's medical condition was stabilized, Dr. Sucre asked him several times what had happened to him. Manes gave conflicting explanations, once claiming, "The people who got in my car forced me to cut my wrist," and at another point indicating that the wound was self-inflicted.

When Sam Samuels reached the hospital at 3:30 A.M.,

Mayor Koch was already there. Victor Botnick, one of the two top Koch aides who were empowered to screen emergency calls for the mayor, awoke him in the middle of the night. Botnick had been given only the sketchiest details by the police and relayed them to the mayor. Although they decided the mayor would not go to Manes, a restless Koch, after calling his press secretary, Bill Rauch, left for the hospital, arriving at about 3:15 A.M. At about 4:00 A.M., Koch informed a group of reporters:

"As I understand it, his wife says he had been on a severe liquid diet. And that it apparently has had some impact that she noticed prior to the accident in his functioning. I talked to him briefly, but he clearly was in shock."

The mayor added: "You don't know about these liquid diets. They'll kill you. Stay away from them."

By the time the mayor held his impromptu press conference, the situation at the hospital was becoming chaotic. The police had sealed off the emergency room and trauma room area. Only Manes's wife, children, brother, his deputy Claire Schulman, the Reverend Coleman Costello, and the mayor were able to see him. At some point in the middle of the night, undetected by the press, Stanley Friedman and Andy Capasso had slipped into the hospital through a back entrance, but it is unclear if they actually got to see Manes.

Tom Russo, the executive assistant to Queens D.A. John Santucci, saw Friedman and Capasso talking to each other at the hospital at about 7:30 A.M.

Manes drifted in and out of lucidity during this period. When he saw Claire Schulman he did ask her how the vote had gone on the homeless shelter on Borden Avenue, and she told him the facility had been reduced to 275 beds.

Sam Samuels set up a command post for the media in an empty administrative office on the first floor that was neither near the emergency room area nor on the route to the emergency room. He had to deal with the growing number of radio and television reporters, print journalists, and photographers without having any information to give them. Samuels never saw Manes that night.

At 9:00 A.M., Dr. Mauro Romita performed microsurgery on Manes to reattach the median nerve and ulnar artery of his left hand. The operating room team also closed a small cut on Manes's left ankle and noticed several bruises on his left arm. At some point before or during the nearly three-hour operation,

Manes suffered a heart attack, and later that day he was placed in the cardiac care unit.

The mysterious slashing of a powerful politician was page-one news in all the New York dailies, and at the top of all radio and television news broadcasts on Friday morning, January 10. A bloody surprise without explanation, the event invited gossip and speculation. Wild rumors began to circulate inside the news media. A tipster called the *Daily News* and claimed to have witnessed a violent quarrel between Manes and another man on a boat docked at the marina near Le Shea restaurant. Several radio stations received calls from motorists who claimed to have seen a prostitute running away from Manes's car.

In this rumor-filled atmosphere of that morning, Stanley Friedman phoned public relations consultant Marty McLaughlin for advice on how to handle the crisis. Friedman's secretary, Rose Mintzer, wrote the following notation in Friedman's diary after she spoke to McLaughlin: "Better make the slash a good story—'a hooker tried to get into car—on Northern Blvd.'—and slashed him when he tried to pull away." Friedman and McLaughlin later that morning discussed three possible explanations to give the media: Manes was attacked by a prostitute; it was a suicide attempt; or it was an irrational reaction to diet pills.

"Whatever it is," McLaughlin urged, "get a good story into the Saturday papers so it can die over the weekend, and that will be the end of it. Whatever it is, you have to come up with a story immediately. The longer you let the mystery remain, with no explanation, the more the press will speculate."

Ironically, independent and simultaneous impetus was being provided for the hooker theory. Political insiders had heard rumors for years that Manes was attracted to prostitutes, and police in the 110th Precinct told reporters that the area where Manes was stopped was near a well-known cruising strip for female and transvestite prostitutes. On Friday morning, WNBC radio went on the air with a single-source report that a prostitute was involved in the stabbing of Manes. (By the following Tuesday, the theory had gained enough momentum that Mayor Koch was announcing at a City Hall press conference that the voters would not hold it against Manes even if he was "with a hooker" when he was hurt.)

The scene at Booth Memorial Hospital on Friday and Saturday was half political caucus, half vigil. Queens district attorney John Santucci had waited for three hours to see Manes on Friday but was denied permission by doctors, a veto that was also extended to the police and to Manes's close political advisers, including Richard Rubin, Alan Gershuny, and Mike Nussbaum, who milled around the hospital lobby but could not get to see him. No one had any information to give reporters, who were also waiting for news. When Gershuny, who had managed Manes's first campaign for the city council in 1965, told reporters, "He wants to run for mayor in 1989," speculative debates arose between Manes's staff and the press corps over how much this still mysterious event might limit Manes's political future. One Manes aide went so far as to argue that the event had "heightened Manes's name recognition among voters."

Peter Vallone told reporters, "There's no way that Don Manes could have tried to kill himself. He had too many friends and too much to live for."

Even Barbara Ross did not connect the slashed wrist of Donald Manes to the PVB story she was writing with Brian Kates at the *Daily News* that Saturday afternoon. Ross still thought of Manes as "the lovable bear." She was still guessing that Stanley Friedman had to be the mastermind behind the PVB racket, that Donny was not corrupt, that his accident was just coincidental to the words on her computer screen.

On Saturday, the one person allowed to speak with Manes was Sid Davidoff, who had flown up from Florida on Friday after Marlene Manes called and said her husband wanted to see him. Manes told Davidoff a story of being kidnapped by two men he could not describe who had hidden in the back seat of the Ford LTD when it was parked in front of Borough Hall.

"The story was not credible," Davidoff says now. "In that Saturday meeting I realized that I would be ineffectual as Donald's lawyer. He needed a professional criminal lawyer. I didn't believe his story, and Donald got all huffy when I tried to cross-examine him about it. It was a difficult circumstance. There were tubes sticking out of him. He was hooked up to all kinds of medical machines and bells kept going off. I couldn't get the real story out of him. It was bizarre. I'm his friend, his lawyer, his confidant, and I couldn't communicate with him. Something had snapped in his mind. His judgment was gone."

The Barbara Ross–Brian Kates story was finally published on Sunday, January 12, under the headline: FBI INVESTIGATING

PAYOFFS TO CITY PARKING OFFICIALS. It revealed that Sandow was cooperating with Giuliani and the FBI, but that a sting attempted by Sandow had produced little evidence. Although Sandow had admitted paying "local officials" up to $4,000 a month for the last four to five years, the story quoted Lester Shafran, the director of PVB, as saying: "It's absolutely outrageous. To the best of my knowledge there has been no impropriety by anyone at PVB."

Although the Manes story continued to be reported as an unrelated incident, one person who did think there might be a connection between the PVB investigation and the cutting of the borough president was Rudy Giuliani. The possibility of a suicide attempt had occurred to him immediately, and with the rest of the media picking up the Sunday story in the *News*, Giuliani and the FBI decided to go overt.

On January 10, FBI agents had visited Lindenauer in his home and tried to convince him to cooperate, without success. On Tuesday morning, January 14, FBI agents sealed his office at PVB, changed the lock on his door, and seized his diaries, phone logs, Rolodex, and a number of documents. At 7:15 P.M. the same day, Lindenauer voluntarily submitted to arrest by the FBI at the office of his lawyer, Irving Seidman. Again, an effort was made to flip him, but Lindenauer refused.

On Wednesday morning, January 15, Lindenauer was arraigned in federal court, charged with extorting a $5,000 bribe from Bernard Sandow at Hisae's restaurant on November 26, 1985. And using the information provided by Sandow, Giuliani alleged that that payment was only one of a series of payoffs exceeding "several hundred thousand dollars" since 1981.

With the failure of the potential shortcut of the sting operation, Giuliani was back to his original strategy of grinding out a case with subpoenas, documents, and grand jury testimony, as well as continuing to apply the maximum pressure to make Lindenauer cooperate. Without Lindenauer's testimony, Giuliani didn't see how he could make a case against Manes, and wondered how to create an atmosphere that would frighten Lindenauer into becoming a government witness.

The first access law enforcement was given to Manes was on Monday, January 13, under restrictive ground rules set up by Manes's top aide in running the Queens organization, Richard

Rubin. Only two people could see him, and the interview could last only fifteen minutes. No stenographer could be present, no tape recording could be made, and no questions asked about PVB.

This first interview was conducted by Tom Russo, the executive assistant to Queens D.A. Santucci, and Detective Lt. Michael McAuiliffe of the 110th Precinct. Manes's counsel, John Milano, was present in the room, and Rubin waited in the hall.

"He looked sick," Russo recalls. "He had tubes and monitors in his nose, chest, and arms. His voice was feeble. He seemed groggy. And he told us a vague story about being abducted by two men who popped up out of the back seat, and put a knife to his neck, and ordered him to drive to Flushing Meadow Park, to rob him. He was confused about the time. He told us he left Borough Hall between 7:30 and 8:00 P.M., when it was 6:30 or 6:45. He couldn't tell us if the men who abducted him were black or white. He said he thought he was headed home but didn't sound sure of it. I did not express any disbelief because he looked so sick, and I assumed this was going to be the first of several interviews with him. Manes never described how his wrist was cut. But we didn't press him on details because we were told by his doctors that he might die."

The police and the district attorney had not turned up any independent evidence to corroborate Manes's account. Dozens of interviews had already been conducted, and no one had seen the borough president during the seven hours he was missing. Credit card receipts at restaurants and motels were checked. Passengers lists of private airplanes were scrutinized. Three of his mistresses were questioned, and all denied having seen him. (The police laboratory had initially reported detecting traces of semen on Manes's underwear, but later that finding was retracted.)

And the police department and D.A. were developing divergent theories of the event. The police thought it was a suicide attempt, while Santucci was treating the episode as an assault. On January 15, after a second fifteen-minute interview with Manes, Santucci told reporters:

"I believed last Friday and I believe now that these wounds were inflicted upon him. This is not the universal feeling in law enforcement, and I'm no forensic specialist. But I know the man's temperament. He's not violent by nature. There was no note. He's a family-oriented man, and he would not do something like that, particularly in that manner."

This created the irony of Manes's own lawyer doubting his story and the Queens district attorney tending to believe it.

At 3:00 on the afternoon of January 15, the Queens chief of detectives, Joseph Borelli, a tough veteran cop, arrived at Booth Memorial Hospital with two detectives, expecting to conduct a third interview with Manes. The attending physicians said Manes was well enough to be seen, but Manes sent out word that he was "too sick." Chief Borelli then asked to speak with Marlene Manes, who declined, claiming she needed to be with her husband while he was suffering from "complications."

At that point Chief Borelli's cop's instincts told him he was facing a stonewalling cover-up. He had also had the benefit of reading a detective's interview summary with Martin Gans, Manes's driver. Gans, who had followed Manes for two-tenths of a mile on the Union Turnpike, stated clearly there had been no intruders lurking in the back seat of Manes's car. He could see into the car, and Manes was the only person in it.

An hour after Chief Borelli was turned away, Donald Manes was smuggled out of Booth Memorial Hospital in a private ambulance, and taken to NYU Medical Center on First Avenue in Manhattan, where his close friend, Martin Begun, was the dean. He was wrapped from neck to toe in white blankets, and a towel obscured most of his face. On his arrival the medical staff at NYU Hospital informed the Police Department that Manes was too weak to be interviewed.

The professional medical staff at Booth Memorial Hospital, however, was telling reporters that Manes had, in fact, recovered sufficiently to be questioned again, explaining that his blood volume had been restored, he was no longer delirious, and he had eaten three good meals on January 14, and breakfast and lunch on January 15. Booth Hospital spokeswoman Nancy Simington told the press: "He was recovering well from the M.I. [myocardial infarction, or coronary]." In contrast, the spokeswoman for NYU Medical Center told reporters: "He was so worn out from his experience, and he already spoke with the police. Doctors thought it would just be too much for him."

The Manes phone logs show that Martin Begun had called the borough president on January 8 and 9, and indeed, Begun was a friend who would use every effort to shield Manes because he viewed the injury in personal terms. As he would later acknowledge:

"I was nervous that the admission of Donald to my hospital would be perceived as a political transfer. But Marlene had asked for help. She told me that Booth Hospital was a zoo and a circus. Marlene, Donald, and their son-in-law were all friends of mine. I felt I couldn't reject their request for assistance at a moment when they were caught up in a family crisis."

Begun saw to it that Manes had "privacy" at NYU Hospital. Two of the facility's security guards, and two plainclothes New York City police officers, were posted outside Manes's fifteenth-floor room in the coronary care unit. That evening, Manes met with his new lawyer, Michael Armstrong, who had been chosen and retained by Davidoff.

January 16 had once been anticipated as a special day in the life of Donald Manes. For six weeks the Queens Democratic Party had been planning a gala birthday celebration and fundraiser in his honor for that night at Antun's restaurant in Queens Village. More than 800 tickets had been sold in advance of the occasion. The mayor had confirmed he was coming, just as he had come to the annual dinner of the Queens Democracy the year before, when he hugged Manes and proclaimed him destined for higher office. But this date would prove to be memorable only for the misfortune it brought Donald Manes.

Over the course of the previous week, Manes's family and doctors had tried to insulate him from the alarming news in the media. He had been prevented from learning that Lindenauer had been arrested and that Sandow had turned into a wired government witness, and had not been allowed to see the *Daily News* headline that morning, which asked: PVB LINK TO MANES' CUT? The lead of the story read:

> Federal investigators are trying to determine the whereabouts of several suspects in the Parking Violations Bureau scandal on the night that Queens borough president Donald Manes suffered a nearly fatal knife slash, an informed federal source said yesterday.
>
> That disclosure is the first acknowledgment that the mystery of Manes' slashed wrist and the burgeoning parking bureau bribe scandal may be related.

Sometime that morning police detectives again attempted to question Manes but were told by executives of the hospital that they could not, and that Manes's doctors agreed with this decision, although the police could not speak directly with these doctors. This further incident of stonewalling was a last straw for the detectives, who had been patient for five days, and shortly after 5:00 P.M. Richard Nicastro, the police department's chief of detectives, held a press conference at 1 Police Plaza in which he announced that the police department did not believe Donald Manes's account of how he was kidnapped and knifed. "We cannot accept the sequence of events given by Mr. Manes," Nicastro said, and declared that Manes's injury was "self-inflicted."

"Based on our investigation," he continued as perhaps a million people watched live coverage on three local television channels, "Mr. Manes became aware of two people in the rear of his automobile before making the right turn at Union Turnpike. We have a witness who was directly behind Mr. Manes's auto at Union Turnpike and Queens Boulevard, and did not see anyone but Mr. Manes in the auto. . . . There's no forensics, no forensics at all, to indicate an assault on Mr. Manes. Our opinion is that the injuries occurred inside the vehicle on the driver's side."

The press conference sent shock waves through a city that had already been confused by so many contradictory claims made by high officials. With its statement, the New York Police Department had, in effect, proclaimed the borough president of Queens a liar. Police Commissioner Benjamin Ward had agreed with the judgment and participated in the decision to go public with it, and it had been cleared with the mayor. Even after Nicastro's announcement, however, Queens D.A. Santucci said, "I still lean toward the belief that the wounds were inflicted by others." But Nicastro's definitive words, accepted as credible by all news organizations, had to end any illusions Manes might have been clinging to about evading or postponing his fate.

The Queens organization's birthday party for Manes began forty-five minutes after Nicastro's press conference ended. Only half the people who had purchased tickets showed up. The mayor stayed away. There was more drinking than dancing, even when the band struck up the obligatory "New York, New York." Many among the patronage job-holders and vendors of city contracts had the sense of a wake about to begin. *The King was finished, long live the Party,* seemed to be the prevailing mood among the rank and file.

But from the podium came an outpouring of sentiment, loyalty, and defiance. Politicians who wrapped themselves in law and order and police endorsements when they ran for office were now calling the police liars.

"Until Donald says otherwise, I believe what he said," proclaimed Congressman Gary Ackerman.

Geraldine Ferraro, who had been a Queens assistant district attorney and congresswoman before she ran for vice president, came to the microphone wearing a bright yellow jacket and black skirt.

She began by berating the media for jumping to "conclusions too hastily," and then attacked the police department directly; "Nicastro is giving a medical conclusion. I didn't know he was a doctor. . . . Donald Manes is my buddy and I'm proud of him."

Filled with people who had gotten jobs, or money, or power out of Queens politics, the room resounded with desperate cheering.

Donald Manes could not hear it. He lay in his hospital room with the television unplugged, floating in and out of lucidity, tubes sticking out of his body, regretting the past, and fearing the future.

CHAPTER THREE

"I Am Shocked,"
the Mayor Said

THE SMALL-TIME, small-town world of Queens Boulevard was home base to Jimmy Breslin. He knew it the way Saul Bellow knew Chicago, or the way the young James Baldwin knew the storefront churches and the tenements of Harlem. Breslin knew all of Queens, its mix of Irish, Italian, Jewish, and German neighborhoods, its ethnic rivalries and intermarriages, its working-class bars, its fear of blacks. But best of all he knew the Boulevard. He knew the four short, seedy city blocks that contained Queens Borough Hall, the courthouse, the offices of 130 lawyers, the always-crowded OTB betting parlor, the Pastrami King, the Part II bar, where Charles Bronson's photo once occupied the place of honor behind the bartender. He knew the law clinic that advertised the values of the Boulevard in its prices: "Buy/Sell house, $199. Misdemeanor, $169. Divorce, $99."

The Boulevard was the common meeting ground for the lawyers and judges from the courthouse; for clubhouse politicians working in or visiting Borough Hall; for horse players from the racetracks located in Queens; for the hoodlums and their private investigators who had business in the courts. In this provincial subculture, Reagan, the Sandinistas, and the Pope were remote abstractions. The giants were Donald Manes, John Gotti, and Bold Ruler.

For years, great journalists went to Cambodia, South Africa, Poland, and Lebanon to find and write prize-winning stories. But Jimmy Breslin mostly stayed close to home, to his beloved Boulevard and the coterie of friends he had known for twenty and twenty-five years. But in January 1986, Breslin's old friends, in whom he had invested trust and faith, became the story that found him. And Breslin, the most popular columnist on the city's bestselling newspaper, became a participant in the story himself. He went into a titanic rage when he found out that friends he thought were amusing rascals had crossed the shadow line behind his back and become "scum gangsters stealing from the people of my city."

Jimmy Breslin is one of those contradictory, larger-than-life characters—a moral cynic, an egalitarian egotist.

Breslin's father was an alcoholic who vanished when Breslin was six and later died a pauper's death. Breslin's mother was a substitute English teacher who supported Breslin and his sister by working for thirty years as an administrator in New York's welfare system; she was manager of the Harlem office, where her sensitivity and flexibility touched many people who would later tell Breslin about it. She had a feeling for the English language and an empathy for underdogs and casualties.

Breslin struggled through John Adams High School in Howard Beach, Queens, where he played second-string guard on the school's football team. It took Breslin "the regulation five years to graduate." Breslin dropped out of Long Island University after accumulating only ten credits. By then he was covering police stations and sports for the *Long Island Press*, and spending all his spare time at Queens's three racetracks (Jamaica, Belmont, and Aqueduct) and two boxing clubs (Jamaica Arena and Ridgewood Grove).

The 1960s politicized Breslin. He covered the civil rights movement in the South, went to Vietnam, saw black poverty and hopelessness in Watts, Newark, and Detroit. He became close to civil rights lawyer Paul O'Dwyer and to Robert Kennedy, and was a few feet from Kennedy when he was shot. Breslin learned from these experiences. He had grown up poor. He had his mother's bloodline. And he resented authority.

Breslin is an intellectual disguised as a barroom primitive, a Robert Caro sounding like Jackie Gleason. He read poetry by Auden and essays by Montaigne and hid the books in the bottom of his desk drawer so no one would see them.

Breslin is also classic Black Irish—melancholy, romantic, with a sense of life's tragedy. He is also a Christian of Mercy. Normally he is self-absorbed and irresponsible about keeping appointments. But let a friend be in trouble or in a hospital, or suffer a death in the family, and Breslin will suddenly become the most faithful visitor.

Over the years, hundreds of Breslin's columns opened with a funny story, an idea, a person, a tip, a stray phrase heard over morning coffee at the Pastrami King, or a late afternoon drink in the Part II or Forty Yards on the Boulevard. The Boulevard people were his writer's gold. He minded and filtered them. They were all his friends—judges, gangsters, cops, honorable politicians, ghastly politicians, bookmakers, horse trainers, fighters, civil servants, private investigators for the mob, writers, bartenders, bail bondsmen. He didn't impose his own moral code on them, and they all gave him material for three implacable deadlines per week.

On May 9, 1983, Jimmy Breslin had been called upon to deliver the eulogy for his favorite Boulevard person, Sheldon Chevlowe. The service was to be held Sunday morning at the Schwartz Brothers Funeral Home on the Boulevard, ten blocks from Queens Borough Hall and the Pastrami King. Chevlowe had died of cancer; two years earlier Breslin's own wife, Rosemary, had died of the same disease, and Chevlowe's wife, Maxine, had nursed Rosemary Breslin through the worst part of it, through the chemotherapy trips to Boston, through the painful, lonely evenings.

The royalty of the Boulevard came to Chevlowe's funeral. Donald Manes was there, as were Mike Lazar, Lester Shafran, Bernie Sandow, and Mel Lebetkin. Mike Dowd was there, crying like a baby. Geoffrey Lindenauer came, too. The Schwartz Brothers chapel was overflowing with five hundred mourners.

Breslin stood at the pulpit of the hushed chapel and nervously started to read remarks he had typed out:

"Dying is no big deal. The least of us can accomplish that.

"The trick is to live.

"And live Shelly Chevlowe did. And with exquisite taste. . . .

"He laughed while everybody else frowned.

"He paused and told a story while everybody else was in the dreary pursuit of absolutely nothing.

"He lived as much as he could each day, while everybody else died a little each day. . . ."

By the time Breslin came close the end of his eulogy he was crying.

"His days consisted of being interested in other people. Then, by marvelous use of his tonal range, he could say something in such a way that he forced a smile onto your face.

"What a valuable gift to give to others.

"I don't think I ever heard of him turning down anybody for anything. If you take a moment out and do something for somebody, then perhaps you implant a little goodness in the person, and he or she will, in turn, help somebody else out some day."

On Saturday morning, January 11, 1986, Breslin came to the Boulevard to work. He had a Sunday column to write and a detested early 1:00 P.M. deadline. Breslin working against a deadline is Mike Tyson annoyed.

Breslin had gone first to Booth Memorial Hospital, where he saw Marlene Manes. He had known Donald Manes and Marlene for more than twenty years; their children knew and visited one another. Breslin had never written unkindly about Manes, as he had about Governor Carey, Mayor Koch, Senator Moynihan, or Senator D'Amato. Marlene Manes took Breslin's hand and said urgently, "I have to talk to you. Donald is in rough shape." But Manes's political handlers steered her away, and the conversation was never completed.

Breslin went to the hospital coffee shop to think and calm his nerves. Sitting at the counter he overheard a nurse complaining to a friend: "The nerve of this FBI agent. He takes my parking place and I ask him to move, and he just looks at me."

The accidental revelation that FBI agents were stealing parking spots at the hospital that housed Donald Manes propelled Breslin to the Boulevard to find Lebetkin.

Lebetkin had been a character in Breslin's 1972 novel *World Without End, Amen.* As the inadvertently funny shyster,

Klein the Lawyer, Lebetkin had been the fictionalized subject of dozens of Breslin columns. The previous autumn Lebetkin's wife, Rosalie, had died of cancer, and the frequently morose Lebetkin had slipped into a depression that required psychiatric treatment. Ten days earlier, on New Year's Eve, Breslin and his wife, Ronnie Eldridge, had taken Lebetkin and Chevlowe's widow, Maxine, out to dinner at the Plaza to cheer them up. Lebetkin couldn't say "no comment" when a manic Breslin found him on the Boulevard.

"I got no time to fuck with you, Mel. Tell me the fuckin' truth about what's going on," Breslin demanded.

"Donny was supposed to bleed to death. It's PVB. Maxine is home sick in bed."

"Where's Bernie Sandow?"

"How could you even mention a name like that to me? I warned Bernie not to go to Chicago. Al Capone was in Chicago."

For an hour Breslin and Lebetkin walked back and forth, up and down the Boulevard, past the OTB and the Pastrami King, talking. Lebetkin did not want to sit down in a restaurant or a bar because he was afraid somebody might overhear what he was saying.

Lebetkin gave Breslin the sketchy outlines of the conspiracy. It involved kickbacks based on a percentage of the receipts by collection agencies for contracts from PVB. Lindenauer was the bagman. Sandow was part of it. Manes was behind it and sporadically he would ask Lebetkin, "How is our thing going?" And Lebetkin told Breslin: "Shelly started it. I paid him money."

Breslin had no lofty civic incentive at this point—merely an early deadline. A gigantic story was developing in his Queens, in his home ball park. He couldn't let anyone else beat him on his own turf. Ego and the territorial imperative drove him on this day.

"I felt like the Celtics about to lose a game in the Boston Garden," he says. "I needed a steal in the last ten seconds. I had to prevent the worst possible crime from occurring—public embarrassment to Breslin. I couldn't allow any other writer to beat me on a Queens story. Later I felt rage, and betrayal, and politics came into the picture. The first day it was pure survival."

Breslin returned to the *News* and composed a column in code, a column of subtle hints. He decided to hold back some of the information, to work it up until it became a grand slam home run.

The column he wrote did not mention either Mel Lebetkin's or Lindenauer's name. It used a couple of Lebetkin's funny comments about Manes and Sandow, but the attribution was fudged. The no-name column did convey a sense of scandal about to strike the rotting Queens Democratic Party.

Breslin ended the column with his own recollections about Donald Manes.

> There was the evening in 1982 when Mario Cuomo, who had decided to run for Governor, stopped at the Manes home in Jamaica on his way home to Holliswood and said that he had decided to run for governor.
>
> "You make me very happy," Manes said.
>
> "I'm happy that you're happy," Cuomo said.
>
> "And I'm so happy that you're happy," Manes said.
>
> He grabbed Cuomo and they both beamed.
>
> "We will be together forever," Manes said.
>
> About two weeks later, Edward Koch, Mayor of New York, decided that he, too, wanted to run for governor. "I support Ed Koch," Donald Manes said. "We are together forever."
>
> Cuomo won. On the day Cuomo was inducted into office in Albany Donald Manes stood in the aisle talking to somebody, and he kept the guy standing in the aisle, and all the while Manes' eyes were riveted on the aisle. When he saw Cuomo start marching down to the podium, Manes put both hands on the guy he was talking to. He pushed the guy into a seat. Now as Cuomo came along, here was Manes alone in the aisle. Both of Manes' hands shot out and he clutched Cuomo. "I'm so happy!"
>
> Cuomo smiled.
>
> "We're together forever!" Manes screamed as Cuomo went down the aisle to become governor.
>
> He danced and waved his hands in the illusion that day, and it was where he belonged, a cheerful man nearly impossible to dislike. And now yesterday it was all different. There was too much reality. The county organization was in shock, and, if he thought there was a chance for illusion, all Manes had to do was turn his head in his bed and look at the bandages on his left wrist.

Breslin's column ran on page three, next to the Barbara Ross and Brian Kates story about the FBI investigating PVB and Sandow cooperating with U.S. Attorney Giuliani. The story and the column together provided the city with its first clue to the extent of the scandal.

On Monday morning, January 13, Barbara Ross approached Breslin at the *News*. She had a computerized printout in her hand which listed all the collection agencies that had received PVB contracts and the amounts each company had collected in commissions by harassing citizens who owed money on parking tickets.

"Look how much money your friend, Klein the Lawyer, is making," Ross said as gingerly as she could.

Breslin scanned the rows of names and numbers. Next to Standard Collection was the figure "$1.1 million" in commissions for the 1985 fiscal year.

Breslin started calling places on the Boulevard to find Lebetkin. He wasn't in his law office or any of his usual haunts. Then the cunning Breslin played a hunch. He dialed Harold Borg's law office and asked for Lebetkin.

"I'm gonna kill you," Breslin screamed.

"You don't understand," Lebetkin whined.

Breslin returned to studying the computer printout. He saw the name of Mike Dowd and a company called Computrace. Next to it was the number "$601,000" under the column listing commissions for 1985.

Breslin did not get around to calling Dowd, whom he had known around the Boulevard for fifteen years, until Friday, January 17, as he had been distracted by the velocity of events during that week.

At 7:30 on Friday evening, Jimmy Breslin and Mike Dowd, two old Irish friends from Queens, sat down at a rear booth in Costello's journalist's bar on East 44th Street. They both ordered bowls of New England clam chowder.

Breslin didn't know it, but Dowd had already been agonizing for a week about whether to confess his role in the scandal and become a witness for the government. Dowd had consulted with friends and lawyers, and when he sat down in Costello's, he assumed Breslin already knew the whole story of his involvement from Lebetkin, a co-conspirator.

The conversation in Costello's was not between a writer and a target. Dowd immediately revealed he had paid $30,000 in bribes for PVB contracts, and the discussion became, in part, a counseling session between friends. Dowd wanted advice. Breslin wanted a column that would be a grand slam home run. Dowd was completely open with Breslin. He admitted that he was frightened that Manes and Lindenauer would get together and accuse him of bribery before he could accuse them of extortion. He wanted Lebetkin to go into the prosecutor's office with him, so it would at least be "two against two."

"This is a bar fight," Breslin said. "The guy who lands the first punch wins. You gotta throw it."

Breslin urged him to get a lawyer and turn himself into Rudy Giuliani, and "make a deal right away." Dowd asked him to call Giuliani from the bar, but Breslin said he couldn't do that. Dowd then asked him to call Lebetkin, whom Breslin found at the Tutu Bene restaurant on Queens Boulevard. He likewise encouraged Lebetkin to make a deal with Giuliani and tell the truth about everything with Dowd. But Lebetkin stalled. He couldn't decide what to do.

When Breslin returned to the booth he asked: "Do you have anything directly on Manes?"

"Yes. You were there," Dowd replied.

Breslin looked blank.

"Remember the funeral we were all at?"

Breslin thought of the funeral for his Rosemary, the one for Rosalie Lebetkin, and then of the funeral where he had eulogized Shelly Chevlowe as the man of "exquisite taste."

"Do you know what happened right after the funeral was over?" Dowd asked.

"Tell me."

"I got told, 'From now on you start paying Geoff.' "

"Who told you this?"

"The guy in charge. Who else is supposed to tell me things? Manes."

This was perfidy to Breslin. A funeral for a friend, where he wept the tears of a mourner, where Dowd cried, had meant nothing to Manes. In Breslin's mind Manes became someone incapable of grief, someone incapable of sincere human emotion because he was consumed by greed.

Breslin felt a rush of anger at his own gang, at Shelly and Mel, for not telling him what they were doing behind his back, for violating the social contract between friends.

"I was so crazed at Shelly I wanted to scream," Breslin remembers. "But how can I yell at a dead guy? Mel was pathetic. So I had to aim all my anger at Manes and the Queens Democrats."

Breslin figured out a strategy for himself. The fact that Manes had personally ordered Dowd to pay kickbacks to Lindenauer was a smoking gun, proof of extortion, usable in court. He had it exclusively. But Breslin did not want to write a column that was only a charge, or an allegation. He had promised Dowd that his confession would be kept "off the record." But he decided to both wait and cheat a little bit. Like Giuliani, Breslin understood that timing was everything in a situation like this.

The next morning Breslin and Dowd met again for breakfast. Breslin again tried to reinforce Dowd's own inclination to tell his story to Giuliani.

"You can't let that guy in the hospital start saying, 'Mike Dowd, Mike Dowd.' You gotta throw the first punch," Breslin advised.

By the end of the breakfast Breslin calculated it would take Dowd two or three more days to choose a lawyer and go in.

When Breslin got to the *News* to confront his early deadline for the Sunday paper, he called Giuliani.

"There's something I'm putting in the paper tonight. Read it and then we'll discuss it."

Breslin then wrote, on the last manual typewriter the *News* owned, his Sunday column. He used most of what Dowd had told him in Costello's, but he used it anonymously, without Dowd's name, without Lebetkin's name, without the source of the information identified. The first column had been a clue; this one was a road map.

Breslin's January 19 column appeared under the headline BOULEVARD OF BROKEN SCHEMES. Its final paragraph was a promise, and a covenant with his readers:

> This is the scandal of our time, and from now on I
> will bring it to you first, and with the most fury,
> because I am personally aroused. I have been betrayed
> by my own boulevard, Queens Boulevard, and in future
> days I will give neither quarter or comfort.

Giuliani read the column and was "pretty sure" the anonymous source was Lebetkin, for he had not even focused on

Dowd. Breslin says: "My use of the word 'betrayed' was a message from me to Lebetkin."

The morning after the column appeared, Breslin called Giuliani.

"Did the witness come in yet?" Breslin asked with his characteristic gruff ambiguity.

"You mean the guy in your column?"

"Yeah."

"No, he hasn't," the prosecutor replied.

Breslin cursed and hung up.

During the traumatic, sleepless week it took Mike Dowd to make the most difficult decision of his life, remorse made him want to confess and cooperate, remorse so strong that Dowd called it "a sense of sin, of shame, and of failing my father's advice to me when I was young that I must never do anything in my life as a result of a threat, because the person will feel that he owned me."

But paralyzing Dowd were any number of fears.

He was afraid of Donald Manes, who to him had always seemed an awesome political force. From his law office directly opposite Borough Hall, Dowd had seen Jimmy Carter as president of the United States walk arm in arm with Manes down the Boulevard. The first days after Manes was found bleeding, Dowd did not believe it was a suicide attempt, and suspected him of "faking, playing possum, or else someone might have tried to kill him." Not realizing Manes had suffered a breakdown, Dowd worried that Manes might retaliate against him, through the courts, through the press, or through the mob.

Dowd suspected that Manes was connected to organized crime. He had never known how high up the PVB corruption went, whether Manes was sharing his money with mobsters who had given him a franchise. As Dowd struggled through his week of decision, he had nightmares and fantasies of his daughter being harmed, of his car being blown up, of a mob hit man walking up behind him on the Boulevard.

As a combative defense lawyer, undefeated in trials for the previous two years, Dowd trusted no prosecutor. He felt that if he went to Queens D.A. Santucci, "Manes would know about it before I got back to my office," and the defense bar had so demonized Giuliani that Dowd was equally suspicious of him.

Even if he were able to find a trustworthy official, Dowd worried that nobody would believe him. He had no witnesses to his conversations with Manes. He was just a 43-year-old political lawyer who had once run for the assembly and lost a primary, who had helped manage Mario Cuomo's losing campaign for mayor in 1977. Who would take his word over the king of Queens?

And Dowd had "the Irish thing" against informing. As a lawyer, he had defended and won the acquittal of IRA supporter Eamon Meehan on gun-running charges. Even after being tortured in Long Kesh prison for almost three years, Meehan had refused to inform; so how could Dowd, who had become close to other IRA sympathizers through this case, make peace with the image of an informer?

On Tuesday night, January 14, Dowd had had dinner with his law partner Joann Harris, a former federal prosecutor, to whom he told the story of his extortion payments in the strictest confidence.

"I wanted to see if she called me a weak piece of shit and walked out on me," Dowd explained. "But she told me that I was right to have stopped paying."

Dowd and Harris weighed the pros and cons of cooperating as would two lawyers, not two friends. Harris was able to offer an interesting perspective because she and Giuliani had been bitter enemies within the justice department. Harris had been the chief of the department's Fraud's Section when Giuliani was an assistant attorney general. They clashed so sharply that Harris left to become the executive assistant to John Martin, the U.S. Attorney in the southern district. When Giuliani came back to New York to replace Martin, Harris resigned rather than work for him.

Despite her history of disagreement and personal conflict with Giuliani, Harris told Dowd that Giuliani was "honest, loyal, and relentless."

Dowd made a dinner date with another lawyer, Barry Sheck, for Friday night, January 17, to solicit his advice. Sheck was a radical intellectual, the head of the Cardozo Law Clinic, a close friend who had been co-counsel with Dowd in the IRA case. They were scheduled to meet at 6:00 P.M. at Bruxelle's restaurant in Greenwich Village, but when Breslin called Dowd, and Dowd agreed to meet Breslin immediately, Dowd reached Sheck and asked him to wait until he got there. Sheck ended up waiting almost five hours.

"You're all a bunch of crooks," Breslin started telling Dowd. "You got a collection agency. You're making millions of dollars."

Dowd tried to explain that he made very little money, partly because he had to pay the bribes out of the proceeds of the company.

Breslin then gave Dowd the most direct advice anyone would give him: "Run in, save yourself, inform."

Dowd was "almost crazy," Sheck recalls, by the time he arrived in the Village. "He was scared to death."

Unlike Harris, however, Sheck did not feel that Dowd should cooperate: "I told him there was no evidence against him, that he could probably avoid an indictment, that Rudy couldn't make a case from the financial records, and that if indicted, he could win a trial with the defense of extortion."

"What do you think about Giuliani?" Dowd asked.

"I don't trust him," Sheck replied. "I think he is unscrupulous."

"Who would you recommend I use as a lawyer?" Dowd asked.

"Mike Shaw," said Sheck.

When Dowd had asked the same question of Joann Harris, she had suggested Charles Stillman. Harris had successfully prosecuted the Reverend Moon for tax evasion in a complicated case that had involved issues of separation of church and state. Her chief adversary in that trial had been Stillman, and she had been impressed by both his character and his competence. Stillman and Mike Shaw were law partners.

"Mike was giddy on the ride home," Sheck recalls. "He was reminiscing in a funny way about all the corrupt politicians he knew in Queens—Judge Brennan, Gene Mastropieri, Troy, Manes. He was almost relaxed for the first time that night."

As Sheck rode back to Manhattan in a taxi at about 2:00 A.M., he thought that Dowd probably would not cooperate.

The next night, Saturday, also at 2:00 A.M., Dowd called Sheck and asked him what was in Breslin's column in the *News*. Sheck went out and bought the paper, but Breslin's column was not in the early edition because of a computer breakdown. The next morning Dowd read his words attributed to a nameless person. This increased his panic.

On Sunday morning, after reading Breslin's road map, Dowd called Charles Stillman at home. Stillman's wife told him her husband was playing tennis, but agreed to call him at the court when Dowd explained that it was an emergency.

After playing the third set, Stillman reached Dowd and asked, "Can it wait?" When Dowd said no in a way that made his stress apparent, Stillman invited him to come directly to his home in Merrick, Long Island, in an hour, leaving Stillman only enough time to pick up bagels and shower.

As Dowd told his story, Stillman's reaction was that Dowd was a victim of extortion. He had been granted the original contract in 1980, which was worth $29,000 in commissions, legitimately. He had had to pay to get more contracts, and financed the bribes with taxable cash from the company. He had stopped paying in 1984. And now he felt his contract with the city was going to be terminated.

After an hour Stillman said, "I think we should ask Giuliani for complete immunity, or else we will go to trial with an extortion defense." Dowd, anxious to end the anxiety of indecision, urged Stillman to call Giuliani at home that afternoon, but Stillman thought it would be better if Dowd "slept on the decision for a day."

When he reached home in the late afternoon, Dowd called his friend Peter Maas, author of a string of bestselling books about informers and whistleblowers—*The Valachi Papers, Serpico,* and *Marie.* In 1985, Dowd had strongly implied to Maas, without being explicit, that he had paid off Queens politicians, and had stopped. So Maas was a logical person for Dowd to call for a second opinion on going in to Giuliani.

Peter Maas had been close to many prosecutors and he held Giuliani in the highest esteem. "You're making the right decision," he told Dowd. "I'm very proud of you."

"What makes whistleblowers do what they do?" Dowd asked, grateful that Maas was being a friend when he could easily have been a journalist.

"Whistleblowers are not your ordinary citizens," Maas explained. "They often have to be a little bit crazy, because a lot of bad things happen to them afterward."

At 9:30 Tuesday morning, January 21 (Monday was Martin Luther King's birthday, and state and federal offices were closed), Dowd, Stillman, and Mike Shaw convened to analyze all the options. Everyone agreed on the decision to call Giuliani, to whom Stillman offered tantalizing information: "I have to see you on an emergency basis about the Manes investigation.

I represent a client, a Mr. X, who can give you an extortion case against Manes and a bribery case against Lindenauer, involving PVB contracts."

"How soon can you come in?" Giuliani asked.

As Dowd waited in Stillman's office at 521 Fifth Avenue, while Stillman went downtown to meet with Giuliani later that afternoon, he began to write down his reflections in a notebook: "It's almost unreal. This isn't happening. It's someone else's life. . . ."

At about 6:00 that evening Stillman met with Giuliani, Benito Romano, Charles LaBella, and Denny Young. A few hours earlier Donald Manes had admitted from his hospital bed that his abduction story had been a hoax and that he had slashed his own wrist. But he had offered no further explanation, no motive for his suicide attempt. The Manes case was on the front pages every day, but the government's investigation had lost momentum. Lindenauer had refused to cooperate; Sandow's sting had only limited success. Giuliani needed a break to turn the massive publicity to his advantage, to convert it into pressure on targets and witnesses rather than pressure on his staff. So the timing of Stillman's proffer couldn't have been better from the point of view of both Giuliani and Dowd.

Stillman told the story, emphasizing what Manes said to his client after Chevlowe's funeral, and ended by asking for complete immunity not only from Giuliani but from "all other law enforcement agencies."

"Who is your client?" Giuliani asked.

"I can't tell you until we have an agreement on immunity," Stillman said.

At about 7:00 P.M., Giuliani asked Stillman to step out of his office while he discussed the proffer with his three assistants. Stillman left, and for about ten seconds the room was silent, with each prosecutor waiting for the other to make the first comment.

Suddenly, Giuliani made a fist, pumped it once, and said, "Let's do it!"

"It was a wonderful moment of euphoria and exaltation," recalls Romano. "We realized this was the first direct evidence against Manes, that it would have taken us a year of investigative work to get to this proof."

Giuliani invited Stillman back into his office and told him,

"If your client tells us the same story tomorrow under a grant of informal immunity, we have a deal on complete immunity," and again asked the identity of his client, still thinking it was Lebetkin.

When Stillman revealed it was Dowd, everyone was stunned. "We didn't have anything on Dowd at that point," Giuliani recalls. "There was no evidence implicating him. We hadn't focused on him at all. It was rare for a witness to come in cold the way Dowd did."

Stillman was relieved. He had been fearful that Giuliani might try to negotiate for a one-count guilty plea, or that he might stall a decision for a few days while he consulted a range of advisers. But Giuliani was able to see the larger picture, sense the moment, and act on his instinct that this was the evidence that could break open the scandal.

At about 7:30 Stillman called Dowd in his office. Dowd answered the phone and Stillman said, "Bingo! We got it."

The next afternoon at about 5:00 Dowd and Stillman arrived at the U.S. Attorney's office at Foley Square. Dowd signed in as "John Smith." Later he would describe this moment in his crisis journal:

> I'm scared. How can I trust these people I fight all the time? I am in no man's land. I'm about to expose one of the most important political figures. My instincts tell me the establishment will try to destroy me. There is no morality attached to the retribution. I am totally distracted and lost. I am standing in the lobby of the U.S. Attorney's office and I can't believe it. I'm a client, not a lawyer.

Of his feelings a few minutes later, as he waited outside while Stillman talked to Giuliani and his aides, Dowd wrote: "Will they believe me? Will something go wrong? I believe I can hear them arguing. My mind is playing tricks. After a while Benito Romano comes out, tells me to relax, everything will be all right." Dowd had met Romano at a Mets game during the season of 1985 and had liked him, and now seeing this familiar face with a friendly smile helped calm his nerves as he was summoned into the room.

For two hours Dowd was questioned by Romano, LaBella, assistant U.S. Attorney Mary Shannon, and FBI agent Joe Persichini.

Dowd, who had not slept in two days, began the meeting with an emotional, almost messianic speech:

"I want you people to understand that I am staying with this to the end. These fuckers are coming back after me a hundred different ways that you won't be able to protect me from because you don't know Queens. I'm afraid of them, out there in Queens, not of you. But I will not back off. I know the Palace Guard will get me, even if you get the king. But I won't quit. I'm in this to the very end. I just hope you guys are, too."

As Dowd told his whole story to the federal government he felt liberated.

He began with the first bribe he had paid to Chevlowe in 1982, and how Manes instructed him at Chevlowe's funeral to start paying Lindenauer. He described the meeting in Manes's office at Queens Borough Hall where he told Manes he wouldn't pay anymore, and how Manes told him to send his partner over with the money if he wasn't prepared to do it himself. He described Lindenauer hounding him for kickbacks within the last month and implying his contract would not be renewed if he didn't pay.

After Dowd ended his narrative, he was ushered into Giuliani's office for his first face-to-face meeting with the prosecutor whom he still didn't trust. But the first thing Dowd noticed was Giuliani's Yankee baseball memorabilia: a photograph of Babe Ruth and Lou Gehrig. An old Yankee Stadium bleacher seat. A baseball autographed by Billy Martin and Yogi Berra. They helped personalize the demonized prosecutor for Dowd. But as these two native sons of New York's working class—both lawyers, both divorced, both in their early forties, both parochial school graduates—began to talk, they slowly discovered their common ground. Giuliani had gone to Bishop Loughlin High School in Brooklyn, and Dowd had gone to Xavier in Queens. Giuliani had contemplated becoming a priest, and Dowd had been an altar boy. They both suffered gnawing guilt over failed marriages. There was empathy between the two men, educated by priests and nuns, who brooded over their mortal weaknesses.

"The key was that I instinctively believed Dowd's story," Giuliani recalls of their conference. "He had all the right attitudes and reactions. He felt bad about what he had done. His remorse was sincere. The other key was that he had stopped paying voluntarily, and he had come into our office voluntarily.

This made it possible to offer him immunity. But our agreement on immunity was conditioned on Dowd telling us the whole, complete truth. If he lied about anything, the deal was nullified."

Before Dowd and Stillman left the U.S. Attorney's office they were assured their cooperation would be kept secret as long as possible, that Dowd would have a period of tranquil transition to prepare his friends and family and to secure his law practice.

But when Dowd arrived home at about midnight his daughter told him he had a message from Barbara Ross of the *Daily News:* he would be on the front page of the next day's paper. Jimmy Breslin had written a column about his going to the U.S. Attorney and giving evidence against Manes.

Dowd scrawled in his journal:

The feds fucked me. I'm frantic trying to think. I can't sleep. My life is changed, but how? I go out at 2:30 or 3 A.M. to get a paper. I just drive trying to understand what's going on, trying to think this out. I can't believe it. I'm on the front page. I lay in bed in a daze. The calls start at about 6 A.M.

At 7:00 A.M., Mike Dowd, an only child, called his father and mother and told them the story they would soon see in headlines. "These two calls might have been the hardest part of the whole thing," Dowd says.

At about 1:00 P.M. on Wednesday, January 22, Jimmy Breslin sat at his desk at the *Daily News,* facing a deadline and a blank sheet of paper. He called Giuliani and left a message that he planned to expose the full PVB story in his column the next day.

An hour later, Giuliani called back and said, "Thank you."

Although Breslin gave Giuliani the impression that he knew that Dowd had come in, Giuliani's gratitude was actually the proof Breslin wanted that Dowd had finally taken Breslin's advice.

Breslin enticed Giuliani into an immediate meeting, telling Giuliani that he had a "second witness" who could also break open the scandal, and they should talk about it. In fact, though Breslin was urging Lebetkin to go in, Lebetkin was stubbornly resisting. Breslin's real purpose for seeing Giuliani was to make sure there was no misunderstanding, to get him to confirm off the record that Dowd was telling the government the same story he told Breslin. Neither had spoken Dowd's name during their oblique colloquy on the phone.

Giuliani said he was planning to pick up his wife, Donna, at 8:00 P.M. after her WPIX newscast, and since WPIX was in the same building as the *News,* Breslin suggested Giuliani meet him for a drink at the Harley Hotel, next to the *News.* Giuliani agreed to meet him there at 7:30.

Breslin started to write his column at about 2:30, striking the keys of his manual typewriter in soaring staccato spurts, like Dizzy Gillespie playing a be-bop trumpet solo.

Breslin wrote, ripped pages out, crumpled them into balls, and rewrote. By 7:00 P.M. he was finished. A libel lawyer named Marge Coleman read the piece and didn't change a word. Gil Spencer, the editor of the *News,* looked at it and ordered the column to begin on the front page, the first time in nearly a decade that a Breslin column would receive such an honor.

At 7:30 Breslin met Giuliani at the bar of the Harley Hotel. The half-hour session was a typical Breslin ramble. He talked about how much he had trusted these Queens politicians, his feeling of being betrayed by Geraldine Ferraro and John Zaccaro, his fury at Queens politicians. This meeting was intended to clear up any misunderstanding, but it gave rise to its own confusion. Giuliani assumed Breslin was writing another no-name piece, like his two previous Sunday ones. But Breslin had already written this column and included Dowd's name. Giuliani had also just been told by Dowd's lawyer that Dowd had a promise of confidentiality from Breslin, and that if the feds protected Dowd, so would Breslin. But neither the attorney nor the witness had taken into account Breslin's code of ethics: "Of course I would betray a friend for the biggest story of the year."

By prearrangement Breslin had city editor Arthur Browne meet him and Giuliani on the sidewalk outside the hotel at 8:00 P.M.

"I didn't want the *News* to go broke because of a libel suit because of me," Breslin explains. "I was nervous. I wanted a second person to hear the same thing I heard."

When Giuliani again thanked Breslin and praised him for delivering a crucial witness—this time in the presence of Browne—Breslin felt he had this confirmation.

Breslin went back up to his office and made a few small corrections in his story. In a compromise with modern technology, he made these editing changes on a computer screen.

By 10:00 P.M. it was done, and Breslin could relax. He asked Arthur Browne to join him for a celebration drink at Costello's, the same bar where Dowd had told him the story.

At Costello's Breslin was in a manic state, waiting for his story to hit the city. "I'm the greatest, I'm J-B!" he roared. "Those bastards, Mel and Shelly, never told me. They made me look bad, so fuck them!"

Breslin and Browne also had a laugh about what the mayor was going to think when he read the story. The night before, Koch had visited Manes in his hospital room, kissed him, hugged him, and assured him: "Don't worry about anything, Donny, we all love you."

At midnight the *Daily News* four-star final rolled off the presses with a giant front-page headline: MANES ACCUSED OF EXTORTION. Under it was the logo of Breslin's column, his smiling face, and his stark and dramatic lead:

> Michael Dowd, a Queens Blvd. attorney, last night told the United States attorney's office in Manhattan that Donald Manes, the Queens borough president, extorted money from him for a period of 18 months.
>
> This revelation causes the city's Parking Violations Bureau scandal to detonate. . . .
>
> It now appears that New York, under Mayor Koch, has the largest political scandal since Jimmy Walker was on the nightclub floor and his people were out stealing even the street lights.

Breslin's column ignited a firestorm, and Mike Dowd was at the center of it. By 8:00 A.M. television news crews and reporters surrounded his house. His telephone was ringing every minute; one caller just said, "Everyone from Xavier is ashamed of you," and hung up. But publicist Marty McLaughlin, an adviser to Manes, Vallone, and Friedman, told Dowd he did the right thing. Giuliani called and assured Dowd he had not leaked the story to Breslin. His former sister-in-law, who hadn't spoken to him since his separation, called to wish him well. Stillman called and said Dowd had better come to his office, as they might have to hold a press conference to deal with the frenzy of instant renown.

Dowd stared at the photograph of himself in the *Daily News,* taken sixteen years earlier, when he had a crewcut. Vanity gave him strength, and he decided to go out and face the media horde and let them take some good pictures. Stepping out onto his porch on Ireland Street, he announced that he had a statement to make, and paused while the cameras were focused and the microphones set up.

"I like the Bears and six in the Super Bowl," he said, and laughter broke the tension. Then Dowd went back into his house.

As the firestorm grew in intensity, Dowd and Stillman discussed their strategy on the phone. Stillman suggested that he read a short statement to the press, but that Dowd not be present. As Dowd would later write in his journal, though: "We'll prepare it, and he will read it. I won't be there. Fuck that. I'm going to be there. I want a message to Manes and his friends. I'm here, you bums. I'm not backing off."

At 1:00 P.M. more than fifty reporters, photographers, camera and sound people, and technicians were jostling for position in Stillman's tiny conference room. Stillman read, and Dowd sat next to him, in a new pinstripe suit. The statement was lawyer's talk:

"Mr. Dowd was pressured by others abusing their official positions. . . . I also want to state that Mr. Dowd independently stopped acceding to these pressures long before the investigation began."

When Stillman finished reading, he and Dowd got up and left the conference room. Before they could disappear, New York's most famous local television reporter, Gabe Pressman, shouted out one question: "The mayor says Manes is a crook, but so are you. What do you have to say?"

Afterward Dowd wrote in his notebook:

The attack is on. They are making me a crook. I'm so tired. I haven't slept in 36 hours. They're going to stop me. The feds will back off. This is too big, better to make me look like a shit. My nerves are shot. They wanna shut me up.

Giuliani wants to talk to me. We drive down the U.S. Attorney's office. Riding down the FDR [Drive] I know I can't bring Manes down. Can't we just surrender and say it was all a mistake? I'm on a battlefield. I just want to get up [and] wave the white flag. I'm not going to get Manes. Already Koch has started. They'll destroy [me] and what for? Nothing will change. I'm so scared.

Seeing how distraught Dowd was, Giuliani arranged for Dowd and his daughter to spend Thursday night in hotel rooms in Manhattan, where they could escape the media frenzy outside their home in Queens. Dowd was grateful, and this small kindness helped to further dissolve the mistrust the penitent felt toward the avenging angel.

Although Dowd had feared that nobody would believe his story, few doubters stepped forward—not even the mayor, who disliked both him and Breslin. Perhaps because he so resented the messengers, Koch gave a strained performance at a long press conference he held Thursday morning in response to Breslin's column. The mayor, who usually was a masterful and intimidating performer before the media, was defensive, groping for the right posture.

"My accountability is what I personally do," he said. "My reputation is adequate in terms of my own personal integrity."

Koch then tried to insulate himself from accountability for Lindenauer, his deputy commissioner: "I said I would limit my appointments to commissioners, and on occasion deputy commissioners, and the commissioners would have the power to make their own appointments. . . . I am very proud of the appointments I made. I believe they were on the merits.

"When I delegated that responsibility to commissioners to do the same, I don't know, and never will know, whether they exercised the same high standards."

Koch had indeed appointed Anthony Ameruso to be the transportation commissioner, but it was through the influence of Brooklyn party boss Meade Esposito. Ameruso, in turn, had accepted the recommendation from Manes, the boss of the Queens Democrats, to appoint Lindenauer and Shafran to top jobs at PVB. While the mayor argued that he had no responsibility for anyone except the commissioner, and that by delegating so much authority he was actually practicing good government, the party leaders in effect had directly controlled a city agency.

In his Thursday press conference Koch also attempted to distance himself from Manes, whom in the previous week he had just called "an honest man" and kissed in his hospital bed:

"I didn't elect Donny Manes. He is elected by the people of Queens. It's not that my administration is tarnished. Donny Manes is independently elected."

The next morning, New York's journalistic Gibbon, Murray Kempton, began his *Newsday* column in this gracious fashion:

> The Mayor and I woke yesterday to see the substantial figure of Jimmy Breslin of the *New York Daily News* shrunk almost to a point of invisibility on the horizon across which he was running so far ahead of us and everyone else. . . .
>
> The Mayor met the journalists in the Blue Room of City Hall yesterday, and the occasion brought them into closer community than has been invariably their experience, because all those present were engaged in the same desperate game of catch-up.
>
> "I am shocked," the mayor said.
>
> And he would say it three times in the next hour until the thought occurred that the Great Seal of New York has gone 300 years without a civic motto, and that the mayor who is the author of so many other novelties, had now remedied that long neglect with whatever the Latin might be for, "I am shocked."

January 26 was Super Bowl Sunday, and Dowd was looking forward to watching the game at Peter Maas's home with a group of friends. At 11:30 that morning he watched Mayor Koch, in a fierce mood, being interviewed live on television by Gabe Pressman.

"I would have staked my life on the honesty of Donald Manes," Koch said. "But nevertheless, even though he is someone whom I would have allowed to be the executor of my estate—I've known him for more than twenty years—I am convinced now that he engaged in being a crook. . . . Dowd is just as much a crook—that the two of them should ultimately go to jail."

The mayor then took the offensive and attacked Jimmy Breslin for his friendship with Dowd: "Breslin was not a good enough reporter to know he was hanging around with crooks. . . . Why didn't Jimmy Breslin investigate Michael Dowd eight years ago?

"There was a city marshal," Koch went on. "His name was Sheldon—Chevlowe—who allegedly . . . was the bagman. . . .

And do you know who delivered the eulogy at his funeral? Jimmy Breslin!"

The mayor then returned to Dowd, calling him a "villain," who came forward only when he felt the "hot breath" of federal prosecutors on his neck.

In an effort to minimize the Manes scandal with a historical perspective, Koch even assaulted his professed hero, Fiorello La Guardia.

"They were stealing cadavers out of the morgue during the La Guardia administration," he reminded viewers. "Cadavers! Out of the morgue!" he added in outraged theatrical emphasis.

While the mayor's performance—his personalizing, his scapegoating, his intense attack on Manes, his attempt to undermine Breslin's credibility—troubled many people, it terrified Mike Dowd. Koch was vindicating Dowd's paranoia about an establishment conspiracy to silence him. The mayor of New York was declaring that he should go to jail after he had received immunity from the federal government. The mayor was calling him a criminal after Giuliani had certified he was a victim of the crime of extortion.*

At the end of the program, Dowd wrote these rambling thoughts in his journal:

> I watched Koch call me a villain, a criminal, and say I should go to jail. It hurts. Hasn't this hurt me? He mis-stated the facts. Well-wishers even talk about a new career for me. It's silly to think he's not hurting me. I'm frightened for my daughter. . . .
>
> I think the machine is trying to protect itself. Koch on the point. How much of a life is left to me? I think, in personal terms, whether this is too high a price to pay. Dear God how long can I hold up? I'll hold up long enough to bring the bastards down, or it isn't worth anything.

Donald Manes would not learn until weeks later that the mayor had called him a "crook," or that a few days after the

---

*In March 1987, when the grievance committee of the appellate division was considering the possibility of disciplining Dowd, Rudy Giuliani wrote a letter in Dowd's support, which rebutted the mayor's comments in this interview. Giuliani wrote that Dowd came forward "on his own volition," and, "unlike any other vendor dealing with Lindenauer and Manes, Mr. Dowd ceased payments voluntarily, well before the initiation of this investigation."

Pressman interview Koch had said Manes was exaggerating his health problems to avoid responding to the charges of corruption. In late January he was still not allowed to watch any television newscasts. His family not only shut off the TV set during football and basketball half-times, to black out any one-minute newsbreaks that might contain a reference to Manes or PVB, but also clipped stories out of the papers that might upset Manes before he could see them. Manes probably was conscious only of fragments of the media's coverage of him, and kept asking visitors, "What are they saying about me?"

Manes's condition had improved steadily; his heart was strengthening, his wrist was mending, his appetite had improved, and his EEG was normal. But his mind was not healing, and he remained in a deep depression. He could not cope with his deprivation of approval and status. He could not cope with his fears that the shameful secrets of his life were about to spill out.

After his discharge from NYU Hospital on January 25, Manes spent his days at home, often alone, when his wife returned to work. He sat in his bathrobe, lost in memory, gazing into space, listening to music, breaking long silences to mutter to himself, "Bad, bad, bad." One visitor heard him mumble, "I shouldn't have let him talk me into it." Another visitor heard him say that Shelly Chevlowe had convinced him to start taking payoffs. A third friend recalls Manes muttering, "I should have stopped Lindenauer." He left the house only to see doctors, a physical therapist, and two psychiatrists.

Manes had tried to kill himself before there was any direct evidence or any witnesses against him. By losing his nerve, he dramatized himself as a suspect. But by early February he had to have learned that there was a witness against him—Mike Dowd. He must also have assumed that since Lindenauer had not run away, and had not hired Harold Borg, that he, too, might eventually turn on him. And he had to be concerned that Lebetkin might make a deal and give him up. He knew that Breslin had attacked him as well, and that the mayor was no longer his friend. He was a man dependent on approval, who was being rejected; a man fearful to be alone, being left alone; a man fearing abandonment, being abandoned.

Around this time an old friend, publicist George Douris, called Manes to cheer him up.

"How are you feeling?" Douris asked.

"It's rough," Manes replied in a weak voice. "When did you get back from Greece?"

"That was in 1971 when we went to Greece with our wives," Douris explained gently.

"Oh" was all Manes said in response.

During the two months when he was recuperating, with reporters permanently camped outside his house, not one member of Manes's staff came to see him. When he reached out for Alan Gershuny, who had managed his first campaign for the city council in 1965, Gershuny was curt and unfriendly. His only regular nonfamily visitors were his lawyer Mike Armstrong; Sid Davidoff; Martin Swarzman, a real estate developer under indictment; and Spike Goldstein, the president of a hospital supply company.

On February 11, Manes formally resigned as both borough president and Democratic county leader. The authority he had acquired during twenty years of maneuver and power plays he surrendered by signing a piece of paper. Manes did not appear in public for the resignation, which was proffered in a one-page statement distributed by his aides that contained the obligatory "I know I will be fully vindicated."

When reporters rang his doorbell, a nurse came to the door and said, "Mr. Manes is in bed right now."

No one can get inside Donald Manes's skin and know what he was thinking and feeling during his season of confinement. One day he was a prince of the city and the next a prisoner inside his own house. One day the mayor was his best friend, and now he had no friends in politics at all. Most powerful politicians caught in scandal survive it, but Manes had been irreparably damaged.

What seems likely is that Donald Manes had a predisposition to depression that was partly hereditary, a predisposition that was expressed in the suicide of Manes's own father.

Manes almost never spoke about the manner of his father's death, nor the suicide attempt of his twin brother Morty, and even his own staff and many of his friends were not aware of it. In November 1985, when Manes sponsored a seminar on teenage suicide prevention, he could not bring himself to mention his own nightmare experience to the mental health professionals and educators assembled in his office conference room. All Manes said was that the public was not adequately informed about suicide because "the issue itself is still taboo—people don't like to talk about death."

During this period the U.S. Attorney avoided applying undue pressure on Manes. It wasn't that Giuliani had any special insight into how mentally disturbed Manes was; he did not. His goal was to convince Manes to plead guilty to one racketeering count, and help clean up New York by becoming a government witness against other corrupt public officials. Giuliani suspected that Manes's criminality was not just limited to PVB but that he was the maypole of graft in Queens, and that he had knowledge of payoffs in the courts, in cable television franchises, and in real estate development. Giuliani took no steps to subpoena Manes before a grand jury, or move to indict him. For his own tactical reasons he accepted Mike Armstrong's representations that Manes was too ill to testify.

But Giuliani had another theory, which grew stronger over time and became his "informed opinion," after Manes killed himself, about why Manes might not be able to work with the government: he suspected that Manes "might have had so many transactions with organized crime that he was too frightened to cooperate," that he feared reprisals against his family. Giuliani studied all the existing law enforcement files on Manes and came to the conclusion that Manes had serious personal and financial entanglements with several known organized-crime associates.

One of these men was Eddie Chan, whom the President's Commission on Organized Crime had named as the Chinatown boss in its 1984 report. Public testimony taken by the commission implicated Chan in the murder of a rival gang leader's bodyguard, and he was described by FBI indices as a "murder contractor" and a "narcotics dealer."

Manes had had many close dealings with Chan. In 1982 Chan arranged for and participated in an expenses-paid junket to Taiwan for Manes and a delegation of Queens politicians and businessmen, including Michael Nussbaum, who was both Manes's campaign manager and Chan's public relations consultant. In Taiwan, Chan brought several hookers to a nightclub where the Queens group was eating, but they weren't interested. Chan raised campaign money for Manes and hosted Chinatown fundraisers for him. After a dinner arranged by Manes between himself, Chan, and the mayor, both Police Commissioner Robert McGuire and Manhattan D.A. Robert Morgenthau warned

Koch and Manes that Chan was a major underworld figure with whom they should not socialize. Koch never saw Chan again, but Manes's logs and diaries show no diminishing of their contacts.* And Nussbaum, one of Manes's closest advisers, continued on Chan's payroll.

One possible emissary from organized crime, Michael Callahan, is known to have surreptitiously visited Manes in his home at least twice during February and early March. These visits, unlike almost all others, were arranged by Manes himself at times his wife was not at home, and were the only ones Sid Davidoff says he was not informed of in advance. After each visit Callahan left the Manes house by the back door, walked several blocks to a pay phone, called someone, and read from a notebook.

In 1982, Callahan had been indicted with Genovese crime family soldier Joe Trocchio for a conspiracy that involved the torching of houses to collect insurance. Callahan eventually pleaded guilty to lesser charges and was sentenced to five years' probation. The case was part of the Abscam investigation, and Mel Weinberg, the government's undercover con man in Abscam, had many meetings with Callahan.

Weinberg told us that Callahan and his mob mentor, Joe Trocchio, brought him to Carlo Gambino's home at a time when Gambino was considered to be the most powerful of all racketeers.

A construction contractor by profession, Callahan had built Manes's summer home in Westhampton and sold it to him at a below-market price. In December 1985, Manes went to Atlantic City to meet Callahan and look at some property. And Manes's office phone logs showed forty calls from Callahan over a two-year period, including messages from the Bahamas and Atlantic City.

Because there were no witnesses to their meetings in the Manes living room in February and early March 1986, there is no proof that Callahan was applying underworld pressure on Manes not to cooperate with Giuliani. It can only be surmised, from the furtive nature of Callahan's visits, from his evasive movements after he departed the Manes home, and from his

---

*Nussbaum was convicted in 1987 of perjury in a case growing out of Manes's attempt to extort payoffs from those seeking cable television franchises in Queens. An appellate court overturned the conviction in July 1988.

Mafia connections, that Michael Callahan's visits may not have been motivated entirely by altruism, but may have had the purpose of conveying a credible threat.

It had taken Bernie Sandow and Mike Dowd a week to decide to cooperate. But for two months Geoffrey Lindenauer engaged in one of the most publicized plea bargainings in New York history, with the ups, downs, terms, threats, and impasses all followed closely by the newspapers.

A primary reason for the delay was, simply, the human element. Lindenauer and Manes were best friends, and the end game of the bargaining would have to be that Lindenauer would walk into a room with twenty-three grand jurors and admit crimes that would put his best friend in prison for ten or fifteen years. Lindenauer's tearful embrace of Manes at the close of 1985 and promise never to testify against him was not a melodramatic fabrication, but a deeply felt culmination of fifteen years of affection and shared experiences.

Lindenauer and Manes first met in the late 1960s, at parties given by the Institute for Emotional Education, the private Manhattan clinic that Lindenauer owned and worked in as a therapist. Marlene Manes was a frequent visitor to the institute, and became Lindenauer's friend before her husband did.

By 1973, Manes and Marlene, and Lindenauer with his wife, bought condominiums on the same day in the same complex in Westhampton Beach. Manes and Lindenauer were speaking nearly daily on the phone, meeting a few times a week, and vacationing together in the summer. They also jointly purchased a small boat for $1,800 but put it in Lindenauer's name, because, Manes felt, "It wouldn't look good" for a politician to own such an extravagance. It was during that year that Lindenauer's father killed himself, which created a tragic bond with Manes.

In 1974, both men celebrated their fortieth birthdays, and Manes secretly invested $25,000 in cash in Lindenauer's clinic. The transaction was predicated on the understanding that Lindenauer would employ Marlene Manes as the co-director but not tell her about her husband's investment, so that she would believe she obtained the job on her own merits. But the cult-like institute was coming under investigation for unethical practices and tax evasion. Not only was Lindenauer having sex with his clients, but all the 135 patients were encouraged to have sex with one another and with the "counselors." Lindenauer had purchased two phony degrees for $500 from a Canadian divinity school, and many of the other therapists on the staff of the clinic also had counterfeit doctorates, bought from the same diploma mill. Shortly after Marlene Manes went to work as its co-director, the institute fell into bankruptcy.

In 1976, at the peak of the fiscal crisis, when cops, firefighters, and teachers were being fired in the name of austerity, Manes, with the help of Stanley Friedman, who was then deputy mayor, got Lindenauer a city job in the Addiction Services Agency. A year later Lindenauer was fired, but he remained on the payroll for two months until Manes found him another position, as assistant director of the PVB. Lindenauer felt a deep sense of gratitude and obligation toward Manes for obtaining these public jobs for him after his therapy clinic went broke.

Geoffrey Lindenauer was a follower, and in the psychobabble of his own pseudo-profession, he can be described as an individual who was "emotionally infantilized." As a follower of Donald Manes, he was faithful and obedient, while at the same time being brutal to those he was extorting money from. Now, in the course of plea bargaining, Lindenauer would have to decide if he could transfer his capacity for subservient loyalty to Rudy Giuliani, as different a man as could be imagined.

The day-to-day plea negotiations for Lindenauer's cooperation were conducted between Giuliani's chief of the criminal division, Howard Wilson, and Lindenauer's attorney, Irving Seidman. Unlike most of the defense lawyers in the case, Seidman had never been a federal prosecutor. A former assistant in the Brooklyn district attorney's office, he rose to become chief of the rackets bureau in 1966, but resigned to enter private practice five years later. Seidman was a stubborn, loquacious, methodical lawyer. The fact that Lindenauer went to him and not Harold Borg was probably one of the watershed decisions in the entire unraveling of the corruption scandal.

Giuliani assigned the negotiations to Howard Wilson, who had a constructive history with Seidman. In 1975 Wilson had been an assistant to Joe Hynes during an investigation into corruption in New York's nursing home industry. During that probe, Wilson worked out an agreement with Seidman that led to a Seidman client's becoming a wired undercover informant for the prosecutors and making substantial cases against crooked vendors. Wilson knew, going into the negotiations, that Seidman was willing to have a client cooperate under some circumstances. He was not one of those criminal lawyers who encourage their clients not to cooperate and then tip off the targets if they do.

Although Lindenauer had refused to flip when the FBI had approached him on January 10 and 14, he was in a stronger position then; at that point, Bernie Sandow was the only witness who could testify he paid him bribes. Also, the federal prosecutor had played for Lindenauer the tape of his November 26 lunch recorded by Burnett at Hisae's, which was incriminating but not devastating. But when Mike Dowd walked into Giuliani's office on January 22, a strong airtight case was locked in against Lindenauer. Then in February, the principals of another collection company that paid off, Sennett and Krumholtz, added vivid grand jury evidence against Lindenauer and inferences that Manes was getting half the bribes. The combination shifted all the leverage to the government's side in the negotiations with Lindenauer. Dowd plus Sandow plus Sennett plus the Hisae's tape equaled almost certain conviction.

The first major meeting between Wilson and Seidman occurred on Friday night, January 24, the day after Breslin's column appeared. Giuliani, Romano, and LaBella were working in their offices and drifted in and out, but it was Wilson's affair. The main item on the agenda was Seidman's proffer, his "show of proof," of what evidence his client could provide the government in return for leniency. From the beginning there was no question of immunity for Lindenauer; the government's non-negotiable position was that he would have to plead to at least one racketeering count and one mail fraud count, and serve substantial time in prison, but Wilson offered flexibility on forfeiture, tax consequences, and civil penalties.

Seidman began by professing that he was "shocked" by what his client had revealed to him, and stated, "I can't believe the city government is running this way."

Wilson then asked for the names of the people that Lindenauer's testimony could help convict.

Seidman said: "Manes, Shafran, Mike Lazar, and Stanley Friedman."

Wilson was not surprised to hear Friedman's name, and it confirmed his belief that Lindenauer was "a dynamite witness."

For weeks after this initial "show of proof" meeting, the two attorneys struggled with the terms of the deal. Much of the bargaining was over financial details, civil tax consequences, and sheltering some of Lindenauer's assets from forfeiture under RICO. Seidman's bottom-line concern was that Lindenauer's family not be destitute when Lindenauer went to prison.

By mid-February the talks had reached an impasse. The media frenzy had not abated, and Giuliani was under pressure to act. Wilson started calling Seidman several times a day with dire warnings that a fifty-count indictment with RICO charges was imminent unless there was progress in the negotiations, and even produced a draft of such a document.

On Wednesday, February 12, both *Newsday* and the *Daily News* carried stories that indictments of Manes and Lindenauer might be voted the next day. Under federal law, Lindenauer had to be charged within thirty days of his arrest. Although February 13 was the deadline, it was circumvented when Giuliani's office filed a sealed application for an extension with federal magistrate Naomi Buchwald, citing "extraordinary circumstances." Seidman agreed to it.

On Friday, February 21, after a week of public conflict with Manhattan D.A. Robert Morgenthau over jurisdiction, Giuliani and Wilson decided to move. They would indict Lindenauer alone, without Manes, although with Dowd's grand jury testimony there was now sufficient evidence to obtain an indictment against Manes. The next day, the *Times* reported that Lindenauer would be indicted on Monday if he did not agree to cooperate. Lindenauer was shaken by the story and spent most of Saturday in Seidman's office, wavering.

On Monday, February 24, at a packed press conference, Giuliani announced a thirty-nine-count indictment of Lindenauer, based on his collecting and extorting $410,000 in bribes. The indictment alleged that Lindenauer had received $313,000 in cash, airfare, and hotel accommodations from Sandow's company, SRS; $68,000 from Sennett and Krumholz; and $29,000 from Dowd's company. The charges included racketeering, extortion, and mail fraud.

But the massed media, expecting Manes to be named as well, seemed disappointed. Most of the questions were about why Manes was excluded from the formal charges. All Giuliani could say was: "I can't legally answer that question. We anticipate further charges."

The thirty-nine counts filed against Lindenauer carried a

theoretical maximum term of more than a hundred years in prison, millions of dollars in fines, and mandatory forfeiture under RICO, an array of penalties that was sufficient to break the logjam in negotiations. Over the next week Seidman became a less leisurely bargainer.

Count thirty-eight in the federal indictment of Lindenauer stated that

> Lindenauer and his co-schemers would and did make and cause to be made false and fraudulent representations and omissions in connection with the consideration and selection of Citisource, Inc., to manufacture a hand-held computer device for the purpose of issuing traffic summonses.

This was a reference to Citisource fixer Stanley Friedman, and by now D.A. Morgenthau had staked out the prosecution of the Bronx party boss as the piece of the scandal over which he had jurisdiction. Eager to prosecute, Morgenthau resorted to an unorthodox tactic to force Giuliani to give him the Friedman-Citisource case. On February 28, as Lindenauer came up the steps of the federal courthouse for his arraignment, detectives from the staff of the Manhattan D.A. handed him a subpoena to testify before a state grand jury.

At 10:05 A.M., the clerk in the federal court's arraignment part called the first case on the day's calendar—*The United States of America v. Geoffrey Lindenauer.*

"The government is ready, your honor," answered prosecutor Chuck LaBella.

After a long silence, Judge William Connor said: "No one here representing Geoffrey Lindenauer? I guess he forgot."

Five minutes later, in the middle of the arraignment of another defendant, Seidman and Lindenauer, clearly agitated, entered the courtroom, and recruited the judge and prosecutor to a nearby conference room. After ten minutes, LaBella came out, leaving defendant, lawyer, and judge behind closed doors. The mass of reporters began to assume the long-awaited plea bargain was at hand, knowing nothing of the state subpoena served on the steps.

At 10:55 Lindenauer and Seidman marched grimly into the

courthouse. The clerk asked how the defendant pleaded to the indictment.

"Not guilty," replied Lindenauer.

Then LaBella announced that the government wished to make "an application," and all the parties marched into Judge Connor's robing room, with the reporters still in the dark about these unusual private conferences.

When he emerged from this second meeting, Seidman announced to the assembled media: "My client intends to go to trial. . . . There is no deal."

In the afternoon, from 3:15 to 4:00, a full legal argument over the state subpoena took place in Judge Connor's robing room. With Lindenauer and Seidman present, lawyers on the staff of the federal and state prosecutors made their cases to win the tug-of-war over their defendant.

At the end of the private meeting, the record was sealed, the parties bound to silence by the judge, and no resolution was announced to the perplexed press corps.

What happened in the sequence of closed-door debates was that the federal lawyers had succeeded in convincing Judge Connor to stay the state subpoena. This thwarted Morgenthau's attempt to bring Lindenauer before a state grand jury before Giuliani could complete negotiations and put him before a federal grand jury. Morgenthau believed he had the stronger case against Friedman, and he was determined to assert his local jurisdiction.

The next day, Saturday, March 1, Giuliani (accompanied by Howard Wilson) and Morgenthau (accompanied by his low-keyed, academic chief assistant Robert Pitler) held a face-to-face summit peace conference. The two principals were opposites in many ways. Morgenthau was a German-Jewish Our Crowd aristocrat, the son of Franklin Roosevelt's Secretary of the Treasury, a lifelong liberal Democrat, a shy, reserved man now in his sixties. Giuliani was more than twenty years younger, the son of a tavern owner, a Democrat turned Republican, a man whose adrenaline flowed faster when the cameras were on him. But they both had a strong sense of public service and law enforcement professionalism, and it was not hard to work out a satisfactory compromise.

They agreed that first Giuliani would indict Manes, Shafran, and Lazar, after which Morgenthau would be free to use Lindenauer's testimony to indict Friedman on rigging the Citisource contract. Then Giuliani would in turn indict Friedman in a broader racketeering conspiracy. Morgenthau agreed to withdraw his subpoena of Lindenauer, honor any plea worked out by Giuliani, and not prosecute Lindenauer on any state charges.

The Saturday summit resolved the sideshow and paved the way for the final hard bargaining between Wilson and Seidman.

Monday, March 3, was a marathon negotiating session between the two attorneys, both in Wilson's office and back and forth by telephone. By the end of the day Seidman had a promise that no one else would prosecute, or sue Lindenauer for civil damages, once he pleaded guilty in federal court. State attorney general Robert Abrams agreed he would not sue for back state taxes on the bribe money. City corporation counsel Fritz Schwarz agreed New York City would not sue Lindenauer for damages or try to collect city taxes. The U.S. Attorney in the Eastern District, Ray Dearie, promised he would not prosecute Lindenauer. Lindenauer agreed to plead guilty to racketeering and mail fraud, pay back all the bribe money he kept, and pay federal taxes on it.

On Thursday, March 6, the front page of the *New York Post* announced LINDENAUER SET TO COP A PLEA, a report that was premature. Seidman would not sign the official agreement until he had the oral promises from eight other prosecutorial agencies in legal writing and fine detail. He further held up signing on Thursday because he did not yet have a written guarantee that Lindenauer's home was exempt from any forfeiture. Wilson kept saying, "Trust me," and Seidman kept saying, "Put it in writing."

On Friday, March 7, the page-one headline in the *Post* read: LINDY AGREES TO TELL ALL, followed on the second page by: IT'S A DEAL—LINDENAUER AGREES TO BE A SQUEALER. Even before he formally pleaded guilty on Monday, March 10, however, Lindenauer spent the entire weekend of March 8 and 9 in Giuliani's office, telling his story in full detail to five members of Giuliani's staff (Wilson, Romano, Mary Shannon, David Zornow, and Bill Schwartz), to FBI agents Persichini and Jaco, and to John Moscow of Morgenthau's office.

Recalls Wilson: "It was an amazing performance. The weekend was half a debriefing, half a proffer. He told us things we didn't know about, like the $58,000 payment from Manes on

New Year's Eve. He told us all the details about how Friedman fixed the Citisource contract. He was clear, precise, and unsparing. It was then that I knew the two months of negotiations were worth it."

Giuliani had initially intended to indict Manes the day after Lindenauer testified against him in the grand jury, since Dowd had already given his testimony, but as he recalls, "Mike [Armstrong] was so persuasive about Manes's mental condition, I changed my mind."

A sheet of paper taped to the door of room 129 in the federal courthouse on March 10 listed three cases for pretrial conference, the middle one of which said: "1:30 A.M. 86 cr158 US v. Lindenauer. PTC."

The "A.M." was a clerk's mistake; it was 1:30 P.M. when Geoffrey Lindenauer came into Judge John Sprizzo's courtroom. The "PTC" was an understatement. This was not a pretrial conference. This was history. And like most real history it was as dry and dull as possible.

Sprizzo asked Seidman, "Do you know any reason why he should not plead guilty?"

Seidman responded: "Your honor, I have spent the past sixty-five days reviewing this case with my client, and there is no doubt in my mind that he is doing this of his own free will."

Lindenauer then put on his glasses and read the lawyer's words on the piece of paper. First he read his guilty plea to count one, racketeering, then he read his plea of guilty to count thirty-nine, the mail fraud charge:

> Sometime in 1983, in order to assist Citisource, Inc. to fraudulently obtain a contract from the City of New York to manufacture hand-held computers to issue summonses, I made false statements to the contract selection committee, including a statement that I had seen a prototype when, in fact, I had not seen such a prototype. In the course of the contract selection process and the performance of the contract, mailings were made between the City of New York and Citisource, concerning the contract selection.

When it was over, the court stenographer, William Cohen, admitted that he had felt "a little dizzy" as he was taking down the plea. A half-hour of scripted legal language had set into motion the fall of two Democratic leaders, of two men who had sat in the first row at the mayor's inauguration just ten weeks earlier.

The forlorn Donald Manes remained in the solitude of his house during the final stages of his best friend's public plea bargaining. He was taking an antidepressant medication, but since its doses were limited as a result of his heart attack, it had little effect.

By March Manes was no longer shielded from television and newspapers, and he was growing more despondent as time passed. Lindenauer was about to testify against him; Dowd had already named him as an extortionist; the mayor had called him a crook. He was in disgrace. His indictment was imminent. He saw a hopeless future and couldn't face the options of prison or cooperation. More and more Manes began to talk openly about making a second suicide attempt as the strain on him mounted.

On March 6 Manes had gone to NYU Hospital for a stress test on his heart. Security guards had placed Manes in a rocking chair in his friend Martin Begun's private office while he waited for the test to begin. When Begun arrived he was surprised to see Manes, who didn't get up, but pulled Begun down toward him and hugged him.

"How are you feeling?" Begun asked.

"Life isn't worth living," Manes answered.

"That's silly. You have your family. Think of Marlene and your children. Politics isn't everything."

But Begun could see that Manes, his head down and his mind wandering, wasn't even listening. Begun, dean of the medical school, was frightened. That day he called several experts in the field, including the state commissioner of mental health, asking for the name of a facility where Manes might be placed. A number of people recommended the Four Winds Psychiatric Hospital in Poughkeepsie, New York. Begun relayed that proposal to Marlene Manes with his own opinion that Manes should be committed to a sanatorium, even if it was an involuntary commitment.

Manes was, in fact, already under the care of two psychiatrists, Dr. Robert Cancrow, the chief of psychiatry at NYU Hospital, and Dr. Elliot Wineburg, whose office was five blocks away in Jamaica Estates. Manes was supposed to see Wineburg three times a week, but he kept these appointments only sporadically. Sid Davidoff thought Manes was "manipulating the shrinks." One of the psychiatrists thought Manes needed to be hospitalized immediately, and the other believed he was better off in the caring, supportive environment of his family. With the professional medical opinion divided, and Manes unable to focus on anything, the situation drifted without a decision being made.

At least three of Manes's closest friends—Sid Davidoff, Martin Swarzman, and brother-in-law Bill Warren—saw him frequently in February and early March, and independently came to the same conclusion: Manes was thinking that, although it might be harder on his family at first if he killed himself, it would be better for them in the long run. Manes feared that a year of legal fees and a conviction under RICO would leave his family broke. And a trial with prolonged publicity would leave his wife and children with emotional wounds. Suicide may have appeared to him as a rational—even clever— economic choice, one that would preserve his assets for his heirs and cheat the government out of forfeiture, restitution, and back taxes.

On Wednesday night, March 12, Queens state senator Emanuel Gold visited Manes at his home. Gold had known Manes for more than twenty years, since they were both young lawyers together in Albany on the staff of assembly majority leader Moses Weinstein.

Gold tried to lift his friend out of his depression, but couldn't. Manes was lying on a couch with his eyes closed part of the time, as Gold told him how wonderful his family was and how much he had to live for. After a while Gold went over to him, and said, "I'm still your friend."

On the morning of Thursday, March 13, Manes arrived at the offices of his lawyer, Michael Armstrong, at 26 Broadway about 11:30 A.M. Their appointment was supposed to be a working session between lawyer and client to prepare a legal defense, to consider alternative strategies, to review documents and diaries that prosecutors were seeking. But Manes could not focus.

"He paced back and forth all day," recalls Armstrong. "He kept picking things up and putting them down. He took a placemat on my table and folded it, then refolded it repeatedly. He tore off a piece of Scotch tape, and wadded it up, and then he started to chew on it. . . .

"He said things about the futility of life that indicated to me he was thinking about taking his own life. I was so upset that I moved our meeting out of a conference room with windows into a room without windows. I thought he might jump."

At one point Armstrong left Manes with his assistants, Mary Corrarino and Charles Gerber, and placed a call to Manes's psychiatrist Elliot Wineburg to discuss institutionalizing him as soon as possible. Wineburg was inclined to hospitalize Manes for severe depression, and suggested New York Hospital's Payne Whitney Clinic as a likely place. He also mentioned to Armstrong that Manes had failed to keep his last three appointments with him.

Armstrong next called Marlene Manes, whom he told, "Donald should be in a hospital now, today. Don't wait for the weekend. He's suicidal."

Marlene, a psychologist by profession, had resisted the idea of committing her husband, but now she seemed to agree that the time had come to take this step.

When he returned to the office, Armstrong even told Manes directly that he should seriously consider checking himself into a psychiatric hospital.

"Maybe I should," Manes replied.

At about 5:30 Armstrong reached Sid Davidoff, who was at La Guardia Airport waiting to board a plane. The two lawyers were in complete accord that Manes had to be placed in a hospital immediately. Davidoff had visited Manes at home early that morning and could see how extreme his despondency was when he had asked how he was feeling.

At 4:00 P.M. Manes was picked up by his brother-in-law Albert Robbins and driven directly to Robbins's Flushing, Queens, home for a family dinner. They were joined by his sister Edith Robbins, his 25-year-old daughter Lauren, and Marlene.

The family dinner was tense. For long stretches he sat in sullen, morose silence, barely picking at his food, as his family discussed what to do about his mental state. At other points Manes roamed around the familiar house, picking things up and absentmindedly twisting them into odd shapes, just as he had in Armstrong's office.

When the family arrived home at 9:00 P.M., Manes started to prowl his own rooms and couldn't seem to sit in one place. Marlene told her daughter, "Keep an eye on your father, stay with him," and went into the bedroom and called Dr. Wineburg to say she thought her husband should be admitted that night to Mount Sinai Hospital in Manhattan.

Manes had by now paced from the kitchen into the bedroom, where he listened for a few minutes to his wife's half of the conversation. He then went back into the kitchen, with Lauren following him. Manes opened the kitchen drawer where all the carving knives were kept and reached for one.

"What are you doing there?" Lauren called out.

Manes quickly closed the drawer and paced back into the bedroom, back into the kitchen, and again opened the cutlery drawer. Lauren forced it closed while Manes stood motionless next to it.

Lauren shouted to her mother that her father was acting very strangely and that he had to be committed this very night to a hospital.

Marlene shouted back to her husband to pick up the phone and speak to Dr. Wineburg. Patient and therapist spoke briefly, but then Wineburg's doorbell rang, and he asked Manes to wait a moment while he answered it.

Donald Manes's back was to his daughter, the phone cradled between his shoulder and ear, abandoned for an instant by his psychiatrist. Suddenly Lauren came into the kitchen and noticed a strange look on her father's face, and then blood, just as Manes had seen his father's blood thirty years before. Lauren screamed, "I think Daddy cut himself!"

Dr. Wineburg heard the scream over the phone five blocks away on Tryon Place and started to run to the Manes home. Marlene ran into the kitchen, where she saw her husband facing the wall, a knife sticking out of his chest, his white shirt showing blood, the phone receiver dangling from the wall. As Manes slumped toward the floor, Marlene pulled the knife from her husband's punctured heart and flung it across the kitchen. She shouted for Lauren to call 911 for emergency assistance and then tried to breathe life into her husband's mouth. Donald Manes did not speak as his wife knelt over him on the floor of their kitchen.

"Donald Manes stabbed himself," Lauren screamed to a 911 emergency operator. It was 9:52 P.M.

"Donald Manes?" repeated a confused operator.

"Yes. Donald Manes. He just tried to commit suicide."

The operator asked for a phone number, and Lauren gave him two numbers at her home. The operator said he couldn't hear her, and Lauren repeated the numbers and the address.

Police officers Rourke Camoin and Anthony Laviero of the 107th Precinct were in their patrol car when they heard crackling over their radio: "10-54. Man stabbed. Sensitive location. 80-65 Chevy Chase Street." They arrived at the Manes home at 9:54.

"He stabbed himself," Marlene Manes told the two police officers and pointed to her husband, lying face up on the kitchen floor. At 9:58 two EMS paramedics—Debbie Wolf and William Bender—arrived. They were able to detect no sign of a heartbeat or breathing. Donald Manes was dead.

At 11:00 P.M. Detective Frank Ahern phoned Dr. Wineburg, who had returned to his home after trying to console the Manes family, but the psychiatrist refused to answer any questions about his last conversation with Manes. He invoked doctor-patient confidentiality and declined to cooperate with the police.

At 1:00 A.M. the body of Donald Manes was loaded into the morgue wagon and transported from Booth Hospital to the Manhattan Medical Examiner's office. Through a thin mist, a hard rain was falling.

Fourteen hours after Donald Manes was pronounced dead, Mayor Koch appeared at Antun's catering hall, on Springfield Boulevard in Queens, to speak at the annual luncheon of the Queens Chamber of Commerce. Antun's had been the venue of all Manes's political dinners. Many of those at the lunch had been friends of the late borough president, and there was genuine grief in the room. The new council majority leader Peter Vallone was on the dais in somber mourning, unable to eat the pre–Saint Patrick's Day dish of corned beef and cabbage placed in front of him. He had told a reporter that this day was "the low point of my political—no—make that entire—life."

But the mayor arrived in an exuberant mood. The mayor seemed liberated, perhaps believing the tragedy of Manes's death would signal the end of the scandal that was preoccupying his administration. Wishful thinking had, in fact, been the tone of interviews the mayor's two most media-sophisticated advisers—Dan Wolf and David Garth—gave the day after Manes's death.

Wolf told Joyce Purnick of the *Times:* "The fact that this is the end of a chapter, that someone's been punished, he's paid a price, a big price—people are going to be a bit more under control. They got their victim."

Garth's message was similar: "Unfortunately the man is dead, and the appearance of his being hounded and the investigation being the cause of it, even if it is not true, is going to have a sobering effect. It's got to slow it down."

In his coverage of the Chamber of Commerce banquet for *Newsday*, however, Mike McAlary reported that Koch "surprised many onlookers . . . by choosing to test his popularity with voters and book readers."

"How many people here read my first book?" Koch asked a stunned audience. About half the arms in the room went up.

"How many people read my second book?"

Only about twelve hands remained in the air.

"You should be ashamed of yourselves," Koch joked, and then launched into his old *shtick:* "How'm I doing?"

Most of the arms in the room went up in affirmation.

"Let me ask this," he went on. "If you were to have an election tomorrow, would you vote for me, raise your hand."

About one-third of the audience raised their hands.

"How many wouldn't vote for me?"

Just a few hands went up.

Koch looked at the minority of dissenters, and as Joyce Purnick wrote in the *Times*, "the seemingly euphoric Mayor" shouted, "You lose!"

The mayor went on so long in his giddy fashion that Kaye Kelly, Governor Cuomo's representative at the luncheon, was bumped from the program. Kelly had planned to read a traditional Irish blessing for Manes:

May the road to heaven rise gently with you.
May the wind of the Lord's mercy be always at your
    back.
May the rain of the Lord's fall gently on the fields of
    your soul.
May God in His judgment deal kindly with you.

Because the mayor had taken up so much time polling the guests about his literary and political popularity, the blessing for Donald Manes went unspoken.

The Sunday morning funeral had an ironic symmetry to its tragedy. The service was held at Schwartz Brothers on Queens

Boulevard, the very place where the downfall of Donald Manes had begun on the Sunday morning he walked over to Mike Dowd at the close of Shelly Chevlowe's funeral and instructed him to start paying his bribes to Geoffrey Lindenauer now that Shelly was gone.

About 600 mourners filled the chapel, and another 500 stood outside behind police barriers. Inside, in the front rows, were Governor Cuomo, Mayor Koch, Comptroller Goldin, Council President Stein, Vallone, the entire Board of Estimate, Stanley Friedman, Richie Rubin, the news Queens borough president Claire Schulman, former council president Carol Bellamy, former Manhattan borough president Percy Sutton, and state attorney general Robert Abrams.

The opinions among the Boulevard people outside were mixed. One man, paraphrasing Shakespeare, said, "The evil that men do lives after them, and the good is buried with their bones. So it was with Caesar. So it is with Manes."

A secretary who had worked for Manes in Borough Hall, tearful and bitter, told a *Times* reporter: "We can't get in to pray for his soul, and we worked with the man. And Koch gets in, and he was his worst enemy."

Some folk philosophy was also heard among the Boulevard mourners. One man, standing behind the barricade, said, "Maybe it's better not to be important," while another in the line offered, "Some people are weaker than others."

Inside the chapel, Queens assemblyman Alan Hevesi delivered a eulogy to a hushed room where the only sound was choked sobs.

"How unbelievable it is that we're here," Hevesi began. "Such a terrible waste. . . .

"I must tell you there may be some confusion because of recent events, but it doesn't have to be.

"Forget that—that's not Donald Manes. And forget the image of Donald for the past two months—a man who was profoundly ill with life-threatening ailments, more than one, and emotionally ill—life-threatening as we have seen.

"Forget that image. The real Donald Manes was an outstanding public figure. Donald Manes made me proud to be a New Yorker. He made me proud to be a resident of Queens. He made me proud to be a public official.

"And he made me proud to be his friend."

At the end of the service, the line of grim and ashen-faced

leaders of the city waved off reporters as they got into double-parked official cars, choosing to keep complicated thoughts private.

But Mayor Koch—who had convicted Manes before he was indicted, and had come to the funeral only after receiving his widow's permission—only Mayor Koch had a prepared statement for the media.

The mayor had had the foresight to arrange for his aides to bring along his own microphone stand to the funeral. Afterward the mayor held forth in what George Arzt in the *Post* called a "press conference." His comments dominated the television coverage that night of the funeral.

"God will be his ultimate judge," Koch told the cameras and microphones. "I hope that on His scales that God will be merciful and give him his rightful place in Heaven. . . . His family, his children, his wife deserve support, sympathy, compassion, love, from all his friends, who are their friends, of which I am one."

The death of Donald Manes was not an ending, and the mayor's sense of relief was short-lived. On March 26, Giuliani announced racketeering indictments of Mike Lazar and Lester Shafran. The indictments named Manes as an unindicted "co-racketeer," who took $285,000 in cash bribes.

The next day Morgenthau announced a twenty-seven-count indictment that accused Friedman and five Citisource company executives of obtaining their $22.7 million city contract through "bribery, fraud, and coercion."

The following week, Mayor Koch was a guest on Larry King's popular interview program on the Cable Television Network. A national audience in the millions saw the mayor of New York, under the pressure of renewed scandal, reveal part of his fantasy life.

> KING: Are you going to run again?
> KOCH: For a fourth, fifth, and sixth term.
> KING: Sixth term?
> KOCH: Yes.
> KING: Then what?
> KOCH: Then I'll give the eulogy at Jimmy Breslin's funeral.

CHAPTER FOUR

The Rise of Ed Koch

ED KOCH'S RISE TO POWER in New York City is the story of fierce will, shrewd opportunism, and good luck. It is a study in the transformation of a Woody Allen character into a Saul Bellow character.

Ed Koch was a working-class child of the Great Depression. The second of three children, Koch was born on December 12, 1924, and grew up in the Morrisania section of the Bronx, in an elevator building facing Crotona Park. Both his parents worked. His father, Louis, moved up from being a pantsmaker to a partner in a small fur company, spending his days bent over a sewing machine. Koch's mother, Joyce, labored equally hard as a designer of women's blouses. Koch's mother was dominating and feisty, and as a child Koch was closer to her than to his more passive and resigned father.

The Depression made the Koch family downwardly mobile. Furs became an irrelevant extravagance few could afford, and Louis Koch's business fell into economic ruin. When Koch's family could not meet the rent payments in 1931, they were forced to move to Newark, to be taken in by Koch's uncle, who had two children and two bedrooms. At age eight, Ed Koch was living with eight other people, in a $45-a-month apartment, at 90 Spruce Street, in an area that was about half black.

Louis and Joyce Koch began to run the hat check concession at Kruger's Auditorium on Belmont Avenue. Customers were charged twenty-five cents to check their coats and hats, and at the end of the night there would be a long, impatient line demanding service. If they were satisfied, they left a dime tip. When he reached the age of twelve, Ed Koch started working at the concession, staying as late as 2:00 A.M. on Saturday nights and then waking up early on Sunday morning to count the dimes and then roll them in paper. Koch had unusual energy and discipline for someone so young. The experience of feeling dependent on the whim of a tip left Koch with a strong childhood memory of feeling demeaned.

Koch enrolled at Newark's South Side High in 1937. A good student, he graduated seventeenth in a class of 229. Koch had a sharp sense of humor, but is remembered by both teachers and classmates as an outsider who was a failure at forming friendships with his peers. His body movements were clumsy, and he was not good at sports. And the work ethic of his parents had been instilled in him; after school Koch worked at the delicatessen counter of a grocery store.

Koch's homeroom classmate Frances Gendel told the authors of the excellent *I, Koch* (Arthur Browne, Dan Collins, and Michael Goodwin) that the teenage Koch was an "immature little boy." Another contemporary, Julius Lehroff, commented: "He was an egghead, a square, a loner, and very bright. He wasn't with the dancing and the cars and the running around with girls." But at least one perceptive classmate had noticed a distinctive quality in the young Ed Koch, which was captured in the motto under Koch's graduation photo in the South Side senior yearbook: "Strong in will to find, to strive, to seek, and not to yield."

In a small surge of wartime prosperity, Louis Koch was able to relocate his family to Ocean Parkway in Brooklyn in 1941, around the time of Koch's graduation from high school. Ocean Parkway was middle-class and Jewish, but here, too, Koch had difficulty fitting in, being accepted by a peer group. Still poorly coordinated, he tended to avoid playing ball on the shaded, tree-lined streets. And had no interest in Brooklyn's collective passion—the Dodgers, who won the pennant in 1941 with Peter Reiser hitting .343 and Dixie Walker batting .341. Koch didn't have any girlfriends. He kept to himself, studied hard at City College (where he was eligible for free tuition), and worked on Thursday nights and Saturdays as a salesman of women's shoes at Oppenheim-Collins.

In 1943, Koch dropped out of school when he was drafted. A good soldier, he was in combat for a month and performed well. He was shot at; he rescued buddies who were wounded; he slept in foxholes; he was a grunt who did his job.

After he was honorably discharged in 1946 as a sergeant with two battle stars, Koch returned to his parents' home and graduated from City College. He then attended New York University Law School, finishing in the middle of his class. In 1949 he was admitted to the bar and settled into a small general law practice of no distinction—matrimonials, wills, minor negligence cases. A former law partner remembers Koch as having had the perfect personality for acrimonious divorces—"vengeful, punitive, thriving on personalized conflict, even if it was vicarious."

Finally, in 1956, unable to bear any more of his mother's nagging about why he wasn't getting married, Ed Koch moved out of his parents' home in Brooklyn to a small apartment at 81 Bedford Street in Greenwich Village. When he came to write his bestselling book, *Mayor,* his parents were granted only four sentences.

In 1956 a new phenomenon was consolidated in American politics in the person of Adlai Stevenson. The Democratic candidate for president against Dwight Eisenhower, Stevenson never really had a chance to defeat the popular incumbent, but he did become an inspirational leader to millions of young, white, educated, urban professionals—1950s Yuppies. His style, his persona, motivated young reformers from San Francisco to New York to become involved in his honorable but doomed campaign.

Stevenson was a curious kind of liberal hero. He was not a champion of the workers, of "the little guy," like Harry Truman or FDR. He did not come from a labor or populist tradition, like his rival and 1956 running mate Estes Kefauver. He was not especially progressive on the great moral issues of racial integration, which divided the nation in the wake of the 1954 Supreme Court decision outlawing segregation in public education.

Stevenson's appeal resided more in his intellect and wit, his patrician gentility, his melancholy dignity. He seemed willing to lose for his principles, and at some level was ambivalent even about being a politician. He would not pander for votes. A politician above the grubby chicaneries of politics, he had an

elegant purity that appealed to intellectuals, and to young ideal-
ists like Ed Koch.

Yet the local political clubhouse in Greenwich Village, the
Tamawa Club, wouldn't even try to elect Stevenson. The local
district leader from Tamawa was Carmine DeSapio, first
elected in 1939, who had by then become the most powerful
Democrat in all of New York City, and probably in all of New
York State. He had helped elect Robert Wagner mayor in 1953,
and Averell Harriman governor in 1954. DeSapio was courte-
ous, gentlemanly, and immaculately groomed. The other Democratic county leaders deferred to his leadership; he was the
strongest Tammany boss since the 1920s.

Although he had a grander vision than Charley Buckley,
the Bronx party leader, and was more sophisticated than James
Roe of Queens, DeSapio still had a machine mentality. He had
an interest in an insurance company that received government
contracts, as well as ties to organized crime. His bedrock concern was jobs, judgeships, and contracts for his friends. Adlai
Stevenson and his literate speeches about nuclear testing didn't
mean much to DeSapio, and for most nights during the fall
campaign of 1956, his club was not even open.

With Tamawa uninterested, Ed Koch and a small band of
about twenty-five white, middle-class Village professionals
were forced to work directly with the Stevenson campaign
headquarters uptown. Koch stood on Village street corners and
gave speeches for his candidate—good, witty speeches—rang
doorbells, and handed out leaflets. After Stevenson lost, his cult
in Greenwich Village met right after the depressing election
and tried to decide how to keep alive their hero's values, to
bring Stevenson's lofty ideals into local politics. The group
viewed the dark, closed Tamawa Club as the symbol of a dark,
closed Democratic Party but were split on how to challenge it.

Some wanted to create an independent political club to
challenge DeSapio and Tamawa; others thought it wiser to
work internally, to join Tamawa as a bloc and try to reform it
from the inside. Ed Koch was among the latter, perhaps because he had attended a few meetings at Tamawa before he
became a Stevenson volunteer.

The majority, however—represented by Herman and Carol
Greitzer, Ed Gold, Richard Kuh, and Charley McGuinness—
voted for independence, and the Village Independent Democrats (VID) was founded early in 1957. Richard Kuh, who had

been the co-chair of the Village Committee for Stevenson, was elected the VID's first president, by a vote of about forty to twenty. Ed Koch had supported Kuh's opponent, and when his candidate lost, Koch went back to Tamawa and started attending meetings at DeSapio's club in the spring of 1957.

Tamawa did not have any formal membership, so it is impossible to chart with precision Koch's arrivals and departures. Although the club's 1958 dinner journal listed him as one of its captains, Koch decided to leave Tamawa late in 1958, a choice about which he once told a humorous story.

Koch was talking to State Supreme Court Justice Thomas Chimera, who was something of the house intellectual in Tamawa, and the figure who could talk most easily to its younger members. Koch had asked Justice Chimera how long it would take for him to become a judge if he hung around the tight-knit, hierarchical club and loyally worked in all the elections for the candidate blessed by DeSapio.

"About twenty years," Chimera replied.

"That's when I decided to quit Tamawa," Koch explained.

Koch rejoined VID in 1959, in time to work in Charley McGuinness's primary challenge to DeSapio, in which the VID won 47 percent of the vote. Given the demographic trend in the Village toward more educated, middle-class voters, and the growth in VID's vote from the 36 percent in 1957, it seemed probable the club would be able to topple DeSapio as district leader in the next election. VID was no longer considered an amateurish fringe, but a rising political force.

In the fall of 1960, Koch ran for vice president of VID against Ed Gold. Gold, who has remained a friend and supporter of Koch throughout his career up to the present, recalls their brief rivalry:

"We both made terrible speeches to the membership, but Ed's was worse. Ed's speech was untypically defensive. He kept saying that he wouldn't apologize for quitting VID to join Tamawa. Most of the people at the meeting didn't even know that Koch had defected from VID in 1957. They were new members. But Ed's curious speech told them history that they were not aware of. I beat Ed by a margin of about three to two."

When asked now how he interpreted Koch's motives in shuttling back and forth between the two clubs, Gold is surprisingly skeptical:

"I think Ed felt the VID was not going to be successful back in 1957 and 1958. I think Ed wanted to run for political office, as far back as 1957. This ambition was the biggest thing in his makeup. For a while he thought he might have the best shot through DeSapio's club. Ed felt a little excluded by the clique that founded the VID. He was experimenting for a way into both clubs, and for a while he couldn't make up his mind. At first he questioned whether there was a political future for VID. By the time he ran for club vice president against me in 1960, he had made up his mind that VID had a future. . . ."

In 1962, Ed Koch decided to run for the state assembly in the Democratic primary against incumbent William Passannante in the old first assembly district (Greenwich Village and Murray Hill). The membership of VID had not been eager to mount a primary against Passannante, for although he was a member of Tamawa and his father had been close to DeSapio, Passannante himself was a liberal legislator. Some VID members did want to appear anti-Italian, and the club was expending the bulk of its effort to elect Bentley Kassal to Congress against incumbent Leonard Farbstein. But Koch wanted to run for office, and since no one else was willing to oppose Passannante, he entered the race—without any clear issue against the incumbent, or any coherent rationalization for his candidacy. Koch's platform was based on three social issues: repeal of the state laws decreeing sodomy a crime; making abortions more accessible; and liberalizing the state's divorce laws. His critics called it "Koch's 'SAD' campaign," taking their cue from the Sodomy-Abortion-Divorce acronym.

Late in the elections, whatever slim chances Koch had were destroyed when former senator and governor Herbert Lehman, the spiritual father of the city's reform movement, endorsed Passannante. He was followed by Mayor Wagner, then by Jim Lanigan, VID's male district leader, who had beaten DeSapio in 1961 and resigned from VID after the Lehman-Wagner endorsement of Passannante, accusing the club of "extremism."

When the votes were counted on Thursday evening, September 6, Passannante had 5,048, and Koch had 3,703. Passannante had received 58 percent of the vote. In the Greenwich Village portion of the district, covered by VID, Passannante beat Koch 4,072 to 2,694.

But the defeat turned out to be a blessing in disguise for Ed Koch. The primary led to Lanigan's resignation as district leader and his withdrawal from politics, thus creating a vacancy for the district leadership election the next year. And the "betrayal" of Koch by Lehman and Wagner transformed him into a martyr to the most radical wing of the reform movement. Ed Koch became the symbol reformers loved best—purity in heroic defeat.

Koch had by now developed an enemies-list mentality that almost spoiled his new role as a reformer. Within VID he went on a rampage against those he felt did not do enough for his campaign. But rather than focusing anger on his opposition, he turned on those whom he considered insufficiently loyal, men like Steve Berger and Ed Gold, who had devoted their efforts to Bentley Kassal's losing campaign for Congress.

Recalls Ed Gold: "Koch was very critical in open meetings of the club of those individuals who didn't drop everything and work exclusively for him. His comments had a small tinge of McCarthyism, of loyalty tests for reform purity. He started to blame people who supported him for his loss. Ed stopped just short of becoming seriously divisive."

What may have halted Koch's recriminations was his decision to run for president of VID in December 1962 as the leader of the militant faction. His opponent was a 26-year-old stockbroker named John Herzog, who was backed by the moderates. The week before the vote, in a front-page article in the December 27 edition of the *Village Voice*, Mary Perot Nichols captured the flavor of factional tumult inside a club where moderates looked like extremists to everyone else in politics:

> The organization of the moderates has brought forth a near-violent reaction from those who regard themselves as the reform purists of the clubhouse. This group, known as the "hardnoses," has, in reaction to moderate caucusing, begun stomping about on white chargers and making more intransigent noise than usual. . . .
>
> The moderates' first test of strength came last month when they organized and captured three out of four vacancies on the club's executive committee. . . . The "hardnose" reaction to this move was characteristically belligerent: "They're a bad bunch!" one of them told the *Voice* angrily. "They have secret meetings, and now they are trying to stack regular meetings!" . . .

It is the contention of the moderates that the self-righteousness of the "hardnose" group is not only offensive to members of VID, but even to the club's ideologically close brethren among Manhattan's West Side reform leaders. . . .

The hardnoses say that the only way to keep the public interested in VID is to retain its purity of image. "It's not our job to wheel and deal in order to win elections," said one hardnose, "our job is to clean the political stable."

The following week the *Voice* carried a lengthy letter from Koch, complaining that "Mrs. Nichols failed to fully grasp the significance of the great debate now being waged in the ranks of the Village Independent Democrats."

Koch ended his rebuttal with an eloquent summation of his political philosophy of that moment, a credo that would have ironic echoes decades later:

> . . . it has become clear to me that the reform movement is a new name for the old game of musical chairs: a substitution of one group seeking power and jobs for another, with little difference in methods or goals. That is why the VID, if it is to have any meaning, must continue in its role as the hairshirt—as the beacons of light, pompous as that might sound. Not that we will effect any change in the City Politic, but there is always the hope that some day the voting public will say that politics need not be the dirty game that it always seems to have been; that it need not contain within it moral lepers who will sell their integrity for the promise of a job, or public or party office designation.

Koch was, in fact, clearly a person of greater speaking and organizing skill, energy, and intelligence than Herzog, and he won the vote for club president, 120 to 105. This triumph improved his self-confidence by certifying his leadership as the purest of the pure, and enabling him to put the brooding bitterness of the Passannante loss behind him. And Koch made an astute move that unified VID: he named George Delaney as the club's campaign manager. Delaney was a popular moderate in VID, who had been a captain in Tamawa as late as the 1959 primary for district leader, and was also one of Koch's closest friends in January 1963.

Throughout the winter and spring of 1963, the first months of Koch's tenure as VID president, the issue that most concerned the club was the search for a candidate for male district leader against DeSapio, who was preparing for a comeback after his 1961 loss to Lanigan. Lanigan himself had tried to form a third club in the Village, but failed. Carol Greitzer, who had been elected the female district leader with Lanigan in 1961, remained a popular figure both in the club and in the community, and her presence on the ticket was almost assured.

Koch said he would not run under any circumstances. Stanley Geller, the past president of VID, rejected repeated invitations to become the candidate. Geller was a successful lawyer whose wife opposed his running because she feared red-baiting over her husband's student radicalism. Ed Gold, who was an editor at Fairchild Publications, declined to run because he had no desire for a career in politics.

"Shortly before the petitioning period was about to begin, we finally found a candidate willing to run," Ed Gold recalls. "It was Lloyd Hauser [now deceased], who was the treasurer of the club. Hauser was a brilliant real estate developer who could raise a lot of money for the campaign. He was not the caliber of campaigner that Koch was. When Koch heard that Hauser was willing to become the candidate, Koch immediately changed his mind. He agreed to run right away and asked me to be his campaign treasurer. Hauser quickly withdrew his name and the club was delighted to endorse Koch as our candidate against DeSapio."

In July Koch appeared as the guest on the WNBC-TV Sunday morning interview show "Searchlight," and went halfway toward mending his fences with Lehman and Wagner. He said he regretted calling them "bosses" the year before. But when asked if he would support Wagner's candidate for judge, Investigations Commissioner Louis Kaplan, Koch stated flatly that VID was "not going to carry Kaplan's petitions." When asked how he could expect the mayor's backing against DeSapio when he would not back the mayor's friend for a judgeship, Koch replied that he didn't think the mayor wanted a "sycophantic" club in the Village.

In the course of the interview, Koch also staked out a strong position on equality for blacks, declaring that he favored "total integration" of the public schools as soon as possible. He added that he supported the busing of Village public school children to other neighborhoods of New York City as part of an overall school integration plan.

Six years after its inception, VID was still viewed as a hotbed of extremists by the liberal and labor establishment of the city, and even by many other reformers. The club seemed to institutionalize the rigidity and hostility of a certain reform style, and had further isolated itself with Koch's personalized attack on Lehman. As a result, a separate parallel structure had to be created to accommodate Lehman, and his cohorts such as Lloyd Garrison and Telford Taylor. These respected liberal wise men were needed to reassure the older generation of mostly Jewish voters who lived in the apartment buildings along lower Fifth Avenue that Koch was not a radical. Koch's base was the middle-class professionals and bohemians, while DeSapio had the Italian working class of the South Village

On Thursday, September 5, Ed Koch defeated Carmine DeSapio by forty-one votes, and Carol Greitzer outpolled DeSapio's candidate for co-leader, Diana Hall, by 650 votes. With the victory, Koch would be remembered for years as the pure reformer who conquered the boss DeSapio, and Lanigan's earlier and larger defeat of the same candidate would recede from consciousness.

Through a disciplined will for political advancement, Ed Koch had transformed himself from a mistrusted interloper at VID into the tribune of the most radical reform club in New York. Koch's gift was his ability to see history's flow and to accommodate himself to it, from DeSapio to VID, from moderate to hardnose. He had the determination to survive the rejection of losing for club vice president, and then for the assembly, and still bounce back, as the motto in his high school yearbook had anticipated.

Even his supporters recognized in Koch a streak of something that was less than political idealism. Sarah Schoenkopf (now Kovner), who served as Koch's campaign manager in both 1962 and 1963, sees his rise to the top of VID in these terms:

"It was primarily opportunism. Ed never had the broad social vision of Stanley Geller, or so many of the other people in VID. He was motivated by power, not ideas, and certainly never money. I can still remember how every night we were at the club, Ed would stop whatever he was doing at 11:00 and buy the morning papers at Sheridan Square. He would always look first for stories about himself, even though he was not yet a citywide figure."

If Ed Koch was unknown to most New York residents in 1963, that decade of liberalism would see him accomplish election to the New York city council in 1966 and to Congress in 1968. Politics remained his whole life. His idea of leisure seemed to be greeting voters at a subway stop.

His popularity grew, as did his talent as a humorous story-teller and his reputation as a serious urbanist. He became a star in the small world of reform politics, and in Greenwich Village civic, artistic, and bohemian circles.

From 1963 to 1970 Koch remained the model liberal. He opposed the Vietnam War in 1966, and called it "immoral" during the race against Republican Whitney North Seymour for Congress in 1968. He not only campaigned for a civilian complaint review board to investigate brutality allegations against the police but also wrote a letter to the New York Civil Liberties Union offering to serve as a *pro bono* lawyer in such cases. He broke with his party to back liberal Republican candidate John Lindsay for mayor in 1965, over Democrat Abe Beame. In 1968 he supported Robert Kennedy for president. He was a steady champion of tenants' rights and even proposed a national system of commercial rent control.

After reaching Congress, he voted for school busing amendments to facilitate integration, urged amnesty for all American draft resisters who fled to Canada, and sponsored legislation to create a presidential commission to study the possibility of legalizing marijuana. He also proposed "immediate action to grant an exemption from military service to young men who are conscientiously opposed to the Vietnam war." There was hardly an issue, cosmic or exotic, during this period on which Koch deviated from the liberal orthodoxy.

From 1963 to 1970, the Village was liberal, and New York City was liberal. John Lindsay had been reelected mayor in 1969 on the Liberal Party ballot position, over conservative Democrat Mario Proccacino, and over John Marchi, who had beaten Lindsay in the Republican primary. Robert Kennedy had been a liberal senator until his assassination, and Jacob

Javits was no less so, especially in matters of civil rights, foreign policy, and economic opportunity.

Below the surface, however, a racial backlash was brewing in the middle class, one that had begun with the defeat of the civilian complaint review board in a 1966 referendum, and was reinforced by the bitter 1968 school strike that pitted a Jewish union against black community activists. Proccacino's victory in the 1969 Democratic primary for mayor suggested the potential of this turn to the right, but Lindsay's triumph in the general election revealed its limits and held it in temporary abeyance. At the heart of this backlash was the fear of crime, which expanded into an antagonism against black people moving into white, middle-class communities. It was the issue that, in 1971, proved to be the turning point in Ed Koch's political career, that marked his break with 1960s liberalism and the start of his quest for one great emotional issue that would make him acceptable to the white middle class of Brooklyn and Queens.

The specific case that provided him impetus was a tumultuous conflict over a proposed 840-apartment "scatter site" housing project in a liberal, Jewish community. The Lindsay administration wanted to build three twenty-four-story buildings of low-income housing at a long-vacant site at 108th Street in Forest Hills, Queens, next to the Long Island Expressway. The concept was a virtuous one. The ghettos were filled with vertical slums, public housing high-rises in communities awash with drugs, where children went to inferior schools. To encourage integration and to provide decent accommodations in better environments, the city had started to construct low-income housing at sites scattered in middle-class neighborhoods.

One such project was Latimer Gardens in Flushing, Queens, which contained 423 units, of which 141 were reserved for senior citizens. The buildings were ten stories high, and the proportion of blacks among the tenants was 31 percent. Latimer Gardens was well integrated into the larger Flushing community, with no complaints of crime or racial tension.

The Forest Hills project, as originally conceived, had similar Housing Authority guidelines: its tenancy was to have been 35 percent black and Hispanic, with a preference for Queens residents, and 40 percent of the apartments were set aside for the elderly. But the Lindsay administration misjudged the fear level in Forest Hills, and took several missteps in carrying out its policy. It failed to negotiate with the community's religious and civic leadership in advance. And it didn't anticipate the emergence of a local demagogue named Jerry Birbach, a loud bull of a man with political ambitions who organized a direct action protest movement against the project.

Birbach founded a group called the Forest Hills Residents Association and started calling the housing proposal a "welfare project," warning that Forest Hills would soon be invaded by hordes of vandals, addicts, muggers, and violent, antisocial teenagers who would flood the schools and shops of this stable neighborhood.

Birbach's message of fear became a contagion, even though the local elected politicians, such as Congressman Benjamin Rosenthal and State Senator Emanual Gold, tried to be responsible and show good sense in handling the issue. Birbach started to lead marches of Forest Hills residents—mothers pushing strollers, businessmen in suits and ties—to the chain-link fence around the excavation site. A few TV cameras showed up. Then there were boisterous public rallies with inflammatory racial rhetoric, and more TV cameras arrived. When the *New York Times* put the story on the front page, still more TV cameras appeared, and in their wake, fringe politicians from across the city, among whom were Vito Batista, a perennial candidate of the right, and the Jewish Defense League, which formed a picket line with torches outside the home of Simeon Golar, the chairman of the Housing Authority. Golar, who is black, said his family felt as if the Ku Klux Klan was outside his home.

Through the fall of 1971, the controversy became more intense and more racially polarized. The well-dressed residents at Birbach's rallies started waving placards carrying the word "nigger." Other signs equated Lindsay with Hitler, which raised the specter of the extermination of the Jews. Birbach began to suggest that Forest Hills had been chosen for the project because Lindsay believed liberal Jews would be more passive and timid in their resistance than the Irish, Italians, or Germans of Queens.

Enter Ed Koch.

In the November 25, 1971 issue of the *Village Voice*, Clark Whelton, a journalist who subsequently became Koch's speechwriter, wrote an article in opposition to the Forest Hills project, in which he quoted Koch as saying:

The residents of Forest Hills are expressing two very real and rational fears. The fear of crime is a very real one, and second, it's absolutely rational to believe property values will decline in the area of a high-rise housing project. Fear moves in and people move out.

The Whelton article also reported that Koch did not believe the city's official statistic that 16 percent of public housing tenants were on welfare: "Congressman Edward I. Koch thinks 30 per cent is closer to the truth."

Three days later, on November 28, 1971, Ed Koch, who had once supported busing Greenwich Village public school children to Harlem, came to Forest Hills and spoke to a rally organized by Jerry Birbach. Racist placards were carried by a crowd of 2,000 people to whom Koch said that they were not racists for opposing the project: "You can turn City Hall around. Keep up the fight!"

Koch's friends were astounded. It wasn't so much that he opposed the project—sound planning arguments could be made against its density, size, and design. What was shocking was that Koch had attended a racist rally and stood with a racist demagogue, and that he had asserted publicly that property values would decline if low-income housing were to be built in the community. What was also troubling was that his motive for such unexpected public behavior seemed to be ambition, since he had already spoken of his plans to run for mayor in 1973.

Victor Kovner was one of Koch's most loyal friends. He had been Koch's law partner, and his wife, Sarah Schoenkopf, had been Koch's campaign manager. Kovner had seen "Niggers Go Home" signs in the television coverage of Forest Hills. When he heard a radio news report that Koch had addressed the Birbach rally, Kovner called him, and they had a tremendous quarrel.

Koch told Kovner his appearance at the rally was accidental, a spur-of-the-moment decision based on the fact that he happened to be in the area. He also insisted that the residents of Forest Hills had to defend their interests, and that they were justified in opposing the project. The issue, he declared, had nothing to do with race.

In the 1960s, Stanley Geller was regarded as Koch's adviser and benefactor within VID. But Geller was so appalled by

Koch's opposition to the Forest Hills project that he drafted a resolution endorsing it and condemning Koch's conduct. The VID membership approved Geller's resolution by a margin of ten to one. Koch had been scheduled to speak to the membership before the vote, but at the last minute he sent word that he was "unavoidably detained" in Washington.

The week after the VID's vote, Geller and Koch engaged in a loud argument about the merits of housing integration in front of dozens of people at the annual Christmas party of the *Village Voice.* The dispute was so insistent that Geller and Koch became estranged for six years, until Koch enlisted Geller's help in the 1977 mayoral race.

In his book *Politics,* Koch described a telephone conversation in which he set up Geller as an elitist foil for his own populist lecture. Koch claimed that Geller had called him in Washington, and in the course of a disagreement, told him, "The Jews in Forest Hills have to pay their dues."

Koch then quoted himself as telling Geller off:

> You have this brownstone in the Village, and I wish I had one like it. And you have this marvelous home in the Hamptons with this near–Olympic size pool, and you've invited me there, and I wish I owned one like that. On the day your kids were born you registered them in private schools. And you're telling me the Jews of Forest Hills have to pay their dues. I am telling you they are willing to pay theirs; they are just not willing to pay *yours.*

Geller likes Koch and has supported him in every election he has ever run in, but he says that he never called Koch in Washington, and the conversation recounted in the book never occurred.

"Ed never stooped to say those things to my face," Geller says.

Jack Newfield was a part of the same liberal/Village circle of old Koch friends as the Kovners and Stanley Geller. And Newfield was equally repelled by Koch's having gone out of his way to confer legitimacy upon the bigoted Birbach.

In the December 16, 1971 edition of the *Voice,* Newfield published an article taking issue with Koch's intervention in Forest Hills, adopting a tone of disappointment rather than anger:

I think Koch is trying to exploit people's understandable fears to further his own ambition to be Mayor. . . . It is Koch's rhetoric that troubles me, his failure to see the issue in human terms, from the point of view of those 400 elderly people, and those poor people who will live in the project once it is completed. . . .

It is not easy for me to write this, because I have affection for Ed personally, and he has done much good work. I feel like grabbing him and saying, "Wake up, Ed, and be a *mensch.*"

The following week Koch responded with a letter to the editor written in the same spirit as the offending article. Koch concluded:

Finally, Jack worries that "ambition has spoiled better men than Ed Koch." This is a reference to the possibility I may be a candidate for Mayor in 1973. I have never programmed my political goals and to do so prior to an immediate campaign for re-election to Congress would be folly. But rather than deal with the reasons for my opposition to Forest Hills, Jack has simply dismissed my motives as "ambition," and distorted my past record. That is not what I would expect from Jack, who is normally such a good writer.

A few weeks later Koch and Newfield had dinner together to patch up their friendship, which had been strong since Newfield came to work for the *Voice* in 1964. Newfield had written several laudatory articles about Koch during the 1960s. Koch had been the lawyer for the *Voice* and regularly dropped by on Friday afternoons for casual gossip. They had been to each other's homes, and shared similar tastes in Italian restaurants and popular music (Joan Baez and Paul Simon). And they would remain friendly for several more years. As a favor, Koch would obtain for Newfield a file from the House Internal Security Committee in 1974, by writing to the committee's chair, Richard Ichord, in Newfield's behalf. In 1975, Newfield would give Koch his files on nursing home racketeer Bernard Bergman so Koch could crusade against him.

At their dinner, Koch essentially took Newfield into his confidence and revealed his intention to run for mayor in 1973, stating that his main political problem was the stereotype of him as "a liberal bachelor from Greenwich Village." Koch asked for understanding from a friend, for his need to shed that liberal, oddball stereotype if he was ever to win the trust of middle-class voters outside Manhattan.

Koch did make it clear that he would support a compromise solution for Forest Hills, that his objective was not the elimination of all the low-income units, which was Birbach's goal, but to modify the density of the project. He also said that it was a form of McCarthyism to hold Birbach's views against him, and to argue that he shouldn't speak at the same rally as Birbach because Birbach's views were abhorrent. Koch did not want to be prohibited from demonstrating against the project just because Birbach was also opposed to it.

The complexity of Koch's motives in shifting to the right became apparent in the course of the evening's wide-ranging discussion. Koch made some justifiable criticisms of radical tactics, styles, and absolutist vocabulary. He seemed to resent, quite personally, the small amount of anti-Semitic literature distributed by blacks during the 1968 school strike over decentralization. He was also angered by the anti-Israel pronouncements of some black leaders, although at this point Koch was a dovish supporter of Israel's Labor Party, not switching his allegiance to the militaristic Likud faction of Begin and Sharon until after they were elected.

While not an intellectual, Koch was alert to intellectual fashions and, much like Norman Podhoretz, was going through a personal backlash against the radical excesses of the 1960s. Nevertheless, over the course of the evening Koch repeated several times that he was still basically a liberal, that his views were unchanged on privacy, civil liberties, tenants' rights, human rights, military spending, integrity in government, judicial selection, mass transit, and exposing Mafia influence in government.

At this point—early 1972—Koch's lurch toward the right over scatter-site housing seemed to combine elements of ambition, trend-spotting, a personalized overreaction to black revolutionary rhetoric, and possibly an exhaustion with the role of powerless maverick.

After two years of careful preparation, Koch announced for mayor at a press conference at the Biltmore Hotel on February 12, 1973. He stood in front of the blue, white, and orange flag of New York City, abandoned a written five-page text, and spoke with feeling about what he said was the most vital issue facing the city: crime.

Koch argued that the middle class was fleeing New York because of its rising crime rate, and the middle class was taking the city's tax base with it to suburbia. He insisted, somewhat defensively, that a tough stance on "crime in our streets, crime in our schools, crime within our government" was not at all incompatible with his liberal philosophy. "Crime is not a left-wing issue, or a right-wing issue," he said, "but a problem that needs a realistic approach." He announced his crime prevention program—and never mentioned capital punishment.

Koch's campaign, however, never got off the ground. Not only was he unable to raise any money, because he had no credibility as a possible winner, but ideologically he stood in the middle without a core constituency or a distinct image. Abe Beame and Mario Biaggi were running on his right, with Biaggi an ex-cop preaching law and order. Albert Blumenthal and Herman Badillo were running on his left, with Badillo emphasizing equal opportunity for minorities.

Koch dropped out of the race after only forty-five days, regarding his brief effort as an audition for his next attempt. The Forest Hills issue had failed to ingratiate him to the middle class in Brooklyn and Queens; yet he still half-desired the approval of some liberals, and he still had a remnant of social conscience that imposed a sense of limits on what he could comfortably say in order to win votes. In 1973, Ed Koch was still in transition, as he returned to his duties as a congressman representing Manhattan's "Silk Stocking" district.

The Forest Hills conflict remains a watershed in New York's tortured recent history of race relations. Years later Koch described it as "my Rubicon." Lindsay's popularity never recovered, and in 1972 he was followed to Miami by Forest Hills residents who campaigned against him in the Florida presidential primary. After Birbach ran against Emanual Gold in a state senate primary in 1972 and lost, he moved out of Forest Hills to Long Island. In 1972 Mayor Lindsay appointed a little-known community lawyer to act as a mediator in the ongoing controversy, the first governmental assignment Mario Cuomo ever had. Cuomo's compromise solution of cutting the project in half—three buildings of twelve floors—was accepted and approved by the Board of Estimate. The place was also converted into a low-income cooperative, the only one in the nation.

The Forest Hills project was built on the smaller scale and became a success. The neighborhood thrived with greater diversity. Crime did not increase. Real estate values went up, not down. About a thousand residents did move out but were replaced mostly by immigrant Soviet Jews and younger orthodox Jews, making Forest Hills "feel" even more Jewish than before. The population of the project is now 750 whites, 175 blacks, 100 Hispanics, and 135 "others," mostly Asian and South American. Two percent of the tenants are welfare recipients.

In the December 11, 1984 issue of the *Voice*, Barry Jacobs published a marvelous retrospective on the project and the hysteria evoked by its birth pains. Jacobs, a Queens resident, wrote:

> The place is well-tended, peaceful. It's a Saturday and old men sit in the playgrounds reading Russian newspapers. White, black, and Hispanic kids play stickball against a building wall. Black-suited Orthodox Jewish men chat in clusters. It's heartening to see how wrong the anti-project people were in thinking that these "poor" people would bring drugs and crime into their neighborhood. It's also maddening.

During all of Ed Koch's years as mayor, no scatter-site public housing was constructed in New York City.

When Ed Koch announced his second candidacy for mayor, on March 4, 1977, he was fifty-two years old. His value system by now was fully developed: he knew what he was doing, and precisely what he wanted.

Once again, almost no one gave him a chance to win at this second bid for the mayoralty, if only because 6 percent of the voters outside his congressional district had ever heard of him. In the second paragraph of its report of his declaration, the *Times* said that Koch would have to "scotch skepticism over the seriousness of his candidacy." The *News* treated his entry into the race even more negatively, running a fourteen-paragraph story that focused on Bella Abzug's possible candidacy, not even mentioning Koch's declaration until the twelfth paragraph.

Throughout April and May Koch campaigned in cheerful

earnestness, promising repeatedly that his first priority would be "getting the hacks off the payroll." And, indeed, he had again chosen an attractive issue. The Beame administration had been shaped by the clubhouse ethic, just as Beame himself had been shaped by it, ever since he had begun his career as a methodical doorbell ringer for the Madison Democratic club.

Most of Beame's commissioners had been clubhouse products. He had made Mike Lazar the transportation commissioner; Stanley Friedman, deputy mayor; Queens district leader Ralph DeMarco, deputy sanitation commissioner; Moses Kove, an old DeSapio crony, chairman of the Taxi and Limousine Commission; Gerald Esposito, a Bronx district leader, deputy commissioner of Marine and Aviation; Abe Goodman, a Meade Esposito crony, first deputy commissioner of the Economic Development Administration; and Anthony Ameruso, Esposito's protégé, highways commissioner.

In May 1974, four months into his term as mayor, Beame had been the guest of honor at Esposito's annual Brooklyn county dinner and given a ringing defense of clubhouse politics:

"We are sometimes accused of running a strong county organization. Critics call it a machine. But Brooklyn has demonstrated that effective party organization need not be synonymous with smoke-filled rooms. Rather, it is a vital force in the American party system. . . . I have been a member of the Brooklyn Democratic organization for the last forty years. I have always been proud of my membership and my pride has increased. No one, no one need apologize for being part of this kind of party organization."

From the start, Koch's campaign did have one secret weapon, one prized asset—Bess Myerson, the first Jewish Miss America, the city's consumer affairs commissioner in the Lindsay administration, a magnet for cameras, a honeypot to fat cats, a star in the neighborhoods. She was cast in a special role in the Koch campaign: as girlfriend for the unmarried candidate. That role was scripted by Koch's media adviser, David Garth, who had worried about rumors that Koch was gay. He was, in fact, so concerned that he investigated them himself before he agreed to accept Koch as a client of his company. He even asked Koch directly if the rumors had any scintilla of validity, and Koch assured Garth they were vile and baseless.

Garth, a student of mass psychology and symbolism, made

certain that Myerson stood next to Koch at his announcement, that she accompany him to large public events, and that she hold his hand when the media could notice the affection. He even placed Myerson in Koch's basic campaign poster, the only example in anyone's memory of a non–family member being given equal prominence with the candidate.

Early in the campaign, Garth began to circulate the rumor that Koch and Myerson were sexually involved with each other, and they might marry after the election. Soon gossip columnists were printing this fancy as fact. Garth had, in effect, taken Koch's most dangerous negative, his bachelorhood, and converted it into his biggest positive—the idea that voters might get Bess Myerson as the First Lady of New York, a two-fer if they voted for Koch for mayor.

There never was any sexual relationship between Koch and Myerson. They were good platonic friends. The idea of an affair was an Immaculate Deception.

Early in the campaign, Garth implicitly conceded this in a conversation with Jack Newfield. Garth told Newfield he had to cancel a meeting with him because he was having lunch with "the Smith Brothers."

Newfield asked who were the Smith Brothers.

"Oh, that's my nickname for Ed and Bess," Garth explained.

"I don't get it," said Newfield.

"Two beards, schmuck," Garth said, and laughed.

As the campaign evolved, the play-acting by Koch and Myerson became more extreme. In rally appearances with Myerson, Koch would say to audiences, "Wouldn't she make a great First Lady in Gracie Mansion?"

On television Koch was asked if he planned to marry Myerson, and he said: "It's always a possibility, but I don't want to talk about it. She is an incredible person, a warm human being that I truly adore."

Late in the campaign, after gossip columnists speculated about a marriage, political reporters started to ask Koch and Myerson about a real romance. They would give coyly misleading answers such as "Anything is possible," or "We may have an announcement after the election."

But all that would come later. In June, Koch was still the tortoise, inching along the road in his honorable and determined style. Most of the private campaign polls showed him in fifth or sixth place, with the colorful former congresswoman

Bella Abzug in first, helped by high-name recognition from her narrow loss in the Senate primary the year before. Abzug, however, would stumble when she supported the rights of cops and firefighters to strike, as would Mayor Abe Beame, placed in second place in the polls, when he was severely criticized for his handling of the city's fiscal crisis in a report issued by the SEC on the eve of the primary. Mario Cuomo was in third place, just above a second tier consisting of Koch, Manhattan borough president Percy Sutton, and South Bronx congressman Herman Badillo. Koch's latent strength was that he had fewer negatives than Abzug and Beame and that a large portion of the population had no opinion of him yet. He was a new face, one that television commercials had yet to define.

In June and early July, Garth started to air his solid, issue-oriented commercials for Koch. Garth wisely made a long rather than a saturated media time buy. A few spots each might spread over several weeks, so the voters would slowly get acquainted with Koch.

The commercials featured Koch stating there were only fifteen hundred cops on the city's streets on an average shift, and that someone had to stand up to the Patrolman's Benevolent Association; that the Board of Education was filled with waste of taxpayer dollars; and that teachers' salaries were exorbitant. These first two advertisements, while stressing opposition to waste and implying the need for tough management, also managed to attack two municipal labor unions, which Garth's continuous polling of voter attitudes had detected were growing unpopular.

The commercials also had a catchy tag line—"After eight years of charisma, and four years of the clubhouse, why not try competence?"—which positioned Koch as independent of the clubhouses, as a break with the past, as a hardnosed manager. These were all qualities that Garth's polling had indicated that Democratic primary voters were looking for.

In July 1977, two extraordinary events occurred that transformed both the mood of the city and the dynamics of the election for mayor. During a Con Edison power blackout at 8:30 P.M. on July 13 that sent the city into a night of darkness, serious rioting, looting, and arson erupted in several black communities. During a single night of pillage, 3,800 persons were arrested, and property damage was estimated at more than $100 million.

That same month New York City was alerted to the presence of a deranged serial killer. Thirteen young people had been shot with a .44 caliber revolver over a fifty-four week period, and six of the victims had died. In 1977 the killer had struck on January 29, on March 8, on April 17, and on June 26. The *New York Post* had published a page-one headline that screamed NO ONE IS SAFE. When the mystery killer, who called himself "Son of Sam," left a taunting, crazed note to the police when he killed Stacy Moskowitz on July 31, the city was sent into a new paroxysm of hysteria.

These two simultaneous events did more than just make crime the biggest concern in the city. They generated enormous frustration, confusion, fear, and rage for revenge. The law-abiding citizens of the city felt violated. They longed for a Charles Bronson or a Clint Eastwood to set things right and punish the predator, like in the movies. A Death Wish Fever raced through the hot city during the summer of 1977.

Enter Ed Koch, again.

A few days after the blackout looting, Koch began to make a public issue of capital punishment. In visits to nursing homes and senior citizen centers, he opened his remarks with the question: "How many of you favor capital punishment? Raise your hands." Koch would quickly raise his own hand first, and then his audience, the elderly, the most frightened and vulnerable of voters, would follow suit. Immediately sensing the powerful appeal of the issue, he took it to voters in middle- and working-class outer borough neighborhoods with the greeting, "Hi, I'm Ed Koch. I'm running for mayor. I'm for capital punishment. Are you?"

In *Flatbush Life,* a community weekly newspaper in Brooklyn, Sheryl Meccariello reported a typical Ed Koch campaign appearance during the summer of 1977:

> [He] stopped a woman at the corner of 48th Street and 13th Avenue. "I'm for capital punishment, are you?" he asked her. The woman's disinterested face became animated. She furrowed her brows and nodded. "I'm for capital punishment and I voted for capital punishment in Congress," Koch told her. "I think society has the right to show its outrage against the reprehensible crimes being committed against it. Did you know that

Beame was against capital punishment until three weeks ago?"

Here, at last, was the transcendent issue that would finally put an end to the stereotype of the "liberal bachelor from Greenwich Village"; the electric chair would make him appear tough.

With the success of the new platform, the Koch campaign began to print two different types of promotional literature. The first, distributed only in liberal Manhattan, offered "FIVE REASONS WHY MANHATTAN NEEDS ED KOCH AS MAYOR: 1) Safe and Affordable Housing; 2) preserving middle class neighborhoods; 3) safe streets and neighborhoods; 4) a fair shake for your tax dollar; 5) safe schools that teach."

The basic campaign flier distributed to the four other boroughs was identical but for the five additional reasons denied to the resident of Manhattan: "1) the blackout and the National Guard; 2) policemen and firemen do not have the right to strike . . . ever; 3) the death penalty . . . for good reasons; 4) protect our senior citizens; 5) New York employees should live in New York City."

Koch was not bothered by the fact that the mayor had no jurisdiction over capital punishment, nor power to institute such a policy, which belong solely to the state legislature. He was fully aware that Governor Hugh Carey had already vetoed a capital punishment law, and that the two-thirds vote of both houses of the legislature required to override that veto would be almost impossible to achieve. Yet he kept on campaigning on the volatile issue, sometimes justifying it as a deterrent to crime, and at others invoking the "Judeo-Christian ethic," quoting the Old Testament counsel of "an eye for an eye, a tooth for a tooth" as God's sanction. He was no longer as defensive or halfhearted as he had seemed in 1973. He was going to ride this issue all the way, and if he had any private doubts he kept them to himself.

Some of Koch's own supporters did have doubts, however, and not so much about his position in favor of capital punishment as about the way he was using the issue. During the summer of 1977, the liberal congressman from Queens, Benjamin Rosenthal, accompanied Koch to a senior center in his district, where he proceeded to conduct his ghoulish plebiscite.

As Rosenthal later told Jack Newfield and Nat Hentoff: "Ed

asked, 'How many here are for the death penalty?' as he raised his own arm. Something must have shown on my face, because Ed leaned toward me and whispered through his teeth, 'Listen, this is the only way I can get in.' "

The primary was scheduled for September 8, with a runoff mandated between the two top finishers if no candidate received at least 40 percent of the vote. By the first week of August the polls started to show Beame and Abzug slipping, and Koch and Mario Cuomo creeping up. The voters seemed to be searching for a fresh face.

In what had by now become a key issue in the campaign, Cuomo was opposed to capital punishment. The two pillars of his intellect—religious faith and legal experience—had convinced him the remedy was a hoax, that it did not solve the crime problem. Twice as a lawyer Cuomo had been assigned to handle appeals for men sentenced to die in the electric chair. Each time, after years of appeals and legal argument, he had gotten the death sentences commuted. He had come to know these men, he had seen the electric chair at Sing Sing, had concluded the legal system was capable of making an error.

In the white ethnic neighborhoods of the city, however, Cuomo's opposition to the death penalty brought him under frequent attack. His campaign pollsters warned him the issue might cost him the election, that 70 percent of New Yorkers wanted the restoration of capital punishment, and even his mother advised him to endorse electrocution. But Cuomo wouldn't—or couldn't—compromise his beliefs on an issue that was irrelevant to the office he was seeking but that Koch and fate had made central to the election.

In August, Koch took a decisive step toward consolidating his position by applying his flexible philosophy toward capturing the editorial endorsement of the *New York Post.*

During the summer of 1977, Steven Berger, the director of the city's Emergency Financial Control Board, was a confidant of both Koch and *Post* publisher Rupert Murdoch. Berger came away from a discussion with Murdoch about whom the *Post* should endorse for mayor with the impression that Koch had a good chance to get the paper's approval. All Koch needed to do was to convince Murdoch that lawyer Edward Costikyan was going to play a major role in his administration. Murdoch had some doubts about Koch's management skills and would be reassured if someone with Costikyan's experience and efficiency was part of the government, handling the bureaucracy, being tough with the municipal labor unions.

Within a few days of Berger's report of Murdoch's concerns back to Koch, Koch and Garth had summoned Costikyan from a court hearing and were driving him down to Murdoch's office. As they headed uptown, Koch asked Costikyan to tell Murdoch that he was going to be in charge of Koch's transition team, and that he was considering an offer of becoming first deputy mayor in a Koch administration.

Costikyan was troubled that Koch would say whatever Murdoch wanted to hear in order to win the *Post*'s endorsement, but he complied with the script written for him. A few days after their initial meeting Costikyan assured Murdoch that he would be willing to serve as Koch's first deputy mayor for at least a year. On August 19, the *Post* endorsed Koch in a front-page editorial.*

The paper not only supported Koch; it actively campaigned for him, running favorable stories about him every day, and unfavorable coverage of Beame, Abzug, and Cuomo whenever it could. Koch press releases the other papers didn't see fit to print became large headlines in the *Post,* while trivial embarrassments to other candidates became *Post* headlines—BELLA OWED $1000 PARKING FINES was a typical example.†

The *Post*'s slanted coverage and the popularity of the death penalty had provided Koch the momentum he needed. Jewish voters had switched to Koch from Beame and Abzug, and when the votes were counted on September 8, the results showed that he had managed to take the lead:

Koch	180,914
Cuomo	171,033
Beame	164,813
Abzug	151,913
Sutton	132,640
Badillo	101,036
Harnett	13,787

---

*Costikyan was, in fact, never appointed to a position in the Koch administration. After the election, Koch refused to create the office of first deputy mayor for him and asked him to take a less influential job. Costikyan would not accept anything less than what he had been promised.

†In October, after the primary, fifty *Post* reporters presented the publisher with a petition accusing the paper of biased, pro-Koch reporting during the election.

Abe Beame, the incumbent mayor, backed by the political machines of Brooklyn and the Bronx, had been eliminated, even though he had finished first in Brooklyn. Koch had won a majority in no borough but had run second in both Manhattan and Queens, and third in Brooklyn.

A runoff election between Koch and Cuomo was announced for eleven days later, and it was immediately clear that the key to winning would be the machine vote in Brooklyn, and to a lesser extent, the Bronx. The Democratic machine on Staten Island supported Cuomo, who had won the original primary on the island and had its substantial Italian vote. But as the smallest borough, Staten Island netted in the first primary a total of only 30,000 votes out of the 910,000 votes citywide.

In Queens, county leader Donald Manes officially endorsed Cuomo but allowed his district leaders and elected officials to divide along ethnic lines. Most Jewish leaders (except Assemblyman Saul Weprin) worked for Koch, and most Italian leaders for Cuomo. Cuomo, who often described his meetings with the shifty Manes as "fishing in shallow waters," was not surprised that Manes was keeping a toe in each pond.

With Beame defeated, the party bosses in Brooklyn and the Bronx would have to choose between Koch and Cuomo. The largest vote was in Brooklyn, where Beame had finished first with 63,000 votes. This vote was now orphaned. Beame had finished second in the Bronx (to Badillo), and this vote was now also up for grabs. The Beame constituency in Brooklyn and the Bronx would now look to their local politicians for guidance on how to cast their crucial votes in this short runoff period.

In the Bronx, county leader Pat Cunningham and his top associate, Deputy Mayor Stanley Friedman, jumped to Koch within hours of Beame's loss. Friedman also played a pivotal role in convincing Beame himself to endorse Koch, and made sure the relevant players knew he was doing it. As deputy mayor, Friedman was now out of a job, and both his political and financial future was on the line.

After a series of preliminary discussions, Beame held one final meeting in Gracie Mansion to decide what course he should take. His son, Buddy, and publicist Howard Rubinstein wanted Beame to support Cuomo, while his press secretary, Sid Frigand, advised him to make no endorsement. But Friedman argued insistently for Koch and, according to one participant, "had a cash register look in his eyes. He played on Beame's resentment of Governor Carey, and he kept saying that Carey would benefit from a Cuomo win. He also argued that Koch was going to win. Beame liked Cuomo, and felt he was more decent, more of a gentleman."

A brilliant judge of character, Stanley Friedman could see that behind Koch's antimachine rhetoric of rectitude lay a desperate pragmatism. And he recognized that behind Cuomo's exterior of the outer-borough ethnic was a moralistic loner. Apparently, Friedman's instinct told him that Ed Koch was more the sort of person he could do business with.

With Beame's endorsement guaranteed, Friedman started both pressuring Meade Esposito to bring the Brooklyn machine over to the Koch camp and rallying his own Bronx organization. With help from Herman Badillo, Cunningham and Friedman easily lined up most of the Hispanic leaders of the South Bronx for Koch. When Bronx assemblyman John Dearie decided to endorse Cuomo, though, Friedman and Cunningham went after him, for the Irish vote was the borough's swing vote. Cunningham called Dearie a "prick" and tried to force him to participate in a press conference of Bronx Irish pols backing Koch; Dearie refused. Cunningham and Friedman responded by deploying workers from other districts to saturate Dearie's district with Koch sound and Koch literature.

The largest vote, however, was in Brooklyn, where Cuomo had finished behind Beame but ahead of Koch. Brooklyn was unquestionably the ballgame in the runoff: its organization was disciplined, and would follow its leader with near-monolithic cohesion. For both candidates, Meade Esposito was the man to see.

Yet for Ed Koch, turning to the Brooklyn boss for support meant allying himself to a man he had long disdained, a man he had described as a "gangster" to his friends. Esposito was the avatar of the machine politics that Koch had been fighting for the past fifteen years, the personification of the system of patronage and bossism that the young Koch and VID had vowed to eradicate. In January 1974, Jack Newfield published a lengthy exposé of Esposito in the *Village Voice* called "Meade, the Mob, and the Machine." Koch called Newfield up to congratulate him, and urged him to follow up his investigation. There was no mystery about Esposito's identity, and he himself made no pretense of being a statesman interested in urban policy. He was a neon sign that said MACHINE BOSS. He ran the party, doled out jobs, socialized with racketeers, made judges, and became a millionaire by using his political influence to obtain jobs for his insurance company, much as his friend and mentor Carmine DeSapio had done before him.

It was on the day after the first primary that David Garth asked the ubiquitous Steven Berger to call Esposito and try to arrange a meeting between him and Koch, which Berger set up for Sunday morning, September 11, in the basement of Esposito's mother's home in Canarsie.

Esposito had, in fact, probably already made up his mind to support Koch, for as one of his advisers recalls:

"A lot of people worked on Meade to endorse Koch. Tony Genovesi [the district leader from Esposito's home club in Canarsie] was strongly for Koch. Genovesi told Meade that Koch would be more 'pliable' and more 'flexible' than Cuomo. Stanley Friedman told Meade the same thing. And Abe Beame was coming out for Koch. On the other hand, Meade felt he couldn't talk to Mario, that Mario was too inflexible, too pure."

Tipping the balance even more in Koch's favor was the fact that Cuomo refused even to ask for Esposito's support, for, as he recalls, "I knew there would be a price attached to Esposito's endorsement. I couldn't fool myself. I had known Meade for a long time. I knew that he wanted more than just a public display of deference. He wanted jobs, he wanted control. So I never asked him for help."

Meade Esposito also had a specific reason to feel more comfortable with Ed Koch, to feel that Koch, for all his public rhetoric about "getting the hacks off the payroll," was more "flexible" than Cuomo. Esposito remembered that Koch had testified as a character witness at a trial for two Brooklyn clubhouse congressmen. Although both Frank Brasco and Bert Podell were convicted of public corruption in the mid-1970s, Congressman Ed Koch had taken the stand for each, to swear to their reputation for honesty.

On the Sunday morning that Koch was to meet with Esposito, the Brooklyn boss was having breakfast with Judge Milton Mollen. Mollen and Esposito had been good friends for years, and they often met for breakfast on Sunday mornings at Esposito's mother's house. Mollen, however, was not a product of the machine, and had, in fact, infuriated the clubhouse in 1965 by running on John Lindsay's reform mayoral ticket against Brooklyn Democrat Abe Beame. At one point during their meal, Esposito casually mentioned that Koch was about to arrive and invited Mollen to remain and quietly observe the meeting.

Koch arrived with Garth, Victor Botnick (who drove the car and got lost on the way), and John LoCicero, his campaign manager, followed a few minutes later by Tony Genovesi. Mollen's recollection is that Esposito told Koch at the outset of the meeting that he would endorse him for mayor. The only condition voiced by Esposito was: "I want to know you will return all my phone calls," and Koch assured him that he would have all the direct access he desired.

Koch then advanced his own condition. He wanted to keep Esposito's support a secret. He wanted Esposito to tell reporters that he was neutral, despite the fact that the Brooklyn machine was working for Koch. As always, Koch was sensitive to the difference between appearance and reality, and Koch knew that any open endorsement from Esposito would cause him to look like a hypocrite and turn his anticlubhouse campaign slogan into a joke. Koch's deal with Esposito was the second Immaculate Deception of his campaign.

Esposito boasted expansively of his arrangement with Koch two years later, in May 1979, at a dinner with Jack Newfield at the Tiro A Segno, an exclusive "members only" dining club on McDougal Street in Greenwich Village:

"I get whatever I fuckin' want from [him]. I told him not to dump our captains, and he said no problem. He promised me access and that he would be a good mayor. He kept his word on both scores. He promised me he would promote Tony [Ameruso] and he did. He told that bullshit screening committee to fuck off when they tried to say Tony wasn't qualified. I admire that kind of balls. I told Koch that Tony is my guy, and he showed respect for my judgment. . . .

"That Garth didn't want to use my name in public. So I agreed to send a message that Brooklyn was with Koch. Harold Fisher [MTA chairman and Brooklyn lawyer] endorsed Koch [officially]. But everyone knew I was calling the shots. . . ."*

---

*Koch offered a somewhat different version of how he obtained Esposito's endorsement in his book *Politics:* "After the primary and before the run-off, Meade Esposito, the Brooklyn Democratic leader, made it clear that he was for me over Cuomo. So we set up a meeting with Meade at his home in Canarsie. . . .

"We wanted to get Meade not to endorse me formally, because I was running without the endorsements of the county leaders . . . we made it clear that the one thing we didn't want him to do was to endorse me in any public way . . . he agreed to pull strings, very discreetly."

While Koch and Esposito made no legal, commercial contract, their agreement was, for all practical purposes, equally binding. For his part, Esposito received an assurance of access. He took this to mean patronage—that he could pick commissioners as he had at the start of the Beame administration, that clubhouse loyalists who had high-level jobs in city agencies would keep them in a Koch administration. Koch, in turn, received an assurance of political support, in the very real terms of campaign contributions, phone banks, posters, mailings, hundreds of primary-day workers, taxicabs, soundtrucks. This meant the influential politicians of Brooklyn would work their home districts for Koch, that they would direct the members of their political clubs to ring doorbells for him. Only one elected official tied to the machine in Brooklyn defied Esposito—State Senator Al Lewis—and Esposito threatened him that his law firm would lose clients if he did not obey the Boss, and that he would face a primary in the next election.

This transaction between Koch and Esposito was the beginning of a relationship. It would evolve and have its ups and downs like all relationships. It grew because each profited from it. It grew because each one knew how to play the other. Esposito knew how to flatter Koch and use his vulgarity to make Koch feel like one of the guys. As Koch came to detest reformers, he came to need the approval of former enemies like Esposito, people Koch suspected knew things about real life that he did not. Koch knew how to play up to Esposito's need to be treated as a *padrone*, with respect. And Ed Koch had the kind of blind ambition that allowed him not to see what was obvious about Esposito. Koch cynically induced himself into a state of innocence.

And all during the runoff period, Esposito kept his word, lying that he was neutral, thereby living up to his own motto, "Never leave fingerprints, never dent the charlotte russe."

The day after the Esposito breakfast, Monday, September 12, was Rosh Hashanah. To observe this Jewish Holy Day marking a new year, Koch declared a moratorium on politics and went to synagogue with Bess Myerson, where they were both conspicuously photographed, with Koch wearing his white yarmulke. But late that night Koch took another decisive step toward strengthening his position and met with fifteen black political leaders to seek their endorsement. Because of the Jewish holiday, the meeting had to be held in secret, and the only place Koch felt secure from notice was David Garth's office, at 745 Fifth Avenue.

Cuomo's continuing ineptness had created another opportunity for Koch, especially with the Harlem political leadership. The day before, all the city's black elected officials had convened in an effort to decide whom to back in the runoff. They had been united behind Sutton's candidacy, and with Sutton now eliminated, they wanted to remain unified and bargain from strength with the two white candidates. It was decided that Congressman Charles Rangel would meet with Koch, and Sutton with Cuomo, and then both would report back to the larger group.

Koch promised Rangel that blacks, picked by the black political leadership, would be given high-level jobs in his administration. Cuomo responded only by asking how black leaders could even consider endorsing a candidate who opposed housing integration and favored capital punishment. The Cuomo campaign had already made a blunder by not including in its inner circle experienced blacks who would be sensitive to the tensions between black leadership in Harlem and Brooklyn, or to the etiquette involved in courting the more senior Harlem leadership. When the disorganized Cuomo campaign had announced on Monday morning that it had obtained endorsements from various black leaders from Brooklyn, including state senator Vander Beatty and Bernard Gifford, Rangel and part of the Harlem leadership were offended. They felt Brooklyn had broken unity by negotiating directly with Cuomo behind their backs. They saw betrayal where there had only been disorganization.

By about 11:00 P.M. on Monday, most of the city's influential black leadership had arrived in Garth's office. The group included Congressman Rangel, Democratic national committeeman Basil Paterson, and city clerk David Dinkins, all from Harlem. Coming from Brooklyn were state senator Major Owens and district leader Ed Towns.

The office was decorated with giant posters of past clients of this grandmaster of political image-making: John Lindsay, Hugh Carey, Dan Walker, John Tunney, Richard Ottinger, Adlai Stevenson III. As the meeting opened, Bess Myerson took a seat at a desk with a little address book and began making phone calls to potential contributors. She punctuated the meeting with shouts of how much money each person had pledged, adding an element of bandwagon psychology to the room.

Koch opened his speech with an unequivocal promise: "I will have more minorities in my administration than my three predecessors combined. Blacks will have jobs at the highest level of a Koch administration."

Several of the Harlem leaders asked about Sydenham Hospital. Harlem was one of the most medically needy communities in the entire country, and it had the infant mortality rate of a Third World nation. There had been rumors that Sydenham would be closed because of fiscal crisis austerity, and the community was worried.

Koch again promised "I will keep Sydenham open. It will not close so long as I am mayor," and pressed further on Sydenham, he agreed to hold a public press conference on the steps of the hospital before the runoff, repeating this vow to the Harlem community.*

Carl McCall and Major Owens next asked about the fate of poverty programs and Koch's uses of the phrase "poverty pimps" during the campaign. Both McCall and Owens had helped administer the citywide antipoverty programs during the Lindsay administration, struggling to clean up bureaucratic corruption in the process.

Koch answered, "If the phrase 'poverty pimp' is offensive to you, I won't use it any more," and he promised not to dismantle the programs.†

After about an hour, Congressman Rangel, who had come to the meeting wanting a Koch endorsement, was confident enough to announce, "We were going to wait till tomorrow morning to endorse, but I can tell by the faces here, we'll go with you."

The rest of the event was spent in a logistical discussion of how to release the endorsements, and on reaching a further agreement that the *Amsterdam News,* the Harlem weekly owned by Sutton and Carl McCall, would endorse Koch in its Thursday edition.

With the city black and clubhouse leadership now aligned

---

*Although Koch did hold this press conference five days later, he closed Sydenham Hospital in 1979, sending a phalanx of city policemen through a community picket line to place a padlock on its door.

†This pledge, too, he violated a year after he was elected.

behind him, Koch took his campaign to the streets. Although Bess Myerson had been absent from the Koch entourage during July and August, she now appeared with Koch daily, and was in effect his co-candidate. She accompanied him to the crowded beach clubs in Brooklyn, charming the older women sitting around the pool, gently reminding them that Koch favored the death penalty and Cuomo opposed it. On Pelham Parkway and in Lefrak City, Myerson introduced Koch and held his hand. Any place where voters were likely to congregate—in parks, at subway stops, at shopping centers, in big housing developments—Myerson was there, trying to transfer her charisma, her credibility, to her friend Ed Koch. They even did a press conference together, where Koch promised to appoint Myerson to be the chief of the city's Economic Development Administration. (He never did.)

Myerson was almost too passionate a campaigner for Koch. One evening they were together at a rally in Sheridan Square, across the street from VID, when several older Italian men from the South Village began to heckle Koch in a mild way. Myerson took the microphone and announced the hecklers were from "the mob," and "part of the criminal element." The microphone had to be firmly recaptured from her strong hands before she started a riot.

And in a characteristically canny move, Garth also had Myerson—not Koch—make the final television commercial for the campaign.

On Wednesday, September 15, Cuomo had started to air a commercial made by Jerry Rafshoon and Pat Caddell. Rafshoon and Caddell had analyzed polling data that showed Lindsay was still unpopular and decided to exploit that sentiment by making a commercial that linked Lindsay with Koch through the coincidence of geography. This tactic was criticized, for not only was Koch quite different from Lindsay, but Lindsay had given Cuomo his start in government when he appointed him to be the mediator in Forest Hills.

Garth's retort was a last-minute, thirty-second spot of the regal Myerson looking straight into the camera and saying: "Whatever happened to character, Mr. Cuomo? We thought your campaign would do better than that." The Koch campaign spent more than $50,000 during the final weekend of the election, playing the Myerson commercial in every available time slot.

The day of the runoff—Monday, September 19—was humid, and in spite of sporadic showers, hundreds of clubhouse members fanned out across the city to work for Koch. This was his patronage army, people placed on city payrolls by the Beame administration and given the day off by their commissioners. They were joined by club members on the payroll of Assembly Speaker Steingut, who was Beame's friend and Esposito's partner in his insurance business at that time. Every doorbell in the high-rise Trump Houses in Coney Island was rung, and Koch literature was slipped under every door in the massive Parkchester development in the Bronx. Soundtrucks drove up and down Kings Highway and Ocean Parkway in the late afternoon as voters poured out of the subways on the way home from work. Phone banks kept busy calling lists of favorable voters, as the final pull began at 7:00 P.M.

Koch's runoff-day operations in the Bronx and Brooklyn were designed and directed by two consummate professionals, Stanley Friedman and Tony Genovesi. Friedman, with his sidekick Murray Lewinter, spent the day roaming the Bronx in a command car, checking on polling locations, positioning soundtrucks and patronage mercenaries. Like a field general calling in air cover, he devoted the most troops to the two high-voting areas where the elected legislators endorsed Cuomo—Oliver Koppell in Riverdale and John Dearie in Parkchester. Friedman and Genovesi each had thousands of dollars in cash to distribute to their patronage army. Genovesi received $11,000 in such traditional "street money" from Koch's headquarters, money the Koch campaign later listed as "delivery expenses" on its disclosure filings with the Board of Elections.

Taxi commissioner Jay Turoff from Brooklyn and Herb Ryan from Queens arranged for the Koch campaign to have the use of hundreds of radio cabs donated by the taxi fleet owners he regulated. This fleet carried elderly pro-Koch voters to the polls and then returned them to their homes, free of charge.

The Democratic machine in New York is often indifferent to party candidates at the top of the ticket in general elections for Senate and president, as DeSapio had been indifferent to Stevenson in 1956. Rather, the Democratic machine justifies its permanent existence in local primaries, where its patronage jobs are at risk. On this particular runoff day, the machine spent itself to the point of exhaustion. It proved that all the obituaries composed for it by professors and journalists were premature.

It delivered. And Ed Koch defeated Mario Cuomo, 432,000 votes to 355,000, or 55 percent to 45 percent. Esposito delivered Brooklyn to Koch 131,000 to 113,000. Koch won 56 percent of the vote in the Bronx, sweeping Riverdale and Co-op City two to one.

Ed Koch had been a great racehorse. He would never become a governmental giant of creative complexity, like Robert Moses, for he was a politician motivated by winning rather than by ideas or a vision. But he had succeeded in inventing a majority coalition, an improbable combination of Manhattan reformers and the clubhouses of Brooklyn and the Bronx; of Jews, blacks, and Hispanics; of political, real estate, banking, and media elites; and of voters who felt populist resentment against these elites. He had run against municipal labor unions, and in favor of capital punishment, and still carried Greenwich Village, Harlem, and the West Side of Manhattan—among the most progressive precincts in America.

An exultant Ed Koch made his victory statement to a hotel ballroom in bedlam, with Bess Myerson next to him on the chaotic platform. Over the crowd's chanting of "Edd-ee, Edd-ee, Edd-ee," photographers shouted for him to kiss Miss Myerson. He obliged them, and that moment, frozen in time, was memorialized on every television station, and in all the newspapers.

It was a lower-class Camelot come true: Ed Koch, the pantsmaker's son from Ocean Parkway and City College, and the beautiful Bess Myerson, the house painter's daughter from the Sholom Aleichem housing project and Hunter College, looking like the new king and queen of New York.

Under normal circumstances, winning the Democratic Party nomination for mayor in a one-party city like New York would make the general election a predictable formality. In the 1977 race, both the Republican candidate, Roy Goodman, and the Conservative Party nominee, Barry Farber, were unknown citywide and had no money to gain exposure through television. But when Mario Cuomo, undaunted, decided to join the ballot, running on the Liberal Party line, he made a fight of it, bringing the name recognition and ethnic base he had developed in the runoff.

Cuomo's vigorous challenge forced Koch to get all the

prominent Democrats who had backed Cuomo in the Democratic primary to defect to him in the general election. As the Democratic nominee, Koch had no trouble winning endorsements from Governor Carey, state attorney general Robert Abrams, Congressman Mario Biaggi, and Queens county leader Donald Manes.

During the general election, it was Manes who made an extra effort to ingratiate himself with Koch. He directed his closest associates to work in the Koch campaign, including Richard Rubin, the secretary of the Queens organization, Mike Nussbaum, and city taxi commissioner Herb Ryan, the president of Manes's home club in Queens.

Bess Myerson also remained Koch's designated companion. On October 10, the pair marched for forty blocks, hand-in-hand up Fifth Avenue, at the head of the annual Columbus Day parade. Their fingers uncoupled only when they waved to the crowds along the route.

However strong his initial showing, Koch needed all the help the bosses could give him. He beat Cuomo in the general election by only 50 percent to 42 percent, with Goodman and Farber splitting the remaining 8 percent of the vote.

In December 1977, mayor-elect Ed Koch was preparing for his inauguration and recruiting his administration. This period was the first ripening of his alliance with the three Democratic bosses—Friedman, Esposito, and Manes. They had all delivered in the general election and now they expected their share of the spoils.

Meade Esposito urged the mayor-elect to appoint his protégé, Anthony Ameruso, as transportation commissioner. Esposito stressed that Ameruso had gone to Yale and that Koch needed a highly visible Italian-American commissioner because Cuomo had received such a large share of the Italian vote. Ameruso was an active member of Howard Golden's Borough Park clubhouse, and his father had been a captain in the same political club.

The transportation assignment would be a large step up for Ameruso, then just forty years old, after having been the highways commissioner in the Beame administration. The transportation commissioner was in charge of several smaller city agencies, including PVB, highways, and the traffic department. The transportation commissioner also regulated certain municipal functions that Esposito, and his colleagues, had a particular interest in—monitoring truck weights for the private carting industry, regulating street improvements by construction companies, and distributing port and ferry contracts and franchises.

One of Koch's first official acts after he was elected was the appointment of ten "search committees" to find, interview, and recommend commissioners for his administration on the basis of "merit and competency." To the citizens' search committee for transportation Koch named an exceptional collection of independent experts. The panel included: Sally Goodgold, the head of the transportation committee of the West Side's Community Planning Board and a Koch supporter; defeated mayoral candidate and City Club president Joel Harnett; lawyer Myron Cohen, who had chaired Mayor Lindsay's subway watchdog commission; and David Schoenbrod, co-director of the transportation project of the Natural Resources Defense Council. The committee was given the mandate to propose candidates for the jobs of transportation, highways, traffic, and taxi commissioner. "I have only one guideline to offer you," Koch told them. "Bring me the best. And he—or she—must live in New York City."

The search committee began to function with serious purpose. They wrote letters to state commissioners of transportation throughout the country, inviting them to apply for the transportation job in New York with a new administration. They contacted the Regional Plan Association, asking for suggestions of candidates. They asked the two prior city transportation commissioners to compose their own job descriptions as a guide. (The third prior commissioner—Mike Lazar—was pointedly not invited to contribute.) The committee then drafted a long, detailed, substantive questionnaire that all applicants would be required to answer.

About a hundred people were finally considered for the position, one of whom was Anthony Ameruso.

Ameruso was interviewed by the search committee in early December 1977, about three weeks before Koch would be sworn in as mayor. The first question he was asked, pursuant to Koch's guidelines, was: "Are you a New York City resident?"

"Look me up in the Brooklyn phone book," Ameruso replied.

Sally Goodgold, the co-chair of the committee, had information from the staff of the Department of Transportation that while Ameruso indeed maintained a Brooklyn apartment, he had a call-forwarding device attached to his telephone and actually lived on Long Island. She repeated the residency question, asking Ameruso to supply more specific detail to the committee.

But Ameruso made the same reply: "Just look up my name in the Brooklyn phone book."

The remainder of the session persuaded the entire committee that Ameruso was not qualified. Not only had he no satisfactory explanation for the poor record of the highways department in filling potholes—one of his main duties—but members of the committee found him lacking in administrative skill and temperament.

By the end of the month the list of applicants was winnowed down to twelve finalists, whose names were sent to the mayor-elect. In the first week in January, Koch met with the committee and said he was considering two finalists—planner and professor Sig Grava, and Peter Stangl, the assistant commissioner for public transportation to Governor Brendan Byrne of New Jersey. He intended to name one of them transportation commissioner, and the runner-up would be offered the post of traffic commissioner. In the meantime he asked the search panel to do more checking of their references and background. The members of the committee were delighted, since both men had been impressive.

Sally Goodgold went so far as to speak with Brock Adams, the Secretary of Transportation in President Carter's cabinet. Adams told her Stangl would be a wonderful choice, and that if he were selected, Adams would see that New York received its maximum possible allocation of federal mass transit funds. The secretary said he was pleased New York City was going to have "a professional and not a politicized Department of Transportation," and suggested that Goodgold arrange for Koch to call him personally in Washington.

Goodgold went straight to City Hall with this exciting news, and encouraged John LoCicero to have Koch speak to Adams. As patronage chief and liaison for the new administration with the county leaders, however, LoCicero knew what Esposito was expecting, and so he was not thrilled by the information that Stangl* was thought of so highly in Washington, or that Secre-

---

*Peter Stangl is now the director of Metro-North, the commuter transit system.

tary Adams was anticipating a phone call from the mayor of New York.

As Goodgold recalls her encounter with LoCicero: "I got no response from John. He wanted to know how I had managed to reach a member of the president's cabinet. But otherwise he just thanked me and suggested I go. . . . I sensed something bad was happening. I was distressed. As soon as I got home, about two hours later, I received a phone call from *New York Post* reporter George Arzt."

"What do you think about Ameruso as the new transportation commissioner?" Arzt asked her.

Goodgold replied, "I don't respond to rumors."

"This is a fact, not a rumor," the *Post*'s City Hall reporter explained.

"It can't be," Goodgold said. "I would know who the new commissioner is going to be."

"Well, I just got an advance copy of a press release from Koch's office. The mayor is announcing Ameruso's appointment tomorrow morning."

By awkward coincidence, the search committee was scheduled to convene in the Blue Room of City Hall at 8:00 the next morning, two hours before Koch was going to introduce Ameruso to the media. Sally Goodgold arrived in a fury. For two months she had worked hard, in good faith, trying to determine the most qualified person in the country to serve the mayor she believed in. She now understood that she had been a dupe: her conversation with Brock Adams had forced the mayor's hand, and Koch had always intended to appoint Ameruso. She realized, too, that if the appointment was being made public, Ameruso had already passed a lengthy background check by the Department of Investigation (DOI), that his name had been submitted to the department even before she called Brock Adams. Peter Stangl had never been under serious consideration by anyone outside the committee.

"We are at least entitled to an explanation by the mayor," Goodgold told LoCicero. "Ed should at least meet with our committee this morning." Koch did appear before the group, to inform them officially that he had decided to appoint Ameruso, and to declare that Ameruso would be a superb commissioner.

Most of the members of the committee were bewildered by their participation in a process that had been a charade all along. Myron Cohen's comments to the *New York Post* were typical in their indignation: "I'm not going to participate in playing games. It was a futile exercise because we weren't overruled. We were ignored." After several members of the committee spoke to the press in a similar fashion and indicated they were going to resign, Koch rushed out an announcement disbanding his own talent search committee.

At his press conference announcing the appointment of his new transportation commissioner, the mayor supported his decision with the assertion, "The ablest person for the job is Tony Ameruso. I believe that he will prove that my judgment is right." But the appointment was so transparently the result of a deal that it received immediate and widespread criticism. A *New York Post* editorial, one of the last Sam Kaplan wrote for the paper before he left it, argued:

> Selection by Mayor Koch of Anthony Ameruso as Transportation Commissioner is inexplicable and indefensible.
>
> As the present Highways Commissioner, Ameruso displayed little initiative and less imagination. . . . Koch's own screening panel bluntly judged Ameruso not qualified for the key transportation post. No wonder they were "dumbstruck" when told of his appointment.
>
> Conceivably, Ameruso's ties to Brooklyn Democratic leader Meade Esposito counted more than the opinions of Koch's respected panel.

Builder and civic gadfly I. D. Robbins wrote in his *Daily News* column: "This was an obvious political pay-off to the Brooklyn regulars who went for Koch."

Finding himself under attack, the new mayor decided to take the offensive, and did so in what would become his signature style—the scapegoating assault, the high-minded rationalization for the low-minded act. At a dinner honoring Meade Esposito at the Hollywood Terrace Ballroom in the Bensonhurst section of Brooklyn, and before a crowd of some 1,400 people, almost all of them Italian-Americans, Koch denounced his own screening panel as elitists from Manhattan. He told the audience he wanted Italian-Americans in his administration, and affirmed that Ameruso had been appointed on his merits. Following Koch to the podium, Esposito cursed the screening panel in both English and Italian and thanked the mayor for standing by Ameruso in the face of such bigoted attacks.

That night, as Sally Goodgold and her husband were watching the eleven o'clock news, a film clip of Koch's speech was featured in the day's coverage.

Sally Goodgold saw Koch ask the crowd, "What do you think of a committee that doesn't want an Italian commissioner in this city?"

He was answered with a cascade of boos.

"What do you think of a mayor who does?"

There was wild cheering now for Ed Koch.

Sally Goodgold, sitting in her living room, was devastated. She felt as if she had just been accused of anti-Italian prejudice by the mayor, and she had no way ever to deny that insinuation to all the people who saw it.

Sally Goodgold, tough citizen activist, began to cry. Tears rolled down her face as her husband tried to comfort her.

CHAPTER FIVE

Early Warnings

ED KOCH LIKES TO TELL THE STORY of how he got the Beames out of Gracie Mansion, the mayor's luxurious official residence. Mary Beame called him, he recalls, in December 1977, and said, "Ed, Mr. Beame told me not to ask. But I must ask you, if we can't get out at the end of the month, could we stay over?" *What do you say?* Ed questioned himself, afraid that they will never get out. Gracious Ed replied that it was okay. Then he telephoned a reporter, told him about the Beame request, and added, "But I am also moving in on January 1, and I don't know who is going to be whose guest. I will be there with or without them." When the Beames heard this, Koch chirps, they made a special effort to leave quickly.

But ebullient Ed Koch, sweeping into City Hall in 1978 as a singular new force in the life of the city, wasn't nearly as forceful about getting Abe Beame out of his government. By the time Koch entered office in January, the clubhouse he once attacked for ruining his predecessor's administration had become his own silent partner. Quietly, and perhaps at times even unconsciously, Koch began making the invisible personnel choices that would, eight triumphant years later, be the undoing of his administration.

The city's transportation department fills 111,000 potholes a year, collects $32 million from 62,000 parking meters, cares for 26,000 miles of roads, 1 million street signs, and 1,400 tunnels and bridges, tows 70,000 cars, carries 22 million ferry passengers, and earns $170 million on parking tickets. When Ed Koch put Tony Ameruso in charge of all this, he didn't just deliver a job to the clubhouse; he delivered an empire. In the early days of the administration, Ameruso picked his top deputies and sent them across the street, one at a time, for ratification by City Hall. Deputy Mayor David Brown, who had been Koch's congressional chief of staff, interviewed many of them, including three with close ties to Donald Manes.

Brown found Ameruso's nominee for first deputy commissioner, David Love, "a real stiff," but thought that Lester Shafran, the candidate for PVB deputy commissioner, was pleasant and impressive. He approved both, knowing they had the backing of Manes, who had roamed the corridors at City Hall, joking and gladhanding, telling Brown that he had "heard" Brown was "gonna interview" them and confiding that Shafran and Love were both "good guys."

When Shafran then picked a new assistant director for PVB, Geoffrey Lindenauer, neither Ameruso nor City Hall questioned his choice. The unnoticed result was that a man who had been unable to hold a steady job since his quack sex clinic collapsed years earlier was suddenly the number-two man in an agency that was the city's second greatest revenue producer (after Finance, which handled property tax collections). It alarmed no one that Lindenauer, who'd been fired from his previous city job, had never run anything larger than a group therapy session.

Down the line within Transportation, Ameruso protected the preexisting preserves of each county organization. The Bronx contingent had long controlled the agency's legal department, and Ameruso made no move to replace General Counsel George Salerno, whose wife was a Bronx district leader. But Ameruso's most important, and immediately controversial patronage decision was the retention of Leon Tracy, a member of Meade Esposito's Jefferson Club, as head of the Bureau of Ferry and General Aviation Operations, a little-known agency that ran the Staten Island Ferry and had already been severely criticized for its mismanagement of a lucrative portfolio of parking lot and ferry concession leases. An Ameruso decision that would prove even more controversial was the retention of Rick Mazzeo, who ran the bureau's leasing section.

Though initially he had been connected to Esposito, Mazzeo's current sponsor in city political circles was power-broker attorney Roy Cohn, who invited this $15,000-a-year petty bureaucrat to his ballyhooed birthday parties at Studio 54, where Mazzeo dined with federal judges, ambassadors, borough presidents, celebrities, and multimillionaire developers. Mazzeo's close relationship with Beame adviser and fixer Cohn was the key to his freewheeling power during the mid-1970s.

A Cohn maneuver had helped elect Beame mayor in 1973. It was Cohn who convinced the *New York Times* that Congressman Mario Biaggi, then the leading candidate for mayor, had taken the Fifth Amendment before a federal grand jury the year before. Cohn knew it because Biaggi had come to him for legal advice and told him that he'd refused to testify. When the *Times* story came out, Biaggi vigorously denied it and, in a grandstand play, went into court seeking the release of his testimony, certain that the court would never divulge it. The testimony was released, however, and revealed that Biaggi had indeed taken the fifth, destroying his candidacy. Cohn's betrayal of Biaggi made him a fixture in Beame's government. A few months before Beame left office in 1977, Cohn agreed to make Beame's outgoing deputy mayor and closest political adviser, Stanley Friedman, a partner in his midtown law firm.

Not only did the Cohn firm represent a host of concessionaires who had leases with Mazzeo, but some of these businesses were actually headquartered in the firm's East 68th Street townhouse and could be reached on its switchboard. Cohn's firm also represented Mazzeo himself, who had become, by the time Ed Koch took office, the subject of at least three criminal investigations. The investigations were the result of a series of devastating audits assailing the bureau for favoritism in the awarding of the leases, particularly those given companies Cohn represented.

Little of the intrigue in this case was known to the Koch team when it took office. But the comptroller's audits were available, as were the initial findings of a year-old probe by the city investigations department. Brown became convinced early in the administration that the ferry agency was "a political dog," but he was never asked to review the Ameruso decision to retain its top staff.

With all the controversy surrounding the ferry bureau, it was particularly surprising that Koch decided to allow its former head, Vito Fossella, who had hired Tracy and Mazzeo, to remain in a new post Beame had given him just eleven days before leaving office—chairman of the Board of Standards and Appeals (BSA).

Fossella had run the ferry bureau through most of the Beame years until he was appointed to a six-year membership on the BSA, and then in December was named its chairman. Shortly before Koch took office, he had gone to lunch with the two other citywide officials, Council President Carol Bellamy and Comptroller Jay Goldin. During the meal, Goldin had launched into a tirade about Fossella's running of the ferry bureau, calling it a "sewer" that awarded no-bid concessions to the connected and deprived the city of millions in revenue that could be earned if the leases were handled in open competition.

Goldin was disturbed by a conversation he had had with Fossella after the second audit in mid-1977. He had never before been told by a commissioner: "I know what's going on. I can't do anything about it. It's beyond me." Fossella had asked the comptroller if he was going to audit the bureau again, and when Goldin said he was, Fossella had replied, "I'll just have to get out then." That's when Fossella moved to the BSA, and Tracy became the ferry director, leaving the 27-year-old Mazzeo, who trekked constantly back and forth in his city-chauffeured limo to Cohn's law office, effectively running the agency.

Goldin did not mention this conversation to Koch, but he did stress his audit findings, which included one highly unusual recommendation—that the only real way to straighten out ferries was to replace the key staff, a commentary on Fossella, Tracy, and Mazzeo. The mayor listened to Goldin's report and announced: "Terrific. We're going to get into that."

But the ferry bureau remained in the same hands, and in June 1978, Ed Koch swore ex–ferry chief Fossella in as BSA chairman for a second time. Although the mayor had the power to dump him, reappointing the 39-year-old Fossella, a graduate of the Newark School of Engineering who had never held a private engineering job in his life, was the mayor's way of making him a Koch commissioner. And the mayor understood that his investment would pay political dividends, because Fossella represented a powerful mix of clubhouse interests. He and his brother Frank were Democratic kingpins in the city's smallest county, Staten Island. The Fossellas were also closely connected to Esposito, who had long viewed Staten Island as a Brooklyn colony. With Fossella at BSA, the party bosses had the critically placed leverage they needed to maintain their interdependent relationship with the city's leading political industry—the real estate interests.

Manhattan real estate dons, who are to New York politics what oil barons are to Texas, had long been a primary source of contributions for the party organizations, precisely because the party controlled key parts of the city development approval process, none more important than the BSA. Developers were dependent on their ability to win discretionary variances from the zoning and building codes granted by the obscure BSA. Beame's midnight appointment of Fossella was an effort to protect this instrument of party power.

Under Fossella, the BSA became an agency staffed and chaired from top to bottom by the machine. Its executive director, Alan Gershuny, had managed Manes's first campaign for city council in 1965 and every local race since. Its deputy director and counsel were also both Manes appointees, and a small circle of clubhouse-tied lawyers practiced there. Manes's phone logs revealed a pattern of hundreds of calls from Fossella and other BSA members, staff, and lawyers, sometimes including messages that referred to apparent BSA items.

The BSA was not, however, the only point in the city's development process where the clubhouse got a new hook. Koch had strengthened the independence of the seven-member Planning Commission by appointing a new chairman, Robert Wagner, Jr., the scholarly son of the former mayor and a man unmoved by the party influence peddlers. But he then ignored Wagner's advice, and the vigorous opposition of the American Institute of Architects, by naming a Staten Island lawyer with no planning background, John Gulino, to the other vacancy on the commission. Gulino was the law chairman of the island party, and its headquarters were housed in a three-story building he owned and used as his law office.

Another outpost of the party machines was the city's Taxi and Limousine Commission (TLC), which regulated the city's 30,000 cabs. A notoriously troubled agency, with commissioners appointed on the recommendations of Democratic and Republican county leaders, the nine-member TLC had long been the reason that the taxi industry cozied up to the party organizations, buying tables by the dozen at their dinner dances and turning over free fleets of cars and drivers for primary-day transportation. Its new head, Jay Turoff, a weekly visitor at Esposito's office and the leader of the regular club in Brooklyn's Bensonhurst, was another last-minute Beame appointee. A small businessman who had taken over his father's hardware store, then started his own novelty shop, Turoff had no knowledge of the taxi industry or the agency.

Fossella's and Turoff's were two of seventy-eight appointments Beame made in his final month in office, in sharp contrast with the total of two he'd made the month before. To create the vacancy for Turoff, Beame had given a family court judgeship to the outgoing taxi chief, another Brooklyn pol named Richard Huttner, a few days earlier. When a small army of Esposito's clubhouse soldiers showed up at City Hall for Turoff's swearing-in, Huttner was among them, standing outside Beame's office, joking with his friends.

"Did you see what Koch said?" he asked. "It was in the paper. Said the judges who weren't approved by the bar association shouldn't buy extra robes, because he won't reappoint them when their terms run out." What about you, someone asked Huttner. "Can't touch me. I'm 1982," Huttner replied, referring to the fact that Koch's term would run out before his. That very morning, the comptroller released an audit of Huttner's reign at the TLC, finding that the agency had lost $3 million in fines because "the records associated with summonses were so poor that the entire regulatory process was rendered ineffective."

Beame's eleventh-hour shuffling of clubhouse chairmen was then used to persuade the incoming Koch administration that Turoff, who could have been replaced by the new mayor at any time, wasn't responsible for the prior disaster and deserved a chance to prove himself. Koch gave Turoff, who'd helped organize the Trump Village campaign rally in 1977 when Beame first appeared with Koch, a 120-day trial period, just enough time to get his foot in the door.

Koch fell into the same "let things be" pattern, as David Brown characterized it, with several other key agencies. For example, though Brown opposed the retention of sanitation commissioner Tony Vaccarello, a close personal friend of Esposito's, Koch decided to keep him. Just as he had with Ameruso, the mayor disregarded the recommendation of his screening panel for sanitation, which had not cleared Vaccarello for appointment.

Esposito also influenced the handling of appointments at the Department of Ports and Terminals, another longtime sinecure of the Brooklyn organization. Beame's commissioner, Louis Mastrianni, had been picked on the recommendation of Anthony Scotto, regional president of the International Longshoremen's Association (ILA) and publicly identified by the FBI as a capo in the Gambino crime family. Scotto's extraordinary fundraising abilities and personal charm had made him the state's most powerful labor leader, an intimate of Governor Carey's. He had even recruited many of the city's liberal journalists as allies in denouncing the FBI depiction of his mob ties as a new form of McCarthyism. During the 1977 mayoral race, the Koch camp used Scotto, who was a major force behind Cuomo, as a measure of the character of their opposition and heaped scorn on the politicians and journalists who defended him.

As Koch took office, the *Times* ran a front-page story revealing that an FBI undercover operation was about to snare Scotto and much of the national ILA leadership. At Scotto's federal trial, which did not occur until the end of 1979, he testified about the control he had exercised at the port agency while Mastrianni was commissioner. Scotto acknowledged that he was so close to Mastrianni that he'd bought him $1,000 tickets to political fundraisers, and that Mastrianni lived in a swank Manhattan building that Scotto partially owned. Information obtained from a federal wiretap also indicated that Scotto was splitting some bribe payments with the port commissioner, though Mastrianni was never indicted.

Finally, Scotto conceded on the witness stand that, in a monitored conversation he'd had with Meade Esposito on December 21, 1977, he'd asked Esposito to intercede for Mastrianni with the incoming Koch administration. The federal prosecutor asked Scotto if he'd told Esposito that he "would like to have Mastrianni kept on long enough to finish up some things" that Scotto wanted done at the agency. "Exactly," Scotto replied. "I was concerned about an orderly transition in that department."

Scotto himself tried to set up an early private meeting with Ed Koch to discuss the port agency, and although Deputy Mayor Brown blocked it, Scotto managed to get exactly what he asked for. Mastrianni lasted longer—six months—than any other Beame holdover who wasn't being rehired, and when Koch finally did replace him, he appointed Tony Gliedman, who routinely ran the election-day operation out of Esposito's home club in Canarsie.

As extraordinary as Esposito's share of these top-level appointments was, the Brooklyn leader added a handwritten list of fifteen or so middle- and upper-level bureaucrats close to his party organization whom he wanted protected or promoted. The list, without a cover letter, was delivered to John LoCicero's cubicle at transition headquarters before Koch took office, and included a Ports and Terminals official from Turoff's club who was promoted to assistant commissioner, the Building Department's deputy commissioner, and the executive director of the city's Industrial Development Agency, which dispensed millions in subsidized loans to industrial and commercial applicants. All of them were protected.

Also on the Esposito list was Abe Goodman, president of the city corporation that ran the Brooklyn Navy Yard. The 261-acre yard, which was owned by the city and leased to private users by a mayorally appointed board, was packed with Esposito jobholders, including the corporate secretary, who was an Esposito district leader; the counsel, who had been staff attorney for Assembly Speaker Stanley Steingut; and the administrative assistant, who was the wife of a Supreme Court judge. As soon as Abe Beame left office, Goodman gave a $1,500-a-month public relations contract to Beame's son Buddy, who had managed his father's campaign. The Koch administration left this entire network in place.

Esposito and the other party leaders were also deeply interested in maintaining their foothold at the Department of General Services (DGS), which handles city purchasing, leasing, and contracting. Koch's new commissioner, Peter Smith, had been one of the only political professionals involved in the mayor's primary victory. An associate for fifteen years in the law firm headed by Bill Shea (the power broker for whom Shea Stadium is named), Smith had used his close ties to Manes to line up support for Koch in Queens. Although Manes had endorsed Beame in the primary and Cuomo in the runoff, surreptitiously he paved the way for Smith to get several key Queens leaders to back Koch.

Once at DGS, Smith hired one Manes associate in a top job, appointed a first deputy with Bronx organization credentials, kept as chief counsel the son of a Queens judge, and promoted a lower-level bureaucrat high on Esposito's secret list, Alex Liberman. A major fundraiser for Meade's home club in Canarsie, the 53-year-old Liberman—a brusque and uneducated man—smiled only when someone mentioned Esposito's name. Four months after Koch took office, Liberman was put in charge of one of the city's most sensitive and politically coveted bureaus, the $80-million-a-year unit that leased office space from private owners for city use. Peter Smith quickly became Koch's first commissioner to fall. When a city background probe uncovered the fact that he had embezzled client funds from his law firm, Smith was asked to resign in August 1978, and eventually was indicted and sent to federal prison.

With decades of preying on city government under his belt, Esposito knew what parts of Koch's government he and his clubhouse allies wanted to control. Koch could have the prestige positions, the ones with great visibility; Esposito wasn't interested in naming the police commissioner. Politics was a business, Meade boasted from behind his cigar, and he was interested only in the shops that could deliver a profit. Esposito's profit was in insurance—his small brokerage firm, Serres, Visone, and Rice, represented clients such as the concessionaires at the ferry bureau and industrial tenants at the navy yard. "I've been very successful in business," Esposito told reporters candidly, "and I owe it all to politics."

Esposito's brokerage business had already gotten him in trouble with the law. When Ed Koch took office, the newspapers were filled with stories about the state attorney general's investigation of the brokerage firm's potentially illegal involvement with a Long Island racetrack. Despite these reports, the wily old boss established a personal rapport with the new reform mayor, smoozing at long dinners at the Rifle Club in the Village, a restaurant open only to members and frequented by many of the city's most powerful mob figures.

In the year after Koch's victory, his appointment diaries listed eight meetings with Esposito, including a private dinner at Gracie Mansion and a Saturday breakfast in Koch's Greenwich Village apartment. No other political leader approached that total, and Meade immediately tried to turn the relationship to his business advantage, bringing his largest insurance client, builder Fred DeMatteis, to one dinner where the mayor was accompanied by the planning commissioner who would be ruling on DeMatteis projects, Bobby Wagner, Jr.

One reason Esposito was able to turn these contacts into

patronage was that he had a direct conduit to City Hall in the person of Tony Genovesi, the district leader who had helped broker Meade's endorsement of Koch at the 1977 Canarsie breakfast. Genovesi had become a Koch insider, one of John LoCicero's closest friends and a constant visitor at City Hall. Many of the Brooklyn appointments were attributable as much to Genovesi as they were to Esposito.

Under these circumstances, other party bosses like Manes had to get most of their own early patronage through Esposito commissioners rather than directly from the mayor. For example, Manes pressed to get the counsel at the Department of Environmental Protection, a Queens district leader, appointed commissioner, but was unsuccessful. When Koch decided to eliminate Beame's Office of Neighborhood Services, which had served as a sort of in-house political unit at City Hall, Manes fought to get his man there, Michael Nussbaum, appointed to head the city's Youth Board, which allocated millions for recreational programs. Nussbaum was told he would get the job and stayed on the city payroll for months waiting for it to open up. But Esposito was pressing Koch to keep the incumbent, and eventually Esposito won.

Koch and Manes were then only beginning a feeling-out process that would last for much of the mayor's first term. Koch did not hesitate to convey his mistrust of Manes to close advisers, telling his deputy mayor Phil Trimble during the first year of the administration that Manes was an SOB. Faced with his impotence at City Hall, Manes asked Queens city councilman Ed Sadowsky, who had backed Koch in the runoff and was the chairman of the council's finance committee, to set up a dinner with Koch, and the three met at an Upper East Side restaurant near Gracie Mansion. At the start of the meal, Sadowsky sensed a tension between the two, each expecting the other to ask for something specific. It was only when Bronx boss Pat Cunningham, who was eating at the same restaurant, stopped by their table that the ice was broken.

Stanley Friedman, who would later become a county leader and play a central role in the Koch administration, had a minimal impact on the early appointments. Since he'd helped deliver the Beame endorsement and the Bronx organization to Koch during the runoff campaign, his recommendations on which Beame staffers to keep were considered. While still Beame's deputy in the final days of the administration, he snatched a last-minute perk for himself, getting Beame to appoint him to a lifetime sinecure as chairman of the city's Water Board. The part-time post paid Friedman $25,000 a year and included a chauffeured limo, secretary, and staff. That, along with his new career as Roy Cohn's law partner, was keeping him busy. His new office, on the fifth floor of the Cohn townhouse, had a cathedral ceiling, bar, outdoor patio, a greenhouse where Friedman's secretary worked, and an adjoining apartment with kitchen, living room, fireplace, and loft bedroom.

Cohn's job offer to Friedman was as much a reward for services he'd performed for clients of the firm while still in government as it was an expression of confidence in Friedman's ability to generate future business. In the closing weeks of the Beame administration, Friedman had frantically forced city bureaucrats to tie together all the loose ends of a package for Cohn client Donald Trump's renovation of the old Commodore Hotel on 42d Street. With the help of a forty-two-year, $160 million tax abatement, Trump planned to convert the tawdry hotel into the elegant Grand Hyatt. Trump was trying his first Manhattan deal, but did not have his private financing in place; yet Friedman signed and sealed a wide-ranging agreement with him in late December, putting it in escrow pending Trump's obtaining his funds.

Not only did this unprecedented maneuver give Trump the largest tax write-off in city history, but, on the final day of the Beame administration, Friedman signed an additional special permit allowing Trump to build his hotel restaurant, the Garden Room, overhanging 42d Street. All the while that Deputy Mayor Friedman was out hustling for Trump, he was already on his way to the Cohn firm, having cut a deal with Cohn a month or so earlier. Trump, largely because of the success of this deal, would become one of Cohn and Friedman's prize clients.

Similarly, Friedman had played a key role in getting Board of Estimate approval in 1976 of one of those coveted ferry bureau leases for a Cohn client. This kind of dutiful service earned Friedman a spot on the letterhead of Saxe, Bacon & Bolan, the only Manhattan law firm whose senior partner (Cohn) had been indicted more often than any of its clients, including mobsters Anthony "Fat Tony" Salerno and Carmine Galante.

In addition to rewarding Friedman, Cohn brought him into

the firm because he believed Friedman could achieve his own lifelong ambition—the takeover of the Bronx Democratic Party. As the son of a Bronx Supreme Court judge, the teenaged Cohn had regularly joined his father's dinner parties, which were often attended by Bronx boss Ed Flynn and the king of Tammany, Carmine DeSapio. As an adult, he rarely missed the annual dinner dances of the Bronx Democratic Party. His law partner Tom Bolan was a powerful force in Conservative Party politics, and he and Bolan were both influential in Republican circles. Cohn understood that Stanley Friedman, who'd been secretary of the Bronx Democratic Party for years and then its chief patronage appointee at City Hall, represented his own best chance of making the party an asset of the law firm.

The Cohn-Friedman union was thus a marriage of deeply personal visions. The 42-year-old Friedman had been reared inside a Bronx clubhouse; a county leader was a king to him. It was all he'd ever wanted to be. Cohn and Friedman sensed that they would not have to wait long to make their move. By the time Friedman moved in on 68th Street, Pat Cunningham was suffering through his third consecutive year as a target of prosecutors. Cohn, whose principal Bronx clients were mobsters, suddenly had his eye trained on a new prize.

Pat Cunningham had ruled Bronx politics for almost a decade when Ed Koch arrived at City Hall. The last of a long line of Irish county leaders, dating back to the 1930s, he was contemptuous of the black and Latin majority that had come to dominate the ranks of his party and occupy most of the Bronx's neighborhoods. Before becoming county leader, he had run for Congress in the 1960s against the Bronx's most liberal and independent public official, Jonathan Bingham, in a campaign that was one protracted race-bait. On election day the returns demonstrated, even to Cunningham, that like most backroom dealers he had no popular appeal. Unable to get elected, he got a handful of district leaders to make him the boss of people who could.

Like Esposito, he quickly parlayed control of the party into a personal fortune, collecting law clients who were looking for a fixer. He steered a $100 million renovation of Yankee Stadium through city government, and even became president of the Yankees when his client, George Steinbrenner, had to step aside to deal with a criminal case involving illegal contributions to a presidential campaign. He obtained a lease for the private operators of the city-owned, thirty-two-acre Bronx Terminal Market, the largest Hispanic food market in the country, and the manipulated bid and final deal were so scandalous they were blasted in a subsequent grand jury report.

After Hugh Carey made him state party chairman in 1974, his street swagger took on a haughty downtown air. He was now, in his own head, bigger than his borough. He practically lived in a Manhattan steakhouse, Smith and Wollensky, when he wasn't in his Madison or Third Avenue law offices. He rarely talked to the district leaders back home. Instead, as state boss, he played a pivotal role in bringing the 1976 Democratic National Convention to Madison Square Garden and fancied himself a national political force.

By then Cunningham's arrogant use of party power had, however, attracted the attention of a new prosecutor in town, Maurice Nadjari, appointed by the governor to examine corruption in the criminal justice system. Alleging in an unproven affidavit filed in court that Cunningham sold judgeships, Nadjari launched a series of leaked probes of Cunningham, indicting the boss, as well as judges, public and party officials, and attorneys close to him. Stanley Friedman, among dozens of other Cunningham associates, was hauled before a grand jury. When Cunningham was introduced at the DNC podium by national chairman Bob Strauss that August, two indictments were already hanging over his head.

In the middle of the investigation, Carey bounced Nadjari, and the indictments, one after another, were dismissed. But by the time Ed Koch and Mario Cuomo met in the mayoral runoff in 1977, Cunningham was estranged from Albany, disgraced by scandal, and just one more rider on Beame's dead-end train. Almost immediately after Beame lost, Cunningham convened a meeting of the Bronx district leaders and sought a Koch endorsement. Privately he told the leaders to ignore the "outsider" signals Koch had been sending about the machine and forget his history as a reformer. "I know we can talk to this guy," Cunningham said. "We can do business with him." The executive committee endorsed Koch, and Cunningham ran a stronger election-day effort for Koch than he'd put together for Beame—posters, literature, and phone banks. One key Cunningham aide who helped run the field operation was Stanley Friedman.

The IRS, meanwhile, had quietly opened a file of its own on Pat Cunningham. It started with a newspaper clipping placed in the file on January 7, 1976, while Nadjari was in hot pursuit. When the Nadjari cases ended, the IRS intensified its probe, questioning Cunningham clients, tracking every dollar of possible income. In late January 1978, a few weeks after Ed Koch was sworn in as mayor, a beleaguered Cunningham, fearful that the IRS was closing in on him, persuaded two friends to falsely tell IRS agents that they had made cash payments to him for legal services he'd performed. At the same time, according to government documents, he concocted fictitious cash receipts for these payments in an attempt to conceal fees he was illegally splitting with attorneys who received politically arranged appointments from the Bronx surrogate. He then decided to lower his profile, hoping that his cover-up and reduced public attention would combine to throw the IRS off his trail.

On April 5, Cunningham assembled the leaders of the Bronx party at Smith and Wollensky and unexpectedly announced his resignation. His plan was to serve for a few more weeks, until the party's annual dinner dance in May, and shortly afterward to hold a meeting of the executive committee, consisting of the elected leaders (one male and one female) from each of the borough's assembly districts and several countywide officials he'd appointed. This group would vote on his successor. Cunningham would keep his designee's name close to the vest as long as possible, allowing several candidates to believe they could get his support, and thereby ensuring that no coherent opposition would galvanize.

Cunningham's plan was to nominate Alan Solomon, a loyal associate with no base of political support other than him. He had manufactured in his own mind an educational requirement for his successor: the new county leader could not have a law degree. Cunningham wanted the best of both worlds: someone he controlled would become leader, reducing the adverse public attention he'd been living with for years, and he'd still get the legal fees that went with the leadership.

When Stanley Friedman came to see him shortly after the announcement and told him that he was interested in the leadership, Cunningham was standoffish. Although Friedman had served as party secretary and had become a deputy mayor on his recommendation, Cunningham had deliberately kept him in the dark about his sudden resignation, haunted by a vision of all the party-connected law business rushing over to Roy Cohn's townhouse.

Cunningham had become the county leader because he knew how to buy and sell loyalty, a valued skill in the culture of the clubhouse that required a sense of timing. One had to know how to inspire loyalty in others, and how to give it to the bosses who could nurture your career. But a player in this game also had to know when to jump ship, abandoning career-long friendships suddenly, without emotion, and with a ready and usually petty alibi. And finally, a leader had to have a sixth sense that warned him when he was about to be abandoned. His last days as Bronx boss would prove that Cunningham couldn't smell betrayal.

After his cool reception by Cunningham, Friedman started meeting with district leaders one at a time and building a base of tentative support. And even though Koch confidants such as Deputy Mayor David Brown were warning him to "stay away from Friedman," whom they considered a "sleazebag," the mayor and Friedman began an intricate dance of mutual support played out over the coming weeks in the pages of the daily newspapers. Koch himself would remain publicly neutral, but LoCicero, Koch's prime political operative, and Herman Badillo, Koch's only deputy mayor from the Bronx, were committed to rounding up support for Friedman.

Badillo—who had announced in March that he and reformers such as Assemblyman Oliver Koppell were putting together a campaign to oust Cunningham by electing anti-Cunningham district leaders in the 1978 elections—had lunched at least twice with Roy Cohn to discuss the Friedman candidacy. The one-time reform borough president of the Bronx agreed to take charge of pulling in the minority leaders on Friedman's behalf. He arranged a meeting near City Hall with Frank Lugovina, Ramon Velez, Fernando Ferrer, and Al Goodman—politicians who, between them, controlled virtually all the black and Latin votes.

In late April, Cunningham had met with LoCicero and Koch, coyly informed LoCicero that Solomon was "the leading candidate," and carefully described this view as an assessment, not a preference. LoCicero informed Cunningham that he felt that Friedman was "the quality candidate," and just as carefully explained that he was speaking for himself, not Ed Koch. The *Times* reported this exchange of deceptions ten days before the vote in a story written by its City Hall bureau chief, suggesting that the Friedman forces at the Hall wanted to get the message of their support out in the open. LoCicero was described as telling anyone who would listen "that the Mayor likes Stanley Friedman and trusts him and thinks he can work with him." In the same story, LoCicero fed Cunningham's stultifying overconfidence by predicting a winner: "If I was betting, I'd bet it would be Al Solomon."

LoCicero's phone calls to selected leaders after the *Times* story were almost redundant, but he made them anyway, and some had an effect. Two LoCicero calls were to George Salerno, the counsel to the city's transportation department whose wife was a district leader. When LoCicero urged Salerno to back Friedman, Salerno at first explained that he didn't know Friedman as well as he knew Solomon; but that he and his wife hadn't made up their minds. By the second call, he told LoCicero he was leaning toward Friedman.

LoCicero's unexpected candor in the *Times* story about his lunch conversation with Cunningham also caused the boss another problem. With the publication of Cunningham's apparent endorsement of Solomon, the cat was out of the bag long before Cunningham intended it to be. The party's secretary, Murray Lewinter, who held the same title Cunningham had held before he became leader, had been urging Cunningham to designate him, citing the precedent of Cunningham's own elevation. At first Cunningham had not discouraged Lewinter. Then he'd told him that he had to pass the leadership on to a black, Joe Galiber, the chairman of the party's county committee. Now it was clear that the Galiber ploy was merely designed to hold Lewinter and Galiber, both of whom had votes, in check. Cunningham did not know just how angry Lewinter was. He continued to rely on Lewinter to act as his head-count man and to work the leaders for him.

The day before the vote, the unsuspecting Cunningham told Lewinter, who visited him at his law office, that he'd heard "rumblings" that some leaders were drifting toward Friedman, and Lewinter said he'd heard them, too. Lewinter did not, however, acknowledge that a rather noisy train had been running through his own head. Cunningham was still certain that the force of his own personality would prevail. After all he had just presided, only a few days earlier, at his final Bronx organization dinner dance, where the 1,100 paying guests, including the mayor and the governor, had turned the evening into a tribute to him. He planned to make a few key phone calls that night, making clear his still half-concealed support for Solomon. But when Cunningham got to his house and began dialing leaders, he couldn't find anyone at home.

Almost the entire Bronx leadership, as it happened, was at a meeting in the law office of district leader Jerry Esposito. Calls for the meeting had gone out only hours before, in an attempt to conceal it from Cunningham. The invitation, at least to leaders who weren't already with Friedman, was open-ended; just come to talk, the Friedman camp suggested. The undecideds who went were astonished to see the breadth of the support that had assembled for Friedman. Even Mario Biaggi, the congressman whose mayoral candidacy had been submarined by Friedman's law partner Cohn, was there, as was Cunningham's aide Lewinter.

It was clear to everyone at the meeting that Friedman (who had just registered to vote in the Bronx earlier that day) had enough executive committee votes to become the county's number-one Democrat.* The discussion dragged on deep into the night, and a strategy was carved out for the next day.

Stanley Simon, the Riverdale district leader and councilman, would be the floor leader. His actions were scripted one step at a time, carefully crafted on the advice of the lawyers who had written the party rules. The group agreed to meet at 7:00 A.M. at the Grand Concourse apartment of Ted Teah, a South Bronx pol whose appointment to the City Planning Commission had been engineered by Friedman in the final days of the Beame administration. Then they would travel together to the county headquarters, a few miles up the Concourse. They could only trust one another if they could see one another. If

---

*Friedman hadn't actually lived in the Bronx for a dozen years, at first living in suburban Rockland County even while he held Bronx party posts and key jobs at City Hall, and later, after leaving his wife and two children in the midseventies, moving into a luxury apartment in Manhattan. He had used his parent's home in the Bronx as a voting address for most of those years, claiming to live there even after his parents died, but had finally switched to a Manhattan registration. Then, on the threshold of becoming the Bronx leader, he had reregistered from the one-bedroom apartment of his 92-year-old grandmother, who lived in the desolate heart of the Hunts Point section of the Bronx.

all of them were quarantined, Cunningham would be unable to pick off leaders.

At 2:30 A.M., Pat Cunningham was awakened by a phone call. The whispering voice told him that the caller had been to a meeting that night and that Friedman had everyone. It was over. The caller hung up after warning him that the leaders were coming en masse to headquarters in the morning.

Cunningham howled. He bled. He remembered every small favor he'd ever done for the people who were abandoning him now. He wailed about a mayor who'd betrayed him. He called his loyal friend, district leader Johnnie Whalen, who'd beaten a Nadjari indictment of his own, around 3:00 A.M. and cursed. Then he came up with a new plan. He would withdraw his resignation, cancel the meeting, and go on being leader. Later he would cripple anyone who had crossed him. Cunningham rose, got in the Lincoln the county organization rented for him, and drove to headquarters at the Wagner Building, his jaw set in concrete.

The Friedman group began arriving at Teah's house before the sun came up. The young Ferrer, whom Cunningham had just appointed to a leadership vacated by a retirement, sat nervously amid the more seasoned pols such as Biaggi. Outside waited a luxury liner from Ed Arrigoni's company, New York Bus, whose city express bus franchises had been personally executed by then Deputy Mayor Stanley Friedman. The group of twenty leaders and other pols boarded the bus and rode to the headquarters, on time for the 9:00 A.M. meeting. The group would not even divide up to take elevators; they walked up the stairs together.

Cunningham was hiding in the back office with a handful of supporters and aides. As the group reached the floor, a secretary peered out into the empty meeting room and closed the door. They quietly filed into the room as a group and got seated. The secretary stuck her head out the door again and seemed shocked to see everyone seated and waiting. "Full house?" she asked of no one in particular. Frank Lugovina, who had become the point man for the minority leaders, blurted back: "No. Royal flush."

When Cunningham emerged from his office, he abruptly announced that he was not retiring and that the meeting was adjourned. All he had left, standing beside him, were three leaders. Cunningham railed that the Friedman forces were "staging a coup to prevent the orderly transition of the leadership." He charged that "threats" had been used, and "lies" spread to put pressure on district leaders. Friedman's designated floor manager, Stanley Simon, began shouting that Cunningham couldn't withdraw his resignation. The two officers of the party—Lewinter and parliamentarian Paul Victor—ruled that a quorum was present and that the meeting was legal. Cunningham retreated to his office, and the vote for Friedman was ratified with only a couple of dissents. Cunningham, Solomon, and Whalen then stormed out.

A few days later, in mid-May 1978, Ed Koch held a press conference with Stanley Friedman at City Hall. "Stanley Friedman won the job on his own," Koch said. "He did a brilliant job putting the votes together." LoCicero was standing nearby, so reporters asked if he hadn't helped a bit. "Look, I spoke to a couple of people," LoCicero said. "People hear my name and they think the mayor's for Friedman." Wouldn't LoCicero have thought so himself, under similar circumstances? "Yes, I would have," LoCicero said with a broad smile. Didn't he want people to get that impression? "Yes," he admitted.

At the same press conference, Friedman and Koch tried to put a reform face on the new reign of Beame's old patronage chief. Friedman announced that he would voluntarily surrender his lifetime sinecure on the Water Board, a plum that Candidate Koch had labeled an "outrage."*

Friedman also pretended, in the weeks that followed, to meet two other City Hall demands. The *Times* reported that when Friedman came to Koch and Badillo before the election seeking support, both had "expressed concern that the party leadership might be used to solicit business" for the Cohn law firm, a charge, they told Friedman, that frequently had been leveled against Cunningham by reformers. Shortly after the election, Roy Cohn told the *Times:* "The firm has no intention of seeking any politically related business—in the Bronx or anywhere else." Friedman also vowed to change the party rules to conform to longtime reform demands, opening up its financial records and eliminating the extra voting positions on the executive committee that Cunningham had created for unelected officers appointed by the party boss. The democratiza-

---

*A month after Friedman resigned, the legislature abolished the board at the mayor's request, making Friedman's gesture meaningless.

tion of the party and promises about the law firm quickly proved to be charades.

The alliances formed to get Friedman the leadership would have a lasting effect, continuing until the scandal exploded eight years later. Murray Lewinter was almost immediately awarded Al Solomon's patronage job on the assembly payroll, leaving the near-boss Solomon unemployed. George Salerno was named chairman of the State Board of Elections. His position as Ameruso's chief counsel was passed on, at Friedman's urging, to a member of Stanley Simon's club. Substantial state- and city-connected legal business was steered to Biaggi, Jerry Esposito, Paul Victor, and other leaders who'd backed Friedman.

Though Candidate Koch had cited Velez as the sort of "poverty pimp" he would drive out of city government in 1977, Friedman convinced the city administration to begin refinancing the Velez empire. Koch wound up turning over a $16-million-a-year antipoverty empire to Velez, who was drawing $210,000 salary from publicly funded corporations. Velez, Lugovina, and Teah were also given pieces of the city's Bronx cable franchise, and Lugovina's job-training company contracts reached the millions. Teah, whose planning commission job was part time, went to work for Friedman's law firm as an associate.

But the biggest beneficiary of the Friedman win was Stanley Simon, who became the new borough president just ten months after Friedman won the party leadership. The opportunity arose when incumbent Bob Abrams resigned after he was elected the state's attorney general in 1978. Friedman got the Bronx members of the city council to pick Simon as Abrams's successor in January 1979—an appointment that would last until the next election in September.

The 1979 primary contest for borough president pitted the plodding Simon against energetic reform assemblyman Oliver Koppell. Simon, who was appointed to a council vacancy in 1973, had never been elected to a public office. Like his sponsor, Friedman, he'd been registered from a phony address—in a decimated South Bronx tenement—for years, moving into the Bronx only after he became a councilman.

Early in the race for borough president, Friedman hired a Manhattan speech therapist to try to get Simon—whose public persona was characterized by blank stares, long pauses, and forced smiles—to begin to communicate. The therapy effort was abandoned midway through the campaign, and instead Friedman kept Simon as far away from a debate with Koppell as possible. Bronx reformers had controlled the borough presidency, but little else, for a dozen years. For them, as for the newly elected Friedman, winning the beep's post was a question of survival.

Once again, Ed Koch was nominally neutral. But both LoCicero and Denise Sheinberg, a member of Koppell's club who worked at City Hall, tried to talk Koppell out of running. Koch made repeated public appearances with Simon in the Bronx, carefully orchestrated for maximum campaign impact. When Koppell tried to make an issue out of a massive illegal dumping site located in a residential neighborhood, Simon came in behind him with an armada of city sanitation trucks and cleaned it up. The transportation department rushed to satisfy neighborhood demands for new stoplights, with Simon getting the credit.

In addition to these campaign assists, Koch's deputy mayor, Herman Badillo, was once again playing a key role for Friedman. Badillo encouraged a Puerto Rican attorney, Victor Marrero, to run. Marrero's candidacy was specifically authorized by Friedman at a meeting with Velez, Lugovina, and others, and when Velez's club got the bulk of the nominating signatures to get Marrero on the ballot, a Friedman organization lawyer protected his petitions during the legal challenges. Friedman feared that without a viable Puerto Rican candidate in the field, the Latin vote could go to Koppell. With four candidates in the race (including a black), Friedman thought his candidate Simon could slip through the cracks.

The campaign was financed with $50,000 in loans and contributions from Ed Arrigoni, the bus company executive who had retained Friedman as his lawyer, and with another $50,000 in loan guarantees from Cohn, others associated with Friedman's firm, and ferry bureau concessionaires so close to the firm they were headquartered there. Friedman deliberately filed the financial disclosure statements late in an attempt to delay the disclosure of last-minute contributions of $10,000 from Donald Trump and $5,000 from longshoremen's union president Anthony Scotto, whose racketeering trial was scheduled to begin the day before the primary. Simon won with less than a third of the vote. Confronted by reporters about Simon's violations of election law requirements and questionable contributions, Koch refused to comment.

The victory gave Friedman a controllable vote on the Board of Estimate, guaranteeing him clout at City Hall. Since Simon's appointment nine months earlier, he had already become the mayor's most dependable ally on the board. When Simon entered his own victory party that night, arm and arm with Biaggi, the crowd of 500 greeted him with the repeated chant, "Mario, Mario." Friedman then took over the mike and hosted the party. Even on the biggest night of his political life, Simon was a prop for the two most powerful men in the Bronx.

The loser in the Bronx showdown, Pat Cunningham, was indicted in July 1981 for tax evasion, obstruction of justice, and making false statements to federal officials. His cover-up attempts in early 1978, just before his resignation, unraveled when the feds flipped the associates he had persuaded to lie about cash payments to him. He was convicted at trial, was sentenced to three years in prison, and lost his license to practice law.

Just as Ed Koch had worked out a deal with Meade Esposito in 1977 that included a promise that Esposito's runoff support would remain covert, he had also bargained secretly with the Bronx bosses twice by the end of 1979, helping to elect Friedman and Simon without ever publicly committing himself to them. His neutral poses were designed to give him plausible deniability when accused of having become a machine mayor. But beneath the facade, the first mayor ever elected from the reform wing of the Democratic Party had gone with the regulars whenever faced with a concrete political choice between the two. The cost of this compromise—affecting even judicial politics, the once sacrosanct center of the reform agenda— would become apparent before Koch's first term was over.

When Ed Koch was a struggling young lawyer in the midsixties, working out of a small office with his apolitical new partner, Allen Schwartz, he and Schwartz shared a single article of faith: a commitment to an independent judiciary, selected on the basis of merit. Koch had just been elected district leader in his classic Village confrontation with Carmine DeSapio, who saw judgeships as prizes to be awarded to the pliant. Koch's unlikely partner Schwartz had been in a clubhouse only once, to hear his and Koch's mutual friend Leonard Sandler debate the death penalty. As young lawyers, Schwartz, Koch, and Sandler—who would later become a Supreme Court judge with the help of Koch's old club—often mulled over together the complicated politics of judicial selection. Later another Koch partner, Victor Kovner, would become a maven of the judicial process.

Party bosses across the state had invented a vehicle designed to virtually guarantee them control of the selection of judges in the Supreme Court, the court that first handles felony and significant civil cases. The vehicle, created under state law, is called a judicial convention. The state is divided into a large number of judicial districts, and each party holds a convention in every district, nominating candidates to run locally for fourteen-year terms on the Supreme Court. The delegates who actually vote at the convention and nominate judicial candidates are elected locally in primaries run by each party.

This arrangement means that the overwhelmingly Democratic voters in the city never get to vote directly in a Democratic primary for the judges they'd prefer. All the party bosses have to do is win the widely ignored delegate races (delegates do not run committed to a named judicial candidate), and the Democrats these delegates nominate at their party judicial convention are virtually assured of success in the general election.

Manhattan and Bronx had long been joined in the same judicial district, just as Brooklyn and Staten Island had been. By the mid-1970s the growing reform movement in Manhattan was strong enough to nominate judges, aided by a sister movement in the Bronx that elected just enough delegates to reduce the machine bloc at the convention that Cunningham and the old-line Tammany leaders in Manhattan controlled. Manhattan and Bronx reformers were united for years around a simple program: their delegates would support only candidates who had been approved by an independent judicial panel. The leaders in this movement came from Ed Koch's Village Independent Democrats. After Koch gave up his party leadership post and went to Congress, his successor John LoCicero, and female district leader Miriam Bockman, carried on the war.

When Koch became mayor, one of his first acts was to establish a high-quality panel to make judicial recommendations. As mayor, he had the power to appoint Criminal and Family Court judges directly, and he made it clear to the party bosses that their longtime influence over the selection of these lower-court posts was at an end. In addition, his victory in the primary in 1977 positioned him to name the new county leader in Manhattan, and he helped install Miriam Bockman. Bockman had been Ed Koch's friend for more than thirty years and had worked as a volunteer coordinator in every one of his campaigns. With a spiritual leader of reform like Bockman at the helm, merit selection of judges had never seemed more achievable.

Bockman's first convention as county leader in 1978 was also Stanley Friedman's first. She engineered a sweep for the reform slate. But when the two county parties convened again the next year, Ed Koch had become a working partner of the new Bronx leadership—Friedman, Biaggi, and Simon. The convention pit these new alliances against Bockman and the mayor's longtime reform friends in Manhattan.

The issue over which the two factions clashed was Friedman's attempt to nominate Anthony Mercorella, who had been indicted three years earlier by Maurice Nadjari. Nadjari had charged that Mercorella had tried to buy a judgeship from Cunningham, making a $10,000 payoff to the Bronx party. But Judge Leonard Sandler, Koch's old friend, had thrown out the indictment, adding in a written opinion that he wanted to "make it emphatically clear" that he regarded Mercorella and Cunningham's actions as "a shabby and cynical maneuver" that was not "appropriate or acceptable behavior for a judicial candidate or a major political leader."

Because of this language and another instance of alleged unethical behavior, the screening panel had strongly rejected Mercorella when Friedman first floated his candidacy. A few days before the convention, Bockman relented on another Friedman nominee, and went to City Hall, where the mayor phoned Friedman with her compromise. Friedman, who controlled only a third of the convention's 175 delegates, rejected the peace offering, insisting on Mercorella. Bockman explained to Koch that she couldn't support Mercorella, and Koch said: "I know you can't go outside the panel, and I understand." Bockman thanked the mayor for his support and told him that he was the only one not trying to interfere in the process. She left City Hall, confident that the mayor was with her.

But pressure on Koch from Biaggi, and the mayor's intricately arranged relationship with Friedman, pushed him, in the intervening days, toward Mercorella. He told LoCicero to make a few discreet calls; not even Bockman was to know.

LoCicero called an old-line Manhattan district leader named Jim McManus and asked McManus to deliver delegates to Mercorella. McManus replied angrily:

"I'm boxed in by the rules of the county party that require me to vote only for candidates approved by the screening panel. I opposed those rules when they were adopted, but you were the VID leader and you stuffed them down the party's throat. Now you want me to go against them."

Nonetheless, two McManus delegates did vote for Mercorella. LoCicero instructed McManus to "forget that the conversation occurred." At LoCicero's request, another City Hall aide, Pete Piscitelli, went on the convention floor and tried to get a Bronx reform delegate he knew well to switch to Mercorella.

Then, a few hours before the convention, LoCicero contacted Marty Begun, the ex–East Side leader, and asked for a couple of votes. When Bockman later saw two votes switch in Begun's old district, she crossed the convention floor and asked the delegates why. She was told that Begun had called. When she finally reached Begun from a pay phone during the vote at the convention, all he would say was that he had acted on a request from "a high source in City Hall." Miriam Bockman, who had spent a lifetime at Ed Koch and John LoCicero's sides, began to shake with rage.

She phoned LoCicero, who admitted having made the calls. He tried to explain why she hadn't been informed by claiming that it was a last-minute decision. "I was reachable at all times," she murmured in reply. When Mercorella won by a single vote, Bockman refused to talk to Koch for days. Although LoCicero and Piscitelli started out denying to reporters that they or the mayor had been involved, Bockman, McManus, and others were talking freely to the press. With the cover story unraveling, Koch finally decided to go public, acknowledging that he "asked some friends" to help Mercorella. He went on the offensive, denouncing the screening panel he'd helped create as dominated by "Legal Aid sympathizers who won't approve tough judges."

With the demise of the resistance to Friedman, many Manhattan reformers abandoned their opposition to a bill introduced in Albany at Friedman's behest to separate the joint district and give the Bronx its own convention. Governor Carey had vetoed the same bill in 1980 at the urging of its reform opponents in Manhattan and the Bronx. In 1981, he signed it, and Roy Cohn and Stanley Friedman had their own judicial district. That same year a war-weary Bockman resigned her party leadership.

The Koch collapse on judicial selection was only one instance of the deepening alliance between the reform mayor and the party bosses. In the fall of 1979, shortly after the debacle at the judicial convention, the mayor and Meade Esposito began talking favorably in print about the same potential candidate for the 1980 Democratic nomination for Republican Jacob Javits's seat in the U.S. Senate. The candidate was Bess Myerson. Koch was repaying the debt he owed his 1977 campaign date.

Esposito was interested not just because he saw Myerson as a possible winner but because he was determined to deflate the candidacy of a reform Brooklyn congresswoman who'd long been a thorn in his side, Liz Holtzman. Myerson would be just the antidote to the stridently independent, intellectual, and insular Holtzman, who'd made a national name for herself during the Watergate hearings.

The Koch-orchestrated campaign for Myerson became so intertwined with Esposito that at one point, when a frantic Myerson called City Hall officials inexplicably afraid she would be shot by PLO assassins, a Koch commissioner turned to an Esposito insurance client to get bodyguards for her. Coastal Dry Dock, Esposito's number-two customer and the occupant of virtually all the usable pier space at the city-owned Brooklyn Navy Yard, provided the security guard services Myerson wanted in the summer of 1980, during the thick of the primary campaign.

While Stanley Friedman joined Esposito on the Myerson bandwagon, only Donald Manes bucked his fellow leaders and Koch to back Holtzman. His move outraged Esposito, who saw Manes's support of a reformer from his county as a violation of the turf understanding that underlay the loose arrangement between the party bosses. When Holtzman won, Manes crossed the border into Brooklyn to celebrate at her victory party, further enraging Esposito. Although Manes and Koch had, by then, established a collegial rapport, Manes's endorsement of Holtzman was a clear message to the mayor: he made his own political choices; the mayor would have to deal with him as a peer.

Even as the political interdependence between Koch, Esposito, and Friedman intensified during the year-long Myerson race, the mayor was receiving ever-clearer indications that his ties with the two might mean trouble for his government. One of the warnings came in the person of Vito Fossella, the Esposito ally whom Koch had gone out of his way to appoint chairman of the Board of Standards and Appeals. In December 1979, Fossella became the subject of a city's investigation department probe, which found that he had acted to expedite an appeal for a Staten Island architect.

The architect was seeking BSA approval to use plastic piping in an island condo development. The architect had filed the application on behalf of the owner of the condo project, a Staten Island plumbing contractor. At the same time that this application was pending, Fossella wrote an extraordinary letter to a judge in a criminal case involving the plumbing contractor, who had been found guilty on thirty-one misdemeanor counts of installing the illegal piping in hundreds of already completed homes in a different project. Fossella's letter sought to delay the sentencing of the plumber, falsely stating that the full BSA—which had actually never discussed the matter—recommended the adjournment until it could rule on the plastic tubing issue.

DOI eventually found that the architect and plumber were trying "to make legitimate" in the second project "what had been ruled illegal in the first," and thus retroactively extricate the plumber from his criminal conviction. Fossella, whom DOI described as "an advocate for the defendant" in the criminal case, "became the means through which this was almost accomplished."

When confronted with these actions, Fossella told three different stories in three different interviews with city investigators, two of which were sworn depositions. His final version, which was close to the truth, was proffered only after Fossella learned that another witness from his own agency had told DOI the whole story. DOI found that, at a minimum, Fossella had displayed a "reckless disregard for the facts," and considered a perjury referral to a district attorney. The architect, whom Fossella had known for ten years, took the fifth on every DOI question.

DOI commissioner Stan Lupkin and an aide then went to see the mayor. They told him what Fossella had done and outlined the alternatives they faced, including the possibility of bringing administrative charges against Fossella. Koch, who would have to decide to press charges, was noncommittal. "Where can this go?" he asked. Lupkin, who was also familiar with the allegations about Fossella's management of the ferry bureau, urged the mayor not to worry about the impact of the case on Fossella. "You are not being well served by this man," Lupkin said. The meeting ended with the disposition of the case up in the air.

DOI proceeded, actually drawing up administrative charges. But since Fossella's recanting made a perjury case difficult, and an administrative hearing could be held only at the discretion of the mayor, Lupkin just had to wait. Although DOI did not discover a single new fact about the case after December 1979, it was not closed until February 23, 1981. Throughout that fourteen-month period, Fossella remained in charge at the board, while DOI, in repeated contact with City Hall, remained confused. Lupkin, who had in the beginning championed at least some disciplinary action, vacillated in the face of City Hall's stonewall, expressing uncertainty about whether the charges justified removal.

One City Hall official who did want to move against Fossella was Bob Wagner, Jr., the ex–Planning Commission chairman who had become deputy mayor at the start of 1980. Wagner was outraged at the state of the BSA, which he called "the most dominated politically and least responsive agency" in city government. Wagner knew that the entire commission and its staff came from the clubhouse, and that lawyers such as Stanley Friedman could call Fossella and get agenda items expedited or postponed, even minutes before they were supposed to be presented. So when DOI came to him, he welcomed their probe as an opportunity to finally get the mayor's ear about changing the BSA. In the end, with the Mayor's approval, Wagner went to Sylvia Deutsch, a Brooklyn Planning Commission member, and asked her to replace Fossella. But a few weeks later he returned to tell her that Fossella would stay on the commission and become her vice chairman. That was the deal that City Hall had struck.

DOI's 1981 closing memo reviewed all the actions that could be taken against Fossella, but recommended nothing. A few weeks after the memo was written, a *Times* story announced the switch at BSA, attributing it to policy differences within the administration. When Fossella actually stepped down in May, Koch said that Fossella "has served the city with distinction," adding that he asked him to remain as vice chair because of "his proven administrative ability." No one said a word about the DOI report. And no one told a disappointed DOI why Fossella had been treated so gingerly.

Before the Fossella switch was made, Wagner paid homage to Meade. Over lunch, he informed Esposito that Fossella would have to go, and that the administration would like to put Deutsch in as a replacement. Esposito indicated that Deutsch was "an independent and difficult person," but he "gave in." Wagner then asked Deutsch, who had been a member of the old Madison Club in Brooklyn that had produced Abe Beame, to make a courtesy call to Esposito, telling him of her new appointment. Since Deutsch had nominal Brooklyn clubhouse connections and annually attended Meade's dinner dance, he could claim her as one of his own, a face-saving deception.

Around the same time that Fossella's BSA problems first surfaced, the long-simmering ferry bureau scandal, with its ties to Esposito and the Friedman law firm, finally exploded. As early as June 1979, Comptroller Goldin wrote Koch a letter about the bureau, reiterating his charges and announcing that another, damning audit would follow. Esposito's clubmember and Fossella's successor, Leon Tracy, was summoned to City Hall and told to reply to the latest allegations. The answer the agency put together conceded many of Goldin's points.

The mayor dallied again, but this time something had to happen. DOI had begun working on the ferry probe while Beame was mayor and, together with the two D.A.'s offices working on the investigation, had put together the beginnings of a tax case on fast-track Mazzeo. Mazzeo drove a Mercedes with the license plate "Gatzby" and lived in a mansion he rented on the Long Island shore for $20,000 a year, more than his total city salary. He owned a house on Staten Island, land in New Mexico, and a Long Island farm. He set up several food brokerage businesses, using the same lawyer who represented a half-dozen of the ferry concessionaires. He actually ran the food businesses right out of his ferry bureau office, using a phone he kept in his desk drawer and listing it in the Yellow Pages.

The DOI team was also intrigued by the intense representation this low-level bureaucrat was getting from the high-powered criminal attorneys in Cohn's law firm. The investigators knew that the worst deals Mazzeo cut were with the concessionaires headquartered at Cohn's office. A DOI informant had also told them that Mazzeo bragged that Cohn was his "rabbi," and said that Cohn's friends had acquired control of one of the parking lot companies after the former principal was found with two broken knees. Federal probers would later determine that Mazzeo's account of how corporate takeovers occurred at the ferry bureau was true.

DOI closed its case on Mazzeo in May, saying in its memo that Mazzeo was "reportedly the bagman" at the ferry bureau, and referring possible tax violations to federal and state prosecutors. The memo specifically stated that the purpose of a tax case on Mazzeo would be to squeeze him, and that if Mazzeo's cooperation was obtained, DOI would reopen its probe of ferry concessions.

With Goldin's and DOI's new findings, Koch finally announced a series of changes. On August 28, 1979, Tracy was demoted, and resigned. The mayor also issued a statement saying he would submit a reorganization plan to the city council, transferring the concession function at the ferry bureau to another city agency, Ports and Terminals. A few months later, following yet another blistering Goldin audit just of the "disgraceful" leases held by Cohn's clients, the city's law office moved and brought the first of what would become a series of eviction proceedings. Mazzeo hung on at the bureau, but in a powerless limbo. It had taken two years for the mayor to do what Goldin had suggested before Koch took office.

With the demise of his ferry empire now a certainty, Roy Cohn struck back at his nemesis Goldin. In November 1979, Cohn wrote an extraordinary letter to Goldin's executive assistant that became big news in the city papers. He indicated that he was considering a libel suit because of the audits and complained that "people around this city who do not comply with the requests of the bagmen for Goldin's office have been subjected to this type of treatment, while those who buckle under and give him noncompetitive sweetheart deals are rewarded with public praise." Cohn, who subsequently began scouring the city for a candidate to oppose Goldin, accused him "of the most crooked political scheme attempted since the days of Boss Tweed." If there was ever any doubt about the importance of the Mazzeo cash cows to Cohn, that letter ended it.

Shortly after this letter hit the papers, the *Daily News* published a five-part series on Cohn, offering the first detailed account of the lawyer's apparent use of the parking lot principals as a front. One part of the series focused on the ferry bureau, describing Mazzeo's frequent visits to the Cohn office, the friendly leases he'd given the firm, and the civil servant's outlandish lifestyle. Even after this coverage, however, Mazzeo stayed on the city payroll, although he did not get a new assignment. Finally, in mid-1980, he went on leave of absence.

By then the city was bringing a second wave of eviction proceedings against Cohn's clients, charging that they had underreported cash receipts, short-changing the city at a single lot by over $700,000. Cohn's legal maneuvers managed to protect the parking lot leases, denying the city hundreds of thousands in revenue while in some cases friendly judges gave him adjournments. Friedman got involved as well—asking his man in the DOT's counsel office to keep an eye open for anything affecting the Cohn companies, and even appearing on court papers filed for the concessionaires. It was not until 1983, deep into Koch's second term and seven years after Goldin's audits had started, that Cohn's cash empire collapsed.

In the years after he left the city, Rick Mazzeo disappeared into a host of private businesses until the Brooklyn federal prosecutor finally indicted him in late 1982 for putting $564,000 into his food brokerage firms during three of his ferry years, when his city salary never exceeded $15,000. He pleaded guilty and got a six-month jail sentence. Even while he was in jail, the feds kept the pressure on him, indicting three of his old concessionaires in hopes of flipping them and making a new case against him. If they could turn Mazzeo, they believed they could make a case against Cohn. They knew Cohn was at the center of the Mazzeo scams—one employee at a Cohn parking lot had conceded that he personally skimmed $5,000 every week, carried it in a paper bag to the East 68th Street townhouse, and gave it to either Cohn or an aide.

When Mazzeo came out of jail in late September 1983, the feds were looking at him again. An FBI confidential informant who had helped make several major mob cases in New Jersey, Harold Kaufman, told them that he had been present when a mob-connected dress shop concessionaire at the ferry terminal paid Mazzeo a cash bribe. The Kaufman tip was putting some new heat on troubled Rick Mazzeo.

Mazzeo had long had a taste for cocaine, but now it was becoming a compulsion. He was broke, unemployed, living out of his mother's house, and consuming $600 to $700 a day up his nose. He began suggesting that if he wasn't taken care of, he just might talk. He pushed Cohn to "get him back in" with the city, and even began talking to reporters, telling one that Stanley Friedman had "done all he could to protect" the Cohn leases.

Then, in November, police found his body in the trunk of a rented 1981 Oldsmobile Cutlass parked for days on a street in Greenpoint. He had been shot four times in the head; one wound in the center of the forehead was large enough to stick a pencil in. His body was wrapped in a plastic bag. He was wearing a Manhattan College ring inscribed with his name and had thirty-seven dollars on him. Though the FBI began their own probe, questioning Cohn-connected concessionaires, no one was ever arrested for the murder.

The Koch administration learned little from the ferry bureau saga. Koch eventually named a new commissioner, Leonard Piekarsky, a lifelong friend of Stanley Friedman's who had gone to high school with him. Ameruso, who knew of Piekarsky's close ties to Friedman, recommended him to City Hall. Mazzeo's replacement was Felice Saccone, a Village pol close to Carmine DeSapio. While the bureau never again sank to a cesspool and even improved its concession operations, Piekarsky did decide to give a new concession to a client of the Cohn/Friedman firm, but when it was revealed that the principals had been convicted of bribing an Amtrak official, the decision was reversed.

Just like the PVB, the ferry bureau, a subdivision of Ameruso's transportation department, had been run by clubhouse minions and a bagman, Mazzeo. All the ferry bureau shots were called from the Cohn townhouse on East 68th Street or from Esposito's headquarters on Court Street in Brooklyn, just as Queens Boulevard ruled the PVB. Instead of collection contracts, parking lots were the currency of the ferry bureau. The evidence of the bureau's corruption was widely available—contained in the indictments, civil suits, audits, and memos. But no one knew yet that PVB was as corrupt as the ferry bureau, and no one at City Hall wanted to see the scandal for what it was: a warning about the danger of turning an agency over to the clubhouse.

Ed Koch was reelected with 75 percent of the vote in November 1981, and was backed in the Democratic primary by Friedman,

Manes, and Esposito. Yet by the time he began his second term, his government was already in the grip of an unacknowledged ethical crisis. Hailed as the new La Guardia in the media, Ed Koch could hardly be blamed if he didn't notice it. As shrill as the warnings were, they were disagreeable pockets inside a vast government that had earned a near-historic mandate.

Since Ed Koch became mayor, the city had moved from virtual bankruptcy to a delirious boom. His dancing eyes looking straight into the TV news cameras each night, Koch had talked for a term directly to the people of his city with zest and humor, the personification of a newly revived metropolis. The self-confidence he had inspired in this one-time town of doubters was the essence of his government, he argued, undisturbed by warning signals from its sinister side.

So Koch barely noticed when Stanley Friedman, whose partner Roy Cohn had promised that their firm would never capitalize on the county leadership by obtaining city legal business, was pleasantly profiled on the front page of the *Times*'s local section boasting about his insider approach to the law. In September 1981, the *Times* described Friedman as "increasingly close" to Koch and reported that he numbered among his clients Donald Trump, who was making another effort to get a city tax abatement; the taxi fleet owners, who lobbied the city for everything from fare increases to looser regulation; and Ed Arrigoni, the private bus operator with city express franchises and school bus contracts.

Noting that Friedman had become "a sought-after lawyer although he never goes to court or draws up a document," the *Times* let Friedman describe his own special skills. Asked if his law practice had benefited from his government contacts, Friedman said:

> Absolutely it should help. Everyone wants to think they're getting an edge. I'm in a position where I know a lot of people. You go to a travel agent to get tickets for Christmas because you think he knows a lot of people and he can get you on the planes when they're all booked. You hope he's going to be able to use his influence.

Earlier that year, Koch had gone to Friedman's wedding at the Saint Regis Hotel and stayed for hours. Everyone was there—Meade, Manes, Cohn, Biaggi, commissioners, contractors, and all the important elected officials from the Bronx. Friedman married Jackie Glassberg, who had worked with him in Beame's City Hall. Two months after Friedman was selected county leader in 1978, his longtime companion Glassberg, who had been carried as a stenographer on the environmental agency's payroll for years, was promoted to an administrative manager, put on the City Hall payroll, and assigned to the mayor's office of special events. After her marriage to Friedman, she was promoted to deputy director of the office and given four raises totaling $9,500 over a fourteen-month period. Just as Koch had attended their wedding, Friedman and his wife were subsequently part of the small group of the mayor's close friends invited to the 1981 preinaugural party at David Margolis's house on New Year's Eve. These social occasions advertised for all to see the growing relationship between these two—Friedman had charmed his way into the inner circle.

Koch's relationship with Esposito, despite the frequency of their early meetings, lacked the personal flair that characterized the mayor's bond with Friedman. To be sure, Koch and his corporation counsel Allen Schwartz did pay a visit to the Christmas party at Serres, Visone, and Rice one year, sending Esposito's insurance clients the same sort of familial message as the Friedman social appearances. But despite Esposito's conspicuous efforts to be casual at all times, elevating vulgarity to a public art form, an unbridgeable distance remained between him and Koch. They had too little in common. Each expected the other to court him, whereas Friedman was perfectly willing to play the supplicant. Only a mutuality of interests kept Esposito and the mayor together.

A classic expression of the mayor's dance with Esposito was his skillful juggling of the navy yard scandal, which by the 1981 campaign had resulted in several indictments and the near bankruptcy of the city corporation set up to run the yard. In July 1981, the city reached agreement with Esposito's client, Coastal Dry Dock, on the terms of a forty-year lease that gave Coastal, without any competition or bidding, control of two-thirds of the rental space in the yard. A few weeks later, the chief negotiator of the lease, Terry Moan, met with the mayor to ask that Koch fire the board of directors of the city corporation charged with running the yard.

Moan brought up the rampant criminality exposed by the February 1981 indictments, which revealed that two of the five top management positions had been given to the same soldier in the Columbo crime family, who had been hired at the yard just a few days after his release from a six-year jail term. The hotdog vendor at the yard had cashed hundreds of thousands of dollars in city checks made out to fictitious vendors and employees, and then turned the cash over as kickbacks to the administrators who were running the yard. Moan cited the chaos that had continued under the new board Koch had appointed in 1980, when he'd made a former Beame deputy mayor, James Cavanaugh, chairman in a halfhearted cleanup attempt prompted by Goldin audits. These events were the legacy of thirteen years of Esposito dominance, four of them under Koch.

Koch immediately agreed to Moan's request, adding that LoCicero would pick a new board. Moan then met with LoCicero, who explained that this shakeup "cannot happen in the middle of an election." So LoCicero slowly put his list together, and included such Esposito stalwarts as Tony Vaccarello, the former sanitation commissioner. The mayor picked a no-nonsense lawyer, David Lenefsky, to chair the new board; but none of the changes were implemented until November 24, 1981, right after the mayor got his kingly electoral mandate.

The mayor's first-term relationship with Esposito culminated in Koch's surprise last-minute endorsement of Meade's candidate for Brooklyn district attorney, Norman Rosen. The race was a classic contest between the machine and reform elements of the party, who were backing Liz Holtzman again (she'd lost the general election for Senate in 1980 after beating Bess Myerson in the primary). The Rosen endorsement was a jolting indication of just how far the Village reformer had gone.

The mayor also began to ridicule the New Democratic Coalition (NDC), the citywide reform organization that had backed his candidacy in 1977 and honored him at the start of his term. He called the NDC the "fringe" and derided them as politically "irrelevant." He went further with the Liberals, a party he'd once carefully wooed, denouncing them as "slime."

Koch even became a public ally of the ILA, the waterfront union he'd once sneered at as a mob instrument. The city's port agency had made a host of concessions to the Scotto-tied operators of the city-owned port in Brooklyn, and Scotto's locals began to make major Koch contributions that would, over the next few years, total almost $70,000. A few days before the primary in 1981, Koch attended a dinner honoring Scotto's successor at the union. The dinner was arranged by Scotto's wife, and Scotto, who was in a federal penitentiary, was warmly toasted by several speakers.

But none of Koch's first-term compromises was as fundamental as his move to the Republicans. He began by backing a number of far right Republican state senators, including Friedman's friend in the Bronx, the borough's GOP leader John Calandra, who had gaybaited him in 1977. His coy support of Ronald Reagan and Republican U.S. Senate winner Al D'Amato in 1980—inviting them for photo sessions at City Hall while shunning and even attacking their Democratic opponents—endeared him to the city's Republican leaders. They repaid him with the GOP line in 1981. He became the first mayor in city history to run on both of the major party lines, paving the way for what he wanted the most: a record-shattering victory margin. Roy Cohn, a pivotal player in the Reagan and D'Amato camps, would later claim that he'd brokered the GOP's deal with Koch.

Another broker was Vince Albano, the Republican county leader in Manhattan whom Koch had described in 1969 as "a contract man in the same sense as DeSapio," adding that Albano was "no different in terms of political corruption." Incredibly, Koch had made these comments in an attempt to hang Albano around the shoulders of the then Mayor John Lindsay. "It's not a case of guilt by association," Koch had explained, "but you've simply got to hold a mayor responsible for his associates and their actions." To win Albano's support in 1981, Koch began making patronage appointments sought by the leader, including naming the president of Albano's East Side club to the Alcoholic Beverage Control Board.

The dollars rolled into the 1981 Koch campaign coffers in the millions, primarily from the very real estate interests that had gotten fat on the tax abatements granted by his administration. It didn't hurt that the man collecting contributions as Koch's campaign finance chairman was the former deputy mayor who'd awarded the abatements, Peter Solomon. This kind of cynicism in the mayor's own campaign reinforced the cynicism of his clubhouse commissioners and party pals. The mayor who had burst on the city scene in 1978 as a new and uncontainable force for change had become, by the time he won his second election, a savvy and self-serving player in an ageless game.

1

1 and 2. Ed Koch's gift was his ability to
see history's flow and accommodate
himself to it. From 1960 to 1968, when
the country was liberal, he was liberal.
Above, Koch holding VID banner at
an anti-war demonstration. John
LoCicero is at left. Below, Carmine
DeSapio, symbol of bossism, whom
Koch the reformer defeated in 1963,
by just 41 votes.

2

3. Bess Myerson was a trailblazing heroine—the Jewish, feminist Jackie Robinson. In 1977, she campaigned with Koch as unofficial co-candidate.

4. Ed Koch (*left*) and Mario Cuomo, tired of each other, waiting for their last debate of the 1977 campaign for mayor of New York.

5. Media consultant David Garth, who dreamed up the Immaculate Deception of a Koch-Myerson romance. Privately, he called Koch and Myerson, "the Smith Brothers" because they were "two beards."

6. The King and Queen of New York. Koch and Myerson holding hands, leading the Columbus Day Parade up Fifth Avenue, during the 1977 election. A new era seemed about to commence.

7. The working class Camelot. Koch and Myerson kissed on the platform the night Koch was elected mayor.

8. Koch impressed almost everyone with the quality of the most
visible commissioners he appointed
during his first term as mayor. At
left, Robert Wagner, Jr., his planning commissioner.

9. Koch's alliance with the party bosses ripened gradually until it reached
maturity when he ran for governor in 1982. Below, the bosses confer: (*left to
right*) Stanley Friedman, Meade Esposito, Donald Manes, and power broker
attorney Harold Fisher.

10. Civic heroine Sally Goodgold. She unsuccessfully tried to save Koch from himself by blocking the appointment of Anthony Ameruso as transportation commissioner in January 1978.

11. When Koch put Anthony Ameruso (*below*) in charge, he didn't deliver just a job to the clubhouse, he delivered an empire. Koch predicted Ameruso would vindicate his judgment, but Ameruso ended up a convicted felon.

12. Pat Cunningham. A leader had to have a sixth sense that warned him when he was about to be abandoned. Cunningham's final days as Bronx boss would prove that he couldn't detect betrayal.

13. Michael Lazar. The ex–city transportation commissioner who invented the Parking Violations Bureau became a multimillionaire developer whose city projects were backed by his close friend Donald Manes.

14. Authors Barrett and Newfield clown with Meade Esposito at the 1980 dinner dance of the Brooklyn Democratic organization. "Come on, write my memoirs with me," Esposito would later tease Newfield. "We'll both get rich."

5

and 16. Roy Cohn, legendary fixer and law
partner of Stanley Friedman, lectures his
client Donald Trump at a Bronx Democratic
dinner. In his final days as deputy mayor,
Friedman frantically tied together the loose
ends of the largest tax abatement in city
history for Trump's Grand Hyatt Hotel (*right*).
In fact, Friedman had already struck a deal to
join the Cohn firm, which represented Trump.

17

16

17. Harlem's Sydenham Hospital. Candidate Koch promised black leaders who
endorsed him in 1977 that he would keep it
open, but in 1979 he sent a phalanx of city
cops through community picket lines to
padlock its doors.

18 and 19. A city's real estate for sale. The changing skyline of Manhattan between 1978 and 1987 documents overdevelopment. Campaign contributors got tax abatements and zoning changes to invade the heavens and block out the sun.

20

20. Bess Myerson, the self-described "Queen of the Jews," lost her Koch-backed bid for the Democratic nomination for U.S. Senate in 1980 to another Jewish woman, Brooklyn reform congresswoman Liz Holtzman.
Former mayor John Lindsay also ran in the primary.

21

21. Koch earned the Republican line in his 1981 reelection campaign with his virtual support of Ronald Reagan in the 1980 presidential race and of GOP senate winner Al D'Amato.

22. The subject of a glorifying lead story in *Time*, the mayor became a national celebrity, with a book that was a number-one bestseller for twenty-one weeks, and appearances on "Tonight" and "Saturday Night Live." *Parade* magazine profiled him under the subtitle: WHY SOME PEOPLE THINK HE COULD BECOME THE FIRST JEWISH PRESIDENT OF THE UNITED STATES.

23

3. Koch's first endorsement press conference of the 1982 gubernatorial campaign against Mario Cuomo featured the city's four Democratic party bosses: Manes, Friedman, Esposito, and Staten Island's Nick LaPorte. Cuomo commented: "The last time four political leaders got together to endorse someone who won was in the Iroquois Confederacy."

24. The relationship between Koch and Friedman deepened when the Bronx boss backed Myerson in her 1980 senate campaign.

25. Investigations Commissioner Stan Lupkin engineered the undercover operation that snared Taxi Commissioner Herb Ryan, but was blocked by Koch when he tried to prolong the 1982 probe in the hope that Ryan would take them to Manes.

26. No episode better illustrated Koch's acquiescence to Manes than his handling of the borough president's determined scheme to use Flushing Meadows Park in Queens as a site for a Grand Prix. The three-year fight against the plan was led by a 54-year-old lawyer, Ben Haber, who lived ten blocks from the park.

27. Transportation Commissioner Tony Ameruso's secret interest in this Greenwich Village parking lot, in partnership with a mobster and a crooked judge, finally forced Koch to regret his appointment.

28. "Everybody else has their own thing," Taxi Commissioner Ryan told investigators. "I just wanted to get my own thing." Before he uttered this implicit motto of the clubhouse clan, Ryan was nabbed on videotape taking bribes from star undercover actor, Eddie Gruskin.

29

29. Koch's extraordinary 78 percent triumph in November 1985 gave him a feeling of invincibility. He had bombarded the public with jokes, foreign policy speeches, personal vendettas, restaurant suggestions, opinions on pending court cases—all delivered in perfect, pithy 30-second sound bites

30

30. The 1986 inaugural at City Hall, attended by 3,000 of the city's elite, was a ritual of ratification, the certification of Koch's popular authority. The mayor's entrance was timed to coincide with Sinatra's singing that he was "king of the hill, top of the heap."

31. Salesman Stanley with the Computer-that-never-worked. Friedman cajoled and blustered his way, with City Hall intervention and support, to a $22 million contract for a handheld computer that would supposedly enable meter maids to automatically record parking tickets. The only ticket ever written on this device was a federal indictment.

32. With the PVB scandal exploding around him, Koch and the city's corporation counsel Fritz Schwarz canceled Friedman's Citisource contract. It took only a few hours for Schwarz to determine that the city process that had led to the award of the contract was a farce.

33. Michael Burnett. Flipped by the FBI after a Nashville gun and burglary bust, his tape-recorded conversations with PVB contractor Bernie Sandow and deputy director Geoffrey Lindenauer led to the uncovering of the PVB case.

33

34

34. Geoffrey Lindenauer. Manes's bagman and psychoanalyst, he engaged in the most publicized and protracted plea bargains in New York history. When Lindenauer finally sealed a deal, Manes killed himself. Lindenauer wound up with a three-year prison term.

35. "I don't think there is anybody worse than a public official who sells his office and corrupts others," crusading U.S. Attorney Rudy Giuliani once said, "except maybe a murderer."

36. Queens D.A. John Santucci launched probes of everything from Manes's first suicide attempt to his Board of Estimate deals, winding up with several cases involving Manes bribes for cable contracts.

37. Manhattan D.A. Robert Morgenthau convicted Transportation Commissioner Tony Ameruso of perjury for lying about his hidden real estate partnership with a developer who had a stake in a Hudson River ferry permit Ameruso had awarded as commissioner.

39. Breslin's friend Shelly Chevlowe, who started the PVB racket. The corrupt royalty of Queens Boulevard wept at Chevlowe's funeral in 1983. After the funeral, Donald Manes switched bagmen as coldly as a manager changing pitchers.

38. Columnist Jimmy Breslin became a participant in the story. He went into a titanic rage when he found out his closest friends, who he thought were amusing rascals, had become "scum gangsters stealing from the people of my city."

40. Official mug shot of master extortionist Alex Liberman. Liberman was a concentration camp survivor who coerced bribes from a fellow survivor. Before Koch was sworn in as mayor, Meade Esposito recommended that Liberman be promoted.

41

41. Peter Vallone, who got his
job as council majority leader
as a result of the last deal
between Donald Manes (*left*)
and Stanley Friedman.

42

42. Mike Dowd (*right*) faces the press the day after he agreed to cooperate
with the government and named Donald Manes as an extortionist, and Geoffrey Lindenauer as his bagman. Next to him is his lawyer, Charles Stillman.
Seated at the center of the table is New York's premier television journalist,
Gabe Pressman.

43

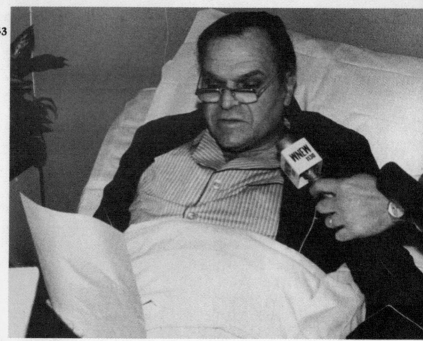

43. Donald Manes, in his hospital bed, admitting his story of being kidnapped was a hoax. He told reporters he had tried to kill himself but never gave a reason.

44

44. Chief of Detectives Richard Nicastro went on live television to announce that the Police Department did not believe Manes's account of how he was knifed.

45. Marlene Manes is escorted out of her husband's funeral service, held in the same Queens chapel where Manes's downfall had begun.

46. Mayor Koch arranged for his aides to bring his own microphone stand to the Manes funeral. Koch, who had called Manes a "crook" before he was ever charged, said after his death that "God will be his ultimate judge."

47. Tom Sheer (*left*) and John Pritchard. Sheer was the head of the FBI's New York office, and he made the pursuit of politicians and power brokers a top priority. Pritchard was in charge of the squad that was investigating the Genovese crime family. He heard the first wiretaps that led to the prosecution of judgemaker Meade Esposito.

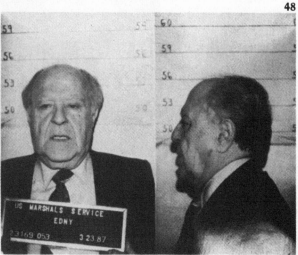

48. Meade Esposito's mug shot. He helped make Koch the mayor and became a millionaire during Koch's reign.

49

Duty, Valor and Honor

ANTHONY J. VENDITTI

"A Cop's Cop"

679

In Lasting Remembrance

of

ANTHONY J. VENDITTI

Detective

New York City Police Department

Born MARCH 11, 1951

Police Trainee 1970 - 1972

Appointed to Police Department

MARCH 15, 1972

Designated Detective

MAY 4, 1984

Assignments

50 PCT. – 1972-1974

48 PCT. – 1974-1982

Organized Crime Control Bureau

BROOKLYN SOUTH PMD - JULY 29, 1982

HQ PMD – APRIL 25, 1983

JOINT ORGANIZED CRIME TASK FORCE

SEPTEMBER 3, 1985

RECEIVED 17 AWARDS OF BRAVERY

SLAIN – JANURAY 21, 1986

"Take Care Anthony"

"Always......."

49. Detective Tony Venditti, the father of four, was murdered while on an undercover assignment. Meade Esposito's hoodlum friend, Fritzy Giovanelli, was charged with the killing.

50 and 51. In 1974, Giovanelli told a grand jury he was too sick to testify and was under a doctor's orders not to leave his home. But then the *Daily News* published a picture of Frank Sinatra singing at Madison Square Garden. Fritzy was visible sitting in the front row, and he was indicted for contempt of the grand jury.

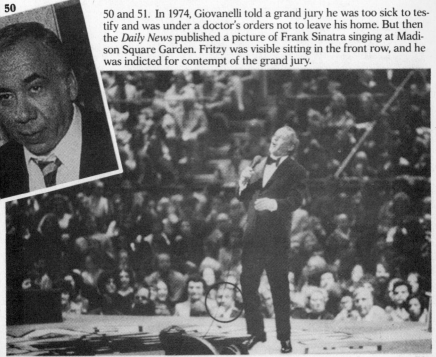

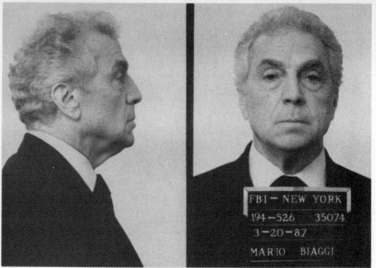

52. Mario Biaggi's mug shot. He was a hero cop and the senior member of New York's congressional delegation, but then turned up on Meade Esposito's wiretap, taking a free vacation with his mistress, while his wife was receiving chemotherapy treatments.

53. Ed McDonald (*left*) and Len Michaels. They prosecuted Biaggi and Esposito in a case many skeptics thought they wouldn't win. Michaels lectured the FBI agents on the importance of Esposito's civil liberties. McDonald, the head of the Organized Crime Strike Force in Brooklyn, was less concerned with publicity than his Manhattan counterpart, Rudy Giuliani.

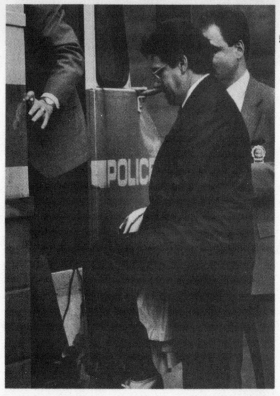

54 and 55. The son of a cabdriver, Friedman, nicknamed "Bugsy" as a kid, went through a series of state and federal arrests on an array of charges in early 1986. The maypole of city corruption, he had become a millionaire off city legal business. He used his underworld ties as just one more weapon in his influence-peddling arsenal, saying of one **PVB** contractor: "He will not fool around with me. He knows me, and if he does, he'll wind up in the river."

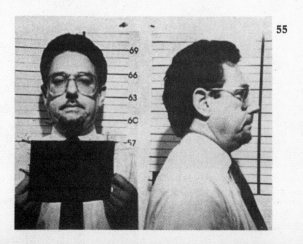

55

56

57

56. With daily scandal revelations, the press conferences Koch had once lived for were suddenly a torture test, and the exuberance he had once conveyed through the lens so easily became just as communicable a sadness.

57. In 90 rapid-fire days in early 1986, federal investigator Tony Valenti spearheaded probes that exposed the taxi commission as another PVB.

58. An hour after Turoff was ordered to leave his taxi commission office by a chagrined City Hall, he was overheard on a federal wiretap informing his mentor Meade Esposito: "Chief, I've been assassinated." Like Ameruso, Liberman, and others, Turoff had both come to power and kept it because of his clubhouse liaison with Esposito.

59

. Longtime Koch aide Victor Botnick,
esident of the city's billion-dollar
ealth and Hospitals Corporation, dis-
lved in a sea of lies during the whirl-
nd summer of 1986. His downfall, and
e probes that engulfed him, meant
at the scandal had at last penetrated
och's guarded private world.

60. Alone before dawn at a long breakfast table in Gracie Mansion with a piece
of fruit. The mayor had for years devoured the happy history of his previous
day in the newspapers, but now, after the Manes explosion, the morning ritual
suddenly deteriorated into a daily bout with indigestion. The newspapers were
finally biting back.

61. Former Abscam prosecutor Tom Puccio, whose victory in the Claus von Bülow murder trial had elevated him to the top ranks of the criminal defense bar, represented Friedman at the New Haven trial. A longtime friend of Rudy Giuliani, he was dumbfounded by disclosures at the trial that Giuliani had bugged him, as a possible target in a probe of grand jury leaks.

62. Having traded in the long-cultivated look of a slick city king-pin, Friedman was remade by Puccio in the image of a cheeky, clean-cut small-town lawyer or businessman, designed to appeal to the only audience that now mattered in his life—the twelve Connecticut jurors who would decide if he was a racketeer. With him every day in court for the ten-week trial was wife Jackie, on paid leave from her City Hall job as a mayoral assistant.

63. Giuliani, who tried the Friedman case personally, took daily beatings on the courthouse steps from Friedman and Puccio, but rarely responded. Friedman regularly derided him as a political prosecutor, motivated only by ambition, and then sneered at his raincoat-covered appearance before the cameras, as if it betrayed Giuliani's amateurish sense of the media packaging business.

64. Government witness Bernie Sandow, the PVB contractor Giuliani had converted into a walking microphone. The Manes gang had become so suspicious that the PVB director had mouthed the question "Are you wired?" when Sandow met with him.

65. Citisource chairman, Friedman friend, and co-defendant Marvin Kaplan became the sugar daddy of the defense team, picking up parts of almost everyone's tab. A last-minute attempt to get him to become a government witness, engineered during the final days of the trial, failed.

66. The Bess Myerson case, with all the elements of tragedy and farce, touched the mayor so personally that it became a torment, visible in his face.

67. *Daily News* City Hall bureau chief Marcia Kramer wrote stories that broke open the Myerson case. One night she was scared, she asked a copy boy to start her car.

68 and 69. Bess Myerson was crowned Miss America in 1945, the year her lover, Andy Capasso, was born. Capasso used a Mafia don as the beard for his affair with Myerson.

70. Nancy Capasso felt that she had been mistreated by two judges and felt she was taking on the entire power structure of New York. But she resolved not to go quietly.

72

71. Judge Andrew Tyler. He presided over the Capasso divorce trial. His findings of fact in the divorce proceedings were taken word for word from the brief submitted by Andy Capasso's attorney.

72. Nancy Capasso's appeals lawyer, Myrna Felder. She did the legal research and wrote the briefs for a fee smaller than usual.

73. Judge Hortense Gabel (*left*) and her daughter Sukhreet, who were both manipulated by Miss America.

The Mayor
Ed Koch
Birthday
Dinner
Dance!

"My doctors tell me that I've got the body of a 63 year old, the brain of a 29 year old, and the energy of a teenager!"

Come dine and dance with our high-stepping Mayor!

Thursday, December 10, 1987
Cocktails 7:00 pm
Dinner and Dancing 8:00 pm
Grand Hyatt New York
Park Avenue at Grand Central
Black Tie
R.S.V.P.

74. The program for the 1987, $2,000-a-plate, Koch birthday fundraiser, which pulled in hundreds of thousands of dollars for the 1989 reelection campaign, was part of the orchestrated pretense that the scandal at last was over, and the song-and-dance days were back. Instead, new trials and revelations continued into 1988.

CHAPTER SIX

Taxi Commissioner "On Call"

DONALD MANES ARRIVED at the San Juan airport before 7:00 A.M. on January 1, 1982. He was starting the new year with a flight to New York, interrupting a week's vacation and leaving his wife Marlene behind in Puerto Rico. He reached Kennedy Airport just in time to make it to lower Manhattan, where Ed Koch was being sworn in for a second term as mayor. When Manes got to City Hall, he discovered that the steady and chilly downpour had forced the inaugural inside, to the auditorium at Police Plaza, the coldly modern headquarters half a block away. Manes had left the sunshine of Puerto Rico for this formal routine in New York because he sensed that 1982 might be the most important year of his own political life, and he could not miss this opportunity to schmooze with the powerful.

The cause of Donald Manes's optimism was Hugh Carey, who was up for reelection as New York's governor. The man that Manes had helped put in office back in 1974 was by now a target of virtually universal ridicule. He'd dyed his hair red. He'd remarried—a Greek millionairess from Chicago whose family firm had grown rich by driving middle-class tenants out of apartment buildings so they could co-op them. His new wife had lied, apparently even to him, about how many times she'd been married. His government was such a neglected shambles that Jimmy Breslin had dubbed him "Society Carey."

Such troubles might be expected to concern a Carey friend and ally such as Donald Manes, but Manes in fact saw each new cross for Carey as a potential opportunity for himself. He knew that in politics, an opening at the top had a multiplier effect: others near the top would reach for it. Using his Queens base as leverage, Manes saw his chance to move up, out of the behind-the-scenes obscurity of the borough presidency. Manes was so certain that something would present itself that he'd raised $160,000 for his 1981 reelection that he'd never spent—a nest egg for a future run he openly discussed. Manes wanted Ed Koch, and the city elite who had come to celebrate the inaugural, to be with him if lightning struck that year.

Four days later Manes hosted his own inaugural—at Borough Hall in Queens. It was his fourth, marking ten years in office, more than any other member of the city's powerful Board of Estimate. But at forty-seven, the Queens borough president was still younger than most of his colleagues. Manes had endorsed Koch's reelection in 1981, the first time he had backed Koch, and he opened his speech with praise for the mayor's first-term record.

Koch, who had taken a while during his first four years to warm up to Manes, returned the praise. Manes also hinted at loftier ambitions, pledging his commitment to continue to work for the betterment of the people of Queens, but adding: "I am not certain in what ways I can fully bring this about, or what paths I may follow to achieve that goal."

A few hours after being sworn in, Manes was rushed to a hospital for an emergency appendectomy, and stayed there for nine days. By the time he was ready to be released, the pressures on Carey were heating up in Albany, and the only callers who were getting return calls from Manes's hospital room were his fellow connivers Meade Esposito and Stanley Friedman. The party bosses could smell blood.

The day Manes left the hospital Hugh Carey met privately with his cabinet but did not invite his lieutenant governor, Mario Cuomo. Carey had been reading Breslin columns about himself for months and seeing Mario Cuomo's byline (the journalist and Cuomo, who had already announced he was running for governor even if Carey sought reelection, were close friends and talked on the phone regularly). The next morning, Carey held an Albany press conference withdrawing from the 1982 race. That night Mario Cuomo, a Queens Democrat seeking his county leader's support, visited a still bedridden Donald Manes at his Jamaica Estates home.

Cuomo wrote in his diary that Manes told him he was "with me all-out" and that Manes was "hoping" that Cuomo, if elected governor, would be "able to help Manes run for mayor in three years." An elated Cuomo wrote: "This is a real big break. There are so many ways Donald helps my effort." But in fact, as he had in the 1977 mayoral campaign, Cuomo soon discovered that when dealing with Manes, he was "fishing in shallow waters." A few days later, Manes told reporters not only that he'd back Cuomo but that he might even run with him on a statewide ticket. Manes said that if state attorney general Robert Abrams decided to run for governor against Cuomo, he'd run for Abrams's vacancy. At that moment, an Abrams gubernatorial candidacy seemed quite likely, and a state ticket with two Queens pols on it was not exactly what Cuomo had in mind.

In addition to putting himself forward as a possible candidate for the state's highest law enforcement post, Manes was watching City Council President Carol Bellamy, who was publicly speculating about a run for statewide office. Her job—with two Board of Estimate votes and City Hall visibility—was an attractive alternative to Manes.

Within hours of Carey's dramatic announcement, Ed Koch, Dave Garth, and a small Koch entourage had taken off on a preplanned joint vacation to Spain. During the eight days that the mayor was away, Rupert Murdoch turned the *New York Post* into a running, page-one advertisement for a Koch gubernatorial candidacy. By the time Koch returned, Murdoch's Draft Koch movement, abetted by the quotable encouragement of observers like Stanley Friedman, had gained enough momentum to fill an airport press conference with hungry reporters.

"I don't think there's a person who voted for me who got a contract that I'd serve four years," said the newly reelected mayor. "I haven't put a lock on the door." Reminded that he'd pledged at the Wailing Wall in Jerusalem never to seek an office higher than the mayoralty, Koch replied: "That was a pledge between God and me—not with you and me."

A few days later, Koch said he would take thirty days to decide whether to run. That same night, Donald Manes went to a cocktail party at La Biblioteque for Mario Cuomo, the only potential Democratic candidate for governor openly vowing to stay in the race even if King Koch entered it.

By February 22, when Koch announced that he would run, news stories had made him so invincible (a thirty-point lead in the polls) that even the state's leading Republican, Comptroller Ned Regan, dropped out of the race, as did Abrams and other leading Democrats. Carol Bellamy decided to stay put, since she would legally succeed Koch as mayor—at least for the ten months until the next election—if he was elected governor. With Koch in the race, Manes realized that his own choices had suddenly dwindled. If Koch became governor, Manes could run against Bellamy for mayor in 1983, but he knew that was a risky reach. If he helped Cuomo become governor, Cuomo might back him for mayor in 1985, but Koch would probably still be a formidable opponent.

On February 24, Cuomo went to breakfast with Manes at the Forge Diner on Queens Boulevard, directly across the street from Borough Hall. Manes had made a Forge breakfast a Queens clubhouse tradition, entertaining city commissioners and city contractors together there. He would arrive each morning around 8:00, sit in the sixth or seventh table down the diner aisle in the back, and order half a grapefruit or occasionally a melon, two poached eggs on an English muffin, and coffee. He never picked up the tab.

That morning Manes listened. Cuomo had already called Esposito and Friedman to make it clear that he intended to see the race through to the end, but he wanted to speak to Manes face to face. He wanted him to understand that if elected he would remember both those who stuck with him and those who abandoned him. Manes replied that everything was on hold, but Cuomo wrote in his diaries that he doubted whether Manes, or the other two party bosses, would hold for long, "given the realities of politics in New York."

One of those realities, unknown to Cuomo, was that Manes had a flourishing business to protect: his PVB and cable profits were dependent on his clout at City Hall. The lawyer for a cable company seeking merely a quarter cut of the Queens cable pie had been informed a couple of months earlier that the company would have to pay a "substantial bribe" to Manes, as much as a million dollars. This information came from the husband of a Queens congresswoman,

Geraldine Ferraro. Another company was simultaneously told by a Manes associate that they'd have to pay $250,000 for even a smaller section of the county. At the same time that Manes was deciding whom he'd back for governor, he was meeting with one cable executive in his private office at Borough Hall, soliciting a bribe in pantomime.

Manes's control of the cable franchises, like his dominance of the PVB, was dependent on his relationship with City Hall. Despite the pressure of these "business" considerations pushing him toward Koch, Manes agonized over his choice with top aides, telling one that he "just had a feeling" about Cuomo, who he said had a "magical sense, like a Kennedy." If Manes needed a reminder about that Cuomo magic, especially in Queens, he got it when he introduced both Koch and Cuomo to a thousand Democratic women at the Queens Women's Luncheon at Antun's Restaurant on March 6. They stood as one and cheered for Mario. Manes worried out loud that he had "screwed up last time," a reference to the 1977 mayoral, and that he "couldn't do it again."

On March 12, Manes and Cuomo met again at the Forge. This time Manes brought Mike Nussbaum, his 35-year-old, in-house campaign consultant. Nussbaum's public relations firm had just handled Manes's reelection campaign, designing a glossy brochure about the virtually unopposed candidate's grand achievements. In addition to campaigns, the Nussbaum firm had gotten into the political brokerage business and was frequently retained by companies seeking the sort of city business particularly vulnerable to Donald Manes's influence. Hired by one bidder seeking a Queens cable franchise only a few months earlier, Nussbaum was later alleged to have solicited a $250,000 bribe from his own client for Manes.* Cuomo brought two of his top campaign advisers to the breakfast—Bill Stern, a millionaire businessman who chaired Cuomo's finance committee, and Jerry Weiss, a longtime Cuomo aide.

Cuomo and Manes sat together at one table, while three staffers, separated from their principals by the peculiar protocol of politics, were a few tables away. Cuomo and Manes had co-chaired the Carter campaign in the 1980 presidential pri-

---

*Nussbaum was convicted in 1987 of seeking this bribe, but the conviction was overturned on appeal. The Queens D.A. is now seeking a reversal of that decision at the state's highest court.

mary, and the staffers they'd put in charge of it, Weiss and Nussbaum, had worked together for months. Weiss had recommended that Cuomo hire Nussbaum to manage his own campaign, and Stern was now assessing him. Were Nussbaum selected for such a role, he would be the embodiment of Manes's commitment to the Cuomo candidacy. Nussbaum himself assured Stern and Weiss that everything would be okay, telling them "not to worry about Donny."

The jovial Manes, who lived on quips and small talk, sank into a conversation without a point. He was noncommittal, hesitant, ambiguous. He would not say he was going to switch to Koch, but Cuomo sensed it. Koch's recent *Playboy* interview, which featured him dumping abuse on suburban and rural voters, had clearly damaged the mayor upstate where the Catholic Cuomo had a vast potential constituency; Cuomo reminded Manes of it and pressed his case. When he left the meeting, he told his aides that Manes had made no clear statement of his intent, but Cuomo felt him slipping away.

Still, three weeks after Koch's announcement, Manes had not bolted. Stern made a note in his own daily record: "Pretty good meeting with Manes." In the weeks that followed, through March and into April, Manes hung onto the Cuomo candidacy, drifting toward Koch out of a reluctant practicality.

The night of Manes and Cuomo's second meeting at the Forge, Herb Ryan, the president of Donald Manes's Stevenson Democratic Club, was waiting in his Queens home for his 5:30 dinner appointment. One of eight unpaid members of the city's Taxi and Limousine Commission, Ryan had hurriedly arranged the meal with a businessman he'd met only two days earlier. Ryan had called Ed Rosen, president of Stern Consulting Company, to set up the appointment within hours of Rosen's first appearance at the TLC seeking permission to run an experimental taxi service in Queens and Brooklyn. "I think you and I should get together," Ryan had told Rosen on the phone. "As soon as I looked at you, I knew that we could talk." When Rosen said he wanted to bring his business associate, Bob Casella, Ryan objected, saying: "Nobody has to know about this." Ryan then asked this total stranger: "Would you want a third party to hear what we have to discuss?"

Ryan did not know that his brazen approach had been

taped. He did not know that Ed Rosen and Bob Casella were actually undercover detectives Ed Gruskin and Bob Lamarata, and that they would be wearing Nagra recorders strapped to their bodies when they came to his house in a few minutes. He certainly had no idea that he was at a turning point in his life. Nothing would ever again be the same for this 61-year-old clubhouse foot soldier who had invested the last seventeen years in Donald Manes.

Ryan had been associated with Manes since the 1965 campaign, when Manes was first elected to the city council. He'd worked on Manes's council staff. And when Manes became borough president in 1971, his successor in the council, Morty Povman, had kept Ryan as a part-time aide at Manes's request, supplementing Ryan's meager income as a distributor for *Newsweek* magazine. After Manes was named the Democratic leader in Queens in 1974, he got Mayor Abe Beame to appoint Ryan to the TLC, an influential post overseeing the politically aggressive taxi industry. Ryan's subservience to the industry's interests had translated into thousands in political contributions, both to Manes's home-base Stevenson Club, whose annual dinner dance Ryan chaired, and to Manes's countywide Democratic organization. With Manes's support, Ryan's name had just been submitted to the mayor by the Queens city council delegation for reappointment to a five-year term. On February 19, just before the undercover sting on Ryan began, Ed Koch had rubberstamped the Manes nominee, sending the appointment to the full council for its advice and consent.

Like his mentor, Ryan sensed, as he looked out his Electchester apartment window for Gruskin's new gray Caddy, that 1982 could be a decisive point in his own career, such as it was. Ryan believed that if Manes were elected mayor, he would appoint him TLC chairman, the only paid member of the commission, with a $62,000 a year salary (Ryan's current three jobs brought in a combined $35,000). Ryan was so anxious to make these Manes connections clear to Gruskin that he'd told the detective—in the first few seconds of their only phone conversation—that he was meeting "the BP" the same afternoon he scheduled the meeting with Gruskin.

Noticing a commotion in the street below his twentieth-floor apartment—the police were barring traffic from his block—Ryan headed outdoors. The decapitated body of a burglar who'd fallen from a nearby roof was stretched across the top of a parked car. Ryan, wrapped up in a cashmere overcoat and wearing a plaid Tote hat, made his way through the crowd that had gathered, looking for the man he knew as Ed Rosen. Gruskin and his partner Lamarata, dressed in hoodlum garb with black shirts, sports coats, and boots, had left their car where the police had stopped traffic and were walking toward Ryan's building when Ryan found them.

Ryan directed Lamarata through Electchester, the vast housing complex built by Local 3 of the Electrical Workers where Donald Manes's political career had begun. Manes's father-in-law, Joseph Warshofsky, was a lifelong Local 3 member and one of the first residents of the project decades earlier. He had gotten Donald and Marlene an apartment there when they married in 1955, and he'd used his network of union and Electchester contacts to give Manes his first political base a decade later. Since Manes left Electchester even before he was first elected its councilman, Ryan had become Manes's liaison with the neighborhood and its union for years.

While Lamarata drove toward a nearby Italian restaurant, La Venenezia, Ryan bragged about his four-and-a-half room, air-conditioned apartment with all utilities for "two and change." He said that the complex, with its 15,000 voters, "can elect whomever we wish." Because Ryan was a city commissioner, he explained, Koch "feels that I belong to him." But, in fact, "I'm very close to Donald Manes. He wants loyalty in the worst way and God forbid that one of his people should look elsewhere."

The restaurant, empty and garish, was preselected by Gruskin's supervisors from DOI, which had instigated the Ryan sting. Another team of detectives was parked outside, listening to Gruskin, the city's top undercover actor in corruption cases, convince Ryan that he was a construction contractor "brand new to the taxi business" and ripe for plucking.

Dubbed "the man of a thousand faces," the 41-year-old Gruskin had played in the course of his work a loan shark, drug dealer, real estate agent, supermarket manager, private detective, buyer at city auctions, consumer affairs inspector, building superintendent, Housing Authority caretaker, out-of-town tourist, and Jewish consigliere of an organized crime family. His scorecard included 97 Housing Authority employees busted for false elevator repair submissions; 20 city marshals, auctioneers, and buyers arrested for sham auctions; and 9 consumer-affairs inspectors and 57 supermarket employees apprehended for taking bribes. "You give me a suit and a tie, a few gold chains, a couple of rings, and a pocketful of money," the glib, paunchy Gruskin once boasted, "hey, there's nobody I can't get to. Everybody takes."

DOI had been so eager to have Gruskin do the Ryan caper that they let him use an artfully constructed phony identity, and shell construction companies, that they'd already spent a hundred thousand dollars inventing for a deep undercover operation that was now getting close to several powerful Brooklyn politicians. DOI's decision to borrow the Rosen identity from the Brooklyn operation and use it to try to catch Ryan ran the risk of prematurely exposing the Brooklyn sting—especially since DOI told the TLC chairman, Jay Turoff, a well-connected Brooklyn politician himself, that Rosen and his companies were a DOI fiction. Turoff was told because it was he, and his inspector general at the TLC, Robert Mackasek, who had come to DOI on March 4 and suggested a sting on Ryan, citing nothing more than their suspicions that he might be corrupt.

One of the reasons DOI was willing to risk the Brooklyn operation in pursuit of Ryan was that, from the beginning, a number of investigators in the department saw Ryan as a route inside the powerful Queens Democratic organization. Ed Siedlick, DOI's chief investigator, had heard rumblings about Donald Manes for at least a decade. He'd been involved in a separate investigation of Manes's former deputy Robert Groh in the mid-1970s while Groh was city sanitation commissioner. Groh wound up indicted (and subsequently acquitted) for soliciting a $10,000 contribution for Manes's campaign in exchange for a zoning variance. Siedlick remembered that the grand jury that had nailed Groh had to be dissuaded by the prosecutor and a judge from indicting Manes himself, since it was Manes who would both benefit from the contribution and act on the variance.

Siedlick also remembered Matty Troy, Manes's sidekick and county leader. When federal prosecutors were closing in on Troy in the midseventies, Troy's lawyer had toyed with the idea of his cooperation and had offered criminal hypotheticals about Manes as part of the negotiations. In the end, the negotiations collapsed, but the hypotheticals left a lasting impression on Siedlick. The detective had also been picking up recent feedback from a police gambling investigation about Manes's sordid relationship with Eddie Chan, head of the Chinese Mafia in America. Siedlick knew that Manes's public relations man, Michael Nussbaum, had been retained by Chan. He knew that Manes met with Chan frequently and tried to open doors for him in city government. For Siedlick, any suggestion that Manes wasn't the ultimate target of a Ryan probe was "pure nonsense."

As the three—Gruskin, Lamarata, and Ryan—sat around a table at La Venenezia that night and the drinks arrived, Ryan lifted his J&B and soda and answered Gruskin's toast "to our luck" with his own: "and good business and making money." Promising to help Gruskin obtain the five commission votes he would need on the nine-member TLC board to get exclusive rights to run a hundred-cab experiment, Ryan said: "I just want to make sure I'm taken care of. That's all. Something up front and then I want to make sure I get income." Just before he placed his order for veal francese, Ryan vowed: "I will do everything I can as commissioner, talk with everybody I can." He said it would cost him money to make the right connections for Gruskin and added: "I do it for the borough president." He then asked for $1,000 a month until the experiment was approved. "I'm not greedy," he explained. "I'm not a pig, 'cause I'm in this politics business for twenty-five years."

Gruskin argued that a grand was too much, and they shook hands on $700 (precisely the amount that Gruskin, who had a knack for predicting a man's price, had taken in payoff money from his DOI control unit). "When it comes to increasing it," Ryan said, seeking a weekly payoff once the project began making money, "that will be up to you. A lot of people tell me I got too much faith. I've done this before and I've got hurt."

Before the night was over, Ryan had implicated himself in a veritable catalogue of possible criminal cases. He offered, for example, to get Gruskin city construction contracts at General Services and Housing Preservation and Development using an inside Manes ally. He indicated that he was "being taken care of" by the city's largest supplier of cars to the cab fleets. He said he was involved in the cable business and had already helped one company win its Queens franchise. He stressed how close he was to Manes, identifying himself as Manes's "chief fundraiser" and said that he "brought shopping bags of cash" to Manes from the taxi industry. He made it clear that Gruskin would have to grease the clubhouse by buying tables of dinner tickets and giving contributions to the Queens party. Referring to his Brooklyn construction contracts, Gruskin told him, "Look, this is a way of us doing business now." Ryan replied, almost with a sense of history: "It's a way of life."

When they returned to the car after dinner, Gruskin counted out $700, handed it to Ryan, and said: "That's the first one." Ryan said: "Fine. We never met. We never talked."

The tape that Gruskin brought back to DOI that night was a rarity in the corruption business: an entire case contained in a single meeting. Gruskin's boss, DOI commissioner Stan Lupkin, couldn't have been happier. Since Ed Koch appointed him in 1978, Lupkin, whose agency developed corruption cases for federal and state prosecutors, had been unable to convict anyone as high as a commissioner. He had helped with the case against former General Services commissioner Peter Smith, but the charges against Smith predated his arrival in government. Although Ryan wasn't much of a commissioner, he did at least have the title.

Lupkin had just taken an awful public beating over the highly publicized bus shelter case. City Comptroller Jay Goldin had allegedly rigged the specifications for the lucrative bus shelter franchise in an attempt to deliver it to a contributor. Lupkin's investigation had dragged on for almost three years. Manhattan city councilman Henry Stern, a close personal friend of the mayor's, took to delivering birthday cakes marking the anniversary of the probe to Lupkin's office. Stern had also nicknamed him Inspector Clouseau, and the name hit the papers. When the case ended in late 1981 without a Goldin indictment, a defeated Lupkin issued a report that was a thousand, limp pages long.

A stiff, large man with a forced smile and a caterpillar air, Lupkin was as honest as he was awkward. He had been at DOI for eleven years, preceded by six in the Manhattan district attorney's office. In 1981, he'd become the first law enforcement official with less than the full powers of a prosecutor to win the criminal justice service award of the state's bar association. By the time the Ryan case came to him, Lupkin had in fact already resigned as commissioner, and in his final weeks in office, was actively looking for a job with a private law firm. In the preceding months, Koch had harangued him over the bus shelter bungle, not only because of its duration but because Lupkin, who was working with the Manhattan federal prosecutor on the case, would not brief the mayor on its developments. Federal rules would not permit him.

The mayor grew so impatient with Lupkin's stubborn silence that he blurted out in one session: "What are you talking about, federal rules? I pay your salary." Shortly after the shelter case finally ended, Lupkin and Koch agreed that Lupkin would resign. Although Lupkin told his friends that the resignation was his idea, a wide assortment of City Hall and DOI officials believed that Lupkin had merely jumped before he was pushed.

Lupkin had tried to get the mayor to name his deputy Ron Russo, who had run the public corruption unit in the Brooklyn U.S. Attorney's office before coming to DOI, as his successor. Lupkin, after all, had been elevated to commissioner from the deputy spot by Koch in 1978, and Russo's appointment would give the office continuity. But shortly after he announced his gubernatorial candidacy in February, Koch gave the position to Pat McGinley, a criminal court judge who had endeared himself to the mayor by jailing a leftist who'd hit Koch with an egg, packing him off for thirty days at Riker's Island. McGinley, who had no connections within the federal law enforcement establishment, was scheduled to take over in mid-April. Though McGinley was a bit of an unknown quantity, City Hall expected that he would be more responsive than the meticulously proper Lupkin.

As pleased as Lupkin was with Gruskin's tape of his meeting with Ryan, it presented an immediate problem. When the TLC's chairman, Jay Turoff, had come to him to suggest this sting a few days earlier, Turoff had stressed the time factor involved. He'd pointed out that Ryan's name had already been submitted for reappointment and expressed his "concern that the mayor might soon be reappointing a crook." What Turoff had proposed, and what Lupkin had agreed to, was a "quick test" of Ryan's honesty. Now that Ryan had failed it, Lupkin decided to act quickly to inform the mayor. Gruskin's dinner with Ryan had taken place on a Friday evening; the next Monday, Lupkin called City Hall for an emergency meeting with Koch. He brought some of his staff and Turoff with him. In an uncontentious late afternoon discussion, everyone agreed that Ryan would not be allowed to keep his position and that the case would be wrapped up rapidly. But Lupkin was already unsure whether this was the best course.

Having broken off relations with the federal prosecutors in Manhattan because of their handling of the bus shelter probe, Lupkin had deliberately set up the Ryan sting in a Queens restaurant so that Russo's old boss—Brooklyn U.S. Attorney Ed Korman, whose jurisdiction included Queens—could handle the case. With Gruskin's tape in hand, Lupkin called Korman and told him about the Ryan payoff.

Korman and his Organized Crime Strike Force chief Tom Puccio were quite simply the most successful corruption prosecutors in American history. They had fought all the Abscam cases together, convicting eight congressmen and the first U.S. senator in a century. They had convicted the Republican boss in suburban Nassau, the most powerful GOP leader in the state. Korman was then embroiled in cases against two Brooklyn congressmen, and like Lupkin, was nearing the end of his term. The Ryan case did not loom large on his agenda.

On Monday, March 15, the same day that Lupkin spoke with Korman, Ryan called Gruskin. In a taped conversation, he suggested that Gruskin contact Jay Turoff to press the case for an exclusive contract. He told Gruskin that he'd spoken with Turoff and with another commission member, Marvin Greenberg. Both, Ryan said, had made encouraging comments about Gruskin's project. Gruskin knew, of course, that Turoff and Greenberg, the only commission members other than Ryan to attend the TLC meeting when Gruskin first pitched his project, had been fully briefed on the sting and coached to encourage it.

A chatty Ryan also predicted that he would be sworn in for another term in April, invited his new partner to the Blue Room in City Hall for the occasion, and renewed his promise to swing General Services construction contracts for Gruskin. He called Gruskin back the next day to give him the name of a Manes-connected official at General Services, who he said was waiting for a proposal letter from Gruskin and would "start, uh, passing it around" at the agency. Ryan ended the conversation by notifying Gruskin that he was going to Jamaica for a week's vacation, giving the investigators time to figure out their next step.

Lupkin, Russo, and the DOI supervising attorney on the case, Dan Karson, then met with Korman and an assistant, Richard Guay, to discuss both the evidence against Ryan and the powerful suggestions in the taped conversations that Ryan might be a horse, or at least a mule, that could carry them to

Manes. At this and the series of meetings that followed, DOI and the federal prosecutors agreed that Manes could wind up a target, as might a Queens public official who both represented and had a contingency interest in a company that was seeking TLC support for a mandatory new meter in all taxis. Asked during his dinner meeting with Gruskin if he had a meter company, Ryan, who had been lobbying at the TLC for the company, said: "I'm looking into it. Somebody in Queens has one." It was Turoff's suspicions about Ryan's possible connections with the Queens meter company that had sparked the Ryan probe in the first place.

Despite the potential of these leads, Lupkin said that the investigation would have to be shut down quickly. He explained the mayor's concerns, noting that as Ryan's name was already before the city council for reappointment, Koch would have to give the council a reason for withdrawing the nomination, which would kill the undercover operation. Lupkin also explained that Koch was "receiving requests from intermediaries for Ryan" to make the appointment as well as complaints that it was taking too long; so that he couldn't stall, not even to give the prosecutors a little time to string Ryan along.

Korman's staff, and subsequently Gruskin inside DOI, began pushing for at least one more payoff meeting with Ryan. The federal prosecutors felt that if the intent was to bust Ryan quickly and try to flip him, they needed two payoffs, one right before they picked him up, to "make him psychologically vulnerable." Lupkin was persuaded.

But that decision triggered a reexamination of the larger issue of whether or not the operation could be sustained for a longer period. Lupkin, who had originally acceded to the mayor's desire to close down the investigation, decided to bring it up again at a City Hall session on another subject, but Koch was curt and clear, dismissing Lupkin's request.

After the second rebuff, Korman and Tom Puccio spoke privately with Lupkin and urged him to go back to Koch a third time. Puccio predicted that Ryan could take them in short order directly to the king of Queens. Like DOI's Siedlick, Puccio had been hearing stories about Manes for years. Lupkin, who had worked with Siedlick on the Groh case years earlier and had his own "instinctual" sense about Manes, agreed.

Lupkin was to tell the mayor that Korman wanted the operation to continue, hoping to explore the tantalizing leads Ryan had offered. He was to explain to Koch that the feds wanted to jointly create a scam that Gruskin could throw at Ryan that would be designed to test Ryan's boasts that he could bring Manes into the game. And finally, Lupkin was to urge the mayor to keep Ryan on as a holdover for a while if he was unwilling to reappoint him. (Puccio recalled that Senator Harrison Williams, whom he'd indicted in Abscam, and all the congressmen, had been allowed to remain unexposed in Congress for years after they'd first taken bribes from Puccio's wired Arab sheikhs to protect the undercover operation.)

On March 24, Lupkin, with Russo and Karson, arrived at the mayor's private office and found him waiting with his City Hall counsel, Bob Tierney. Tierney's presence, rather than that of the city's corporation counsel, F. A. O. Schwarz, reduced the possibility that the mayor would be willing to openly consider their arguments and seek an inventive solution. Schwarz, who is to the law what his family's store has long been to toys, had taken over in January as New York City's top lawyer, in charge of its massive legal department, the second largest law firm in America (after the Justice Department). In complex legal situations like the Ryan matter, he had peripheral vision, and could see the whole court with the eye of a Larry Bird. On the other hand, no one at the meeting, including Tierney, could remember a thing Tierney said at it, if indeed he did speak. The mayor did not even seek his opinion after Lupkin and Russo presented the case.

In addition to never discussing the matter with Schwarz, the mayor ignored the time factors surrounding Ryan's reappointment that would have easily justified an attempt to delay it. Ryan's term had expired way back in January 1980, and the city council had taken twenty-six months before sending his name to Koch for reappointment. Koch, in fact, had ratified Ryan in less than a month and transmitted the reappointment, together with four other TLC nominees, back to the council for a final, full vote.

At the time Koch and Lupkin met to discuss Ryan, none of the prospective appointees had yet appeared at the mandatory council public hearing. Contrary to Ryan's tape-recorded anticipation of an April swearing-in, the appointment process could still take months without any interference. The mayor's office could have slowed the process down by inventing any one of a variety of obstacles, including the fact that DOI background checks had not been completed on any of them. These possibilities weren't even considered.

At the start of their presentation to Koch, Lupkin and Russo took turns making the arguments to justify a sustained Ryan probe. "Let us work with it," the two requested. "We don't know where it will take us. The U.S. Attorney wants to work it. They're ready to invest resources. This guy has clubhouse connections all the way to the top of the Queens Democratic organization. He may lead us right to Donald Manes."

Though Koch loves to stretch his long frame out in his reclining office chair, he did not sit during this session. For virtually all of the half-hour meeting, he stood, musing. He did not pace. He was ruminating silently, as if searching his memory.

The mayor had his own reasons to suspect Manes. He knew about the Groh case and the runaway grand jury that wanted to indict Manes. It had been Koch's close friend Judge Leonard Sandler, and his eventual Criminal Justice Coordinator John Keenan, who had been criticized by the appellate division in 1977 for talking the grand jury out of indicting Manes and convincing them to indict Groh. Indeed Koch's recently departed press secretary Tom Goldstein had written the *Times* story that first revealed the near Manes indictment.

In fact, when Koch had first hired Keenan in 1979, taking him out of the special prosecutor's office and hiring him to run the Off Track Betting Corporation, Keenan had raised the subject of Manes's criminal case in a personal conversation with the mayor. Keenan, a trusted Koch adviser who would eventually become a federal judge, told the mayor that he had put Manes in the grand jury twice. He believed at the time that Manes had committed a crime, and he settled for the indictment of Manes's deputy Groh, hoping that a convicted Groh might take them to Manes. He told the mayor that he was concerned that he might have great difficulty dealing with Manes if he took the OTB job because he'd gone after Manes so aggressively. Though Keenan was obviously a well-informed source on the possible criminality of Manes, Mayor Koch never sought his advice while considering the closing of the Ryan probe.

Koch knew, too, that Ryan was not the first Manes appointee to wind up in trouble. Two years earlier, the mayor had awakened to banner headlines in the *New York Post* about Nicky Sands, a man Koch had appointed in 1978 to the board of the city's Public Development Corporation (PDC). The story, which reported that Sands had been shot eight times as he left his Queens home the day before, also revealed that Sands was actually a convicted embezzler named Dominick Santiago, the former president of a mob-tied carpenter's union local. Santiago, according to a 1967 justice department criminal division report, "reportedly was closely associated with several Columbo family members" prior to that time.

The mayor's chief of staff Diane Coffey immediately asked City Hall staffers to determine how Sands had gotten on the PDC board. Everyone was relieved to learn that the appointment did not originate with City Hall; it was on Manes's recommendation. Manes had also made Sands a Democratic state committeeman, and just three months before this shootout had signed off on a Queens project Sands was developing. Sands survived the attack and refused to cooperate with police efforts to find his assailants.

More recently, Manes and his public relations sidekick Michael Nussbaum had tried to get City Hall to appoint Eddie Chan to the city's Youth Board, which controls millions in recreation funds. The two had also helped put together a Chan fundraiser for Koch's reelection in September 1981. The Youth Board appointment had been blocked only when Koch learned from police and prosecutorial sources that Chan was a notorious underworld figure.

This history of Manes associations, most of them well publicized, hovered over the room as Russo and Lupkin made their plea to the mayor. He began questioning the DOI officials, but more in the manner of a debater with a fixed position searching for arguments than a decisionmaker listening to advice and considering options. The heart of the objection he raised was whether they had any real evidence from the first payoff tape and the two phone conversations that Manes might be involved in a conspiracy. They repeated the specific lines about Manes from the tapes, but acknowledged that the barely begun probe had not unearthed hard evidence, only nuance. Of course, they'd begun the probe of Ryan a couple of weeks earlier with less than nuance. "The only way to know," if the case could lead to Manes, said Lupkin, "is by testing it, by letting the string run out."

But Koch was adamant—the one word every DOI participant would later use to describe him. "I want Ryan arrested," the mayor announced. Russo tersely replied: "That's not a decision we can make. We'll pass that along to the U.S. Attorney."

A disappointed Lupkin lumbered back to the DOI offices a few blocks away, even this farewell triumph having been transformed into a headache.

Lupkin and Korman agreed that if the mayor wouldn't keep Ryan on as commissioner, the operation couldn't go forward. They would go through with the plans for a second payoff meeting and would pick up Ryan the same night on a search warrant. They could then try to flip him without the complications of an arrest.

Ryan called Gruskin on March 29, back from his Jamaica vacation. Though he didn't owe Ryan another payment for several weeks, Gruskin pushed the schedule up in an effort to get an early, final meeting before the case was closed. He told Ryan that he was leaving shortly for three weeks in Florida and that he wanted "to meet certain obligations before" he left. Gruskin agreed that he and Lamarta would pick him up at his Electchester building at 4:00 the next day. They'd go to the nearby Palace Diner for a quick bite and conversation. This time, in addition to the body Nagras, Gruskin would be traveling with a video crew hidden in a van.

The following afternoon, as soon as Ryan got in the car, he started complaining about Gruskin's failure to contact his friend at General Services, assuring Gruskin that it "doesn't cost anything to open the door." When they got to the diner, they pulled into a space right beside the van and were videotaped leaving the car and entering the restaurant. Inside, when Gruskin raised the problem of insuring the new cabs, Ryan offered to contact a "very dear friend who got his job through Donny"— an official in the state's insurance department. Then, almost on cue from prophet Puccio, Ryan said: "I want to introduce you to Donald, I want to get you to know Manes."

When the three returned to the car, Ryan once again took his $700, this time on camera, talking about Manes all the time. After Gruskin dropped Ryan off near his house, he headed back to DOI, where Turoff's aide Mackasek, who had encouraged the Ryan probe from the beginning, was waiting with a case of beer.

A DOI detective, meanwhile, walked up to Ryan where Gruskin had dropped him, introduced himself, and showed Ryan his badge. Ryan tried to shake the detective's hand, but the cop told him: "I believe you have some Department of Investigation money—$700." Ryan sheepishly removed it from his inside coat pocket. "I believe it would be in your best interest to come with me to the U.S. Attorney's office," the detective continued, and Ryan, who instantly began crying and begging, agreed.

Brought to a large conference room in Korman's office, Ryan began a stream-of-consciousness monologue about his family and about how he "can't go to jail." The brassy business-man of the tapes dissolved into a hyperventilating, teary peni-tent, who kept apologizing to Lupkin, as if Lupkin's forgiveness were all he needed to end the nightmare. But Lupkin ham-mered away at him, so hard that Korman's corruption chief had to move in to try to soften the pressure. The attempt to break Ryan dragged on for four hours. A large number of cops, agents, and prosecuting attorneys walked in and out of the room during the questioning, while Ryan kept running to the bathroom.

"What if I just gave you some things?" a weakened Ryan asked at one point, forcing Lupkin to make it clear to him that he was "either in or out"—that his cooperation could not be partial. Mostly, Ryan just threw Lupkin's questions back at him: "Give us some names," Lupkin would say; "What names do you want," Ryan responded. "What do you know about Manes?" brought the reply "What do you want to know?" Finally he moaned: "Everybody else has their own thing. I just wanted to get my own thing." Unwittingly, Ryan had uttered the motto of the clubhouse clan that had established itself within the Koch administration.

Lupkin closed the session with advice: Ryan should speak to no one, not even his wife, if possible, about the case and should consider cooperating. He urged Ryan, if he sought legal advice, not to go to a clubhouse lawyer, stressing that such an attorney would enter the case to protect the clubhouse, not him. Lupkin made it clear that if Ryan elected not to cooperate, Korman's office would move to indict him.

When Ryan arrived home that night, his wife, Molly, knew immediately that something was wrong, and the whole story soon tumbled out. Ryan remembered that Manes had told him if he ever had a problem, he should go to Harold Harrison, a Queens Boulevard criminal lawyer who had once been Manes's partner. The next day Ryan called Lupkin, said he'd told his wife about the whole affair, and announced that he was going to a lawyer. Ryan had invested his life in the clubhouse network; he believed, even now, that it had the power to save him. He went to Harrison, whom he'd known for years, and told him that the feds had tried to flip him against the borough president.

Although Harrison, still a friend of Manes's, said that it might be a conflict of interest for him to represent Ryan directly, he nonetheless called Richard Guay, told Guay he was representing Ryan, and said he'd be bringing in another lawyer. Since he was scheduled to go to Florida for a long stay, Harrison suggested that Ryan see another Queens Boulevard lawyer, Paul Vladimir, and promised he would work with Vladimir on the case. Ryan left Harrison's office with Molly and went straight to Vladimir. Harrison's call was interpreted by the feds as the end of any realistic possibility that Ryan would cooperate.

Though Ryan was in hiding from his own daughter's calls and would not discuss his nightmare with anyone else, he called Donald Manes the day after, as soon as he got back home from his first meetings with Harrison and Vladimir. He told Manes that he'd been set up—that the U.S. Attorney really wanted information about Manes—and that he'd already seen Harrison and Vladimir. Manes replied that he liked Vladimir, who was close to Manes's PVB bagman Shelly Chevlowe. He urged Ryan to "take two Valiums," and promised him that everything would be okay.

Herb Ryan learned that he'd been formally indicted the next Monday morning, April 5, when he started getting press calls at his apartment. Lupkin and Korman had gone to the Blue Room to announce the indictment with the mayor, and everyone at the conference praised everyone else for his cooperation. Lupkin refused to answer questions about the origins of the probe and was quoted in that day's *Post* as saying: "I won't comment on what the targets were." But the *Post* story left little doubt that Manes was involved, pointing to Ryan's ties to Manes's home club.

During the period immediately before and after the indictment, Donald Manes's phone lit up with calls from people connected to the Ryan case, including the DGS official Ryan had referred Gruskin to for construction contracts, and the Queens official whose meter company was mentioned repeatedly by Ryan on the tapes. Also calling Manes in the days after Ryan's arrest was Marvin Greenberg, the TLC commissioner close to Turoff who'd known about the sting and had long been a personal friend of Manes.

Of course, the newspapers also called. Manes's statement was reminiscent of the one he'd made when his PDC appointee Nicky Sands was unveiled two years earlier and anticipated what would one day be said about him. "I am really shocked. I have known Herb Ryan for a long time. He has been extremely active in the civic and political life of Queens County."

On April 5, the same day that Herb Ryan's indictment was announced, Mario Cuomo, who had formally announced his gubernatorial candidacy on March 18, recorded a telephone conversation with Donald Manes in his diary. For the first time, Cuomo reported: "All indications are that Manes is going to go with Koch." Cuomo was not surprised, and made what he called "a last effort" to talk Manes out of it. He argued that the polls showed "a softening of support for Koch," and contended that "if Manes went for Koch, he would probably never get to be mayor even if Koch won." Koch, he said, "would have to go with Bellamy, or Biaggi, whom he was trying to reach, or Goldin, who was helping him . . . or remain neutral." On the other hand, Cuomo promised, "If Manes was with me, his chances would be excellent." For the moment, Cuomo reported to himself, "I may have made him think, but only for the moment."

Cuomo's call was prompted by a *Times* story the day before written by Frank Lynn, a reporter whose early coverage of the campaign was perceived by Cuomo as designed to suggest that Koch was unbeatable, drying up money and political support for his own effort. Cuomo believed that Lynn was being lobbied by Koch's media adviser, David Garth. His story, appearing in a column of political notes in the Sunday edition, led with the assertion that four of the city's five Democratic bosses would endorse Koch. Lynn made much of the supposed support for Koch in Cuomo's home county, where even Manes was said to be now backing Koch. Manes wasn't quoted; no one was, not even a blind source. Manes's support for Koch was printed as an unattributed yet uncontested fact.

What no one knew at the time was that Garth and Manes had apparently sealed this deal at a lunch listed in Manes's diaries on March 26 at the Palmcourt Restaurant in the Plaza Hotel, Garth's favorite watering hole. Garth told top Koch campaign strategists that Manes had made a commitment, though no one could be certain, with the ever-shifty Manes, just what it meant. The Lynn story was intended to turn the luncheon promise into hard type, and as Manes's logs reveal, the reporter called him the same day as Garth's lunch and again on April 1 ("re politics" was Lynn's phone message).

Lynn repeated his assertion in a front-page story on April 6, writing that Manes, Friedman, and Esposito were threatening to tie up enough delegates at the upcoming June state convention that they might deny Cuomo even the 25 percent vote he would need to qualify for the primary. However, Manes was the only one of the big three who had yet to be quoted in any published story as favoring Koch.

A week later, Manes left the country for two weeks in Taiwan, still having made no public statement of support. During his absence, not only did Koch formally announce his candidacy in a major statewide campaign swing, but *New York* magazine reported that unnamed federal law enforcement officials were angry at the mayor (and Stan Lupkin) for torpedoing the Herb Ryan case. The source was quoted describing Ryan as "a way to open a wide-ranging probe of the Queens Democratic machine." Lupkin called Korman and asked him to write a response, and while Korman's letter split hairs, denying that the investigators had been barred from trying to turn Ryan, as the story had alleged, it did concede that there was "a difference of opinion as to the most practical way of achieving the objective." Korman did not mention Koch's shutdown of the undercover operation. Apparently unpersuaded that Korman's version materially contradicted the original story, *New York* refused to print the letter. But Koch had a figleaf for the file.

One of Manes's first visitors when he returned to his office from Taiwan on April 28 was Donna Ryan, Herb's hot-tempered and determined daughter, who had once worked at Borough Hall for Manes. Donna Ryan was convinced her father had been set up by Jay Turoff, who she believed was a crook determined to force her father off the TLC because Ryan had raised questions about his corrupt deals. She suspected that Manes had been tipped to the sting, and she was upset that no one was helping her father now. Manes was moving to distance himself from Ryan, and wary of Ryan's daughter, he insisted that his secretary join the conversation. Without citing any evidence, Donna Ryan told Manes that she would never forgive him because he "knew it was a trap and should have told her father to keep cool." She said Ryan was "thinking about suicide," adding, "I hope your daughter winds up the same as me." Manes said he would try to help and asked if Herb Ryan was "saying anything about anything."

The Ryans did not know how accurate many of their hunches were. It would not become clear for years that at the time Turoff came to DOI about Ryan, confiding his suspicions about Ryan's connections with the meter company represented by a Queens elected official, Turoff himself was deeply involved with a competing company. He had deliberately delayed TLC's approval of the other meter for months, putting it through a second round of tests in cabs he selected. One of the test cabs was owned by Turoff's son's Little League coach, and in late 1981, Turoff had called the driver and asked him to allow a group to examine the Queens meter. The group included Hy Schwartz, a longtime friend of Turoff's from the same Brooklyn club, Zenek Podolsky, a politically connected investor, and an engineer the two had hired to design their own meter. Podolsky would subsequently claim that shortly before this clandestine raid on a competitor, Turoff and he had agreed that Turoff would have a 10 percent hidden interest in the meter company.

Herb Ryan, who was the only advocate of the Queens company at the commission, was viewed as an obstacle to any plan to deliver the meter business to Hy Schwartz. So Turoff and Mackasek began taping Ryan, even strapping a recorder on Turoff for a lunch meeting with Ryan. But all he got out of Ryan was what Mackasek described in a memo as "very strong lobbying" for the other meter. When this strategy failed, the two went to Lupkin, without telling him about their own taping. Mackasek had worked for Lupkin before being appointed the TLC inspector general and was regarded at DOI as one of their own. He helped develop the sting and, as a participant in DOI meetings during it, pressed for its early shutdown.

Indeed in the aftermath of Ryan's indictment, at the very time that Donna Ryan was pressing Manes for help, an emboldened Turoff was acting to deliver a temporary corner on the potentially lucrative meter market to Schwartz's company, even though the competing company had come to the TLC a year ahead of Schwartz. A last-minute TLC edict, issued when the new meter was finally mandated by the commission for use in all cabs, put the other meter out of compliance.

Donna Ryan knew little of this detail when she threw the

family's suspicions about Turoff at Donald Manes. She knew that her father had been a thorn in Turoff's side, not only about the meter contract but about a highly profitable diesel taxi experiment championed by Turoff. Herb Ryan had even gone to City Hall—an appointment arranged by Manes—to complain about Turoff, who subsequently learned of the meeting and confronted Ryan about it. The more the Ryans thought about the sting, the clearer it was that Turoff had orchestrated it. Why else would Turoff have called Herb at home and cajoled him into coming to the TLC meeting where Gruskin first appeared?

However angry they were, the Ryans understood that Turoff, a loyal soldier of the clubhouse, would not betray the appointee of another county leader unless it was a sanctioned hit, and they believed that Meade Esposito had authorized it. Turoff was so widely regarded as an Esposito appointee that when his reappointment was in trouble in 1981 because of his mismanagement of the taxi agency, John LoCicero was heard to worry out loud among friends about Esposito's reaction if Turoff was bounced. (In fact the mayor moved to reappoint Turoff in 1982, at the same time he nominated Ryan.)

Esposito and Manes had never really liked each other—an antipathy that grew stronger after Manes's backing of reformer Liz Holtzman in the 1980 Senate race; moreover, Esposito regarded Ryan's intrusions at the TLC as a turf violation. The regular party leaders were not unlike the five crime families—they did business together, but each had his own piece of the action, which the others were supposed to respect. Esposito might have been willing to okay Turoff's initiation of an investigation, especially one that would be brought down quickly and contained.

The best evidence of Esposito's possible knowledge of the Ryan sting is that when Turoff was told by DOI about Gruskin's undercover construction company in Brooklyn, Esposito found out. An Esposito district leader ultimately indicted in the scam testified at the trial that Esposito had warned him to stay away from Gruskin, asserting that he was a cop. An Esposito-backed congressional candidate was videotaped a few days after Ryan's first payoff meeting stuffing $1,300 that Gruskin gave him in his pockets, and promising to steer construction contracts to Gruskin's company. A few days later, the candidate returned the cash to Gruskin.

But the Ryan suspicions about the origins of the sting did

not help the Ryans find a way to cope with its result. Morty
Povman, the Queens councilman Ryan worked for and a lawyer with an exclusively civil practice, thought Ryan had a
chance at trial—he'd taken only $1,400, his TLC position was
unsalaried, his wife was a diabetic, and even the tapes indicated
that he was confused about whether he was functioning as a
commissioner, since his term had expired. Povman called
Manes and made those arguments to him, but Manes said that
Ryan ought to plead guilty, as did Harrison once he got a look
at the tape transcripts. Ryan believed Manes was speaking to
him through Harrison. He incorrectly believed that Harrison
and Manes could get to the federal judge assigned to the case,
who had Brooklyn machine ties, and that they could win for
him what he wanted most—no jail time. His faith in the clubhouse's power in the courthouse had reached the level of the
mystical.

Though Vladimir opposed a plea, Ryan, urged on by Harrison in the hallway of the federal courthouse, decided to admit
his guilt and spare himself the agony of news stories during the
trial filled with quotes from the Herb Ryan who appeared on
the tapes, a Herb Ryan he couldn't bear to hear talk in a courtroom. Though Harrison brought a sheaf of letters from Manes
and other Queens officials to the sentencing hearing, the judge
gave Ryan a six-month jail term. Manes's subsequent phone
logs reveal a torrent of calls from Ryan, who was beside himself
with fear.

Of course, Ryan's decision to plead not only had spared
him from humiliating trial publicity; it had protected Manes
from a week of possible headlines. The plea completed a circle;
a sanctioned and contained investigative hit had wound up with
the foot soldier it had targeted in the beginning. Yet Ryan's
demise was apparently enough to send Manes the message Turoff intended. The next TLC appointee from Queens was a low-
key and dependable Turoff vote. The Queens official who represented the competing meter company dropped his client and
never again tried to do TLC business.

It was a gloriously sunny day in May when Donald Manes went
to Ed Koch's office for a brief morning meeting with coffee and
danish. Joining Manes were the other three county leaders—
Friedman, Esposito, and Staten Island's Nick LaPorte. The

mayor and the boys were together, cocky, casual, enjoying a contest of one-liners.

When Koch and his friends finished their chat at his office that morning, they walked out of City Hall together and stood on its steps. This was Ed Koch's first endorsement press conference in the gubernatorial campaign. When Deputy Mayor Robert Wagner, who also functioned as a campaign adviser, asked why the campaign was beginning with the May 6 endorsement of bosses, he was told: "To lock in Manes." Koch's press secretary for the campaign, Marty McLaughlin, was told by Dave Garth that the conference was necessary because "there was a feeling of nervousness about Manes jumping off the reservation."

The courtship of Manes, which had begun a few months earlier and continued through all the events of March and early April, was at last over. Koch could now be endorsed by a Manes who was not the target of any ongoing undercover investigation. The critical meeting that had led to the endorsement, Garth's March 26 lunch with Manes, had occurred two days after the undercover probe had been ordered shut down by the mayor in his final meeting with Lupkin.

Mario Cuomo, who called Manes the day before the endorsement for one last conversation, wrote in his diaries that the support of the four leaders had "nothing to do with what they believe," but was instead a "practical judgement." An angrier Cuomo told the *New York Times* that the four leaders were "intimidated" because even if Koch lost, he would be mayor for three more years. Cuomo said that "Donald has done what's good for him." And he attempted to belittle the significance of the endorsement: "The last time four political leaders got together to endorse someone who won was in the Iroquois Confederacy."

Four days after the endorsement, Ed Koch appeared at two dinners on the same night. One was held in the Heisman Room at the Downtown Athletic Club, a farewell for Stan Lupkin, at which the mayor saluted the man he'd prodded to resign. The other was at Antun's Restaurant in Queens, the annual dinner dance of Donald Manes's Queens Democratic organization. The gubernatorial candidate and the supportive boss bear-hugged. It was the first county dinner that Herb Ryan had missed in twenty years.

Several weeks later, on May 26, Esposito held his own

county dinner dance, which was attended by Friedman, Manes, and the mayor. The taxi fleet owners had their tables. And Jay Turoff had a table of his own. Among the ticket purchasers listed at Turoff's table was supposed corruption buster Robert Mackasek, a convert to the clubhouse culture whom Turoff could now bring to its annual ritual. Turoff would soon promote Mackasek to deputy commissioner and would ultimately obtain a $100,000 loan for him from a politically wired credit union. Also listed at his table were two owners of a cab company in Yonkers that Turoff allegedly owned a part of, and a new partner in Hy Schwartz's meter company.

Seated at another table was Marvin Greenberg, whose reappointment to the TLC had been approved by the council only the day before. Since his name had been transmitted to the council by Koch at the same time as Ryan's, the council would not have gotten around to finally voting on Ryan either until late May. So if Koch had let Lupkin go forward while the council dallied before voting on Ryan's appointment, the sting operation on Ryan could have continued for two more months. There's no telling how close to Manes it may have taken investigators in that time.

Throughout the spring and summer of 1982, Herb Ryan hibernated. In August his lawyers worked out a deal with the government that permitted him to stay out of jail while they appealed a technical issue in his case. Then in September, his friends threw a fundraiser to help cover his legal defense costs. Manes listed the fundraiser on his appointment diary but went instead to a party for Koch.

On primary day later that month, a panicky Ed Koch called Manes midway through the afternoon, concerned about the low turnout in Forest Hills, a symbol of Koch's Jewish base in Queens. It had taken a few hours for Koch to get Manes, who reassured him that voters in Forest Hills came out late. In fact, Manes had sent workers out in some critical districts with instructions not to push any gubernatorial candidate, hedging his bets again. Once Cuomo had started narrowing what had appeared to be Koch's insurmountable lead in the polls, Manes had started fidgeting. Even though Manes could become a mayoral candidate himself if Koch won, he could not make a full-fledged effort to elect him, for he was fully aware that a governor from Queens who was determined to damage Manes could knock him out of the party leadership and the borough presidency.

Indeed, when Cuomo pulled his stunning upset, losing Queens by only a thousand votes and winning statewide, Manes told reporters that he'd backed "the right candidate in the wrong year," reminding everyone of his support for Cuomo in 1977. "This time I picked Koch," he said, "but I didn't make life miserable for anyone who supported Mario. I never acted with malice, never said Mario wasn't a quality candidate."

Unlike Manes, Stanley Friedman had thrown himself enthusiastically into the gubernatorial race, working with Koch's closest advisers and strengthening his personal ties to the mayor. The word in the Koch camp before the debacle was that a victorious Koch would make Friedman the new state Democratic chairman. But the large black turnout in the Bronx, overwhelmingly against Koch, prevented Friedman from delivering more than a thousand-vote margin.

Similarly, Meade Esposito had boasted during the campaign of his personal commitment to the mayor, saying that he'd decided to stay on as county leader as long as Koch was in politics because he liked working with Koch so much. But Koch's Brooklyn margin of 13,000 votes was less than he needed to counterbalance Cuomo's upstate strength. The bosses Koch had wooed couldn't produce for him in a race where television exposure shaped voter preferences.

After Herb Ryan did a four-month jail stint in 1983, a year after Koch's defeat, he had to start over again, already in his sixties. He wound up with a distribution job for a male pornography publisher in New Jersey.

He also went back to the Stevenson Club, which made him a vice president again. He began selling tickets for the club dinner dance once more. And he renewed his friendship with Donald Manes. Manes helped get Donna Ryan a position with Warner's cable subsidiary in Queens, and also offered Herb Ryan employment but at salaries he wouldn't accept. The only city job Manes ever came up with, though, which Ryan likewise rejected, was that of a low-level manager at another city transportation agency, the Parking Violations Bureau. Herb Ryan's name appeared on the borough president's phone logs on a weekly basis until the day Manes tried to kill himself.

CHAPTER SEVEN

From Auschwitz
to Allenwood*

Meade was God.
—*Alex Liberman,
during his
debriefings
with prosecutors in
1986*

BY THE SPRING OF **1983** the city's leasing czar, Alex Liberman, was becoming the same sort of problem for Meade Esposito that Herb Ryan had been the year before for Donald Manes. Liberman's mouth was quickly making him a magnet for prosecutors, and some of what he was saying was damaging to Meade and winding up on tape. The difference was that Liberman made Ryan look like a piker. Just as Ryan raised contributions for Manes from the cab industry he regulated, Liberman dunned the landlords he gave city leases. But in addition to his role as breadwinner for the clubhouse, Liberman, like Ryan, had branched out into a more personal line of business: extortion. Before the year ended, the evidence that would surface about Liberman would sound the shrillest warning yet about the character of his leader and sponsor. But no one at City Hall, where Meade remained a friendly insider, could hear the siren.

The 60-year-old Liberman, who had been put in control of the city's leasing bureau shortly after Koch took office in 1978, solicited ads for the dinner dance journal of Esposito's home base, the patronage-rich Thomas Jefferson Club in the Canarsie

---

*This is the title of a fancied autobiography Liberman began talking about in jail.

section of Brooklyn. A member of the club's executive committee, he sold tables for its annual affair as well. His key city job,
which gave him the power to pick sites and negotiate leases for
use by all city agencies, also positioned him to deliver large
contributions to the Brooklyn county organization. A Jeff Club
vice president, he sometimes chaired its dinner dance. He was
also one of the select few invited regularly to the basement of
Meade's mother's house in Canarsie for Sunday morning "business breakfasts." And everywhere he went in government and
political circles, he announced that he was Meade's man, as if
he were a property, on perpetual lease to the boss of bosses.

The year before Liberman was appointed leasing director,
the Jeff Club had honored him as its "Man of the Year" at its
October dance at the Palms Shore Club along the waterfront at
Sheepshead Bay. The five-foot-three-inch Liberman, a balding,
cold man with large, flapping ears and a mugshot face, was
seated at the head table with his wife Sylvia, next to Meade and
U.S. Senator Pat Moynihan. He and Sylvia were given a gift and
flowers by the club's female district leader, Shirley Weiner.
Two hundred and fifty of the club faithful filled the room.
Moynihan spoke, then Meade, and finally Liberman, stumbling
through a thank you in his heavily accented, immigrant English. Liberman, who ordinarily wore a snarl, beamed. It was
the high point of Alex Liberman's life.

Born in Breslau, Germany, in 1923, Liberman was the son
of a well-to-do coal broker, but he and his family were forced
to flee penniless across the Polish border in 1938 by the Nazis,
settling in the city of Lodz, where Poland's largest concentration of Jews lived. When the Germans invaded Poland in 1939,
they encircled the Jews of Lodz with an electrified fence,
banned religious services and newspapers, and began a reign of
terror and starvation that would ultimately cost 70,000 Jewish
lives. A few days after the Nazis created what would become
known in history as the Lodz Ghetto, 16-year-old Alex was
awakened at 2:00 A.M. by the SS knock at the door. The family,
including his father, brother, stepsister, and stepmother, were
taken to the town square, Balliter Platz. When they arrived,
they saw three nooses dangling from gallows the Nazis had
erected for a rabbi, a banker, and the elder Liberman, who had
become a local Zionist leader. Forced to watch, along with
thousands of ghetto residents, Alex and his family stood shriek-
ing until his father hung limply in the square.

For three days, Abraham Liberman was left hanging under

a sign that read simply "For Disobedience," a warning to the ghetto residents. Alex visited each day, saying the mourner's kaddish from a discreet distance until finally the body disappeared. For the next four years, Alex Liberman lived in the ghetto, watching his stepmother and half-sister die of starvation. Sixty-eight other members of his family also perished in the ghetto before August 1944, when the Germans, under pressure from the Russian army, closed the ghetto and shipped its survivors to concentration camps. Liberman and his brother Harry were taken in a cattle car to Auschwitz.

Fed only soup poured into a small hat they'd been given to wear, the two Libermans were slowly starving, until a tormented Harry suddenly broke free from the group, raced to the electrified barbed wire, and electrocuted himself. Liberman stood in the yard motionless when the camp commander bellowed over the loudspeaker that Harry had tried to "escape," and demanded to know the identities of any of his relatives. Liberman had to deny his brother to stay alive himself. During the final year of the war, Liberman went from a tire factory to an underground munitions factory to two more concentration camps.

On the morning of April 11, 1945, the camp commander at Verdun awakened Liberman and his fellow prisoners with a 5:00 A.M. announcement that the "Jewish" president of the United States—"Rosenfeld"—had freed them, that the war was over. Liberman scoured Germany, found only one remaining surviving relative, his cousin Sylvia, and married her. In 1947, at the age of twenty-three, he came to America and took a furnished room in the Borough Park section of Brooklyn.

Ten years later, after a series of jobs as everything from a carpenter to a painter, Liberman became part-owner of a small Brooklyn dairy. He later made enough off the sale of the dairy to the city in a condemnation proceeding to start a small business in nearby Canarsie—a deli called Shop and Spot. By that time, Liberman had already become a captain in the Democratic clubhouse in Canarsie that preceded the Jeff Club and was a founding member of a new Jewish temple in Canarsie, the Remsen Heights Jewish Center. The synagogue, which began in a tent, was able to move into a simple one-story building in 1958 when Liberman personally signed a note to the lending bank.

When reapportionment combined Canarsie with the East New York section of Brooklyn, forming a new assembly district in 1966, the Jeff Club, which had dominated East New York for years, became the regular club in Canarsie as well. Liberman joined and quickly attached himself to the club's district leaders, Esposito and Weiner. A year later, he told his friends at the club that he was "bored," sold his deli, and asked for a municipal job.

In April 1968, the same year that Meade Esposito became Brooklyn's county leader, Liberman went to work as a real estate manager with the city's housing agency. He was hired as a "provisional," outside the civil service system, and assigned to the Atlantic Terminal Urban Renewal Project in downtown Brooklyn. His job was to supervise a low-interest loan program that allowed homeowners to rehabilitate their houses, financed by thirty-year federal mortgages. Liberman was responsible for picking the materials, selecting the contractors, and overseeing the construction.

In 1972, John Lindsay's investigations commissioner released a report that blasted Liberman's handling of the loan program, noting that he had allowed contractors to install inferior materials and that he and the homeowners gave "conflicting accounts" when asked why. Newspaper coverage at the time noted that DOI had recommended departmental charges be brought against Liberman and two other inspectors. Though the city housing commissioner wrote DOI that Liberman had "already been relieved" of his duties "pending further appropriate action," in fact he stayed with the agency another year. When he finally left in mid-1973, his personnel file made no reference to any disciplinary action and listed the reason for his departure as "budgetary considerations."

Mysteriously, a month later Liberman appeared on the payroll of the General Services Agency, again as a provisional, this time as a manager in the city's real estate department. Earlier that year, with the support of Esposito and the Jeff Club, he had also become chairman of Canarsie's planning board, an appointive position with substantial influence over neighborhood zoning.

Liberman remained a real estate manager and planning board chairman throughout the Beame years. He continued acquiring his own commercial and residential properties all over Canarsie, building a personal real estate empire. In the final year of Beame's term, he went to Meade to ask for a promotion on his city job. Esposito questioned Liberman about how much he was making, and Liberman understated his city salary by a few thousand dollars. When Meade checked and learned Liberman's real salary, he challenged Liberman about the false statement. Liberman coolly informed Esposito that he was so wealthy he never paid any attention to what the city was paying him. It was so unimportant, he explained, that he had arranged for his paycheck to be routinely forwarded to his accountant. What he wanted Meade to get him was a job title with clout; the salary didn't matter. That request led to Liberman's name being placed on the handwritten list of Esposito jobholders that Meade submitted to the Koch transition team in late 1977.

Four months after Ed Koch took office in 1978, Liberman got his title. As director of leasing he had sweeping discretion over an $80 million annual leasing budget, and millions more in renovation funds. The position was a sensitive one, and a clubhouse plum; the previous director under Beame had been convicted on bribery charges and had arranged millions in leases for private landlords connected to Esposito and the other party bosses.

At the moment that Liberman received his promotion, however, he was under investigation again by DOI. Despite this active case, which involved Liberman's attempt to sell a piece of city land, DOI inexplicably gave him a clearance for the position. The case wasn't officially closed until March 1979, with DOI finding "insufficient evidence to establish whether a corrupt relationship existed among any of the principals involved in this transaction." With the investigation ended, Liberman was given another title—director of negotiations, a "lateral move" in new commissioner Jim Capalino's reorganized DGS structure—as well as a 6 percent raise. Capalino had received a call on Liberman's behalf from patriarch Meade Esposito.

By this point in his career, Liberman was already taking advantage of his discretionary public power and demanding an assortment of kickbacks for city leases. Landlords were writing checks to his synagogue at his suggestion, and Liberman was pressuring his fellow directors at the temple to split the contributions with him. At first, the synagogue's president rejected the idea, and Liberman got no part of the initial small donations. But Remsen Heights Jewish Center had a working-class, struggling congregation, and when Liberman began dangling larger and larger contributions, the temple's leadership weakened.

They began giving part of the money Liberman raised back to him—sometimes in cash, sometimes in checks written to fictitious names provided by Liberman, sometimes in large quantities of liquor, and sometimes in Panasonic VCRs. Eventually the synagogue was laundering $10,000 checks; by 1983, it had collected almost $64,000 from seven different landlords, and returned $28,000 to Liberman.

Liberman also concocted other circuitous forms of payment. One landlord, David Twersky, gave him $25,000 in State of Israel bonds in the name of Liberman's grandson. On another occasion, Liberman asked Twersky to make out a $25,000 check to a Rabbi Bernard Harold, but told him not to write "rabbi" on the check. When the canceled check was returned to Twersky, it was endorsed by a small brokerage firm, Bernard Harold and Co.; it had been credited to the account of Liberman's daughter. Liberman also induced Twersky to write five $5,000 checks over a seventeen-day period in October 1982 to fictitious individuals. Liberman himself cashed all the checks.

The managing agent for an office building near City Hall filled with various municipal agencies, Twersky was utterly dependent on Liberman's lease renewals. A retired toy store owner, Twersky had been in the real estate business for only a year; his firm was new, and marginal. When Twersky initially hesitated to make any illegal payments, Liberman taunted him: "What I give you I can also take away."

The fact that Twersky was a 68-year-old Jew who had survived four years in the Krakow Ghetto, the sister city of Lodz, as well as a stay at the Mauthausen concentration camp, was irrelevant to Liberman, apart from its value as a bargaining tool. In one early conversation, Liberman acknowledged his and Twersky's common heritage of pain—"You're a survivor and I'm a survivor"—and Twersky was astonished that Liberman had cited their mutual experience as a reason why they should do business together. The beleaguered managing agent, who would later describe his dealings with Liberman as "the worst moments of my life," finally balked at further payments to Liberman in April 1983. When he did, Liberman snapped at the suddenly noncompliant Twersky, promising to "teach you a lesson" by pulling all the city's leases out of his buildings.

Liberman's favorite forms of conduit payment, begun in 1981, were large real estate brokerage fees, handed over to various fronts. These fronts, who agreed to pose as brokers though they'd had nothing to do with the deals involved, would pay taxes on the fees and then split the profits with Liberman. Liberman picked his bagmen carefully. Among them were two politically connected lawyers who had their own firm, Saul Radow and Helaine Brick. Both were also staff attorneys on the payroll of Assembly Speaker Stanley Fink, who, like Radow, was a member of the Jefferson Club. Brick was on the board of directors of Donald Manes's Stevenson Club, making their small firm a marriage of two of the most powerful Democratic clubs in the state.

Liberman sought out the firm because of Radow, using it to help on minor matters relating to his own commercial properties. Then, in early 1981, at Liberman's suggestion, the two attorneys got broker's licenses. In November 1981, Liberman told Radow to draw up a brokerage agreement on three properties rented to the city and owned by the same landlord, Albert Corwin. Three months later he had Radow draw up a revised agreement, this time specifying a $421,000 fee and naming Radow and Brick as the brokers. Neither had ever met the landlord, seen the properties, or reviewed the leases. Both were astonished when their secretary called them in Albany several days later and told them that three checks, totaling $210,000—the first half of the fee—had arrived at the office. Liberman had sent Corwin the revised brokerage agreement, with Board of Estimate resolutions approving each of Corwin's three multimillion-dollar leases attached to it. Radow and Brick hurriedly opened a new corporate account and deposited the checks.

At Liberman's direction, Radow and Brick then began to make a series of cash payments to him, totaling half of the brokerage payment. One way they generated cash was through a series of transactions with a mysterious shell company run by mob-tied, cash-rich businessmen suspected by federal law enforcement officials of involvement in narcotics traffic. Awaiting Liberman's periodic visits, the two young lawyers, both in their thirties, hid their cash hoard in the radiator cap in their office. A year after the first payment, Corwin sent the second $210,000, and the two again began paying Liberman.

This system worked so well that Liberman used it with other landlords, including David Twersky. In mid-1982, he got Twersky to write three checks totaling $250,000 to a leading Brooklyn Republican named Ray McKaba, who shared a law office with the minority leader of the city council. McKaba split the "fees" with Liberman.

As circuitous as he made these payoff routes, Liberman was not averse to direct cash transactions. He told one bribe-payer to meet him in front of the Jeff Club and give him $2,500 in cash, which he would later claim he gave to club officials. Another landlord, Robert Steele, dealt almost exclusively in cash payments, totaling over $50,000, most of it in envelopes wrapped in newspapers handed to Liberman in the city parking lot behind the criminal court building, a block from Liberman's office. Samuel Goldfarb paid Liberman in Krugerrands, giving him a total of sixty gold coins, worth $52,600. Liberman, who was expecting a $55,000 payment, checked that day's newspaper for a listing of the Krugerrand's exchange rate while Goldfarb waited, and then demanded the $2,400 Goldfarb had shorted him. Goldfarb paid it in cash. In another shakedown, Liberman actually agreed to initial a slip of paper every time he took a cash payment, so there would be no dispute about how much he was owed.

Especially in cash situations, but in other circumstances as well, Liberman repeatedly explained to the bribe-payers that he was not keeping all the loot himself. When he took a $20,000 payment from Steele in a parking lot in July 1981, he pointed at his beatup 1974 Chevy and asked if Steele would buy him a new one. A shocked Steele, who had just borrowed the money to make this payoff, asked why Liberman couldn't buy it himself with the cash he'd just given him. Liberman, almost matter-of-fact, explained that the cash was not for him. When Liberman first demanded a payment from Steele, he repeatedly referred to "people who had to be taken care of," demanding that Steele produce "good faith money" before the Board of Estimate voted on his lease so that Liberman could convince "the people upstairs" that Steele was "a serious person."

A doubting Steele, unconvinced that Liberman had the power to kill his lease, finally came through with the cash payment when, as Liberman predicted, the board took no action on a resolution authorizing the lease even though it was on the calendar for a vote. Steele finally understood what Liberman had meant when at their first meeting months earlier, he pointed at the photo of Meade Esposito on his office wall and told Steele that he and Meade were "close friends."

Despite this vast bribery network, Liberman lived modestly

in a Canarsie home, on the same block as Alan Silver, his fellow Jeff Club member who had become a secret partner in the taxi meter company favored by TLC chairman Jay Turoff. Though he boasted that he was rich, Liberman wore shiny plastic shoes and cheap plaid sports coats. He hid his wealth, keeping the bonds he'd extorted from property owners and the Krugerrands in a safe in his basement. Also concealed behind a drape in his basement was a furtive cache of canned food and other staples, piled up over the years in apparent preparation for some undefined future holocaust. When pressed later by a psychiatrist to explain why he'd set up this hidden grocery in his basement, he couldn't. "I know it's crazy," he said, "but I must."

Liberman's secretive bearing attracted suspicion wherever he went. Even many of his fellow clubmembers thought he was a crook, said so among themselves, and stayed away from him. Lawyers connected with the club declined his business. Capalino and other top officials at DGS said he was "up front about his sleaziness." A wary DGS inspector general, Steve Kline, had followed repeated leads he had received about Liberman, but got nowhere. When Kline confronted him about one of the allegations, involving a TLC lease, Liberman appeared wounded. "You suspect me?" he asked. "How could you wonder about me?"

But early in 1983, Steve Kline finally got a solid tip. The DGS commissioner who had replaced Capalino, Robert Litke, told Kline about a landlord who'd complained that Liberman had been shaking him down. The landlord had complained to an official at another agency, Ed Gitkind, who managed the facilities used by the Department of Environmental Protection (DEP). One of his responsibilities was to work with Liberman on any new leases DEP needed, and at that point, DEP needed a garage site in Queens for its motor pool. Liberman had been negotiating a lease for months with a garage owner, Sol Heiferman, who was an apolitical and philanthropic civic leader.

Heiferman and Gitkind had gotten to know each other in the course of their dealings over the garage site, and suddenly, in one chat, Heiferman began telling Gitkind about Liberman's insatiable appetite. The elderly Heiferman acknowledged that he had made payments to the Remsen Heights Jewish Center at Liberman's instructions, and blamed his heart attack on Liberman's relentless pressure for payoffs. It was his unwillingness to fully satisfy Liberman's greed, he said, that was holding up the lease.

A savvy political operative who had known the mayor personally for years and had backed Koch in the 1973 campaign, Gitkind did nothing with Heiferman's information for weeks. Finally, he went to Liberman's boss at DGS. It was a curious choice: he never told his own commissioner or inspector general, although that was the chain of command such information was supposed to travel. Nor did he go to DOI or to a district attorney. Subsequently, the DGS commissioner went directly to Kline, who brought the case to DOI.

DOI then decided to send a detective out on a surprise visit to Heiferman's office in Queens, and dispatched Bill Kilgallon, a longtime narcotics and homicide detective to whom corruption work was kid's stuff. As a street cop, Kilgallon had done wired dope deals on Mulberry Street in Little Italy; had handled hacked-up johns in seedy midtown hotels; and had made the first brown rock heroin purchase in Chinatown. When he walked into Heiferman's two-story brick building and found him in the back office—a small, graying man with glasses—he decided to try a street bluff. He implied that Heiferman had been overheard on a wire complaining about a shakedown. When Heiferman denied that he'd been shaken down, Kilgallon expressed skepticism and left.

Shortly after Kilgallon got back to his office, he received a call from his former boss, ex–DOI commissioner Stan Lupkin, now in private practice. Lupkin said that Kilgallon had just spoken to a client of his, Sol Heiferman, and asked if Kilgallon had indeed told Heiferman that he'd been picked up on a wire. Kilgallon, who wanted to continue using this device to get Heiferman to cooperate but wasn't willing to lie to his friend Lupkin to do it, carefully answered: "Yeah, that's what I told him."

Lupkin and Heiferman, who was a personal friend and neighbor of the former commissioner's, met the next day in Lupkin's den and discussed Heiferman's options. Lupkin's children had gone to the Solomon Schechter Hebrew Day School, which Heiferman had founded, and his wife had become the school's board president. Heiferman was almost a father to him. Lupkin was horrified when Heiferman told him the story of Liberman's shakedown.

Heiferman told Lupkin that he'd rejected Liberman's demands for cash or bonds but eventually agreed to make a $25,000 contribution to Liberman's temple. He had written the center two checks, and the co-owner of his building had written one, for a total of $17,500. Though the synagogue had immediately transferred half of these contributions to Liberman, he still would not approve the lease until he received the balance of $7,500. In the meantime, Liberman and Heiferman had begun discussing another lease, for an industrial building in Brooklyn that Heiferman owned alone. Heiferman balked at direct payments but did not resist the alternative of paying a broker selected by Liberman. Liberman had given him Raymond McKaba's name.

Lupkin worried out loud about the emotional and physical strain on the frail Heiferman if he told this story to DOI, and warned Heiferman that they might want him to wear a wire. "You mean cops and robbers?" asked Heiferman, his eyes lighting up. So Lupkin went to DOI to meet with Kilgallon, Kline, and others in the department, and they decided to use Heiferman on a number of wired phone conversations with Liberman but to try to get him out of the deal as fast as they could. Heiferman would then tell Liberman that he was too ill and that he had to turn over their negotiations to his son-in-law Sam Siegel.

Siegel was actually Sam Millman, a DOI undercover who was the antithesis of Eddie Gruskin. Millman looked like a son-in-law, with close-cropped hair, a baby face, and an accountant's suit. He projected a naïve innocence as artfully and unconsciously as Gruskin advertised sleaziness. Millman believed that Gruskin's demeanor was an invitation to graft, an implicit form of entrapment, and he studiously avoided behaving like a crook. The suspect, he said, would have to make the first move. Millman had just finished a case that caught a councilman. Now, in early May 1983, he was sent in as a replacement for Heiferman. He would have to gain Liberman's trust.

As Millman was entering the investigation, the Board of Estimate approved a temporary agreement for the lease of the Brooklyn industrial property. Heiferman subsequently got a letter from Liberman's bagman McKaba, stating that he had shown the building to the city and was entitled to a brokerage commission. The letter convinced DOI that Heiferman's information was on the mark.

For the next few months Liberman ducked Millman, speaking to him only about technical questions on the leases and making no reference to a payoff. Neither would he say anything to Heiferman in the taped phone conversations DOI arranged. Finally, on June 20, Heiferman reminded Liberman that he'd given "at least three-quarters of the money . . . at least $17,500 for the *shul*" and Liberman said he'd go along with the garage lease. When a wired Millman went to see Liberman the next day, Liberman complained that Heiferman was "stupid" for discussing money on the phone. He said that any future discussions had to take place in his office. Millman had broken the ice.

By then, an FBI unit that had targeted Meade Esposito had joined the Liberman probe. Kilgallon, DOI investigative attorney Seth Kaufman, an FBI agent, and others began having predawn meetings near Liberman's office before sending the wired Millman in for another meeting with the leasing director. Kaufman worked out scenario after scenario, anticipating every possible turn that the next conversation might take. Kilgallon and the agent also began camping out in Heiferman's office, awaiting Liberman's next call. Slowly, over the course of thirty-two taped conversations, Liberman moved toward demanding an actual payment.

On July 25, Liberman told Millman that he was getting Heiferman a dollar per square foot more on the Brooklyn rental than Heiferman had asked for—which would total an extra half-million in Heiferman's pocket over the fifteen-year life of the lease. The Board of Estimate approved the lease that day.

On August 1, in his first rambling and unguarded conversation with Millman, Liberman described the entire brokerage commission scam. After Millman provoked such candor by expressing a reluctance to pay a broker he'd never met, Liberman acknowledged that "there was no broker," yet insisted, almost in a rage, that Millman pay McKaba's fee: "This is the understanding I have with your father-in-law, and he said have an attorney send me in a commission agreement and I will gladly pay it, so I went ahead." When Millman said that Liberman was talking "in the neighborhood" of $50,000, Liberman replied: "No, fifty-seven."

Arguing that the property was unrentable until he and Heiferman cut their deal, Liberman spelled out just what he'd done to earn the payoff: "Heiferman said, Liberman, do whatever you have to do to rent the space. I don't want the building to sit empty; the tenant is moving out in January. I says, don't worry, I'll find you. I'll dig up a corpse. I dug up an agency. I prepared a resolution and the minute they went out, we went in."

Millman next introduced the subject of a third Heiferman property that needed a tenant. Liberman instantly recognized it and said that it had already been rejected by an agency that needed space. The agency had argued that any employees assigned to the 150,000-square-foot facility wouldn't be able to get there by public transportation or find a restaurant to eat lunch. "I don't take no for an answer," said Liberman. "If there's a remote possibility, I'm gonna lease this space."

Then, in the presence of Millman, Liberman called the agency that had already turned down the site.

"Molly, let me tell you something," Liberman bellowed into the phone. "When I got a job I kissed the goddam ground, and I went to work no matter how many fares I had to pay. And if I didn't have a restaurant around the corner from the place where I worked, so I walked seven blocks lunchtime to buy myself a sandwich. And they're gonna have to learn to do the same goddam thing, okay? I'm not gonna prepare restaurants for them around the corner and give them transportation. I think it's a lot of bullshit, okay?"

Liberman ended by threatening to write a detailed response to the agency's rejection letter, "and it's gonna go straight to the mayor's office."

When he got off the phone, Liberman told Millman that once he delivered a lease on this third property, it didn't matter what problems developed with the facility. "Once I feed this into the computer, all hell breaks loose. That computer never stops for the next fifteen years. It keeps throwing out a check every month." Millman asked about a price per square foot, but Liberman said the question was premature and presented his own strategy: "When I sell the idea and move down on them and says, yes, you're gonna eat this, then I will have coffee with you and I will sit down with you."

Three weeks later, when the two met again, Liberman explained that he was "holding off" on the new deal "until everything is finished" with the first two. "Let's not have three strings hanging in the air," he said, reviving the long dormant discussion of the unpaid $7,500 synagogue donation, as well as the McKaba fee. Suggesting once again that he was a collection agent for others, he said: "When I come to them and say I have

150,000 square feet from the same owner, they say, Liberman, do me a favor, will ya finish up with the other two?" He stressed how he had to go to "the borough president's office" to get Heiferman's earlier Queens lease approved, a reference to Donald Manes that he coupled with the question: "Do you think it's that easy to consummate a lease like this?"

But Liberman also stressed that he used his own arbitrary power: "The mere fact that you can walk in and talk to me like this over here don't minimize the importance of my signature on a piece of paper. I say yes, it flies. I say no, it doesn't fly. I don't care if it's your father-in-law's building or anybody else's building. The only thing he has to do is slap me once dirty here" and he showed Millman his open palm. But if he wasn't paid, he warned: "The day will come, the day of reckoning will come when you'll have to come to my office once more in this lifetime." Liberman closed the session with a simple, patronizing lesson: "You have to understand what makes Johnny run. This makes Johnny run." And he rubbed his fingers together.

On September 7, 1983, Millman delivered a $55,455 check to Liberman. It was drawn on a Heiferman account, and Kilgallon had gone to the bank with Heiferman before the check was issued to make certain that it would not be honored when McKaba deposited it. Since DOI could not cover such a large payoff with their own undercover funds, the delivery of the check meant that Liberman would have to be arrested soon.

In their final conversation before the bust, Liberman and Millman again discussed their new deal. "We're talking big money—a half-million dollars a year in rent," Liberman estimated, offering a twenty-year lease. He said Millman would have to pay 6 percent of the total lease amount to a broker or some other designee of his. Liberman and Millman computed the bribe together, and arrived at a half-million-dollar figure, but Liberman offered to inflate the lease to cover the bribe. "You and I are going to get along very well," Liberman said.

A few days later, Kilgallon and the FBI task force director on the Esposito case, Sid Casperson, waited for Liberman to arrive at the parking lot where he had taken cash bribes. Liberman always appeared between 6:30 and 7:30 A.M. They wanted to pick him up without anyone's being aware of it, because they believed they had him so cold he would agree to cooperate and that they could wire him for conversations with bigger targets. For everyone in the case, from DOI to the FBI, the elusive

Meade, who had survived a lifetime of probes, was the goal. When Liberman arrived, they quickly arrested him.

Once at the U.S. Attorney's office in Brooklyn, Liberman declared that he wanted a lawyer. Kilgallon told him: "Do yourself one favor. Get a lawyer who will look out for you, not someone else." But like Ryan, Liberman turned instinctively to the machine and said he wanted George Meissner. Casperson again advised him: "Meissner's a member of the club. Think about it." But Liberman insisted, Meissner was called, and the investigators knew from that moment on that Liberman would not cooperate. Meissner was Esposito's personal attorney and had served briefly as the Canarsie district leader. He was also a partner with Liberman in a flea market.

By the time Liberman was arraigned late that afternoon, the banks were closed, so he had to send his son home to get bearer bonds hidden in the basement safe to bail him out. His wife didn't know how to get the bonds out of the safe or, apparently, even that he had secreted them there. Not even a signatory on some of his biggest bank accounts, she had no idea how wealthy her husband was. Indeed, investigators would later learn that when she asked for new curtains, Liberman poormouthed her.

Once Meissner arrived, Liberman was brought into a conference room and, surrounded by seven or eight law enforcement officials, told that his conversations with Heiferman and Millman had been taped. The government, which knew only about Liberman's shakedown of Heiferman at that point, offered to allow Liberman to plead to a single mail fraud count with the maximum possible sentence of five years if he would help them make other cases. Liberman protested that he knew nothing, that the Millman deals were his only questionable transactions. He and Meissner appeared stunned when questions about Esposito were raised, and said that "Mr. Esposito" had nothing to do with such "little people" as Liberman. They expressed disbelief that the government actually thought Liberman and Esposito knew each other well.

Both sides walked out of the room and went directly to work. As soon as Liberman was released on bail, he called one of his phony brokers and instructed him to call back on a public phone. He told the broker to go to the landlord who had made the bogus commission payments, David Twersky, and get him to support their story that the broker had done legitimate work on the deal. The broker agreed, but Twersky refused. So, the day after his arrest, Liberman contacted Twersky himself, asked to meet him near his Canarsie house, and insisted that if Twersky were questioned about the five checks to the fictitious names, he should claim they were contractors. When Twersky asked about the $250,000 payment to the phony broker Mc-Kaba, Liberman replied: "Hell with him—he's an Arab." (McKaba is in fact of Syrian descent.)

Finally, when Liberman suggested that Twersky take back the $25,000 in State of Israel bonds, Twersky refused and replied, "I am going to tell the truth." The next morning, when Twersky arrived at his office, he found the bonds stuffed in his mailbox.

On the day of Liberman's arrest, DOI and FBI investigators also visited the Remsen Heights Jewish Center to review its records. When Liberman arrived the following day, temple officials told him he was too late. Informed that the agents had noticed that the entries relating to the liquor disbursements had the initials A.L. next to them, Liberman told the group that, if asked, they should say that Liberman picked up the liquor for the synagogue. But more important than the liquor entries, the temple records taken by Kilgallon also contained a list of landlords whose contributions to the temple had been attributed to Liberman. Kilgallon and assistant U.S. Attorney Ken McCallion began matching that list with city leases. In every instance, the dates coincided.

The investigators also got an unexpected break when Meissner wrote a letter to the Department of General Services asking to review their files on about a dozen leases Liberman had negotiated. DOI's Seth Kaufman, a tenacious digger whose decade of work at the department had equipped him with a mental list of every suspect city bureaucrat and clubhouse pol, used Meissner's letter as a road map. With the Meissner and Remsen Heights lists in hand, Kilgallon and company fanned out over the city, surprising landlords with sudden visits.

When confronted, landlords and brokers immediately cooperated. McKaba, a wealthy, skiing bachelor in his late fifties, just said "Ya got me" when approached. Tracking McKaba's brokerage fees brought them to Twersky, who also opened up. The synagogue donations led them to Albert Corwin, and he immediately named Saul Radow and Helaine Brick, together with another broker he'd paid. When Radow told the probers about his cash kickbacks to Liberman, the pattern rang a bell with Kilgallon, who retrieved a scrap of paper he'd found in Liberman's wallet on the day he was arrested. Scratched on it were a series of dates and amounts that matched Radow's account exactly.

The biggest of the immunized bribe-payers was Seymour Cohn, the principal owner of Sylvan Lawrence, Inc., a major force in Manhattan real estate. The company and its principals, who leased more office space to the city than any other landlord, had given Koch $40,000 in campaign contributions and let him run his gubernatorial campaign rent free out of one of their buildings. It had been no less generous with other city officials—giving Comptroller Jay Goldin $178,000 (he had never audited one of their leases) and Manhattan borough president Andrew Stein the free and exclusive use of Cohn's luxurious Hamptons home for a summer, a personal benefit valued at more than $50,000 and the subject of a previous, critical DOI report. The investigators found that Cohn had also kicked back $150,000 to Liberman, and was a major source of Jeff Club ad purchases and contributions through Liberman.

But potentially more important than the Lawrence payoffs was the information the investigators gathered about George Klein, whose designation to do the office tower development in the multibillion-dollar Times Square project made him the city's most prominent developer. The synagogue records indicated that Klein, a nationally prominent Republican donor friendly with President Reagan, had contributed $5,000 to the synagogue after Liberman leased three floors in a dilapidated Brooklyn building of Klein's that had not had a tenant in a decade. When Klein was confronted by Kilgallon and an FBI agent at his Park Avenue office, he admitted he had handed Liberman the check but insisted it was unconnected with the lease he and Liberman had just negotiated.

Klein also had discussions with Liberman who was seeking a $100,000 brokerage payment on the Brooklyn lease for a broker unknown to Klein. When Liberman's broker died a month later, Klein took seven months before finally rejecting the widow's, Liberman-backed, claim for payment. Assistant U.S. Attorney Ken McCallion did not give Klein immunity or put him before the grand jury. Instead he decided that if Liberman ever cooperated, they might try to make a case against Klein (they never did).

One other property owner with a lucrative city lease who had made two contributions to Liberman's temple was Donald Manes's close friend and favorite developer, Michael Lazar. DOI ultimately put Klein and Lazar under oath, but their repeated denials that their contributions were connected with city leases made them unusable in the Liberman case, and meant that, unlike the landlords who conceded that Liberman had shaken them down, the two would not be named as bribe-payers in the new, omnibus indictment announced in early 1984.

The indictment against Liberman ran to thirty counts and included $2.5 million in actual and attempted extortions. The Public Integrity Division of the Justice Department announced that it was "the largest extortion case ever brought against a public official by the government." Almost a million dollars in bribes went to Liberman himself, with a half-million going to his designated brokers. Another million was extorted, but never received, such as the Millman deal discussed just before the undercover operation was brought down. The government also charged Liberman with several obstruction-of-justice felonies. In his memo on these charges, U.S. Attorney Ray Dearie described Liberman as the "ultimate arch thief and extortionist, the very personification of public corruption."

Despite the extraordinary scope of the Liberman case, it was barely noticed in the New York daily press. The *Post* gave it six paragraphs, the *News* nine, and the *Times* fifteen; the papers put it inconspicuously inside their local coverage. Ed Koch was asked if he wanted to join the press conference announcing the indictment, but he uncharacteristically declined. DOI's press release contained a short quotation from the mayor, praising it for its role in the case. No reporters pressed the mayor about how Liberman was able to get control of the leasing bureau and turn it into a "racketeering enterprise," as the indictment called it. The daily stories also made no mention of Liberman's ties to Esposito.

Koch had actually been briefed about the case sometime before it surfaced by DOI commissioner Pat McGinley. By the time the final indictment was announced, McGinley had made a point of telling Koch that "the conduct of the landlords" was as bad if not worse than Liberman's, citing specifically the involvement of the city's biggest leasor, Sylvan Lawrence. McGinley had also briefed the mayor explicitly about the conduct of the powerful developer George Klein. He wanted Koch, whose close ties to Klein were public knowledge, to be aware that Klein "did business" with Liberman, as he put it in his private meeting with the mayor.

Noting Liberman's clubhouse ties, McGinley also told Koch that the leasing director "may well have information about other people who come from that club, including other city officials." McGinley mentioned Esposito in particular because he believed he should inform Koch about "cases that might implicate some of his friends," so that the mayor could avoid "potentially embarrassing relationships." The mayor had little reaction to the Liberman news from McGinley, assuring him that the city would consider legal options in dealing with the bribe-paying landlords.

The Liberman connection to Meade was well known to John LoCicero and the political wing at City Hall. But none of them saw Liberman's greed as a reflection on Esposito, or thought his conduct should diminish City Hall's enthusiasm for job applicants referred by the Brooklyn boss. The relationship between City Hall and Esposito was not even disturbed by the repeated written statements of prosecutors that they did not believe Liberman was acting on his own. Ray Dearie referred publicly to the "likelihood," on the basis of information in the government's possession, that "in fact the cooperation of other public officials was essential to the success of Liberman's corrupt practices."

The government took an even stronger stand in meetings with Liberman's new attorney, Tom Puccio, the former head of the federal organized crime unit. As Puccio wrote in a defense memorandum, prosecutors had taken the position that Liberman "would have been unable to wield such tremendous arbitrary authority without the complicity of others in the Brooklyn Democratic machine." Puccio added, "the government suggests that since Liberman knew or knows 'powerhouses' in the Thomas Jefferson Club, his corrupt activities were done at their bidding."

In the aftermath of the Liberman case, the city made no move to cancel any of the leases that had been corruptly negotiated. Instead, it gave new leases to some of the same landlords identified by the government as bribe-payers and co-conspirators, including Seymour Cohn. McCallion was contacted by state leasing officials, asking him what sort of safeguards they should institute to see to it that their own lease processes weren't susceptible to corruption, but their local counterparts didn't call.*

The mayor also reappointed George Klein to an unsalaried post at the city's United Nations Development Corp., and his chief of staff actually called DOI's McGinley to ask him if the agency could make an exception of Klein, and not require him to comply with the financial disclosure portion of DOI's routine background questionnaire for all appointees. The city proceeded with Klein's Times Square project as if nothing had happened, delivering to him, with the state, one of the greatest grab bags of tax abatements ever assembled for a private project.

Finally, the city failed to take any action on a charge in the federal indictment that implicated another top official in a Liberman scam. The count focused on a $5,000 cash payoff that a pharmacist who cooperated with the government conceded he had made to Liberman. The city official apparently involved in the fraud with Liberman was transportation commissioner Tony Ameruso's executive assistant, Joel Stahl. The pharmacist wanted to stop DGS from selling a parking lot adjacent to his Brooklyn drugstore, which he was renting cheaply from the city. Liberman had no authority to block such a sale, but he came up with a strategy to prevent it.

Liberman was a friend of Tony Ameruso's, and the two lunched together often. He took Ameruso on trips upstate and bought him expensive suits. He saw Ameruso sometimes at the Sunday breakfasts at Meade's mother's house. Ameruso had hired Liberman's son-in-law, and given him a top managerial job at the scandal-ridden Bureau of Ferries and General Aviation.

It was Ameruso's aide, Stahl, who in September 1980 wrote DGS asking that the pharmacist's lot not be auctioned, claiming that the transportation department was conducting a feasibility study to determine if the land should be turned into a municipal parking lot. Liberman used the document to extort a $2,500 payment from the pharmacist. A year later, Stahl wrote a sec-

---

*The only affirmative action the city took was to file suit in 1985 against Liberman and the landlords and brokers, seeking civil damages.

ond letter, saying that the feasibility study "had not yet been completed." In fact, as the investigators noted in their pre-sentencing memo in the Liberman case, "no feasibility study was ever conducted or even considered by the Department of Transportation." Liberman nonetheless used the second letter to collect a second payment, and the lot was never auctioned.

It was the story of this parking lot that had initially drawn the FBI into the Liberman probe. The Bureau had first heard about the scam from a confidential informant close to Esposito, who claimed that the county leader had helped broker the deal. The pharmacist wound up cooperating with the government, but Stahl wasn't helpful. When McCallion closed down the Liberman case, he discussed the Stahl matter with DOI and received assurances that the agency would pursue it, but nothing ever happened.

The Stahl letters were merely the latest in a series of probes that raised suspicions about Ameruso. His award of special no-parking privileges to a Little Italy restaurant run by Matty the Horse Ianniello had alerted DOI and the State Investigation Commission (SIC). His handling of towing contracts had prompted damaging audits, lawsuits that featured charges of a political cartel (represented by Donald Manes's ex–law partner), and at least one state investigation. But the mayor stuck with Ameruso, despite repeated pressures from his top deputies to replace him. And he just as doggedly stuck with Ameruso's political sponsor, Esposito, ignoring the evidence that two Esposito appointees—Ameruso and Liberman—might have been associated in the same extortion plot. Just as City Hall had dismissed Esposito's connections with the scandals of the first term—Fossella at BSA, Goodman at the navy yard, and Tracy and Mazzeo at the ferry bureau—it was undisturbed by the party boss's associations with the Liberman and Ameruso scandals of the second term.

In June 1984, Alex Liberman pleaded guilty to racketeering charges, agreeing to forfeit $500,000 to the government and facing up to twenty years in prison. Tom Puccio wrote an impassioned presentencing memo to Judge Joseph McLaughlin, detailing dramatically Liberman's history under the Nazis and including a psychologist's report that Liberman was suicidal. Between his arrest and his sentencing, the unemployed Liberman had put on twenty-seven pounds, drinking himself to bed each night.

Puccio also submitted a handful of letters on Liberman's behalf, including one from the Remsen Heights Jewish Center rabbi, commending Liberman for his generosity, but it had been written in 1968. In fact, the government's check of the synagogue records revealed that other than the kickback contributions Liberman had fostered, he never gave more than $200 to the temple. The only rabbi who wrote a letter for Liberman dated later than the 1960s was one recruited by the still-loyal Esposito, who also produced a letter from the pastor of a Brooklyn church.

At a hearing before McLaughlin on September 11, the government attorney, McCallion, hammered away at Liberman's stoic refusal to cooperate, asking McLaughlin for the maximum sentence. McLaughlin, citing the need to deter other public officials, almost granted the government's request, giving the stunned Liberman twelve years—one of the toughest sentences ever handed out in a New York corruption case. Puccio then moved to hold the sentence in abeyance pending psychiatric reports from the Bureau of Prisons about the likelihood of a Liberman suicide. McLaughlin granted the motion, and Liberman began months of observation.

On April 12, 1985, forty years and one day after Liberman was freed from a Nazi concentration camp, he was before Judge McLaughlin again for final sentencing. "This defendant is asking for mercy," his new lawyer, Jay Goldberg, pleaded. "He stood before another government and asked for its mercy forty years ago. He got no mercy. His parents got no mercy. His brother and sister got no mercy."

Goldberg's strongest weapon before McLaughlin, however, was the psychiatric report issued by the Bureau of Prisons. One doctor, supported by others, concluded: "While I do not believe his Holocaust experiences excuse his antisocial behavior, I do believe that they, coupled with his current financial, social, political, spiritual, relational, and emotional demise, will accomplish what the Nazis did not, his death."

McCallion answered that the prison bureau found, just as the prosecutors had, "a particularly manipulative individual who very often lied to the staff and attempted to pit one staff member against the other." He reiterated the government's belief that Liberman was withholding information about the criminal activities of others.

McLaughlin, noting that Liberman's crimes were "a carefully contrived plot where many people were manipulated for many years," modified the sentence in one respect: he would not require Liberman to serve a minimum prison term (usually one-third of the sentence); he would be eligible for parole at any time. The new terms of the sentence created an incentive for Liberman to cooperate.

So Liberman began a bizarre odyssey, weaving through the federal prison system, moving again and again because he alternately teased and then stonewalled prosecutors, cooperating ever so slightly at the beginning of his prison term, then opening up more, but never coming completely clean. His suicide threat was a hoax: after Auschwitz, Allenwood could never kill him. His son managed his commercial real estate empire, while he defaulted on the remainder of the forfeiture funds he had agreed to pay the federal government.

Liberman told the prosecutors, during debriefings that went on for days, that he'd kept his cash bribes in the trunk of his car, and had parked it, cash and all, in the airport lot for weeks at a time, while he vacationed at his summer condo in Florida. He said that he removed $250,000 from the trunk after he was arrested, all of it still concealed in the original wrappers given him by bribe-paying landlords, and used it to pay the fine levied on him by McLaughlin.

His rationale for his corrupt activity was that he was in a sea of "sharks"—his own description of the major real estate moguls. He insisted that he had always negotiated leases that were in the city's interest. All he wanted to do, he said, was to harpoon the sharks. Liberman detailed thirty-five separate criminal allegations against a wide variety of politicians, leading citizens, developers, and others; most would never be investigated. Because of his cooperation, one more day in the sun awaited him—when Donald Manes's bloody scandal would make what Alex knew so important that the government would cut a deal for it.

When the Liberman case broke in late 1983, Meade Esposito was embarrassed. He started telling friends that he knew Liberman was a crook and that he'd been warning the city about Alex for years. Behind this public bluster, he quietly gathered letters for Liberman's presentencing submission to the judge. It wasn't just Liberman that had Meade percolating, however, for by the beginning of 1984, the Esposito gang was awash in criminal cases.

Three of its loyal district leaders were under indictment, including one, Vander Beatty, who doubled as a state senator and had been charged in three different cases. He had already been convicted of orchestrating the forgery of thousands of voter registration cards at the Brooklyn Board of Elections in an attempt to steal the election for the congressional seat vacated by Shirley Chisholm. In addition to this trio of troubled leaders, the husband of a fourth had recently pleaded guilty to federal tax charges, lost his supervisory post with the state tax department, and been sentenced to a two-year jail term.

One Brooklyn congressman, Fred Richmond, was in a federal penitentiary, having pleaded guilty to a wide variety of charges, including payoffs for navy repair contracts for Esposito's second-largest insurance client, Coastal Dry Dock. Richmond's plea prompted the forced resignation of one of the top civilian officials of the U.S. Naval Sea Systems Command, whose daughter's college tuition was subsidized by Richmond in exchange for inside information for Coastal's use in winning repair contracts at the Brooklyn Navy Yard. The Richmond case had launched a full-scale federal probe of Coastal's navy contracts.

Another close associate of Esposito's, Tony Buffalano, a former law secretary to a state judge, was convicted of taking $3,500 from a wired federal informant and promising to use it to bribe a federal judge. Buffalano revealed at his sentencing hearing that the prosecutors had promised him leniency if he would wear a wire on Meade Esposito. What City Hall knew, and the reporters who covered Buffalano's explosive sentencing hearing did not know, was that at the very time in 1982 that Buffalano was taped by prosecutors discussing coke deals and bribery schemes, the beefy assistant district attorney was under consideration for appointment as the police department's deputy commissioner for trials. An aide to John LoCicero had sent the police commissioner referral letters seeking Buffalano's selection. LoCicero's office was fully aware of Buffalano's ties to Esposito.

Once prosecutors learned of Buffalano's possible appointment, they called the police commissioner and warned him to stay away from Buffalano (he said he wasn't picking Buffalano anyway). LoCicero was questioned by prosecutors about the referral. But, like the rest of these early warnings, the administration's toying with the appointment of Buffalano to this sensitive post set off no Esposito alarms at City Hall.

Meade's greatest problem during this period, though, came in mid-1983, when he figured out that the government finally had a pigeon. Early that year, the FBI had begun listening to a loquacious and well-connected informant, a disbarred Brooklyn attorney named Spencer Lader, who had married into the upper echelons of the county party. Lader's wife was the niece of Shirley Weiner, the Jeff Club's female district leader. First elected with Meade back in 1960, she also held the titles of vice chair of the county party and deputy clerk of the Brooklyn Supreme Court. Lader, indicted on fraud scams totaling $600,000, had brutally cheated some of Meade's closest friends, and then, faced with some tough state time, had decided to plead guilty and cooperate.

Some of the Lader schemes provided penetrating evidence of the Esposito gang's inside track at City Hall. For example, Lader had convinced other highrolling insiders, including another Weiner relative and a Brooklyn civil court judge, that they should put up front money to buy city-owned properties that Lader said he could get at bargain-basement prices because of Jeff Club hooks inside the Koch administration. In fact, the city did not own the properties Lader was marketing, but the perception of Esposito's and Weiner's influence at City Hall was so pervasive that he lassoed a half-dozen investors, promising a fast turnaround on the properties and large profits.

The 31-year-old hustler became such a familiar figure at City Hall that when impressing a potential customer in one of his real estate scams, he could park in the spot next to the mayor's in the City Hall lot and walk into the offices of top DGS officials, one of whom actually got on the floor with him and searched maps for the properties Lader was shucking.

Convinced by his early polygraph results, the FBI and Ray Dearie began debriefing him. He helped them almost immediately on a high-society Philadelphia mob murder contracted through a politically connected Brooklyn private detective. He gave them one count against Liberman, involving the drugstore parking lot. And Lader's information about Shirley Weiner's no-show job at Brooklyn Supreme Court led to a stakeout which determined that Weiner almost never went to work. Weiner was allowed to plead, repaid a portion of her salary, and resigned. Lader, though, would eventually burn himself out with the feds, misleading them on a murder case. He wound up discarded, and did his time in the roughest state prisons.

In addition to all these cases so close to him, Meade Esposito was haunted by one of his own. While not criminal, it was a protracted civil action that Meade knew he would ultimately lose, costing him his county leadership. Back in 1978, the state attorney general had brought suit charging that Esposito's mortgage, insurance, and printing businesses were all illegally involved in a Long Island racetrack, violating a state law that barred party leaders from doing business with tracks regulated by the state. The penalty was forfeiture of office.

The court record of the suit against Esposito was a scandal. Judge after judge had granted Esposito's lawyers stay after stay. At one point a state judge had dismissed the suit on the inventive grounds that Meade was not actually the county leader but merely chairman of the county's executive committee, an obscene ruling it took years for two appellate courts to reverse unanimously.

Finally, after five years of masterful delays, Esposito was forced to testify. But his lawyers said he was legally blind and couldn't read the documents he was shown. His memory was so bad he drew blanks again and again. His lawyers would not permit him to answer certain questions intended to resolve the issue of whether or not he performed the functions of a county leader, such as: "Can you tell us whom you recommended to the mayor for jobs?" In late 1983, he was at last ordered to answer the questions and produce his business records.

In the midst of these court and prosecutorial pressures, Meade hired a PR man and granted a lengthy interview to the *Daily News*. Asked about the FBI probes, Esposito boasted: "The only way they can get a guy like me is by setting me up or framing me. These fucking FBI guys have some nerve. A lot of them tried it over the years. I defy anybody to point a finger at me and say, 'You did this.' "

The boss also described Ed Koch as "about the best of the lot of the mayors" he'd known and said Koch was "a good friend" who "came up to hold my hand in the fucking hospital" when Esposito had a severe intestinal disorder in 1980. "Every call I make to him," Esposito announced, "he always calls me right back." He also explained his mayoral and gubernatorial endorsements of Koch over Cuomo. "I waited three days for this guy Cuomo to call me in 1977. He never called. Then I got a call from the Koch people." And in 1982: "Guys like me couldn't go for Cuomo," he said. "Hell, I've got to have doors open for me to service my constituency. The patronage system, a lot of people laugh at it, but it's very important to any organization. It keeps it going."

During the same period, Esposito appeared at a Sheraton Center forum sponsored by the *New York Post.* All five of the city's Democratic leaders were present; but when asked, only Esposito and his longtime colleague, Staten Island's Nick LaPorte, were willing to endorse Koch for reelection in 1985. Stanley Friedman and Donald Manes took the position that it was too early, two years before the next election, to commit themselves. Friedman said that it would be a bad political move to come out for Koch now: "any pot of money lying around" in 1984 or the spring of 1985 would "not go to the borough that's already in somebody's pocket."

News stories revealed several days later that the mayor had "passed on his feelings of disappointment to Manes and Friedman" and "expressed his appreciation to Esposito and LaPorte." The mayor also rebutted Friedman's pot-of-gold statement: "Most people don't realize that this administration is pretty unique in running a city without using patronage." The same day that the mayor's gratitude to Meade was reported, the new indictment of Alex Liberman, superseding the first set of charges and raising his extortion total into the millions, was unsealed. But neither this nor any other message from the criminal side of Meade's life mattered at City Hall. The boss could blow away the criminal cloud that hung over his organization with a single word of praise.

In January 1984, Meade Esposito called a press conference at a restaurant in Brooklyn, and resigned. No daily newspaper or TV station mentioned the indictments that engulfed his organization or the probes and suits that threatened him personally. He was serenaded, rather, with complimentary editorials. He anointed borough president Howard Golden to succeed him, which meant that Golden, like Donald Manes, would hold the most powerful city and party posts in his county.

The announcement stunned Tony Genovesi, the district leader from the Jeff Club, who'd been promised the leadership for years and as recently as the weekend before the Golden endorsement. A tearful, embittered Genovesi, betrayed by his mentor with no explanation, decided that he would challenge Golden when the succession came to a vote among the party's district leaders in February. Genovesi's camp told reporters that Meade had bypassed Genovesi because he "would not do business Meade's way." This analysis of Meade's character, repeated by those who knew him best, was the theme at City Hall, which served as a virtual headquarters for the Genovesi campaign.

Ed Koch, who had become so close to Genovesi that he'd run the mayor's field operations in two campaigns, worked the phones personally for him, pressuring district leaders who held city jobs. But Meade's clout among the party insiders was too much for Genovesi and Koch. Vander Beatty, the leader with three criminal cases, cast the deciding vote for Golden just days before trooping off to jail. When Genovesi lost a second attempt to defeat Golden that summer, the mayor moved quickly to patch up his differences with Esposito and Golden.

That May the Brooklyn machine threw Meade a farewell party, making him guest of honor at their annual dinner dance. On the dais were Ameruso, City Hall aide Joe DeVincenzo, Housing Authority chairman Joe Christian, and the mayor. Donald Manes, Stanley Friedman, Mario Biaggi, Jay Turoff, Carmine DeSapio, and a host of top city officials appeared. Four of the landlords who had paid off Alex Liberman, including Seymour Cohn of Sylvan Lawrence and Albert Corwin, the largest bribe-payer, bought tickets. There was a table of PVB contractors, including Datacom's Joe DeLario and Citisource's Marvin Kaplan. The Longshoremen were listed, as were Marion and Roseann Scotto, the mother and daughter of the jailed ILA leader. Roy Cohn and Donald Trump shared a table, next to the crowd from Coastal Dry Dock. Meade was going out among friends. Only tough Tony Genovesi and his wing of the Jeff Club failed to show.

With his own anointed successor in place, Meade thought he had the best of both worlds: influence without investigations.

Within days after Alex Liberman lost his suicide appeal for a reduced sentence and went off to federal prison, in April 1985, the mayor released his just-filed 1984 tax returns. The figures were a striking commentary on what had become of his mayoralty. He collected a city salary of $111,601, more than any other mayor in the country and far more than the $60,000 he'd earned when he took office, before he could give himself a raise. But Koch had also earned another $205,185 in fees for personal appearances and for writing a book. *Mayor,* co-written with his press secretary, appeared in January 1984 and rapidly rose to the top of the bestseller list, where it remained for twenty-one weeks.

Mayor did not mention Alex Liberman, Herb Ryan, or Rick Mazzeo. Meade Esposito was named once, for his assistance in the appointment of the schools chancellor. Donald Manes appeared only because he and the mayor had competed in a weight-loss contest in 1980. The sole reference to Stanley Friedman was a critical assessment of his patronage delivery of summer youth jobs during the Beame years, quickly compensated for by a parenthetical bow to him as "one of the smartest, ablest, most loyal people I know." This trio went unmentioned in the mayor's "no-holds-barred" chronicle because virtually everyone who was discussed was ridiculed, blasted, or blamed. Even Koch's friends, such as loyal aide John LoCicero, came in for criticism.

The bulk of *Mayor* was written in the year after Koch's gubernatorial debacle, when even those close to him said he was so crushed he "could only talk about himself." It may have been that depression that accounted for Pat McGinley's feeling that he was "intruding" when he broke through the Koch haze with the disturbing 1983 news about Esposito's man Liberman and the landlords. Koch had spent two successive years campaigning—for mayor and then for governor—followed by a year of pouring his spleen onto the printed page. He hardly had the time, let alone the inclination, to undertake an in-house ethics check of his government and his political relationships.

Koch claimed, in the concluding chapter of his book, that he had come to terms with his loss to Cuomo. In truth, however, his gubernatorial aspirations were only a prelude to an imaginary national candidacy that had long run through Ed Koch's mind. He could envision himself at center stage as a national political force, possibly a vice presidential nominee. It was hard, after all the media speculation about these grand ambitions, for Koch to come back to earth, where Alex Liberman and Meade Esposito lived. But with the blockbuster success of his book, he could go on floating above the daily tedium. He could be a cocky celebrity again, and take possession, at least temporarily, of what he had always wanted, a national stage.

The closing words of *Mayor,* written in late 1983, took Koch "on to the battle of the third term," adding that lately he'd been saying: "Eight good years deserve four more." In fact, he had been mayor for only six years and was only halfway through his second term. He had two years of governing to go before the next election, but terms in office had become interludes between campaigns to him. Vindication at the polls was the only motivation that could get him to work. This combination—the 1982 race, the postdefeat depression, the book, the new celebrity status, and the obsession about a 1985 win—created a second-term moral vacuum at City Hall, when the petty compromises of the first term loomed larger and the clubhouse sharks moved in for the kill.

CHAPTER EIGHT

Twin Towers

DONALD MANES AND STANLEY FRIEDMAN spent their teenage summers in the Catskills, working as waiters. But while Manes's father owned a fifty-unit bungalow colony, a farm, and a natural swimminghole near the Tamarack Lodge where Donald worked, the senior Friedman was back in the hot city driving a cab and Stanley lived on the tips he hustled at a hotel. Both young men went to Brooklyn Law School, just a year apart, with the son of the taxi driver finishing near the top of his class and the son of the well-to-do dairy distributor near the bottom.

Manes began his career in politics as an instant success, winning a city council seat and founding his own club. He was the beneficiary of a network of hereditary political connections to power brokers at the top of the citywide Democratic leadership,* plus his father-in-law's electrical union and grassroots contacts within the council district. Friedman, in contrast, was a clubhouse grunt whose politically active father sent him

---

*David Malbin, a Brooklyn Supreme Court judge tied to the top leadership of the county party, was Manes's father's closest friend and became Manes's adopted uncle. Malbin carefully guided Manes's political career, getting him on Abe Beame's citywide slate in 1966, though Manes was an unknown insurgent for a vacant council seat. A Manes adviser until his death in 1980, Malbin was indicted in the 1970s on a federal conspiracy charge involving the acceptance of a Miami trip from a union that had a matter before him. The federal judge who eventually dismissed the case criticized Malbin for "back scratching."

across the street to the regular organization storefront while he was in law school. He sat in the club one night a week for years, listening to citizen complaints about sewer clogs and traffic lights, making out white index cards on each constituent, and trying to jolt the city into responding to at least some of the problems.

Friedman eventually graduated from a series of low-level patronage jobs, including one as an assistant district attorney in the Bronx secured by his club, to becoming associate counsel to David Ross, the majority leader of the city council and the dominant figure in Friedman's Bronx club. Friedman's first day at the council, January 1, 1966, was the same day that Manes was sworn in as a city councilman.

In 1971, Donald Manes became Queens borough president without having to compete for what was the most powerful public office in the county. The position was his prize in an inside game played out among the several dozen politicians who controlled the county cartel; the incumbent was enticed with a judgeship into resigning, and Manes got the appointment. Friedman by then was midway through his eight years as a council staffer, and secretary of the Bronx Democratic Party, making him Pat Cunningham's top aide and apparent successor as county leader. Both careers were on the clubhouse fast track—Friedman as an in-house mover of the party's contracts, Manes as the party's public face.

Friedman had also attracted the attention of law enforcement for the first time, becoming a DOI target. Acting as the city council's liaison with the transportation department, he had helped draft the legislation that created its Parking Violations Bureau. After convincing the bureau to hire his father as its administrative assistant, he began sending selected parking tickets to him, and the elder Friedman was caught fixing them. Friedman beat the case when his father died six months after the probe began, leaving Stanley with the option of claiming he had no idea what his father was doing with the tickets he was giving him.

"Had Moe Friedman not expired," the DOI report concluded in 1972, "the facts developed in this case would certainly require referral to the D.A.'s office for a determination as to whether they warranted criminal prosecution of Moe Friedman or any other persons." Stanley Friedman's sworn testimony before DOI was described in the report as having "strained credulity," and his conduct was found to have been "improper."

At the same time as the DOI report on Friedman was completed, Manes and his deputy Robert Groh were engaged in a series of campaign financing activities that would soon attract the attention of prosecutors. The solicitation of a $10,000 Manes contribution from a developer seeking a zoning variance for an airport motel would eventually lead to Groh's indictment. Seven thousand dollars was actually contributed to Manes through conduits, and the borough president narrowly averted indictment himself.

In September 1974, Abe Beame pushed enough district leaders to make Donald Manes the county leader of Queens, and two months later, Beame named Stanley Friedman deputy mayor. During the remainder of the Beame mayoralty, Friedman, who presided at Board of Estimate meetings, and Manes, one of the board's most powerful members, collaborated on deal after deal. One example was the plan for an amusement park on city-owned land on Staten Island advanced by one of Manes's closest friends, developer Marty Swarzman. In 1976, Manes, described by the *Staten Island Advance* newspaper as "the prime mover" in the amusement park deal, met with Beame development officials and Swarzman at his Borough Hall office and selected a site that abutted on land owned by the law partner of his former deputy Bob Groh.

When Staten Island elected officials raised objections to the plan at a Board of Estimate meeting, Friedman, according to the *Advance*, "began to fight for the developer's cause, hammering away at the park's economic advantages." At one point Friedman, who was then living in a luxury apartment in an East Side Swarzman building, set up a meeting for Swarzman with a leading opponent of the project, city council president Paul O'Dwyer. Swarzman told O'Dwyer that if the city didn't approve his project soon, he was going to take it to Edgewater, a small town in New Jersey right across the river from Manhattan. The exposure of a phony appraisal of the city site, the mob links of the arcade operator selected by Swarzman, and the start of state senate hearings probing the deal eventually combined to kill the Staten Island proposal.

A subsequent financial disclosure statement filed by Manes revealed that he acquired a half-million-dollar interest in the Edgewater project, joining Swarzman and the same two partners who had first proposed the Staten Island park. Friedman also eventually acknowledged having become a business partner of Swarzman's, contending, like Manes, that it wasn't until a couple of years after the demise of the Staten Island project. A multimillionaire, Swarzman owned three houses, a dozen racehorses, planes, a yacht, and a helicopter. In fact, it was on the tennis court at Swarzman's Hamptons home that Manes first introduced a friend of his, Geoffrey Lindenauer, to Friedman. In the early 1970s, a few years after this meeting, Manes brought Lindenauer to Friedman at City Hall and got the then deputy mayor to give Lindenauer a city job.

By the second year of Koch's first term, Manes and Friedman virtually owned party politics in their boroughs. Manes had the advantage of leading a middle-class county that had replaced Brooklyn as the largest Democratic constituency in the country, while Friedman controlled an area that was part prairie and part occupied by the nonvoting poor. Although the Bronx was the weak sister of the city's tricounty party structures, Friedman had a way of making do. Like the ballhawking, five-foot-seven-inch college basketball guard he once was, Friedman played politics with a boldness that made him seem larger than life. With a kingmaker capacity to raise political money, he had become the luminary of deals, sought after because he had just the right mix of connections and intuition to make the unlikely happen.

The two party potentates bought luxurious homes in the Hamptons only a few miles apart, and spent their summers playing and partying together. Their lives were increasingly intertwined; they shared an election day palmcard in the 1981 and 1982 Democratic primaries, backing the same citywide and statewide candidates, with the mayor at the top of the ticket. And ironically, when their candidate lost the gubernatorial race in 1982, their hold on city government, especially in the moral vacuum of the immediate aftermath of the Koch defeat, grew even stronger. They had become the twin towers of insider trading.

As early as the spring of 1982, while the gubernatorial race was in full swing, these career bookends began to formalize their long-standing casual partnership in municipal plunder. Their target was the biggest contract ever handed out by the city department that Friedman through his father had once corrupted and that Manes, through his agent Lindenauer, now controlled: the Parking Violations Bureau. This coveted $22 million contract was for a portable computer that traffic enforcement agents could use to record every ticket they issued. The corporate vehicle they would set up to seek the contract had no assets, no employees, no computer, and, as they conceded in their own prospectus, "no history of operations." The leverage they would need to give the shell company credibility was the clout the two bosses had inside the government of their colleague, Ed Koch.

Their attempt to win the PVB contract originated with Friedman soon after he, Manes, and the other county leaders met at City Hall to endorse Koch's gubernatorial candidacy in April 1982. Within a week of that publicized endorsement Friedman arranged a meeting with the first deputy commissioner at the Department of Transportation (DOT), Larry Yermack, who'd just been installed as City Hall's efficiency expert inside Tony Ameruso's notoriously sloppy operation.

Friedman arrived at Yermack's office with his wife's lifelong friend Marvin Kaplan, the chairman of the still unincorporated company that was seeking exclusive rights to produce the handheld computer. Kaplan had already secretly promised Friedman, who was ostensibly acting as Kaplan's lawyer, a substantial stock interest in whatever entity was formed to secure the contract. Friedman did not even sit at the conference table where the details of the planned computerized system were discussed but relaxed in a couch, and barely spoke. Yermack expressed interest in Kaplan's concept but rejected the notion of any negotiated deal with him at this early point. Rather, he wanted a Request for Proposals (RFP) to be issued by the parking bureau, a wide-open search for bids.

Kaplan, a balding, remote, and mechanical man in his early fifties who had made millions in the data processing business, had actually been dealing with one man at the meeting, PVB's Lindenauer, for years. Another Kaplan company had been handling the $1–$2-million-a-year manual keypunch contract with the agency since 1979. Kaplan's move to the handheld computer was as much an effort to protect his existing PVB business as it was a leap forward in technology; if anyone else sold a computer to the city, Kaplan would lose his keypunch deal.

Shortly after the Yermack meeting, Kaplan met alone with Lindenauer in Kaplan's East Side office. Lindenauer's reputation preceded him: he was known to have taken cash bribes for himself and Manes for years, and the bribe-payers included Marvin Kaplan's close friends at another PVB contractor, Datacom. Kaplan now told Lindenauer that if his company were to win the handheld contract, he would give stock to Manes and Lindenauer, a minimum of a half-million apiece.

After promising to get back to Kaplan, Lindenauer went to Manes's home the next day and pitched the deal. Manes commented that Kaplan was indeed talking "serious money," and worried that "the real problem would be who would be holding the stock for us," adding, "this is the kind of problem I like." Lindenauer replied: "Okay, you handle that aspect of it, and I'll handle the contract." A day or so later, Manes contacted Lindenauer again and told him he wanted Friedman to hold the stock, which meant that the shares for the two would be issued in Friedman's name.

Lindenauer expressed surprise. He knew that Manes and Friedman had been fighting each other over control of the presidency of the Board of Education. "Geoffrey, you don't understand," Manes responded. "That's business. Stanley hurt me, and he understands that I'm going to get him back for that. But that has nothing to do with the friendship itself. I know Stanley. I trust Stanley."

Manes and Lindenauer then agreed that they wanted the stock issued to Friedman in three blocks, one for each of them, so that it could be sold off as each participant wished. It would be Friedman's job to "generate the cash" when the stock was sold. Lindenauer went to meet with Friedman at his midtown law office, and Friedman readily agreed.

Friedman had begun, by May 1982, to alter his professional life radically. Since joining Roy Cohn's firm in 1978, he had been its employee. Though Cohn and Friedman referred to each other as law partners, Friedman did not receive a partnership share but was instead paid a salary—one that was substantial enough when he left government, but by 1982 not commensurate with what his insider influence could command. As a central player in both Koch's government and Koch's then heavily favored gubernatorial campaign, Friedman decided to form his own professional corporation; and though he remained physically located at the Cohn firm, he was now in a position to take home his own earnings. A month after Fried-man went into business for himself, Marvin Kaplan began pay-ing Friedman a thousand-dollar-a-month retainer to represent the handheld computer. He also began paying him thousands more in fees for other conduit corporations.

Lindenauer, meanwhile, began his work inside the PVB. He told the agency's research director, who was in charge of the handheld project, that he would like to co-chair the commit-tee that was examining the issue. He met with Kaplan and the man Kaplan had hired to run the handheld project, Robert Richards, an imposing technocrat whose six-foot-three-inch, blondish arrogance captivated the physically unprepossessing Lindenauer. Richards and Lindenauer began to discuss the RFP that the agency would issue, skewing it to favor Kaplan's new company. Richards drafted critical sections of the RFP and gave his handwritten notes to Lindenauer, who in turn passed them on to PVB staffers, instructing them to include these pas-sages. But Lindenauer held off issuing the completed request until after Ed Koch lost the gubernatorial primary, releasing it several weeks later. Manes and Friedman had been unsure just what the politics of the contract process would be if Koch won and vacated the mayoralty in January 1983 to become gover-nor.

Once the RFP was public, Kaplan officially formed his com-pany, Citisource, and filed his computer proposal. Citisource's submission listed Friedman as the company's special counsel, but it made no mention of Friedman's equity position. This omission was carefully orchestrated at Manes's suggestion; he said he didn't want Friedman's stock holdings to surface yet, fearing they would cause "too much grief" and attract media attention. Kaplan and several other partners were listed as shareholders, though no stock had yet been issued.

Nine other companies bid on the contract, including such giants as Motorola. At Richards's suggestion, Lindenauer took the originals of their proposals uptown to Kaplan's office, where they were photocopied. Richards was going to prepare a brief, written evaluation of each bid, summarizing strengths and weaknesses in such a way as to stack the deck for Citi-source.

At the same time, a PVB technical unit headed by a 33-year-old systems analyst, John O'Connor, had been evaluating the proposals. At a spring meeting with Lindenauer and the director of the agency's research division, O'Connor announced that the team had ranked Motorola's application first. Lindenauer stared coldly at O'Connor and, without smiling, said carefully: "I want Citisource. If you don't go along with me, you will be fired." Lindenauer then had Richards's handwritten evaluations of the proposals typed at PVB and turned them over to the research team with instructions that they were to become the opinions of O'Connor's evaluators.

O'Connor, furious, went to the research director and protested that he had "done an in-depth evaluation and Motorola was the best." The selection committee, which was co-chaired by Lindenauer but consisted of a variety of city officials inside and outside PVB (including representatives from the budget and comptroller's offices), was scheduled to make its decision soon. "I'm going to present my findings to the committee the next time we meet," O'Connor told his supervisor. "I know I'm going to get fired, but I'm going to put it on the table anyway." Shortly after this speech, O'Connor went on a long weekend vacation to Lake George. When he returned, he discovered that the committee had met and unanimously picked Citisource.

While Lindenauer was carefully steering the contract through his agency, he was also periodically checking with Marvin Kaplan and Stanley Friedman to make sure that the stock was issued. In April, Kaplan explained that he, Manes, and Friedman were each getting 57,500 shares, and promised that the stock would be issued to Friedman soon. A week later Lindenauer went to Friedman's law office and warned him, "It's important that you get the stock from Marvin before the selection committee vote." Friedman held up his hand and wrote out the number 57,500 on a piece of paper. Then he tore the paper to pieces, put them in a large, plain ashtray on his desk, and set them afire with his cigarette lighter.

The stock was finally sent to Friedman on May 3; Lindenauer went to Friedman's office to see it a week later. Friedman pulled three blocks of 50,000 shares out of his desk drawer. Lindenauer said it was supposed to be 57,500 shares apiece, and Friedman said Lindenauer shouldn't worry about it, that another block would be issued totaling 21,000. Lindenauer brought the news to Manes, told him he would now get the contract through PVB, and that it would now be Manes's job to get it through the Board of Estimate.

On June 7, Lindenauer persuaded a reluctant selection

committee to go with Citisource by falsely assuring them that he had been to the Citisource plant and personally observed the working printer they had developed for their computer. But after the PVB vote, the project hit a snag. The transportation department had to send it to the Board of Estimate for a vote, but questions were suddenly being raised. Yermack's assistant was concerned about the publicity that might result if Friedman's role as "special counsel" leaked once the contract was submitted to the board, and city operations officials wanted language that would permit the city to get out of the contract without creating legal problems.

Friedman now set out to push the city bureaucracy to get the contract approved, dogging Ameruso, Yermack, a budget overseer, the head of the mayor's operations office, and City Hall. Finally, in May 1984, Friedman met with the new first deputy mayor Stan Brezenoff. An ex–Ford Foundation executive, Brezenoff had held a passle of important titles in the Koch administration—he'd run the Department of Employment, the Human Resources Administration, and the Health and Hospitals Corp. Brezenoff was cut from the same public service cloth as Fritz Schwarz, Nat Leventhal, Bob Wagner, and other top city officials appointed by Koch. He was, like the mayor himself, unapproachably honest, and just as ambitious. A genius at bureaucratic protocol, he had committed the crosscurrents of government process to memory. But unlike his predecessor Leventhal, Brezenoff had made himself part of Koch's political apparatus, playing an up-front role in the mayor's 1985 reelection campaign.

Friedman got John LoCicero to arrange the meeting, and Friedman started the session with a county leader agenda, complaining about what he described as the administration's lack of responsiveness on patronage decisions. Twenty minutes into the meeting, however, he suddenly switched gears and began talking about the problems a law client of his was having at DOT, explaining that the Citisource contract had been "dragging on for months and months." Brezenoff agreed that "a decision ought to be made on this" and promised to look into it. Friedman never mentioned his substantial financial interest in the company but repeatedly referred to Citisource as his client.

Brezenoff soon discovered that the delay was due to a dispute over the cancellation clause of the contract. When he notified Friedman of the problem, Friedman agreed to permit the city to cancel the contract at its discretion. Once Friedman made that concession, the contract was immediately put on the calendar for a June Board of Estimate vote. On June 16, PVB sent a package of materials on the contract to every member of the board. Once again, the list of Citisource principals did not include Stanley Friedman.

The day before the board formally voted on the contract, it met at its customary executive session. A representative from the office of Manhattan borough president Andrew Stein resisted the Citisource project and threatened to lay it over. But Stein had no real problem with the contract and was merely trying to use his vote on it to force a recalcitrant transportation department to give him a stoplight at a Manhattan intersection where citizens had complained about the lack of one. When Marvin Kaplan learned of Stein's resistance, he notified Lindenauer and left a message that the problem was a traffic light, and Ameruso unexpectedly materialized at the executive session. In an unusual personal appearance, the commissioner pledged that the light would be installed, and the Citisource contract routinely, and unanimously, passed.

The day after the board approved the contract, Kaplan entered into an agreement with a brokerage house to take Citisource public. A company that had no assets and employed one person was suddenly ready to make a public offering on the stock exchange at five dollars a share; three weeks before the contract was approved, Citisource's privately held stock was valued at twenty-three cents a share. The plan, which Friedman, Kaplan, Richards, and Lindenauer had discussed for months, was that the public offering would raise $4.2 million, part of which would be used to develop and manufacture the computer system called for in the contract.

It was a perfectly drawn circle: Kaplan and his colleagues would not have to invest anything. They had enticed the city into giving them a $22 million contract by claiming they'd developed a new technology; now they would use the contract to lure investors on the public market to finance the development of that technology. There was even a bonus for the Kaplan insiders—whatever was left over from the millions raised at the public offering, beyond what it would cost to design the minicomputer, could be siphoned off as legal payments to Friedman, or consultant disbursements to other Kaplan companies.

One problem remained, however. Citisource could not conceal from the Securities and Exchange Commission what they had successfully hidden from the city: Friedman's interest. So a draft of the disclosure statement—filed with the SEC on the same day the contract was signed in late August 1984—was the company's first official document to describe Friedman as a "director," and one of a half-dozen "organizers and parents of the company." The prospectus also listed him as having 167,500 shares in Citisource, almost 19 percent of all privately held stock.* Friedman held 57,500 more shares than Kaplan, the chairman of the board, and was by far the company's single largest shareholder.

A reporter for a Wall Street tip sheet who had read the Citisource prospectus noticed the Friedman holdings and called a City Hall reporter for the *New York Post,* David Seifman, who immediately asked the mayor's press office for an interview. At their meeting, Koch expressed no surprise about Friedman's massive stake in this city contractor. "So what?" he asked cryptically. "There's nothing illegal here." Though Seifman's story apparently did not disturb the mayor, it sent shockwaves through the PVB. Lester Shafran and the agency's counsel, who had just sent the inaccurate list of shareholders to the Board of Estimate, asked a nervous Lindenauer if the PVB had ever been informed of Friedman's holdings. He said he had not been told.

Fearing that the nondisclosure could be a basis for canceling the contract, Lindenauer called Manes, who tried to calm Lindenauer down. "Geoffrey, this is exactly the reason why Stanley was given the stock," he explained. "It's his job to take the heat. He'll be able to deal with it." In the meantime, PVB dashed off a letter to Citisource asking when Friedman had become a director and a shareholder, and why the bureau hadn't been informed. Friedman convened a meeting of the Citisource principals, and they composed a reply that falsely claimed that Friedman had first become a shareholder in September 1983, six months after he had in fact received the stock. This particular date enabled them to argue that Friedman hadn't been a shareholder when PVB approved the contract that June, and therefore that Citisource hadn't misled the agency.

As Manes had anticipated, the controversy surrounding the

---

*Kaplan gave Friedman a fourth block of 17,500 shares, not the 21,000 promised.

contract just seemed to vanish. PVB was apparently satisfied by the Citisource response, even though it meant that Friedman's stock position had been kept secret from the city for the nine months before the Board of Estimate vote. The company's response, however, also raised an obvious, new question: if Friedman had been with this company from the beginning, his large holdings might have been explained as a reward for getting in on the ground floor. But since the company was now claiming that he came in at the end, why did he get more of the private stock than anyone else?

The incongruity of Friedman's stock position passed unquestioned by city officials, including Brezenoff, who now knew that Friedman had repeatedly misled him when he kept referring to Citisource as his client. Likewise, the mayor who had raised questions years earlier about Friedman's possible use of his party post to fatten his law firm now raised no objection to such gross conflicts as Friedman's becoming the principal owner of a company with a major city contract. The ethics issues, as Koch would himself demonstrate at a public forum, were a giant yawn.

In October, the mayor appeared as the guest speaker at a luncheon sponsored by the City Club, a small good-government citizen group. Koch was introduced to the couple of hundred members by chair Sally Goodgold, the former transportation task force head whose panel had rejected Tony Ameruso back in the beginning of Koch's mayoralty. Waiting in the audience was a questioner who had carefully read the Citisource prospectus—gadfly and clubmember Jim Smith.

Smith, thirty-seven, was the founder and publisher of several stridently independent and profitable weekly newspapers in gentrified Brooklyn neighborhoods. He also owned a very successful printing business, but he rode a bike and rarely wore a suit. A Choate alumnus who had spent five years at MIT without graduating, Smith was an iconoclast with a clean-cut, Clark Kent look—including the dark-rimmed glasses. He was quaint enough to think that politics was a contest of ideas and principles. He had put himself forward as a candidate against Koch in 1981, but, an unknown, he couldn't get enough signatures on nominating petitions to qualify for the ballot. One of the central issues of his platform was the administration's destruction of the civil service system—and Smith assailed it for contracting out for services that could be performed by municipal employees and filling thousands of civil service jobs with non–civil service provisionals.

Smith had recently started his first citywide newsletter, a journal of political opinion called *Talking Turkey*. In an issue published a few days before the City Club luncheon, he wrote an article analyzing the Citisource contract. A stack of the newsletters had been distributed at City Hall to the press and top mayoral aides. In the article, Smith posed the unanswerable question that no one in city government was asking: "What did Stanley Friedman do for Citisource that merited his becoming the biggest shareholder?"

He also examined the political implications of the cancellation clause that Brezenoff had insisted on—a clause that gave the city the power to terminate the contract at its "sole discretion." What the open cancellation language meant, reasoned Smith, was that Friedman "has to support Mayor Koch for reelection," or risk losing both the contract and his multimillion-dollar capital gain.

When the questioning session began at the City Club, Smith launched a barrage on Citisource: "You voted with the Board of Estimate unanimously to award that contract to a company in which Stanley Friedman is the largest shareholder, making him an overnight millionaire. Were you aware that this company had no money to fulfill that contract, in comparison with, say, Motorola and McDonnell Douglas, which did not win the contract? And that they subsequently, like two weeks after winning the contract, went public, which is when Friedman became the millionaire?"

By the time Smith had finished, Koch was in a fury. He would not meet Smith's eyes but pursed his lips and glared straight ahead. He had been a hairshirt himself once, and now nothing bothered him more than having to listen to one, much less having a questioner, even temporarily, steal the show. It was time to take the offensive: "You know what we have is, ah, is what we have all the time by—ah, those who would really seek to malign and implicitly convey corruption. That's exactly what that statement is intended to do."

Koch began ridiculing Smith without ever addressing the specifics he'd raised: "Is everybody on the Board of Estimate corrupt? Are they all criminals?" he asked rhetorically. "The fact that it's Stanley Friedman—you know it's so easy to libel people—and that's what I perceive is the implication of what you're saying," he continued. "Do you know of any criminality on his part? If you do"—and he interrupted himself by warning Smith "don't answer"—then "rush to the D.A." But "if you don't, how dare you say those terrible things about him?" Koch ended by absolving himself of any responsibility for the details of the contract, stating, "it is decided on by a commissioner." The audience belly laughed at the mayor's banter and applauded him.

Although City Club rules barred Smith from replying, his nagging questions did eventually provoke a response. Friedman himself sent an answer to *Talking Turkey*, ghostwritten by Robert Richards, charging that Smith's "knowledge of business and free enterprise is questionable and truly reflects that of a turkey." On stationery that featured a cartoon of Friedman smoking a huge cigar, Friedman penned a "Dear Ed" note to the mayor that simply said: "Thought you might be interested in my response to Jim Smith of *Talking Turkey.*" Attached to the note, signed just "Stan," was a copy of the letter he'd sent Smith's paper.

Sometime after the showdown with Smith, Brezenoff and the mayor discussed the Citisource deal and the newspaper articles that had appeared about it. They decided to order investigation of the process that had led to the contract. But they did not ask the Department of Investigations to do it, nor the Board of Ethics, nor even Fritz Schwarz, the corporation counsel who was often brought in to make judgment calls. Instead Brezenoff asked the mayor's Office of Operations to do a "background check," which elicited a two-page memo outlining how the contract had woven its way through city government. The April 1985 memo, and twenty-three pages of enclosed documents, were a predictable defense of the process.

By the time the Brezenoff memo was completed, Citisource stock was selling for nearly fifteen dollars a share. Friedman was holding $2.4 million worth of stock for which he'd paid a penny a share, or a total of $1,675. Yet the company was blithely breaking every production schedule deadline in its contract. Robert Richards, emboldened by the knowledge that the contract was politically invulnerable despite the open cancellation clause, had taken to verbally abusing the PVB staffers who raised questions about the company's performance. Richards got so bad that in mid-1985, Friedman, who was then actively involved in the mayor's reelection campaign, had to step in as Citisource's direct liaison with the agency.

By the year's end, Citisource had yet to develop a functioning computer, and hadn't even begun to set up the contract-mandated hub stations and mainframes that the minicomputer would feed into; yet the city had taken no action against the company. Almost four years after the initial meeting with Larry Yermack, when Richards talked optimistically about a ready technology and brought with him a black metal box that was supposed to be a prototype, Citisource had failed to deliver anything approximating a working system.

The Citisource deal aside, it was apparent to the politically savvy at City Hall that PVB had become, during the second Koch term, a major arena of Friedman and Manes activity. "The Hall" knew, of course, that Manes controlled the key positions at the top of the agency, and that these administrators staffed it down the line from Queens clubhouses. But no one ever questioned why a politician who actually had to face the voters every four years wanted to control the most hated agency of city government, a department notorious for dunning the innocent at ticket prices higher than anywhere else in the country.

Manes's involvement was by now so pervasive and personal that he was able to call City Hall officials and request that a key PVB contract be broken into two parts, so that a bribe-paying company could get a share of it. His direct intervention on a matter that was unrelated to his public or party obligations was a signal of how entrenched in the agency's business he had become. When Shelly Chevlowe died, Manes pressured City Hall to appoint Chevlowe's widow to his vacancy as a city marshal, transforming an important and lucrative public position into a family legacy. Like bounty hunters in the Old West, city marshals are responsible for enforcing judgments issued by the courts, and can earn hundreds of thousands of dollars a year by taking for themselves a percentage of the amount they collect. The Chevlowes were given a virtual corner on the marshal business generated by PVB scofflaw cases.

Stanley Friedman likewise did not limit his interventions at PVB to the Citisource deal. In 1983, he began representing Datacom, another major PVB contractor that had previously used Manes's friend Michael Lazar as its PVB influence peddler. Datacom paid $245,000 in legal fees to Friedman over the next few years. When Datacom wanted part of a new scofflaw towing contract, Friedman brokered a deal involving it and two other companies that were already paying bribes to Manes and

Lindenauer. One of the executives of the two companies already in line for the towing contract said that Friedman appeared "like a ghost out of a machine" when the negotiations bogged down.

The contract for this three-way joint venture was so large that PVB estimated it would exceed Citisource's and generate $50 million in business. When Lindenauer at one point told Friedman that Manes and he would cut him in on the kickbacks they were already collecting from the other two companies, Manes exploded, screaming, "You schmuck, where the hell do you get off telling Stanley about this? He's a goddam pig, he's only in this because we brought him in." In the end, asserting his own dominance over PVB profits, Manes forced Friedman to collect his payments for this contract from Datacom alone, and to split even Datacom's kickbacks with him and Lindenauer, who was supposed to be paid directly by the other two companies.

Friedman also represented Datacom in an effort to obtain the agency's lucrative data processing contract. Friedman, Manes, and Lindenauer had agreed to divide up evenly a Datacom bribe on this deal that equaled 10 percent of the company's earnings. But because of previous problems with Datacom over the efficient delivery of payoffs, Lindenauer and Manes required, and received, an up-front $30,000 cash bribe from the company, paid directly by Friedman.

PVB evolved into a booming clubhouse business during 1984 and 1985 partly because the one-man system of checks and balances introduced at the transportation department by Nat Leventhal in early 1982 had been abandoned. Leventhal's mole in Ameruso's agency, Larry Yermack, found it increasingly difficult to get Brezenoff's ear, and when Yermack returned from a 1984 vacation, he was abruptly told his authority over the traffic department had been taken away. As surely as Yermack's influence was in decline under Brezenoff, Ameruso was in the ascendancy. The 1981 attempt by ex–deputy mayor Bob Wagner to dump Ameruso had failed; the 1982 Leventhal strategy of surrounding him with City Hall–designated aides had been effective only so long as Leventhal had stayed at City Hall. By the summer of 1984 a frustrated Yermack had decided to quit, but it took him a year of jobhunting to finally leave. Ameruso, for most of this period, was back in charge, with no one keeping guard. The agency had once again become the plaything of the clubhouse.

PVB was hardly the only arena in city government where Stanley Friedman did big business. His wife's job at City Hall made it seem perfectly natural for him to spend time there, and he became a familiar fixture all over the three-story building. Friedman would drop in on Ken Lipper, Koch's deputy mayor for economic development from 1983 to 1985, and roll up his sleeve, showing Lipper the ten project items he'd scrawled on his arm. "I know you're going to say no to nine out of ten, but maybe you'll say okay to one," he teased. "And you don't know which one I really want." Since Friedman had convinced borough president Stanley Simon to make him chairman of the Bronx's city-funded economic development corporation, Lipper frequently couldn't tell whether Friedman was working on behalf of a client or for a project of the borough corporation.

Just as he had inherited the Yankees as clients from ex–county leader Pat Cunningham, Friedman wound up representing the operators of the city-owned Bronx Terminal Market, whose lease had been negotiated ten years earlier by Cunningham and had become in the late 1970s the subject of a highly critical state grand jury report. A renegotiated city lease with the same operator had languished for four years, unable to get final approval, until Friedman entered the picture in late 1982.

At one four-hour bargaining session involving a top city official, Friedman resolved a key issue that was preventing the city from submitting the new lease to the Board of Estimate. A few months later, in a classic demonstration of the way Friedman mixed his political and business roles, he endorsed the same official who attended the meeting for commissioner of the city's Department of Ports and Terminals. Within four months of Friedman's retention, the logjam had broken, and a long-term lease for the market—where fifty subtenant distributors do a half-billion dollars worth of business a year—quickly passed through the board.

Friedman also began representing several major Manhattan developers, including one, Harry Macklowe, who leveled a "single room occupancy" (SRO) hotel, occupied by the poorest of the poor, in a midnight attempt to beat the deadline on a new law that barred converting these dwindling housing resources into luxury co-ops. Friedman relentlessly pressed city planning officials first to approve a controversial zoning variance for a thirty-nine-story apartment building Macklowe was building along the East River, and then to allow a modification of the permit they'd granted when Macklowe overbuilt. Planning officials not only had to bargain with Friedman; they had to resist pro-Macklowe pressure from one of their own commissioners, Ted Teah, who shared a law office with Friedman.

Another major real estate firm, Newmark and Co., retained Friedman in 1983 for a very specific governmental purpose: to convince Donald Manes to change his position on several city leases, including one for the offices occupied by Ameruso, Lindenauer, Shafran, and much of DOT's headquarters staff. Newmark, which had just purchased a sixteen-story office building at 40 Worth Street that housed DOT and other agencies, wanted the city to prematurely cancel leases covering half the 500,000 square feet the company rented, and sign new ten-year leases at more than double the previous rent. Manes had said he would not vote for such a large package of downtown leases until the city made a commitment to move some of its agencies to Queens and rent space there.

Newmark's press spokesman would later claim that Friedman had been retained to lobby the board members opposing the new lease, but in fact he never contacted the comptroller or the council president, both of whom had joined Manes in a coalition demanding more outer-borough leases. Friedman spoke only with Manes, and Manes's nine-month opposition suddenly evaporated. The mayor and Manes reached an agreement that the city would relocate several agency offices to Queens, and the biggest new city lease was for a Jamaica building owned by Manes's close friend Michael Lazar. The well-connected principals of Newmark, just like their counterparts at Datacom, already understood what everyone else would learn over the course of the following two and a half years: if you want to get to Manes, you hire Friedman.

The special and expensive influence of Stanley Friedman—whether over Donald Manes or over a host of city agencies—became a quiet scandal among political insiders. When the Koch administration contemplated a new tax on movie admissions, the Metropolitan Motion Pictures Theatre Owners hired Friedman as their lobbyist and beat the tax. Because his control over the city council's transportation committee (it was chaired by a Bronx council member) gave him the power to block any reform legislation targeting the taxi industry, the taxi association retained him as their lobbyist. One of the changes Friedman blocked was an increase in the number of taxi medallions, meaning that the number of cabs would remain the same as that permitted under a 1937 law. This decision blocked minorities around the city, including Friedman's Bronx, from breaking into the lucrative and virtually all-white medallion cab business—as well as denied the residents of the county Friedman was ostensibly representing any possibility of better cab service.

As Meade Esposito's influence faded during the second Koch term, key city officials that the old boss had installed, particularly Jay Turoff and Tony Ameruso, became closer to Friedman, gravitating toward the new center of clubhouse clout. Ameruso recommended Friedman's express bus clients for desirable new routes, while opposing franchises for operators without heavyweight lawyers. When a 1985 state probe began focusing on a multimillion-dollar experimental diesel program that had distributed free taxi medallions to a company whose principals were represented by Friedman, Turoff and his inspector general Robert Mackasek actually went to Friedman's law office to secretly brief him on what they knew about the investigation.

Friedman was able to influence many top-level appointments at another agency, the Department of Environmental Protection, responsible for such massive construction projects as the $5 billion third water tunnel, a water pollution control plant, and new sewer construction. Jeff Sommer, a former Friedman aide at City Hall in the Beame days and a close personal associate, was brought into the agency in a top administrative post three months after Friedman became county leader in 1978. Sommer was promoted to deputy commissioner in late 1979, and in April 1982, at the urging of City Hall, to first deputy. DEP commissioner Joe McGough was also forced to promote the son of a former Bronx district leader to another deputy commissioner post by an insistent Brezenoff, who told him at one point "the mayor really wants you to appoint this guy." The agency was also awash with Friedman law clients including sewer contractors and the key participant in the consortium that won the water tunnel project.

Friedman's mounting influence at DEP, the taxi commission, the port agency, and DOT was clearly a product of his direct ties to the mayor, who seemed unaffected by Friedman's increasingly outrageous public performance as a party boss. In the fall of 1983, for example, Friedman refused to allow two sitting Supreme Court judges with unblemished records to be renominated by the Bronx judicial convention, dooming them to defeat. One of Friedman's replacements—a former PVB director forced out by a DOI investigation involving improper fundraising on the job for a Bronx club—was found unqualified by the Bar Association, but Friedman dismissed the opposition as "the ravings of Manhattan reformers."

City Hall was not only tolerant of Friedman's judicial gyrations; it was oblivious to his mob ties. The perception that Friedman was connected to the underworld was so widespread that he used it to intimidate—as if it were a weapon in his power arsenal. He once told Lindenauer, who was worried about whether Datacom's president could be relied on to make the promised payoffs, that the executive wouldn't go back on his word. "He will not fool around with me," Friedman said. "He knows me, and if he does, he'll wind up in the river."

The river is exactly where one enemy of a client of the Friedman firm did wind up. Vinnie DiNapoli, a capo in the Luchese crime family and the most powerful mobster in the Bronx, was represented by Friedman's firm in a 1982 federal racketeering case when one of his co-defendants suddenly disappeared. No body was ever recovered, but the car he was driving was found in the Hudson River. DiNapoli owned several drywall construction companies and managed to obtain $25 million in noncompetitive, federally funded subcontracts for Bronx housing rehab projects between 1978 and 1981 (his competitors got the remaining $3 million). A confidential police department report on corruption in Bronx construction projects, quoted by the *New York Times* in a front-page story in 1981, concluded: "Nothing moves in the Bronx without DiNapoli's authorization."

When DiNapoli was convicted, Friedman's law firm put together a well-publicized presentencing submission asking for leniency that included letters from a half-dozen elected officials from the Bronx. Paul Victor, Friedman's right-hand man and the law chairman for the Bronx party, represented DiNapoli's brother and DiNapoli's right-hand man, Steve Crea, who partied with Friedman at Victor's house. In fact, Victor, who advised Friedman on the selection of judges, was really Paul Viggiano, the son of "a close associate of numerous organized crime figures," who changed his name and built a law practice that included the biggest drug dealers in the Bronx.

Friedman's most prolific source of mob contacts was his mentor and partner Roy Cohn. Fat Tony Salerno, head of the Genovese crime family and a partner with Vinnie DiNapoli in a concrete company, had been a Cohn client for years. Friedman's phone logs revealed that Salerno would sometimes make it a point of setting up an appointment with Friedman when he was at the firm's townhouse visiting with Cohn.

Cohn's office was such a hub of mob activity that one federal indictment charged that an associate of Salerno's, while out on bail in Missouri, justified three trips to New York by "misrepresenting" them as consultations with his attorney Cohn. The indictment said that Cohn was merely an excuse for the man to meet with Salerno.* One Cohn biographer goes further and cites reports that the Commission itself—the heads of the five crime families—sometimes met at the Cohn townhouse where the lawyer-client privilege would prevent any FBI electronic intrusions.

Friedman could move so casually from this nether world, where he would help a friend of Tommy Gambino (son of Carlo) obtain a real estate broker's license, to City Hall, where he would drop in on a deputy mayor to seek a favor, that he disarmed even the wary. He craved respectability at the same time that he advertised himself as an influence peddler who hovered in the darkest shadows. Occasionally, with a roguish glint in his eye, he wondered out loud why his ethics were so often suspect. He even developed a way of brusquely defusing critics that was so compatible with the mayor's that those who dogged either of them with questions about their character were met with similar sneers, a shared contempt. It was enough to make him an indispensable part of the scenery at City Hall.

Like Friedman's, Donald Manes's influence over Ed Koch's government mushroomed in the aftermath of the mayor's 1982 gubernatorial defeat. The mayor installed a Manes associate as head of the city's Public Development Corporation, and

---

*These counts were dismissed after Cohn's death.

Manes's friends, such as Michael Lazar and Sid Davidoff, began building empires in various parts of the city's development apparatus, from PDC to the port and housing agencies. But no episode during the second Koch term better expressed the mayor's acquiescence to Manes, and his willingness to ignore warnings about Manes's ethics, than the handling of the borough president's ambitious and determined scheme to use Flushing Meadows Park in Queens as a site for a New York Grand Prix. Ed Koch went as far as he could to make this nightmare project a reality, but it unleased such grassroots opposition that the fight dragged on for three years, led by a 54-year-old lawyer who lived ten blocks from the park, Ben Haber.

Haber had long been a park militant. He and his son were hikers who went wherever it was green. He quoted the works of naturalists to anyone who would listen. The yard surrounding his cozy colonial home in Kew Gardens, a plot that was only eighty by a hundred feet, was his personal park. While the rest of his neighbors hired gardeners, Haber tilled his own soil. He never wore gloves; he liked the feel of dirt on his hands. The azaleas, petunias, dahlias, rhododendrons, and impatiens in the front were such a masterpiece that when the daughters of his neighbors' children got married, the wedding party invariably wound up using Haber's yard as a color photo background.

But Donald Manes looked at Flushing Meadows Park and saw a different kind of green than Haber did. Since its typical users were poor, often immigrant minorities, battling each other in international sandlot soccer matches and lolling on the summer grass, Manes viewed it as a politically defenseless, unclaimed territory. He envisioned converting it into New York's Meadowlands, a sports center littered with ticket stubs from every kind of televised game. The ideas kept pouring out of him—a domed stadium to be built by Donald Trump on the park's outer rim, a sixty-concert-a-year rock center to be run by his old mob-connected buddy Michael Callahan, a restaurant concession on the lake, and now, a racetrack. When Manes was called by one top city official in the mid-1980s and told that many people were suggesting that the park be renamed after a beloved Queens congressman who had just died, Manes replied: "No. I'm saving that one for myself."

Manes's Grand Prix plan, the details of which were unveiled in early 1983, called for the elimination of 113 trees that surrounded Meadow Lake, and the construction of a roadway thirty-five feet wide and 2.5 miles long, in place of the strolling paths, just forty feet from the lakefront. He also wanted to shut down large portions of the park for a summer month every year for the next decade, so preparations, including temporary grandstands, could be completed for the three-day race. Twenty-six cars would wind up roaring through the park, doing seventy-five laps at speeds of up to 160 miles an hour. When Ben Haber heard this, sitting in his yard in the hills off the park, he could almost hear the engines spitting into the park air. It was as if the massive wheels on the soapboxlike Formula One cars were rolling through his petunias.

Haber had fought Manes before. A few years earlier, a major developer wanted to build a huge apartment complex on the edge of the park. When Donald Manes refused to respond to the heated opposition Haber helped stir up against this project, Haber knew where to go. He went to the Board of Elections and got lists of the campaign contributors to Donald Manes. He found the developer, as well as his architect and his lawyer. They had given thousands of dollars to Manes. The contribution list became a weapon in Ben Haber's hand, and the project died.

So when the Grand Prix plan surfaced in mid-1982, Haber and his small group of park activists were already veterans of a Manes war. They soon discovered, however, that this Manes scheme was rooted in a year-old deal that would make it very hard to stop. In the spring of 1981, Manes and his executive assistant, Dan Koren, began talking with Bernard Ecclestone, the London-based head of the Grand Prix network. After a couple of face-to-face meetings, the two took Ecclestone and his partners over to the Parks Department to float the idea. Then that June, Koren suddenly wrote the Board of Ethics, which rules on conflict-of-interest questions involving city employees, and asked if he could legally leave his job with Manes and "become a principal owner of an entity to be formed for the purpose of organizing and promoting a Flushing Meadows Grand Prix."

Koren contended that there was no conflict because Ecclestone would not have a financial interest in the new venture, contending that Koren's corporation would be "independent of the abortive effort of the former promoters." In fact, Ecclestone had introduced Koren to a Canadian shopping center developer who'd pledged millions for the project. Ecclestone's firm would collect almost $4 million a year in fees from the race for actually staging it. Nonetheless, the ethics board's counsel wrote an opinion in record time, finding that Koren's Grand Prix was "a new matter and not a matter in which he was involved in his official capacity."

The ethics decision did suggest that if Koren was going to go ahead with the Grand Prix, "he should promptly resign" from Manes's staff. So Koren quit even though the Grand Prix entity wasn't yet prepared to pay him a salary. Manes instantly created a new, interim, paycheck for Koren, persuading the city's Department of Cultural Affairs to make a $25,000 grant to a group Manes said was promoting a cultural center in Queens. The city awarded the contract to Manes's cultural group four months before it was even incorporated. Manes added $10,000 from his own borough budget. The only employee of this invisible organization, Koren was supposed to determine the feasibility of such a center. The city grant ended in the summer of 1982 without results.

Meanwhile, the Canadian financier put up enough seed money to cover Koren's salary and costs; so he went to work for the Grand Prix, immediately retaining Manes's publicist Michael Nussbaum and his personal attorney Sid Davidoff. Pressured by Manes, the mayor informed his parks commissioner, Gordon Davis, that he supported the project, and the skeptical Davis prepared a Request for Proposals. The RFP went out in December 1982; applications were due in February 1983 (almost precisely the same postcampaign schedule as the Citisource RFP). With only a few weeks to respond, Koren was, unsurprisingly, the only applicant.

Gordon Davis was his usual straightforward self, publicly declaring that the project would now have to pass through the city charter–mandated Uniform Land Use Review Process (ULURP), which requires a vote by the community boards of each affected neighborhood, the planning commission, and the Board of Estimate. But somehow Manes knew he'd be able to sidestep ULURP. Way back in 1981, Koren's ethics letter had asserted that the Grand Prix "would not be required to win approvals from any department or body" where he was employed. In fact, if ULURP was required, Manes would have voted on the project at the Board of Estimate. As predicted in the Koren letter, a top city attorney decided to waive ULURP. Davis then said he at least wanted a vote from the Queens

Borough Board, consisting of the chair of every Queens community board, the city council delegation, and Donald Manes.

Ben Haber and much of his Stop the Grand Prix committee went to the April 1983 Borough Board meeting. They had assiduously worked seven community boards near the park and had forced public hearings at each. Four boards had voted against it, two were for it, and one voted to require ULURP but took no position on the race itself. Haber argued that only the chairs of boards that had held a public hearing should vote at the Borough Board, since the others had no idea how their members felt. But the chair of the Borough Board, Donald Manes, ruled otherwise. All seven of the representatives of boards that had never held hearings voted for the Prix, including one who was already on record signing a letter opposing it. One chairman whose board voted 24 to 2 against the Prix abstained.

A confident Manes, who preferred dealing with the chairmen rather than the full boards, celebrated when he won a 15 to 7 mandate after six hours of debate that carried into the morning. From then on, whenever Haber and his legions would confront the mayor about the project at Town Hall meetings, he would invoke the Borough Board vote as a "home rule" statement in favor of it, even though the vote was in fact a substitute for the ordinary home rule process under the city charter.

A few weeks before the Borough Board vote, Davis had resigned, quietly telling the mayor that he opposed the Grand Prix. The new decisionmaker was Henry Stern, a lifelong personal friend of Koch's known during his days on the city council for the "nose test" he frequently applied to seamy city deals. The first challenge Stern faced, as the new parks chief, was whether or not the Prix project required an environmental review. Haber believed it had to be approved by two city environmental agencies charged with examining the effect of "significant, discretionary" government actions. But Stern said he didn't think a review was necessary, prompting a confident Koren to declare that the race was set for September.

Then the bubble burst. A news story pointed out that, though Koren had won his ethics clearance by claiming that his Grand Prix was a new venture begun after he left government, he'd actually incorporated it in 1981 while he was still Manes's executive assistant. Another story detailed the way Manes had invented the cultural group to keep Koren on the tab. Suddenly the Queens district attorney opened a case. So did DOI. The Board of Ethics decided to take another look. And Henry Stern found himself besieged.

From the moment his appointment was announced, head-line-hungry Stern had been saying all the things a parks commissioner should say, but his support of Manes's race contradicted these pronouncements. He had called Central Park "sacred soil," leading Ben Haber to wonder out loud why Flushing Meadows was any less so. A *New York Times* editorial, the single column of newsprint that meant the most to Stern, threw his own words back at him in a blast at the Prix, reminding him that he'd promised to "maintain the city's open space against incursions." The self-described "commissioner of good times for people, plants, and animals" was on the hot seat.

So Stern reversed himself and asked for a legal opinion on the environmental questions from corporation counsel Fritz Schwarz. The request launched an unspoken conspiracy including Stern, Schwarz, and other top city officials to find ways to slow the Manes steamroller without incurring the mayor's wrath. When Schwarz ultimately ruled that an environmental review was necessary, the race was dead for 1983. Ed Koch got on the phone to Bernard Ecclestone in London, told him not to lose heart, and publicly prejudged the planned environmental review, saying that he hoped his agencies would find the race "do-able."

The criminal investigations then took on steam of their own. By mid-1984, DOI's Pat McGinley met with the mayor and told him that the Koren job "appeared to be a ruse" so that "Manes's executive assistant could put together the Grand Prix while on a public payroll." McGinley told Koch that the Queens D.A., and the Brooklyn U.S. Attorney, were looking at the case. McGinley noted that the case "might not result in an indictment," but that DOI had nonetheless concluded that Koren's city job had been improperly concocted. In the heat of these probes, the project ground to a halt temporarily.

The city's environmental review dragged on into the spring of 1985. In the end, the report found that joggers, cyclists, and ballplayers might lose large chunks of the park for up to four months a year, and that the concrete roadway around the lake "would have a significant adverse aesthetic impact on that section of the park." Though the negatives far outweighed the positives, the report was not a bar to the project, and suddenly

Koren began to move forward again. The investigations had simultaneously receded, though they were still technically open. As McGinley had predicted, the questions were ethical, not criminal.

One final hurdle remained: the city's Arts Commission, an eleven-member body appointed by the mayor to review and approve any structures erected on city property. In a tumultuous July meeting, Henry Stern, sitting in for the mayor, cast the decisive vote in a 6–5 squeaker for the Prix. It was Haber's most depressing moment. He had met with commission staff and members and felt he was dealing at last with people who were unintimidated by Manes and the mayor. Haber assailed Stern for his vote, but Stern would later tell a reporter: "I couldn't come out against it if I wanted to remain Parks Commissioner. I am not elected, I serve at the pleasure of the mayor."

The commission's decision was not, however, an undiluted victory for Koren. Like Stern, the commission and its staff were waging an invisible war on the project. Their public vote acceded to the mayoral mandate, but they also tacked on a tough set of new requirements: the Prix backers were barred from eliminating more than sixty trees, and would have to show how they would return the park to its original condition after the race. Koren was told to come back to the commission once more with a plan to meet these requirements.

Still, at the end of 1985, after three years of ugly wars and open probes, the Grand Prix was alive, moving slowly toward a possible 1986 race. McGinley's warning to Koch about Manes's job for Koren hadn't stopped it. Neither had any of the other issues—the acknowledged environmental damage to the park, the rigged Borough Board vote, the confluence of Manes power brokers attached to it, the opposition of everyone in the administration who examined it. To the mayor, who complained to deputy mayor Nat Leventhal about the delays, the project was just one more clause in the mutual service contract he and Manes had implicitly executed. No finding short of an indictment could diminish the mayor's enthusiasm for it.

At the start of 1986, with Koren readying his final plan for the Arts Commission, Ben Haber believed he'd lost the battle with the Koch administration and that only a lawsuit could now prevent the Prix. He knew that Manes had great power in Queens Supreme Court, too, but his group had been raising money to cover appeal costs as well, and Haber believed that

Manes's influence did not extend into the highest state court. He had already made it clear that he would not take a cent to represent the group, and had supported the retention of another lawyer. Haber would assist the lawyer, but he did not want anyone to infer that he'd made this war to get his law practice press notes. Manes flunkies were saying it anyway.

Then, on the morning of January 10, Haber woke to the radio news of Manes's wounded body found in a car parked just off his park. To Haber, it was both a tragedy and a mystery. But as the revelations exploded in the press over the succeeding days, he could feel the mythical bleachers around Meadow Lake coming down. He could smell the park grass even though it was a frigid winter and the turf was like stone. The trees around the lake seemed to stand taller. Ben Haber knew that Donald Manes had finally stopped himself.

CHAPTER NINE

Under Siege

FROM THE MOMENT Donald Manes was discovered by police in the early hours of January 10, 1986, Ed Koch's third term became a nightmare. Alone before dawn at a long breakfast table in Gracie Mansion with five empty seats and a piece of fruit, the mayor for years would devour the happy history of his previous day in the newspapers. But after Manes, this morning ritual suddenly became a daily bout with indigestion. The newspapers were finally biting back. Throughout the early months of 1986, each morning's new revelation cast a shadow over the day that faced him, and probably stirred buried memories of compromises he once thought would never be discovered. On weekends and in the evenings, he now frequently pattered about his mansion, which he'd spent $6 million renovating, accompanied only by police guards and the ghosts that haunted his government.

As the days dragged by that January, and the two men he'd helped make king in the Bronx and Queens sunk under the weight of criminal allegations, he lay in his oversized bed, looking out his bullet-proof bedroom window at a distant Triboro Bridge that joined his home Manhattan to the boroughs Friedman and Manes had corrupted.* The bridge, lit at night and

---

*Arthur Browne, Dan Collins, and Michael Goodwin, in the book *I, Koch* (Dodd, Mead, 1985), sketched the physical layout of the mayor's bedroom and bathroom.

pointing in three directions, connected the gold coast of East Side Manhattan to South Bronx prairies and the Archie Bunker rowhouses of Queens. Even the mayor could no longer see the Triboro as merely the link between a rich variety of communities; it had become a metaphor for his government. As the stunning details emerged of what was now called simply "the scandal," Ed Koch's administration was depicted more and more as the bridge that had carried the criminal contracts from Manhattan, where they were routinely approved, to the sister counties of Queens and the Bronx, where the mayor's friends sold them for cash, stock, legal fees, or campaign contributions.

Adjoining Koch's bedroom is a bathroom that had been converted years earlier, for security reasons, into a bunker, just like the one that was now taking over Ed Koch's mind. Koch could disappear into the bathroom with his newspaper and his fears, and slam shut four long steel bolts behind him. By pushing the buttons on a high-tech combination lock, he could open the door to a closet inside the bathroom and remove sufficient survival gear to sustain him long enough to at least read the voluminous indictments that would dog his administration through 1986 and 1987. If he wanted to get the latest break in the scandal story without emerging from his personal vault, he could pick up the phone directly connected to police headquarters that is hidden in the bathroom closet, or order more newspapers on the two-way police radio. And if it all became too much for him, there was a rope ladder he could throw out the bathroom window, descend, and abdicate into a New York night.

The mayor had gone to the same real estate barons and investment banking insiders who had financed his campaigns to get them to pick up much of the tab on the restoration of the mansion. The dramatic new entranceway, the hand-painted wooden floor, the marbleized woodwork on the main staircase, the antiques, the rebuilt front porch were paid for by the Gracie Mansion Conservancy, a privately funded benefactor that answered to a solitary interior decorator, the mayor himself. Even the conservancy wound up the subject of rumors early in the year of the scandal. In February, when the infamous Alex Liberman began cooperating and was brought to the Manhattan federal prison for debriefing, he told investigators that one of his bribe-payers had shown him a list of the conservancy donors and told him that not all of the contributions were actually being spent on mansion improvements. The Liberman list of allegations was by then so long that investigators were too preoccupied even to probe this latest claim.

In the aftermath of the Manes explosion, the mayor took his bunker mentality with him each morning, in his black Lincoln Town Car, down the FDR Drive, alongside the East River esplanade whose recent improvements had been shaped by Stanley Friedman's secret machinations with the city on behalf of a developer client, past the 60th Street Heliport parking lot, whose lease with another Friedman client had led to the conviction of city real estate director Rick Mazzeo, and by the city-owned pier at 23d Street, where the yacht owned by Meade Esposito's insurance firm docked to entertain a coterie of influence merchants and pols.

With two police guards in the front seat, and the mayor alone in the back bracing himself for another day under a cloud, the car looped around the waterfront site of the long-delayed Riverwalk project. This massive residential and office tower complex had been undertaken by a Koch-designated developer who was using Esposito's top insurance client as his builder, prompting an FBI probe—of a losing bidder's allegation that he had been told by top city officials that he would get the designation if he used the same builder and Meade's brokerage firm.

Finally, the police driver would steer off the drive and past Police Plaza, whose electrical work would become the subject of a federal fraud indictment in early 1987, and up to City Hall, where Donald Manes once skillfully maneuvered deals later revealed as crimes through the Board of Estimate, kibitzing all the while with his one-liner colleague Ed Koch.

Inside the hall, as the mayor rushed through the columned rotunda and past the metal detectors, he could see straight into Stan Brezenoff's office. The first deputy mayor was as likely now to be talking to a federal or state investigator as he once was to be dealing with a county leader. Koch walked by the small section of crowded offices occupied by aides such as Herb Rickman, a longtime friend who would soon wind up a government witness against another longtime friend, the city's cultural affairs commissioner Bess Myerson.

Waiting for Koch in the mayor's impersonal and uncluttered private office was 32-year-old Victor Botnick, a frequent companion and adviser during the early months of the scandal, the chairman of the city's $2 billion Health and Hospitals Corporation and a Koch assistant since high school. Botnick had stayed at the mansion until late the night before, as he had many nights since the scandal began, just sitting with the mayor, the two of them silently watching television.

Although the mayor rejected every newspaper's description of Botnick as his surrogate son, there was little doubt, especially after the early death of Botnick's father, that Ed Koch had shaped the Victor Botnick most people knew. And just as the mayor's surrogate wife, Bess Myerson, would let a life of private excess drag her into the swirling city scandal, so, too, in the coming months, would the mayor's mirror-image Botnick.

The mayor spent more and more of his days slouched in his black leather-bound armchair, listening impatiently to advisers and waiting for the scandal to end. He knew it had to end. He thought it would conclude with the shocking death in March of Donald Manes, a dramatic curtain closer if there ever was one. But the thing seemed to have a will of its own, and a hundred faces as well. A moment of Hollywood drama had triggered the scandal, but after that initial shock, its almost two-year run on television, in the papers, and in the courts was a testament to how deeply the sickness had insinuated itself into Koch's government. The beast had almost as many lives as the mayor had shameful memories; each hidden blot seemed determined to be found.

The mayor's office became the center of the storm, and again and again he took the fifteen-step walk from it to the Blue Room for a press conference as though he were heading to the gallows—his shoulders stooped, his eyes down, his heavy body drooping, his face white. In the boom years, he had collected hundreds of news videotapes of his own performances, shown the best tapes to guests at the mansion, and kept a library under lock and key at the investigations department; but now the camera revealed night after night an aging face in anguish. The press performances he'd once lived for were suddenly a torture test; and the exuberance he had once conveyed through the lens so easily became a just as infectious sadness.

Ten days after the first Manes suicide attempt, and with Manes still contending from a hospital bed that he was the victim of a mysterious assault, Ed Koch announced that the city was canceling PVB's $22 million handheld computer contract with Stanley Friedman's Citisource. Geoffrey Lindenauer had been arrested a few days before, on a paltry $5,000 bribe, and he, Lester Shafran, and another PVB official had already been forced out of the agency by burgeoning federal and state probes. News stories pointed out that Lindenauer had played "a key role in the selection of Citisource," a fact that convinced a mayoral task force headed by corporation counsel Fritz Schwarz to spend the weekend after the arrest examining all the documents available at PVB about the contract.

It took Schwarz only a few hours to determine that the award process was a farce, as was the company's performance; he persuaded the mayor to immediately nullify the agreement. At their joint press conference, the mayor stressed the performance default as the basis for the cancellation, but Schwarz determinedly emphasized Friedman's misrepresentations to the city on the company's disclosure filings and his attempt to conceal the fact that he was Citisource's largest single shareholder.

With the mayor standing silently at his side, Schwarz also assailed the "curious process that was used to obtain the contract." He described how the request for proposals had been transparently stacked in favor of Citisource, and how the company had falsely claimed it had a working model of the computer. Neither Stan Brezenoff nor the mayor had informed Schwarz that the study he'd just completed of the contract was actually the second one commissioned by them. Schwarz, who was also kept in the dark about Friedman's deceptive description of his ties to the company in the 1984 meeting with Brezenoff, was not told that the earlier operations office review had concluded—just a few months before the scandal exploded—that everything was just fine. This face-saving report remained a secret for several more months, until it was unearthed by a *Newsday* reporter's freedom-of-information request.

Schwarz's assault on the contract clearly went further than the mayor had intended. Even now, Koch was trying to protect the long-standing mutual service agreements he had with Donald Manes, the invisible hand that hung over Schwarz's "curious process," and Stanley Friedman, the known beneficiary of the process. Indeed, the next night, shortly after Manes finally conceded that he'd tried to kill himself, Koch went to visit him in the hospital, brought him Chinese food, kissed him on the forehead, and reassured him: "Don't worry about anything, Donny, we all love you."

Friedman was treated no less tolerantly. The mayor issued a prepared statement the day after the press conference that went unquoted in the newspapers but effectively repudiated Schwarz. Instead of Schwarz's unambiguous declarations, the mayor's statement claimed that "the extent and nature of the disclosure" of Friedman's relationship to Citisource "has been and is being reviewed." The statement tried to dispel any suggestion that the cancellation was connected to suspected wrongdoing—asserting that the city has "no reason to believe" that the contract was even under investigation—and stating flatly that the city had "simply" exercised its rights "for failure to comply."

The mayor's extraordinary, and unnoticed, backstepping closed with an appeal to the man who Koch knew had lied to get this contract: "Stanley Friedman is a friend of mine and has been a political supporter," he said, adding, "I hope he still is." Koch even apologized to Friedman for having killed his sordid deal: "I regret the notoriety brought to Stanley Friedman as a shareholder in Citisource," he said, "which can be attributed to the cancellation of the contract at this particular time."

But the best barometer of the mayor's commitment to Friedman was Brezenoff's continuing reticence. The day after the cancellation, Friedman cited his 1984 meeting with Brezenoff to reporters as evidence that "everybody in City Hall knew" of his ties to Citisource. Instead of revealing Friedman's deceit at the 1984 meeting about his ownership interest in Citisource, Brezenoff merely told the *Times* that all the two had talked about was why the contract was being held up. Even while Koch acted to kill the contract that expressed in monetary terms the political alliance between him and Friedman, City Hall was still of two minds about how to handle this scandal, which was moving so quickly it could maim a career in a day.

Friedman himself had no trouble figuring out whom to blame: he zeroed in on Fritz Schwarz, telling reporters that he was a victim of a "Schwarz vendetta." In fact, Schwarz's widely reported comments about Friedman's deceptions, coupled with the documents he'd discovered, had attracted the attention of prosecutors who, up to then, had not really focused on the Citisource contract.

Ironically, the news stories at the time of the cancellation also quoted two of the city's top operations officials as conceding that the bid process "seemed to favor Citisource" and denying that either the operations or the budget office "ever gave their blessings" to the project. Brendan Sexton, the director of operations and author of the earlier and still secret memo to Brezenoff defending the award of the contract, was quoted as saying: "I don't think we ever thought this was the right way to do this contract or conduct this experiment."

But Sexton's shift in position was minor compared with the events of the next day. Jimmy Breslin's revelation that morning on the front page of the *Daily News* that Michael Dowd was cooperating with federal prosecutors suddenly pushed Manes to center stage again, forcing Citisource and Friedman temporarily into the background. The mayor held three consecutive press conferences, running a total of almost four hours, in a day described by the *Times* as one "of high tension and feverish activity at City Hall unlike anything since the fiscal crisis of a decade ago." Koch declared that Dowd's allegations had "a credibility," said the man he'd just hugged and kissed should consider stepping aside, and tried to put distance between himself and Manes, and even between himself and his own agency, the PVB.

Over the weekend that followed, the mayor began publicly pressing for Manes's resignation or impeachment, and denounced him as a "crook" on a Sunday morning television interview. The mayor was more circumspect about Friedman in the same interview: "As it relates to Stanley, I am not aware of any corruption. I want to make that clear. And it may turn out that there is, but I'm not aware of that."

On Monday, with Governor Cuomo caustically assailing Koch's rush to judgment on Manes, the mayor took off for California on a two-day swing to promote his latest book, *Politics*, published at the end of 1985.*

The book failed, in spite of publicity such as his appearance during this California tour on the "Tonight" show with Joan

---

*Ironically, his new book's first chapter—entitled "On the Merits"—began with the mayor's claim that he had "decided early on," and "never deviated from this," that "patronage was not going to be helpful to providing the best government for the city." He revealed that he gave the county leaders this bad news at his first meeting with them at City Hall in 1978, and it was met with "a silent gasp." The mayor wrote that he made his several hundred top appointments, especially commissioners and deputy mayors, "without regard to the political consideration of the county leaders and other political people who had helped me and now wanted me to select their choices."

Rivers, where he urged: "If you read it aloud, it's as if I'm in the room with you. Don't read it aloud in bed." But even as far away as California, reporters hounded him about Manes, especially after the borough president's one-sentence note announcing a leave of absence became public on Tuesday.

After two days in California, the mayor rushed back to City Hall to announce the resignation of transportation commissioner Anthony Ameruso, the embodiment of Koch's central contradiction. It was Ameruso's initial appointment, in defiance of the mayor's screening panel recommendations, that had caused panel chair Sally Goodgold to weep in her living room when Ed Koch attacked her selection process as bigoted. It was Ameruso whom Meade Esposito had publicly claimed as his own commissioner, and whose eight-year term as the longest-reigning Koch commissioner had been possible only because of his protective clubhouse connections.

When Koch and Ameruso went to the Blue Room for a farewell press conference that Wednesday, what the mayor knew, and the press didn't, was that Ameruso had, only a few months earlier, told City Hall that he had decided to name Lindenauer PVB director, replacing the retiring Shafran. With pressure from Manes, Ameruso had brushed aside the objections of the budget and operations offices, which regarded Lindenauer as parochial, secretive, unaccountable, hidebound, and "impossible." Rumors that Lindenauer also might not be honest had been circulating in and around City Hall for years, and concrete criminal allegations involving him had been conveyed directly to Ameruso. Brendan Sexton, who had been fired by Lindenauer from a low-level city job during the Beame administration, was so incensed about the possibility of Lindenauer's promotion that he went to Brezenoff's office, argued strenuously against it, got on Brezenoff's phone in front of the deputy mayor, and, with Brezenoff's support, told Ameruso that he had to withdraw the Lindenauer recommendation.

"He's first rate," Koch said of Ameruso at the press conference. "He's impeccable. He's honest. I'm sad that he's leaving, and I recommend him without reservation. I can't make it any stronger than that." After this litany was repeated several times, one reporter asked Koch if he hadn't said the same things about Manes just a week or so earlier. "What you've just done," the mayor replied, "is really quite offensive to Tony Ameruso. I honestly think that your question is out of order." The position that Koch and Ameruso took at this conference was that the PVB disaster had occurred on Ameruso's watch, and that he would have to be held accountable for it, even though he was unconnected with the crimes that had apparently occurred. Ameruso, who effusively praised the mayor and said he would work with Koch when the mayor ran "for his fifth, sixth, and seventh terms," claimed that he could not have "detected" the corruption that had long gripped his agency.

Both Ameruso and the mayor ducked repeated questions about the clubhouse origins of Ameruso, Shafran, Lindenauer, and other appointees within the agency. Koch said he had "no personal recollection of Meade Esposito calling" to press for Ameruso's appointment, though Esposito himself certainly recalled a direct conversation. Koch's hazy memory was a step clearer than his position just a few days earlier, when he had firmly declared, "No Brooklyn leader ever urged Ameruso's appointment or retention."

Then, when a reporter raised a question about damaging references to Ameruso on FBI mob tapes, Koch interjected, "You're smearing this guy." Pointing at the reporter with a quivering finger, a flushed mayor said: "I consider what you've done the pits."* Another reporter countered: "If Donald Manes is not convicted of any crime, can we conclude that you have smeared him by calling him a crook?" The mayor came unglued, rambling on about how "citizens spoke out about Nixon during Watergate and there was no conviction," and trailed off into non sequiturs.

The day after Ameruso resigned, Ed Koch met in the late afternoon with Pat McGinley, the city's silver-haired investigations commissioner. McGinley, the 48-year-old former judge who had been running DOI since 1982, was told he would have to resign or be fired. McGinley was in shock. He knew he had a problem but thought it was under control. Manhattan district attorney Robert Morgenthau had begun a probe of him three weeks earlier, examining the disability claim of a DOI detective who had supposedly hurt himself installing an air conditioner in McGinley's apartment. The detective's claim for a maximum city pension, however, attributed his injuries to other incidents, and was backed up in a letter to the pension board supposedly sent at the behest of McGinley.

---

*The denounced reporter was Wayne Barrett.

City Hall had been aware of the probe from the moment it started, and an already scandal-skittish Ed Koch was suddenly confronted with the possibility that his own anticorruption supercop could wind up indicted. He called Morgenthau personally, and the D.A. confirmed that his office was now intensively examining the case. After ordering McGinley to go to Morgenthau and answer all his questions, Koch had Fritz Schwarz monitor developments. Schwarz got McGinley's version of events—the detective had volunteered to install the air conditioner because of his wife's severe asthma, but McGinley had not heard that he was hurt doing it. Morgenthau, however, wasn't satisfied with McGinley's answers and would not give Schwarz a direct answer about whether he'd move to indict McGinley.

Alarmed by indications that a reporter was on to the story, Schwarz went to Morgenthau's office for a full briefing on the evidence against McGinley. The prosecutors implied that a criminal case was likely. More important, at least from the mayor's point of view, the leads they were following almost guaranteed that the investigation would drag on for a protracted time. McGinley had privately offered to step aside pending the outcome of the investigation, but the mayor never seriously considered that option. He wanted to be out front on this matter, not forced to fire his own top investigator in reaction to a news story. Schwarz and Brezenoff concurred—McGinley had to go.

McGinley saw himself in part a victim of intramural law enforcement antagonisms. He had offended Morgenthau by referring key cases to his rival, Rudy Giuliani, and had done a devastating report in 1984 on police commissioner Ben Ward's use of his office for late-night meetings with a woman (it was Ward, in turn, who had referred the air conditioner case to Morgenthau). But he believed that the mayor would hardly have been in such a rush to get rid of him, without even giving him a chance to respond to Morgenthau, had he not become such a pain in the ass in recent years.

Just a few months earlier, at the end of his second term, Koch had seriously considered firing McGinley, a decision Brezenoff favored as well. Their concern was that he had become a headline hunter, an increasingly independent scourge. Koch was still irate over McGinley's public report that Staten Island borough president Ralph Lamberti, a valued Koch ally, had broken the law. McGinley's 1985 report not only referred the criminal case against Lamberti to the island D.A.; it revealed that the city's Public Development Corporation was willing to pliantly turn over fifty acres of city land to Lamberti's friend and secret business partner, even though the developer had no plans for half the parcel.*

Both Lamberti and Koch had been in the middle of reelection campaigns when McGinley dropped his bomb, and though the mayor was certain to win, he did not let a criminal charge get in the way of an alliance. He was photographed hugging Lamberti and was quoted describing Lamberti as "honest, straightforward, and honorable" in "all" his dealings with him. Koch endorsed the reelection of a man his investigations commissioner had accused of misconduct.

The Lamberti case was one of a series, ranging from conflict charges against the port commissioner to misconduct allegations involving Bess Myerson's chauffeur, that had strained the relationship between Koch and McGinley. But at the end of 1985, Koch, Brezenoff, and Fritz Schwarz met with McGinley and told him he would be reappointed, insisting, though, that he temper the language of his public reports. With those events fresh in his memory, McGinley believed that City Hall was using the air conditioner probe as a pretext, and that if the mayor hadn't come to view him as a wild card, this case would hardly have been enough to finish him.

The mayor made no attempt to mimic his praise for Ameruso at McGinley's farewell press conference that Friday afternoon. He leaned on the podium and said little, while McGinley bitterly observed that "in normal times, a situation like this is resolved easily." When a dejected McGinley returned to his office after the resignation, he got what would turn out to be even worse news than the pink slip.

A *Times* reporter was waiting on the phone, writing a story that quoted an unnamed former DOI official who claimed that McGinley had failed to act a year earlier on suggestions from senior staff that he open a broad inquiry into PVB. The source also said that DOI had received numerous reports about corruption in the parking bureau during McGinley's tenure. McGinley

---

*A Staten Island grand jury refused to indict Lamberti. News accounts later reported that federal prosecutors also declined prosecution, citing a change in court interpretations of the mail fraud statute.

declined to respond directly. The next day's paper carried his resignation on the front page, and inside, the story of the unheeded PVB warnings.

The mayor had been claiming since the scandal began that he had no way of knowing what was going on at PVB, and now the *Times* was reporting warnings at his own back door. In his tense resignation meeting with McGinley on Thursday, the mayor had just shrugged his shoulders when McGinley had at one point warned that if he quit now, "everyone will think it involves PVB." No one had ever mentioned any DOI shortcomings in uncovering PVB corruption as a reason for McGinley's departure, but suddenly it was the companion story to his dismissal. When Koch appeared on a Sunday interview show that weekend, he was ready to sharply criticize McGinley's running of the department, questioning the value received for the millions in city funds that had been spent on investigations, and announcing that he was going to have someone look into the *Times* allegations about the failure of DOI to follow up on information about PVB.

Koch then asked former U.S. Attorney John Martin to conduct this probe. He had named Martin to head an amorphous "commission" he'd established a few weeks earlier, shortly after the PVB story broke, saying then that Martin would undertake an "independent" examination of the municipal contracting process, exploring how the city got into this mess and how it could protect itself against a recurrence. Though no one was clear about exactly what Martin was supposed to do, Koch had decided to establish this "commission"—as he called the one-member body—to preempt the naming of a real investigative body by the governor. Martin had a prestigious title and the look of a boy scout, but other than his successful prosecution of ex–Bronx boss Pat Cunningham, concluded four years after Cunningham quit politics, he hadn't brought a significant public corruption case while U.S. Attorney. A next-door neighbor of Allen Schwartz—Koch's former law partner, ex–corporation counsel, and close adviser—Martin had actually represented Koch *pro bono* on one personal legal matter.

Koch's delivery of the DOI cover-up probe to Martin enabled him to keep in house the element of the scandal most threatening to him: what he knew about PVB, and when he knew it. Over the next few months, news stories appeared sporadically about other early signals at DOI that all was not right at PVB, but Martin's own DOI probe and McGinley's very expensive air conditioner largely disappeared from the scandal coverage. However, Koch's choice to succeed McGinley, Ken Conboy, a social friend of the mayor's and the first DOI commissioner ever appointed from a mayor's personal staff, began an almost immediate drumbeat of harsh criticism of the McGinley reign, publicly calling it "ineffective" for not having uncovered the trouble at the parking bureau. The battered McGinley, who only a few months earlier had been privately assailed by the mayor for behaving like a bulldog, suddenly found himself under attack from the same quarters, but this time as a lamb.

By the beginning of the second month of scandal, the mayor was publicly acknowledging that he was so depressed he was having trouble sleeping. (Normally, Koch could take a doze at a red light.) He canceled his annual State of the City speech, planned for February 5. Reeling from daily punches, he was not ready for a strategic overview.

When Donald Manes turned his leave of absence into a resignation in mid-February, the mayor said little, and took off to Boston for a one-day book tour. When Koch got back to New York, he found himself, for the first time, besieged by questions from reporters about his role in the demise of the 1982 sting of Manes's old friend, taxi commissioner Herb Ryan. The case, which had never before attracted much attention, suddenly surfaced because one of the local TV stations, WNBC, had managed to get a copy of the videotape of Ryan offering to introduce Eddie Gruskin to Manes. During a quick press conference, the mayor acknowledged ordering Ryan's arrest, and bringing the sting down, but said he had no recollection of Manes's name ever having come up at his meeting with then DOI chief Stan Lupkin and others. Although Koch's denial temporarily stymied reporters, Lupkin himself then made it clear that not only had Manes been mentioned but that the taped references to Manes were "described in detail" to the mayor.

In a second press conference the following day, Koch admitted that Manes had been named during the meeting, but said he did not consider the reference significant. "There was never a statement to me, an inference, or an implication that Donny Manes was the target of any corruption," he explained. "And if there had been, and if they told me that, obviously I would have had a different point of view." Lupkin's response was that the investigation was at "too early a stage" for that sort of charge, and that "no one was targeted," at least in a formal, law enforcement sense. But he said that prosecutors were all "very excited" over what Lupkin called "the potential of exploring where else it might go." A rueful Lupkin recalled: "Ideally, when you get a situation like this, you want to run out the string."

While each paper did a Saturday story on the new Ryan issues, none put the mayor's sting-killing decision in the context of his simultaneous wooing of Manes's gubernatorial endorsement. It became a one-day story.

The next assault occurred only a few days later. On February 18, the *Village Voice* published a front-page story by us and Bill Bastone, disclosing that the "impeccable" Tony Ameruso, who was still in office and was scheduled to be until the end of the month, had secretly invested in a Manhattan parking lot with the head of a mob-tied carting company, a Queens Supreme Court judge just convicted of fixing mob cases, and three close associates of Meade Esposito. Our *Voice* story revealed that Ameruso had cleared $100,000 when the group sold the lot in 1985, and that he'd never reported either the investment or his share of a mortgage on city financial disclosure forms. Ameruso's department regulated the carting and parking industries.

When confronted about the allegations on a Tuesday evening news show, a stunned Koch said that if they were proven true, "it would be more than distressing, an enormous shock. . . . I believed him to be an honest man." At first Koch indicated that he was referring the matter to DOI, where McGinley was still serving out his final days, but he quickly placed the probe under the authority of John Martin and ordered Ameruso to appear "forthwith" for questioning. Martin and Ameruso spent hours together the next day with Ameruso's lawyers. "It has shaken us up, shaken us up," Koch said of the latest revelations. "And maybe out of that we can make some progress."

Without questioning anyone other than Ameruso, Martin gave Koch a quick report that adopted the essence of Ameruso's argument. Ameruso claimed he had deliberately invested twenty-five dollars less than the $20,000 threshold required on the city's disclosure form. And though he was a signatory and personally guaranteed the $250,000 mortgage he and his partners obtained to finance the purchase of the lot, Ameruso argued he didn't have to list it as a loan on the city's forms because it was a liability of the parking lot company. Once Martin agreed that Ameruso had effectively dodged the requirements of the disclosure statutes, all he could find was that Ameruso had "violated the spirit of the law." Martin stressed that his findings were preliminary, and promised a more detailed report in the future.

Pressed by reporters about the vote of confidence he'd given Ameruso on the day of his resignation barely two weeks earlier, Koch said that if he'd known then what he knew now, he would not have made those remarks. He volunteered that the daily scandal developments were making him angry. "I'd like to open up the window and yell: 'I'm not gonna take it anymore.' "

Effortlessly, Ed Koch had converted himself, at least in his own mind, into the scandal's primary victim. A number of weeks before the Ameruso revelations, the mayor had told a group of new judges at a swearing-in ceremony: "You know it's easy to become overwhelmed by the corruption of others and the feelings of betrayal. It's easy to start feeling sorry for yourself, and I try not to. But occasionally . . . I start saying to myself, 'Geez, what did I do to deserve this?' " Or, in mid-January, shortly after PVB was first uncovered, his stream of consciousness public posture was: "Here I was thinking I was running the most honest government in the history of the world, and suddenly, like it's a fish smack in your face."

Such statements were not a public relations gimmick, a strategy crafted by skilled advisers designed to shift elsewhere the onus for the exploitation of his government. This was Ed Koch saying out loud the only thoughts about the cause of the disaster that he would permit to stir in his head. Those who sat with him for hours, then weeks, then months, wrestling with the unraveling scandal and possible reforms, cannot recall a single reflective moment when he surrendered to self-examination and criticism. Doubt was a disease he had immunized himself against for years, with a daily dosage of camera-induced, poll-sustained, ego indulgence. He was, in his own eyes, as innocent, and as consistently vulnerable to unprovoked attack, as a punching bag. Anyone who suggested otherwise was just being that old bugaboo again—his enemy.

But it became clear even to Koch that he had to rise above

the daily headlines, and move the issue to a higher plane. He had to figure out a way of assuming some degree of responsibility without accepting any hint of blame. He had to convey concern and a willingness to act, or at least appear that he was willing. A summons to Gracie Mansion was issued to a host of top advisers. The regulars—Brezenoff, Schwarz, his counsel Pat Mulhearn—were there. Dave Garth, the campaign media wizard, told Koch that his greatest "vulnerability" was that he would begin to "look like a schmuck" for not having known, to look as if he'd been manipulated by a den of seedy flatterers.

Bob Wagner, Jr. was there, too, long departed as a deputy mayor, the boyish look of his early Koch years lost in tired eyes. Wagner urged the mayor to focus on his relationship with the county leaders. He knew that the speech they had gathered to design had to examine this issue, which lay at the heart of the scandal, and he knew that the mayor had to be prepared to make some admissions about the nature of his alliances. But Wagner, whose quiet loyalty to Koch during his years in the government had often been rewarded with abuse and spiteful indifference to his views, understood that he could only convince the mayor to go so far in this direction. He clearly could not get him to admit what Wagner himself had publicly: "What Ed did was create a climate for commissioners, and they all sort of try to read the tea leaves, that accommodating borough presidents and county leaders was the order of the day."

The speech that emerged, delivered on February 24 in the Board of Estimate chamber where Manes and Friedman had once exercised power, was a jigsaw puzzle of admission and defense, sounding in its broad strokes like an expression of regrets but wrapped masterfully in a caveat of justification. "I am embarrassed, chagrined, and mortified that this kind of corruption could have existed and that I didn't know of it," Koch proclaimed, and admitted that his administration had "lost the distance and controls I had hoped to maintain in order to avoid the undue influence of party leaders on the workings of government." But he attributed the rise of the party bosses within his government to his need "to work with the established political structure to resolve the fiscal crisis"—not to any self-serving political alliance.

Koch noted that he'd fought against the influence of the clubhouse all his life and claimed that as mayor "I have tried to continue that fight," a statement at odds not only with the eight-and-a-half-year history of mutual, back-scratching political endorsements but at odds with what he had written in his own books. His concession, "We let our guard down and now we're paying the price," was mitigated by his simultaneous contention that, to obtain assistance for the financially troubled city from Washington, from Albany, from the city council, from wherever, he had let the party leaders in.

Koch delivered the speech in his shirt sleeves at the swearing-in of Ken Conboy, the new DOI commissioner. After his description of the roots of the scandal, the mayor announced a series of reforms, including the creation of a merit selection panel to appoint members to politically plagued bodies like Standards and Appeals and the taxi commission. He also said he would seek state legislation to bar party leaders from profiting from city business, a reform that only a few weeks earlier he had scornfully dismissed.

The most effective rebuttal of the alibis offered in Koch's speech came quietly, in the form of an unnoticed speech several months later by David Brown, the mayor's former congressional aide and top deputy mayor in the first year of the administration. Once extremely close to Koch, Brown had long been unhappy with the direction of his government, but had never become a public critic. He'd slipped into an academic, very private life, teaching some at Yale and living year round in the Hamptons. In a lecture at the Yale Club of New York City, Brown challenged the Koch analysis of the scandal's origins: "He is wrong to imply that no one could have figured out that the political conditions developing in New York City over the past eight years were likely to promote the kind of corruption that is now finally being uncovered."

"From the outset of his first term," Brown observed, "Koch started to indulge himself in the arts of charisma and reaching out to the clubhouse. Early on Koch realized that the threat posed to his reelection in 1981 would come from reformers on the left in his party. . . . So being an astute politician, he started cultivating the Democratic county leaders through the practice of patronage. . . . I have read recent remarks of the mayor that his dealings with the county leaders were inspired by his need for their help in moving the city beyond the fiscal crisis. It's a plausible explanation, but I don't recall it ever being discussed on those terms in his first term when the fiscal crisis was our major preoccupation. What I saw was a former reform councilman and congressman from Manhattan mending his political fences with the regular party organizations in the outer boroughs."

Brown pointed out that the names everyone was reading now—and he listed Ameruso, taxi boss Jay Turoff, Alex Liberman, and PVB's Lester Shafran—were "holdovers" from the Beame years. "Many of the holdovers did keep their jobs, which encouraged the county leaders that you could do business with the new mayor." This deal "removed the threat of any solid political opposition to his reelection," Brown concluded, "and paved the way for his big victories in 1981 and 1985. . . . His agencies . . . got the message that it was OK to work closely with the party establishment."

"As it turned out," said Brown, who once headed the State Investigations Commission and had somewhat of a law enforcement perspective of government, "the blessing of county leader support for Koch has proved to be a curse. The county leaders grafted their borough monopolies onto his successful administration. They also became his pals at a political cost now to Koch that is hard to calculate."

Two days after his own scandal speech, Koch announced the resignations of three more commissioners—Jay Turoff, housing commissioner Tony Gliedman, and general services chief Robert Litke. This time the mayor held no press conference, but merely made terse statements about Turoff and Litke's departures. Unnamed mayoral sources were quoted in news stories conceding that Turoff's demise was connected with an ongoing state probe that had begun attracting press attention. Litke, too, had been assailed in recent stories for his facilitation of questionable city leases for friends of Manes and Esposito, but no one acknowledged that they were a factor in the departure.

Gliedman's resignation was casually revealed by the mayor, to the surprise of everyone in the Blue Room, at a press conference with the commissioner to announce a new housing program. Even more shocking was Gliedman's answer to a reporter who wanted to know about his future plans: "Well, what I'm doing, frankly, I'm joining the Trump Organization," explaining that developer Donald Trump had offered him a top post. Contrary to what Koch officials said at the time, a senior aide later acknowledged that all three men had been asked to resign. It was hardly a coincidence that Turoff and Gliedman, like their departed Brooklyn clubhouse brother Ameruso, had been publicly claimed by Meade Esposito as his appointees. While this designation had always been hotly disputed by the capable Gliedman, he did not deny that he and Esposito had long been close.

Then, on the last day of the second month of the scandal, the mayor held a hastily arranged news conference around a hallway radiator at City Hall to announce the departure of the nineteenth high-ranking official since the end of 1985. He had dismissed the city's commissioner of business development, Larry Kieves, he explained, because he'd discovered that Kieves owned stock in a company that was obtaining relocation assistance from Kieves's own office. The company had come to the city's attention, and was receiving an array of costly subsidies, through Kieves.

The same day as the Kieves decision, subpoenas were served on several development agencies for documents related to a host of projects approved by the city for Donald Manes's favorite developer, Michael Lazar. The probes were now reaching into the city's public development process. Ed Koch was coming to understand that his problems were as formidable as his alliance with Manes, Esposito, and Friedman had once been, and that the scope of this trio's former influence inside his government was now a minimal indicator of just how widespread the corruption was. It was a scary thought.

Though March would bring the death of Donald Manes and the indictments of Michael Lazar, Lester Shafran, and Stanley Friedman, the most frequent newsmaker was taxi czar Jay Turoff. Although he had resigned in the final days of February, he was scheduled to stay in office until April 30. During that period, the Taxi and Limousine Commission suddenly shoved the PVB aside as the scandal agency of the moment.

The State Investigation Commission (SIC), which funnels public corruption cases it develops to state and federal prosecutors, had been probing Turoff since 1984, driven by the same allegations raised two years earlier at DOI by fleet owner and whistleblower Barbara Myers. A 1960s hippie and antiwar protestor who'd wound up running her own small cab company, Myers had appeared on a television show with a special assistant to the mayor and charged that the taxi commission was "corrupt." In later briefings at DOI, Myers provided specific details on Turoff's suspicious manipulation of a taxi meter contract and the distribution by the commission of 100 new taxi medallions—each worth $80,000 at the time—to a few favored fleet owners for an experiment on the use of diesel fuel that she called "a fraud."*

What Myers did not know, and the subsequent investigation uncovered, was that the same lawyer who had worked as a lobbyist for the taxi association to keep the number of taxis frozen had also represented the principals of the favored firm that received Turoff's new, experimental medallions: Stanley Friedman. Myers's warnings were ignored at DOI, and picked up later at the state commission only because they fit a pattern of complaints from cab drivers and others.

By August 1985, when the SIC probe first surfaced in a *New York Post* story, the investigation was moving in several directions. The *Post* reported that the agency was looking at Turoff's Atlantic City gambling habits. While Turoff denied that he had a line of credit there and said he'd only been to Atlantic City "two or three times," he had in fact gambled twenty-three times between June 1982 and September 1984. Not only had he been given a line of credit; he'd received complimentary accommodations as well. Turoff told the *Post*, "I don't play cards," when he was actually a fanatical blackjack player who'd lost $2,000 on a single visit.

The same week that the *Post* ran its story, Turoff was ingratiating himself with the mayor by working in Koch's primary reelection campaign. His former top assistant, Robert Mackasek, the one-time inspector general who had helped him nail the bumbling Herb Ryan in 1982 and was now in private practice representing taxi operators, acted as a transportation coordinator for the mayor's reelection committee. Turoff himself helped arrange for more than thirty taxi and car service companies to drive Koch voters and volunteers to the polls, an in-kind campaign donation worth an estimated $45,000. He also raised $30,000 in direct contributions. And he spent the two election days—primary and general—at Koch's campaign headquarters acting as a cab dispatcher.

---

*Every legal cab in the city has to carry a medallion bonded to its hood. Since the 1930s, the number of medallions available has been frozen by law at 11,700 to keep the supply limited and the value rising.

As a longtime protégé of Meade Esposito, and a campaigner for Koch, Turoff maintained a hold on his TLC job that was unshaken by the SIC probe—at least until the Manes scandal heated everything up. In February, SIC chairman David Trager, the former U.S. Attorney from Brooklyn, began talking with Brooklyn federal prosecutors about a criminal case against Turoff. By March, the acting U.S. Attorney, Reena Raggi, and Tony Valenti, the agency's longtime top investigator, were beginning to work with SIC staff. Without the FBI, without wiretaps, and against a racing time clock, the pair uncovered two separate Turoff scandals in ninety days.

Late in the first week of March, Valenti and Raggi learned that a break-in had occurred at the offices of the TLC, located on 42d Street in an otherwise deserted office building owned by former TLC chairman Michael Lazar. New DOI commissioner Ken Conboy was alerted as well. Investigators determined that the records of the experimental medallion program had been tampered with and that some of the medallions themselves were missing. Turoff claimed that after the break-in, he'd discovered some of the missing medallions in a trash can at the office—a retrieval almost no one believed.

While no one could sort out exactly what had happened, Turoff was summoned to City Hall and told to depart immediately, six weeks ahead of schedule. An hour later the now ex-commissioner was heard—by federal agents wiretapping the phones of Meade Esposito in an unrelated investigation—informing his mentor: "Chief, I've been assassinated."

On March 13, the same night that Donald Manes killed himself, another break-in occurred, this time at the TLC's offices in Queens. Neither television sets, typewriters, nor tape recorders were stolen, but a cabinet had been opened with a key, and records of the medallion experiment were taken. The next night, Valenti led a raid on the cab companies that had been given the experimental medallions. When he reached the office of Donald Sherman, a cab industry titan close to Friedman and Turoff, he saw "tens of thousands of dollars in cash" lying around—on shelves, in drawers, on his desk—mostly in $100 bills. The stacks of money had rubber bands around them, not bank tape. It didn't look like payroll money; it looked like loose cash.

Valenti's search warrant stipulated "books and records," so he wasn't authorized even to count the cash. But he did find what he was looking for—actual taxi medallions and log books listing medallions by number. By law the medallions should have been either on a cab or at the TLC offices; the logs established that Sherman had in fact had custody of all 123 medallions. A former cab driver himself, Valenti knew that he'd hit a home run.

Two weeks later, Valenti led another search party into a credit union on Coney Island Avenue in Brooklyn, near Turoff's old clubhouse. The credit union had forged documents, made improper loans, and covertly financed Compumeter, the company Turoff had given a temporary monopoly on taxi meters. Valenti instructed Edmund Lee, the founder and director of the union, to leave the premises while the loan records were searched. Lee, who had built an empire out of IRS dodges, taxi loans, and bogus books, tried to leave with a folder under his arm, but a state investigator with Valenti stopped him. "What's that under your arm?" she asked. "My personal tax returns," Lee answered. The investigators seized Lee's folders and discovered the documents that led to his arrest and to Jay Turoff's eventual indictment.

Lee soon pleaded guilty to embezzling $15 million from his credit union, which prospered principally on the deposits of underpaid hospital workers and taxi drivers. He also claimed that he had paid Turoff a $30,000 bribe for aiding Compumeter by making a computerized cash transfer to a secret account Turoff maintained at the credit union. Filled with mysterious cash deposits and described by the government as an equivalent of a "Swiss bank account," the account had been used to hide thousands in interest payments from the IRS. Turoff had obtained this protection in exchange for providing Lee with a confidential TLC list of medallion owners.

New revelations about Turoff hit the newspapers almost daily during March and April, culminating in an SIC public hearing, at which Turoff and Donald Sherman both took the Fifth Amendment. SIC's chairman, David Trager, a friend of the mayor's who also chaired Koch's judicial nominating panel, was so disturbed by the findings of the Turoff probe that he publicly called for the disbanding of the taxi commission, charging that Koch's agency was hopelessly corrupt and mismanaged. Trager also announced that Turoff had masterminded the diesel experiment scheme, getting the cooperation of another city agency (the Department of Environmental Protection) to deliver $20 million in extra revenue to Sherman's company, which got the fraudulent medallions.

In May, the mayor admitted that he had known of Turoff's helpful role in his 1985 campaign, and DOI eventually issued a report condemning the thousands of dollars' worth of taxi time contributed to the Koch reelection effort and not reported, as required under law, on campaign disclosure forms. Turoff's meter indictment didn't come until June, and the medallion case, charging him with conspiracy and massive obstruction of justice, until the spring of 1987. He was eventually convicted on tax and conspiracy charges in the meter case, though acquitted of a $30,000 bribe; his co-defendants, the principals of the meter company, were convicted on all counts. The medallion case has been repeatedly postponed, but the combined findings of the SIC and the federal jury left little doubt that the taxi commission, like the PVB, had been allowed over the Koch years to become an emblem of the clubhouse's criminal class, prized and plundered.

The Turoff revelations were only part of a spring offensive that seemed to revive every forgotten scandal of the Koch years. Even former parking lot lease king Rick Mazzeo, whose conviction and death had attracted virtually no press attention in 1983, became a *New York Post* banner headline that asked three years too late: WAS CITY AIDE KILLED TO KEEP HIS MOUTH SHUT? U.S. Attorney Ray Dearie was quoted as saying that Mazzeo "was possibly killed to shut him up," and that "we have been aware for some time that his death may have been related to his city duties."

Several weeks after that story appeared, Stan Brezenoff announced that the administration had discovered a "cluster" of politically appointed officials at the top of the ferry bureau, and was now moving to "break it up" by transferring personnel out of it. Brezenoff said the transfers were a "precaution" against the kind of corruption found at the PVB. While the parking bureau was staffed down the line from the Queens Democratic organization, the ferry employees were attached, said the *Times,* to its Staten Island counterpart. And, once again contrary to the Koch claims that there was no patronage in his administration, the ex–environmental commissioner conceded that he'd been enlisted by City Hall to hire hundreds of sewer and water laborers on the recommendation of county leaders, principally Stanley Friedman.

In late March, parks commissioner Henry Stern pronounced the formal demise of the Grand Prix. Manes's former assistant and Grand Prix president Dan Koren said he was "surprised" by Stern's comments, attributing them to "nervousness" over Queens investigations. A *Times* editorial recalled that Koch had said, "We've got to do this for Donny," and had silenced all objections. "Such good riddance for a bad idea still leaves a sour taste," said the *Times*. "How many of City Hall's earnest arguments masked a cynical agenda? All New Yorkers should mourn their leaders' loss of credibility."

Even Alex Liberman returned to public prominence. His name first began to turn up in news stories amid speculation that he was talking to federal prosecutors. Then his information became a count in the indictment against Michael Lazar, whom Liberman accused of bribing him to get the taxi commission lease. DOI was given dozens of such tips from Liberman and began following them up with new probes of suspect leases.

In late March and early April, a series of state and federal indictments was announced—Friedman, Lazar, Shafran, Citisource president Marvin Kaplan, other Citisource principals, and other collection company executives and lawyers, including Manes's old law partner. By then, the mayor's earlier backpedaling on Friedman's behalf had been abandoned. Once an indictment appeared likely, Koch announced with great fanfare that he would not be attending Friedman's annual Bronx dinner dance, where he had at one time told the assembled dignitaries, "At least I know where my commissioners are tonight."

Again the *Times* editorial page, where Ed Koch had enjoyed eight years of reflected glory, said that the indictments painted "an appalling picture of self-enriching influence-peddling by politicians who distracted the normally shrewd Mayor Koch with their vote-getting services for him." The *Times* disputed Koch's excuse that he hadn't personally hired the wire pullers. "Letting unelected, unappointed alumni of city bureaus run them for private profit was the system."

In April, the *Village Voice* revealed that the city had granted $20 million in plumbing contracts, including prison and precinct jobs, to a small firm headed by Manes's next-door neighbor and friend, who was also under indictment in a federal racketeering case for laundering mob narcotics profits. The firm employed John Gotti, the most notorious gangster in the city and head of the Gambino crime family, who was listed as a salesman for the plumber. In the uproar that followed the story, Koch moved to cancel pending contracts for the company, and the Brooklyn D.A. indicted and convicted it for false filings with the city.

The Queens D.A. now opened a probe of yet another Manes offshoot. The city's Public Development Corporation had approved, at Manes's urging, the no-bid sale of the air rights over a city parking garage located behind Manes's Borough Hall office. The developer had made an illegal $10,000 contribution to Manes's campaign, twice the corporate campaign limit, as well as hired Manes's son and his personal lawyer Sid Davidoff. The D.A. learned that the developer, who wanted to build a $75 million office tower, had agreed to pay Davidoff a $750,000 finder's fee for this deal, even though the PDC had advertised the site in a 1982 brochure. Not incidentally, Manes was telling his close friends before the PVB scandal that he was planning to leave office and become a partner in Davidoff's firm. The city moved to cancel the mysterious Queens office deal, as well as all of Michael Lazar's PDC-assisted projects.

As the investigations gained momentum, key Friedman appointees, lodged at various city agencies, found themselves in trouble. Planning commissioner Ted Teah, named in connection with the cable and other probes, resigned. Transportation counsel Robert Shaw, a leading member of Friedman's Riverdale club, refused to waive immunity and testify about the long-term no-bid monopoly on highway towing contracts by an association represented by Manes's ex–law partner. He, too, resigned.

DOI, meanwhile, found that a whistleblower at the Department of Environmental Protection who had suggested that corruption was involved in the handling of a billion dollars in water tunnel construction contracts had been improperly demoted and harassed by a top deputy in the agency appointed on Friedman's recommendation. Friedman also represented a principal in the water tunnel consortium. The whistleblower, Ed Nicastro, had tried unsuccessfully for years to draw attention, first to the corruption, and then to the retaliation against him. In fact, his wife, who'd acted as Koch's volunteer driver in the first mayoral campaign of 1977, had written the mayor a personal letter on the matter in 1985, but received only a form letter in reply. As a result of the new DOI findings, Nicastro at last won salary and title restorations. The deputy commissioner who'd harassed him was demoted, and eventually quit.

The picture that emerged from these repeated revelations

was that the administration was rife with fixes. But as the taint spread from agency to agency, it grew less intimate, and less shocking. By late spring, it had become a blur of scandal stories, with the mayor receding into the background. Nevertheless, one episode, less venal than most of the other crimes uncovered during the period, took on a special prominence precisely because it brought the news focus squarely back on the mayor. By June, it became the galvanizing event of the scandal calendar, and led to the resignation of the closest associate of Koch yet to fall before this whirlwind: Victor Botnick.

The Botnick debacle began with the announcement in April of the indictment of former city hospital chief John McLaughlin. McLaughlin had actually already been indicted once, in the summer of 1985, and had resigned then to defend himself against charges that he had pillaged the assets of a law client. When he was indicted again, the new charges included a $150,000 bribe that prosecutors alleged he'd taken in the form of cheap stock from a hospital contractor.*

Botnick was first publicly connected with this case in May, when it was discovered that the mayor's youthful health adviser had made eleven trips to California, at a city cost in excess of $21,000, to visit with the same consulting company that had allegedly bribed McLaughlin, and that he and McLaughlin had occasionally traveled there together. That news in turn revived a forgotten story from 1984, when it was reported that Botnick had solicited a $5,000 campaign contribution from the company, called NuMed, shortly after the city's hospital corporation had, with Botnick's support, awarded NuMed a million-dollar contract.

Now, in light of the NuMed trips, reporters began to take a closer look at this longtime Koch aide and new hospital corporation president, described by Koch's closest government advisers as having a unique relationship with the mayor. Ed Koch liked Botnick's singleminded toughness in the face of carping critics; it reminded him of his own. He appreciated the cutting humor and commonsense directness of this man he called his "avenging angel"; they, too, reminded him of his own. But what Ed Koch valued most about Victor Botnick, who he openly boasted he had "created," was that unlike many in his close circle of advisers, Botnick was nothing without him.

---

*McLaughlin was ultimately acquitted on the bribe count, but convicted on several lesser charges.

It had long been known that the mayor rarely traveled without Botnick as a companion, whether it be on vacation trips to Israel, Egypt, Lebanon, Germany, and Italy, all paid for by the host countries, or on several book promotion tours, financed by the publishing house, or on personal appearance swings, covered by the campaign kitty. What was not known was that Botnick had also taken 106 trips around the country at city expense, ostensibly on hospital corporation business, and that the amount of money he spent on his travels was "shocking," according to the state comptroller. A week after these excesses made the news, it was revealed that Botnick had failed to list his wife's employment on city disclosure forms. He explained this oversight as an "inadvertent error," though she worked as an administrator of a private medical center that had a $31 million contract with the city hospital corporation Botnick had run for years, first as a behind-the-scenes mayoral adviser and most recently as its president.

The mayor paid little attention to these stories, but in late May, the volatile Botnick, who was licensed to carry a thirty-eight-caliber Colt and a twenty-five-caliber Beretta semiautomatic, got into a shoving match with the head of the doctor's union in his corporation office. While preparing a routine story on the assault charges the doctor had filed against Botnick, Kevin McCoy, a *Daily News* reporter, asked Botnick where he'd gone to college. Botnick repeated what he had been telling reporters and the city for years: he was a graduate of Mercy College in Dobbs Ferry. When McCoy noticed that another newspaper's story indicated that Botnick had graduated from Fordham, he began checking the records and discovered that Botnick had actually attended four colleges, without graduating from any of them.

When this deception was exposed, the mayor insisted at a press conference that McCoy had misquoted Botnick, that his loyal friend had not misled the reporter, and that the mayor had always known that Botnick had not graduated from college. Reporters asked for a copy of a résumé Botnick might have submitted to the city before his appointment. The mayor said none had been required; apparently, Botnick had taken over the nation's largest hospital system, and was spending $2 billion a year, employing 45,000 people, and running sixteen hospitals, without a degree or a résumé.

Finally, on June 5, the mayor and Botnick appeared together at a second press conference. They revealed that Botnick had himself secretly taped the phone interview with the *Daily News* and that when the mayor asked Botnick if he had, Botnick had conceded that his tape verified McCoy's account of the conversation. Koch now acknowledged that Botnick had lied, not only to the reporter but to him, about what he'd told the reporter.

But even during this public display of penitence, with the mayor next to him, Botnick lied again, by stating that he'd never claimed a bachelor's degree when he filled out a city background form. At a second press conference later the same day, Botnick admitted he'd done just that, but had forgotten about the false 1978 form until after the earlier conference, when he'd decided to check with DOI. Incredibly, at a third press conference on the same day, Botnick conceded that Koch's counsel had discovered the old DOI form two days earlier, and that he'd been participating in discussions about it ever since.

This extraordinary performance was followed by revelations that Botnick had lied on the written statement prepared for the press conference about where he'd graduated from high school, and also exaggerated his height by four or five inches. And he'd even fabricated a story, repeated over the years in published profiles of him, about how he met Koch. Botnick had described a dramatic, chance encounter at the Wailing Wall in Jerusalem when in fact Botnick's father had introduced them on a Manhattan street.

The following day, Koch announced a punishment crafted by Fritz Schwarz—Botnick was to serve 240 hours of orderly duty in a hospital, caring for the terminally ill. Later that afternoon, Koch attended a budget meeting at City Hall with D.A. Robert Morgenthau, who was prosecuting the McLaughlin case, and other city officials. He greeted Morgenthau with a boast about the punishment he'd devised for Botnick. But Morgenthau, who knew a great deal more about Botnick's deception than the press was yet reporting, was not at all satisfied with the mayor's plan.

The next day Morgenthau met with Fritz Schwarz to detail a disturbing story of Botnick's involvement in the McLaughlin case. Morgenthau said that Botnick had agreed in late 1985 to help the then ongoing investigation of McLaughlin's stock bribe from NuMed. He'd said he was willing to try to draw NuMed president Maurice Lewitt into a phone conversation Morgenthau's office could tape. Morgenthau's office wanted Botnick to get Lewitt to discuss the stock given to McLaughlin. But when the call was placed to Lewitt's California office, with a detective listening on an extension phone in Botnick's City Hall office, Botnick did not ask Lewitt the questions Morgenthau had anticipated. At one point Lewitt volunteered to discuss the matter and Botnick hushed him up, insisting they talk later.

When Botnick was subsequently subpoenaed by Morgenthau's grand jury and presented with his taping lapses, he protested that he had been distracted by a long-standing and painful back problem (he was, in fact, operated on shortly after the taping). But later Botnick admitted to the jury that he was afraid Lewitt would "lie" and implicate him in the stock offer, which he claimed under oath to know nothing about. In fact, McLaughlin contended that Botnick had been present when the stock arrangement was made. Through a California attorney, Lewitt eventually tried to steer a neutral course—agreeing with McLaughlin that Botnick was in the room, but adding that there was a lot of "noise" and that Botnick might not have heard the brief conversation. Botnick's dealings with the D.A. were so shabby, Morgenthau said, that he was unusable as a trial witness against McLaughlin. He was also now the subject of a possible perjury case.

When Fritz Schwarz brought this news back to the mayor, it did not appear to surprise the mayor at all. In fact the mayor had been deeply involved in the initial planning of how Botnick would handle the Morgenthau matter. Koch had suggested to Botnick that he use as his own attorney in the case, the mayor's unofficial personal lawyer and ex-partner Allen Schwartz. Allen Schwartz had been present during the aborted taping, and it was he who had instructed Botnick not to pursue the line of questioning planned for the Lewitt conversation.

That weekend the mayor agonized. He told reporters, who knew nothing about Morgenthau's briefing or Botnick's taping performance, that this was "probably the most painful period I've ever been through in my life." When Botnick's departure was announced the following week, everyone at City Hall went to great lengths to describe it as a resignation, but the mayor had forced him out. Koch then went on a rampage, calling reporters "sharks," a one-time Botnick nickname. He said that the press was "out of control," and began demanding that reporters and editors release disclosure statements. "You make policy," he told them accusingly, and before the week was out, the mayor was vowing in banner headlines: MY ENEMIES WILL DIE BEFORE I QUIT. Bob Wagner observed in one story that a "low ebb" had been reached at City Hall. The mayor went from one newspaper editorial board to another observing that "some people obviously would love me to resign," and shouting a defiant "No!" in response.

The Botnick stories briefly disappeared, but returned in 1987 as part of a whole second cycle of scandal. This time DOI had found various discrepancies in Botnick's city expense reports. All of it was petty, but more serious was his apparent lie in sworn testimony at the department. He had denied knowing a stewardess whose accommodations had been paid for as part of a Botnick trip to California. The case was referred to Morgenthau, but DOI had erroneously concluded that Botnick had double-billed the city, and Morgenthau decided not to indict him.

Botnick had, by then, cut off contact with Ed Koch. Wounded and embittered, he skipped the mayor's private birthday party in 1986 and, for a while, didn't return Koch's calls. Months after Botnick's departure, at an end-of-the-year press conference, Koch was still complaining about how unfairly his closest friend had been treated by the media. At last, the scandal had taken a deeply personal toll on him.

But even the Botnick bloodletting did not kill the scandal.

In August of 1986, the McGinley controversy reappeared. Morgenthau announced that his seven-month air conditioner probe was ending with no criminal charges being brought against anyone. Then, in early September, John Martin issued his long-awaited report on DOI. Martin had actually resigned in March, the day after Donald Manes killed himself, and his mythical "commission," partially invented as a way of bypassing McGinley when the PVB scandal began, went out of business shortly after Conboy took over DOI. Nonetheless, the mayor asked Martin to finish his work tracking the early warnings about PVB. The report Martin finally presented—drafts of which were circulated at City Hall before they were released— had immediately damaging impact on the mayor, but in the long term would prove to be a boon.

The report blamed "the failure to investigate properly PVB allegations" by DOI on "mismanagement, poor judgment, administrative errors, improper or inadequate record-keeping, and a lack of adequate communication within DOI itself." It concluded implicitly that the furthest any early information about PVB corruption had reached up the chain of command was McGinley; no information had ever been conveyed to the mayor. Koch recognized that he now had the report that gave him an answer to the Watergate question of what he knew and when he knew it. "You ask whether I should have personally known of this particular investigation?" he told reporters. "The only way I could know of this investigation is if somebody told me about it."

Koch was quoted as saying he'd wished one of several informants who'd gone to DOI about PVB over the years had come to him. "Dear God, if only he had," the mayor said. "Had he brought those charges to me, you can be sure it would not have been an Inspector Clouseau operation."

But Martin's report hadn't really answered the question of what the mayor knew. One informant identified by Martin, ex–PVB comptroller James Rose, told several top officials at the Department of Transportation the same story he'd given DOI, and one of those officials, Larry Yermack, later said that he had found Rose's detailed tale of PVB corruption "chilling." Martin knew this, and never questioned the officials to determine whom they spoke to about what Rose had said. Martin also never interviewed anyone at City Hall about whether they'd heard anything of possible PVB corruption over the years. Not Koch, Brezenoff, Leventhal, or LoCicero. In fact, as was later revealed at the PVB trial, Brezenoff had stronger evidence of wrongdoing at PVB than any of the early informants ever delivered DOI: Stanley Friedman had lied to him face to face about the agency's biggest contract. Despite these shortcomings, the Martin report cleared the mayor, and at the same time, gave him a fall guy.

That October the major news was a series of three cable indictments announced by Queens D.A. John Santucci. Supreme Court Judge Frank Smith, the top judge in Queens and son of a former Queens county leader, was indicted on perjury charges for lying about his attempt to broker a cable contract with Manes. Michael Nussbaum, the Manes public relations consultant, was charged with soliciting a $250,000 bribe for Manes from another cable contractor. And John Zaccaro, the husband of former congresswoman and vice presidential candidate Geraldine Ferraro, was indicted for seeking a million-dollar cable bribe for Manes.

From Koch's standpoint, the disastrous assumption of the

cable indictments was that the multimillion-dollar selection process he himself had set up was an utter sham. The prestigious outside law firm that had been paid over $4 million, the cable working group of technical professionals and honest bureaucrats—all of it had no meaningful impact on the selection process. As Hadley Gold, the city's in-house lawyer who monitored the process, admitted to prosecutors, "whoever Manes wanted" would "very probably" have gotten the Queens franchise. The biggest winner in Queens, not surprisingly, was Warner's, represented by Manes's attorney and future law partner Sid Davidoff.

One other long-brewing Koch scandal now culminated quietly. Vito Fossella at last departed as both vice chairman and a member of the Board of Standards and Appeals, the fourth of the big four Esposito appointees to resign in 1986, following Ameruso, Turoff, and Gliedman. Press questions about the fate of the 1981 findings about Fossella's mishandling of a piping variance for a Staten Island architect forced a DOI review of the file. Without doing any new investigative work on the case, DOI simply recommunicated the five-year-old findings to the mayor, and a few days afterward, Fossella resigned. No one in the press was told the reason, and just as in the days of the earlier cover-up, Fossella's change of status was allowed to appear unrelated to his conduct.

As the first year of scandal drew to a close, the elusive Tony Ameruso was at last indicted, on charges that he'd committed perjury while testifying before Martin's commission in February. At that time, Ameruso had repeatedly claimed that the parking lot was his only investment, though he was in fact a secret investor in another real estate venture with a partner who had a stake in a Jersey-to-Manhattan ferry service that Ameruso had to approve. Martin's four-month probe of Ameruso never uncovered this other investment, even though the Jersey venture was where Ameruso put the proceeds of the parking lot sale, which was precisely what Martin was supposed to be investigating.

The day Ameruso was indicted Koch acknowledged that he'd "made a great mistake" in rejecting the advice of his screening panel in 1977 and picking Ameruso. He even conceded that "there's no question but that Meade Esposito would have been a supporter of Ameruso," adding, contrary to his previous recollections about whether Esposito had urged him to appoint or retain Ameruso: "I can't give you any particular conversation, but I couldn't doubt but that he would have raised his name."

By the time Ameruso was indicted, he was working out of an East Side townhouse in a variety of bizarre businesses, including the tax shelter sales of frozen cattle embryos. His partner was Robert Steele, who'd admitted that he'd paid $50,000 in bribes to Alex Liberman for a city lease. Liberman, meanwhile, was telling investigators that he had done the appraisal of Ameruso's infamous parking lot at his old friend's request years earlier. The criminal circle of predators was just that interconnected.

Several days after Ameruso was charged in early December, Wedtech, a munitions manufacturer with national and local political connections, closed its South Bronx factory. The company had been buffeted by a flurry of negative news stories, but the national implications of the reported criminal investigations into it—involving Attorney General Ed Meese and presidential adviser Lyn Nofziger—dwarfed those elements of it that were connected to the city scandal. In 1987, a host of Giuliani indictments named the company's principals, and then Congressman Mario Biaggi and borough president Stanley Simon, both of whom had been allegedly bribed in part to deliver favors to Wedtech from city government. Wedtech had obtained four parcels of city-owned property and, in one deal, gained control of a crucial piece of waterfront land, owing in part to the direct intervention of the mayor in a civil suit seeking the eviction of the tenant then renting it.

The first several months of shame had left the mayor shaken and searching for a way to cut off the stream of foul revelations. At times, Koch even had to take on the rumor of his own impending resignation. His experience told him that the media, and New Yorkers, have no electoral memory; each new crisis evokes amnesia about the one that preceded it. He believed that his greatest blessing was that the scandal had occurred so early in his term that it could not last until 1989, when he could rise above it and win a fourth term, transforming it into an anecdote in the triumphant history of his mayoralty. But still, it would not stop.

While the cable, Ameruso, and Wedtech cases broadened the scope of the scandal during the final months of 1986 and through 1987, the central events of this new period, rattling the mayor with disturbing and almost daily disclosures, were the surfacing of the FBI investigation of Meade Esposito in mid-1986 and his eventual prosecution, the explosive Friedman trial in late 1986, and the two indictments brought against city contractor Andy Capasso, which, by the end of the second year of scandal, had implicated Capasso's lover, Bess Myerson, in an apparent criminal conspiracy.

Fittingly, the backdrop for Esposito's crimes was the familiar felony turf of the city's leased piers at the Brooklyn Navy Yard, where Esposito's insurance company had made millions. The Koch administration had ignored the early warnings about what it meant to turn the yard over to the party plutocrat. Now the navy yard giveaway would come back to haunt him, and the case against Esposito would ultimately demonstrate that his administration had looked the other way while Meade's insurance client bilked the city.

Though the Friedman trial was a seminal event in the life of the scandal, it did not, as the mayor flatly predicted before it began, draw the curtain on the drama that had begun with Manes's unsuccessful suicide attempt. But it was, unlike either of Ed Koch's books, a true chronicle of his government, a minute-by-minute account of its ignominious side.

And the Myerson case, with all the elements of a tragedy and a farce, touched the mayor so personally that it became a torment that tugged at him visibly—almost as if he'd believed himself the love story he and she had invented in the 1977 campaign. The awkward kid from Ocean Parkway in Brooklyn—always with his mother, belittled by his peers—had grown up to a life that included the only Jewish Miss America at his side, and she was still beautiful, still wanted by men twenty years younger. Ed Koch would prove damagingly slow in separating himself from that fantasy. Even though his relationship with Myerson was a fraud, just as his reform government had been, the mayor survived—secure behind both the bulletproof windows of Gracie Mansion, and the reality-proof shield of a business establishment and ethnic popular base that protected him from himself.

CHAPTER TEN

Denting the Cherry

FRITZY GIOVANELLI IS A GANGSTER, a career wiseguy. He steals for a living, and by 1985, he had a record of eleven arrests and three convictions, including two for assault. Fritzy had a no-show job at the Sumo Container Corporation at Kennedy Airport, but spent his days running a citywide illegal gambling empire that grossed $400,000 a week. He also was in charge of some loan-sharking and debt collections.

The Mafia has never issued a printed organizational chart like the Ford Foundation, or a published roster like the New York Mets. It is a secret society. In 1983, a U.S. Senate subcommittee released a chart that listed Giovanelli as a soldier in the Genovese crime family. FBI analysts in charge of studying the Genovese group, however, believe that Fritzy had in fact become a capo in the mid-1980s, when the boss of the family, Anthony (Fat Tony) Salerno, was facing a trial under the RICO statute for his role in the Mafia's ruling national commission. (Salerno was convicted in November 1986 and sentenced to 100 years in prison.)

With Salerno absent, the Genovese family leadership vacuum was filled by Vincent Gigante. At the time he took command Gigante was in his late fifties, an ex-boxer who had been convicted with Vito Genovese, the original boss of the family, for smuggling heroin in 1959. Despite his goonlike résumé and physical appearance, Gigante was the prototype of an old-fashioned Machiavellian crime boss. He was highly secretive, usually going out onto the streets only at three or four in the morning to discourage surveillances, and obsessively avoided being bugged or wiretapped. Some law enforcement officials believed that it was Gigante, and not the more charismatic and violent John Gotti, who was the most influential crime boss in New York. With forty years of experience, Gigante had a more supple view of leadership and fiduciary responsibility.

As a respected member of middle management in Gigante's criminal organization, Fritzy Giovanelli ran his own crew in Brooklyn and Queens. His responsibility was overseeing the efficiency of the family's illegal gambling empire. He made sure the "writers" taking down the bets, the runners delivering them to a store, and the pickup men delivering the slips to the controller were all doing their job. He saw to it that the controllers took the slips to the "policy bank" and the bank workers honestly reported if any bettor hit the number—usually the last three digits of the handle at a local racetrack. Fritzy had to make certain that anyone who did hit the number was paid the correct amount, and to verify that the bet had been placed before the last race was run. He had to be vigilant to prevent the number being rigged, or one of his locations being raided by the police or robbed. He also had to guarantee that the designated share of the profits collected was passed along to his superiors in the family—Dom Canterino and Chin Gigante. To accomplish all this Giovanelli had to keep in regular phone contact with his main gambling locations.

Most evenings, Fritzy reported to the Triangle Social Club at 208 Sullivan Street in Greenwich Village. A members-only storefront club with dim lighting, no heat, and an old campaign poster for former Bronx city councilman Father Louis Gigante, the Chin's brother, in the window, this drab outpost served Vincent Gigante as headquarters, from which he directed in his authoritarian fashion all the rackets in the domain of the Genovese crime family.

Despite his two convictions for assault, violence was not Fritzy's game, although he used it when he had to. When a rival named Vinnie Bontovigma had tried to set up a competing gambling operation on Fritzy's monopoly turf, Bontovigma was found dead in the trunk of a car at Kennedy Airport. When debtors were laggard in loan repayments, Fritzy was known to slam car hoods on their fingers.

Fritzy, a "good earner," had the respect of other crime families, had a reputation of being someone who knew people. His nephews, Patsy and Danny Giovanelli, were main-event television fighters during the 1950s. He was especially reputed for his acquaintance with politicians and celebrities. He was a friend of John Gotti. He knew Jimmy Breslin. He was sometimes seen in Frank Sinatra's entourage.

In fact, Fritzy's relationship with Sinatra led to one of his arrests. In July 1974, Fritzy was subpoenaed to testify before a Brooklyn grand jury investigating organized crime. Fritzy's wife told the Brooklyn district attorney's office that her husband had suffered a tragic fall and was under a doctor's orders not to leave his home. In September Giovanelli did manage to stagger into court for a hearing. He was wearing a neck brace, limping, and clutching a bottle of pills. His lawyer assured the court that Fritzy was much too sick to testify. On October 15, two doctors' letters arrived at the Brooklyn D.A.'s office verifying Fritzy's severe medical problems. Fritzy's lawyer maintained that his client was in such agony that he never left his bedroom.

But on October 13, Frank Sinatra had performed a concert in Madison Square Garden. The *Daily News* had published a photograph the next morning of Sinatra on stage. And visible in the very first row, wearing a jaunty smile and no neck brace, was Fritzy Giovanelli. The D.A.'s office got blowups of the picture and presented them as evidence to the grand jury; Giovanelli was indicted for contempt of the grand jury.

Although he had only an eighth-grade education, Fritzy was a sophisticated wiseguy. He could provide a body bag for an execution or a bank mortgage for a friend with a criminal record. He knew how to manipulate stocks, divide an estate when a Mafioso died, obtain city contracts, get a union book for a friend, mediate a dispute over injured pride, or come by free tickets to the fights.

In New York there are perhaps two thousand people like Fritzy Giovanelli, dinosaurs from the old world. But Fritzy had one distinction that raised him above the criminal rabble. An investigation into the Genovese crime family would lead the FBI to him, and through him to the prosecution of two of the most powerful politicians in New York. Fritzy Giovanelli would unwittingly prove what law enforcement officials, investigative reporters, and Hollywood script writers have fantasized about for years: that there exists a direct connection, an unholy alliance, between the world of the bookmaker and the world of the judge-maker, between the mob and the machine.

During the summer of 1985, John Pritchard was in command of a joint FBI-NYPD task force created to crack the Genovese organization. Pritchard had served for eleven years at the NYPD and for nine as an agent at the FBI. He was now the highest-ranking black in the Bureau's New York office, and an officer of NOBLE, the national organization of black law enforcement. Eighteen FBI agents, and eighteen New York City police detectives, worked under Pritchard on the joint task force. Pritchard had been promoted to this assignment after working on the public corruption squad, where he had spent two years helping to make the case against labor leader and mobster Anthony Scotto, who was convicted of taking more than $300,000 in bribes.

In May 1985, Pritchard's task force members began to follow Fritzy as he visited his gambling locations and reported to the Triangle Social Club late at night. A pen register was placed on Giovanelli's home phone, which traced and identified the phone numbers of every outgoing call he dialed. Most of these calls were to members of the crew that ran his gambling empire. But Pritchard noticed that Fritzy also called Meade Esposito, the former Brooklyn county leader, almost every day. Pritchard knew of Esposito's ties to organized crime from his Scotto investigation, and he made a mental note that he just might get lucky on this case.

Quickly enough, "probable cause" for a wiretap on Giovanelli's home phone was assembled. An affidavit detailing the illegal gambling evidence was drafted. On August 26, 1985, federal judge Leo Glasser, the former dean of Brooklyn Law School, signed a court order authorizing the FBI to intercept wire communications for thirty days over telephone number (718) 894-2311. This phone was listed in the name of J. Schaich, at 63-62 75th Street, Queens. (Schaich is the name of Giovanelli's in-laws.)

The FBI and Ed McDonald, the chief of the federal organized crime strike force in Brooklyn, actually had a motive for their pursuit of Fritzy Giovanelli that was more significant than just their interest in his gambling empire. Fritzy was the main suspect in the theft of one of the most sensitive documents ever stolen from law enforcement by the Mafia.

In November 1981, the FBI had managed to install a hidden microphone in the home of Angelo Ruggiero, a key member of the Gambino crime family and allegedly involved in heroin traffic. The bug proved to be a technological goldmine. It caught the leaders of the mob at ease, committing crimes and hatching conspiracies in a living room over drinks and cigars. Conversations about heroin smuggling were recorded, as were plans for bribing a corrupt Nassau County police officer for mob intelligence reports. Ruggiero was taped telling mob lawyer Mike Coiro, "You're not our lawyer, you're one of us."

But on July 6, 1982, the FBI learned from an informant that Ruggiero and Gotti had obtained a copy of a thirty-page draft of an affidavit asking a federal judge for a thirty-day extension on the listening device in Ruggiero's home. The affidavit summarized all the information about Ruggiero gathered on all the previous thirty-day extensions for the bug. It contained the names of all the judges who signed the previous orders extending electronic surveillance. It outlined the criminal case being built against Ruggiero for conspiracy to distribute heroin—a commerce to which the boss of his family, Paul Castellano, was opposed. The affidavit also made it clear that Eugene Gotti, John's brother, had incriminated himself on tape and would be indicted along with Ruggiero for heroin trafficking.

The same trusted FBI mob informant who had found out about the stolen affidavit indicated that it was Fritzy Giovanelli who had obtained it and passed it along to his friends. The informant also reported that Giovanelli didn't even tell Gotti the truth about how he had come into possession of the affidavit but made up a story to protect his own source.

For three years the FBI and Ed McDonald had tried to solve the mystery of how Fritzy had obtained so sensitive a document. Eugene Gotti's lawyer, John Pollok, claimed in a court hearing that his client had found it where a drunken FBI agent had left it in a Queens bar. In February 1985, FBI agents, understandably incensed by this alibi, secured a search warrant and raided the Howard Beach home of Anthony Moscatiello, the accountant and record keeper for the Gambino gang, and in his basement found a copy of the affidavit. The investigation into Fritzy's embarrassing penetration of the FBI had therefore already been on the front burner in August of that year when Judge Glasser authorized the first Title III wiretap.

.   .   .

John Pritchard usually arrived at his cubicle at 26 Federal Plaza before 8:00 A.M., and each morning he would find a cassette waiting on his desk. This tape would contain all Fritzy Giovanelli's conversations from the night before. By the end of the first ten days of recording, it was clear that Giovanelli was involved in a suspicious stock deal with Meade Esposito and a New Jersey company named Lopat Industries.

Lopat manufactured a product, an environmental cleanser that could remove asbestos from walls and could be used in cleaning up toxic waste dumps. Giovanelli and Esposito had been discussing transactions with Lopat that seemed to involve manipulating the stock, financing a private placement, getting city contracts, and possibly extorting a distributorship from Lopat in exchange for influencing Transportation Commissioner Anthony Ameruso to help the company. These conversations disclosed an extraordinary intimacy between the wiseguy and the power broker. Esposito agreed to hire Giovanelli's son at his insurance company, Serres, Viscone, and Rice (SVR). Giovanelli often visited Esposito's home in Brooklyn for matters too sensitive for the telephone. Esposito even knew Giovanelli's mistress, and once confused her with Giovanelli's wife. Esposito and Giovanelli spoke with the affection and trust of brothers.

So great was the respect Giovanelli showed to Esposito that Pritchard wondered whether Esposito might even be a "made" member of the Mafia. It was, on its face, an almost inconceivable notion, but Pritchard began to consider whether it was possible that Esposito had been inducted into organized crime years earlier, when he was a bail bondsman for the mob, before he entered politics.

Pritchard was also aware of a famous tape that his FBI squad had made during the investigation into Anthony Scotto. Recorded on September 12, 1978, it revealed Scotto's waterfront partner in crime, Mike Clemente, talking about Scotto's career as a union official and mob capo on the Brooklyn docks: "That's when Anthony [Scotto] come to see me: 'Hey Mike, I hope you don't put me, pass me, like my father-in-law [Anthony Anastasio].' I said, 'Anthony you prove you're a man, you're a man. You're a button.' They made him a wiseguy. Then they made him a captain. Hey, I got a politician that they made a wiseguy."*

Pritchard now asked himself if that politician might be Esposito.

By the end of September 1985, Esposito had spoken so freely to Giovanelli on the phone that Pritchard had to transfer jurisdiction of the Esposito investigation to the FBI's political corruption squad, as his charter was restricted to the Genovese family. He didn't mind giving up the case, for the public corruption squad was supervised by his friend Sid Caspersen, and he knew that Caspersen had been studying Meade Esposito since 1982. By now Caspersen knew more about Esposito than Esposito remembered about himself.

With 1,200 agents, New York was the largest of the FBI's fifty-nine field offices. Since 1978, it had been gradually shifting its manpower priorities, assigning younger agents who were "self-starters" and "go-getters" to the public corruption squad instead of to the more typical bank robbery or auto theft units. At first these agents met with frustration, partly because the U.S. Attorneys for the southern district—especially John Martin—did not seem to have any great desire to probe politicians and power brokers. For a time, the FBI, which was feeling its way in this new realm, collaborated with the more aggressive (or perhaps less naïve) federal prosecutors such as Tom Puccio and Ed Korman in the Eastern District, winning convictions against Queens judge William Brennan, Brooklyn state senator Vander Beatty, Teamster union leader John Cody, and Alex Liberman, the City of New York's director of leasing.

By 1983, however, all the elements of a championship law enforcement team had finally fallen into place: Rudy Giuliani had become the new U.S. Attorney for the Southern District; the low-key, almost academic Tim Dorch, the chief of the FBI's public corruption section; Sid Caspersen was the leader of the first squad created to develop an intelligence base on New York City's culture of corruption; Ed McDonald was the head of the federal organized crime strike force in the Eastern District; and Tom Sheer was the new director of the criminal division of the FBI's office in New York.

It was Sheer, more than anyone else, who was responsible

---

*This tantalizing quotation was included in the report by the President's Commission on Organized Crime.

for transforming the FBI's image during this period. Although he had played football at the University of Florida and had been a Marine Corps first lieutenant, Sheer was far from being the stereotypical FBI jock. An intellectual who got ideas from books, he recruited minority and female agents and helped to break down the Bureau as a white male bastion. He was a natural leader by example—neither a publicity hound nor an empty suit. He also helped change the FBI's philosophy in New York, helping to turn the Bureau away from mechanistic statistical accomplishment toward targeting the infrastructure of white-collar and organized crime. He argued that it was more important to focus on corrupt politicians, or to spend five years wiping out the leadership of one crime family, than to produce a press release saying auto thefts were down by 2 percent.

Late in 1982, 38-year-old Sid Caspersen was invited into the office of Tim Dorch and given a new, long-term research project—Meade Esposito. Caspersen was possessed of an unlikely combination of polite Southern manners and New York street savvy. A former police officer in Anniston, Alabama, he joined the FBI in 1978, and after four years in the Birmingham office was transferred to New York.

As Caspersen recalls receiving the assignment: "My job was to study the systemic, pervasive political corruption in Brooklyn. This meant the judiciary, the patronage system, and Esposito, who was then the party leader. We got very close to Meade when we convicted Alex Liberman, Saul Radow, and Shirley Weiner. We got close to him in other cases. But we were always a day late, or a dollar short. People were always *afraid* to talk to us about Meade. Everyone who could have given him up had one or more relatives who owed their jobs to Esposito. Everyone had a son, or a cousin, or parent, or sister whom Meade had placed on a public payroll. He did favors, and he was in a position to call the favors back. So he was protected that way. From the beginning, Dorch and I believed the only way we were ever going to make a case on Esposito was by doing something covert, by using electronic surveillance. He was too powerful and too insulated to be caught any other way."

What the white whale was to Ahab, Meade Esposito became to Sid Caspersen. For three years Caspersen worked on, and successfully solved other white-collar cases. But all the while he was amassing and storing information on Esposito. He became an expert on Serres, Viscone, and Rice, the insurance brokerage company of which Esposito owned 50 percent. He learned that the company did $2.5 million a year in commissions and that Esposito took more than $250,000 a year in salary, as well as another $70,000 in travel and entertainment expenses. He discovered that Esposito owned the building at 108 Greenwich Street in which SVR was located. And he realized that Esposito himself was ignorant of the insurance business; his partner, Joe Martuscello, actually ran the company, while it was left to Esposito to pressure people to do business with them.

Caspersen also studied the Beaumont Offset Company in Farmingdale, Long Island. Esposito owned the building and the printing press, and controlled the company, although it was kept in the name of his daughter Phyllis. Once again, Esposito knew nothing about this particular business; Harry Dickran managed the company, and Meade simply opened doors. He saw to it that candidates from Ed Koch to Abe Hirschfield to Norman Rosen gave Beaumont hundreds of thousands of dollars in printing work from their political campaigns. Koch's 1985 mayoral reelection campaign committee, for example, paid Beaumont $117,000 for its services.

In the course of his research Caspersen found that law enforcement archives contained a good deal of circumstantial intelligence linking Esposito to organized crime. From 1948 to 1960 Esposito had been a bail bondsman, and had supplied funds for members of Joe Columbo's crime family and Jimmy Napoli. In the late 1950s Esposito had entered the pharmaceutical business with Dr. Mario Tagliagambe, a close associate of Carlo Gambino. The mysterious "Dr. Tags" had been secretly filmed by the Waterfront Commission leaving an organized crime social club. In the mid-1960s, FBI wiretaps intercepted two organized crime figures discussing how they had to stay away from Esposito for a while because he was about to make a move to become Democratic county leader in Brooklyn.

During the late 1960s Esposito was vice president of the Kings Lafayette Bank in Brooklyn, during a period when several organized crime figures were prosecuted for lying on loan applications to that bank. After he became county leader in 1969 Esposito remained in contact with Jimmy Napoli, Paul Castellano, Anthony Scotto, and Paul Vario, all high-ranking mobsters. According to FBI informant Henry Hill (the subject of Nicholas Pileggi's bestselling book *Wiseguy*), Esposito and

Vario, a Luchese family capo, met regularly to speak in private on a bench in Marine Park in Brooklyn. Hill told the FBI that he had always been allowed to participate in Vario's other meetings, and that Esposito was the only person whom Vario insisted on meeting alone.

In January 1984, when Esposito retired as Brooklyn county leader, Caspersen did not give up, shred his files, or abandon his quest. Knowing that Esposito still had influence and was not about to change his way of life, he was determined to continue the case, and could only smile when he read Roger Starr's *Time's* editorial valedictory: "Many are incredulous that Mr. Esposito was content with the rewards of power, prestige, and friendship instead of wealth. . . . this boss was not brought down by scandal."

This boss, Sid Caspersen had discovered, had in fact become a millionaire through his political influence. He owned four homes: one in Brooklyn; an estate valued at $900,000 in Quogue, Long Island; a $120,000 condominium in Fort Lauderdale, Florida; and a $350,000 villa, in Beaumont's name, on the Caribbean island of St. Maarten. He had a $250,000 yacht and a 5 percent interest (with Charles Montanti, Joe Martuscello, and Harold Fisher) in a Queens apartment complex called Surfside Park. In 1984, Esposito's net worth was more than $5 million—almost all of it accumulated since Ed Koch had become mayor.

One day in May or June 1985, an agent working on the early surveillances of Fritzy Giovanelli asked Caspersen, as the resident Esposito expert in the office, who Harry Dickran was. When Caspersen explained that Dickran ran Beaumont for Esposito, the agent told him that Dickran had been meeting often with Giovanelli.

From that day forward, there was an informal coordination, a pooling of knowledge, in the FBI office. Over morning cups of coffee, and over beers after work, Caspersen and Pritchard talked. By September enough conversations had been recorded about the Lopat distributorship involving Esposito that Caspersen, as squad supervisor, was able to take over the Esposito part of the investigation. He immediately began to plan an affidavit to submit to the court for electronic surveillance—the covert opportunity he had been waiting for since 1982.

Caspersen code-named the top-secret Esposito probe "Runnymede." It was a pun resurrecting the site in England where the Magna Carta was signed, the landmark democratic document that transformed the long autocratic reign of an evil king.

Caspersen's counterpart in the Esposito investigation was Ed McDonald, the 39-year-old chief of the federal organized crime strike force. McDonald was a different style of prosecutor from Giuliani. Less concerned about publicity, and more of a liberal on issues of law and social policy, McDonald was an advocate who did his best to understand the defense's point of view. But he could also be determinedly aggressive. He loved to play and watch basketball, and his approach to law enforcement suggested the style of one of his favorite players, Bill Walton—fierce but fair, with a strong collaborative spirit.

McDonald was a registered Democrat, born and raised in Brooklyn, but he had never belonged to a political club or met Meade Esposito. He had come closest to the latter one day in 1984. McDonald was having lunch in Foffe's restaurant, near the Brooklyn courthouse, with the writer Nicholas Pileggi. Esposito happened to be in another booth having lunch with Congressman Chuck Schumer.

From his booth, McDonald watched a procession of deferential judges wait on line just to say a few words to the ex-boss. McDonald knew every hood in Brooklyn, but he didn't recognize the judges acting so obsequiously to the old bondsman. So Pileggi served as a spotter, whispering the names to McDonald.

"It was like a scene straight out of the *Godfather*," McDonald thought.

As strike force chief, McDonald was primarily responsible for prosecuting organized crime bosses, and only unusual circumstances had given his office jurisdiction over a politician such as Esposito. McDonald's small staff of thirteen attorneys was already overwhelmed preparing for trials and indictments of the top executives of the Mafia—Paul Castellano, Phil Rastelli, Joe N. Gallo, Sonny Franzese, Aneilo Dellacroce—and the Esposito case placed a strain on their limited resources.

McDonald eventually assigned the Esposito probe to Len Michaels, a lawyer whose strongest talents lay in the investigative realm of creative research. As an assistant in the Brooklyn D.A.'s office, Michaels had grown familiar with the players in Esposito's orbit, and had even successfully prosecuted several corruption cases at the Brooklyn Navy Yard, where Esposito's behind-the-scenes influence was considerable. Because Michaels's wife was a busy lawyer and they had no children, it was thought his schedule might be flexible enough to handle a long-term electronic surveillance project like Runnymede. But Michaels soon found himself consumed by the project, working six days a week, twelve hours a day. He no longer had a free night for his favorite leisure activity, attending the opera. In October 1985, Michaels moved out of his own strike force headquarters in Brooklyn and took up residency in a windowless cubbyhole next to Caspersen's office at the FBI in Manhattan. This one investigation began to dominate his job.

Late on October 14, Ed McDonald made the decision to apply to the court for one day of electronic surveillance of Meade Esposito at Beaumont Printing. This required the submission of an affidavit that offered proof of probable cause to believe that criminal activity was being committed by specific people at a specific location. Most of the proof that had been gathered in the case consisted of conversations between Esposito, Dickran, and Giovanelli that had been recorded on the Giovanelli wiretap. Time had been the major factor in McDonald's decision to press ahead with the new surveillance: a key meeting appeared to have been scheduled at the Beaumont premises that Friday, October 18.

Michaels and Caspersen convened in Caspersen's office at 7:30 A.M. on October 15 to begin drafting the affidavit for a wireless microphone and transmitter—a bug—to be installed at Beaumont. Working to exhaustion compelled a recess at 3:00 A.M.; they met again after a few hours of sleep on October 16 and pushed straight through until 7:00 that evening. At that point, they had a draft of a fifty-page affidavit.

At midnight on October 16 the phone rang at Len Michaels's home in Greenwich Village. FBI agent Claudia Thornton, who was deputy case agent on Esposito and would be chief monitor of all the electronic surveillance during the investigation, told the fatigued Michaels there had been a problem in preparing the final draft of the affidavit. His handwriting couldn't be deciphered. No typist was available, and the material could not be transferred from one word processor to another. When Thornton told Michaels that Caspersen was driving in from New Jersey to handle the crisis, Michaels said he was going back to sleep.

Caspersen stayed up all night making certain the affidavit

was properly completed. In the morning Claudia Thornton flew to Washington to personally deliver three copies of the documents. She took one to the FBI headquarters, where several officials had to approve it, including Director William Webster. Her next stop was the Department of Justice, where one copy was given to Paul Coffey, the deputy chief of the organized crime section, who in turn passed it along to Steve Trott, the chief of the criminal division. The final copy was for the Office of Enforcement Operation, the specialists in Title III electronic surveillance. Thornton caught the next shuttle back to New York, where she waited with Caspersen and Michaels for the legal go-ahead. Federal District Judge Leo Glasser had been notified in advance that his signature would be required immediately on a court order, because the bug would have to be installed that night if the October 18 meeting were going to be recorded.

In the early evening, a facsimile of Trott's signed approval was wired to 26 Federal Plaza, which signified that both the justice department and the FBI had signed off on the one day of surveillance. By now Judge Glasser had left the courthouse, and Caspersen and Michaels had to drive to his home for his signature. Caspersen then contacted the Title III technicians by walkie-talkie in Farmingdale, to inform them that they had received the legal authorization to enter the Beaumont offices and install the bug. The installation was completed after midnight.

Every electronic surveillance has a "plant"—usually a room where a reel-to-reel tape recorder and a receiver are set up and the original tape is made. A pen register is attached to the recorder, a device that indicates the number, time, and date of any outgoing call. An FBI agent is always present as the monitor at the plant, and shuts off the recorder if the subject matter of the conversation doesn't fall within the court's authorization for interceptions.

The Beaumont plant had been placed in a cemetery behind the building, and the FBI agents staffing the plant were surrounded by open graves, grieving mourners, caskets, and gravediggers. They were so uncomfortable they couldn't eat their lunches.

The particular meeting that was expected to take place on October 18, a discussion that was supposed to deal with Lopat's receiving city contracts through the Department of Transportation, never materialized. But the normal chit-chat between Esposito and Dickran contained more than enough incriminating references to justify another application to the courts for expanded electronic eavesdropping on Esposito.

Caspersen and Michaels labored the entire weekend of October 19 and 20 drafting a new affidavit for permission to wiretap Esposito's home at 2600 National Drive in the Mill Basin section of Brooklyn, and to continue to monitor the phones at Beaumont. By the end of November these taps had provided enough probable cause to intercept the phone calls at Serres, Viscone, and Rice as well—the main number and seven rollover numbers. On the night of December 2, the bureau's Title III specialists gained entry to 107 Greenwich Street (where the "box" was located for the insurance company next door) and attached eight lines to tap into SVR's phone system.

By early December 1985, the FBI had more than sixty agents assigned full time to Runnymede. Thirteen phone lines were being tapped in four different counties. Each line had to be monitored by an agent, with eight posted at SVR, because it was impossible to predict which line Esposito might pick up. Each location had its own plant. All the tapes had to be duplicated overnight at the FBI's offices at 26 Federal Plaza, so that Caspersen and Michaels could listen to them as soon as they arrived at their offices. Potentially significant tapes were rushed from the plant and transcribed word for word within three hours. Each new character on the phone had to be identified, each new transaction mentioned had to be researched.

Other agents had to log and input into a computer the names of the parties, their phone numbers, and the specific times of all calls intercepted. At the end of the investigation, nearly a thousand individuals would have to be notified that their conversations had been recorded.

Still other agents had to prepare reports every ten days to the court, summarizing the criminal activity that had been discovered through electronic surveillance.

In addition, whenever Esposito made a date for a meal where an important conversation might be held, agents from the specialized surveillance squads often had to be rushed to the restaurants on short notice to try to overhear fragments of the conversation. When Esposito met with a Brooklyn judge in Junior's restaurant to fix a civil case for a friend over breakfast, FBI agents were at the next table, as they were when he met

Mafioso Jimmy Napoli for dinner in Crisci's restaurant in the Greenpoint section of Brooklyn.

In a quasi-military bureaucracy like the FBI, a working force of this magnitude isn't allocated without a command decision. On this case it was Tom Sheer who backed up Caspersen, expedited the paperwork, and let it be known that Runnymede was exactly the sort of project the Bureau should be sponsoring. It also helped the case that Sheer kept getting promoted during the life of the investigation. In May 1985 he was named the deputy assistant director of the New York office, and in September of the following year, director.

The group of agents working on the public corruption squad were all young enough to have joined the Bureau after J. Edgar Hoover retired in 1972, and were not infected by the Hoover era's lawless anticommunism and paranoid cult of personality. This was a different generation, and a different breed, from those agents who had routinely framed or defamed people because of their political ideas, did black bag jobs, or spied on the bedroom of a Nobel Peace Prize laureate.

In fact, on October 28, just before the electronic surveillance on Esposito was expanded, Len Michaels gave a lecture on the minimization law to thirty FBI operatives who would be monitoring the phones, and their supervisors.

"You are not authorized to intercept constitutionally protected speech," Michaels told them. "You must shut off the tape when the political process is being discussed. Political conversations must be minimized. Don't violate anyone's privacy. I don't want this to become an intelligence gathering mission. If you are going to make a mistake, then err on the side of minimization. Shut off the microphone when you are in doubt about what to do. I would rather miss some evidence than violate Esposito's rights."

When Meade Esposito resigned as county leader of Brooklyn in 1984, he was confident that he had beaten the system. He had outwitted prosecutors and conned journalists for a generation. He had developed a deceptive act that worked. He talked dirty, waved a cigar he never smoked, and played the vulgarian with the heart of gold, relying on the same rehearsed aphorisms again and again:

"Today's reformer is tomorrow's hack."

"I danced on a charlotte russe and never dented the cherry."

"Don't say I was honest, just say I never got caught."

And, after a few drinks, "Don't trust anyone you haven't stolen with."

When Esposito retired, almost all the mass media bathed him in sentimentality, to the point that he might have been a Jimmy Durante retiring from vaudeville. Typical of the press's farewells was a *New York Post* editorial published on January 19, 1984:

> They don't make politicians like Meade any more and we can't imagine the prospect of being without his earthy wit and wisdom. Politicians, mere mortals, come and go. The Meade Espositos, for whom a man's word is his bond, go on forever.

At seventy-eight, Meade was a lion at twilight. He could have sold his partnerships in SVR and Beaumont, really retired, enjoyed his three grandchildren and four great-grandchildren, and lived happily ever after, still boasting that he had never been caught. But that was a choice Meade Esposito was not prepared to make. He had, in his own mind, resigned only a formal title—county leader. He was not about to hand over any real power, for his ego wouldn't allow it. He enjoyed seeing people jump too much; his self-image as a padrone required that he continue to demonstrate to his old friends that he could still impose his will on government. And ironically, now that he was officially retired, he finally felt safe from investigative scrutiny. After years of vigilance, he was able to drop his defenses a little, certain that his advanced age, failing eyesight, and heralded departure were a veil protecting him.

Because the old boss's guard was down, the electronic surveillance was immediately amusing and productive. For Caspersen and Michaels it was an exhilarating experience to put on earphones and actually hear Esposito's profane voice and listen to his philosophy of life, not the rehearsed routines he performed for reporters and college kids.

One day Esposito told Giovanelli: "You know, when Moses went up to Mount Sinai for the Ten Commandments he made a mistake. There should have been an eleventh: Think of Thyself."

Esposito also explained on another early tape why he never attends wakes: "I don't wanna go. Fuck 'em. They're dead. Fuck 'em."

In their hours of surveying the tapes the investigators heard Esposito boast that for six years he had been "the boss of the fucking state." They heard his weary, self-important complaint, "Every fuckin' place I go, contracts, contracts!" They heard him reminisce how he had "picked mayors." They heard him brag how he always insulated himself and let middlemen and intermediaries do the dirty work for him. They listened to him skillfully use patronage debt he had built during twenty-five years of sending résumés to four different mayors. Esposito never forgot whom he placed where, and how far he could go in asking for a favor.

As early as the first day of the wiretap on SVR, Caspersen and Michaels heard Esposito fix a civil case in Brooklyn. Esposito had called Sam Plotkin, who was both the public administrator of Kings County and the vice chairman of the Industrial Development Agency (IDA), two powerful jobs that Esposito had helped him secure. Esposito, who often used public officials as his messengers, told Plotkin he wanted to see Civil Court Judge Irving (Red) Levine at 8:45 the following morning at Junior's restaurant, a popular breakfast meeting place not far from the courthouse. "It's important," he barked. That night Levine called Esposito at home and told him he would comply with the breakfast summons. Levine had been a law secretary for many years before he was made a judge by Esposito.

The next morning FBI agents seated near their table overheard Esposito ask Levine to do a favor for a "dear friend" who owned Randazzo's restaurant in Brooklyn. The owner's lease had expired, and the landlord had been trying to evict her and recover back rent. Esposito wanted to make certain that the restaurateur got an extension from Judge Levine, to give her sufficient time to open at a new location.

The following day Esposito told his friend not to worry, because the judge was going to grant her three or four months of extensions. Judge Levine, in fact, granted a series of adjournments, until March 13, 1986. While not a federal crime, because no money changed hands, such behavior was certainly unethical. But it was fairly standard procedure for the way Meade Esposito exercised power on an average day in retirement: the legal fix based on a line of credit at the Favor Bank. Esposito proved once again that the real scandal in New York politics was what's legal, not what was illegal.

But Meade's power base, the investigators discovered, was

not limited to his own party, for they quickly learned how friendly this old Democrat was with certain Republicans. In New York, above a certain level of power, above a certain level of wealth, there are no Democrats, and there are no Republicans, except on election day. When there is money to be made or favors to be traded, the political battlefield is transformed into a bipartisan fraternity of fixers and power brokers. Some of Esposito's influence-peddling conversations were with Republicans, such as Joe Margiotta, the convicted boss of Nassau County; Long Island Republican leader Edmund Marino of Babylon; Senator Alfonse D'Amato; and Robert Curcio, Jr., the executive assistant to the Republican county leader of Suffolk County.

Caspersen and Michaels also heard, for the first time with their own ears, Esposito's dealings with the mob. They heard him add the son of one mobster to his payroll as a favor to the father, and then put the son of Fritzy Giovanelli, whom he called "Freddy Boy," on the SVR payroll. They listened as SVR acted as the broker in placing a $430,000 surety bond on the estate of Thomas Bilotti, the bodyguard and capo, who was assassinated with Gambino family boss Paul Castellano in December 1985. Esposito also spoke frequently with the Gambino capo and convicted labor racketeer Anthony Scotto, for whom he secured a line of credit at a bank, and quashed a jury notice for one of Scotto's employees.

On the second day of surveillance the Esposito tap was almost exposed. Esposito himself had been warned his office telephone was bugged, but he refused to believe it. The tip had come from an employee of the telephone company that serviced SVR's system, who also happened to be a close friend of Frank Brasco. Brasco had been Esposito's driver when Esposito had been party leader, and now he held the title of controller of SVR, although his functions were more those of an office manager and traveling crony for Esposito.

The plant heard Brasco being told, "Thirteen are up," meaning thirteen lines were being tapped; his contact apparently knew that eight lines had been attached to the box at 107 Greenwich. Brasco then brought this phone company employee directly to Esposito's third-floor office, to give the boss this confidential information in person.

But Esposito dismissed the warning, saying that it was probably "a bunch of bullshit," that he had been hearing his phones were tapped for twenty years, and since he had never been tapped in the past, why would anyone start now, when he was retired?

Esposito's logic was not shared by his partner Joe Martuscello, who after the alert had been sounded became consistently discreet on the phone. Esposito himself would waver between self-discipline and recklessness in his discussions, but Martuscello never again had a totally open conversation when phoning from SVR.

Even though Esposito chose to ignore the warning, the threat of its surveillance being uncovered was a crisis for the Bureau's technicians. It was decided that the tap would have to be removed from 107 Greenwich and placed on SVR's lines at another location, and that a hidden videocamera would be installed over the box. Indeed, a few hours after the tap was moved, Brasco's phone company friend was videotaped checking the lines.

By pure luck, the FBI was back on Esposito's phones by December 17. On that day a conversation took place between Esposito and Bronx Congressman Mario Biaggi that sounded as if it might be an illegal transaction in progress.

At 10:39 A.M. Biaggi responded to a message Esposito had left at his Washington office earlier in the morning.

"Give me the name of that young lady," Esposito said.

"Barlow," replied Biaggi.

It quickly became apparent that Esposito was making arrangements for Biaggi and a mistress to take a vacation at the Bonaventure Hotel in Florida during the Christmas–New Year's holidays.

After the travel days were worked out, the conversation shifted:

ESPOSITO: What else is doin'?
BIAGGI: By the way, we've been doing wonders for Montanti [president of Coastal Dry Dock].
ESPOSITO: What'd you do? Let me know.
BIAGGI: On the city side, we've been working very hard with them. And on the federal side, we've been getting them money.
ESPOSITO: You got money?
BIAGGI: They got one million, two.
ESPOSITO: When did they get that?

BIAGGI: Well, they should have gotten it last week, and with that money they'll be able to . . . pay-off on the city. So it takes the sting out.

ESPOSITO: How much do they owe?

BIAGGI: . . . They owe the city about two or three hundred thousand dollars.

ESPOSITO: Mean for the utilities?

BIAGGI: Yeah.

ESPOSITO: Well I can . . . I can help there.

BIAGGI: But I think . . . that's been reduced.

They've been helped on that score. . . . They know they're being helped . . . I've been bird-dogging it right along.

At the close of the conversation, Esposito told Biaggi: "And when you go down [to Florida], don't get your balls wet."

After laughing, Biaggi closed with: "I gotta call Charley [Montanti] now."

Biaggi did not know that Esposito had an economic incentive for lobbying for Coastal Dry Dock, and may have assumed that good old Meade was just trying to do a friend a favor. In fact, Coastal paid Esposito's insurance brokerage company $1.8 million in premiums and about $250,000 in commissions annually. On a single premium of $220,000 to Lloyds of London, SVR collected a $44,000 commission from Coastal. Through Coastal, Meade Esposito made money on every ship that docked at the Brooklyn Navy Yard. Despite these advantages, Coastal Dry Dock by late 1985 was in severe financial jeopardy. The company had been awarded $460 million in ship rebuilding contracts by the navy department over the last six years, but its work had been shoddy. Now it faced $26 million in disputed claims and invoices—cost overruns—being contested by the navy department. Coastal also owed New York City $3 million in back rent and utility charges, and Esposito's company an additional $280,000 in commissions.*

Moreover, the navy yard itself had long been an Esposito plantation for business, patronage, and influence peddling. It was Esposito who had helped Coastal get its sweetheart forty-year lease at the navy yard without any competition or bidding. Esposito also met personally with the two top city officials over-

---

*In May 1986, Coastal Dry Dock filed for protection from its creditors under chapter eleven of the U.S. Bankruptcy Code.

seeing the yard and pressured them to do the deal. This lease gave Esposito's brokerage client control over two-thirds of the rental space at the 261-acre yard.

The Koch administration disregarded a written suggestion from investigations commissioner Stan Lupkin that a clause be added to the lease voiding it if Coastal's principals, Charles and Vincent Montanti, were indicted. Lupkin wanted this unusual provision included because he knew the feds were probing Coastal's naval contracts. Shortly after Lupkin's departure in the spring of 1982, and in the midst of Koch's campaign for governor, the city reached an agreement with Coastal that gave the company a $500,000 rent credit later blasted in city audits as exceedingly generous.

At the same time that the city was cutting this deal with Coastal, federal prosecutors were revealing that a Brooklyn congressman had paid the college tuition of a leading naval official in exchange for inside information about navy contracts Coastal was seeking. This same congressman, Fred Richmond, had hidden an escaped felon, who was also his homosexual lover, on a Coastal payroll under an alias. Congressman Richmond quickly pleaded guilty and went to prison; the navy official resigned. These episodes were part of a tangled history of Esposito-related scandals at the yard, including the 1981 state indictments that disclosed Mafia influence over the city corporation that administered it.

Once Coastal had its lease, the company proceeded to blithely ignore its obligations to the city year after year, provoking occasional ire from Koch officials but little concrete response. The city adopted what it called a "two-tier" rental policy. It went into court swiftly against any of its fifty other navy yard tenants if they failed to make a single payment owed to the city. But the Koch administration tolerated a constantly mounting Coastal debt that by late 1985 had reached $2.5 million. City officials would later concede that lobbyist Esposito had never mentioned any tenant other than Coastal during his periodic conversations with them about problems at the yard. Like his counterpart Stanley Friedman, who had concealed his ownership interest in Citisource while lobbying for its handheld computer contract at City Hall, Esposito hid his financial stake in Coastal from the city officials he lobbied.

When one new deputy mayor, Ken Lipper, failed to return Esposito's calls in behalf of Coastal, the mayor's special assistant, John LoCicero, not only urged him to do so but also insisted that Lipper make an appointment to meet with Esposito. Lipper did have dinner with Esposito twice but refused to accede to Meade's demand that Coastal be allowed to go off the yard's expensive electric and steam system, and cut its own cheaper deal with the utilities. Coastal tried to win this exclusive concession from the city for years, even though they had signed a lease that obligated them to pay the yard's energy costs. The company used Lipper's unwillingness to grant this favor to justify its refusal to make lease payments to the city. Eventually Coastal's nonpayment led to a threat by Con Edison to cut off service to the entire yard, forcing the city to pay the utility bills Coastal wouldn't pay.

The city's response to Coastal's multimillion-dollar stonewalling was to offer them access to every kind of government assistance program in its arsenal. After Lipper left the city in early 1985, the city also decided to spend at least $33 million modernizing the yard's energy plant, meaning that cheaper electricity would be delivered to Coastal and other yard tenants. Twice the city also forced Coastal to sign explicit repayment agreements with detailed schedules spelling out when Coastal would clear up its debt. Within weeks, Coastal broke both agreements. But City Hall authorized no legal action against Esposito's client.

As soon as the Esposito-Biaggi call was completed, Virgil Adams, the FBI agent supervising the plant, called Caspersen and Michaels. He played the tape back for them over the phone, and then sent it to FBI headquarters for immediate transcription and duplication.

At 10:55 A.M. Esposito called the law office of Jimmy La Rossa, a friend as well as Esposito's attorney in many matters. La Rossa had been Esposito's lawyer when the state attorney general filed a civil suit in 1978 to remove Esposito as county leader, because his business transactions with a racetrack violated state law. He was now on a $2,000-a-month retainer from Beaumont, and was also the criminal lawyer for Esposito's mob contacts, Anthony Scotto and Paul Castellano. Like Esposito, La Rossa owned a villa at Bonaventure; he was also a member of the Bonaventure Spa, and as a member could gain Biaggi and Barlow access to its facilities, at a cost of $185 per day.

ESPOSITO: Remember the arrangement I made for Biaggi, down at the Bonaventure thing.

LA ROSSA: Yeah.

ESPOSITO: And you billed me.

LA ROSSA: Yes.

ESPOSITO: I want to repeat that. . . . Charge it to yourself, and then you, you charge Beaumont.

A few minutes later, when Stella Paone, La Rossa's executive secretary, called Esposito for the details of the vacation, he explained:

"Listen, you recall we made an arrangement for Mr. Biaggi last year? . . . All right, take this down. Barbara Barlow. B-A-R-L-O-W. Make reservations for her at the Spa between December the 22d through January 3d. And Mario Biaggi, December the 27th through the 3d. And you send the bill over to Beaumont."

At 11:21 A.M., Esposito called Montanti, Coastal's president, and told him: "I just spoke to Washington. . . . Mario is doing his best."

What prosecutors would discover months later, through a subpoena of airline computer records, was that at 11:04 that morning, Congressman Biaggi's personal secretary had made flight reservations to Miami on December 26 for Biaggi. Biaggi would later bill the taxpayers for this plane fare, claiming the purpose of his Florida trip was legitimate government business—which he justified by citing a visit he paid to a health maintenance organization for two hours. The timing of this reservation phone call would establish that Biaggi had made it ten minutes after he confirmed that Esposito was taking care of his—and his girlfriend's—second annual gift trip to the Bonaventure.

Out of his own moral weakness, Mario Biaggi had wandered into a net never meant to entangle him. Biaggi was cheap, and not very bright. His wife of forty-five years, Marie, was seriously ill with Hodgkin's disease, and was then in New York undergoing painful chemotherapy treatments. An aging Don Juan, Mario Biaggi at age sixty-eight had many mistresses; some of these relationships were notoriously public, like the one with the 45-year-old redhead Barbara Barlow.

Barlow was a spoiled former model with expensive tastes. She had introduced Biaggi to a fancier class of restaurants and started buying his clothes for him in better shops. Biaggi had taken her to the Bonaventure Spa Christmas week of 1984, and she had badgered him for months to repeat that escape to luxury. Eager to please her, Biaggi complied by working out the gift transaction with Esposito. Biaggi's motive was sex, while Esposito stood to gain $280,000, plus $250,000 more every year in commissions, from the continued existence of Coastal. Also, Esposito would be able to placate Montanti if Biaggi would carry the lobbying burden, a necessary task, since Coastal's longtime champion, Congressman Joe Addabbo of Queens, was dying of cancer.

As soon as Biaggi was certain the arrangements were definite and complete for his gift vacation, he redoubled his efforts in behalf of Coastal. On the very same day—December 17—late in the afternoon, Biaggi called New York City deputy mayor Alair Townsend to urge it be given favorable consideration.

At 9:42 P.M., Friday, December 20, Martuscello called Meade Esposito at home. It was a relaxed, rambling end-of-the-week talk between two old partners. At two points during the conversation, the monitoring agent at the plant minimized the call by shutting off the tape recorder, as Michaels had instructed the agents to do. When the agent turned the tape back on the second time, he reentered the discussion in midsentence:

ESPOSITO: . . . guest at the Spa, you know.
MARTUSCELLO: Yeah.
ESPOSITO: Mario is.
MARTUSCELLO: Right.
ESPOSITO: And hey, that's good money invested. . . . I did it last year, too.

It was just twenty-two words, five seconds of conversation. The next morning Michaels and Thornton listened to the tape but missed the significance of what Esposito had said. Caspersen heard it on Monday, but noticed nothing unusual either.

It was not until the following Saturday afternoon, when Michaels was working in his cubbyhole at the FBI, that he decided to listen to the December 20 tape again. This time its meaning was clear, and the phrase "good money invested" registered.

"I just heard something that sounds like a smoking gun," Michaels said after he reached Caspersen in New Jersey.

By the time the relevance of this exchange was recognized, the FBI had already dispatched a team of thirteen agents to Fort

Lauderdale to follow and photograph Esposito and Biaggi. One of the group was a female undercover agent assigned to find out as much as possible about Barbara Barlow.

The agent signed up for the same aerobics class as Barlow, and started asking her questions about whom she was with and what her plans were for the day, so that the surveillance squads could be alerted to Biaggi's movements. Barlow revealed that she was a successful businesswoman who worked for a designer of coats marketed under the Bill Blass name; that she lived in a luxury high-rise on West 57th Street in Manhattan; and that she had been "dating" the congressman for three years. She went on to describe her visit to the Bonaventure with the same congressman the year before.

This information proved to be the most substantial the surveillance would yield, for as it happened, Esposito and Biaggi saw each other only once in Fort Lauderdale, for a drink. Otherwise they went their separate ways, Esposito with his daughter Phyllis, and Biaggi with Barlow.

On his return to Washington, Congressman Biaggi billed the taxpayers for his round-trip plane fare to Florida by having his House Select Committee on the Aging pay for the ticket. Barbara Barlow's fare was paid by the law firm of Biaggi and Ehrlich, which was involved in many of Biaggi's deals. Before Biaggi arrived at the Bonaventure Spa, Barlow called up and hustled a 50 percent discount on their room on the basis of Biaggi's being a VIP—a member of Congress. She also finagled an upgrade of their room to deluxe, so they ended up getting a $250 accommodation for $60 a night.

Because the couple believed that others were picking up the bill for the Spa, while Biaggi was covering his own costs at the hotel, they both loaded up Esposito's charges. Barlow spent forty-five minutes with a desk clerk switching $850 in expenses—meals, three beauty salon treatments, the aerobics classes—to the Spa expenses. In a separate visit to the desk clerk, Biaggi analyzed a computer printout of his bill and transferred $150 in expenses to the Spa portion. He then paid $500 of his own $836 hotel bill with a Biaggi and Ehrlich law firm credit card. After Biaggi and Barlow checked out, they had an $18 breakfast. They even loaded this final meal onto the bill for the Spa.

Perhaps because of all the confusion caused by these transfers, the clerks at Bonaventure mistakenly sent Biaggi's bill to the Biaggi and Ehrlich firm instead of to Jimmy La Rossa. The accountants at Biaggi and Ehrlich automatically processed the bill and paid it, just as they had paid so many other expenses incurred by Biaggi, who had no formal relationship with the firm, other than that his son Richard was a partner. Biaggi thus left Florida believing that Meade Esposito had paid his bill, just as Esposito had paid in 1984–85, by laundering the payment through La Rossa and Beaumont. The FBI and the organized crime strike force also believed that Esposito paid the $3,800 tab for the Spa.

Esposito returned from Florida chipper and refreshed on January 4. Six days later Donald Manes tried to kill himself, and the first inklings of the PVB scandal started to surface in the media. When Lindenauer was arrested on January 14, all those who moved in the same circles as Esposito realized it was time to retreat. The smart sharks of politics started to avoid him. His friends grew more circumspect. Anthony Ameruso announced he was resigning as transportation commissioner, and the Lopat discussions about contracts with the city stopped. The wiretap started to dry up.

In this abrupt new era, Deputy Mayor Townsend sent a memo to the mayor laying out the problems with Coastal. On January 20—the same day that Ed Koch canceled Stanley Friedman's Citisource contract—he wrote a memo back to Townsend with new instructions on how to handle the five-year-old problem of Coastal's stiffing the city. Koch now instructed Townsend to "never again" allow Coastal to be in default. He recommended that while continuing the discussions with Coastal, the city require the company to post security in case ultimately they didn't pay their back rent. He noted that "there may be people who think Coastal Dry Dock has political clout," but he was now, half a decade late, saying there was no clout, and that if "anyone called to try to pressure us to do anything untoward on behalf of Coastal, we should disregard those calls." At last, in the new climate, the mayor was getting tough.

January 21, 1986 was a watershed in the unfolding of the city's scandal, the day that Donald Manes admitted that the story he had given to the police about being abducted was false, that in fact he had tried to kill himself. At about 7:30 that evening, U.S.

Attorney Rudolph Giuliani granted immunity from prosecution to Mike Dowd, clearing the way for Dowd to reveal the truth about PVB by admitting that he had paid bribes to Manes to obtain city collection contracts.

At that same time, in the Ridgewood section of Queens, two New York City detectives, Anthony Venditti and Kathy Burke, were on a routine surveillance assignment, tailing Fritzy Giovanelli. They were members of the joint FBI-NYPD task force. Because they were part of an investigation that involved federal wiretaps, they had both been sworn in as deputy marshals, deputizing them as federal agents.

Through the wiretap that was still on Giovanelli's phone, FBI monitors could tell that January 21 was not an average day in the life of Fritzy Giovanelli. Although he conducted his conversations in code, it was clear from the tension in his voice and from his unusual behavior that he was involved in a crisis.

At 8:41 A.M. Vito Perrone, one of Giovanelli's numbers workers, had called to say that "the tall guy in Brooklyn" had established 644 as the daily number, when actually it was 187. An angry Giovanelli answered that the tall guy "can't be trusted no more."

At 12:15 P.M. Giovanelli left a message on his girlfriend's answering machine, apologizing for not being able to see her that night, since "something came up, very important. . . . Love you." So demonstrative an expression of affection was out of character for Giovanelli, and likely indicated a further sign of his emotional stress.

At 1:41 P.M. Giovanelli called Joey Ida, a Genovese family soldier, and asked, "Remember that stuff I gave you? When can you get it to me? I'm going to the city right now because the quicker I get that tonight, the better, because I got to put it together quick." Ida agreed to meet Giovanelli "in the park around the corner" from Benny (Eggs) Mangano's social club at 101 Thompson Street, a mob hangout that kept an old poster of Pope John Paul II in the window. The FBI monitors believed that Giovanelli was getting a gun from Ida, and possibly a police scanner, used to intercept police radio transmissions.

At 1:53 P.M. Frank Condo, a Genovese member, called Giovanelli and told him that Chin Gigante wanted to see him at 7:00 that night at the Triangle Club. Giovanelli said he might not be able to be there, because his children were getting sick, and he had to see Dom Canterino, a family capo.

The FBI agents, who had never heard Giovanelli fail to comply with a summons from Gigante, interpreted his reference to his children being sick as code for a problem with members of his crew. And they surmised that he wanted to see Canterino to get permission to kill somebody. In the rigid hierarchy of the Genovese family, Giovanelli would need formal permission from Canterino for a hit. The week before, one of Giovanelli's gambling locations had been robbed by an Hispanic male-female stickup team. The Bureau operatives suspected he might have felt he needed to avenge the robbery himself, since the Chin was holding him responsible for the loss of the income to the family.

At 1:59 P.M. Frankie Condo called back with Canterino's home phone number in Brooklyn and reminded him again that Gigante wanted to see him at the Triangle at 7 P.M. Giovanelli answered, "We're in the middle of something," and promised he would come if it were at all possible.

At 4:04 P.M. Giovanelli reached Canterino at home. "Remember when my wife was sick?" he asked. "I want to come and see you because I need a doctor." When Canterino questioned, "What kind?", Giovanelli told him he would explain when he arrived at his house. Giovanelli was then driven by his crew member Steve Maltese to see both Canterino in Brooklyn and Joey Ida in the park at the corner of Thompson and Spring streets in Soho.

Tony Venditti and Kathy Burke, dressed in funky plainclothes, began their surveillance of Giovanelli at about 6:00 P.M., unaware of his tense emotional state. Giovanelli quickly "made" their unmarked brown car, and not only gave them the slip but managed to come up behind them. It is likely that Giovanelli believed he was being tailed not by detectives but by potential robbers—perhaps the very ones that had struck at his gambling location. With his drooping bandito moustache, Venditti could have passed for Hispanic, and Burke, who had a wild perm, looked convincingly like a junkie.

At about 8:20 P.M. Venditti stopped to buy a container of coffee and use the men's room at Castillo's Diner on Myrtle Avenue in Ridgewood, a block from Fritzy's social club. Burke circled the block to see if Giovanelli's car would follow her, but by now it had stopped.

When Burke arrived back at the diner, three men were holding guns aimed at Venditti.

"What are you going to do with that thing?" Venditti asked Giovanelli. Venditti did not identify himself as a police officer, unwilling to sacrifice the surveillance. Burke says she did shout she was a cop.

Burke testified at trial that she saw Giovanelli shoot first, hitting her partner in the head, his blood spurting over his face and out of his ears. She fired but was almost immediately shot in return. One of Giovanelli's cohorts wounded her in the lung and ribs, she said. She also testified that as she went down, she could see one of Giovanelli's associates pump two more bullets into her partner.

Tony Venditti, the father of four daughters, the youngest only a month old, lay dying on the frozen Queens pavement. Giovanelli tried to flee but was identified by a teenager and arrested by a uniformed police officer in a radio car less than a block away. At the 104th Precinct, police found $4,700 in his pocket and recovered a police scanner from his car. Two days later, the police arrested two suspects as Giovanelli's accomplices—Steve Maltese and Carmine Gualtieri.

At his arraignment Giovanelli was represented by George Meissner, a very close friend of Meade Esposito. Meissner had been the Democratic district leader from Esposito's home club in Canarsie, and he was the lawyer Alex Liberman called the day he was picked up by federal and city agents. Meissner announced to the large group of reporters that had assembled that Giovanelli had no connections to organized crime, did not know the two men charged with him in the case, did not fire any weapons, and "was not involved in any criminal activity whatsoever."

At 8:29 A.M., the day after the murder of Detective Venditti, a man called Vito (presumably Perrone) called Giovanelli's house and spoke to his wife, Carol. Vito reported that "Meade" would honor Carol's home as bail, even if she were unable to find the deed. That same morning Meade Esposito sat in his office at SVR and talked about the need to help Fritzy make bail.

Tony Venditti was the first police officer to be killed in the line of duty in more than a year. The police and FBI drew on all their resources to interview witnesses and analyze the physical evidence. There was a professional resolve within law enforcement to cement this case against Giovanelli. Although many in the FBI wanted to see a federal prosecution, the Queens district attorney's office took jurisdiction for the case.

In the course of this investigation, the executive staff of the Queens D.A.'s office and the top commanders of the police department had to be informed of the electronic surveillance that had been placed on Giovanelli on the day of the murder. Copies of the tapes were turned over to Queens D.A. John Santucci.*

Ed McDonald rightly feared that, amid this tumult and dissemination of confidential information, the wiretaps on Esposito would be revealed. More people now knew there was a tap on Giovanelli, and they would inevitably wonder why. McDonald, Caspersen, and Michaels held their breath for a week, and somehow the secret held. There was no leak either to the media or back to Esposito. Luck was still on the side of the hunters.

The heavily publicized arrest of Giovanelli caused even more of Meade Esposito's appointees and cronies to shun his telephone. Many people were aware of Esposito's comradeship with Giovanelli, whom he always took care to describe as "just a gambler."

One of the few men of power not made mute by caution was Congressman Mario Biaggi, who continued to report to his benefactor his exertions to get Coastal Dry Dock at least some of the $26 million the federal government was impounding. On February 10, 1986, Biaggi phoned Esposito, and the two veteran politicians engaged in a conversation that opened a wonderful window on their closed community of cynics.

BIAGGI: Who do ya have in the motor vehicles bureau? Friend of mine has a problem, needs some advice and guidance.

ESPOSITO: Geez, I got nobody there now. What do ya need?

BIAGGI: It's Brooklyn. You don't have anybody there now?

ESPOSITO: No, no. I never bothered with that stuff. The girl used to take care of it. . . . I always kept away from that shit.

BIAGGI: Whatever you did, you did right.

ESPOSITO: I know. *I had other people do it.*

A few moments later, Esposito and Biaggi were reminiscing about how they had tried to get Stanley Friedman to side

---

*In July 1987, Giovanelli's trial for murder in Queens Supreme Court ended with the jury deadlocked after fifty hours of deliberations. A second trial also ended with a hung jury in April 1988.

with Howard Golden instead of Donald Manes in the struggle over the city council majority leadership. They acknowledged that had they known at the time that Friedman and Manes were in a corrupt partnership in PVB, they would have understood Friedman's disinclination to break with Manes in the leadership contest. Ending the topic, Mario Biaggi commented admiringly: "The guy helps put two million dollars in your pocket. Hey, my friend, I would do the same thing."

By late May 1986, the decision was made to terminate the covert phase of Runnymede and to go overt with search warrants, subpoenas, and simultaneous interviews, so that witnesses and targets would be unable to coordinate their stories. The reasons for taking the step were that Esposito was no longer active in any new criminal activities; the labor cost of the project was becoming prohibitive; and the prosecutors believed there was already sufficient evidence to indict both Esposito and Biaggi.

On Saturday, May 31, Caspersen and Michaels drafted seventy grand jury subpoenas and five search warrants. They prepared packets for the interview teams, who would go out and question about fifty people in a single day, including judges, city officials, Mario Biaggi, and Barbara Barlow. The interview folders contained a summary of the relevant telephone interceptions, biographical background information, and a list of suggested questions.

On Sunday June 1, Caspersen and Michaels briefed the key interview teams on what facts needed to be pinned down. Caspersen hand-picked the group that was going up to the Bronx to see Mario Biaggi. He chose agent Nancy O'Shea, because she worked on the public corruption squad and knew a lot about Esposito, and George Bolds, who had four years of experience and a proven expertise in conducting interviews.

The operation of June 2 was as carefully executed as a military exercise. About 150 FBI agents assembled at the office before dawn, were briefed, and were dispatched in all directions. A group of fifteen agents went out to Farmingdale, Long Island, with a search warrant for Beaumont and instructions to find the book that had the guest list for the villa in St. Maarten. Another fifteen agents searched the two floors of SVR on Greenwich Street. A third team flew to Florida with a search warrant for the records of the Bonaventure Hotel and Spa. June 2 was the last day of the electronic surveillance on SVR's phones, and the next-to-last day of court authorization for the listening device in its offices. It is standard law enforcement procedure to maintain electronic surveillance during a blitz like this, for occasionally someone will panic and make a mistake.

At 8:30 A.M. Nancy O'Shea and George Bolds were waiting on the street outside Mario Biaggi's congressional district office on Westchester Avenue in the Bronx. They knew he was due to arrive there about 9:00 A.M. As he stepped out of his car they produced their badges, and he agreed to be interviewed in his office.

Biaggi acknowledged that he and Barbara Barlow had vacationed together at Bonaventure over the last two years. He said he wasn't sure who had financed her plane ticket in 1985. When asked who had paid for the Spa, Biaggi said he didn't wish to identify that person. When asked why another party had paid for his Spa bill, Biaggi replied, "No comment," a response more appropriate to a reporter than to two FBI agents.

Sensing Biaggi was fumbling to hide something, the agents requested that he provide the numbers on his American Express cards. Biaggi reeled off the first five digits, abruptly stopped, and said he didn't wish to give any further information about his credit cards.

When pressed again on who had paid for the Spa activities, he refused to comment, although he did volunteer that he had performed no favor in return for these benefits. He next claimed not to know why this unnamed person would pay for Barlow's Spa activities, and said he did not consider this payment a gift. When asked if he had disclosed the payment on the appropriate ethics forms, he said he didn't think that it was necessary.

Twice during the interview Biaggi called his Washington office and spoke to his administrative assistant of fifteen years, Bob Blancato, to verify particular facts and dates. In neither conversation did Biaggi mention that he was being questioned by two FBI agents.

The well-briefed agents then zeroed in on Coastal Dry Dock, but Biaggi told them he was "certain" that his unnamed benefactor had no financial dealings, direct or indirect, with the company.

Finally, at the close of the ninety-minute interview, the agents pressed Biaggi one last time to identify the individual who had paid the Spa bills. This time he admitted it was Meade Esposito.

Near the end of the interrogation, Biaggi was phoned by Barbara Barlow, who informed him two FBI agents were with her and asking her about their Bonaventure vacations together. Biaggi was not convinced that the FBI already had a great deal of information, and that he was in the middle of something big. At 11:04 A.M., he reached for the telephone on his desk, but rather than contacting his lawyer, he called Meade Esposito.

At the start of the subsequent conversation Biaggi was almost in a state of shock, breathing hard and speaking in a slow, stammering voice. Initially the self-absorbed Esposito did not detect any sense of urgency, and even growled his pet axiom—"Never, never dent that cherry." Biaggi drifted into pointless subtleties as he tried to coach Esposito on how to lie about the vacations. But Biaggi was only coherent enough to incriminate himself with the prosecutors, without being understood by his co-conspirator. Their dialogue was a comedy of misunderstanding that could have been a scene in a play by Harold Pinter or Bertolt Brecht:

BIAGGI: How long have you and I known each other?
ESPOSITO: Quite a long time.
BIAGGI: Say twenty, twenty-five years.
ESPOSITO: At least.
BIAGGI: We're very dear friends?
ESPOSITO: Oh yeah.
BIAGGI: You regard me as a son?
ESPOSITO: No problem. Whatta ya want?
BIAGGI: You're concerned about my health?
ESPOSITO: Absolutely.
BIAGGI: You knew I had some trouble with my heart.
ESPOSITO: When?
BIAGGI: Now just listen to what I'm saying . . . and I needed some relaxation?
ESPOSITO: Yeah . . . what the fuck do you want, pal? Tell me.
BIAGGI: Listen to me, listen to me. This is serious. . . . All, all of this. And that's why you invited me down to the Spa. You're my host.
ESPOSITO: Of course. When do you want to go down?

BIAGGI: No, I did that. . . . You know my friend Barbara Barlow.

ESPOSITO: Sure.

BIAGGI: Remember her name. What's her name?

ESPOSITO: Barbara Barlow.

BIAGGI: Right. You knew her before?

ESPOSITO: I met her before.

BIAGGI: Right.

ESPOSITO: This sounds like a fuckin' grand jury.

BIAGGI: That's, that's what I'm talking about.

ESPOSITO: Go ahead.

BIAGGI: You said I needed my health and all of that? And you invited us both to the Spa, right?

ESPOSITO: Well, you wanna go to St. Maarten?

BIAGGI: No.

ESPOSITO: Then what?

Later in the eight-minute conversation, Biaggi whispered over the phone, "Don't mention St. Maarten . . . cause I didn't mention it . . . we just mentioned the two times at the Spa."

This was the first the FBI and the strike force had heard of Biaggi's also taking a gift vacation from Esposito to spend five days in Esposito's villa on the island of St. Maarten. Months later, the prosecutors discovered that in March 1984 Esposito had paid Biaggi's $639 round-trip airplane ticket with a check drawn on the offshore Bank of N.T. Butterfield and Son in Bermuda, where Esposito kept an account. Shortly after this trip, Biaggi's congressional office opened a file on Coastal; that June Biaggi himself wrote his first letter to Mayor Koch urging lower utility rates for the company.

There was one further moment of drama in the conversation, when Biaggi sputtered the words "Coastal Dry Dock."

ESPOSITO: What about it?

BIAGGI: Do you personally have any business with them? Personally?

ESPOSITO: Well, we handle their insurance.

BIAGGI: But . . .

ESPOSITO: That's about it.

BIAGGI: It's business then.

Biaggi sounded ill; he had apparently never before realized Esposito had an economic interest in the company.

Right after hanging up the phone, Esposito turned to Frank Brasco, his controller, and asked: "How much have we got in fuckin' Mario Biaggi?"

"Ten-two," answered Brasco, a cryptic reply that might have meant $10,200. (The $200 could well have referred to a campaign contribution Esposito had just sent to a curious Biaggi reelection committee located in Fort Lee, New Jersey.)

The FBI agents at the plant had telephoned Sid Caspersen while the Biaggi-Esposito conversation was still in progress, and as soon as the call was completed, they played him the tape over the phone. Twenty minutes later the tape was delivered to FBI headquarters, where three duplicates were made and the original sealed as evidence.

At about 12:30, Caspersen, McDonald, and Michaels were sitting in the offices of Fred Verinder, the chief of the white-collar crime section, when the tape came down from the lab. They played it several times. Parts of it were so accidentally funny they laughed until tears came to their eyes. Esposito offering Biaggi a new free trip got the biggest laugh. The perplexed Esposito growling, "This sounds like a fuckin' grand jury" got the second biggest laugh.

While more than forty people had been interviewed that morning, only one person had panicked and babbled everything out over the phone. Ironically, that one person was a lawyer, a member of Congress for eighteen years, and a former police detective with medals for bravery under fire.

The next day the media were filled with stories about the raids and the news that Meade Esposito had been wiretapped and was the target of a federal investigation. On Wednesday, June 3, at a speech before the Citizens Crime Commission, Mayor Koch attempted a civil libertarian defense of the Brooklyn boss, attacking newspaper accounts of the raids.

"Do you think that's fair?" Koch asked. "Let's assume that he is never indicted. Do you think that he will ever recover from that story?"

But earlier in the same speech, Koch defended his actions in calling Donald Manes a "crook" before he was ever charged with a crime.

"But wasn't I right? Wasn't I right?" Koch cackled twice. "They said he hasn't been proved guilty. He is entitled to the presumption of innocence.

"Uh-uh," Koch said, shaking his head in the negative. "Presumption of innocence is a court matter for the jury. There is no presumption of innocence outside the courtroom."

Ed McDonald might never have been able to bring criminal charges against Meade Esposito and Mario Biaggi had he not obtained the tape of their June 2 conversation as evidence. Without that record, the case was so problematic that a good lawyer might have been able to beat it. McDonald first realized that a prosecution would be difficult when he discovered that Biaggi had in fact inadvertently paid for his own vacation in 1986. But he surmounted this problem by studying the law, which stressed the importance of a *promise* to give a thing of value, and listened closely to the tapes, which clearly indicated that Biaggi believed he had received the vacation as a gift.

In his mind, McDonald compared the decision to prosecute Esposito with the prosecution of Al Capone. The limited parallel was that Capone had been put on trial for tax evasion, not for the dozens of gangland executions he committed and commissioned; he was removed from public life for violating the specific law for which prosecutors had the best evidence against him. Similarly, McDonald knew that the value of the two free vacations Esposito had given Biaggi was only about $4,000. But he was convinced that both politicians had corrupted government for so long, in so many different ways, that they had to be pursued over this comparatively trivial sum of money. McDonald believed it was sometimes necessary "to indict a significant criminal for an insignificant crime."

On March 16, 1987, Esposito and Biaggi were indicted on charges of bribery, conspiracy, illegal gratuities, and interstate travel in aid of racketeering. Biaggi alone was also indicted for obstruction of justice—a result of his June 2 call to Esposito.

At the trial, which was held in September, the government's case took nine days to present, and was based on fifty-three tapes, building to the climax of the June 2 recording.

Meade Esposito never took the stand. He had built his career on his braggadocio style, on his ability to intimidate. He had spent the pretrial months like a boxer in training—taunting the prosecutors, proclaiming his innocence, predicting his own victory. But when the moment of truth arrived, when the witness chair and the Bible awaited him, Meade Esposito did not testify in his own defense. He could not explain his own words on tape, he could not answer questions on cross-examination.

The case went to the jury on September 18—ten years to the week from the Sunday morning that Ed Koch and Meade Esposito shook hands and agreed Esposito would secretly help make Koch the mayor of New York.

After deliberating for sixteen hours over three days, the jury came back with its decision at 1:15 P.M. on September 22.

Jury foreman William McNichol read from the verdict sheets.

"Not guilty," he said three times, on the first three counts of conspiracy and bribery.

"Not guilty," he announced on the fourth count, but as McDonald's heart sank, he stopped himself: "Oops, wait a minute. Guilty on count four."

He then read "guilty" three more times: both men guilty of giving and receiving unlawful gratuities, both guilty of interstate travel to commit a crime, Biaggi guilty on obstruction of justice.

Esposito's hard, craggy face was stoic as the verdict was read, and the only sign of tension he allowed himself was biting repeatedly into an empty cigar holder. Biaggi's face flushed under his distinguished white hair, and his three grown daughters—Jackie, Barbara, and Toni—began to sob.

Before he released the jurors, Judge Jack Weinstein did something unusual. During the *voir dire,* the lawyers for Esposito and Biaggi had accused McDonald of bias, of systematically keeping Italians off the jury. Weinstein now asked each juror, one by one, if he or she was related to anyone of Italian heritage. Seven of the twelve jurors said they had a relative who was Italian—two parents, one parent, a wife, a husband, a stepchild.

One of the jurors who spoke to reporters afterward was Teresa Cataldo, who was 100 percent Italian. "The last tape got them," she explained, referring to the June 2 tape. She admitted that she wanted to convict both the defendants of bribery, but compromised to break a deadlock.

Outside the courthouse, a composed and again cocksure Meade Esposito defiantly claimed vindication. Without fear of cross-examination under oath, the lion at twilight roared.

"I'm happy about one thing," he said, "no charge of corruption—to me that was very important. That means that I maintained and have proven to the world that my integrity and my honor is still great. . . . I am not corrupt. There's no law prohibiting helping a friend. There're three hundred congressmen shitting bricks today."

Meade Esposito's conviction on two felonies was added to

the tally of fallen Democratic Party county leaders in New York, whose collective misconduct was beginning to assume the proportions of a crime wave. The last two county leaders in the Bronx—Pat Cunningham and Stanley Friedman—had been convicted of felonies. The two most recent county leaders in Queens—Matthew Troy and Donald Manes—were proven criminals, with only suicide thwarting the formal conviction of Manes. Five of the last ten Democratic Party county leaders in New York City were corrupt. Three of the four county leaders who endorsed Ed Koch for governor in May 1982 were crooks. The crime rate among ordinary people in the poorest neighborhoods of New York—the Seventy-ninth Precinct in Bedford-Stuyvesant, the Forty-eighth Precinct in the Bronx—is *one per hundred.* Among the county leaders of the Democratic organization in this one-party city, that rate had become *fifty per hundred.*

Ed McDonald did not want to display any personal emotion in the courtroom with Biaggi's children present, feeling it would be unprofessional. When he returned to the privacy of his office, accompanied by Michaels and Caspersen, he was greeted by strike force attorney Bruce Maffeo waving two bottles of champagne. As soon as Maffeo had heard the foreman say the first "guilty," he had run to the liquor store at the corner of Clark and Henry streets. In the quiet of the strike force law library, McDonald raised his glass and offered a toast to the joy of collaborating with Sid Caspersen and the FBI.

Caspersen then raised his own glass and said, "I have never worked with anyone who was so dogged as Len Michaels. And I have never worked with anyone who was so determined that everything be done properly as Len Michaels."

A little later Rudy Giuliani called McDonald from a meeting in Washington. The two prosecutors, who had different methods, were not close; three years earlier they had disagreed about jurisdiction over a case against the leaders of the Columbo crime family. But now Giuliani was telling McDonald, "You should be proud of what you accomplished. It will help everyone in cleaning up the city. It will help my office in our case against Biaggi. You've made an historic contribution."

As the day of his sentencing approached, Esposito seemed lonely, depressed, and apprehensive; a few friends even saw him shed a tear. He was eighty years old (eighty-two, according to some of his friends), and the past eighteen months had taken their inevitable toll. His wife of sixty-two years was now bedridden, and Esposito himself suffered from a degenerative disease of the retina that made him almost blind. Most of his political appointees were still avoiding him. His friend Fritzy Giovanelli was awaiting retrial for the murder of Detective Venditti. No one at City Hall would have lunch with him now, and the mayor was already rewriting history, diminishing Esposito's role in his election and in staffing his administration. And Esposito knew that when he died, his obituary would have to mention he had been convicted of corruption.

Yet, on his judgment day, Esposito collected himself, came to court alone without any family members, and put on one last epic performance, like the great method actor he is. The only hint of the anxiety beneath the bravado was that Esposito was wearing the jacket from one suit and the pants from another.

Before the proceedings began, Esposito stopped in the hallway of the court to fence with reporters.

Coming over to Jack Newfield, he joked, "Come on, write my memoirs with me. We'll both get rich."

"Only if you let me stay in your villa in St. Maarten," Newfield laughed, and Esposito cocked a playful fist.

"How long were you investigated?" Dick Oliver of CBS-TV asked Esposito.

"Twenty-five years. Most of it unfounded."

Judge Jack Weinstein's humane custom at sentencing was to perform this difficult rite in conversational tones, sitting behind a long table, rather than from an elevated bench, looking down at the guilty penitent. When Weinstein asked Esposito if he wished to make a statement, Esposito launched into a spontaneous outburst to the court, arguing for his lost dignity and honor. It was hard not to feel some sympathy, even affection for him as he spoke, even as his unrepentant soliloquy strayed far from the truth.

"I'm angry," Esposito began. "I'm not sad. I'm not bitter. I am just God damn angry. I am in the twilight of my life. As for myself, *c'est la vie.* But I am concerned about the legacy I leave my three grandchildren and four great-grandchildren. . . ."

As Esposito's voice started to rise, and his gestures grew more expansive, he might have been sitting at his favorite table at Foffe's or the Tiro A Segno.

"For your information, Mr. McDonald, I am not corrupt.

And you are not a bigot. I gave everything away. When you say I am corrupt, I don't know what that means. So, I go to bat for someone. What do you mean corrupt? . . .

"He [McDonald] talks about my financial statement. Ten years ago I didn't have any money. I made some money in real estate. On my ability. I was a good insurance salesman. If he wants to see how I made some bucks I will be glad to elaborate.

"I came from East New York and Brownsville. I came from the roughest area in the world. I had sharks all over, but I was a good swimmer. Now, all of a sudden, I'm a mobster.

"Do I know Tony Scotto? So what? I helped him when he came out of jail. I tried to rehabilitate him and get him a line of credit. . . .

"I was the first guy in town to create a judicial screening panel. Now Brooklyn has the best judiciary in the country. . . .

"Corrupt? Never in my life! On my grandchildren, no!"

After a ten-minute recess, Judge Weinstein pronounced his sentence.

"These crimes were bred in greed, arrogance, and vanity," Weinstein observed coolly and precisely. "The desire of the defendant to improve the financial position of his insurance company was demonstrated by the evidence. The arrogance of the defendant in buying the congressman is clear from the transcripts. The vanity of a former political power anxious to demonstrate that he still has some appreciable influence is clear from the record. . . .

"Because of the defendant's age and poor health, and the poor health of his wife, prison is inappropriate. He and his wife probably would not survive any appreciable sentence of imprisonment."

Judge Weinstein then sentenced Esposito to two years' probation, and fined him $500,000.*

---

*In contrast to Esposito's bravura performance, Mario Biaggi cried at his sentencing two weeks later. As his hands shook and face twitched, Biaggi made an almost inaudible speech to Judge Weinstein for fifteen minutes. Weinstein nevertheless sentenced him to thirty months in prison, largely because Biaggi lacked Esposito's mitigating circumstances of "age and poor health."

Biaggi's lawyer, Barry Slotnick, in his presentencing letter to the court, had the perversity to appeal for mercy on the grounds of the health of Biaggi's wife: "We ask that consideration be given to the deteriorating state of his wife's health and her absolute dependence on her husband. . . . When she was in the hospital, Mario visited her every day he was in New York, spending hours at her bedside."

This bathos made little impact on Judge Weinstein, who knew full well from the

Meade Esposito left the courtroom smiling. Ed McDonald thought the sentence was reasonable, that confining Esposito at his age would have been cruel. Sid Caspersen never expected Esposito to go to prison, but he still wished for a symbolic "three-month zinger to teach him a lesson."

In the lobby of the courthouse, engulfed by lights and cameras, Esposito kept up his front. He told one reporter he was "going home to make a baby," another that he was eager to "bounce my great-grandchildren on my knee."

But deep in his heart, Meade Esposito, comrade of gangsters and maker of mayors, knew he had finally overreached and dented the cherry.

---

trial testimony that the cause of Biaggi's downfall was his desire to be with his mistress in Florida, and that he had left his seriously ill wife alone over two consecutive Christmas holidays.

CHAPTER ELEVEN

An Era on Trial

NEW HAVEN IS A MOST UNLIKELY SETTING for the closing scene of a seedy urban drama that began in the urinal of a Manhattan restaurant. A few hours away from New York, it is so much a university town that Yale seems to be everywhere, dominating the city from one end to the other with Gothic elegance. The biggest crowds that gather in downtown New Haven are at the rush-hour bus stop when the secretaries and sales force who work in its shops and offices leave for homes in the outskirts, turning the center of town over to the students and faculty who can afford to live in it.

The trial of Stanley Friedman, a circus culmination of the worst scandal in New York history, came to New Haven in the fall of 1986 because Friedman, who had never faced the people he ruled in a voting booth, decided he'd rather not face them in a courtroom, either. Friedman had taken a poll in the late spring and had convinced some of his co-defendants, principally Citisource chairman Marvin Kaplan, to help defray its $25,000 expense. The poll revealed that the one-time behind-the-scenes party boss had achieved a formidable level of name recognition, virtually all of it negative. He and his attorney Thomas Puccio, the former Abscam prosecutor whose recent victory in the Claus von Bülow murder trial had elevated him to the top ranks of the criminal defense bar, decided that they ought to look for a jury outside the reach of the daily bombardment of the city's scandal coverage.

When Puccio came into court in Manhattan with this surprise motion in June, U.S. Attorney Rudy Giuliani acquiesced instantly. Giuliani, who had just decided to lead the prosecution team personally during the trial and was making his first appearance in the case, needed no poll to tell him that Friedman's act would not play in a Connecticut court. Giuliani had begun to think of the Friedman trial in much the same way as he viewed an organized crime case. He believed that juries were reached corruptly far more often than anyone could prove; and he worried that when the evidence unfolded at trial, an increasingly desperate Friedman might try to get to a juror if the pool were drawn from the city. In the months that his team had been investigating Friedman, Giuliani had come to regard him as a consummate fixer, and he feared the ultimate fix.

One of the reasons Giuliani had decided to try the case himself was that U.S. District Court Judge Whitman Knapp had been letting Puccio dominate the preliminary proceedings and had been very tough on the two young assistants handling it, Bill Schwartz and David Zornow. For almost two years Giuliani had prepared to personally try the "Commission" case—an extraordinary prosecution of the leaders of the five Mafia families that was also about to start, and was virtually a sure winner. While the Friedman case was a riskier proposition, Giuliani thought his office needed a counterweight to Puccio. As soon as he entered the case, Knapp's attitude about Puccio's pretrial maneuvers changed perceptibly.

Friedman saw Giuliani as just one more pol, the sort he'd spent a lifetime inventing, commanding, and sometimes destroying. But this one, Friedman feared, was bent on building a career by ending his own. Friedman was so convinced that his indictment was a naked political act that his daily press interviews at the courthouse consisted of references to Giuliani's purported ambitions. At one point, when the jury was deliberating over a November weekend at the end of the trial and Giuliani brought his eight-month-old son Andrew to court for the first time, Friedman charged that the baby's presence was a ploy in Giuliani's unannounced political campaign.

There was no doubt that this was Giuliani's biggest case ever. Not that he hadn't tried major ones before. As a young assistant U.S. Attorney in the early 1970s, he had convicted a

Brooklyn congressman, who collapsed during his crushing cross-examination and suddenly pleaded guilty. During that first turn of duty as a federal prosecutor, Giuliani also spearheaded the second phase of a spectacular probe of police corruption that ended with the indictment of eighteen members of the police department's notorious shakedown squad, the Special Investigations Unit (SIU).

It was during this two-year probe—the city's previous great corruption upheaval—that Giuliani first crossed paths with the two other stars of the Friedman case. Tom Puccio was then a young prosecutor in the Brooklyn U.S. Attorney's office, coordinating its activities in the SIU cases, and Judge Knapp headed a city commission named after him that was exploring the same charges. Though they came from two different, intensely competitive federal prosecutorial offices, Giuliani and Puccio forged an effective partnership, transcending the petty rivalries that traditionally cripple law enforcement agencies in New York.

This brilliant and brash twosome—both born in Brooklyn just months apart, each an only child of Italian immigrants, and each then in the throes of a difficult separation from his first wife—developed such a relationship of trust that they never had to put anything in writing to each other. Although neither worked closely with the patrician Knapp, the name of the Knapp Commission became newspaper shorthand for the whole explosive probe, and the extraordinary cases put together by Puccio and Giuliani were inevitably associated in the public mind with its revelations. To complete the circle connecting these two major scandals, Knapp's chief counsel from the old commission, Michael Armstrong, was now the attorney and public spokesman for the corpse of Donald Manes, retained by the family.

Giuliani had gone on from the Manhattan prosecutor's office to the first of two stints in the justice department in Washington, with a few years of lucrative private practice in between. Ironically, at least for a man so identified with the issue of public morality, Giuliani quit the Democratic Party immediately after Watergate, became a Republican, and took his first political job during the Ford administration, explaining later that he'd become disenchanted with the global views of the McGovern Democratic Party. He left Washington when Jimmy Carter arrived, to return when the Republicans regained the presidency in 1981. Appointed Justice's number-three man, he seemed destined for as long a Washington career as Republican electoral triumphs would permit.

But even though he was in charge of all U.S. Attorneys across America, Giuliani could not resist taking the Manhattan job himself when it opened up in 1983. He seemed to have a premonition from the beginning of his four-year term that he could make himself into a Deweyesque figure, a prosecutor with political promise.* He rapidly became a public persona, determinedly pursuing a crush of mob, narcotics, white-collar-fraud, and other cases, each announced with great fanfare at a Giuliani-hosted press conference. It was just such headline grabbing (including staged drug buys with television cameras stationed directly behind him and a U.S. senator) that convinced Friedman that his own trial was merely the set for some future Giuliani campaign commercial.

At forty-two years of age, with a year and a half left of his term as U.S. Attorney, Giuliani himself acknowledged when he arrived in New Haven that an acquittal could end, before it began, the possible political career that had long tantalized him. He had been asked in every media interview for the last year or two if he would become a candidate for governor, senator, or mayor, and he had answered that he didn't know but wouldn't rule anything out. His closest friends and colleagues believed this was not a posture; it was as far into his own future as Giuliani would let himself wander. His obsession was achievement in the present, not the anticipation of a powerful new title in front of his name. He wanted to do something important under the glare of the hottest lights he could find.

Giuliani's father had given him a pair of boxing gloves when the boy was two, and had started shadowboxing with him, showing him how to hit and block, telling him never to walk away in fear from a fight. The gloves were as big as Rudy's head, and his dad would sit in a small chair opposite him so that they could poke and duck at the same level. The Friedman case was the kind of contest of wills his father had trained him for: all the chips were on the table, bet on a single hand. Giuliani also had the chance to test himself against his old friend Puccio in an uncomplicated match of good and evil. He did not see the

---

*Tom Dewey became governor of New York and the 1948 Republican presidential nominee on the strength of his prosecution of mob and rackets cases as Manhattan D.A.

case as a path to glory. Trying it was what Giuliani had prepared himself to do all his life.

He couldn't have found a bigger fishbowl. The most immediate, unanticipated result of the decision to move the case out of the city was to turn a trial already certain to be a major media event into one unparalleled in the annals of municipal corruption. The remote location meant that assignment editors couldn't settle for covering highlights; they had to give the trial a permanent priority. Never has each legal move or evidentiary detail in a city corruption case received the kind of press scrutiny the Friedman trial attracted.

Each morning for the ten weeks that preceded a Thanksgiving verdict, Puccio walked Friedman and his wife, Jackie, the five blocks from their hotel, the six-story Colony, to the brick courthouse, taking the longer and more photogenic route across the New Haven Green. And every morning, lunch break, and evening, a couple of dozen reporters, photographers, and cameramen, stationed on the steps of the courthouse, hunted for some new angle. The move to Connecticut had forced the five New York TV stations to assign full-time crews to New Haven, and the reporters, including WNBC's Gabe Pressman, the savviest and most senior of the city's newscasters, had to come up with a story every night. Three radio mikes joined the TV crews everytime Friedman walked in or out of the courtroom.

The four city dailies and two wire services had also assigned reporters to the full trial, sending extras in for the high points. Stories appeared daily, even when the trial had momentarily adjourned, and were often given front-page banner treatment. A half-dozen artists took up a row in the courtroom. Three Pulitzer Prize–winning columnists—Sydney Schanberg, Jimmy Breslin, and Murray Kempton—visited from time to time, as did *Newsday* color reporter Mickey Carroll and *Post* columnist Beth Fallon, the husband-and-wife team that had headed the City Hall bureaus of the *Daily News* and the *Times* when Stanley Friedman was deputy mayor.

For ten weeks, this unprecedented media herd, which Friedman had cited as the reason he had to get out of town for a fair trial, mysteriously moved in his direction. Reporters decided that they were assuming the appropriate skeptical distance from the case by adopting every doubt Friedman and Puccio could concoct about the government's case. Old Friedman friend Fallon openly wrapped her copy around him. Her paper, the *Post,* led the tabloid trashing of every important government witness, spurred by leaks from the defense. Even the *Times* and *Newsday,* seduced by Puccio and Marvin Kaplan's counsel, Gerald Lefcourt, repeatedly understated the force of the blows that Giuliani witnesses were delivering.

Giuliani, whose widely suspected role as a pretrial leaker had fed the scandal furor, became in New Haven a silent saint of due process, refusing to say anything much of substance on or off camera. Friedman and Puccio, on the other hand, were magnets for the microphones, ridiculing the government's case at every recess. Their performance made little apparent trial sense since the jury came from Hartford, which, unlike New Haven, is beyond the range of New York television stations. Knapp nonetheless tried to convince Puccio to stop the show, but the interviews on the courthouse steps, as much as the testimony inside, became a central event in the daily lives of this self-contained community of nearly fifty people—prosecutors, defendants, reporters, lawyers, families, and witnesses.

Besides Friedman and Kaplan, there were three other defendants in the case: PVB director Lester Shafran, who'd run the agency described in the indictment as a racketeering enterprise for eight years; Michael Lazar, the ex–city transportation commissioner and multimillionaire developer close to Manes; and Marvin Bergman, Manes's ex–law partner who was shoehorned into the case because a collection company he'd represented had been one of the half-dozen allegedly paying PVB bribes.

Except for Lazar, the defense entourage took over the tiny Colony. Citisource's Kaplan had secretly agreed to bear the New Haven costs of most of his co-defendants when they objected to Puccio's relocation proposal on the grounds that they couldn't afford the additional cost. This meant, for example, that the hotel expenses of Shafran, who was indicted for subsidizing his personal life with thousands in penny-ante bribes and gratuities from PVB contractors, were paid, at least in part, by a PVB contractor.

In fact, over the course of the trial, Kaplan would quietly become the sugar daddy of the defense team, even paying the lion's share of Puccio's legal fees (the rationale being that it was he who "got Stanley in trouble"). Kaplan also rented a suite with a large-screen television and a bar for everyone to relax in, and converted another room into an office, filled with file cabinets, a photocopying machine, a shredder, and a computer. Puccio's business expenses and those of his two associates, who would jointly run up a $2,000-a-week hotel bill, were also covered largely by Kaplan, as were those of his own attorney Lefcourt and his associate. Kaplan even rented a Connecticut shore mansion near New Haven, where occasionally, when there was a break in the trial, parts of the defense team would curl up around fireplaces.

Friedman had managed to get himself reelected Bronx county leader only a week before the trial began. The party's executive committee, consisting of two leaders from each of the Bronx's ten assembly districts and other officials appointed by Friedman, voted 38 to 6 to grant him another two years in office. The key Bronx Democrats who put the votes together for Friedman—both in the most recent election and in his first, back in 1978—were now themselves targets of Giuliani's far-reaching probes. They included antipoverty sultans Ramon Velez and Frank Lugovina, who'd been implicated in the cable scandal, lawyer Paul Victor and party secretary Murray Lewinter, whose jointly owned printing company had attracted the attention of prosecutors, and Congressman Mario Biaggi and borough president Stanley Simon, both of whom would soon be indicted in the Wedtech case. Many of this long-standing crew of Friedman loyalists would trek up to New Haven to watch key parts of the trial, or lunch with Friedman discreetly away from the courthouse.

Several weeks before the trial began, Friedman shaved off the goatee he'd worn for years. He put away the eyeglasses that had become his trademark—with his initials written in rhinestones on the rims—and put on a nondescript, businesslike pair that matched those of his attorney Puccio, who was choreographing this physical transformation. The once-rangy Friedman hair was closely cropped; no gold chains anymore, no flashy rings. Puccio convinced him to wear conservative suits and white shirts daily, always without an overcoat or sweater. He got Friedman to keep his ever-present cigar in his suit coat pocket within a three-block radius of the courthouse. Friedman had effectively traded in the long-cultivated look of a slick city kingpin for the clean-cut profile of a small-town lawyer or businessman. He had been remade in the image of the only audience that now mattered in his life—the twelve Connecticut jurors who would decide if he was a racketeer.

Friedman started each trial day at 6:00 A.M., when he would knock on Puccio's hotel room door and hand him copies of the city papers. Dressed in a sweater, his growing belly hanging over sweatpants and a cigar juggling between his teeth, Friedman would usually greet the groggy Puccio with a quip and a one-line summary of the morning's coverage. More often than not, he and Puccio would celebrate their latest media coup. They both preferred the news stories to the transcript.

Friedman's wife Jackie, who never wore the same outfit to court twice over the course of the trial, used her accrued time at City Hall to take a paid leave of absence. As the $47,000-a-year deputy director of the mayor's Office of Special Projects and Events, she was responsible for organizing everything from Koch inaugurals to proclamations; the only time she left the trial was the day of the Mets ticker-tape parade, which she had helped organize to celebrate the World Series victory. Otherwise, she remained at Stanley's side, but her face, unlike the usually implacable Friedman's, was frequently a mirror of just how badly things had gone in court that day. She alternately scowled, agonized, sagged, and gaped.

She had come to City Hall as Jackie Glassberg in the early 1970s, and had worked as a secretary in the mayor's office of intergovernmental affairs, a patronage job she'd obtained through her Queens clubhouse. She needed a job because her previous employer and close friend, Queens state senator Seymour Thaler, had just been convicted of selling stolen treasury bonds. As she would do later with her second husband Stanley, she went daily to Thaler's tortuous federal trial. She even took the witness stand for Thaler, testifying that she'd never typed the commission agreements for the stolen securities that Thaler was attempting to portray as forgeries. Another Thaler secretary also testified, and claimed that Thaler and Jackie Glassberg had persuaded her to lie before the grand jury about her role in typing letters connected with the securities.

Once at City Hall, Jackie Glassberg wound up working for Friedman during the Beame years, and eventually the two obtained divorces and married. It was Jackie who got Stanley Friedman together with Marvin Kaplan, a neighbor and long-time close friend of her first husband, Gil Glassberg. Ironically, Glassberg, who himself became a Citisource investor during the boom years, attended the Friedman trial almost daily, just as he had previously observed the Thaler trial. He returned each night to the hotel lobby with Kaplan, his ex-wife, and Friedman, vigorously championing in conversations with reporters the cause of the man who'd taken his wife away from him.

Virtually the entire defense entourage participated nightly in this mutually reinforcing chitchat over drinks in the Colony lobby, followed by a brief meeting of the lawyers in an upstairs suite and a dinner out at a variety of New Haven restaurants. One night Friedman and Giuliani, who was staying at another hotel, wound up at the same restaurant, and Friedman, who managed to remain calm for much of the trial with glass after glass of Absolut, sent a pitcher of water with straws in it over to Giuliani's table, "compliments of Mr. Friedman."

The rhetorical leader of the Friedman crowd, who never tired of rehashing the most inconsequential inconsistency in the government case, was Kaplan's attorney Lefcourt. A short, wiry, dark-haired tinderbox of a sixties' ideologue, Lefcourt brought the same passion to defending this financier of PVB graft as he once had mustered for Lumumba Shakur in the Panther 21 case. The description of Lefcourt offered by an admiring Murray Kempton in *Briar Patch*, the National Book Award–winning chronicle of the Panther case, still applied sixteen years later in New Haven: "He was possessed of that identification with the defendants which violates every tradition. And yet Mr. Lefcourt was somehow likeable, for all of being so engaged with his clients as to have the repute almost of being a co-conspirator."

Puccio had urged Kaplan to retain Lefcourt, though Lefcourt had never before handled a principal defendant in a major white-collar criminal case.* His most recent courtroom experience had been as counsel to a business partner of Matty the Horse Ianniello, and his vigorous and successful representation of the co-owner of an Ianniello carting company had earned him invitations to Matty's parties, a prize he brandished over drinks as proudly as he once had his association with the vanguard of the black revolution. In one corner of Lefcourt's mind, it was all the same struggle against the overweening excess of government. A police raid on a Panther home in the middle of a sixties night was indistinguishable from a subpoena for the records of a looted Kaplan company.† He moved easily

---

*Lefcourt had represented Pat Cunningham's secretary in the earlier trial of the former Bronx boss.

†Lefcourt had even contributed to the American Civil Liberties Union on behalf of

into the vacuum created by the nonchalant, inattentive, and realistic Puccio to become the voice of the defense team's out-of-court (and sometimes in-court) outrage, zeroing in on Giuliani as a prosecutor without a conscience.

Giuliani and his seven-member team of assistant U.S. Attorneys, FBI agents, and a city investigations department attorney stayed at the only other downtown hotel, the Park Plaza, a 19-story tower overhanging the courthouse. While almost the entire press corps stayed at the Plaza as well, none ever discovered that their hotel neighbors included the targets of their daily stories—government witnesses such as Geoffrey Lindenauer, whose anticipated tunnel escape route in and out of the courthouse was monitored unsuccessfully by teams of vigilant reporters and photographers. The photo every tabloid editor was salivating for—a room service meal delivery for the immense Lindenauer—was available for weeks right over the heads of their on-site staff.

Giuliani and his two trial assistants Schwartz and Zornow turned one hotel suite into a rehearsal hall, strewn with transcripts, documents, and notes. They often worked deep into the night, subjecting their own witnesses to practice cross-examinations. Later in the trial, Zornow and Schwartz ran Giuliani through sequence after sequence of his planned cross of Friedman, the one defendant who seemed likely to take the stand from the moment the trial began. On other nights Giuliani walked himself through his summation, a draft of which he'd outlined at the outset of the trial.

As a Yale college grad, Schwartz had signed up with an alumni club, so he could regularly bring the prosecution team as his guests to a university dining hall. Another Yale grad, Judge Knapp, frequently ate a table or two away. Giuliani had to spend months separated from his infant son Andrew, but his wife, television reporter Donna Hanover, often took the two-hour train ride after her show, spent the night with him, watched much of his performance the next day, and returned in time for another show. Her enthusiasm was a potion for Giuliani, who was periodically deflated by the surprisingly favorable press coverage Friedman was receiving and by the media savaging of his own witnesses.

Ianniello and became a mail drop for the alleged mob capo—collecting his ACLU mail and forwarding it to him in jail.

The news stories at the start of the trial billed the Friedman case as a "battle of the titans," focusing on the head-to-head confrontation between Puccio and Giuliani while overlooking the skillful trial work of Lefcourt, Zornow, Schwartz, and others. Despite the media hype, though, the most intricate and significant drama in the usually packed, hundred-seat courtroom was in fact the playing out of the strategic and competitive instincts of these two old friends.

Since their SIU days, Giuliani and Puccio had maintained a close relationship. At one out-of-town judicial conference, they went drinking together, and Puccio wound up bedding down in Giuliani's hotel room. When Giuliani reconciled with his first wife for a while, Puccio and his new wife went out socially with them. And when Giuliani married Donna Hanover in 1982, Puccio was a guest. Giuliani was one of Puccio's few friends to receive a dinner invitation to his Brooklyn Heights home.

When Puccio finally left the Brooklyn U.S. Attorney's office in 1983, Giuliani tried to use his national contacts at the justice department to secure an appointment for Puccio as a U.S. Attorney, first in Washington and then in Miami. Puccio turned down the Miami job, however, and entered private practice, just a few months ahead of Giuliani's decision to become Manhattan U.S. Attorney. In effect, when Giuliani began pursuing public corruption cases, he was competing with Puccio's record: six convicted congressmen, a U.S. senator, and a host of other top pols.

Though both attorneys have an intuitive, though hardly flawless, sense of the flow and tone of a case, their trial approaches are as different as their personalities. Puccio answers Giuliani's intensity with a casualness about his work that at times can be misinterpreted as carelessness. Giuliani is a stickler for detail, seeking out endless layers of proof; Puccio filters out all but the big picture as useless tangents. Giuliani works so hard that he intimidates the people under him into sharing his obsession. Puccio alarms his associates with his coolness; he rarely reads transcripts or case law, and waits until the last moment to prepare an opening, an argument, a witness, or a summation. While Giuliani will try to persuade a disagreeing reporter or observer of his point of view, Puccio will simply greet an opposing opinion with smiling disdain, and the reporter will usually wind up embarrassed by his own courtroom inexperience. Puccio has a way of effortlessly positioning a listener on his side of an issue as the only intelligent place to be, while Giuliani provokes exchange.

They are about the same height—six-footer Giuliani has an inch on Puccio—and both have unwieldy bodies. Giuliani's shoulders hunch forward as if they've been bent over a desk too long, making him look, when he's standing, as if he's leaning into your face. Puccio stands on a slant, with one shoulder tilted higher than the other, suggesting that he is always about to slide away from you. Giuliani is a jogger, but his awkward proportions make one wince for the running shoes. Puccio, likewise, has never made a jump shot in his life, and has been a balding, spectacled, and lethargic ambler since his twenties. Giuliani has always worn the same suburban 1950s hairdo and, though pale and toothy, can be good looking, at least when he isn't rolling his massive eyeballs up and down, as is his habit, seeming to look into his own mind for the next thought. In addition to this frequently televised eye roll, Giuliani has the uncanny knack of blinking less than humanly possible, something he must have practiced to convince others he was really listening to them.

Shortly after the teams of attorneys arrived in New Haven, while they were both systematically sorting through the jury pool, Giuliani quietly informed the court of a pretrial maneuver that stunned even the unflappable Puccio. In a closed-door session with Judge Knapp, Puccio, and Friedman, Giuliani revealed that his office had secretly taped Puccio in a meeting with a wired undercover informant. The only reason this information was now being made known was that Giuliani intended to use the wired informant as a witness against Friedman.

Though the record of the proceeding before Knapp was initially sealed, Judge Knapp released a partial version a few days later, just as Giuliani's key witness, Geoffrey Lindenauer, began his direct testimony. The taping episode upstaged the star government witness and threw the courthouse into shock. Though the jury wasn't told about the taping, it turned the press against Giuliani and boosted the morale of the defense camp, deepening their sense of themselves as victims of a politicized prosecutor. While the full story of the bugging of Abscam's engineer never emerged in New Haven, enough was known to give Puccio the weapon he needed to help shift the early momentum in his own direction.

Puccio, it turned out, had been taped in June at a meeting in the East Side office of Jerry Driesen, the friend of Geoffrey Lindenauer's who had let Lindenauer treat some of his patients. Puccio had been invited to the meeting with Driesen by Queens lawyer Harold Borg, an acquaintance of Puccio's for years. Borg was the attorney whom Donald Manes had advised Lindenauer to retain when the two first got word of the PVB scandal. Borg was also an old friend of Driesen's, and had once used the forensic psychiatrist as an expert witness at a parole hearing for mobster Sonny Francese.

Puccio had arranged this meeting with the psychiatrist because he believed Driesen could be a devastating witness against Lindenauer, or at least provide damaging cross-examination material about him. What he and Borg offered in return was information from well-placed sources that a sealed indictment of Driesen had been voted by a state grand jury in Queens and that the case against him was based on the testimony of his suddenly talkative friend Lindenauer.

Puccio had gotten this tip from Friedman, who had in turn learned it from the *New York Post*'s City Hall bureau chief George Arzt, a longtime close friend. Arzt told Friedman that Queens D.A. John Santucci had inadvertently confirmed the existence of the secret indictment to the *Post*. The *Post* had agreed not to write a story about this court-sealed case in deference to its source; Arzt, however, passed the information along to the already indicted Friedman, though Driesen was involved in a related criminal case.*

Friedman's phone logs revealed that Arzt had periodically left messages for him containing helpful tips about breaking events at City Hall. During the New Haven trial, Arzt wrote three stories that were critical of government witnesses, including one that described in detail Driesen's wild, cocaine-contaminated life.

---

*Asked later if he'd made this call, Arzt said, "I don't think so, I don't recall it happening." He added that he did not even know Driesen's name until Friedman's trial months after the taping of Puccio in June. But Jack Peritz, another *Post* reporter who'd written a story in April revealing that an unnamed go-between close to Manes had been secretly indicted by Santucci, says it was Arzt who "first tipped me to the name in May or June." Arzt asked Peritz, who was the beat reporter at the Queens courthouse, to see if he could get Santucci to confirm Driesen's name.

Peritz says Santucci "panicked" when he confronted the D.A. with the name and, without directly confirming it, asked him not to print a story naming Driesen. Peritz

What neither Arzt nor Puccio knew, at the time of the meeting with Driesen in June, was that Driesen had already been secretly indicted by Giuliani for sharing PVB bribes with Lindenauer, and was now cooperating with the government. When Borg called Driesen to set up the meeting, and said that Puccio would attend, the Giuliani assistant working with Driesen thought there was basis for believing that a criminal obstruction of justice might take place. She brought the matter to Giuliani, who barely flinched at the thought of wiring his old friend. "Record it," he said.

The FBI installed taping devices all over Driesen's office—in the waiting room, the bathroom, the desk clock, and an attaché case, and on Driesen himself. Puccio arrived at Driesen's slightly off-balance: he had just had a few glasses of wine with dinner. Driesen brought Puccio and Borg into the back office where he treated patients and closed the wooden double doors behind them. At the very outset of the half-hour meeting, Puccio told Driesen that the information he had about Driesen's sealed indictment came from a *Post* "editor," adding "these guys speak directly to Santucci."

Driesen, who'd been instructed by FBI agents on entrapment, eased Puccio into a quid pro quo discussion, implying that if Puccio found out precisely what Lindenauer's grand jury testimony about him was, he might give Puccio information on Lindenauer. He repeatedly tried to entice Puccio into suggesting a line of testimony against Lindenauer. When Puccio asked if Lindenauer had ever had a nervous breakdown, Driesen replied: "You want me to say he's crazy, in other words." But Puccio countered: "Yeah, if he were." So Driesen continued: "And if he were not?", provoking Puccio to declare: "Tell me that, too." Eventually Puccio left no doubt that he was uninterested in the trap Driesen was trying to set for him: "Just so we understand each other," he volunteered, "whatever you tell me is going to be the truth no matter what, right?" Each of Puccio's Abscam convictions had withstood an entrapment attack. Now, so had he.

After listening to this tape until 3:00 in the morning, an outraged Puccio argued in Knapp's chambers that the taping had occurred shortly after the judge had rejected a government

---

"knew by the reaction" that he had the right name and told Arzt, but Santucci's office prevailed on the *Post*'s top brass to stop the story.

motion to disqualify him from the case because of his representation of two other critical PVB players. Puccio charged that the government had tried to "set me up," by inducing him to suborn perjury.

Giuliani's response was a hodgepodge of contradiction. At first he claimed that Puccio had not been under investigation, only Borg; then that he and his staff had reviewed the tape and come "to the conclusion that there was no criminal violation" by Puccio; so the FBI "closed that investigation." His third position was that it was "a rather esoteric matter as to whether or not Mr. Puccio was under investigation." The release of this embarrassing transcript by the judge on the second day of the trial left Giuliani reeling.

Giuliani's opening statement the day before had already drawn negative reviews. A flatly delivered dissertation, it was so clogged with the details of a dozen separate conspiracies that there was no room in it for real people or real emotion. Giuliani's theory of an opening is that it should understate the evidence, giving the jury only the barest facts; but this was little more than bones, banging loosely around. He had written it out in his own hand and read it from two large, black looseleaf notebooks with all the charisma of a CPA. The jury of seven women and five men had a glazed look throughout.

Puccio, on the other hand, awed the courtroom. Giuliani had pointed his finger repeatedly at Friedman as he led the jury through his crimes, so Puccio opened with his own finger stabbing in his opponent's direction. "This is Rudolph Giuliani, the United States Attorney for the Southern District of New York. And he stood up here for over an hour this morning, and his mouth moved and words came out. But the words weren't his at all. They were the words of Geoffrey Lindenauer. I want you, when you listen to Mr. Giuliani argue to you, I want you to superimpose Geoffrey Lindenauer's face on his, because that's who's talking to you, not the respected United States Attorney." Bringing only a few pages of barely scratched-on yellow notepaper to the lectern, Puccio roamed the courtroom, painting a gripping picture of the human drama that he claimed explained the indictment of his client.

Despite the bravura of his presentation, Puccio had grossly overstated what he could prove, and did so in images so vivid that there was little question whether the jury would remember what he had promised. He said that the master manipulator Lindenauer had manipulated Manes into killing himself. He said that Lindenauer had then invented the allegations against Friedman to cut a deal with the feds and give them a fish big enough to satisfy them. It was a bizarre theory on its face, no matter how intriguing it seemed, because it suggested that Lindenauer was willing to double his workload—first creating Puccio's "empty chair" by leading Manes to his grave, then rushing to fill it with Friedman. In any event, Puccio himself soon abandoned it, aware all along that Lindenauer had detailed Friedman's role to the prosecutors before Manes's death, destroying any empty chair theory. (The government had turned its debriefing material with Lindenauer over to Puccio as part of the discovery process.)

At the conclusion of the openings, Giuliani brought out his first witness, Michael Dowd. With Manes's death, Dowd had become a mere scene setter. He knew nothing about Friedman; he had paid bribes only to Lindenauer, who was waiting in the wings to testify after him. Dowd's inventor, Jimmy Breslin, arrived to hear him deliver the lines he and Dowd had rehearsed in January, when Dowd had first implicated Manes in Breslin's *Daily News* column. It was one of the columnist's few visits to New Haven, and his friend Dowd sounded appropriately Breslinesque on the stand, offering cinematic scenes complete with crisply recalled dialogue and descriptions of Donny in a sweatsuit and a trenchcoat. Positioned by Giuliani as a kind of expert witness on bribery, he dramatically detailed the shakedown operation at PVB as if delivering a civics lesson in reverse. But he never mentioned the name of a defendant, and when he was barely cross-examined, his superfluous testimony looked like Giuliani's third blunder in a trial that had just begun.

But in fact, though the reporters and observers from New York did not notice it, Dowd had effectively defused a possible defense that Giuliani feared. Giuliani believed that the only way to successfully defend Stanley Friedman was to defend Donald Manes, and to suggest that the payoff scheme originated with Geoffrey Lindenauer. Without Dowd, who testified about direct bribe conversations with Manes, the defense could argue that Lindenauer was a one-man operation. Dowd forced the defense to concede the essentials of the government's PVB scenario and, in Giuliani's eyes, made it inevitable that the jury would eventually see the defendants, almost all of whom were closely connected with Manes, as characters in the same criminal drama.

However, this tactical objective was lost on those who'd come to New Haven from a city where Manes's criminal culpability had long been accepted as an axiom. Instead, all that Dowd appeared to accomplish in his short stay on the stand was to prepare everyone in the courtroom to hate Geoffrey Lindenauer. Dowd testified how in the weeks shortly before the investigation surfaced at the end of 1985, Lindenauer had crushed his collection company for nonpayment of bribes, unswayed by Dowd's plea for a stay of execution because he'd slipped a disc, his mother was an invalid requiring twenty-four-hour care, and his father had just had a heart attack. Since Dowd's anecdote directly preceded Lindenauer's appearance on the stand, Giuliani had chosen a strange way of introducing his lynchpin witness to the jury.

The courtroom was built for a performer like Lindenauer. Unlike most witness stands, which are situated between the judge and jury so that both can see only the witness's profile, the New Haven stand places the witness on the far side of the courtroom, opposite the jury. The jurors thus looked directly at Lindenauer, or, more aptly in his case, this master of eye contact looked directly at them. The defendants sat at tables grouped just to the side of the witness, so that jurors who wanted to see how Friedman and the others were reacting to his testimony did not have to stop looking at him to observe them.

David Zornow, a soft-spoken, almost mechanical Giuliani assistant who had met with Lindenauer over sixty times since he began cooperating with the government seven months earlier, was given the responsibility of questioning Lindenauer. Only thirty-one years old, Zornow had grown up a member of the same Queens temple as Donald Manes and Michael Lazar, and had gone to Hebrew school with one of Lazar's daughters. She made it a point during the trial to brush by him in the hallway and murmur "shame."

For two days on direct, Lindenauer was a spellbinding storyteller. He recounted hundreds of corrupt transactions and conversations, without Dowd's melodrama or any face-saving caveats. He spoke in a fact-filled monotone without changing his blank expression. His voice soothed; his manner assured. As the government would do with each of its troubled witnesses,

Zornow got him to admit the worst about himself during his direct examination, including his counterfeit degrees and his early life as a therapist who prescribed sex with himself. The admissions were almost disarming.

When Lindenauer began his testimony, the government deliberately ushered him to the witness stand before the jury was brought into the courtroom. But after a couple of recesses, Puccio caught on and insisted that he wait until the jury was seated before taking the stand. Puccio wanted the jury to see all of him cross the courtroom. He wanted Lindenauer to feel the glare of a hundred eyes watching this short, 250-pound hulk—hands hanging limply at his side, eyes staring straight ahead at a wall—step slowly forward. Just the movement, Puccio thought, might break Lindenauer's composure, and make him self-conscious and ashamed.

Beneath Lindenauer's layers of flesh was a still handsome face. He was so embarrassed by his body that once, when he went to the Downtown Athletic Club with Driesen, he refused to take his clothes off. He and Manes spent weeks at a time, and thousands of bribe dollars, at various diet clinics in upstate New York and Pennsylvania. The dark suits he wore on the stand, tailored to his large frame, weren't acquired on a bureaucrat's salary. Indeed, he testified that he'd spent thousands in bribe money on clothes to deftly cover the body he'd spent other thousands bloating.

Lindenauer never met Mike Lazar's gaze while he testified about taking his first bribe at Lazar's home, with the white-haired, wealthy Lazar standing in his living room in a red bathrobe. He kept his eyes riveted on the jury when he detailed how Friedman gradually became his and Manes's partner on the grandest PVB scams—the $22 million Citisource contract, the potentially $50 million in-state towing deal, and the Datacom data processing contract. After hundreds of meetings about PVB with Manes alone, he said, he and Manes began to include Friedman as a partner, arranging three-way splits of bribes, even meeting at Friedman's summer home in the Hamptons in 1985. Lindenauer also came close to putting a $30,000 bribe payment in Friedman's hands—up-front money that he and Manes demanded from Friedman's covert client Datacom. But Lindenauer admitted that he got his half of this bribe from Manes, who claimed to have collected it directly from Friedman.

In one damning episode, Lindenauer coolly conveyed Friedman's greed. He told of bringing Friedman the first print-outs of Datacom's earnings on the towing contract, because Friedman's payments were based on a percentage of Datacom's gross. When he tried to explain the numbers to Friedman at the boss's midtown law office, Friedman cut him off: "Will you stop? You're getting me crazy with all this stuff. I don't want to know from the program itself. I just want to know how much to charge them."

Only at the end of Lindenauer's two days of direct testimony, as Zornow took him slowly through the days before Manes's suicide attempts, did his composure falter. He began breathing heavily as he described his meeting in late December with Manes, and Manes's attempt to suggest that he kill himself. "He had tears in his eyes, and I had tears in my eyes," a haunted, emotionally gutted Lindenauer recalled.

As Giuliani's other assistant, Bill Schwartz, sat listening to this testimony, he remembered how Lindenauer had first come to them back in March, a defeated man who believed his life was over. Schwartz had memorized Lindenauer's remarkable first few days of debriefings, and now relived the excitement he and Zornow had felt—when they realized, almost instantly, that this strange man whom no one in the public life of the city had ever heard of was telling them the truth about the sacking of a government.

When Lindenauer testified about the final days, Schwartz recalled his meeting with Lindenauer on March 15, just a few hours after Manes had plunged a kitchen knife into his chest. He could still hear Lindenauer insisting that he wanted to work, he wanted to continue the debriefing. And Schwartz remembered going out to the Queens FBI office on the morning of Donald Manes's funeral and joining a session with Zornow, the FBI, and the somber shell of Geoffrey Lindenauer. Schwartz knew as Lindenauer concluded that the test of all those months of preparation was about to begin.

Zornow did not finish with Lindenauer until late Thursday afternoon, giving Puccio a night to pick the witness's testimony apart in his own mind. By the next morning, he was ready. His shoulder tilt gets worse when he's excited, and at that moment he seemed as if he might tip over, slipping toward the lectern with a few sheets of scratch paper, looking disheveled in an $800 suit.

He started his cross-examination with rapid-fire accusation: "Prior to your ever going to the PVB, is it a true statement that you engaged in lying, deceit, and manipulation?"

"Yes I did."

"On many, many occasions?"

"I did."

"Have you manipulated people?"

"I have not told people the truth."

"What do you understand manipulation to mean, Mr. Lindenauer?"

"That's a difficult—I don't know."

"You don't know what manipulation means. Is that your testimony?"

Lindenauer was already uneasy, bobbing and weaving instead of answering directly. Puccio took him step by step through his twenty-five years of therapy frauds, from his tutelage under quack and convicted tax dodger Jacob List to his association with cocaine user Driesen. Then he led Lindenauer through his career as a bagman, totaling up the payoffs until they reached $600,000, at which point Puccio tried to extract an accounting of how Lindenauer had spent his $250,000 share of the bribes.

Then Puccio shifted to a line of questioning focused on the weakness in Lindenauer that he'd noticed during direct. Even though Lindenauer's account of the final Manes days had virtually nothing to do with Friedman or the criminal charges in the case, Puccio began probing the circumstances that preceded and immediately followed Manes's first suicide attempt. His questions were about the cold shoulder that Lindenauer turned on the frantic Manes, sending what Puccio suggested was a fatal message.

After a long, painful, and seemingly purposeless rerun of the suicide period, Puccio suddenly turned to the facts at the heart of the case against Friedman. Zornow's examination had carefully created a structure for Lindenauer's memory, fitting the bribery events along a timeline. Puccio brought Lindenauer without warning to a single point in the continuum, and asked when his initial conversations with Marvin Kaplan and Donald Manes about a Citisource stock payoff had occurred. It was a disconnected question, casually dropped while Lindenauer was catching his breath after the suicide discussion, but it undid the tenuous lines holding Lindenauer together.

"Just give us the year," persisted Puccio.

"I'm thinking out loud. Eighty-two, eighty-three, I don't remember. I just don't recall right now. It had to be sometime eighty-one, eighty-two. I'm really having difficulty at this point." Next he agreed that the conversations had occurred in the first half of 1983, shortly before the PVB selection committee picked Kaplan's company. This was fifteen months later, it turned out, than he had said on direct.

"So much was happening that the dates really are jumbled," said an anxious Lindenauer, after erring on another point of chronology. "I'm having most difficulty in terms of events. What I do is, I'm trying to construct the time sequences. . . . Basically on the logical sequence of the events themselves. . . ."

A few moments later, Lindenauer wouldn't even attempt an answer about when Friedman had supposedly written the number of shares each party would get on a piece of paper, torn it up, then burned it in an ashtray. His facile performance with Zornow now seemed an embarrassment, and only highlighted the contrast between his rehearsed persuasiveness and his plunge into a mental morass when on his own. Lefcourt followed Puccio with a few minutes of questioning before the judge adjourned for the weekend. While Puccio had let Lindenauer ramble, Lefcourt tried to restrict him to yes or no answers. "I don't know where to go," the lost Lindenauer said at one point. When the three hours of cross-examination mercifully ended, Rudy Giuliani knew he had a problem.

Joe DeLario was riverboat gambling out in Teaneck, New Jersey, at the Glenn Pointe Centre headquarters of his company, Datacom Systems Corporation. Every morning he would sit in his executive suite and read a copy of the prior day's testimony from New Haven, hand-delivered before he arrived. He was looking for references to himself, particularly in Geoffrey Lindenauer's testimony, but he also wanted a grasp of the ebb and flow of the trial. He was paying for five transcripts a day, and he had at least three lawyers reading them as well as another top Datacom executive implicated in the case. He even had a paralegal sitting in the press row in New Haven taking notes and rushing at every recess to call in a minute-by-minute report of the day's events. When she wasn't in court, she was jogging with

Gerry Lefcourt, picking up every available nuance of the case.

And when he wasn't reading the transcript or conferring with his lawyers, DeLario was on the phone with an unpaid observer of the New Haven scene, his close friend Marvin Kaplan. He talked to Kaplan almost as often as his lawyer, Robert Kasanoff, met in a coffee shop with Howard Wilson, Giuliani's top assistant back in New York. Kaplan wanted DeLario to tough it out; Wilson wanted him to step forward and become a government witness. DeLario, who had been formally named by Giuliani as an unindicted co-conspirator in the Friedman case, needed to know as much as he could about everyone else's hand. Either way he went, this was the biggest game of stud poker he'd ever played.

DeLario had the wavy, blondish brown hair, confident smile, slight build, and laid-back style of a modern corporate king. At fifty-three, he was a millionaire at least twenty times over. He couldn't take a drive in a Datacom limo without passing a scofflaw who hadn't fattened his wallet. Thirty years earlier, DeLario, who'd just graduated from Fairleigh Dickinson University, had decided to become a computer programmer trainer. Within four years, he had started the first of several computer service companies that failed. By 1975, however, he was half-owner of a struggling new firm, Datacom, which was just entering the parking ticket collection business. DeLario's first municipal contract was with New York City's Parking Violations Bureau. The city's transportation commissioner, Michael Lazar, signed the contract after its PVB director, Harry Voccola, negotiated it. Within a couple of years, both would be working for Datacom.

DeLario retained Mike Lazar in the spring of 1978, shortly after Lazar's protégé, Lester Shafran, became the head of PVB. He started Lazar on a $500-a-month retainer; by 1982, the retainer had climbed to $11,000 a month. At the start of the Koch years, Datacom was a nickel-and-dime company, with twenty employees and no major contracts other than PVB. By the time DeLario sold the company to aerospace giant Lockheed in 1984, it did $32 million a year in business, served 100 municipalities, and employed 500 people. Lockheed paid $40 million for Datacom, giving principal shareholder DeLario $15 million of its own stock and paying him handsomely to continue running the company.

The secret of Datacom's success was its willingness, in

major cities across America, to retain or employ politicians and bureaucrats who could help it get contracts. In New York, Stanley Friedman's predecessor, former Bronx boss Pat Cunningham, was at first paid as part of Lazar's retainer and then placed on a $4,000-a-month stipend, which he received even while he did his time in a federal penitentiary. Beginning in 1983, Stanley Friedman was covertly paid $120,000 annually, disguised in DeLario's books as computer service expenditures made to a Kaplan company. DeLario set up this circuitous route because, without any evidence of actual legal work that Friedman was supposed to perform, he could not explain such a large fee to Datacom's new investors.

But in the competitive world of municipal collection contracts, the consultant jobs, legal fees, and campaign contributions that Datacom had turned into a national sales technique had long ago ceased to be sufficient. In New York at least, Joe DeLario had been dealing in cold cash for years. The cash for the payoffs to "Fat 1" and "Fat 2," the nicknames given Manes and Lindenauer by a Datacom computer specialist, had at first been concealed in Lazar's ballooning retainer. DeLario, who ordinarily distanced himself from the payoffs orchestrated by his subordinates, had once been confronted personally by Lazar, who demanded a hike in his retainer and justified it by saying he was "taking care of the Lindenauer problem." When DeLario finally dropped Lazar in 1982, Lazar complained in a meeting at a bar with DeLario that he had been forced to dip into his own pocket to pay the fat guys.

DeLario's new bribe-broker, Stanley Friedman, communicated with DeLario about payoffs in the same way he had with Geoffrey Lindenauer: by writing notes in his office—one time merely scratching out a dollar sign—and then tearing them up, burning the pieces in an ashtray. When DeLario and his friend Kaplan decided to jointly seek the PVB data processing contract in 1985, they agreed to a 10 percent take for Manes and Lindenauer. But Friedman had insisted that DeLario had to make an additional good faith, up-front payment of $35,000. Friedman offered to launder the bribe payment as a legal fee, but wanted $70,000 to cover the taxes. This bribe, which was paid directly to Manes by Friedman shortly before the scandal exploded, made DeLario the only potential witness, aside from Marvin Kaplan, who could put a cash payment in Stanley Friedman's hands.

DeLario had been walking a tightrope since Donald Manes's first suicide attempt. A week after it, he'd met with Friedman and Kaplan in a Manhattan restaurant where at first no one spoke, perhaps unnerved by the possibility that one of them was wired. Once Friedman broke the ice, they agreed to a series of cover-up strategies, including altering the underlying paper trail that underlay the cash payment. In late January, he and Datacom vice president Neal Anderson, who'd worked for various DeLario companies for twenty-six years and had been involved in Lazar and Shafran payoffs, were hauled before a Giuliani grand jury. They carefully orchestrated their perjury, and DeLario did the same before a federal grand jury in Chicago probing municipal collection contracts there.

But in late March, the government had turned the pressure on Datacom up one notch. Allen Scott, a burly, curly-headed, 48-year-old Datacom executive who had overseen its towing operations, was arrested by Giuliani's office on a charge of having extorted kickbacks from a Bronx towing operator. He was arrested on the same day that Lazar was indicted. Giuliani had hoped to flip Scott, knowing that Scott had intimate knowledge of the Lazar payoffs to Lindenauer and Manes. More important, at least from DeLario's point of view, Scott had personally delivered a $20,000 towing company kickback to DeLario himself. DeLario's lawyer Kasanoff recommended a close friend of his to represent Scott, and Scott's defense was coordinated with and paid for by DeLario.

Over the next few months, Scott's case would become the background music for DeLario's dance with the government. First, Giuliani and Scott's lawyer worked out the terms of a peculiar standoff. Every thirty days for the next five months, they got together to sign an extension of the speedy trial requirements, which would normally have forced Giuliani to either turn Scott's arrest warrant into an indictment or drop it. Scott's lawyer also indicated that his client would cooperate in exchange for immunity, but Giuliani was looking for a guilty plea. Only when the judge dismissed a key count against Lazar was Giuliani willing to deal for Scott.

DeLario soon learned that Michael Lazar had given him a new and compelling reason to unleash Scott. Lazar had secretly retained another lawyer without telling his own attorney, who was close to Puccio, and in the weeks preceding the trial had begun meeting with the government. He wanted a free ride, and in the clubhouse tradition from which he came, he believed that if he hired the right lawyer, he might get one. So he selected a personal friend of Giuliani's. All Lazar offered the government, however, was information on DeLario. None of this particularly intrigued Giuliani, who wanted a guilty plea and information that would damage Friedman, so the negotiations broke down by midsummer. Joe DeLario's response to the Lazar move, however, was a brilliantly conceived surgical strike.

On September 12, a little more than a week before the trial was scheduled to start in New Haven, Allen Scott came into the U.S. Attorney's office. Scott refused to have any informal conversations with the government; instead, his lawyer offered an outline of what Scott was prepared to discuss—which, coincidentally enough, happened to be only matters that involved Michael Lazar. While no one expressly said so, it was clear that if he was asked about Joe DeLario, his predictably false responses would make him unusable against Lazar. This novel and narrow deal would have to be a very finely cut piece of work indeed.

Scott was granted use immunity, meaning that what he said couldn't be used against him but that the government could prosecute him if they developed a case independent of his own testimony. Although it was too close to the trial date for Scott to go before a grand jury, Giuliani needed to commit him to an explicit story before putting him on the witness stand. So in a creative maneuver, he took a ten-minute sworn deposition from him. Scott detailed the $2,500 monthly payoff, described the cigar box wrapped in brown paper that Lazar's driver picked up from the towing operator, and recounted the events of the night when the towing operator went with Lazar to deliver a "package" to Lindenauer.

After his success with Scott, Giuliani made one last, halfhearted pretrial attempt with DeLario, asking that DeLario plead guilty to three felony counts, and indicating that he wanted DeLario to testify at the Friedman trial. A guilty plea, however, would finish Joe DeLario. Lockheed would have to drop him; lawsuits in all likelihood would cost him the $20 million in stock he'd received on the sale of Datacom. He would also have to testify against Marvin Kaplan, a lifelong friend. So DeLario refused, and Kasanoff told Giuliani his client would take the Fifth Amendment if called to testify. Kasanoff believed that Giuliani would ultimately need DeLario badly enough that he could dictate a deal on his own terms. DeLario decided to wait and see who would flinch first.

He did not have to wait long for the immunity offer he wanted. After the first week of Lindenauer's testimony, a worried Giuliani came back to New York to reassess his case. The rules of procedure barred him from talking to Lindenauer during cross-examination; Lindenauer would have to rehabilitate himself. Giuliani took out the outline he'd done of his summation and reconstructed it, already beginning to deemphasize Lindenauer and stress the corroborating witnesses and documents he had yet to present. He wrote ten new pages of summation notes he would wind up never using.

As the second week of Lindenauer's cross dragged on in New Haven, Howard Wilson intensified his discussions with Kasanoff that had begun months earlier. Wilson had already discussed the possibility of immunity, but now he began pointedly raising the question of what his own recommendation to Giuliani would be. He wanted a proffer from DeLario—a sketch from his and Anderson's lawyer of their possible testimony.

Yet DeLario was not ready, even with the real possibility of an immunity offer, to agree to testify. He was still talking to Kaplan virtually every night, and he dreaded appearing in court against him. While testifying would not be as automatically devastating to DeLario's Lockheed relationship and business life as a guilty plea, his admission on the stand that he had paid bribes to obtain city contracts could be almost as damaging.

With DeLario's demur, Giuliani realized he had two critical audiences to persuade: the jury, and an unseen group of Datacom lawyers and potential witnesses, led by DeLario, who were studying his every move through the transcript. Puccio knew it, too, and as a warning to DeLario of what was in store if he stepped forward, the lawyer and Friedman planted story after story in the papers castigating government witnesses.

But Puccio could not control what happened next in the courtroom. His four defense colleagues kept Lindenauer on the stand for four days, and the longer he talked, the more cogent he became. By the time Lindenauer finished his testimony at the end of his second week on the stand, his hour of floundering with Puccio had been reduced to a faint memory. Lefcourt did a fine job of extracting admissions from him about his sordid life, conceding that his old psychotherapy clinic almost encouraged its troubled patients to have sex with one another and therapists. The admissions, though, only made him look more candid.

Larry Silverman, Shafran's attorney, managed to give him further credibility by doing the impossible: he turned Lindenauer into a sympathetic character. He insisted that Lindenauer stand, take his suit coat off, and demonstrate how the coat had once hung over a chair, exposing an envelope of cash placed in the inside pocket. Silverman was ostensibly trying to get Lindenauer to demonstrate how implausible it was that Shafran had noticed the envelope in Lindenauer's jacket and commented on it, as Lindenauer had testified. But the real purpose was to humiliate Lindenauer, who had been shamed by questions about his weight and his eating habits. ("Have you ever paid for a meal in your life?" was one question.)

When the pocket didn't visibly hang open, an intent Lindenauer said: "It doesn't pull out because there's nothing in it. If you get—let's say—$5,000 and put it in here—" at which point the courtroom broke into laughter. And by the end of Lindenauer's detailed demonstration, it was clear that the incident had occurred just as he said it had.

After Zornow finished his redirect examination of Lindenauer, Giuliani, Schwartz, and Zornow went upstairs to the small U.S. Attorney's office above the courtroom and hugged a grinning Lindenauer. Through seven days on the stand, he had never smiled. The Friedman crowd in the courtroom would periodically taunt him by laughing derisively at his testimony, but Lindenauer remained a stone. Now, with Zornow's arm wrapped around him, he looked like a man in the first moment of a new life. He told the prosecutors that he couldn't believe none of them had tried to circumvent the court prohibition and get a message to him after his early disarray on the stand. "I know how badly you guys want to win," he said, "and I was really impressed that you played by the rules. The difference between you guys and them is you really don't cheat."

Back at the hotel a subdued Friedman roamed the lobby, soliciting the opinions of reporters and silently accepting the judgment that the passage of time had rehabilitated Lindenauer. When Shafran went up to the hotel desk at the start of the following week, the clerk informed him that Kaplan would no longer be picking up his and Silverman's tab. The momentum had shifted.

Allen Scott took the stand at the opening of the third week

of the trial, and a nervous Joe DeLario could, for the first time, read testimony from a top executive in his own company about the bribery he had commissioned. The next witness, PVB's former comptroller James Rose, one of the whistleblowers whose early warnings at DOI were ignored, detailed how Datacom was favored by Shafran, and at various points, Lindenauer. Lazar was implicated again by the testimony of a lawyer who had set up another collection company, with Lazar as a secret partner, and had gone after PVB contracts with Lindenauer's help. Then Bernie Sandow came on for several days, damaging every defendant except Bergman, and corroborating Lindenauer with detailed records of his Shafran bribes. Like Lindenauer, he had once taken a secretive walk around the block with Friedman. He testified about Friedman's awareness of Lindenauer and Manes's stake in the towing contract that Sandow, DeLario, and a third company were seeking in a joint venture.

But the big blow, for the defendants and the watching DeLario, was Robert Richards, the former Citisource president who in January had entered the case as part of the defense team. A few weeks after Lindenauer began cooperating in early March, however, Richards dropped Puccio, got himself another lawyer, pleaded guilty, and became a government witness. He now testified about conversations he'd had with Lindenauer, Friedman, and Kaplan about the stock payoff. Richards also recounted tales from the early 1986 cover-up period, saying that he had met with Kaplan after Manes's suicide attempt and that Kaplan, perhaps mimicking his mentor, had scribbled a note and held up the message: "Stanley still has all his stock." Using Richards to introduce them, the government put the stock certificates into the record, and Bill Schwartz held them up to the jury one at a time. The even, three-way split was a dramatic visual confirmation of the heart of the government's case.

Richards's testimony was the last of the transcript read in New Jersey, for Joe DeLario had closed the book on the case. He knew his friend Kaplan was doomed. And he knew that if he stayed out in the cold, so was he. He had been trying for the last several weeks to talk Kaplan into taking a plea, and testifying against Friedman. Giuliani's office had encouraged these conversations. If DeLario could have persuaded Kaplan, the government would no longer have needed him, and he might have escaped without an indictment, a guilty plea, or testifying. Even when DeLario told Kaplan that, with or without him, he was going to the government, Kaplan refused. When a dejected Kaplan brought the news of DeLario's defection to Friedman, Puccio, and the rest, he muttered ominously that now they would "all be convicted." It was as if he had become a martyr in the crusade against Giuliani.

On October 28, only a few days before Giuliani was prepared to rest his case, Joe DeLario finally made a sketchy proffer, outlining what his trial testimony would be. That day in court, Jerry Driesen testified that Lindenauer had told him all about the Citisource stock deal years earlier, recounting a half-dozen conversations right up to the first Manes suicide attempt. Before Giuliani reached the substantive portion of Driesen's testimony, he took forty-five minutes to get Driesen to spell out every detail of his own sordid personal history. Since Giuliani had usurped the available cross-examination material, Puccio and Lefcourt passed. Driesen was so happy that he hopped on the back of an FBI agent, hugging him in relief, as soon as he was led from the courtroom.

That night, while Giuliani and his assistants pondered their response to the DeLario offer, the Friedman gang went out drinking. Friedman, Jackie, Kaplan, Puccio, Lefcourt, and Kaplan's daughter came back to the Colony lobby about 11:00 in a raucous mood. Friedman was jumping in the air, giving Jackie high fives. He yanked his white sweater up and rubbed his bare belly, laughing boyishly. They all knew by then that DeLario was on his way to court with a death notice, but Kaplan had held, and that seemed to break the tension.

While Howard Wilson had bargained for weeks with Kasanoff and was now recommending that DeLario be granted immunity, the final decision was Giuliani's, and Giuliani was still troubled. He had forced Lindenauer, Richards, Sandow, and others in the case to plead guilty; an immunity bath for DeLario did not sit well with him. He postponed a decision, waiting to meet DeLario, who was due to arrive in New Haven the next night.

At the end of a day of dry and repetitive testimony, a long black limo pulled up to the Park Plaza, where it sat all night. Inside the hotel were DeLario, his lawyers, and Giuliani's top New York staff, who had assembled to hear DeLario finally tell what he knew of the events. Giuliani was surprised at how open Friedman had been with DeLario, and at how damaging the joint testimony of several Datacom witnesses would be against every defendant but Bergman. Schwartz made one last attempt to insist on a plea, and Kasanoff waved it off. Schwartz, Zornow, and Giuliani then took a long walk around the block and through the New Haven Green.

Giuliani said that a decision to immunize the Datacom gang had to be unanimous among the trial counsel; anyone of the three could veto it. And Schwartz was reluctant. Back in the hotel suite Wilson had drawn some parallels to the tense World Series games that the Mets were then playing against the Red Sox, asking if it wouldn't make sense to let Darryl Strawberry swing away with a lead and a man on first in the ninth inning, looking for an insurance run. As they strolled across the green, a previously neutral Giuliani began to pick up the same theme in an effort to persuade Schwartz.

"What are we here for?" he asked. "What's important about the PVB? Is it Joe DeLario? This is a case about politics, and if we have an additional weapon in our arsenal to attack the heart of this case, we have to use it. This guy can put the final nail in the coffin."

The following day, in a chambers conference with Knapp and the defendants, Giuliani announced that the government wished to adjourn at the end of the day Thursday, taking Friday and Monday off to prepare a new, unanticipated group of witnesses. The protests from the defense, then and shortly before DeLario took the stand on Tuesday, were deafening. Lefcourt argued that the government had made DeLario "an offer he couldn't refuse," contending that if he had been indicted under the racketeering statutes, DeLario might have had to forfeit his Lockheed stock.

Giuliani countered this monetary argument by reminding Knapp that the government had in fact waived the racketeering forfeiture provisions with every other PVB contractor who pleaded guilty or was immunized, and that each contractor, including DeLario, was still vulnerable to civil suits from the city and private parties such as Lockheed. He pointed out that three other contractors who testified had been immunized rather than required to plead, suggesting that there was nothing unusual about the Datacom deal. Yet what was unusual about DeLario's free ride was precisely what Lefcourt had argued— the timing. The last man in was getting the best deal. As Puccio would later pointedly taunt Giuliani in his summation: "The best way to describe it is that the prosecution, acting in good faith and trying to do its job, came face to face with a businessman who could take their pants off as easily as he could get up for breakfast. If you're in the U.S. government, you don't play poker with Joe DeLario, because if you do, you're going to lose."

Giuliani was dismayed at the ferocity of the defense response to the DeLario deal, and initially he, Schwartz, and Zornow had some second thoughts, especially after they had to take a marvelously orchestrated bashing in the newspapers. But over the next four days, as they debriefed DeLario and three other Datacom witnesses, their doubts vanished.

Unable to believe his luck when DeLario mentioned during one of several hastily arranged weekend sessions the name of the secretary who had backdated a critical letter after the scandal broke in early 1986, Schwartz immediately sent the FBI after her, and she recalled DeLario's mysterious request as if it had just happened. Giuliani was equally enthused about the cooperation of an unexpected and unimpeachable Datacom executive, who had no involvement with the company's criminal activities but could testify about the repeated vouchering for Datacom reimbursement of the $70,000 payoff for the data processing contract.

But the centerpiece was still crafty Joe DeLario, who had no psychosexual, cocaine, or snakeoil-salesman baggage like some of the other government witnesses against Friedman. Without DeLario, Lindenauer's testimony about the cash payoff through Friedman for the data processing contract would have had to stand alone (and Lindenauer had actually been given his half of the bribe by Manes, not directly by Friedman). The November morning when DeLario at last took the stand was election day, and Knapp had scheduled a late start. Stanley Friedman had already voted by absentee ballot, anticipating, perhaps, that it might be his last legal vote for years, since felons lose the franchise.

The unflappable DeLario had arrived at the Park Plaza the night before his appearance in court in his usual casual way— wearing a sports coat and Adidas. In the morning he discovered that he'd forgotten to bring his dress shoes, and walked into Knapp's courtroom in an FBI agent's wingtips. When DeLario finished his devastating direct testimony, Puccio asked for an early adjournment so the defense could prepare cross overnight. "About six weeks," Lefcourt added in open court. "That's what we really need."

. . .

November 11, 1986 was the most important day in Stanley Friedman's life since the morning bus ride he had arranged ten years earlier to take Pat Cunningham's title away from him. He was preparing to sit where Joe DeLario had sat the week before. A jury that had been looking for weeks directly into the eyes of government witnesses was now going to be sizing him up. Puccio had been working with Friedman for days, orchestrating a disarming direct examination during which Friedman would concede his unsavory influence-peddling, as a way of suggesting both that Friedman was telling the truth, warts and all, and that he didn't need to pay bribes to get what he wanted. Puccio also ran his client through several practice cross-examinations, baiting him, bullying him. In sixteen years of criminal practice, most of it as a prosecutor, Puccio had never before put a defendant on the witness stand. This was as new to him as it was to his client.

Before the trial began, Puccio had believed that he would have to use Friedman, but he had made no firm decision on the matter. Once Lindenauer rehabilitated himself, however, Puccio thought again that he would have to counter with Friedman, but he still hesitated. The problem with putting a defendant on the stand is that the burden of proof inevitably shifts. Though jurors are still instructed that the defense doesn't have to establish anything, they will never acquit a defendant they don't believe. In a juror's mind, the decisionmaking process becomes a choice between two versions of events, rather than a skeptical probing of the government's version, looking for a reasonable doubt. But DeLario's testimony left Puccio with no choice. Without an extraordinary Friedman performance, conviction was a certainty.

Preparing him to testify forced Puccio to come to grips with Friedman's story. Puccio has a simple rule for handling criminal clients: "Only answer questions about the case that I ask you," he told Friedman when Friedman retained him. "Nothing else." Puccio doesn't want his clients denying the undeniable to him; so he tells them from the start not to tell him what they say happened but to relax, and hear the government's version.

Puccio deliberately minimized the amount of time that he spent with Friedman in New Haven, delaying his own exposure to Friedman's detailed account of the events at the heart of the case. For example, the first time that Puccio heard Friedman's contention that he'd gotten the Citisource stock split in three equal parts because he intended, at some future time, to give one certificate to his son Michael and one to his daughter Betty was when he sat with Friedman a few days before Friedman testified. Once this defense emerged, the two children from Friedman's previous marriage, who had appeared at the trial only sporadically, were brought back as exhibits.

Friedman's direct was a friendly tour of this fanciful tale. Why didn't he just put the stock in his children's names? Because he knew that his holdings would one day be public and he did not want to be "put in a position where it looks like we're concealing the stock holdings." Friedman also laid the groundwork for what would become the central theme of Puccio's summation. He acknowledged that Lindenauer had announced at a dinner with DeLario that the three were "partners" in a criminal scam, and conceded that Lindenauer had told him in the famous walk around the block that he thought Friedman was holding Citisource stock for Manes and him. But he said that he then told Lindenauer: "You're out of your mind, or Manes is out of his mind."

Friedman claimed that he called Manes afterward and complained, and that Manes assured him he would take care of the "off-the-wall" Lindenauer. This testimony allowed Puccio to argue that Manes had lied to Lindenauer to get him to fix the Citisource contract, misleading Lindenauer into believing there was an imaginary stock deal with Friedman up the road. The theory was that Manes misled Lindenauer to help Friedman because he needed Friedman's support on other, unrelated political deals, and because Lindenauer wouldn't deliver the contract unless he believed there was a payoff in it for him.

Whenever Friedman becomes anxious, his lower lip quivers, trembling so visibly that over the years he developed a defensive habit of chewing it to hide the shakes. When he took the stand the next day for Giuliani's cross, he was chewing vigorously. During one break, when he poured himself some water at the defense table, he used both hands to bring the small cup to his mouth.

Giuliani began with the stuff of Stanley's life, all off-point, but the sort of tangents that would put Friedman's PVB scams in context. He asked Friedman about the excessive hotel tax abatement package he'd put together for Donald Trump while still deputy mayor, and his subsequent representation of Trump. Giuliani also raised questions about Friedman's fat fees from the taxi industry and his scuttling of taxi legislation that would have produced more cabs for the people in the Bronx. Friedman conceded much of the thrust of Giuliani's questions, differentiating the kind of conflict-of-interest dealmaking he once denied, but now wore like a badge, from the grubby bribery he was on trial for.

Nothing better expressed this tactical decision than a single crucial exchange with Giuliani that captured a lifetime of Friedman arrogance. Giuliani's questions—involving Friedman's attempt to get favorable city leases in a downtown office building—were based on information provided by former leasing director Alex Liberman. Liberman had no incriminating information about Friedman, just memories of two phone calls he received from him on behalf of the owners of a building whose leases were stalled at the Board of Estimate.

Giuliani had determined that these owners had paid Friedman a $10,000 fee for facilitating the lease. Yet Friedman had not lobbied the Board of Estimate about the lease, or any city official other than Liberman. Liberman had been trying out a series of shakedown suggestions on the owners, and the owners had rejected some but not all. Friedman then called Liberman to find out what was delaying the lease, and Liberman insisted it wasn't him but Manes. Friedman responded: "That's my end. I'll take care of that." Shortly thereafter, Manes's position changed, and the leases passed the Board.

Giuliani started this section of his cross by asking about Friedman's two calls to Liberman, and Friedman said he thought it was only one, and purely ministerial, just to determine the status of the lease. Then Friedman confirmed that he'd also called Manes. "You got paid $10,000 for making one phone call to Mr. Liberman and one to Donald Manes?" Giuliani asked. Friedman corrected him: "I think it was just for one phone call," reiterating that the Liberman conversation was merely a status call. Friedman had managed, in a single, snappy retort, to turn himself into a switchboard for sleaze.*

When Giuliani finished with the side issues, he led Fried-

---

*Giuliani tried to use Liberman as a trial witness against Michael Lazar, bringing him up to New Haven for a preliminary hearing before Judge Knapp. Liberman claimed that the lease-hungry Lazar had once dropped a "little brown bag" containing $5,000 in cash in his lap while he sat in his car in a city parking lot. But after hours of legal argument, Knapp barred Liberman's appearance, saying that he had decided not to "unleash this sewer" on his courtroom.

man through a minefield of questions about the Datacom and Citisource bribes, pushing him to explosive denials and shouts of innocence. Pressed about his repeated meetings with Manes at the end of 1985, when the house of cards was crashing, he insisted that they never talked about PVB. "It didn't faze me," Friedman said, though he had contracts worth millions in the pipeline at the agency. "I had no fear of an investigation in Chicago. I had no fear of Sandow being wired. I have done nothing wrong and I will continue to say so."

Giuliani challenged Friedman's stock story with questions that contrasted his secret plan to give the stock to his children with the contents of a footnote in the Citisource public prospectus, which stated that the stock listed in Marvin Kaplan's name "includes the holdings of the wife and one daughter." And he repeatedly hammered away at Friedman's failure to take any action when Lindenauer revealed, as Friedman conceded he had, that he believed Friedman was his and Manes's partner in a bribery conspiracy. In fact, as Friedman's logs and diaries showed, he continued to meet with Lindenauer again and again, even for private breakfasts, after this supposed conversation.

The success of Giuliani's cross was overshadowed in the press coverage by Judge Knapp's morning announcement in a chambers conference with the lawyers that Friedman's direct testimony the day before had featured "a highly improbable story." The latest in a series of unexpected pearls from the 77-year-old Knapp, this one inflamed Friedman and forced Puccio to seek interviews with each juror, conducted by the judge and the lawyers, to determine if any had heard news reports of the judge's candor. Knapp took his own beating in the press for this improper comment.

The remainder of the defense strategy involved an attempt to depict Manes as a liar. Puccio called a former Manes law partner to the stand, who testified that Manes had in fact earned no fees on an old murder case that Lindenauer had described as the source of a $25,000 loan Manes had made to Lindenauer's clinic. Puccio used this testimony, and a few loose threads in the case, to argue at summation that Manes had lied to Lindenauer about Friedman's role in the Datacom and Citisource deals. However, Judge Knapp barred Puccio from showing a videotape of Manes on his hospital bed after the first suicide attempt, admitting that he lied about the incident to the police.

Puccio had once again tried to manipulate the jury with an image—he wanted them to take this unforgettable footage of Manes-the-liar with them when they began deliberations.

The summations themselves were a classic match of hard fact persuasively argued by Giuliani, who abandoned the loose-leaf notebooks of his opening, versus Puccio's intriguing theories, based wholly on inference. Puccio had little real evidence to work with but wound up discovering unnoticed gems in the record, buried even in the forgotten Dowd testimony. He used Dowd to prove that Manes made it a practice to lie to Lindenauer, even about their bribery business. Puccio concluded that the case came down to a question of the credibility of "Stanley Friedman, head to head, against the dregs of the earth."

The jury was out for three days, but spent half of that time listening to testimony being reread to them. Even though Friedman assailed the arrival of little Andrew Giuliani during the deliberations, telling the *Times* that he guessed "the child is very interested in the case" and calling the visit "the kickoff of a campaign," Jackie Friedman and Giuliani's wife Donna stood in the lobby of the courthouse talking about babies, with friendly smiles on their faces.

The day before the verdict was reached was Lazar's fifty-eighth birthday, and a reporter gave him two Hostess cupcakes topped with candles in the lobby of the courthouse. While Lazar blew them out, Friedman joked: "Racketeering count number one, racketeering count number two." Giuliani declined the slice of cake Lazar offered him. Kaplan gave Lazar a box of cigars wrapped in brown paper with a note attached saying the package was "for Lazar's driver." That night the defense team went to Lazar's exclusive club, where he had stayed throughout the trial, and had a birthday dinner. Friedman gave him a red bathrobe—Lazar's wardrobe when he paid Lindenauer the first cash bribe seven years earlier. Lazar had barely socialized with the other defendants for the ten-week trial, partly because of the tension created by his pretrial effort to cut a deal with the hated Giuliani. But in the end, on this night before a verdict, all the defendants were united by the tragedy they all knew awaited them.

A few hours after the jury assembled on November 25, the fourth day of their deliberations, they sent out a note asking for a verdict sheet. Friedman instantly recognized that this quick a decision was deadly for him. When he heard Puccio say that the game was over—"We just don't know what the score is yet"—he countered, "Only those who are fooling themselves don't know what the score is."

Friedman and Kaplan were convicted on all counts, Lazar and Shafran on most. The judge had severed Marvin Bergman from the case when the prosecution rested, and a few months later Bergman was acquitted in Manhattan federal court, where he found a jury that would not believe Lindenauer. But this Connecticut jury told reporters that they had had no real difficulty reaching a consensus about Friedman and Kaplan, and had decided their fate in the first few hours. "Friedman was the easiest," one juror commented, adding that it was some of the counts on Lazar and Shafran that had given them trouble.

A worn Giuliani had arrived in court that morning sporting a burst blood vessel in one eye and a cheek covered with red shaving scars. The waiting had been taking a tougher toll than the weeks of work. When the verdict was announced, Giuliani, Schwartz, Zornow, and crew showed little emotion in the courtroom but quickly charged upstairs, where, out of view of the defendants and their families, they guzzled champagne and hugged one another. They were so angry at the waiting reporters that Giuliani dallied for almost an hour, predicting that the morning stories would be headlined FRIEDMAN APPEALS. When he finally emerged, the restraint that he had shown since Friedman started his daily, increasingly personal attacks was finally abandoned; for the first time, he spoke in the harshest possible terms about Friedman's rape of the Bronx.

Friedman himself was unrepentant, and continued to repeat his charge that Giuliani was overzealous: "When he throws his hat in the ring," Friedman predicted, "I hope you will say somewhere along the line that maybe Stanley Friedman was right." Then he, the lawyers, the family, and the entourage trooped off one last time to the Colony lobby for drinks and lunch, trailed by a camera crew and a *Daily News* freelance photographer. Friedman had courted and used the press throughout the trial, and had even let the same *News* photographer now following them into his and Jackie's hotel room for pictures. But now he had lost any taste for publicity, and when the photographer, a persistent woman in her thirties, wouldn't leave the group alone in the lobby, a loud, sudden pushing and shoving match ensued. The woman wound up on the floor with a cut lip. A waiter and a bartender said that Friedman kicked the photographer after his 21-year-old son knocked her down. A reporter said that Jackie threw a drink in the photographer's face. Suddenly the hotel was filled with police.

"There's obvious evidence from her face that an assault took place," said the sergeant who had restored order. "We're going to handle this downtown." But Friedman refused: "I'm not going anywhere. If you want to arrest me, arrest me." The sergeant replied, "Mr. Friedman, you are under arrest," and Friedman and his wife were escorted to a patrol car with Jackie screaming, "What are we, criminals?" At the precinct, they were booked on third-degree assault charges, and Friedman filed a counterclaim against the photographer. A few weeks later the photographer withdrew her charges, and the case mysteriously disappeared.

When Friedman returned to the hotel, he and the entourage adjourned to the bar, where he spent several hours swallowing glasses of Absolut. At one point he suddenly announced: "I guess I'll call an executive committee meeting tonight," referring to the Bronx party organization. "Tonight?" Jackie asked. "I've got to do it fast," he said, anticipating his own resignation and his maneuvering to name a replacement. Most of the defense camp gradually drifted away, and eventually Friedman sat, virtually alone, in the Colony bar watching the news reports of his own conviction on a giant screen.

He had by now loosened his tie, and unbuttoned his shirt almost to the waist. Rubbing his hairy chest with his hand, he couldn't stop talking about the case that had wrecked his life. Collaring an unfriendly reporter and pulling him aside where they could talk face-to-face, he said, "Let's just assume for argument's sake that there was a quid pro quo with Manes for his delivering the Citisource contract." By now his eyes were filled with desperation; he was chewing his lip frantically. He was about to concede that he had lied on the stand, and that he'd committed a different crime from the one he'd just been convicted of.

"Maybe I had to agree to deliver the city council leadership to Manes. Maybe I had to give him Vallone. Maybe that was the deal," he said, referring to the Bronx city council votes he'd obtained to ensure that Manes's man, Queens councilman Peter Vallone, would be elected majority leader just before the scandal exploded. "But I never agreed to hold any stock for them. Never. You gotta believe me."

. . .

While Stanley and Jackie Friedman were being booked in New Haven on assault charges, Ed Koch was hosting a postverdict press conference at City Hall, fielding questions about his 1984 savaging of whistleblowing publisher Jim Smith, who'd publicly warned him about the Citisource contract two years earlier. "In retrospect," he admitted to the press, "I am sorry that I did not take the information and turn it over to the Department of Investigation." Reminded that he had curtly advised Smith to take his complaint to the district attorney or "stop saying those terrible things about Stanley Friedman," Koch noted defensively that Smith never did go to the D.A. "No," said a reporter, "but he went to you."

Koch now confided that he was going to change his governing style. He had believed, he said, that Manes and Friedman were honest, and "it turned out they were not." This experience had made him "less naïve, less innocent, less trusting, less willing to accept what people say." Corporation counsel Fritz Schwarz expressed the sentiment a bit more candidly: "The next Stanley Friedman is not going to be given the free ride that this one was."

But in some respects, even with the verdict in, Koch's public response to the Friedman case was as ambiguous as it had been during the trial. He blamed the corruption of PVB on Lindenauer, just as the New Haven defendants had. Though he issued a general attack on the "greed" of the defendants, he made none of the patented Koch denunciations of his old friend Stanley. The mayor who'd assailed Donald Manes as a crook on the basis of public statements of a single bribe-payer was silent on the subject of the character of the convicted Friedman.

Indeed, Friedman's colleagues at City Hall continued to thrive. George Arzt, Friedman's old friend from the *New York Post*, who had invited the party boss to his bachelor party, had become Koch's new $85,000 press secretary the same day the jury began its deliberations. His repeated stories assailing government witnesses were among his last. Joe DeVincenzo, the mayor's special assistant whose close ties to Friedman dated back to their City Hall days together under Beame, still operated out of office number one in the basement of City Hall, just a winding stairway from the mayor's private office. During the trial, DeVincenzo assembled press packets on government wit-

nesses, feeding Arzt and others negative material. He spearheaded a three-day search of city files for anything that could
be found on Jerry Driesen, who over the course of a dozen years
had worked as a consulting psychiatrist for sixteen different
agencies. City officials began checking Driesen's credentials to
see if in fact he was a board-certified psychiatrist—a step they
had never taken before he became a government witness. One
agency that still used Driesen as a consultant canceled his contract.

And, of course, there was City Hall staffer Jackie Friedman.
In response to reporters' questions, Koch said on the day of the
conviction that "it would be unfair to judge her by her husband's deeds." Later that afternoon, Jackie told friends in the
Colony lobby that the mayor had scheduled a meeting with her
for the next morning, and that she had been assured by phone
that her job was safe. In conversations before and during the
trial, Friedman had repeatedly indicated to the press that he
had information about Koch, telling them that "we have bigger
fish to fry." But in the weeks following the trial, Friedman was
disbarred, and he disappeared from public view. Jackie's once-
inconsequential salary became a significant factor in a reconstructed family budget.

As DeVincenzo's and Arzt's behavior during the trial suggested, the mayor had a stake in Friedman's acquittal. If Friedman were acquitted, he could claim that the scandal had all
been media hype. The best indicator of Koch's wait-and-see,
bet-hedging attitude during the trial was the behavior of his
deputy Brezenoff, who was called as a witness by Puccio. His
testimony cut both ways, especially after he conceded under
cross that Friedman had misled him in their 1984 meeting
about his holdings in Citisource. But confronted by reporters
after testifying, Brezenoff seemed to make light of Friedman's
deceptive attempt to scratch personal gain out of a meeting
supposedly scheduled for party purposes. "I was surprised, but
it wasn't the first time, or the last," he said.*

In his handling of the PVB case, Giuliani seemed to step
around the mayor as if Koch were a landmine. The mayor's
professed ignorance of Friedman's stake in Citisource could

---

*In sharp contrast to Brezenoff's moral neutrality, Knapp declared, "If you come
to me and ask me to act for that company without telling me that you have an interest
in it, you're defrauding me," and ruled that Brezenoff's testimony was collateral evidence of Friedman's violation of the mail fraud statutes.

have made him a substantial government witness. Koch had been to Friedman's summer home and his wedding; Friedman's wife worked in Koch's office, and Friedman was frequently there. Had Friedman withheld this information from Koch, it would have been a far stronger indication of his determination to conceal it than the omission of his name on a disclosure form. But Giuliani never put Koch before the grand jury and never tried to use him as a trial witness, explaining that no prosecutor could anticipate what the unpredictable Koch might say under cross-examination.

The trial testimony constituted an indictment of the Koch administration—the patronage decisions, the dismissal of whistleblower warnings, the unsupervised autonomy of Manes's PVB operation, the Citisource award and its protection even after the company repeatedly defaulted. Yet Giuliani never focused his public statements on any of these matters—before, during, or after the trial.

Though personally convinced that Koch had to know in the years before the PVB revelations that Friedman was probably a criminal, Giuliani felt that as a prosecutor, he could not publicly hold Koch accountable for the scandal without creating the unwarranted impression that he had some undisclosed evidence of the mayor's own culpability. Giuliani was also, perhaps, affected by his own office's dependence on Koch's DOI for investigative help, as well as his continuing need to get the city to agree to deals on civil penalties that might entice cooperation from bribe-paying contractors.

But beyond the omission of the mayor from his frequent public pronouncements on the governmental implications of the scandal, Giuliani actually went so far as to invoke Koch in the presentencing memo he sent the judge several months after the conviction. He quoted from a victim impact statement—signed by the mayor and submitted to the Department of Probation—that assailed the four defendants for their "betrayal of the public trust," and urged tough sentences.

Judge Knapp found the use of Koch's letter by Giuliani so distasteful that he phoned the prosecutor before the sentencing hearing in March 1987 and advised him not to cite the mayor in his oral argument. "It will do you no good," the irked Knapp told Giuliani. Knapp had listened for months to evidence of the administration's acquiescence in the corruption that had consumed sectors of a city government, and it was impossible for him now to consider the mayor as a victim. Giuliani took Knapp's advice.

On the day of the sentencing, Knapp attacked the administration from the bench, and though the courtroom was packed with reporters, his stunning comments went unnoticed. He said at the outset that he had leaned toward giving Shafran the lightest sentence because he viewed Shafran as having "the least relative culpability." Noting that some might find this a surprising judgment, since Shafran was the public servant in charge of the racketeering enterprise, Knapp posed the question: "What could he have done about it?" Shafran, he said, "had as much power to fire Lindenauer as he had to fire me," explaining that "Lindenauer was appointed by Manes" and that in the real world of power relations in the Koch administration, Shafran had "no power to deal with Lindenauer."

The judge then cited the stonewall that PVB comptroller James Rose met when he tried to tell DOI and other top city officials what he knew about PVB corruption. He argued that "it must have been clear" to Shafran, who had himself once been the transportation department's inspector general, "that whistleblowing wouldn't have done any good." When Bill Schwartz countered that Shafran had once been an assistant D.A., had seen bribe money in Lindenauer's coat pocket, and could have gone to someone in authority, Knapp dismissed the argument: "Rose went to authority and nothing happened. Caught in that box, he acted badly," Knapp scolded. "He should have quit"—an ironic commentary on Ed Koch's frequent sermons about there being no higher calling than public service.

Stanley Friedman and Lester Shafran, both facing a maximum term of fifty years, were at opposite ends of Whitman Knapp's scale of justice: he gave Shafran six months in jail, and Friedman twelve years. Before sentencing Friedman, Knapp commented on the leniency letters he'd received from people whom Friedman had helped. "They showed a side of you," the judge said, "that was not apparent in the courtroom, quite clearly." And Knapp repeated his charge that in New Haven, Friedman had committed "deliberate and blatant perjury."

Knapp reminded Friedman of the great public power he had possessed and pointed, as an example, to Friedman's one-time judge-making authority. He cited Friedman's decision in 1983 to dismiss two sitting judges with such "exemplary records" that even Friedman did not contest their reputations.

Lastly, Knapp challenged the Puccio claim that the verdict had ended Friedman's political career. The judge had clearly seen the photo of Stanley, cigar in hand, peeking through the blinds in the Bronx county headquarters the day after his conviction. He had read the stories that appeared in every daily newspaper citing Friedman's role in putting together the votes six days after the conviction to handpick his successor, George Friedman (no relation). The articles quoted one old-line district leader who had voted against the new Friedman, saying, "I'm tired of walking around with the smell of garbage on me," and reported that the first item on the new Friedman's agenda for his troubled borough was a defense fund for the old Friedman. Reporters had even spoken with the new Friedman's mother, who, when told that her son was about to become county leader, warned her son: "God forbid, don't do it."

Knapp would not be blind to the arrogance of this maneuver: "Although you say your political power is gone, my impression is, you don't act that way," he argued, adding that Friedman's continuing to exercise power in the Bronx was "a continuation of your grievous sin." The twelve-year sentence was as long as Alex Liberman's, the precedent Giuliani had cited in his argument, and as long as any defendant in a municipal corruption case had ever received. The courtroom shuddered.

During a brief recess after Friedman was sentenced, while the others were waiting to learn their fate, Jackie Friedman went to the front where Stanley stood and hugged him, then returned to her seat, and collapsed on the floor. A wheelchair was brought to the courtroom, but by then she had pulled herself together. She had come into court that day with the brother and partner of celebrated appeals lawyer Alan Dershowitz, who was already at work on briefs that would allege, in true Friedman fashion, that Puccio had been paralyzed during the trial by a multiplicity of conflicts of interest—most of which had been raised by Giuliani before the trial and waived by Friedman.

A suntanned Kaplan was given four years. The only defendant with real appeal issues, Kaplan seemed unmoved, except when Knapp added a $250,000 fine. A repentant Lazar got a mere three and rocked and embraced his wife (Lindenauer would subsequently wind up with the same sentence). As always, one of Joe DeLario's lawyers sat inexplicably in court and took notes. In this circle of winners and losers, millionaire

DeLario and lawyer Michael Dowd, whose longtime law partner had replaced Manes as the county leader, had found a way out of the darkest days of their lives.

When it was over, the Friedmans and Puccio, unaware of the coming attack on him in the Dershowitz appeal, went out one last time to face the cameras on the courthouse steps. Wrapped in a long overcoat, his hair again curling up behind his ears, Friedman had lost his New Haven bravado—he'd gotten heavier since the verdict, and his face sagged, the glint was gone from his eyes. He had no more speeches left in him.

CHAPTER TWELVE

The Bess Mess

IN 1980, BESS MYERSON decided to run for the United States Senate from New York. A very popular candidate, she referred to herself as "the queen of the Jews," and indeed many people did seem to regard her as royalty. She had been an effective consumer affairs commissioner in the Lindsay administration. She was thought of as a pioneering role model because she had been crowned the first Jewish Miss America in 1945. A whole generation of Jewish women identified with her the way a whole generation of blacks identified with Jackie Robinson—as their First, a figure who conquered a social barrier and made millions feel the pride of accomplishment.

Within the circles of New York political power, Bess Myerson had a privileged standing. She was not an ally of convenience for Ed Koch, but a friend of choice. She was not a party boss, like Donald Manes or Meade Esposito, but a companion whom Ed Koch took to the movies. They were forever bonded in the public's imagination by Myerson's role in Koch's 1977 campaign for mayor. Ed Koch trusted her because he wanted to, not because he had to.

When Bess launched her senatorial campaign, Koch, Stanley Friedman, and Meade Esposito all actively supported her. David Garth managed her media and strategy. She looked invincible, compared with her three Democratic primary rivals:

former mayor John Lindsay, Congresswoman Elizabeth Holtzman of Brooklyn, and Queens district attorney John Santucci.

But for all her money, endorsements, and celebrity, Myerson faltered as a candidate. Her insecurities showed. She lacked mastery over the issues. She had health problems; she had to undergo chemotherapy treatments during the campaign to consolidate her cure from ovarian cancer. She occasionally smoked marijuana before debates to ease nausea and anxiety. And in the end, she lost the primary to Elizabeth Holtzman—a plainer-looking but more intellectual queen—by more than 70,000 votes.

After her loss in the primary, Myerson's mental equilibrium seemed to grow increasingly precarious. With jealous obsession, she began to harass a former lover who had broken off an affair with her, financial investor John Jakobson, and his new girlfriend, Joan. A private detective hired by Jakobson traced some abusive, anonymous phone calls from Myerson to a pay phone outside Gracie Mansion. Myerson even sent crank letters to herself and went to the police to complain that some unknown enemy was tormenting her.

This compulsive element in Myerson's character had once before been revealed publicly, in her extraordinary diaries, which became part of the court record in her second divorce case, from Arnold Grant. The diaries also portrayed a woman given to misanthropy, and self-loathing of chilling dimension. Myerson put into writing her wish for her husband's death, so she could inherit "the safety and security of a house"; in the meantime, though, Grant was "more like a thing—I must manipulate." Myerson occasionally claimed that these diaries never existed, but she submitted an affidavit during the Grant divorce admitting that she would at times read them aloud to her husband, to show him how she felt. The journals also contained details of her infidelities with several men, all apparently of wealth and some prominence.

Two quotations from Myerson in the book *Miss America, 1945,* by Susan Dworkin, gave further insight into this aspect of her character.

Deep in my heart [Myerson confessed], "I was in awe of my mother for the power she had over Dad. She drove him crazy, but he loved her, committed himself to her, and could not leave her. I believe that when I married, I looked for men who had my mother's controlling powers. . . .

Myerson also admitted, in reference to her mother:

All the praise I received [publicly] couldn't substitute for the praise I had never received from my mother at home. I longed for some wonderful man to come and save me from my life.

The Bess Myerson of such thoughts was at her most vulnerable when she became involved in an affair with sewer contractor Andy Capasso, a virile, instinctual, self-made millionaire. The relationship began in the fall of 1980, shortly after she lost the Senate primary. Myerson was then fifty-six years old, twice divorced, still a role model and heroine to a generation, but with a history of failed romances with men of wealth, some of them married and demonic. Capasso was then thirty-five, with an attractive wife, two children, and three stepchildren. He had grown up hungry on Liberty Avenue in the East New York section of Brooklyn, with a family so poor that the lights in the house were once turned off because the electric bill hadn't been paid. In 1968, Capasso started Nanco Contracting in a hotel room at the Forest Hills Inn. Twelve years later Nanco was a success and about to grow even larger. By 1983, Nanco would have a virtual monopoly on city sewer contracts.

Capasso had met his wife, Nancy, in 1965. She was then twenty-five, separated from her husband and with three children. He was almost twenty, digging a ditch for his father's company outside her home in Queens. After they watched each other for a few weeks, Nancy got up the nerve to invite Andy in for a cup of coffee one morning. There was "instant chemistry" between the Skidmore College graduate and the construction worker, and although they didn't marry until 1971, Nancy had already begun to work for Nanco, keeping payroll records, delivering bids, taking deliveries. She eventually became vice president of the company that was named after her. Nancy had two more children, born in 1972 and 1974, and by 1980 felt she was "living a neat life." Despite occasional volcanic quarrels, she was still in love with her husband.

By 1980 the Capassos had settled into a comfortable new affluence, while Andy maintained his old alliances. They had a large house in Old Westbury, Long Island; a ten-room Fifth

Avenue duplex in the city worth $3 million; seven cars; expensive paintings, including a Cy Twombly valued at almost $200,000. Andy ate at the best restaurants, and fancy cufflinks now adorned the wrists that had once gripped a shovel. He played tennis with Donald Manes and Stanley Friedman, and occasionally had secret, late-night meetings with Manes at odd places such as JFK Airport, where they were unlikely to be recognized. Capasso had similar meetings with Matthew (Matty the Horse) Ianniello, an interesting, well-read Mafia capo who controlled large portions of the construction, concrete, and pornography industries. Capasso socialized often with Teamster union leader John Cody, who would later go to prison for labor racketeering, and attended many early-morning and late-night sit-downs with gangsters who seemed to protect his construction projects from all union strife. Mobster Louie DiNapoli was once recorded through an FBI bug talking about Capasso with a combination of awe and envy: "See, he talks smooth, that guy. I don't know how to talk smooth."

Andy Capasso was first introduced to Myerson by Donald Manes, at a Queens Democratic fundraising party during the spring of 1980. Capasso immediately became active in Myerson's Senate campaign as an aggressive collector of campaign contributions from other contractors. He himself donated $2,000—the legal maximum.

Capasso was a gallant, generous companion to Myerson during the difficult period after her electoral defeat, showering her with gifts, jewelry, and romantic attention. Capasso provided Myerson with an office at Nanco, and the two worked out together several times a week in the company gym. He also gave her several Nanco credit cards.

Early in 1981 Myerson collapsed with a minor stroke while working at the Nanco office in Long Island City. She was rushed to Lenox Hill Hospital in an ambulance and admitted under an alias. Capasso followed the ambulance to the hospital in one of Nanco's limousines. After he was assured by doctors that Myerson would be all right, he left the hospital and ran directly into his wife, Nancy, on East 77th Street.

"I was just visiting a sick friend," Capasso explained.

Nancy Capasso was among the last to know about this eighteen-month affair between her husband and Bess Myerson. Andy Capasso had never been family-oriented, staying home to listen to music and read his kids a bedtime story, but spent most nights out to "see the guys," "meet Matty [Ianniello]," or "keep some appointments."

One Friday night in the winter of 1982 Nancy Capasso was eating with a friend in the Fortune Garden, a Chinese restaurant she and Andy often went to together. Out of the corner of her eye she saw her husband walk through the restaurant into the rear room. She followed him back and found Andy sitting with Bess Myerson at their favorite table. He explained that he was meeting Bess on business, but Nancy wondered whether Andy hadn't in fact wanted to get caught, with a move as blatant as coming to this restaurant.

Nancy subsequently confronted her husband with her suspicions. "You're crazy," Andy replied. "Nothing is going on. You're imagining things. You must be paranoid."

When Andy Capasso put their new Westhampton home solely in his name in 1982, Nancy became alarmed enough to consult with a divorce lawyer, though she remained indecisive, reluctant to make the final break. Andy kept earnestly denying that he was having an affair, and she didn't have any real proof that he was.

On November 5, 1982, Andy Capasso was drinking scotch on the rocks at home. It was a Friday evening and, as usual, he announced he was going out for "an appointment" at about 9:00.

"Daddy, are you going out to see your girlfriend?" his eight-year-old daughter Andrea asked.

Capasso flew into a rage. Nancy Capasso was on the lower floor of the duplex when Andrea had posed her innocent question, and Andy now charged downstairs and threw his wife over a glass coffee table by the hair. She was trapped on her back, draped across the table, as Andy Capasso began to kick her in the groin, in the lower back, and in her stomach with his heavy shoes.

Nancy screamed for her children to protect her, shouting for them to get the doorman. Andy finally stopped beating her and walked out of the apartment, leaving his wife to examine her welts and bruises. She called her lawyers, Raoul and Myrna Felder, and a week later Nancy had an order of protection, signed by Judge Bruce Kaplan, restraining Capasso from any future violence.

The colorful Raoul Felder, with his monogrammed Rolls-Royce and monogrammed shirts, cross-examined Capasso at the hearing. With his flair for the theatrical, he had Capasso remove his shoe, to show Judge Kaplan how heavy a weapon it was. At the conclusion of the hearing, Judge Kaplan characterized Capasso's attack as a "vicious beating."

Seven or eight weeks after this incident, Nancy went to see Matty the Horse, determined to learn the truth. Ianniello was a neighbor of the Capassos, and their children were close friends. Nancy liked the gangster, and came to him pleading for information.

"Andy says he is out with you every night," Nancy told him. "Is that true?"

"Nobody sees Matty every night," the Genovese family capo replied.

Nancy then asked if Matty ever saw her husband with Bess Myerson.

"I can't explain what Andy is doing with that old bag," Ianniello said, after a pause, indirectly confirming the affair for Nancy.

By this time, Andy had sued Nancy for divorce, filing his papers in Manhattan Supreme Court on December 20, 1982. Nancy answered with a countersuit, eventually naming Bess Myerson as co-respondent.

During this legal back and forth, Andy Capasso abused his wife a second time, in February 1983. Andy was about to take the children on a skiing vacation to Colorado when he got into an argument with Nancy. The cause of the dispute was that Nancy had returned to a local drugstore some extravagances Andy had purchased, including a ten-dollar toothbrush and some expensive men's cologne. After losing his temper and throwing a drink at her, he grabbed her by the shoulder and shoved her against the wall.

This second attack violated the order of protection issued by Judge Kaplan, and Andy Capasso was evicted from the Fifth Avenue duplex by Justice Hortense Gabel, who had been assigned jurisdiction over the divorce case. On February 15, Gabel signed an order giving Nancy exclusive occupancy of the duplex. On March 7, 1983, the *New York Post* published a front-page photo of Bess Myerson with the headline: IRATE WIFE EVICTS ESCORT OF BESS MYERSON.

Nancy Capasso had one more shock coming during the winter of 1983. Someone she won't identify, probably a servant in the Westhampton house loyal to her, informed her that Andy had been secretly taping their conversations. This source told Nancy that Andy had installed a sophisticated voice-activated recording system, and then gave her some tapes made with the device, one of which featured Andy expressing his love for Bess Myerson over the phone.

Nancy "almost died," the first time she forced herself to listen to the tape, which was made in September 1982. On the tape Capasso was leaving a tender message on Myerson's telephone answering machine: "Hi, baby. How are you. It's ten after seven. I'm sorry I didn't call. I'm home in Westhampton. I'll be here tonight. I'll try you a little later on. I love you. I miss you. I'm sorry I didn't call you before."

Like Richard Nixon, Andy Capasso had created the evidence against himself by bugging himself.

Bess Myerson wanted the job of cultural affairs commissioner very badly when it became available in December 1982, with Henry Geldzahler's resignation. Her relationship with Ed Koch had cooled noticeably after he declined to offer the position he had promised her, deputy mayor for economic development, after she lost the Senate primary, and Myerson was well aware that it would be difficult for Koch to reject her ambitions a second time. She, as well as Koch, knew just how much he owed her for her participation in the Immaculate Deception of 1977.

But in January 1983, other parties were in the competition as Ed Koch decided whom to appoint to the post. One logical candidate for the job was Geldzahler's top deputy, Randy Bourscheidt, who was well qualified by knowledge and continuity at the agency. Koch also toyed with the idea of placing a superstar in the position, and apparently offered it to both Jacqueline Kennedy Onassis and Beverly Sills, the head of the City Opera.

Koch also must have had some lingering misgivings about Myerson as a result of the face-to-face meeting he had had with his police commissioner, Robert McGuire, in 1980. The subject of that meeting was a secret report on Myerson prepared by the police department's intelligence division, which found that Myerson had harassed John and Joan Jakobson with abusive letters and up to forty anonymous phone calls a day. It suggested that Myerson had acted erratically, and had apparently delivered excrement to Jakobson's doorstep. It also concluded that Myerson had made a false complaint to the police, claiming that she was the victim of harassment and had therefore committed a crime. All this had been considered serious enough for the police commissioner to come personally to the mayor's office in City Hall to brief him about the way his closest female friend was behaving.

But the mayor somehow rationalized, or trivialized, the results of the police report, and Myerson continued to press her claim for the job, now through the close friend she and the mayor shared in common—mayoral aide Herb Rickman. Finally, on February 23, 1983, Koch announced he would name Bess Myerson to the commissioner's post.

The DOI's background check on Myerson never came up with the police department's report on her 1980 conduct. It was one of those missing gaps of government. The mayor knew about it. The police commissioner knew about it. And neither one informed the Department of Investigations.

Shortly after Myerson was named commissioner, and before she started work, she took a celebratory vacation with Andy Capasso to Caneel Bay. By this time Capasso had given Myerson a $41,000 Mercedes with a brass plate affixed to its dashboard that said "Bess Myerson." During 1983, Capasso had also given her a sapphire and a diamond bracelet, and a new fur coat. None of these gifts was ever reported by Myerson on her official financial disclosure forms, as required by the city's administrative code. This information would have been relevant, since Capasso held $150 million in city contracts. Just after Myerson's appointment was announced—and before she took office—Nanco received its largest contract ever from the city, a $53.6 million job to build a "sludge processing complex" at the Owl's Head sewage-treatment plant in Brooklyn—an assignment for which Nanco had no prior construction or engineering experience. But Nanco had submitted the lowest bid.

In April, when Myerson took over as commissioner of the Department of Cultural Affairs, at 2 Columbus Circle, she was practically living at Capasso's estate in Westhampton Beach. Nancy Capasso's possessions were stored in the garage, and Myerson moved her personal belongings into the house. Each Thursday morning, a Nanco limousine would take Myerson to the 23d Street pier, where she would board a rented seaplane and fly to Westhampton for the long weekend of tennis, lobsters, pool-side drinks, and parties.

When Koch appointed Bess Myerson, a private drama of

betrayal, greed, lust, violence, and revenge crossed the line and became entwined with government business and public payrolls. A city commissioner close to a significant city contractor and to the mayor (and perceived as being even closer than she was) became obsessed by a matrimonial case in which millions of dollars—and everyone's pride—became invested. The always murky boundary between public and private became even more confused by the passions of sexual politics.

By spring 1983, both Myerson and Capasso were caught up in the litigation over the divorce. Capasso was enraged by his eviction from the Fifth Avenue duplex, and by the fact that he was now forced to live during the week at the Westbury Hotel. The strain of the conflict was also causing him to drink heavily and lose sleep. During the weekends, the divorce was the main topic of conversation at Westhampton, even when there were house guests, such as Herb Rickman. Pretrial motion papers and legal documents from the case were scattered about the house, and Capasso often had his driver deliver legal papers to Myerson in the city so that she could read them and make editing or tactical comments.

It was during this same period that Judge Hortense Gabel, who was handling the Capasso suit, was desperately trying to find a job for her only child, 35-year-old Sukhreet. Sukhreet was a self-absorbed intellectual who spoke five languages and had completed studies for a Ph.D. in race relations at the University of Chicago. But she was emotionally fragile. During the spring of 1983 she had been a patient in the Payne-Whitney psychiatric clinic, suffering from acute depression. Her marriage to a Dutch diplomat had ended in divorce, and she had been unemployed for more than a year. Judge Gabel, motivated by unconditional maternal love, had sent out Sukhreet's résumé to dozens of her friends in government and elsewhere; eventually more than a hundred people were contacted, including Myerson, who was clearly aware that Judge Gabel was presiding over Capasso's case. But no one would employ Sukhreet, who eventually ran out of money and had to move in with her parents.

In May 1983, however, Sukhreet Gabel's fortunes changed when Bess Myerson began to pay attention to both her and her mother. Myerson and Judge Gabel had been professional acquaintances for twenty years, although they had not seen each other at all socially during 1982, and there is no record of a single phone conversation between them for this period. On May 25, 1983, Mayor Koch hosted a reception at Gracie Mansion to celebrate his appointment of Bess Myerson as cultural affairs commissioner. Myerson not only invited Judge Gabel to the reception; she arranged for a car and driver to take her there. The next day, Judge Gabel attended a function at the City Gallery, at DCA headquarters, at Myerson's invitation. About a week later, Judge Gabel, her husband Milton, Bess Myerson, and Herb Rickman dined together in a Manhattan restaurant.

On June 17, Bess Myerson came to dinner at the Gabels' home, inviting herself, according to some accounts. In the course of the meal, Myerson and Sukhreet had warm, personal conversations and discovered they had much in common, including their pleasure in taking long walks around the city. At the close of the evening, the troubled, overweight Sukhreet gave the celebrity commissioner her telephone number, flattered that she had made a new friend who cared about her for herself.

Less than a week later, Judge Gabel made her second ruling in the Capasso case, again favorable to Nancy Capasso. She signed an order granting Nancy $1,500 a week in temporary maintenance and $350 a week in child-support payments. The order also mandated Andy Capasso to make all mortgage, maintenance, and utilities payments on the couple's Westhampton house and on four other apartments they jointly owned, including one in Palm Beach, Florida.

Soon after this order was signed, Myerson phoned the judge's daughter and invited her out to dinner at a Chinese restaurant on the Upper East Side. In the middle of their meal, Andy Capasso showed up and announced that he had some friends waiting nearby at Abe's Steakhouse and invited Myerson to join them.

"No, I'm having a perfectly good time here," Myerson told her lover. "I'm not leaving. Tough luck."

In the weeks following, these two women of unequal status and different generations saw each other often, always at the instigation of Myerson. They often walked home together, from Columbus Circle to the Upper East Side. They went out to dinner, they went on long walks, they went to the movies and to the ballet.

On July 5, 1983, Andy Capasso's divorce attorney, Alton Abramowitz, arrived at Judge Gabel's chambers with an "order to show cause," seeking an immediate stay (a "TRO") of the

June 23 maintenance and support order. Andy Capasso was also asking for reargument of the substance of the order. Capasso's papers contained no new facts bearing on his finances or ability to pay the maintenance and support costs. He was still a wealthy man, with a construction company worth $3 million and $1 million in annual income, most of it shielded by tax shelters.

Howard Leventhal, Judge Gabel's law secretary, read the papers and noticed that they had failed to even address the status of the support payments while the motion to reargue was pending. He advised Abramowitz that his application for a TRO would probably not be signed by Judge Gabel. While Abramowitz waited in an outer office, Howard Leventhal went in to speak to the judge in private. To his astonishment, she immediately said that she had been too generous to Nancy Capasso two weeks earlier. She was inclined, she announced, to slash Nancy's $1,500-a-week maintenance by more than half. When Leventhal replied that he thought this too drastic a reduction, Judge Gabel agreed to sign an order cutting the payments by exactly one-half—to $750 a week. She lowered child-support payments from $350 a week to $250 a week. Not only was it highly unusual for a judge to make such a dramatic change in response to an *ex-parte* motion, but for years Judge Gabel had had the reputation among matrimonial lawyers of being biased in favor of women in divorce cases.

Two days after this decision, Judge Gabel left a message for Bess Myerson at her DCA office to call her at home after 5:30 P.M. By this time, Judge Gabel had given Myerson the private, unlisted phone number of her chambers, a number that only Judge Gabel's husband had.

After the favorable July 5 decision, Myerson began to take Sukhreet Gabel with her to public appearances in her official capacity as city commissioner. Sukhreet accompanied her to a meeting of the board of directors of the Henry Street Settlement, and was encouraged to ask questions, which she did. Afterward, Myerson told Sukhreet that the board members thought she was "very bright" and that Myerson should hire her.

Myerson's social courtship of Sukhreet was suspended while she and Capasso took a European vacation from July 22 to August 4. They spent a week cruising around Sardinia on a yacht with real estate developer Arthur Fisher and his wife. They spent another week together in the South of France.*

On Myerson's return, she invited Sukhreet to spend two August weekends at Capasso's estate in Westhampton. During the weekend of August 19–20, Myerson said to Sukhreet: "Come on, I'm feeling bored. I want to go someplace. Let's go for a drive. Where is your mother staying? Isn't she on the Island?"

Myerson knew that Judge Gabel was only about forty miles away in Mattituck, at the home of two other judges, Sybil Hart Kooper and William Thompson, and drove Sukhreet, and her own granddaughter, Sammantha, over to see Judge Gabel for a friendly social call.

It was also during this weekend that Sukhreet first learned that her mother was presiding over her host's divorce case. She had risen early one morning and was having tea and toast with Andy Capasso's live-in maid, Shirley Hammond. After a few minutes of talk, Sukhreet decided to formally introduce herself.

"Oh, by the way, I'm Sukhreet Gabel," she said, shaking hands with the maid.

"Isn't there a judge named Gabel connected to Mr. Capasso's divorce proceedings?" Hammond asked.

Sukhreet finally put two and two together and sensed something unsavory about the situation. That night, as soon as she returned to New York, she called her parents, and her father, Milton Gabel, a dentist, answered the phone.

"What the hell is going on?" a livid Sukhreet asked.

"Mind your own business," her father advised. "Your mother knows all about it. Let her handle it. Just don't get involved, don't get confused. Just keep your nose to the grindstone, and maybe Bess will give you a job."

Two days after the Mattituck visit, Sukhreet Gabel filled out the official city personnel forms necessary to process her appointment to a $19,000 job at DCA, a position described as "special assistant to the commissioner" on her business card. No other applicants were interviewed, and Sukhreet was offi-

---

*All through this period, Myerson denied to reporters that she was romantically involved with Capasso. As late as May 1986, Myerson would tell reporters from the *Daily News* that she and Capasso were "friends, that's all." She likewise denied ever having received any gifts from Capasso. On January 18, 1987, gossip columnist Liz Smith would quote Myerson as saying, "I have never taken or received a penny from any man in my entire life!" In a similar vein, Patricia Morrisroe would quote Myerson in her March 30, 1987 *New York* magazine profile as saying, "All my marriages had happy endings."

cially given the job before the formal, legally required vacancy notice was posted at City Hall. In honor of the occasion, Myerson treated Sukhreet, Sukhreet's boyfriend and father, and Judge Gabel to dinner at a Chinese restaurant.

On September 14, Judge Gabel issued another ruling in the matter of *Capasso v. Capasso*. She wrote the opinion herself, which was a rarity; most of her opinions were drafted by Howard Leventhal. This new order reduced Nancy Capasso's weekly maintenance payments even further, to $500, from the original $1,500, retroactive to May 24. The child-support payments were lowered from the original $350 to $180.

In Westhampton, a jubilant Bess Myerson exclaimed, "We got it reduced!" A few days later, her city driver delivered a bouquet of flowers to Judge Gabel's home, at Myerson's instruction.

Around the same time that this ruling by Judge Gabel was decreed, Herb Rickman told his friend Bess Myerson that he was shocked at the appearance of impropriety created by her hiring of Judge Gabel's daughter, but Myerson cut him off, saying, "I don't want to discuss the matter."

A few weeks later, the DCA press officer, Judith Gray, a social friend of Bess Myerson's, asked Myerson how she could have hired Sukhreet Gabel when her mother was the judge handling the Capasso divorce, and made it clear she considered it a mistake in judgment. Myerson responded that she had made the right decision and that Sukhreet would fill a necessary role in the department.

But it was soon apparent to the top management at DCA that Sukhreet was not functioning well in a job for which she was probably overqualified. She was slow to complete projects and misunderstood the point of some assignments that had been given to her. After only a month, the senior staff of DCA began complaining to Myerson that Sukhreet's performance was unsatisfactory. To compound this awkwardness, Sukhreet acted conspicuously as if she had something on Myerson, and that nothing could be done to her because of it. She even told another DCA staffer that she was concerned, "if it ever came out that my mother is a judge and if the papers ever found out."

The papers did find out. On October 17, *New York Post* reporter Richard Johnson called DCA assistant commissioner Richard Bruno and asked whether Sukhreet worked at DCA, whether she was Judge Gabel's daughter, and whether DCA was aware that Judge Gabel was sitting on the Capasso divorce litigation. Bruno promised to check and call back, and then went to speak with Commissioner Myerson.

Myerson told her deputy that the proceedings before Judge Gabel had already been completed (which was not true). She also asked Bruno to lie to the *Post* reporter and say that she had not been involved in the decision to hire Sukhreet, but that Sukhreet had been his own choice. "You interviewed a lot of people, didn't you?" Myerson said, coaching Bruno in the deception.

A few minutes later Sukhreet found a phone message from Richard Johnson on her desk. She sat only about thirty feet from Myerson and could see that the commissioner was agitated about something. Myerson, aware the reporter had also called Sukhreet, invited her into her office, where she made a proposition:

"Why don't you call the reporter back, and Richard and I will be listening on the extension. We'll feed you the right answers to give. I'll mouth the answers to you, after I hear the questions."

Sukhreet was noncommittal but felt demeaned; she felt she was being treated like a ventriloquist's dummy. After lunch she called Richard Johnson back without informing Myerson. When Myerson discovered her talking to the reporter, she made a gesture to terminate the conversation by drawing her finger across her throat. But Sukhreet proved to be enough of a bureaucrat to lie to the reporter on her own.

The next morning, the Myerson-Gabel scoop was the lead item in the *Post*'s well-read gossip column, called "Page Six" for its placement in the paper. The story quoted Bruno as saying: "I interviewed her and I hired her. She was among a number of applicants and she was the outstanding candidate."

The item also reported:

> As for Sukhreet, she said she knew nothing of her mother's cases, or boss's social life, "except for what I read in the newspapers."
>
> "I don't share Miss Myerson's social life. I work for her between 10 A.M. and 6 P.M., and don't normally see her after hours."

"Page Six" also introduced a new claim: that Sukhreet "got the job after Herb Rickman, special assistant to Mayor Koch and a long-time friend of Judge Gabel, arranged for an interview for a job with the economic affairs desk at the city's Office of Economic Development.

" 'The desk wasn't set up yet, so her résumé was sent over to me,' Bruno said."

Rickman was furious at this attempt to set him up as the fall guy and called both Myerson and Bruno to vent his anger. He also informed the mayor that he had nothing to do with Sukhreet's being at DCA.

One person who read the "Page Six" item in astonishment was Nancy Capasso. "It opened my eyes to what was really going on," she recalls. "I went screaming to my lawyers. The item made me realize I was going up against all this power, all these connections."*

The same day the "Page Six" item appeared, Judge Gabel presided over another pretrial hearing in *Capasso v. Capasso.* The judge seemed visibly shaken by the *Post* story, and asked the lawyers if they wished to make a motion disqualifying her from hearing the case. But she did not disclose the truth of her relationship with Myerson, her own role in getting her daughter the job with Myerson, or that her daughter did indeed socialize with Myerson after hours—all facts she knew contradicted the published story. Since Nancy Capasso's lawyer did not know to what extent the *Post* story had been shaped by Myerson's own deception, he chose not to make a motion to disqualify.

On the following day, October 19, Commissioner Myerson sent Mayor Koch a three-page, single-spaced letter justifying the hiring of Sukhreet Gabel, adding further disinformation to her account.

Myerson reported that Sukhreet "sent her résumé to the Department of Cultural Affairs, and an interview was arranged. Both Assistant Commissioner Bruno and Deputy Commissioner Randy Bourscheidt recommended her to me. . . . Among

---

*The "Page Six" item almost didn't appear, according to both Susan Mulcahy, who edited the item, and Richard Johnson, who reported it. "Everyone denied it so vehemently," Mulcahy says, "that I was nervous about running it. I thought it all might be just a coincidence. The fact we couldn't get Myerson to comment also made it harder to use." Richard Johnson admitted, "If we had something better to run that day, we probably wouldn't have used the Myerson item, because it was so hard to write with all the denials." Bess Myerson had claimed for years that Nancy Capasso was the original source for the item, but Mulcahy, who got the tip, denies this.

the two dozen people he [Bruno] interviewed was Sukhreet Gabel."

Myerson also grossly distorted the status of the Capasso divorce case: "Most of what was to be decided had already been decided in the first six months, a major part of it in favor of Mrs. Capasso." A majority of Judge Gabel's rulings were *unfavorable* to Nancy Capasso—including the last five in a row. And Judge Gabel would retain jurisdiction over the case for nine more months, during which she would make seven more rulings, including holding Nancy Capasso in contempt and quashing Nancy's third-party subpoenas.

Myerson concluded her letter by saying of Sukhreet: "Her performance has been excellent. She represents the Department and the city well. I do not regret my decision. A person who is that highly qualified should not be discriminated against because her mother is a public figure."

On October 21, the mayor replied back with a note that said, in its entirety:

> I have your note of October 19 commenting on the hiring of Sukhreet Gabel. While your note wasn't necessary, I do appreciate your having thought to write it. Based on the recommendations made to you, her talent and your own appraisal, you did exactly the right thing in filling an open job with an able person.

The mayor did not independently investigate any of the assertions made in Myerson's letter, nor did he assign any deputy to verify its factual claims, though any of them could have been easily disproven.

Bess Myerson gave Sukhreet Gabel a copy of her October 19 letter to the mayor and told her to go and thank Richard Bruno, who had drafted the document, "because he got you off the hook." Although Sukhreet did express her gratitude to Bruno, she recognized her own hypocrisy, and knew she was thanking him for writing lies. And she was angry that Myerson hadn't even thanked her for her own lies to the *Post* that had saved her boss from serious trouble.

Soon after the *Post*'s item was published, there was a discernible shift in Bess Myerson's attitude toward Sukhreet. Although she continued to offer occasional—and confusing—gestures of friendship, Myerson also began to exclude Sukhreet from departmental meetings, and to assign her meaningless busywork. Myerson even took back the business cards that identified Sukhreet as a "special assistant to the commissioner," and tossed them in a dumpster in front of Sukhreet.

Myerson's mixed messages to Sukhreet were such that on December 19, she agreed to be the guest of honor at a small dinner party at Sukhreet's apartment. Myerson approved the guest list beforehand, which included Sukhreet's parents, Herb Rickman, and DCA counsel Bob Vanni. During the meal Myerson launched into a ten-minute diatribe against Sukhreet, who sat only a few feet away, going so far as to tell Vanni, "I can't stand Sukhreet," in her own house, over food she had prepared.

Sukhreet ran into the kitchen and started to cry, letting the water run over the dirty dishes in the sink to hide the sound of her sobs from her parents and the other guests.

On March 1, 1984, by a vote of 5 to 0, the appellate division reversed Judge Gabel's rulings that cut Nancy Capasso's weekly temporary maintenance and child support payments. The decision noted that Capasso's "yearly gross income was approximately $1 million," and restored the payments to the original levels. The maintenance payments were increased from $500 a week to $1,500, and the child support payments from $180 to $350.

In June 1984, Sukhreet left DCA and took a job her mother secured for her—at twice the salary—as deputy executive director of the city's human rights commission. But she was in a severe depression, could not concentrate or function, and was allowed to resign in August. By then, to treat her depression, Sukhreet received about ten electric shock treatments as an outpatient.

By the summer of 1984, stories about the Capasso divorce were no longer to be found in the newspapers, and no editor, no reporter thought to follow up on the item in the *Post*. But Nancy Capasso kept on fighting for what she believed was rightfully hers—custody of her children and a fair share of the marital property. She could have settled and accepted the small amount of money her husband was offering her, but she resolved not to go quietly.

Andy Capasso, however, felt in complete control of the situation, with the help of his powerful friends. The mayor of New York came to his house in Westhampton for a big party on July 4, 1984. Andy had contributed more than $50,000 to comptroller Harrison Goldin's recent campaigns. His friend and sometimes lawyer Stanley Friedman had his patronage appointees high up in the Department of Environmental Protection, where most of Nanco's city contracts originated. And Friedman had influence over many of the judges sitting in Manhattan, where his divorce case would eventually come to trial.

Nancy hired a new lawyer in June 1984, although she didn't know where she would find the money to pay his fee. Herman Tarnow had had enough experience with city government and politics to have a sense of how much concentrated power was arrayed against Nancy, and one of the first pieces of advice Tarnow gave his new client was to buy a cheap device to record her phone conversations with her husband. After Nancy went to the local Radio Shack and bought "a two-dollar gizmo," Tarnow showed her how to use it and explained what sorts of conversation might be valuable in her struggle for marital property and child custody.

On July 25, Tarnow had Andy Capasso under oath during a grueling all-day pretrial deposition. Tarnow pressured Capasso on his finances, his handling of cash, his reimbursement of insurance claims, his net worth. He asked Capasso to produce an accounting sheet for all the personal expenses that were charged to Nanco. He asked him about all his bank accounts. Tarnow was not after anything specific—he was merely "poking the ashes"—for although Nancy suspected that Andy kept a cash horde, it was just a hunch. Andy Capasso, however, thought Tarnow and Nancy knew more than they were letting on. He became evasive and nasty during the deposition, and began to stonewall and give flippant answers. More and more he answered, "I don't recall" to Tarnow's questions; more and more Tarnow thought Andy was overreacting to his grilling.

On July 31, which was a very hot day, a furious Nancy Capasso began to move all her clothes and summer things out of the garage of the Westhampton beach condo. She had to move out under the conditions of her separation agreement, although no one else was moving into the condo. Most of her fury was directed at Bess Myerson, who she believed was behind this act of spite. Late that afternoon, while Nancy was in the basement of her mother's home, Andy called her, and she immediately put the gadget on her phone. Their conversation lasted for an hour, and was by turns angry, funny, and even affectionate at one point, when Andy admitted, "I basically like you." But it became clear to Nancy that the purpose of Andy's call was to determine whether she actually had criminal evidence against him.

"Your lawyer is on to something," Andy insisted. "You know something that can put me in jeopardy. What do you intend to do? Do you intend to go to the prosecutors, to the IRS, to the authorities? I know what you know, and I even know how you know it. . . .

"Are you going to run to the authorities and put me in jail for four hundred, five hundred years? Your lawyer is pursuing a line of questioning. Do you intend to pursue these questions? I want you to stop your lawyer from asking the questions. I don't want that stuff on the record."

Regaining his composure, Andy then asked, "What will it take for you to settle this case?"

"Make me an offer I can't refuse," replied Nancy, consciously echoing the memorable line from *The Godfather.*

Andy then returned to his fears: "Where is your head with turning canary and putting me in jail for four hundred, five hundred years? If I did anything, I only did it for the common good. Do you want to put me in jail?"

"I said I won't put you in jail," Nancy said.

"There are papers I must provide, testimony I must give," Andy complained. "I'm concerned about something I may have done that may have been illegal, that may have been criminal. I don't want to know that I'm going to continue into this case facing a jail rap."

When Nancy hung up she felt she had suddenly come into possession of "the hydrogen bomb," without knowing precisely what secret it was that Andy was so frightened about. Tarnow agreed that it was a remarkable and mysterious conversation but didn't see how it could advance his cause in the divorce case, which was his sole responsibility. He didn't know how to make use of it. From his point of view, prosecuting Andy Capasso was not in his interest. He wanted the maximum share of the marital property for his client. A criminal prosecution would only diminish the value of the marital property, eating it up in legal fees and putting Nanco itself at risk.

As the case dragged on to the close of 1984, Nancy Capasso became increasingly upset. She felt she was not being treated justly by the courts. No trial date had yet been set, and Andy's lawyers were trying to maneuver all the pending motions back before Judge Gabel. These tactics made her feel more powerless over her own destiny than ever, and brought back all her fears of the influence Andy and Bess could command.

Without consulting Tarnow, Nancy composed a handwritten letter to Judge Gabel, which she hoped would reach her at a human level, beyond all the impersonal briefs and transcripts. Nancy's letter, dated December 22, 1984 and marked "personal and confidential," said:

Dear Justice Gabel

I am the plaintiff in this action. My attorney Herman Tarnow did not participate in the preparation of this letter, and does not even know that I am writing it.

I am appealing to you directly to disqualify yourself from my case because I have no other alternative. Since the inception of this case your decisions have endangered my ability and that of my two small children to subsist pending the ultimate trial of this matter. And I have recently learned that motions in our case made after you left the matrimonial part will be referred back to you.

I do not mean this letter to be accusatory but I think a review of your prior decisions will raise in your own mind the possibility that something might have interfered with your sense of justice and fair play.

(As you know, the New York Post reported on October 18, 1983, that your daughter was employed by Bess Myerson who is my husband's acknowledged paramour in this case. I want to believe that this fact did not interfere with your decisions. Miss Myerson was later named the co-respondent in this case.) . . .

You reduced my temporary maintenance to $500 per week, a decision that was clearly inadequate as the appellate division later ruled.

You denied my application for medical and dental expenses for myself and the children. (Although my daughter Andrea's braces were cutting into her gums and causing bleeding, for four months her orthodontist refused to treat her because Mr. Capasso would not pay the bill.)

That we are surviving this ordeal at all is due entirely to the Appellate Division's reversal of your decisions.

Because we have heard of your fine reputation for protecting women in my circumstances, your decisions in my case are inconsistent with your rulings in other cases, and are inexplicable. I am sure that you can see this.

In sum, the only appropriate action you can now take is to remove yourself from my case. For the record plainly presents, at the least, an appearance of impropriety.

Respectfully yours,
Nancy Capasso

Judge Hortense Gabel never responded to this letter. In May 1986, her law secretary found it stuffed and crumpled in the back of a file.

In the spring of 1985, as the date of the trial drew near, Tarnow finally obtained access to about forty boxes of Capasso's business records. He decided to hire a team of forensic accountants and instructed them to analyze all the raw checks from the last harmonious year of the Capasso marriage, which turned out to be 1981.

In their investigation, the accountants found $200,000 worth of checks converted to cash, some with no bank involved, the remainder cashed at the Long Island City branch of the European-American Bank. About half of the total amount had been paid to individuals with strange-sounding ethnic names. There was no backup for many of these transactions, no vouchers, no invoices, no accounting documents. All this was gradually discovered in a large conference room at Nanco's offices in Long Island City. Day after day, in a tense, unfriendly environment, the accountants, Tarnow, and Nancy Capasso worked around a long table, piecing together the puzzle of the past. At all times, Andy had a family member or an employee in the conference room standing guard over the litigation team. Each time Nancy needed to use the Nanco bathroom, Andy's sister, Sally, insisted on escorting and observing her.

"Do you think I'm going to steal the toilet paper?" Nancy finally asked. Sally did not smile.

After a few weeks of turning over checks, it became apparent to Nancy and her lawyer that the mysterious transactions represented large sums of money being siphoned out of Nanco. This information provided essential support for Tarnow's legal strategy of proving that Nanco's net worth was greater than Andy was admitting. It was also valuable for locating all Capasso's assets that might be defined as marital property for the purpose of equitable distribution. But proving criminality was still not in the legal or economic interests of Tarnow's client, and Tarnow thought that Andy would now be smart enough to settle the case before trial. He informed Andy's lawyer, Sam Fredman, about what he had found, and even let him know that he had a "devastating" tape of Andy. Tarnow duplicated the front and back of each check and waited for a call to negotiate a settlement before trial. But Capasso, driven perhaps by stubborn pride, perhaps by the arrogance of power, perhaps believing that he and Myerson could fix any case, never called.

In June 1985, Tarnow had two meetings at City Hall with the mayor's counsel, Patrick Mulhearn. Tarnow had requested these meetings because he wanted Mayor Koch and mayoral aide Herb Rickman to testify at the Capasso divorce trial, scheduled to start on July 8. Tarnow felt Capasso's adultery with Myerson was central to winning custody of the children, and both the mayor and Rickman were witnesses to the couple's living together at the Westhampton estate.

In the course of the meetings, Tarnow related to Mulhearn the entire history of the 1983 episode in which Myerson hired Judge Gabel's daughter and Judge Gabel made a series of rulings against Nancy Capasso.* Tarnow also told the mayor's counsel about some of the gifts Capasso had given Myerson and the trips they had taken. Tarnow said that he considered the gifts "improprieties" and the basis of "potential wrongdoing," but Mulhearn responded that the gifts were not unethical, because, "after all, they are friends."

The judge selected to preside over the Capasso divorce trial was Andrew Tyler of Manhattan Supreme Court. In November 1977, a jury had found Tyler guilty of committing perjury, a charge that stemmed from the judge's lying to a grand jury about his meeting with a convicted gambler named Raymond

---

*Mulhearn has a different recollection about how much detail Tarnow provided.

(Spanish Raymond) Marquez. But in April 1978, an appellate court had overturned the jury's verdict without ordering a retrial. Tyler had also been indicted for improperly granting bail to a defendant, but this charge had been dismissed before trial. To say the least, Tyler, because of this record, had not established himself as a jurist of great distinction before the Capasso litigation landed on his calendar.

Moreover, Tyler was a close friend of Stanley Friedman, whom he would ask for the names of lawyers to be given receivership appointments. Nancy Capasso was well aware how close her husband was to Friedman, and how close Friedman was to Judge Tyler. Already victimized by Judge Gabel's bias and connections, Nancy wanted to request another judge, but there was nothing she could do about it. "Let's make a record and we will win on appeal," Tarnow told her.

The trial began on July 8 and went on for twenty-one days, spread over four months. On most days Judge Tyler took the bench at about 11:00 A.M., broke for lunch at 12:30, and worked only another ninety minutes in the afternoon before adjourning. He dozed off several times on the bench, and otherwise seemed uninterested in the proceedings, not even making an attempt to mask his boredom. When Tarnow tried to get Bess Myerson to testify, Tyler granted a motion from Myerson's lawyer to quash the subpoena. The July 31 tape was never offered in evidence.

Despite her forebodings, Nancy Capasso was still unprepared for the one-sidedness of Andrew Tyler's opinion, when it was finally issued just before Christmas of 1985. Nancy had contended that the value of the marital property was about $15 million, and an equitable distribution would allow her about $6 million. Tyler granted her $2 million. He ended alimony and child-support payments. He valued Nanco at $268,000, when the evidence indicated it was worth more than $4 million. Tyler denied Nancy any portion of the Westhampton estate or the Palm Beach condominium. He denied her any portion of Nanco, even though the company had been named after her and she had been its vice president. Nancy could plainly see that Tyler's opinion simply regurgitated and restated without change the "findings of fact and conclusions of law" that Sam Fredman had submitted to the judge in behalf of his client, Andy Capasso. Tarnow had submitted a similar request for findings, but his effort was completely ignored.

Nancy Capasso had fought this divorce for three years, and

now a second judge had ruled against her. She had no funds to pay for an appeal. The media had no interest in her lost cause. Most people would have surrendered at this point. But Nancy Capasso would not give in, or give up.

The first week of January 1986, Nancy went back to Raoul and Myrna Felder. Under normal circumstances, Raoul Felder would have asked for a $50,000 retainer to handle an appeal in a matrimonial, and then have billed the client at $450 per hour. But he was sympathetic to Nancy Capasso's cause. He had remained in touch with her since he represented her on the 1982 order of protection and on the pretrial motions decided by Judge Gabel. He knew that Andy Capasso had unlimited resources and was trying to beat Nancy down with the weight of his corporate wealth. He had seen "the smirk on the face of Andy Capasso and his lawyers," and Felder, a populist millionaire, did not like "this kind of gang-up."

"I need help. I've been shafted," Nancy Capasso told Felder. "Judge Tyler just lifted his conclusions word for word from Andy's legal papers."

Raoul Felder found her accusation hard to believe. As a divorce lawyer for more than twenty-five years, he had been involved in thousands of matrimonial cases, and had never encountered a judge who did that. He asked Nancy to send the two documents over to his office so he could examine the alleged wholesale borrowing himself, and discovered that they were, in fact, identical. Not a comma was changed. Felder agreed to waive his standard fee structure and take Nancy Capasso on as a client. Nancy paid a small retainer and signed a promissory note, payable at the end of the case.

While Raoul Felder usually gets the headlines at the start of a divorce, it is his partner and wife, Myrna Felder, who is the recognized expert in appeals. Myrna Felder grew up in Brooklyn, was a child television performer, and was a dancer in the Broadway chorus of *Stop the World, I Want to Get Off*. She then attended law school, and started specializing in divorce law, representing, among others, Ethel Scull, wife of art collector Robert Scull, and Michele Lerner, the wife of composer Alan J. Lerner. Myrna quickly gained a reputation as one of the best in the business, partly because of her mastery of tax law and investments. Myrna knew Nancy, felt, like her husband, that she had been treated unjustly, and was prepared to work to right this wrong without being paid.

The following week, on January 10, Donald Manes was

found bleeding in his car. This event caused an overnight revolution within the media, as well as within law enforcement. There was suddenly a new atmosphere in New York. Donald Manes was suddenly the biggest story in New York, and Andy Capasso was one of the best friends of the biggest story.

Capasso was seen at Booth Memorial Hospital early in the morning after Manes was brought in. His name was among the most frequent callers on Manes's phone logs, and Capasso was one of the few people allowed to see Manes at home after he was discharged from the hospital. Because his company had received $200 million in city contracts, Andy Capasso stopped being a topic for gossip columnists and started being a subject for prosecutors and investigative reporters.

The U.S. Attorney's office opened its investigation into Capasso and Myerson in March 1986. This formal step was not taken as the result of any referral from the DOI. It was initiated, rather, because a young assistant, David Lawrence, had heard about the divorce case from Herman Tarnow (who attended the same fitness center) and brought it to the attention of Giuliani.

Giuliani knew how close Capasso was to Donald Manes and Matty the Horse Ianniello. He knew Capasso had attended Ianniello's victory party when he was acquitted in one of the three federal cases brought against him. Giuliani was aware of a tape, made by the FBI in 1984 in the Palma Boy Social Club in East Harlem, on which Anthony (Fat Tony) Salerno, a member of the Mafia's national commission, could be heard telling mobster Louis DiNapoli that "Andy's looking to build a fucking cement plant." The tape indicated that Fat Tony was suspiciously familiar with many of Capasso's plans and projects. Giuliani was in fact primed to give the go-ahead on a Capasso investigation when Lawrence came to him with information on the Capasso divorce case and Bess Myerson.

Since he had been the source of the original information, 32-year-old David Lawrence was assigned the case. Lawrence had grown up in Manhattan, been a sixties antiwar activist in high school, and graduated from Brandeis University. In 1983 Lawrence was doing products liability litigation for Weil, Gotshal when he decided to apply for a job in the U.S. Attorney's office. He was hired during the last days of John Martin's tenure, and was reinterviewed by Giuliani when he assumed leadership. Lawrence knew he would like Giuliani as soon as he saw the baseball autographed by Yogi Berra on the prosecutor's desk. Giuliani knew he would like Lawrence when he heard the job applicant talk about idealism and explain why he wanted to leave commercial law at a prestigious firm for less money and more work.

By March 1986, Lawrence had worked his way up into the corruption unit after prosecuting motorcycle gangs and drug cases. As soon as he had subpoenaed and studied the sealed state court file of the Capasso divorce, he sensed he had been given a great case.

Assigned to work the case with Lawrence was Tony Lombardi, a former federal agent who was now a special investigator working with the U.S. Attorney on political corruption cases. Lombardi had been the case agent in the successful prosecution of former Bronx Democratic leader Pat Cunningham. He then served on the President's Commission on Organized Crime, and later as the chief investigator for the short-lived Martin Commission. During his stint on the Martin Commission, Lombardi had learned a great deal about Capasso's city contracts and his relationships with Manes, Friedman, Myerson, and Ameruso, information that gave him a head start when Giuliani teamed him up with Lawrence.

After a few weeks of studying the background of the case, Lawrence got a tip that Nancy Capasso had in her possession incriminating tapes that were part of her divorce case but had never been played at the trial. In late March Lawrence sent her a subpoena that only ordered her to speak to him, but not to testify before a grand jury. The next day Andy Capasso called Nancy and politely offered to provide a lawyer for her visit to the U.S. Attorney's office. Nancy rejected the idea, just as politely. Next, Jay Goldberg telephoned, offering to secure her a lawyer without cost. Nancy knew Goldberg was the criminal lawyer for both Andy and Matty the Horse Ianniello. She had no reason to trust her ex-husband or his lawyer, and assumed any attorney they provided would be there not to represent her but to spy on her for Andy. In the end, Nancy met with Lawrence without a lawyer and told him what she knew, which wasn't very much.

On March 31, Nancy Capasso received a subpoena from the U.S. Attorney's office, ordering her to produce by April 14 all documents, tapes, canceled checks, computer disks, transcripts, ledgers, electronic wire transfers, invoices, financial statements, cables, and contracts she had that related to Andy Capasso or Nanco.

Nancy recognized that this was the Rubicon: if she complied with this lawful subpoena, and turned over the July 31 tape and the Xeroxes of the Nanco checks, Andy could go to jail. She had chosen not to use the tape all through her divorce trial, because it was potentially so damaging. But now she felt as if she had no choice. To withhold the tape would be a violation of law, and, believing she had been dealt with unfairly by two judges, she was rightfully bitter. When she surrendered the relevant materials to the federal government in mid-April, the tape was among them.

Marcia Kramer had joined the *Daily News* in 1970, and by April 1986 had risen to become chief of the City Hall bureau, though she was not yet forty. She ran three miles a day and did 600 sit-ups four mornings a week at the same gym the mayor sometimes used for less strenuous exercise.

After the Manes suicide, and after it seemed inevitable that Stanley Friedman was going to be prosecuted, Marcia Kramer tried to figure out where the scandal was likely to spread next. She guessed Bess Myerson and Andy Capasso—the scandal had yet to have an element of romantic passion—and she assigned herself to work on the story at the beginning of April. Her boss, city editor Arthur Browne, who had co-authored a book on Koch, agreed with Kramer's assessment and, relieving her of all other reporting responsibilities, gave her an entire month just to look at the pair. Browne had spoken to Myerson twice for his book, and recalled how she had tried to manipulate the conditions under which she might agree to be interviewed. He knew that she was a big target to be going for, and that the story "had better have the goods" to justify the time spent on it. But he believed very deeply that "none of the dailies had been doing a very good job of covering the ethics of city government before the Manes suicide attempt. The mind-set of the dailies had become accepting of too many things."

Marcia Kramer began her project by trying to reassemble the complete record of the Capasso divorce case. She went down into the basement of Manhattan Supreme Court and found the log book where all the cases were listed, but the clerk told her that the Capasso divorce file was sealed. Forced to piece

together the record on her own, Kramer contacted various lawyers and court employees, and managed to obtain almost all the
decisions, briefs, and transcripts in the four-year history of the
divorce.

Kramer had also heard about Nancy's handwritten appeal
to Judge Gabel of December 1984, and asked her for a copy of
it. At first Nancy, who was inexperienced in dealing with the
press, was reluctant. Her appeal of Judge Tyler's decision was
still pending in the appellate division, and she worried that
publicity might affect it. And even though her lawyer was advis-
ing her to be cautious in talking to reporters, in early April she
finally agreed to meet Marcia Kramer on Madison Avenue;
while Kramer waited across the street, Nancy xeroxed the letter
in a stationery store.

By the end of April, Kramer felt she had gathered enough
information to start a series of articles. She would eventually
write nine stories on Bess Myerson during the month of May,
while the *News* also ran several others by Barbara Ross and
Marilyn Thompson.

The first story in this sequence was published on May 2,
written by Ross and Thompson under the headline: BESS' BIZ-
MAN PAL PROBED.

The lead reported:

> A federal grand jury is investigating a major city
> contractor who provided posh lodgings and
> entertainment to a top Mayoral aide and has been
> linked romantically to Cultural Affairs Commissioner
> Bess Myerson.
>
> Sources said the grand jury has subpoenaed
> witnesses who will detail Capasso's entertainment of
> officials, including Koch's long time special assistant
> Herb Rickman.
>
> The jury is also reviewing records of Capasso's
> recent divorce, in which his former wife, Nancy, has
> charged that Myerson was responsible for the breakup
> of her marriage.

The story quoted Myerson as saying she and Capasso were
"friends and that's all."

This story alone should have alerted the mayor to what
Bess Myerson had become, but in fact Koch had already been
given five serious warnings about the woman to whom he owed

so much. In 1980, the police commissioner had notified him that Myerson had made a false complaint of a crime and had harassed others in a bizarre fashion. In addition to the police commissioner's 1980 report, the Brooklyn D.A.'s office sent a letter to the Department of Investigations the same year reporting that a security guard company at the Brooklyn Navy Yard was improperly being used to protect Myerson during her 1980 Senate campaign. In October 1983, the *New York Post* published its "Page Six" item with sufficient clues about the scandal, and Koch's friend and assistant, Herb Rickman, had told him the implication in the story that he had played a role in hiring Sukhreet Gabel was false.

In July 1984, Koch had been advised by Rickman not to attend the party at Andy Capasso's Westhampton estate on the fourth, as Capasso was under investigation for using fraudulent minority subcontractors on his state contracts. Rickman told the mayor he was terminating his friendships with both Myerson and Capasso and boycotted the July 4 party out of his own sense of propriety. In 1985, Herman Tarnow had told Patrick Mulhearn, the mayor's counsel, about Myerson's acceptance of gifts and free vacations from Capasso, and Koch had been informed of this conversation. But no one bothered to check whether Myerson had disclosed these gifts on her ethics filings.

The fifth warning the Koch administration had received was one that no one outside government had been made aware of. In May 1984, a typed, unsigned letter was sent to DOI charging that Bess Myerson had improperly influenced Judge Gabel by giving her daughter a job. Investigations commissioner Patrick McGinley gave the letter to John Chiaffone, the inspector general for both the parks department and DCA. Because Chiaffone had no staff in his role as DCA inspector general, he asked McGinley either to assign him additional staff or to use his own staff to follow up on the letter. Chiaffone regarded the letter as "credible, rational, and serious." Chiaffone did show the letter to parks commissioner Henry Stern, who had been Myerson's counsel at Consumer Affairs in 1969. Stern read the document and thought it was "not crazy, but contained nothing new," and never mentioned it to Koch or Myerson. In July 1984, Chiaffone returned the letter and the responsibility for any investigation to McGinley. The letter apparently rested in a dead file until it was rediscovered by Giuliani in the spring of 1986.

On the morning of May 2, 1986, Ed Koch held a news conference. The session began with some sharp questions following up the *News* story, which elicited lavish praise for Myerson from the mayor. When more questions were posed about Myerson's relationship with Capasso and her visits to Capasso's Westhampton home, Koch said: "I've thought to myself that have we gotten so low, that this would be the subject of discussion, whether Bess Myerson could spend a weekend at someone's home. I was appalled by it. . . . What I'm trying to convey, there is a certain element of McCarthyism here, in my judgment."

Five days later, on Wednesday, May 7, Marcia Kramer made the first revelation of the full extent of the scandal under the headline: MYERSON HIRED DAUGHTER OF JUDGE WHO CUT BEAU'S ALIMONY. Although Myerson herself would not give Kramer an interview, Judge Gabel claimed she "didn't remember anything" about the Capasso case, and said, "The chances are dollars to doughnuts that the decision was drafted by a law assistant."

The mayor's response to Kramer's story was to recirculate to City Hall reporters Myerson's letter to him of October 1983. This was done after Myerson assured the mayor's chief of staff, Diane Coffey, that the entire divorce case had been settled by the time Sukhreet Gabel was hired, and that most of Judge Gabel's decisions had been made in favor of Nancy Capasso.

Marcia Kramer's next story, published on May 13, clearly disproved Myerson's account to the mayor, and demonstrated the falsity of Myerson's cover-up story. A simple reading of the court record by DOI would have proved Kramer was correct in her assessment, but the mayor never ordered the department to explain to him the discrepancy between her account and the story in the *News*.

The mayor's aides even engaged in a subtle campaign to discredit Kramer's stories and discourage other reporters from following up on them. In fact, none of the dailies did any independent investigations of the disclosures in the *News*, while some of the other daily reporters in the City Hall press room, led by George Arzt, the bureau chief of the *Post* (who would soon become the mayor's press secretary), bad-mouthed Kramer's scoops as "smarmy" and a "re-hash." Kramer thought the criticisms had the narrow, repetitive ring of "a party line." But the silence and sniping by some of her colleagues only made her more determined to prove she was right. Kramer understood Koch well enough to interpret his lashing out with invective like "McCarthyism" to mean that she had struck a nerve and was on the right track.

By early June, Kramer learned about Nancy's tapes, and particularly the one in which Andy pleaded with her not to put him in jail for "four hundred, five hundred years." Kramer began to harass Tarnow to play the tape for her and to try to convince Nancy that it was in her interest to publicize its contents. Tarnow finally let Kramer listen to the tape once, on the condition she not take any notes and she not quote from it in any published story. Kramer now understood why Nancy had considered giving it up as the equivalent of crossing the Rubicon. Any prosecutor who listened to the recording would conclude Andy Capasso had committed crimes.

Kramer kept hounding Tarnow to allow her to listen to the tape a second time, with the understanding she could take notes and write a story in the *Daily News,* until on Friday, June 13, he relented. Kramer left the lawyer's office and walked the two blocks to the *Daily News,* already drafting a story in her mind that she believed would help put Andy Capasso in prison. The plan was to publish the piece in the thick, well-read Sunday paper, and Kramer worked until midnight Friday finishing the writing.

Kramer has a vivid imagination, and she was frightened— so frightened that she asked a copy boy to walk her to her car in the darkened garage at about 12:15 A.M. She requested that the copy boy start the car for her, but he declined the honor, and Kramer turned on her own ignition uneventfully.

The story hit the streets about 7:00 on Saturday evening. It contained direct quotations from the tape, and revealed that it was already in the possession of Giuliani's grand jury. Kramer revealed that Capasso had feared turning over to Nancy's lawyers his records on insurance and damage claims, and that the possibility of these claims being bogus had become a focus of Giuliani's inquiry. When Myerson and Capasso read this story, it was probably the first time they realized that Giuliani had heard Nancy's tape.

On Monday, June 16, the day after Kramer's story appeared, Bess Myerson made a visit, uninvited, to the apartment of Sukhreet Gabel.

Shortly after 9:00 P.M. Myerson telephoned Sukhreet with

the message, "I've got the most wonderful news for you. I'd like to come over and see you. We'll talk about it." As she had seen Myerson only once in the past year, the call surprised Sukhreet, but she agreed to see Myerson in an hour. A half-hour later Myerson was buzzing Sukhreet on the house phone, and Sukhreet, when she went downstairs to meet her, saw that she was wearing a jogging suit, Reebok running shoes, and big purple glasses. Because Sukhreet had not read Marcia Kramer's Sunday feature, or any of the other stories on Myerson and her mother that had been appearing in the *Daily News* for the previous six weeks, she had no context for Myerson's abrupt visit. And for the next two hours the two women walked aimlessly around the East Side, up and down streets in a five-block radius of Sukhreet's 69th Street apartment.

Myerson began the conversation by trying to get Sukhreet to promise that she would tell her everything she was going to say, before she said it, to her lawyer. She then gently tried to coach Sukhreet into accepting a rewriting of history, into believing that she had gotten her job through Herb Rickman. As Sukhreet tried to organize her recollections of 1983, Myerson kept asking her, "Exactly what did you tell your lawyer?" When Sukhreet described how she was shunted aside at DCA, and stripped of her title, and kept away from Myerson, Myerson told her: "Don't you see, they were all out to get you, because they were jealous of our close relationship."

Toward the end of their walk, Myerson became more threatening in trying to pressure Sukhreet into participating in a cover-up: "Just keep your big mouth shut. . . . I need to know what you are going to say so I can say the same thing. . . . You are a fool and you could be very dangerous. . . . Don't talk to anyone else."

Leaving Sukhreet at the door of her building, Myerson left without ever having mentioned the "wonderful news" that had prompted her visit.

On May 22, 1986, Myrna Felder had made her oral argument to the appellate division on her appeal of Judge Tyler's decision. She had four excellent judges on the bench—Arnold Fein, Leo Milonas, Ernst Rosenberger, and Richard Wallach. She felt she was at the top of her game, and sensed the judges were receptive to her factual and legal arguments.

On October 2, 1986, the appellate court released its opinion, reversing all Judge Tyler's findings and ordering him to reconsider his decree. The appellate decision, which was drafted by Judge Wallach for the unanimous panel, chastised Andrew Tyler for his "wholesale, verbatim adoption of the husband's requests for findings," calling this "an error of law," and observing, "these proposals were unacceptable and should have been rejected across the board."

The appellate judges also ruled:

> With respect to the Long Island City commercial properties [Nanco], we reverse the trial court's valuation of $268,000 as of the commencement of the action, and make our own finding that their value as of the commencement of the action was $4,462,119. We do this on the basis of the husband's admissions.

The appellate court also rejected Tyler's finding that Nancy was entitled to only $2 million of the $10–$19 million in marital property. It directed Tyler to give "some recompense" to Nancy because of her direct and indirect contributions to Nanco.

Normally a trial judge would respond to such a stinging rebuke by complying with whatever the superior judges recommended, but Tyler did not. On February 23, 1987, he issued his own fifteen-page opinion refusing to reconsider any of his December 1985 rulings. With unprecedented defiance, Tyler wrote:

> This Court finds and determines that defendant's [Nancy Capasso's] activities during the marriage were limited, and her contributions as a spouse, parent, and homemaker did not contribute to the career advancement of plaintiff or his business.

In May 1986, at about the same time that the oral argument was being presented in the appellate division, Andy Capasso stopped making his child-support and maintenance payments, a tactic that seemed to be part of his battle plan to break Nancy's will. So during this year of uncertainty, while her appeal of Judge Tyler's verdict was pending with a higher authority, Myrna Felder was forced to litigate. She had to draft and argue four enforcement motions before a money judgment was entered, and Andy Capasso was compelled to pay his substantial arrears in child support.

. . .

By December 1986 David Lawrence and Tony Lombardi had succeeded in putting together a criminal case against Andy Capasso. They had interviewed about fifty of the people whose names had appeared on the checks that Tarnow had copied, and every one of them said they had no connection to Nanco, had never made a claim against Nanco, had never heard of Nanco. Moreover, dozens of the checks had been made out to nonexistent people at nonexistent addresses.

Nanco's documentation on the claims also proved to be counterfeit. Release forms had been forged in one handwriting and the checks had been cashed in another. Checks were signed by Capasso, and the signatures on the bank, converting them to cash, belonged to Nanco employees—clerks and drivers. The evidence was clear: Capasso was submitting false liability claims against his own company and pocketing the cash. Between 1981 and 1983 alone, he stole more than $350,000 in this fashion.

An audit of Nanco's books and bank records showed that Capasso had looted his own company of an additional $1.2 million via fraudulent bookkeeping, and used most of the money to renovate and lavishly decorate his two apartments. More than $700,000 was siphoned out of Nanco to the Lennie Construction Corporation, to pay for work on the Fifth Avenue duplex while Andy and Nancy were still living there together.

While the evidence of tax fraud against Capasso was solid, the investigators were unable to trace the fate of another sum, amounting to nearly $500,000, that had been diverted from Nanco. But when it learned that Bess Myerson had about thirty separate brokerage accounts, kept in the names of her daughter, son-in-law, and four-year-old granddaughter, the U.S. Attorney's office subpoenaed Bess Myerson to testify before the Capasso grand jury. Myerson took as her lawyer Fred Hafetz.

On December 22, 1986, Bess Myerson invoked her Fifth Amendment right before the grand jury on almost every question asked of her. She had made a calculated judgment. She must have been fully aware that she could not answer some questions truthfully without incriminating herself or Andy Capasso. She had been a suspect for months, and prior to her appearance before this grand jury, her lawyer had been informed that Myerson was now a potential target as well. Hafetz had been advised in advance that Myerson would be asked about the hiring of Sukhreet Gabel, about her misleading October 1983 letter to the mayor, about the gifts from Capasso she never disclosed, and about her personal finances.

The blunder Myerson made was not telling Koch what she had done. She deluded herself into thinking it could somehow be kept secret. But in June 1986, Koch had declared he would fire any city official who refused to cooperate fully with a prosecutor probing city corruption. Myerson was building a trap for herself.

On Monday, January 5, 1987, Marcia Kramer got her first tip that Bess Myerson had taken the Fifth Amendment, but because she was home with the flu she decided she would wait until she recovered to pursue the rumor. By Friday, Kramer had received two more calls from sources repeating the same allegation. Although Kramer will not identify her sources by name, she places them "close to people in City Hall. These were people trying to protect Koch from himself. The motive of these leakers was damage control. These were people who were aghast at what Myerson had done. People in power wanted this story to get out."

Kramer herself was leery of the story. Without any documents, she had no way of verifying the tip, and she didn't want to write an incorrect account after all her accurate early reporting. Giuliani's office would not comment, or confirm her information off the record, or even wink in code that it was true.

On January 9, however, one of Kramer's sources called back and told her that WNBC-TV reporter Mike Taiibi had the story and was going to air it at 6:00 that evening. Kramer now had to follow it through, and first called Myerson, who, through a spokesman, denied the rumor. She next reached Hafetz, who refused to confirm or deny. After watching Taiibi's report on television, she wrote her story for the January 10 edition of the *News*. It appeared on the first anniversary of Donald Manes's first suicide attempt, the event that shifted the political center of gravity in the city, and provided the impetus for the Capasso/ Myerson investigation.

The mayor learned that his cultural affairs commissioner, campaign companion, and friend of twenty years had taken the Fifth Amendment only when he watched Taiibi's televised report. Although Koch was privately furious, he was forgiving in public, and at a press conference the following morning announced, "I have confidence in Bess Myerson's integrity."

At first Myerson explained to the media that she hadn't notified the mayor of her refusal to testify because she had been so advised by her lawyers. But a few days later, Myerson admitted to one of her favorite newspeople, *Post* gossip columnist Cindy Adams, "The reason I didn't tell the mayor in advance was, I suppose, because I imagined he'd have told me not to do that."

Myerson's taking the Fifth Amendment, and her failure to inform the mayor, either before or after the fact, created another media firestorm. Reporters and editors began to wonder what she had to hide, and rumors of Capasso's indictment began to spread and nourish the media's belated frenzy. On January 13, Myerson announced she was taking a ninety-day leave of absence from her job, and in a statement to the press said: "I have done nothing wrong. I will return to my position in ninety days." She also indicated there would be "a city investigation concerning the subject matters of the grand jury appearance. I agree with the appropriateness of this procedure and expect to testify at this inquiry." She concluded the statement: "I plan no further comment to the media until I return to my position as commissioner."

The following day, Andy Capasso was indicted for evading $774,000 in corporate and personal income taxes.

At his arraignment on Thursday, January 22, Capasso stunned everyone by pleading guilty to all nine counts in his indictment. There had been no plea bargaining with the U.S. Attorney's office, and the prosecutors were not notified in advance of Capasso's intentions.

Capasso tried to make his decision look as if it were based on chivalry and gallantry. After his court appearance, he stood on the steps of the federal courthouse, in a lightly falling snow, and said he wanted the press to know that, despite his guilty plea, Bess Myerson had not provided any assistance "in the conduct of my matrimonial proceeding."

Capasso's strategy had the element of being too clever by half. He had presented his plea to Judge Charles Stewart, who had the reputation of being the softest sentencing judge in the Southern District. Because of the system of two-week rotation, Stewart happened to be sitting in the arraignment part on this day, and Capasso's lawyer, Jay Goldberg, was a scholar on the sentencing patterns of Southern District judges. It looked like an astute, although risky maneuver, but it was too public, too naked. Soon stories were appearing in the press about what light sentences Charles Stewart was known to give out in white-collar cases, including one by Murray Kempton, who wrote that "Stewart was on the calendar bench and Goldberg pressed toward him with all haste short of the ungainly."

In preparation for the sentencing, David Lawrence wrote an incendiary memorandum to Judge Stewart. Lawrence quoted from the 1984 FBI electronic bug that recorded mob boss Anthony (Fat Tony) Salerno talking about Capasso. He emphasized Capasso's refusal to provide any information to prosecutors that might help clean up the city's corruption. He quoted Jay Goldberg's statement to federal prosecutors that his client didn't want to be a "rat," and that "it will take more than a tax case to make him talk." Lawrence was convinced that if Capasso really did feel contrite, and if his guilty plea was not just a cynical bet on a generous judge, he would give important testimony on politicians, and on racketeers in the construction and concrete industries.

On March 30, Judge Stewart pronounced his sentence, declaring:

"Mr. Capasso, as I mentioned earlier, in sentencing you, I am not taking into account any of the information I have received about your alleged failure to cooperate, or any of the suggestions that you are somehow involved in municipal corruption or other mysterious things. I am focusing only on the income tax fraud which you have pled guilty to.

"As Mr. Goldberg has indicated, the income tax fraud involved here is quite serious and indeed I am amazed that someone with your intelligence, your abilities, and your resources, financial resources, found it necessary to engage in such deliberate, ongoing, long-term fraud."

Stewart then sentenced Capasso to four years in prison and fined him $500,000. The attempt at judge-shopping had backfired. Judge Stewart might have resented the expectation he would be an easy mark, and despite the judge's denials, the argument that the penitent was holding back valuable knowledge of municipal corruption probably did influence the comparatively stiff sanction.

Within a week Bess Myerson had begun behaving as erratically as she had in 1980. Without an office to go to, she found her days formless and unstructured. The mayor had named former federal judge Harold Tyler (no relation to Andrew) to investigate the circumstances behind her refusal to testify, and to report back to him in ninety days. Myerson had trouble in mind and time on her hands, and in violation of her vow of silence with the media, she started to contact reporters in an almost obsessive way.

Her first call was to Mike Taiibi of WNBC-TV on February 3, in the middle of the afternoon. "There's no validity to any of the charges," she told him, and began rambling. "Look, I took the fifth because I sat with four lawyers, and that's what they told me to do. And it's the grand jury. Nobody is gonna know, because you can't talk about it. So I didn't. I held up my end of the bargain. But the prosecutors didn't.

"I mean, really. Do you think, really, I'd make any calls to anyone so Andy could get a contract? Christ, I'm not fucking stupid. And I have too much respect for the man I helped get into office. . . .

"The prosecutor wants to ask me, 'What color was the room you were all meeting in?' Hell, I'm gonna say 'blue,' but I know there's those hostile witnesses who have already said it's 'green.' And now the prosecutors are going to charge me with perjury. So the only thing to do is clam up.

"You know what Italians say? Andy uses the expression 'I swear on my daughter's eyes.' Well, I swear on my daughter's eyes all this stuff is bullshit. . . ."

About a month later Myerson contacted Patricia Morrisroe, who was writing an article about her for *New York* magazine, at 9:00 one morning. She kept Morrisroe on the phone for more than seven hours, with a half-hour break for lunch in the middle. Most of Myerson's monologue was about envy, sex, and hostility. She painted herself as the victim of Nancy Capasso, claiming that Capasso wanted to ruin her reputation because she was a celebrity.

"There's a great deal of jealousy because most women haven't achieved what I have, and because they don't have more men in their lives. . . . By the way, have you spoken to any of my lovers? . . . I am not the type of person to go after men. Men go after me. And I choose among them. . . . The reason this is happening is that I'm a woman. I'm a Miss America . . . I'm queen of the Jews . . . I'm a commissioner. I'm the perfect route to the downfall of this administration."

"Is it possible to continue this in person?" Morrisroe finally asked at 5:15 P.M., her ear aching from an entire day of a telephone receiver pressed against it.

"No," Myerson replied. "My lawyer told me I'm not supposed to talk to the press."

A few weeks later, however, Myerson consented to be interviewed by Morrisroe face to face.

"Who have you been talking to? Who? Who?" Myerson demanded, and then, answering her own question: "Look, I don't know who you are talking to. Some poor souls in my department. All you are hearing is riffraff and *National Enquirer* popcorn. I've always had people who have done things through jealousy that have been deliberately injurious to me."

She then countered Morrisroe's question about her tendency to become involved in messy relationships with a personal attack: "Listen, Patricia. Maybe that's why you're not married. . . . You don't take enough risks. Think about that."

During this same period Myerson also called Marcia Kramer at her home and delivered an hour's disjointed monologue, which led Kramer to conclude that Myerson "was drunk or on drugs."

"I've got a big story to tell," Myerson kept repeating, and Kramer thought the implication was that if she would stop writing about Myerson, Myerson would give her information on somebody else. Myerson also began to refer to herself again as "the queen of the Jews."

The mayor received Harold Tyler's report on Bess Myerson on Wednesday, April 8. After he and his top aides read it thoroughly, it was decided to make public only a brief summary of the report's seventy-five pages, even though the mayor had assured the media that its full contents would be released. Giuliani agreed to go along with the decision to keep the report secret, concerned that if he opposed its sealing, he could be accused of trying to generate prejudicial publicity and of willfully violating the fair trial rights of Myerson and Judge Gabel.

At 9:15 on Wednesday night Myerson called Gracie Mansion, and according to Koch, submitted her resignation in a conversation of only "a few moments'" duration. Myerson had not seen the report, but her lawyer, Fred Hafetz, had been informed of its findings by Koch.

The next morning a somber Ed Koch held a press conference to announce Myerson's resignation. In place of the Tyler report, Koch issued a strange 156-word summary, written in generalities. While one of the five sentences of the mayor's statement exculpated Myerson, the summary did state that Tyler had found her guilty of "serious misconduct" in "the hiring of Sukhreet Gabel, and with respect to her subsequent explanation for that decision to the Mayor." It further indicated that "there were improprieties with respect to Commissioner Myerson's use of city employees for personal use and with respect to her failure to report gifts from Carl Capasso."

The last sentence of the summary, which disclosed that Myerson had never kept her promise to testify before Judge Tyler under oath, reported in legalese: "Myerson chose not to speak with Judge Tyler on a voluntary, non-immunized basis."

With the statement the mayor also released a copy of his letter to Myerson accepting her resignation, which assured her, "My affection for you remains unabated. . . . Our personal friendship will continue undiminished."

Throughout his press conference the mayor was careful not to say anything that might irritate Myerson. Although she had lied to him, and betrayed his trust, he did not call her a crook, a wacko, a schmuck, or any other insult in his standard repertoire. Instead, Ed Koch declared that Bess Myerson had been "a superb commissioner," and that he was accepting her resignation out of "duty" and "obligation."

Despite pressure from the gathered reporters, Koch would not divulge any details of the report beyond his bland 156 words. He replied to long, complex questions with three- or four-word monotone answers. He seemed to be struggling not to express his innermost feelings, fearing that he might make vivid the specific acts behind the vague accusations of "misconduct" and "improprieties." It was, all in all, a masterful gambit of public relations.

Koch seemed afraid of Myerson. She was erratic and capable of saying almost anything. She knew many potentially embarrassing secrets about him, and had already been quoted in *New York* magazine as stating, "I'm the perfect route to the downfall of this administration." Some of the mayor's friends read this as a veiled threat of blackmail.

Two days later, with the Tyler report locked away, Ed Koch invited Bess Myerson to be a guest at his Passover seder at Gracie Mansion. On April 13, Myerson was one of fourteen family members and close friends at the mayor's first-night seder.

The *Times, News, Post,* NBC, ABC, and CBS filed a lawsuit under the Freedom of Information Act to make the Tyler report public. On May 8 there was a hearing in Manhattan Supreme Court before Justice Bruce Wright. Arguing for the Koch administration, assistant corporation counsel Doron Gopstein warned that witnesses cited in the report could be murdered by the Mafia if it were unsealed. "One key witness was nearly killed," Gopstein said. "Should we wait until there is another shot?"*

A reasonable compromise of selective disclosure was always available on the Tyler report. The names of any endangered witnesses could be redacted. Portions of the report, or at least a more comprehensive summary, could have been made public. But the Koch administration remained inflexible; the entire report had to remain secret to protect life and safety. And Judge Wright agreed, issuing a fourteen-page opinion on May 18, keeping the report confidential.

May 1987 found Ed Koch in an optimistic mood for the first time in seventeen months. He told his friends, with no small relief, "The scandal is over." He could see that his popularity in his private polling was inching back up: his job approval rating had improved to 55 percent, while his disapproval rating was only 25 percent. He started to taunt his potential electoral rivals that he was still invincible, still destined to serve three more terms. He had just awarded himself a salary increase of 16 percent, to $130,000 a year, and there was hardly a ripple in the polity. The mayor felt confident that at last there would be no more surprises, no more press conferences called to respond to news of yet another indictment.

Late in May, however, Jack Newfield met with a government official who had read the complete Tyler report and was troubled that the mayor's summary was not a faithful reflection of its actual findings, which he described as "shocking." The official was also angered that the mayor had invited Myerson to Gracie Mansion even after he had read the report. The official had too much integrity to violate a court order and leak the

---

*Gopstein's reference was to the Nanco's former bookkeeper, who was shot at after he declined Capasso's offer to provide a lawyer and hired one of his own choosing. The day after this former employee was interviewed by federal agents, several gunshots were fired into his home, with one bullet missing his head by inches.

But all this took place before the witnesses testified before the grand jury, before Capasso was indicted and pleaded guilty. There was no longer any motive to harm or frighten anyone involved with the case.

report directly to Newfield, but did urge him to "drop whatever you're doing" and "find a way to get a copy." This same official, who was in a position to know, said the city's argument in court, that witnesses might be killed if the report was made public, "was bullshit."

Newfield followed the advice of the tipster and contacted a dozen sources who he thought might be able to provide a copy of the Tyler report. He finally found one who was willing, though the source was too nervous to meet Newfield face to face, even on a street corner at midnight. So the source agreed to mail it to Newfield's home on the condition that Newfield say that the report arrived anonymously, and that he didn't know the identity of the sender. Newfield had to promise he would "go to jail" before he named his contact, a promise given with the comforting knowledge that New York State had a strong shield law to protect journalists from naming their confidential sources.

One day passed. Two days passed. The package did not arrive. Newfield became concerned about the legendary incompetence of the postal system. The source swore the envelope had been mailed to the right address.

Finally, the Tyler report arrived in the mail about noon on Friday, June 5. Newfield called Wayne Barrett and suggested they write the story together all through the weekend, if their wives and children approved. Newfield went to the *Voice* offices, duplicated the Tyler report, and he and Barrett read it together for the first time. Before Newfield got to page ten he asked *Voice* editor Martin Gottlieb to hold the front page. Neither Gottlieb, nor *Voice* libel lawyer Victor Kovner, had any hesitation about publishing the story.

The Tyler report was an extraordinary document, written with narrative power and dramatized with vivid anecdotes. It found there had been a "secret understanding" between Bess Myerson and Judge Gabel, and that the job for Sukhreet was a bribe to fix the judge; it stated conclusively that Myerson "intended and did improperly influence" Judge Gabel. It described how Myerson's deputy, Richard Bruno, knowingly lied to the press and drafted the deceitful letter to the mayor. Tyler called Judge Gabel's sworn testimony "unbelievable." He demonstrated that Myerson had repeatedly lied to the mayor, and that she had received "substantial" gifts from Andy Capasso and never disclosed them as is required by law.

The Tyler report contained numerous revealing and inflammatory little details. Myerson used her city driver to deliver money to her stockbroker, and instructed him to falsify the mileage reported on the travel logs he submitted to the city. Myerson had said, "If I don't have a driver, the job is not worth it to me." Myerson told Herb Rickman that Sukhreet Gabel's hiring had been "cleared" by City Hall. In its specifics, the report made Bess Myerson appear to be a schemer of astonishing audacity.

Myerson was depicted as setting out to take advantage of a lonely and vulnerable woman in order to get what she wanted from that woman's mother. She saw human weakness and exploited it, and her manipulativeness was captured in so rich a prose that it seemed intended for an audience wider than just Ed Koch.

On Tuesday evening, June 9, before the *Voice* reached the newsstands, Newfield called Rudolph Giuliani at home to alert him that the story was about to be released and to give him time to arrange protection for any witnesses, just in case the city's justification for sealing the report had any validity. In fact, no witnesses needed any protection, and it was clear from Tyler's conclusions that the principal witnesses had been Sukhreet Gabel, Judge Gabel's law secretary Howard Leventhal, Herb Rickman, and various servants and chauffeurs to Andy Capasso and Bess Myerson. None of these were people likely to be harmed by the Mafia, as Doron Gopstein had luridly suggested in court.

"How Bess Bought Justice" appeared on the front page of the *Village Voice* on Wednesday, June 10. By noon three television news crews were waiting at the *Voice* offices to interview Barrett and Newfield. The city's corruption scandal had clearly not ended. The *Post* came out at midday with a huge front-page headline stating THE BESS COVERUP EXPLODES, which a few hours later was modified to: BESS BLASTED IN "FIX" REPORT, and finally, in the evening edition, to: BESS MESS ROCKS CITY HALL. The next morning the *Daily News* devoted two full pages to excerpts from the report.

On Thursday Koch held a crowded press conference at City Hall. He took his first measured step away from his campaign companion by stating, "It's very sad what's happened to Bess Myerson. Bess Myerson has fallen from grace."

The mayor was asked why he had never referred any of the

allegations against Myerson to his Department of Investigations.

"That did not occur to me," he explained, "because it was not reasonable to assume she was lying."

Why had he invited Myerson to the Passover seder even after he had read the Tyler report?

"I wouldn't turn my back on her," Koch insisted. "She was alone in a state of depression. I was worried about her mental state."

Why had he ordered the Tyler report kept secret?

"There was a need to protect witnesses."

In response to this conference, however, three New York daily newspapers published editorials concluding that Koch was wrong to have sealed the Tyler report, given the seriousness of its revelations. The *New York Post,* for years the most pro-Koch paper, wrote:

> The Tyler Report on the Bess Myerson affair offers damning documentation of serious wrongdoing by a high public official. For just that reason, Mayor Koch should never have sealed it. That report always belonged in the public domain. . . . The argument for keeping Tyler's finding secret did not outweigh the public's right to know. And it's hard to avoid the conclusion that the Mayor's primary purpose was to limit the political fallout from the Myerson episode.

The *Times* took a similar view:

> Mr. Koch, for his part, needs to explain why a Mayor who would stand firmly against corruption in his administration, sought to keep the report secret. . . . Worries that release might jeopardize ongoing prosecutions may have merit, but surely more of Mr. Tyler's story about Ms. Myerson's sordid manipulation of the judge and her daughter could have been safely revealed.
>
> With the report under lock and key, Mr. Koch appeared to deserve praise for sensitive handling of Ms. Myerson's case. Now he needs to explain why he did not provide more information and express more outrage until now.

The *Daily News* said in its editorial:

> At long last, the Bess Myerson rock has been kicked over, and what's crawling out is sickening: arrogance, abuse of power, payroll manipulation, case-fixing, coverup. Small wonder so many people fought so wildly to keep former Judge Harold Tyler's report secret. . . .
>
> The Tyler report also fingers a Myerson aide, Assistant Cultural Affairs Commissioner Richard Bruno, as taking part in Bess's scheme to whitewash the hiring of Justice Gabel's daughter. Mayor Koch has known about this ever since he received the report in April. Why didn't he fire Bruno on the spot? The lapse is shocking.*
>
> So is Koch's blind sympathy for Myerson, which continues to this day. Koch's people have axed whistleblowers without a trace of compassion—or shame. Yet even after he knew the Tyler report's contents, the Mayor allowed Myerson to resign and preserve the fiction *she* was the victim, while she wallowed in the most cynical graft. Friendship is no excuse for tolerating gross corruption.

On Friday, June 12, in the middle of the afternoon, the mayor held a small press conference in his office. Only a few cameras and a handful of print reporters were present. Koch sat slouched in his chair, looking deflated and depressed.

The mayor had called the conference to badger the Board of Estimate and city council about the municipal budget, whose deadline for passage was imminent. But the reporters still wanted to talk about the fallout from the Tyler report. For perhaps the first time in his nine years as mayor, Koch lost his composure. "I don't know," "I don't recall," and "I can't reconstruct that" were his replies to question after question.

After Koch said he had no memory of events in 1983, Wayne Barrett asked him to think back to when he first read the Tyler report two months earlier. Barrett wondered if the mayor could recall whether the report's account of the activities of Herb Rickman rang a bell with him, sounded like something he had heard before, or whether it was news to him—the first time

---

*The day *after* the *Voice* published the Tyler report, Koch announced that Bruno had resigned his position, effective July 1.

he had ever heard that Rickman had warned both Myerson and Gabel not to go ahead with the hiring of Sukhreet. The mayor paused; the mayor grimaced; the mayor grappled; but again, he couldn't remember.

Koch was so furious about the leaking of the Tyler report that he ordered his investigations commissioner, Kenneth Conboy, to track it to its source, and DOI spent hundreds of hours investigating Barrett and Newfield, with what the *Daily News* called "unusual fervor." Over three months, forty-three suspects were interviewed, many under oath. Law clerks in the appellate division were questioned, for the mayor had stated that he believed it was there that the leaker worked. U.S. Attorney Giuliani was questioned, and aides to the mayor were quoted as saying they suspected Giuliani was the source. David Lawrence and Tony Lombardi were questioned under oath. Even Judge Wright, who had sealed the report, fell under suspicion, and he, too, was put under oath and grilled for several hours. Eventually the DOI admitted it could not find our Deep Throat.

Having convinced himself the scandal was over, Koch found himself besieged again, and reeling from the aftershocks of the Tyler report. The reformer who was elected by promising to "get the hacks off the payroll" was reduced to reciting flimsy rationalizations:

"Only five people have been indicted so far."

"Why didn't you reporters know about Donald Manes and Stanley Friedman?"

"Corruption is worse in Chicago, Boston, and Washington."

"None of this has anything to do with me. It's the acts of others."

On July 1, *Newsday* published the results of a Gallup poll of 1,013 New Yorkers, taken between June 19 and 24. Seventy-eight percent of the respondents believed "Koch should have known about the corruption in his administration." When asked, "Do you think Koch has or hasn't done everything he can to investigate and resolve the Myerson situation?," only 28 percent replied that he had done everything he could have. Another question asked: has Koch told all he knows about what's been going on in his administration? By 59 to 29 percent, the answer was no.

The Myerson scandal had done more to erode Koch's popularity and credibility than any preceding event. There was an irony in this; the voters were most disappointed in Koch because he had betrayed an illusion he had sold to them. The Myerson intimacy of the 1977 campaign had been fabricated by Koch and Garth. Koch and Myerson were never lovers, just friends. In 1987, Ed Koch paid a price for the politics of sexual fantasy he had practiced a decade earlier. He and Myerson had remained indissolubly bonded in the public eye by gossip Koch invented to win a long-ago election.

On July 2, the appellate division finally released its decision in the Capasso divorce. This time the appeals judges imposed their own solution. Their forty-two-page decision began by reminding everyone that they had originally reversed Andrew Tyler and ordered him to award "some recompense" to Nancy Capasso. They admitted that they were tempted to remand the whole matter again, "perhaps to a different judge," but because there was such a complete record in the case, they had chosen to make all the final findings themselves, a clear sign of displeasure with Tyler.

In a unanimous ruling, five appellate judges (Wallach, Kupferman, Milonas, Rosenberger, and Sullivan) awarded Nancy Capasso $5.5 million, as opposed to Tyler's $2 million. The higher court found the marital property was worth $15.6 million, not the $4.2 million Tyler had insisted on since December 1985.

But Nancy Capasso had little to celebrate, for she soon learned it would take years for her to receive any of this settlement money. A few days before he went to jail, Andy Capasso signed contracts with the Aetna Insurance Company and the European-American Bank, giving them the right to sell his properties to pay debts owed by Nanco. Although the appellate court had awarded Nancy the $1.9 million bay-front estate in Westhampton and the first $3 million from the sale of the Fifth Avenue duplex, Andy had given the rights of first lien against these properties to Nanco's creditors—to outmaneuver his wife.

Months after this appellate reversal of Judge Tyler, Nancy Capasso had less money than ever. She had to hire more lawyers to fight the insurance company and the bank to collect her legally entitled divorce settlement. "Andy once warned me that he would make me pay for the rest of my life," Nancy Capasso now recalls. "Even from prison, he is still making me pay."

.   .   .

On Wednesday, October 7, 1987, Rudy Giuliani announced at a press conference the indictment of Bess Myerson, Andy Capasso, and Judge Hortense Gabel. Myerson was charged with conspiracy, mail fraud, using interstate facilities to violate state bribery laws, and obstruction of justice. The obstruction count was based on Myerson's visit to Sukhreet Gabel in June 1986, during which she attempted to induce Sukhreet to lie to the federal grand jury. The basic facts outlined by the indictment were in the stories published in the *Daily News* in May and June 1986, which the mayor had deplored as "McCarthyism." The outline of the conspiracy could be found in the Tyler report, which the mayor ordered sealed in April 1987.

Giuliani called the Myerson indictment "a very sad case," a fair assessment of the circumstances. Judge Gabel, nearly blind at seventy-four, once had a luminous reputation but tarnished it, perhaps out of an excess of maternal love. Her own depressive daughter, whom she had tried so desperately to help, had testified in the grand jury against her. Bess Myerson had been the inspiration of a generation, a true working-class heroine. But she was self-destructive in love, and prey to Lord Acton's axiom that power corrupts. Now, with her lover already in prison, she herself faced trial on corruption charges. Andy Capasso had been a self-made millionaire with powerful friends. Now his life and his company were in ruins. Nancy Capasso was still being denied her settlement, twice a victim of the legal system. Sukhreet Gabel was still unemployed and confused about what she had done. There were no winners left standing on this battlefield.

Exactly ten years before, on October 10, 1977, Ed Koch and Bess Myerson had led the Columbus Day Parade up Fifth Avenue, holding hands. The festive crowds lining the sidewalks cheered the new king and queen of New York. Baton twirlers and high school bands marched behind them, stirring martial music filled the autumn air, a new era seemed about to commence. Ed Koch had won the Democratic primary, and his election in November was regarded as a formality; he was already viewed as the mayor-elect. Here was the candidate who vowed to be different from other politicians, the candidate whose slogan had been the promise of competency after years of the clubhouse and charisma.

Now, ten years later, all that glittering promise had crumbled into this sad case. So many of the friends who made him mayor and tried to make him governor were now gone from power. Donald Manes was dead. Stanley Friedman and Meade Esposito were disgraced felons. City commissioners Anthony Ameruso, Jay Turoff, and Lester Shafran had been convicted after trials. And now Miss America, the mayor's commissioner of culture, was in the dock for fixing a judge in a tawdry divorce case.

In the end, Ed Koch had not been different enough. His tragic flaw had been a desire for power, not money. He became the mayor who didn't want to know. Admiring his own performance, he didn't notice anyone else's. While he had been gazing into the mirror, his city had been for sale.

Epilogue

ON A SUNLIT September day in 1988, two years and nine months after his inauguration to a third term, Ed Koch traveled across the Brooklyn Bridge to the borough's Technical High School. Waiting for him were all the nearly 3,000 inspectors from the fire, buildings, health, housing, ports, transportation, and sanitation departments, as well as those from the Taxi and Limousine Commission. The top brass from these agencies were also there, as was Kevin Frawley, the 36-year-old new investigations commissioner who was acting as the master of ceremonies for what was planned as a combination forum and rally for honesty-in-government. The mayor and each commissioner were prepared to address the inspectors, a record number of whom had been busted in recent months on bribery charges. A forty-five-page anticorruption booklet was ready for distribution to the entire inspectional staff, which enforces everything from the building to the health codes.

When Ed Koch entered the Brooklyn Tech auditorium, the packed house instantly broke out in boos. The response started slowly, but built, and by the time he reached the stage, the mayor was buffeted by a crescendo of abuse. Even the hundreds of inspectors hidden in the balcony joined in. Standing in the aisles and sitting in their seats, this army of shirtsleeved bureaucrats, many of them waving their arms in a contemptuous gesture of dismissal, revolted as one at the mere sight of their leader.

No one, least of all the mayor, had anticipated this greeting. Though the appearance had been noted in the mayor's day book, most of the City Hall press corps had not even come, assuming that there would be no story. A single photographer, and no television crews, had accompanied Koch, a sharp contrast to the clicking locusts of inaugural day. "You're all under arrest," Koch grinned when he got to the mike, in an effort to convert the hostility to a joke. "To those of you who are trying to turn this into a circus, you are making an error," the mayor shouted, trying to be heard above thousands of his own employees.

"In this audience," Koch persisted, "you know that there are people who sometime in the coming year will take advantage of their position and steal. We are going to go after every single miscreant in advance. . . . You're on notice. I want to make it very clear. The vast majority of you are honest. But you have a second obligation. Not just to be honest, but to turn in those that are not. If you know that someone is stealing, and you don't tell us, you have violated your obligation and we'll punish you, too."

Likening the jeering audience to "a coliseum of Roman vintage" and jabbing the air with his forefinger, Koch reddened, his lips tightened, his long brow furrowed seemingly to the top of his bald head. "Yes, you can boo," he said hoarsely. "But I want you to know that those who are booing . . . that what you've just displayed is that you think it's okay. It's not okay and we want you to know it. It's not okay for you personally to steal."

Finally he announced to cheers that he was going to conclude, and he reached for his favorite ethics one-liner. He had closed his inaugural with it, but had used it then as an introduction of praise for the dais guests who were facing the January wind with him—Donald Manes, Stanley Friedman, Bess Myerson, Tony Ameruso, Jay Turoff, and many others who had since been swept up in the anguish of the intervening years. "The noblest of professions is public service, if it is done honestly and done well," he said for the thousandth time, but now in a voice strained with resignation. "I believe that heart and soul. I believe that most of you perform nobly, honestly, well. Those that don't, beware."

What Koch could not understand was that the inspectors were tired of being singled out. They knew that at worst some of them were petty thieves in a government consumed at the highest levels with graft. The same day that Koch was lecturing them he told reporters that Manhattan state senator Manfred Ohrenstein, the Democratic leader of the senate under indictment on 394 felony counts, was "personally honest" and "deserved reelection."

Ohrenstein had just won the Democratic primary in a closely fought race the day before. One of four indicted or convicted candidates running in the five contested state senate districts, he had rejected the mayor's offer of a formal endorsement, apparently out of concern that it might cost him more votes than it gained him. But quietly, through his agent John LoCicero, Koch had helped Ohrenstein in his old Village base. Beyond these four tainted candidates, two other incumbent state senators under indictment were renominated without opposition, and a third ran unopposed though he had just been acquitted in his second criminal case.

Also on the ballot again was nine-term Bronx congressman Mario Biaggi. Biaggi had just been convicted in the Wedtech bribery case, and with a previous federal conviction already on his résumé, he had the distinction of being the only candidate in a city race convicted on more felony counts than he had had terms in office. The only other Bronx congressman, Robert Garcia (who was, like Biaggi, a longtime major booster of the mayor's and had co-chaired the 1985 Koch reelection campaign) was still under investigation by Rudy Giuliani's office. Garcia had been named in open court by federal prosecutors as a recipient of Wedtech bribes and would soon be indicted. Nonetheless he won handily, while Biaggi lost, despite a last-minute rally for the ex-cop that included the head of the police union as one of the speakers.

The inspectors that filled the Brooklyn Tech auditorium that morning may not have had the previous day's ballot in mind as they sat in the mayor's mandatory corruption class. But they knew that no one had gathered, then scolded, the Democratic conference in the state senate or the Bronx congressional delegation. When Koch finished, they lined up at a mike to ask questions. One demanded to know how the mayor could stand up there, "talking to us," when his own administration was engulfed in corruption. An inspector from the Taxi and Limousine Commission exploded: "I want to know why we're on one side of the fence and you're on the other side, and you're throwing stones when you live in a glass house?" The boos swallowed up Koch's muted answer. A few months later, the taxi inspector was fired from his civil service post on a technical violation.

. . .

The September honesty rally was in fact only a small part of a Koch campaign to portray himself, in preparation for his 1989 reelection effort, as the aggressor against ingrained corruption. A week earlier he had entered a Brooklyn Supreme Court to appear, for the first time, at the sentencing of eight people convicted of stealing from the city. The defendants—members of a larger group of twenty-eight low-level employees of a company contracted to collect quarters from the city's parking meters—had been charged with pocketing $50,000 over a three-month period.

The judge in the case, 52-year-old Ruth Moskowitz, had attracted the mayor's attention when she promised a few months earlier that if the defendants pleaded guilty, she would give them conditional discharges, sparing them a jail term or even probation. Since cameras had recently been permitted in state courts, the mayor saw this sentencing as the perfect opportunity for a righteous proclamation. Accompanied by nine aides, Koch went to Moskowitz's Brooklyn court to make a fifteen-minute "victim" statement, warning the judge that her leniency represented "an outright invitation" to steal.

Moskowitz reacted much the same way as the inspectors. When Koch finished and started to leave, she asked him to stay. "[Not] unless you order me," Koch replied. "I am ordering you," Moskowitz interrupted. After questioning her power to require him to stay, he complied, and he listened for twenty-five minutes to a judicial heckle. "I will note this is the first time the mayor is in a courtroom. He has never appeared when a commissioner was being sentenced. He has never appeared when a borough president or someone in high political office was being sentenced.

"These are the little people," she said, noting they had no prior convictions, "and the little people commit crimes, too. Little people are going to be treated just the way the big boys are treated. They are human beings and they have rights, too." The judge said Koch should be more concerned about "the crime committed by the city," pointing out that in 1981 a similar scheme had resulted in arrests but that the city had done little to tighten security since then. "The city has an obligation to every one of us to see to it that it isn't easy to steal thousands of dollars. I think the city failed us." Finally, Moskowitz announced that she was going to "release the mayor from custody."

A flushed Koch rushed to the courtroom hallway, where he spoke to reporters in whispered rage, calling Moskowitz's comments a "cheap shot," and pointing to his presentencing letter in the Friedman case as evidence of his willingness to seek tough sentences even when the powerful were involved. He informed a cameraman who had his klieg lights off that his statement was important, and planted his grim face before the lens when the lights went on. The media reacted with condemnations for Moskowitz's sentence, but with some recognition that the judge's comments had hit a raw nerve.

Koch's performance in Moskowitz's courtroom, like his lecture to the inspectors, suggested that the wily old Village chameleon had decided, once again, to cross the street from the Tamawa Club to the VID. Tom Manton, the ex–law partner of PVB witness Michael Dowd, who eventually succeeded Manes as the Democratic leader of Queens; George Friedman, the new Bronx boss; and Howard Golden, the New Brooklyn party head, had by now made public statements hinting that they preferred an as yet undetermined alternative to Koch in 1989. Koch was already attempting to turn these rejections into an ironic reelection theme of opposition to the bosses. As desperate as such a ploy might seem, the polls were telling Koch that he had to come up with something.

A *Newsday* poll at the beginning of 1988 revealed that 69 percent of New Yorkers thought corruption "was worse now" than when Koch became mayor; only 5 percent said municipal government had become more honest under Koch. Forty-six percent blamed Koch "a lot" for the corruption, while only 17 percent said he was "not at all" responsible. In September, just days after the informal poll taken by the inspectors at the Brooklyn Tech rally, *Newsday* reported that Koch's ratings had hit an all-time low of 34 percent favorable, and a new high of 48 percent unfavorable. A few months later, in the spring of 1989, the same poll put Koch below 30 percent favorable for the first time ever.

Damaging as they were, the scandals were not the only causes of Koch's waning popularity. His orgy of verbal assaults on Jesse Jackson during the presidential primary in April 1988 hurt, as did a virtual endorsement of the British occupation of Ireland on a pilgrimage there with Cardinal O'Connor. His flip attacks on beggars, street vendors, and the homeless had taken on such a churlish quality that more and more people began to wonder if, as *New York* magazine put it, "the clutch had slipped." Still owned by Rupert Murdoch, a longtime champion of the mayor's, *New York* ran a cover story in May that nonetheless predicted that Koch's fourth campaign would "devolve into a public tragedy."

However ill-advised his public statements, the principal obstacle to Candidate Koch's effort to reposition himself as a reformer continued to be the municipal scandals, which by now seemed as if they simply would not die. The mayor had convinced himself during the worst months of 1986 that by the time he had to run again, scandal headlines would be a faint memory in a city that moves on ever so quickly. Instead, they continued to haunt him, even taking on new forms. A frightening one—even for the media magic of David Garth—was the emergence of service breakdowns indisputably connected to the moral breakdown of the administration.

In the spring of 1988, the heavily traveled Williamsburg Bridge was closed to traffic, spawning a nightmare of clogged arteries stretching from Brooklyn to Manhattan. The Williamsburg, as well as several other critical city bridges, had become a monument to deferred maintenance, and in its now-dangerous condition it was threatened with prolonged closure.

The commissioner who had neglected the bridges was none other than Anthony Ameruso. A month before the Williamsburg shutdown, tape transcripts released by federal prosecutors revealed that Ameruso's sponsor, Meade Esposito, had been talking to him about buying a Lopat chemical concrete enhancement product for city bridges when the scandal blew. The tapes indicated that Esposito and his alleged mob sidekick Fritzy Giovanelli were engaged in a scheme to extort a lucrative franchise from a New Jersey chemical company seeking city contracts. Prosecutors believed that the Manes explosion in January killed the then-budding bridge deal.

The deputy commissioner under Ameruso who oversaw the bridge maintenance unit for eight Koch years was Henry Fulton, a Queens appointee friendly with Manes. Fulton resigned just before the scandal hit, and it was revealed that he had been for two years a business partner in a real estate deal with the principal of an asphalt firm to whom he had given $3.5 million in emergency asphalt contracts. Fulton, who was also the highways commissioner, went to work as a consultant for the asphalt contractor as soon as he left the city.

It was during the same period that the city was also hit with a catastrophic decline in ambulance service. The newspapers began reporting that people were dying because ambulance response time was slow, and getting slower. As much as half of the 246-car ambulance fleet, the city grudgingly conceded, was out of service at any time, particularly during the heat of the summer. The man who had traveled the country buying ambulances and running up much-investigated expenses doing it was Victor Botnick, who had frequently cited the lowering of emergency response time as his greatest achievement at the Health and Hospitals Corporation.

As if to challenge the record of the long-departed Botnick, Emergency Medical Service dispatchers were suddenly appearing at city council hearings and describing just how they were forced to invent response data. They said the deceptive data practices went back as far as 1984 and were "pervasive." While the dispatchers could not pinpoint the origin of these life-or-death lies, they said they knew they came "from the top." In the middle of the ambulance crisis, Koch was forced to bounce his EMS director.

It was not, however, only the service crashes that resurrected the scandal. The major figures who had dominated the dark days of 1986, each of whom was an all-too public reminder of the mayor's criminal associations, resurfaced with alarming regularity two years later.

● Meade Esposito was indicted again, this time with his 61-year-old daughter, in a massive money-laundering scheme engineered through the family printing business, which the Koch campaign was still paying for 1985 services. The indictment, which charged that Esposito "used his connections and influence to obtain lucrative printing business" for the company, listed $200,000 in Esposito kickbacks. Plea bargaining discussions with the feds revolved around Esposito's apparent willingness to admit guilt if his daughter could be spared indictment. But this gentlemanly gesture, according to law enforcement sources, was withdrawn when prosecutors made it clear that Meade and another partner in the business would have to "come clean" and cooperate fully. Not even a daughter was worth that to the 81-year-old *omertà* loyalist. She wound up

pleading guilty and being sentenced to house arrest, while Esposito used surgery to delay another trial. In the end, the
charges against Esposito were dismissed when the judge found
he was incompetent to stand trial.

● The mayor's old friends Bronx borough president Stanley Simon, who had long been Koch's most reliable ally on the
Board of Estimate, and Mario Biaggi were convicted in Giuliani's massive bribery and extortion case involving Wedtech,
the Bronx defense contractor where a Koch campaign commercial was taped in 1985. The trial testimony was another indictment of the malleability of city government, which delivered
four city-owned sites to Wedtech, including one crucial waterfront property that enabled the company to qualify for a multimillion-dollar navy pontoon contract.

Prosecutors demonstrated at the trial that Simon and
Biaggi's law partner had managed in the space of four days
(including night meetings at City Hall with a deputy mayor and
the port commissioner) to get a commitment that the city
would evict the current corporate tenant on the waterfront site,
another minority business that was not paying its rent, and
install Wedtech. Port commissioner Susan Frank instantly gave
the Biaggi firm a letter agreement promising to lease the premises, as the prosecution noted in summation, "before it was
approved by the Board of Estimate, before a lease [was] drawn
up, before there [was] even an occupancy permit." Simon's
reward for helping Wedtech with this lease and other favors
was a $50,000 bribe—paid in cash, contributions, expenses, and
casino chips.

● Stanley Friedman went on trial again, too, this time on
charges that he bribed state National Guard officials to obtain
a contract for Citisource's handheld computer. While the case
had nothing to do with the city administration and was barely
covered in the press, Friedman once again proved to be an
embarrassment to the mayor. Transferred from federal custody to the city jail at Rikers Island, the thirty-pound-lighter
Friedman, relaxed and resilient, was given a private cell in the
infirmary, segregated from the ordinary prison population. His
wife, Jackie, still a City Hall aide and the recipient of two merit
increases since her husband's conviction, was allowed, unlike
any other visitor, to drive her car across the bridge to the island
prison and right up to the door of the infirmary. (Visitors are
normally required to take a bus to the prison.)

Her escort on her first trip to the prison was none other than Barbara Margolis, the wife of the mayor's best friend, businessman David Margolis. Barbara Margolis could gain entry into any city prison by virtue of her appointment by the mayor to the Board of Corrections. The Margolis family had been the hosts for each of the mayor's preinaugural parties, and the Friedmans had been invited to these very private affairs twice during their heyday. Once Barbara Margolis had gotten Jackie through the door of Rikers the first time, Jackie returned, using her City Hall pass to drive again up to Friedman's quarters. Finally, corrections officials ordered a halt to the special privileges, afraid they would hit the press. They did anyway, and an again redfaced mayor had to publicly forgive the two women. "I think they both understand they embarrassed the administration . . . and I am sure that it will never happen again," he said, noting that Jackie Friedman had supposedly been "taunted" by other prisoners when she rode the Rikers bus. However, her car trips to the prison occurred on the first two days that Friedman had been assigned there.

Friedman waived his rights to a jury, implicitly acknowledging, as he had when he moved the federal case to New Haven, that he could not face the verdict of his peers. Smiling and chatting amiably throughout the trial, he presented no formal defense and did not even challenge the credibility of witnesses he had maligned in New Haven. Brought in and out of court in handcuffs, his thinning body was by now overwhelmed by the same suits he had worn at the Connecticut trial. He had let his dark hair grow out, and, without the nightly toxic of alcohol, his eyes gleamed again. He seemed at ease with himself; even the shakes were gone. It was the third version of Stanley Friedman to go public in as many years.

He was convicted by Supreme Court Judge Marie Santagata, who subsequently added a seven-year state sentence to his dozen federal years. It was a shocking decision, apparently designed to persuade tough guy Friedman to talk. Giuliani had written a presentencing memo to the state judge urging a maximum penalty, citing Friedman's unrepentant silence, as had Robert Morgenthau, the Manhattan D.A. who finally won his own Friedman conviction. Federal and state prosecutors tried repeatedly in the ensuing months to reel Friedman in for briefings, bringing him back to New York from his Missouri prison, but he dickered and stonewalled.

● Even the December 1988 acquittal of Bess Myerson had a downside for Koch, exposing him as a fickle friend who could remember neither his 1977 debt to Myerson when she was in trouble, nor how she had deceived him when she beat a troubled Giuliani case. The mayor's postverdict exultation, after he had himself been a government witness against her during the trial, was unseemly, even for Koch. He said he had "hoped she'd be exonerated and she was," announced that he would be "proud" to have her campaign at his side again, and dismissed as commonplace her repeated lies to him about the hiring of Sukhreet Gabel.

Only months earlier, on the eve of her trial, Koch had begun formally dissociating himself from her in a *Times* story: Myerson would be transformed "from a political embarrassment into a personal tragedy." As Dave Garth and the rest of the mayor's circle contended to reporters, Myerson was "a troubled woman, a fallen heroine whose credibility—and therefore ability to damage Koch" had already nosedived. But there was no way for City Hall to avoid the reality that Ed Koch had made Myerson a commissioner when she was already a troubled woman, and that he had supported her virtually up to the day of her indictment. His verbal support had continued, even after an investigator he appointed, Harold Tyler, had completed an extensive investigation and concluded that she had used a city job to get an alimony reduction. Koch had abandoned Myerson only when an indictment turned Tyler's findings into a criminal charge.

The widely publicized testimony pitting daughter Sukhreet against feeble, sweet mother Hortense Gabel turned the trial into the city's most popular news for weeks. Myerson, ashen and in sunglasses, ran a gauntlet of cameras every day. She kissed Capasso in court, though she had been alternating for months with the new woman in Capasso's life, Betty Bienen, on weekend prison visits to Allenwood. (Nancy Capasso had actually bumped into Bienen on Madison Avenue and noticed that Bienen was now wearing the Cartier diamond circlet Andy had given her, and then taken back when he'd seized the bulk of her jewelry.)

In a preliminary hearing, U.S. District Court Judge John Keenan, the mayor's former criminal justice coordinator, who was presiding at the trial, had ruled that if Myerson took the stand, the government could not cross-examine her about her arrest on shoplifting charges in Pennsylvania just a few months earlier. On a visit with Capasso at Allenwood, Myerson had been busted stealing $40 worth of nail polish, earrings, and sandals at a local store, and had pleaded guilty to the charge. While Keenan barred reference to this misdemeanor conviction, he said the government could question her about an earlier shoplifting conviction in London, since Myerson had omitted it on a sworn statement when she was appointed a city commissioner in 1983.

The revelation of these shoplifting cases, involving a woman whose assets were estimated by her own attorney in his opening statement to the jury at over $10 million, merged with the charges in the government's case to create a new public image for Myerson: she was out of control, pathetic, bizarre. Even her attorney, Fred Hafetz, conceded during his opening that Myerson had "misled" the mayor and the press in her initial explanation of the Sukhreet Gabel hiring, and that she had used aliases, notably "Mrs. Robinson," when calling Judge Gabel's chambers. "Bess Myerson is a complex person," Hafetz explained, "and there are sometimes oddities of behavior in her."

Though Koch and one of his top aides, Joe DeVincenzo, were nominal government witnesses, their testimony was muted and ineffectual, carefully sidestepping the repetition of damaging statements they had made either publicly or in private sessions with the prosecutors. They and other noncommittal administration witnesses were barely cross-examined, while Herb Rickman, the City Hall aide who had blown the whistle on Bess and who testified vigorously against her, was battered for days. City Hall attorneys prepared every administration witness except the independent Rickman, who was treated as odd man out in an apparent fence-straddling inner circle strategy.

A case against Myerson that was built on inference atop inference—without a smoking-gun witness, a cash payment, or a tangible victim (Nancy Capasso carried too much baggage to be put on the stand)—collapsed in the end. Yet the acquittal was hardly the "exoneration" Koch regarded it. In fact, Harold Tyler's conclusion that she had committed "serious misconduct" was still the city's official position, and interviews with half the jurors found a virtually unanimous repudiation of Myerson.

● Even the taxi commission scandal returned to haunt Koch. The former taxi chairman, Jay Turoff, and taxi owners tied to Stanley Friedman, pleaded guilty to federal charges involving the fixing of a diesel experimental program. And when the mayor appeared under oath before a state integrity commission investigating campaign finance abuses, he acknowledged that Turoff had acted as a dispatcher in the 1985 mayoral campaign, operating out of the headquarters, recruiting and sending out on campaign missions cabs from the very companies he regulated. The use of Turoff was just one of the campaign finance abuses leveled at Koch, who claimed he didn't know that Turoff had been given hundreds of free cabs for the reelection effort.

The mayor also conceded that former deputy mayor Peter Solomon had, as finance chairman of his 1981 campaign, raised thousands in contributions from the same real estate developers who had won multimillion-dollar tax abatements from the city board Solomon had chaired. Koch likewise admitted that the finance chairman of his 1982 gubernatorial campaign had, after Koch's loss, been named to head the same abatement board, and had awarded more giveaways to developers he had just solicited for large contributions. Finally, he acknowledged that his consumer affairs and sanitation commissioners had accompanied him at a 1985 Rainbow Room fundraiser that raised over $50,000 from the mob-ridden private carting industry. (After Koch spoke at the fundraiser, the commissioners who regulated the carting industry spoke.)

As difficult as this continuing series of blows from past scandals was, Koch also had to contend with new probes that reached into his private residence, Gracie Mansion, and into the basement of City Hall. The charges against his Gracie Mansion chef were purely tabloid material, though they suggested that Koch had knowingly tolerated a clear-cut ethics violation in his own house. But revelations about the plumbers' operation just a stairwell below his City Hall office finally put the mayor himself on the witness stand and dogged his reelection campaign into the summer of 1989.

Despite a 1988 DOI finding that the mayor's chef, Mitchell London, had violated the city charter for years, ignoring two city ethics rulings, Koch did not fire him. (He ultimately resigned.) DOI found that London, who actually held the $51,450-a-year title of executive administrator and was the only live-in occupant of Gracie Mansion other than the mayor, had "intentionally used mansion staff and resources for his private catering business knowing that such activity violated" the charter. Though the agency found that London had committed misdemeanors, Commissioner Frawley did not send a referral letter to a prosecutor, as is DOI's usual practice, but merely spoke with D.A. Morgenthau, who declined to prosecute.

The Frawley report indicated that London recruited staffers, on city time, to prepare, pick up, and deliver food for his catering business, and sometimes used the mansion kitchen to cook it. DOI did not note that London's company did frequent business with the same vendors who were supplying the mansion, creating an open invitation for collusion, or that customers for the catering business, which was run without health permits or incorporation papers for much of its history, were lined up by London's friends in the mayor's special projects office.

The chef issue faded quickly, however, obscured in part by the media turmoil surrounding two state probes of a secret patronage operation run directly out of City Hall by Joe DeVincenzo, the balding, rail-thin, phantom aide of the mayor who had invisibly wielded extraordinary personnel powers over every city agency for eleven Koch years, without attracting more than an occasional line of newsprint. Throughout 1988, the State Commission on Integrity in Government—a nonprosecutorial body set up by Governor Mario Cuomo and chaired by the effusively fair dean of Fordham Law School, John Feerick—was spearheading a public probe of "Joe D.," as he was known. By December, Manhattan D.A. Robert Morgenthau had started his own criminal inquiry.

While DeVincenzo was the ostensible target of these investigations, the media firestorm that engulfed the DeVincenzo issue could only be explained by the widespread tacit understanding that his operation, and its possibly illegal cover-up, occurred so close to the mayor that knowledge of chilling aspects of it could not plausibly be denied. With a sudden explosion of press interest that began in the spring of 1988, DeVincenzo slowly emerged from the City Hall shadows where he had carefully concealed himself since the days of Abe Beame, when he worked for his longtime friend, then deputy mayor Stanley Friedman.

DeVincenzo had long been the mole for the machine inside the highest levels of the Koch administration, so close to Friedman he had fed reporters negative information about government witnesses during the PVB trial in New Haven, so close to Esposito that he had been given a seat on the dais at Meade's 1984 farewell dinner, and so close to Nick LaPorte, the Democratic boss from his home borough, Staten Island, that he had steered a wholly disproportionate number of discretionary city jobs to the tiniest of the party organizations.

"Joe D." was the only mayoral assistant with a city limo, provided by the sanitation department. He had started as a sanitation worker twenty years earlier, winding up as the $104,000-a-year potentate of city patronage, ruling over everything from parking passes in the City Hall lot to travel vouchers and furniture for commissioners. A master of the arcane bureaucratic rules of city personnel practices, the 46-year-old DeVincenzo traded job favors with other top city officials and political leaders, arranging such a network of IOUs that he made himself indispensable. In a rare August 1987 profile of DeVincenzo published in the *Staten Island Advance* the mayor said: "Loyalty? I think Joe D. is loyal to good government. He's a first-rate administrator, the complete professional." The reporter who wrote the gushing profile got a city job shortly thereafter.

DeVincenzo obtained city jobs for six of his cousins, and though married, put the mother of "a close female companion" on the city payroll. He authorized the expenditure of $11,000 from the mayor's budget to pay for lockers and mirrors at the Police Academy, where he was the only non–law enforcement official to enjoy special swimming privileges. He reportedly even got a city official to tend his garden at his Staten Island home, as well as one at a summer house in Pennsylvania that he bought with $95,000 in cash.

His fearsome temper and daily access to Deputy Mayor Brezenoff, John LoCicero, and mayoral executive assistant Diane Coffey positioned him to dictate hirings and promotions, even to commissioners. Said one former Department of Environmental Protection director: "Joe D. is City Hall. For 230,000 city workers, he is the mayor."

This new picture of DeVincenzo began emerging in great

detail in January 1989, when the Feerick commission held the first of two public hearings about the operations of the Talent Bank, a supposed affirmative action hiring program set up by Koch and run for years by DeVincenzo. The jobs program was announced by the mayor in early 1983—on the heels of Koch's disastrous defeat in the 1982 gubernatorial election, and at a time when he was in such a perceptibly disinterested slump his government became a neon-lit marketplace for the schemes of the clubhouse predators. (Citisource and the Grand Prix began in earnest at the same time as this institutionalized patronage operation.)

The public testimony of a Talent Bank director, several staff members, other aides to DeVincenzo, agency officials from transportation and environmental protection who dealt with the bank, LoCicero, Brezenoff, and the mayor himself pieced together an extraordinary scenario (contested somewhat by Joe D.) that became the culmination of the city's greatest scandal.

What emerged was patronage so pervasive that in certain well-paying jobs from sewer workers to highway repairmen, "if they looked neat and weren't reeking of alcohol," the Joe D. referrals, who usually originated with party leaders, were hired. "We had one guy come in, he was behaving very strangely, rambling, babbling," testified the former personnel director under Transportation Commissioner Tony Ameruso. But Ameruso refused to fire the Talent Bank placement, transferring him to the PVB, and then to the ferry bureau, where he "fell down a ferry hatch," and eventually left city government after collecting workmen's compensation. A Donald Manes referral for a laborer job in 1984 produced a "rejected" notation from a supervisor that interviewed him, and a note that read "fired from last job, poor impression, looks lackadaisical." He wound up hired anyway, as a shop clerk at DEP.

The list of political placements included the nephew and brother-in-law of Staten Island borough president Ralph Lamberti, the son of Queens councilman Archie Spigner, the son of a Conservative Party boss, and the widow of a Manhattan judge. "Hot" referrals at the bank, coming from the most favored political leaders, were placed in color-coded files and forced repeatedly on the most compliant city agencies. Unrelated agency requests to City Hall for promotions, transfers, or whatever were held up in DeVincenzo's office if the clubhouse-connected applicants weren't hired. "If you don't play ball, where do you think your stuff winds up?" asked the DEP deputy who was the agency's go-between with Joe D.

The exposure of this system, involving hundreds of jobs over a period of years, directly contradicted the pious pronouncements of the mayor, in both of his books and at press conferences. "I decided we wouldn't do it that way," Koch had declared. "In prior administrations they turned over the jobs to the county leaders and said, 'You fill them.' Now only the commissioner can fill them." With these revelations, the mayor tried a "much ado about nothing" response, conceding only that he was "the victim of my own rhetoric and hyperbole." When he published a third book in early 1989, coauthored with Cardinal John O'Connor and titled *His Eminence and His Honor,* the index listed a reference to DeVincenzo, but the passage had been hurriedly scratched right before publication.

What turned a mere embarrassment into a possible crime, however, was what happened in City Hall after the Manes scandal exploded in 1986 and a *Village Voice* story identified DeVincenzo as City Hall's best-kept secret and patronage king. Jim Hein, a top DeVincenzo aide, who even the mayor's counsel believed was too meek to have acted without orders from Joe D., walked into the Talent Bank offices with a handful of plastic bags. He initially ordered a computer analyst to "pull the plug" on the agency's computer, but eventually settled for erasing all political referrals from its memory. He also wanted the color-coded files of political referrals dumped in the trash.

Up to five staffers, including Joe D.'s secretary, spent the bulk of a frenzied day tearing résumés, memos, and files in half and stuffing them in green trash bags, while a computer analyst sat in a corner wiping the names of party bosses out of the Talent Bank computer. The doors to the Talent Bank offices, which had been moved to a building directly behind City Hall, were locked at Hein's suggestion, while the giant trash bags were packed and hustled out to his car. Hein, who testified that DeVincenzo had ordered him to destroy the records (a contention Joe D. disputed in his own testimony), said he took the filled bags to his Westchester home and put them out with his garbage the following day, explaining that he did not leave them for a city garbage pickup because he "did not want those papers flying all over Chambers Street the next morning."

A DeVincenzo aide who joined the shredding party midway through wisecracked: "If you think it's bad here, you should see over at City Hall, it's chaos." The Talent Bank director, Inez Padilla-Barham, an Hispanic with a Yale degree, said that after the records were purged, Hein instructed her to tell anyone who questioned her about the hiring system that "it was blind and that we had no knowledge of political referrals." Padilla-Barham would later testify that "a lot of what happened at City Hall" was "unusual," and that she was frequently given "weird instructions," but that despite this acclimation to the bizarre, the events of this frenetic day "shocked" and "scared" her. Padilla-Barham, the daughter of a candy store owner raised in one of the poorest sections of Brooklyn and proud of her City Hall post, eventually left her Talent Bank job after months of depression over the realities of life behind the marble pillars.

DeVincenzo's denials—both of the patronage and deep-sixing operations—were greeted with such widespread skepticism by members of the state commission, as well as the media, that a perjury or obstruction of justice indictment became the topic of open speculation. In the aftermath of DeVincenzo's testimony, he arranged shadowy meetings on street corners with the head of the city's retirement system and set in motion the secretive paperwork that would give him a $1,000-a-week pension for the rest of his life.

Brezenoff and the mayor would subsequently testify that they knew nothing of DeVincenzo's retirement application until shortly before it became a fait accompli. They said they thought it would not be final for weeks, but instead DeVincenzo moved to finalize it without telling them. Just as mysteriously, a notice of the pension application disappeared between the retirement board and the city's investigations department, which is supposed to be routinely notified of retirements. Had DOI been notified, it would have been forced to hold up approval of DeVincenzo's pension, since he was the subject of Morgenthau's and Feerick's probes and a separate DOI probe.

The retirement director who met with DeVincenzo on the streets of Tribeca had received a major salary boost and title change through DeVincenzo, and could recall only one other city official he had met surreptitiously: Tony Ameruso. The pension manipulation was a parting tribute to DeVincenzo's mastery over the bureaucracy and, simultaneously, a crass signal to the mounting Morgenthau investigation.

What the Feerick commission and the media found most disturbing about DeVincenzo's golden parachute was that his aide, Jim Hein, whose testimony had implicated Joe D., was demoted to a civil service title and took a $20,000 salary cut at the same time. The mayor, who relentlessly pressed his counsel and Brezenoff to sack the witness who had undone DeVincenzo, said his rationale was that Hein had changed his testimony, recanting earlier claims (in private testimony before Feerick) that dovetailed with DeVincenzo's.

Demoting Hein but keeping him at City Hall served the dual purpose of punishing him and maintaining leverage over him during the grand jury probe begun by Morgenthau. On a kidney dialysis machine and extremely sick, Hein was for all purposes shell-shocked. Soon after Hank White, the mayor's counsel, said he believed Hein and referred new charges against DeVincenzo to DOI, he suddenly resigned though he'd only been in office five months.

By the time the mayor testified before the commission in April, he was ready to turn this remarkable saga of cover-up and irregular hiring practices into a feisty, self-serving lecture, replete with enough "don't recalls," "not awares," and other murky hedges to detach himself from the worst of it. Despite the overwhelming evidence that a wholesale destruction of Talent Bank records had occurred, Koch was "not in a position" to make "a conclusion" about whether it had happened. He claimed he never heard another word about the hiring program after he had set it up in 1983, until the scandal hit in 1986. Though he described DeVincenzo as "the last signature" on every city personnel decision for years, he could not recall a single meeting with him, claiming he merely "passed him in the hall."

DeVincenzo took the fifth, refusing to reappear before the commission and disappearing from sight. The commission began preparing a written report, scheduled to appear during the summer—a kind of official afterword on the scandal. Morgenthau pursued the DeVincenzo evidence, but the decision on the case could clearly go either way.

While this final episode in a four-year run of sordid chronicles might not lead to a criminal charge, there is no erasing the database of other indictments and convictions. PVB, the leasing bureau run by Alex Liberman, and the city's health inspector unit had all been defined as "racketeering enterprises" in successful federal criminal cases. The second, third, and fourth most powerful political leaders attached to the Koch administration—Manes, Friedman, and Esposito—had all fallen. In addition to the publicized cases against city contractors like Andy Capasso and Mike Lazar and the prosecutions of the party bosses that lived at the city trough, more than 180 high- and middle-level city employees had been convicted of job-related corruption from January 1985 through June 1989. Included among the convicted were twenty cops, dozens of sewer, electrical, restaurant, and fire inspectors, armies of Housing Authority and Board of Education staffers, three officials in the Bureau of Vital Records, the superintendent in charge of waste disposal, and the chief pharmacy buyer for HHC. A federal judge, Thomas Griesa, sentencing one environmental agency employee in an extortion case, said: "If the city administration decides that there will be no corruption in its departments, they can get rid of it. If they tolerate it, there will be corruption. It is up to the city."

But in the face of this sort of judicial challenge to the city, the Koch administration has disarmed its own Department of Investigations, blunting its effectiveness. Kevin Frawley, named commissioner in early 1988, had less law enforcement background than any of his modern predecessors, and was the first investigations chief to have actually been a campaign aide to the mayor who appointed him. Frawley had acted as a Koch advance man during the 1982 gubernatorial campaign, accompanying him on upstate swings, and had worked in the 1985 campaign as well.

Under both Frawley and his predecessor, Ken Conboy, the agency's productivity declined by virtually every measure, despite a claimed tripling of DOI's budget and doubling of its manpower at the peak of the scandal in 1986. The department was doing 1,400 fewer background investigations of high-level appointees than in the last full year under McGinley, and was taking an average of 169 days to complete one, more than twice the McGinley rate. The regular investigative unit closed a hundred fewer cases in fiscal year 1988 than it had projected itself, and 90 fewer than in tumultuous 1986. It even opened 164 fewer cases than the year before.

The much ballyhooed budgetary increase, announced in a major Koch address, was allocated in ways that minimized impact—the investigations unit actually lost thirteen positions between 1987 and 1988, while the executive staff gained twenty. Finally, after making the DOI budget boosts an early centerpiece of his anticorruption efforts, Koch quietly gutted the agency in 1989, slashing forty-six positions. The decimation of DOI, budgetary and otherwise, made Koch's onetime public outrage over DOI's failure to discover the PVB scams little more than a joke.

Stanley Friedman could be heard clucking all the way from his Missouri cell. With prophetic savvy, he had predicted more than two years earlier, when Rudy Giuliani brought his wife and baby to the New Haven courthouse during jury delibera-tions, that the photo opportunity presented by this family ap-pearance was the "kickoff of a campaign." An unbowed Fried-man's post-conviction press conference had consisted of a single request: "When he throws his hat in the ring, I hope you will say somewhere along the line that maybe Stanley Fried-man was right."

On May 17, 1989, two months after he resigned as U.S. Attorney, Giuliani, his wife Donna Hanover, and 4-year-old An-drew made their first joint public appearance since New Haven. Giuliani announced his candidacy for mayor at the fashionable eastside clubhouse where Fiorello LaGuardia had campaigned fifty-six years earlier. Gone was the stern, businesslike profile of the dreaded prosecutor. Giuliani beamed—relaxed, joking, energized, optimistic. No longer the protected embodiment of the public's interest, Candidate Giuliani was entering a new life, exposing himself to the probing pressures of a wide open New York campaign, moving voluntarily from hunter to hunted.

"If you're happy with the way things are," Giuliani directed, "reelect Koch. If you only want to see minimal change, then choose one of the others. But if you want to see real, honest, fundamental change in this city, then vote for me.

"If you offer support or money expecting any special deals, forget about it. Save your money. Let me repeat it one more time—no deals for jobs, no deals for contributors. If you are receiving special favors to which you are not entitled, you had better be willing to give them up, or you better redouble your efforts to defeat me."

Giuliani was but one of eight candidates to announce in the 1989 campaign against the irrepressible Koch, who was deter-mined to win vindication and a fourth term. The field in the Democratic primary included David Dinkins, the black borough president of Manhattan, whose civility and fairness seemed the perfect antidote for twelve years of racial stridency under Koch; comptroller Jay Goldin, who had warned Koch so many years earlier about the breeding ground for scandal that the transportation department had become; and Richard Ravitch, a wealthy builder and banker whose very presence as a candidate was a signal that significant elements of the city's establishment had tired of the tainted mayor.

Giuliani also had three possible Republican opponents, only one of whom, cosmetics heir Ron Lauder, was considered a serious contender. Lauder, who is as awkward and inarticulate as he is wealthy, began weeks before Giuliani even announced to spend millions on television ads that pummeled Giuliani, but virtually ignored the candidate they were ostensibly promoting. Lauder's candidacy was an invention of the state's most powerful Republican, U.S. Senator Al D'Amato, who was so close to Koch that the mayor had endorsed him against a liberal Democrat in 1986. Tied by an extraordinary trail of campaign contributions to the Wall Street bankers Giuliani had indicted for insider trading violations, D'Amato was in fact as much anti-Giuliani as he was pro-Koch.

Many of the other Republican leaders drawn to Lauder had also, indirectly at least, been at the defending end of Giuliani prosecutions. Lauder's campaign chairman was former state GOP chairman George Clark, who had been thrown into Giuliani's Wedtech grand jury and questioned about his role in soliciting $200,000 in campaign contributions for Ronald Reagan. Joe Neglia, a powerful Brooklyn district leader close to Clark and a Lauder backer, had also been implicated in the Wedtech case. Trial testimony indicated that he had introduced Wedtech brass to his son Peter Neglia, who as head of the Small Business Administration was the state party's highest patronage appointee in the Reagan administration. (Peter Neglia was convicted of racketeering and obstruction of justice in the Wedtech case.) The Bronx GOP leader, Guy Velella, another Stop Giuliani general, shared a law practice with his father Vincent, who had represented the business interests of two of the city's most powerful mob bosses for years. Giuliani put both the Velella clients in jail for what seemed likely to be the rest of their lives.

Lauder was not the only Giuliani opponent, however, manufactured by enmities that seemed rooted in his performance as a prosecutor. That became clear when the leadership of the city's smallest party with a guaranteed line on the ballot—the 23,000-member Liberal Party—decided in April to designate Giuliani as their candidate. Republicans have been able to win the mayoralty in Democratic New York only when they run as fusion candidates, after periods of wrenching corruption. John Lindsay was elected as a Republican–Liberal in 1965. Seth Low won as a Republican–Independent in 1901, and LaGuardia duplicated the feat in 1933. Giuliani's designation by the Liberals made him an early front-runner.

In a desperate attempt to block Giuliani, Barry Feinstein, a Democrat, a strong supporter of Al D'Amato, and the leader of a powerful Teamster local that represents thousands of city workers, announced that he would field a candidate against Giuliani in a Liberal primary. Feinstein had to find a registered Liberal, and the only person he could come up with was the 75-year-old former state chair of the party, Donald Harrington, who lived in Long Island and had to suddenly switch his voter registration to a Manhattan address. While state chair in 1985, Harrington had broken from the party to endorse Koch and had put in writing a strategy for dissolving the party.

Harrington's hoax candidacy was run out of the Teamster headquarters and staffed by Teamster officials. Giuliani had brought a civil racketeering case against the Teamsters, and the union had been placed under the supervision of a court-appointed former Giuliani assistant. Feinstein had himself been the target of an unsuccessful Giuliani probe of his diversion of millions in union funds to a company controlled by a Feinstein relative. (Feinstein's mother had been convicted years earlier of a similar scam involving the same local.) The Feinstein strategy was to position Giuliani as the target of simultaneous opposition from the right and the left.*

From the left, Giuliani could justifiably be assailed for his direction as associate attorney general in the Reagan administration of detention camps for thousands of Haitians fleeing the regime of Jean-Claude Duvalier. He could be criticized for his evasive position on abortion, which was less pro-choice than Dinkins. He could also be attacked for his support of the death penalty for 16-year-olds, and his embrace of a Donald Trump

---

*In mid-July, Harrington withdrew after Feinstein's operatives couldn't even collect 1,200 valid signatures to qualify him for the ballot.

advertisement that ran in every city paper following the rape of a white jogger in Central Park by a gang of black teenagers. Trump had issued an explicit call for hatred, and Giuliani was quoted as saying the ad spurred "a healthy debate." (Coincidentally, Trump, the former Friedman client whose relationship with Friedman was critically assessed by Giuliani in his New Haven cross-examination, had signed on as cochair of a million-dollar Giuliani fundraiser.) Ironically, from the right, Lauder was already attacking Giuliani on the airwaves for being an insufficiently vigilant death-penalty advocate and a closet liberal on social issues.

The initial flurry of Lauder ads and negative press focused, however, on the clients of the major Manhattan law firm Giuliani had just joined, White & Case. The stories began to appear on the day Giuliani announced, saying that White & Case represented the government of Panamanian dictator and indicted drug dealer Manuel Noriega, and suggesting that Giuliani should not have joined the 370-partner firm, which has thousands of clients, because it did. In fact, the firm represented the Panamanian bank and, after Noriega's indictment and seizure of the government in 1988, had explicitly refused to participate in a bank legal matter because of Noriega's involvement.

When Lauder ads and the mayor's wagging finger in television interviews taunted him for "taking drug money," Giuliani, who said he didn't know anything about the firm's representation of the bank and that the bank hadn't made a payment to the firm in six months, exploded. Calling Koch "an embarrassment" to the city, he placed himself in the position of any other politician, down in the pit, throwing mud, instead of remaining the avenging angel on a higher moral plane. Eventually, a beleaguered Giuliani had to take a leave of absence from the firm.

Most of the early poll results suggested that the Noriega deluge was mostly inside baseball anyway. On May 27, in the midst of this barrage, the candidate did a walking tour along Steinway Street in Astoria, Queens. In a community of extraordinary ethnic diversity—including Greeks, Hispanics, Italians, Irish, and Asians—Giuliani was instantly recognized and warmly received. No one mentioned the law firm.

"You've got my vote."

"You're my favorite person in the whole world. Koch is crazy."

"I'm a Democrat, but you're the best," the people said.

At a pizza stand across the street, a group of teenagers began the two-beat chant of "Roo-dee, Roo-dee." The embattled candidate smiled.

The anticipated head-to-head combat of a mayor engulfed by corruption pitted against the detective who unearthed it was instead shaping up as a typically blurred New York story, both sides tarnished, one by real scandal and the other by transparent innuendo. In the Darwinian politics of a city gripped by an apparently permanent political commercialism, there was an almost palpable need to damage this white knight, to make him one of the sullied pack. Koch reveled in it, emerging from a longtime shell of somber depression about his prospects. It was as if the opportunity to be vicious got his blood flowing again, as if reducing Giuliani had liberated him.

But Giuliani was not his only problem. Dinkins was rolling up endorsements, winning support from every major municipal union, as well as those of the Manhattan and Bronx Democratic parties. By mid-July, Dinkins was 15 points ahead of Koch in several polls and in a dead heat with Giuliani. Ravitch, who threatened Koch in his Jewish base of support, became a credible candidate when he won the endorsement of the remnants of Donald Manes's Queens organization. When the Brooklyn organization backed Goldin, Koch, who had intensely sought the support of several of the party machines, again tried to transform himself into the candidate who stood up to the bosses. He did this the same month that Jay Turoff was sentenced for his second conviction, and Donald Manes was named in court papers in New Jersey as the supposed recipient of a $2 million bribe for a cable franchise and Melvin Lebotkin finally pleaded guilty in the last PVB case.

The most telling indication of the mayor's troubles in New York took place on the evening of June 1, in a hot, steamy auditorium in Greenwich Village, when the political club Ed Koch founded in 1983 met to decide its 1989 endorsement for mayor.

The setting was like the final scene of a novel. The room was crowded with people who had known Ed Koch for thirty years. There were people who had quit the VID to start this club in his behalf. John LoCicero had organized the Village Reform Democratic Club (VRDC) out of his City Hall office after the more liberal VID had endorsed Mario Cuomo over Koch for governor. There were people who had befriended him when he defected from DeSapio's club to VID in 1959. Alex Mennella, who came to vote for no endorsement, was wearing the "Koch for Mayor" button he had kept from the 1977 campaign. It was a symbol that he was still loyal to what Ed Koch once was, but not to what he had become.

The pro-Koch forces understood the potential political and psychological impact of losing this club, and put enormous effort into winning the endorsement. LoCicero called dozens of members himself and stood at the back of the room with a list of names. Jerry Skurnick, LoCicero's former deputy, now working in the Koch campaign, also made calls. Koch's campaign manager, Paul Crotty, came in person and spoke.

Koch was able to count on the votes of about a dozen of his own appointees who were members of the club, including his speech and proclamation writer Clark Whelton, and Sam Azadian, who worked at HHC and lived in Brooklyn. Azadian was twice indebted; his son, Robert, also got a job at DEP through Joe D.'s discredited Talent Bank.

Peter Smith came to vote for Ed Koch. Smith had been a Koch commissioner who went to prison in 1979 for embezzling funds from his former law firm. When he got out he started the Partnership for the Homeless, yet he came to vote for the mayor who had insulted the dignity of the homeless so often, and who did so little to build them permanent housing.

"I'm voting for Ed," Smith said, "because I owe so much to John LoCicero," though he seemed pained and embarrassed to be admitting as much.

Marty McLaughlin came to vote for no endorsement. McLaughlin had once been Koch's friend, and had been the mayor's press secretary during the campaign for governor.

"I just feel he shouldn't run," McLaughlin said. "I don't dislike the guy. But his time is past. He should have gotten out gracefully, for himself, and for his friends. If he didn't run, everyone could be more forgiving."

The debate lasted for more than an hour. Sid Baumgarten, who had worked for Mayor Beame, set the tone for the Koch side: "Don't turn your back on a man who has done so much for this club. Don't be selfish. Ed Koch had a lot to do with the birth of this club. It would be cowardly and disloyal not to endorse him tonight."

A voice yelled out from the back: "But what about loyalty to New York?"

Elinor Macy spoke movingly: "I canvassed with Ed Koch in 1960. I personally welcomed him to VID when he quit DeSapio. I loved Ed in those days. He once saved my apartment. But he is now a political animal. He has no other interest in his life. I urge a vote for no endorsement."

John Picarello summarized the case for loyalty: "Because of a little turbulence you want to abandon ship. That's the worse thing this club could do. We have to show we stick with our friends. That way people will stick with us."

Then the paper ballots were marked, collected, and counted. Ten minutes later the result spread through the tense room.

No Endorsement 69

Koch 58

In 1981, when Ed Koch defeated Frank Barbaro, he held a particularly graceless press conference. He boasted that he had defeated Barbaro in his own assembly district, that he had won Barbaro's block.

"The people who knew him best, his neighbors, voted for me," Koch crowed.

On this night, the people who knew Ed Koch best—and longest—rejected him. His neighbors, his friends, his oldest comrades in politics told him that his time had passed.

Index